easy
iMac
See it done
Do it yourself
que®

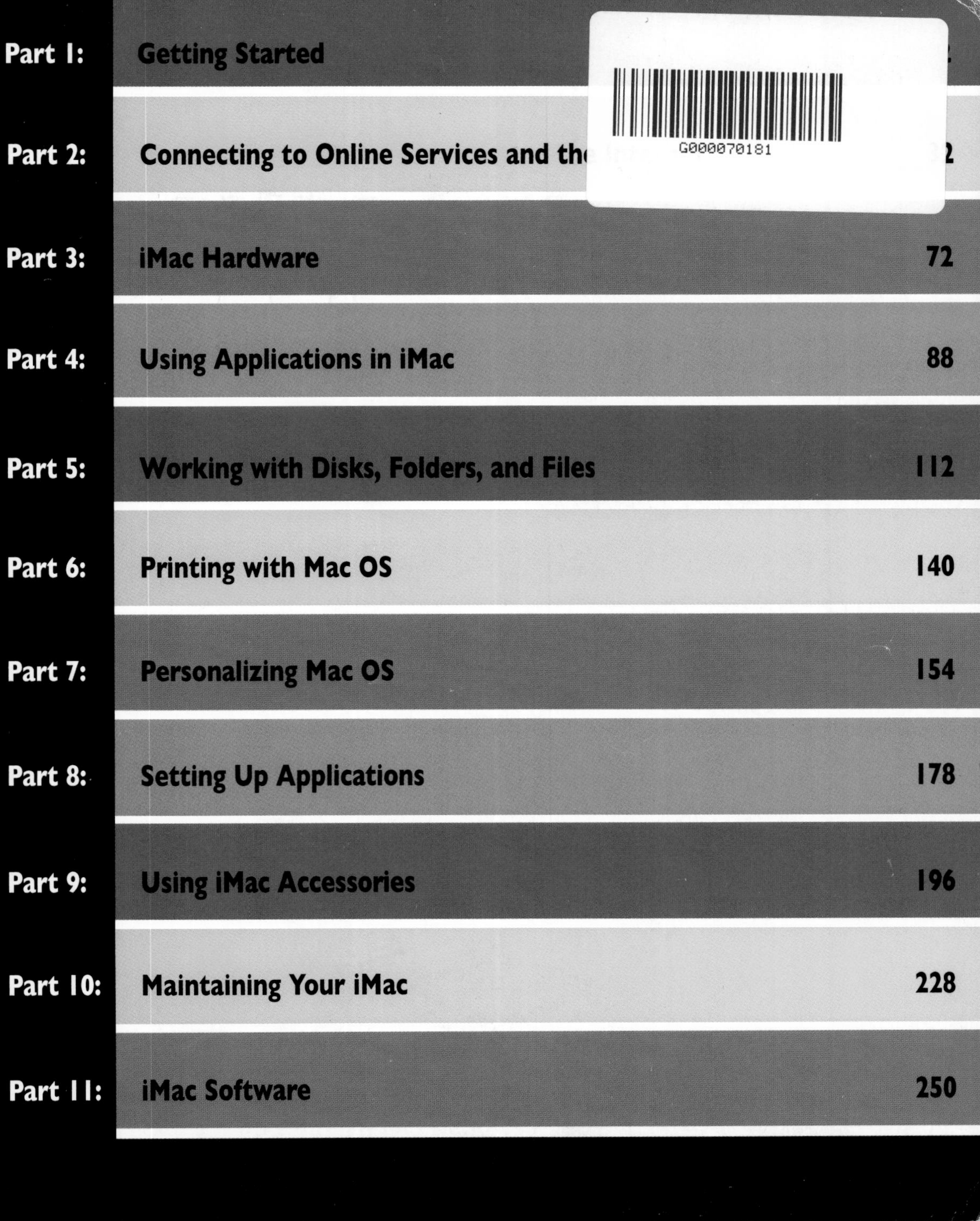

Part 1: Getting Started

Part 2: Connecting to Online Services and the Internet

Part 3: iMac Hardware

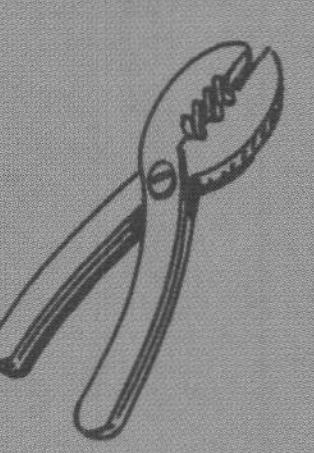

Part 4: Using Applications in iMac

Part 5: Working with Disks, Folders, and Files

Part 6: Printing with Mac OS

Part 7: Personalizing Mac OS

Part 10: Maintaining Your iMac

Part 11: iMac Software

International Standard Book Number: 0-7897-1992-4

Library of Congress Catalog Card Number: 98-89540

Printed in the United States of America

First Printing: April 1999

02 01 00 99 4 3 2

About the Author

Lisa Lee has written *Upgrading and Repairing Your Mac, Guide to Mac OS 7.6 Update*, and co-authored *Sams Teach Yourself Mac OS 8.5 in 24 Hours*. She was also a contributing author for *The Macintosh Bible 6th Edition* and *Zen and the Art of Resource Editing* (2nd Edition). She has helped develop Macintosh hardware and software products for over nine years.

She has been a forum leader on America Online (AFCLisa@aol.com) for over eight years, helping others use their Macs. In her spare time, she uses her Macs to create art, music, and write stories to put on her Web site (http://www.flatfishfactory.com).

Dedication

To Mike Neil.

Acknowledgments

Thanks to Chris Will, who asked me to write this book. I share the credit for this book with the amazingly talented Kate Welsh, my development editor, and the team at Macmillan that helped edit, design, and lay out every page of this book.

This book would also not be possible without Apple's CEO, Steve Jobs, iMac evangelist Mike Shebanek, and the Mac OS and iMac teams who have brought a wonderful product to the world.

Special thanks to all my friends who supported my iMac efforts: Paul Rybicki, Yun Shin, Robert Stones, Greg Schroeder, Terry Rawlings, Brad Reigel, Grace Krueger, Rene Wise, Perry Spitz, Andy Bates, Christianne Petite, Joel Black, Rob Moore, Michael Emery, and Sandy Williamson. And finally, thanks to my family for all their support: Laura, Jackie, Julie, Jason, Ron and Jeanette Lee, and Gary and Beverly Neil.

Associate Publisher
Greg Wiegand

Executive Editor
Christopher A. Will

Acquisitions Editor
Tracy Williams

Development Editor
Kate Shoup Welsh

Technical Editor
Gene Steinberg

Managing Editor
Lisa Wilson

Indexer
Eric Schroeder

Production Designers
Brian Borders
Mark Walchle

Proofreader
Benjamin Berg

Cover Designer
Ann Jones
Maureen McCarty

Book Designer
Ann Jones
Gary Adair

Illustrator
Bruce Dean

How to Use This Book

It's as Easy as 1-2-3

Each part of this book is made up of a series of short, instructional lessons, designed to help you understand basic information that you need to get the most out of your computer hardware and software.

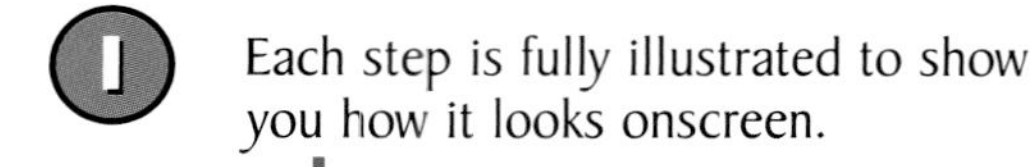

Each step is fully illustrated to show you how it looks onscreen.

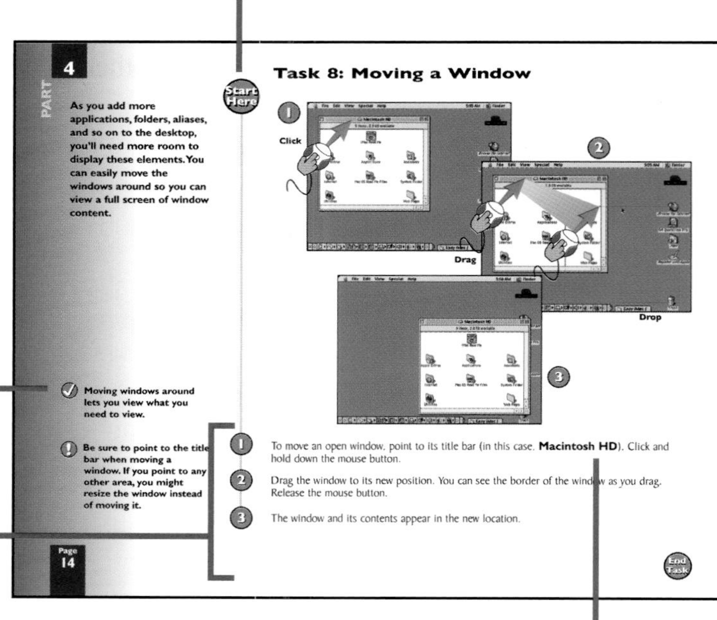

Click: Click the mouse button once.

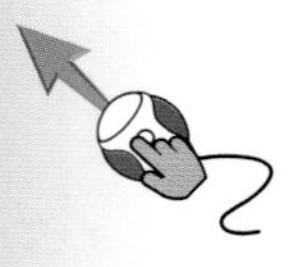

Double-click: Click the mouse button twice in rapid succession.

Pointer Arrow: Highlights an item on the screen you need to point to or focus on in the step or task.

Selection: Highlights the area onscreen discussed in the step or task.

Click & Type: Click once where indicated and begin typing to enter your text or data.

Tips and Warnings give you a heads-up for any extra information you may need while working through the task.

Each task includes a series of quick, easy steps designed to guide you through the procedure.

Items that you select or click in menus, dialog boxes, tabs, and windows are shown in **Bold**. Information you type is in a `special font`.

How to Drag: Point to the starting place or object. Hold down the mouse button, move the mouse to the new location, then release the button.

Next Step: If you see this symbol, it means the task you're working on continues on the next page.

End Task: Task is complete.

Introduction to Easy iMac

One thing the Mac is well known for is its ease of use. The iMac is no exception; virtually every hardware and software feature is visually welcoming and easy to use. Many first-time Macintosh users can put their iMac together and write a letter or balance their checkbook without ever thinking about looking for a manual or a book. However, once you start using your iMac, you will realize, that there's so much to learn.

Easy iMac provides concise, visual, step-by-step instructions, explaining how to use everything on your iMac. You won't have to read through paragraphs of explanations to learn how to get your iMac hooked up to the Internet, send email, or connect printers or other USB devices to your iMac. If you already have a Macintosh computer, you can learn about all the great new features in Mac OS 8.5, including how to customize your system, use the applications installed with Mac OS, and maintain your system. Even if you have never used a computer before, this book shows you what's possible on an iMac.

Easy iMac does not cover the technical inner workings of your iMac. When you are ready to learn more nitty-gritty details about how Mac OS works, you should read *Sams Teach Yourself Mac OS 8.5 in 24 Hours*. Nonetheless, if you have a question about something that is not covered in this book, please send me email at afclisa@aol.com. I will reply to any reader email you send to me (except spam, or mean-spirited ones).

You can read this book cover to cover, use it as a reference when you're trying to figure out how to do a particular task with your iMac, or put it on your coffee table as a conversation piece. Either way, *Easy iMac* lets you see it done and do it yourself.

PART I

Getting Started

iMac is the newest Macintosh from Apple. It is on its way to being the most popular Macintosh ever made. iMac includes the latest version of Mac OS, the Macintosh operating system. It is also missing many of the things previous Macs had, such as serial, SCSI, and ADB ports. Instead, iMac has USB ports in addition to many other easy to use features.

Tasks

Task 1: Setting Up Your iMac

Before you can use your iMac, you need to connect your keyboard, mouse, and phone line to their respective ports. Apple includes a helpful picture guide to walk you through these steps. This task summarizes what you need to connect and where to set up your iMac. Be sure your iMac is on a desk or table top.

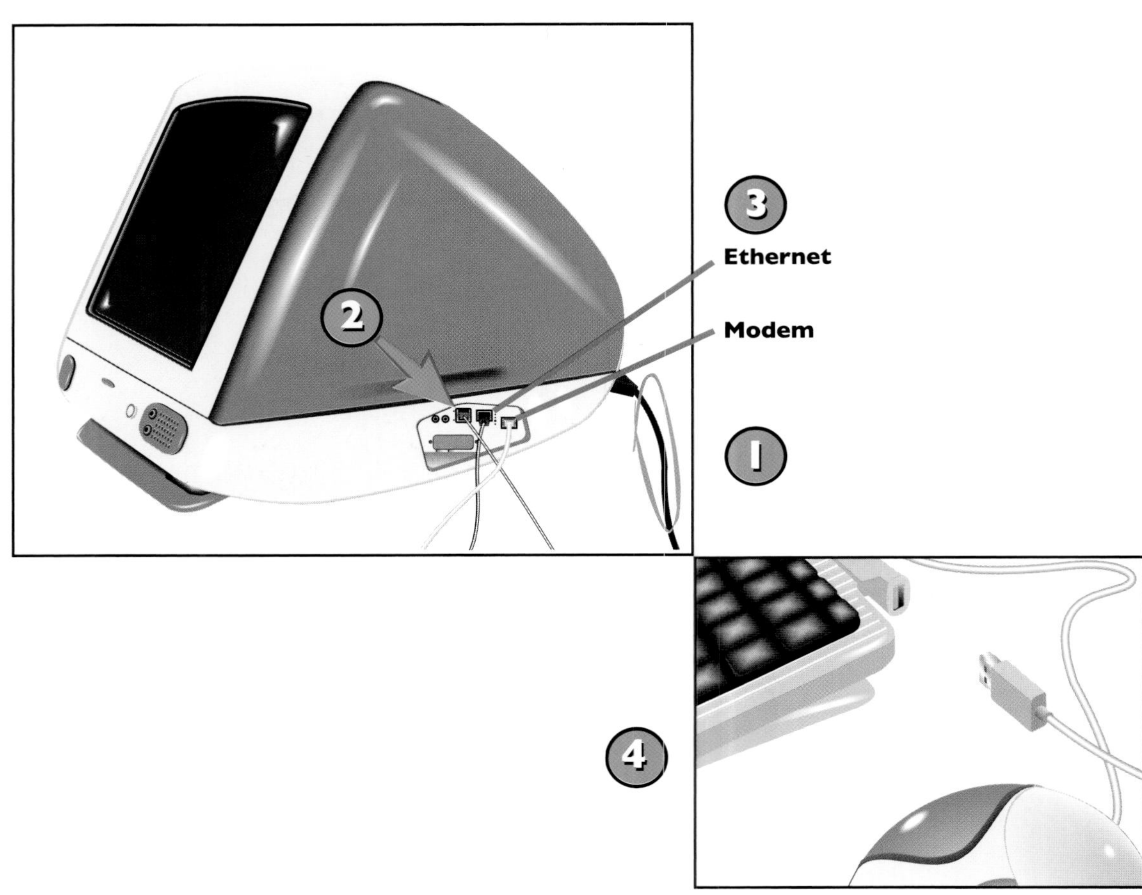

1. Connect the power cable to the back of the iMac.
2. Connect the keyboard to the iMac's USB port.
3. Connect Ethernet or modem cables to the Ethernet or modem port.
4. Connect the mouse to the keyboard's USB port.

Try to place your iMac in a location that is out of direct sunlight, away from moisture or dustiness.

Task 2: Starting Up

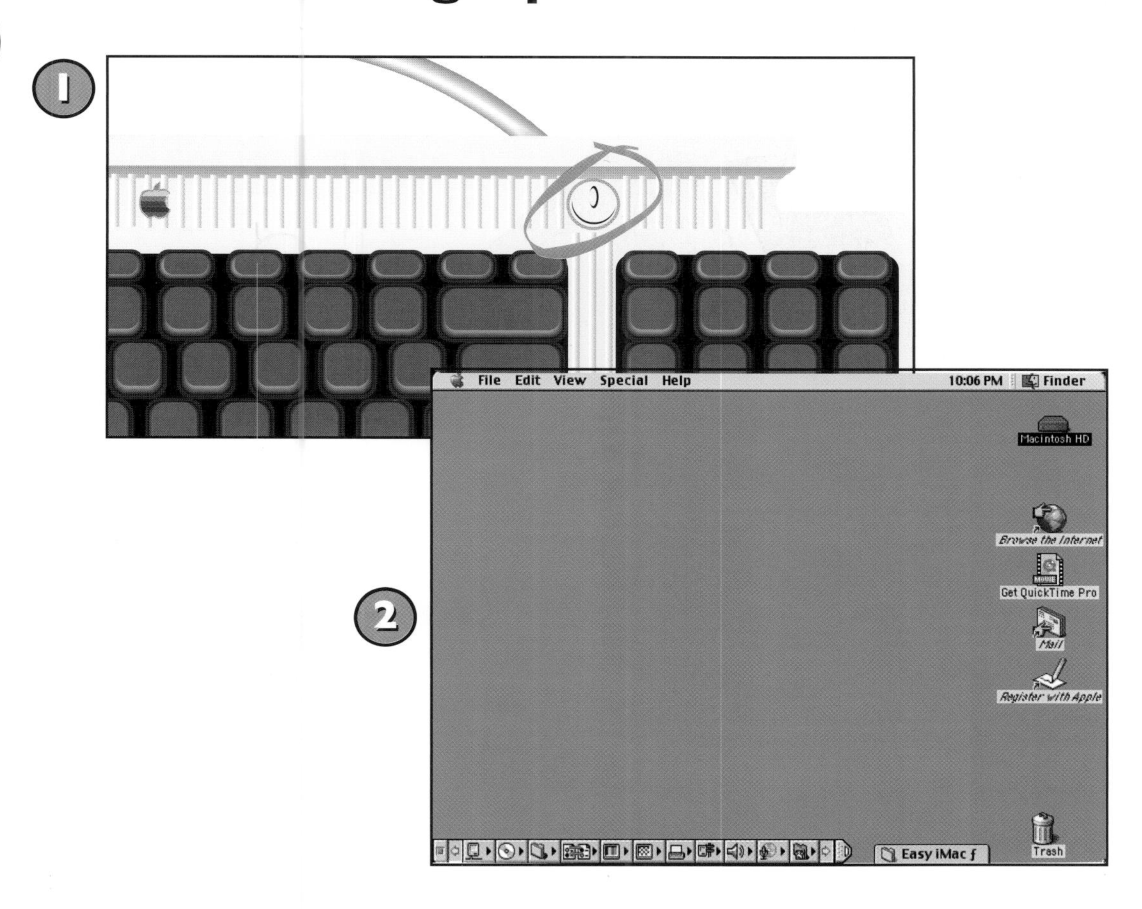

Starting up your iMac involves starting up both the hardware and the software. When you press the power button, it turns the iMac hardware on, as well as the software: Mac OS.

Several things happen after you press the **Power** button. The first thing you will hear is the monitor will turn on. Listen for the iMac chime, then look for the happy Mac icon on your monitor. As Mac OS loads, it will show some of the software loading onscreen until it loads the desktop. The desktop consists of the menu bar and icons.

1. Press the **Power** button.
2. The iMac starts, ultimately displaying the desktop.

The mouse does not light up when you click.

Task 3: Using Mac OS Setup Assistant

Start Here

The first time you turn on your iMac, Apple's Mac OS Setup Assistant application will automatically start. Mac OS Setup Assistant configures several settings in Mac OS, such as the date and time, as well as printer and network settings. Many of the settings in Mac OS Setup Assistant are also covered in other tasks in this book.

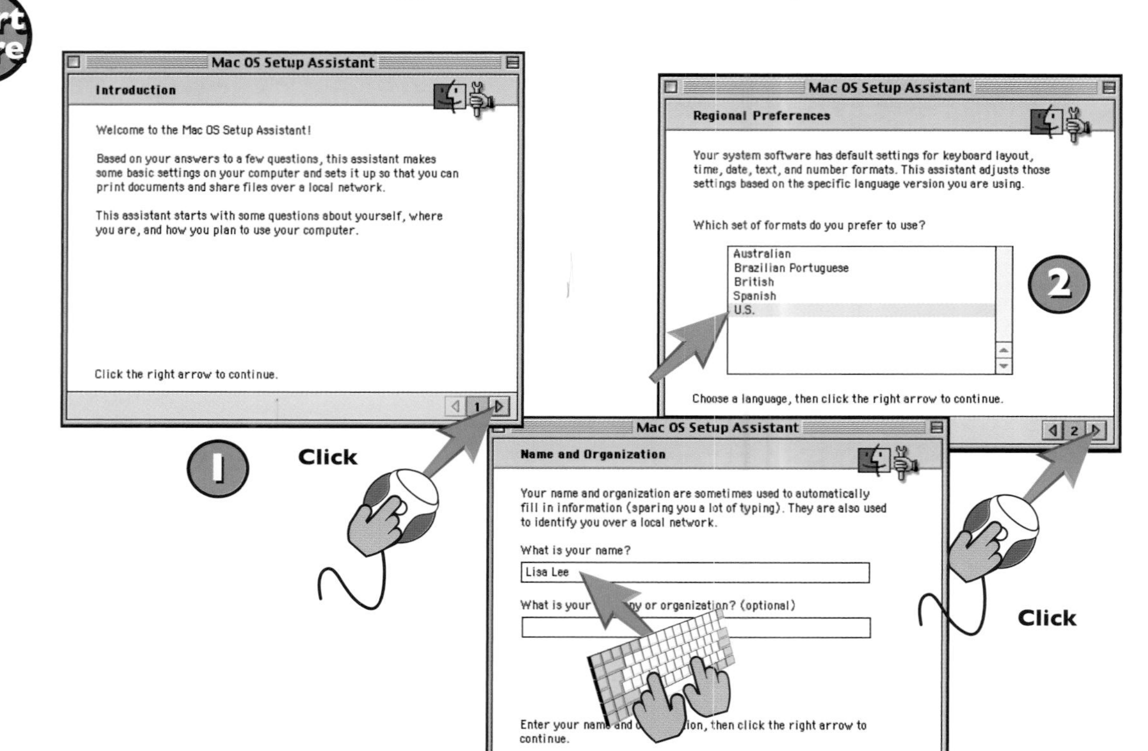

✓ You can start Mac OS Setup Assistant to change your Mac OS settings at any time. The application is located in the **Assistants** folder on your hard disk.

✓ You can quit Mac OS Setup Assistant at any time. However, none of the data you entered will be saved if you quit before you click the **Go Ahead** button in step 11 of this task.

1. Once the Setup Assistant starts, read the **Introduction** page, then click the right-arrow button in the bottom-right corner of the dialog.

2. Select a **Regional Preference** (**U.S.** is chosen as the default), and then click the right-arrow button.

3. Type your name, then click the right-arrow button.

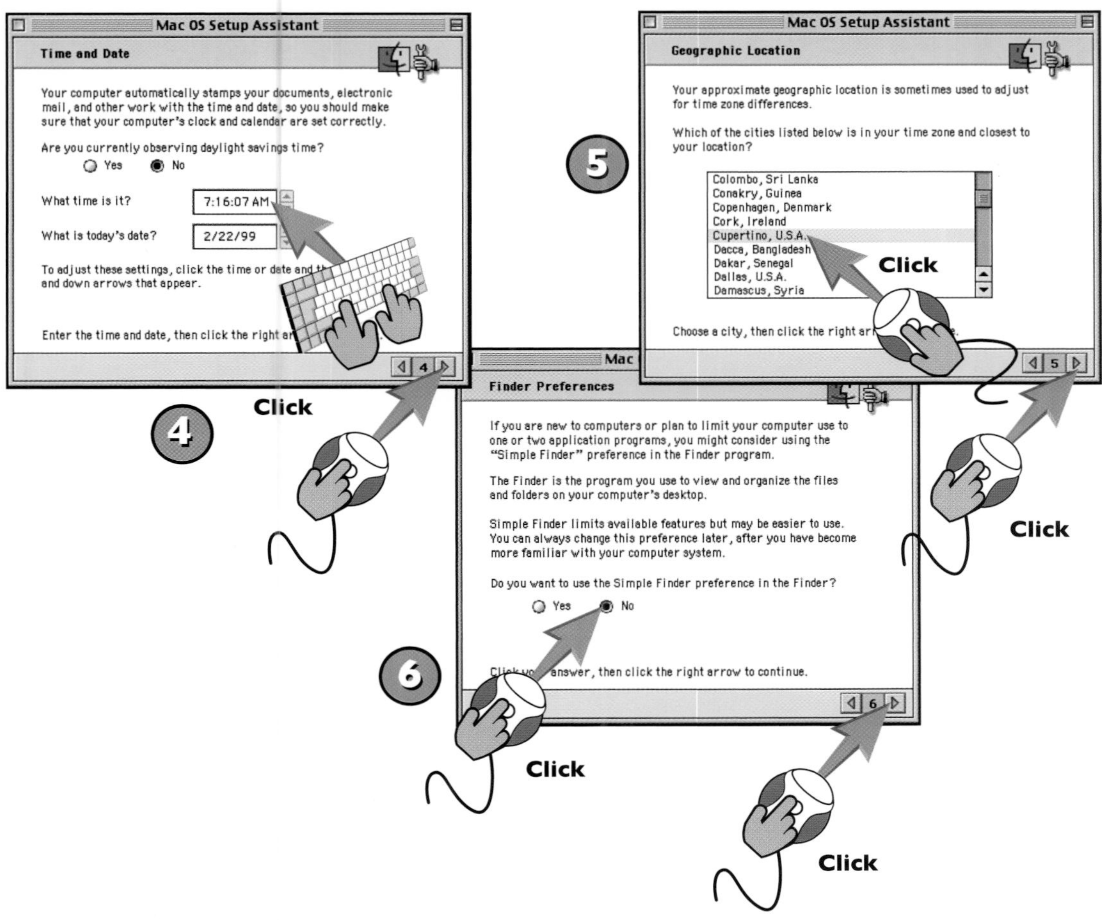

4. Enter the time and date information, then click the right-arrow button.

5. Click on a geographic location from the list. Click the right-arrow button.

6. Choose a **Finder Preferences** setting (the default setting is **No**).

Date and time settings are stored in the Date and Time control panel. For more information about the Date and Time control panel, see Part 7, Task 12, "Changing the System Date and Time."

Simple Finder provides a subset of regular Finder features in Mac OS. For example, Simple Finder contains fewer menu items and no command-key shortcuts.

There are several Finder setting options you can change at any time. To turn Simple Finder on or off, click Edit and choose Preferences, then click the General tab.

Task 3: Continued

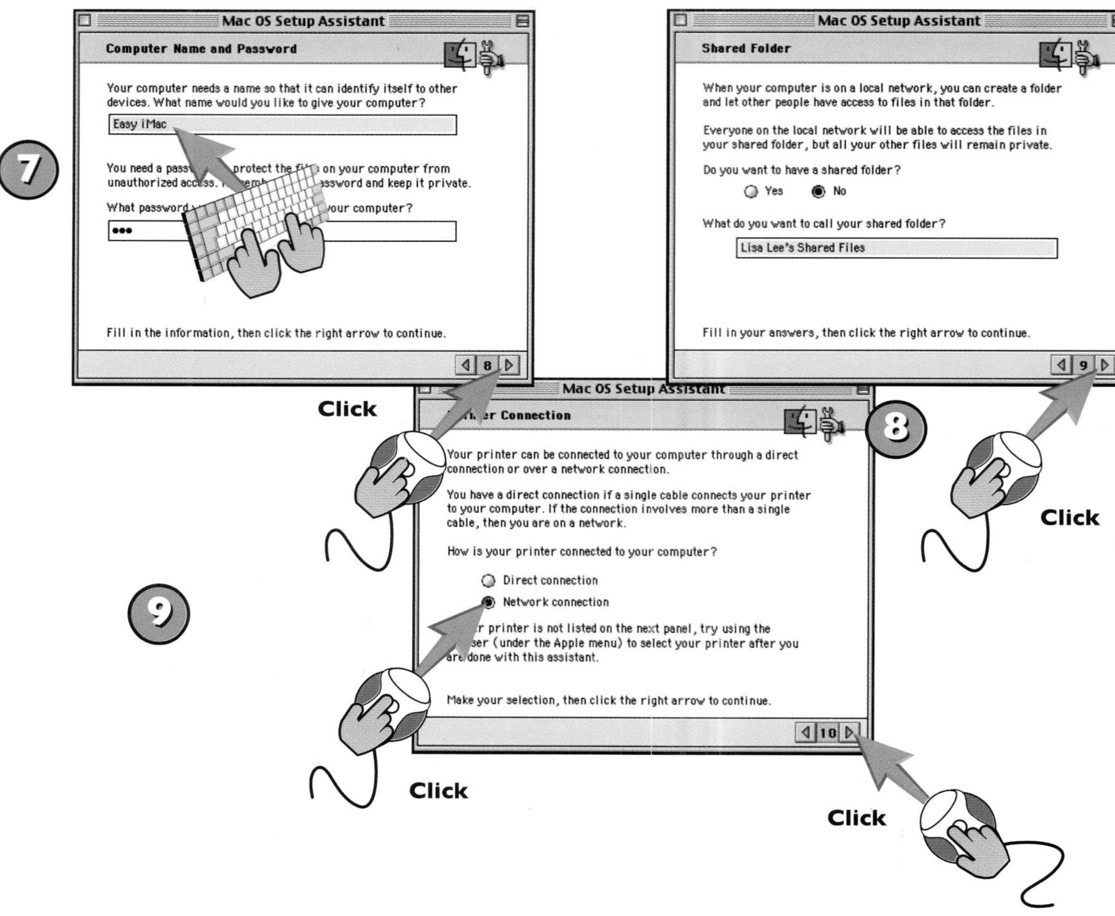

7. Type a computer name and password for your iMac. Click the right-arrow button to continue to the next page.

8. If your iMac is on a network, click **Yes** to share a folder with other computers on the network. Type a name for the shared folder, then click the right-arrow button.

9. Choose **Direct connection** if you have a printer connected to your USB port, or **Network connection** if your printer is on a network. Click the right-arrow button.

If you want to change any of the settings you previously entered while in Mac OS Setup Assistant, click the left-arrow button to move to the previous page.

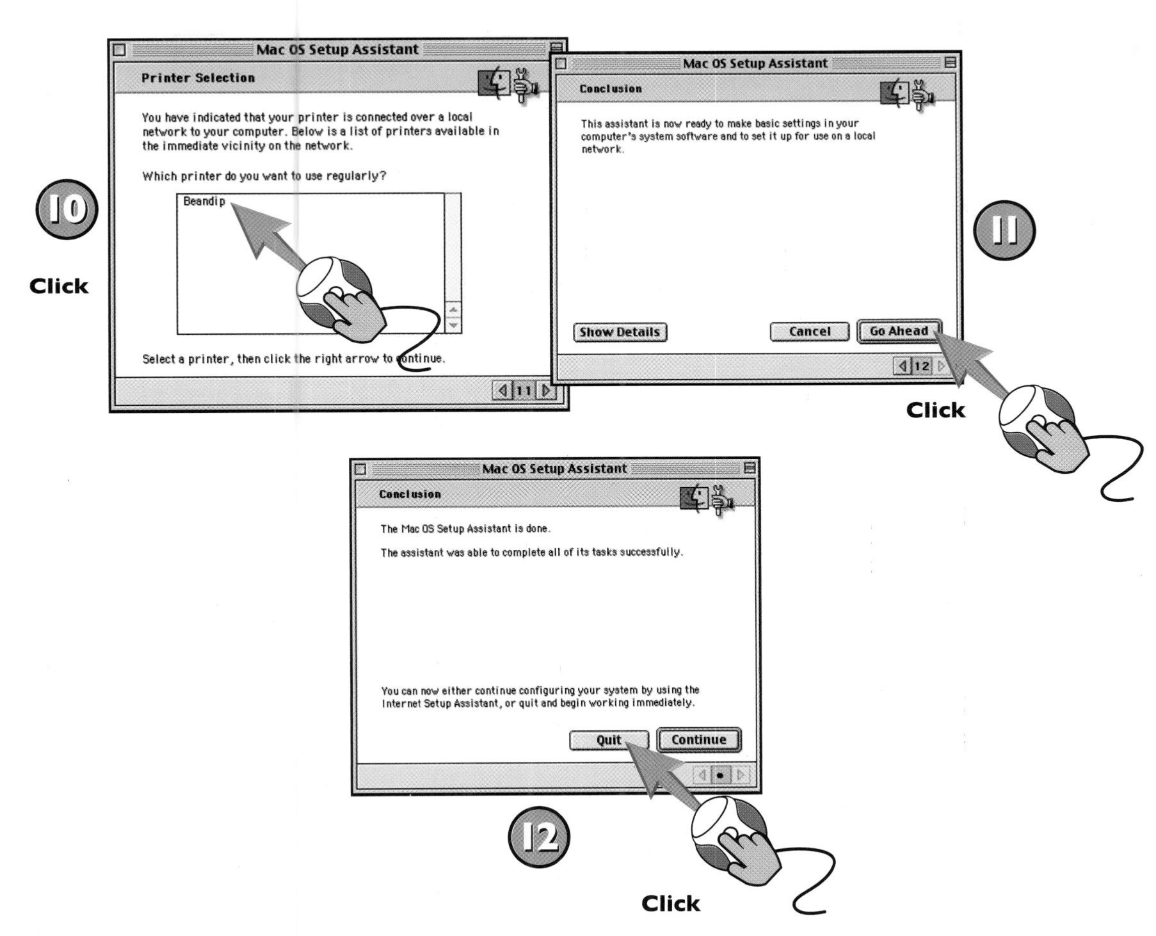

10. Click on a printer name (in this case, **Beandip** is my network printer). Then click the right-arrow button.

11. Click **Go Ahead**. Mac OS Setup Assistant will configure Mac OS. Click **Cancel** to quit Mac OS Setup Assistant.

12. Click **Quit** to exit Mac OS Setup Assistant.

For more information about sharing files and folders on a network, see Part 8, Task 12, "Using File Sharing."

To review all the Mac OS settings you have input, click the Show Details button in step 11.

Click Continue if you want to configure your Internet setup information. For more information about Internet Setup Assistant, see Part 2, Task 3, "Setting Up for the Internet."

Task 4: Opening a Window

Start Here

Mac OS displays all its information in onscreen boxes called *windows*. You need to know how to open windows to work with the information on your computer. Windows are represented onscreen by small pictures called *icons*. You can double-click an icon to display the contents of a window, presented by Mac OS with a folder icon.

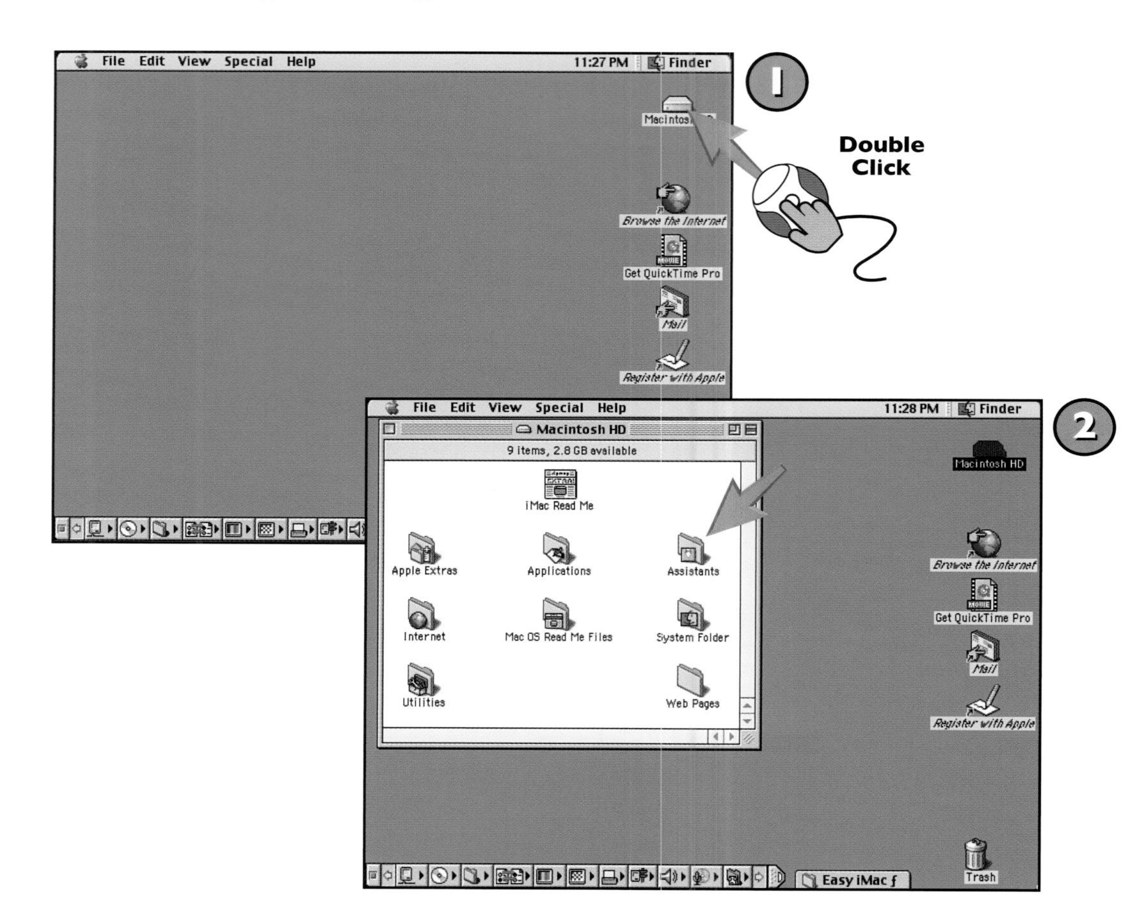

✓ If nothing happens when you double-click an icon, it might be because you did not click quickly enough or because you single-clicked, moved the mouse, and single-clicked again. You have to click twice in rapid succession. A good way to practice using the mouse is to play Jigsaw Puzzle. To open Jigsaw Puzzle, click the **Apple** menu and choose **Jigsaw Puzzle**. For more information about Jigsaw Puzzle, see Part 9, Task 1, "Playing Games."

1. Double-click the **Macintosh HD** icon.
2. The contents of this icon are displayed in a window.

Task 5: Closing a Window

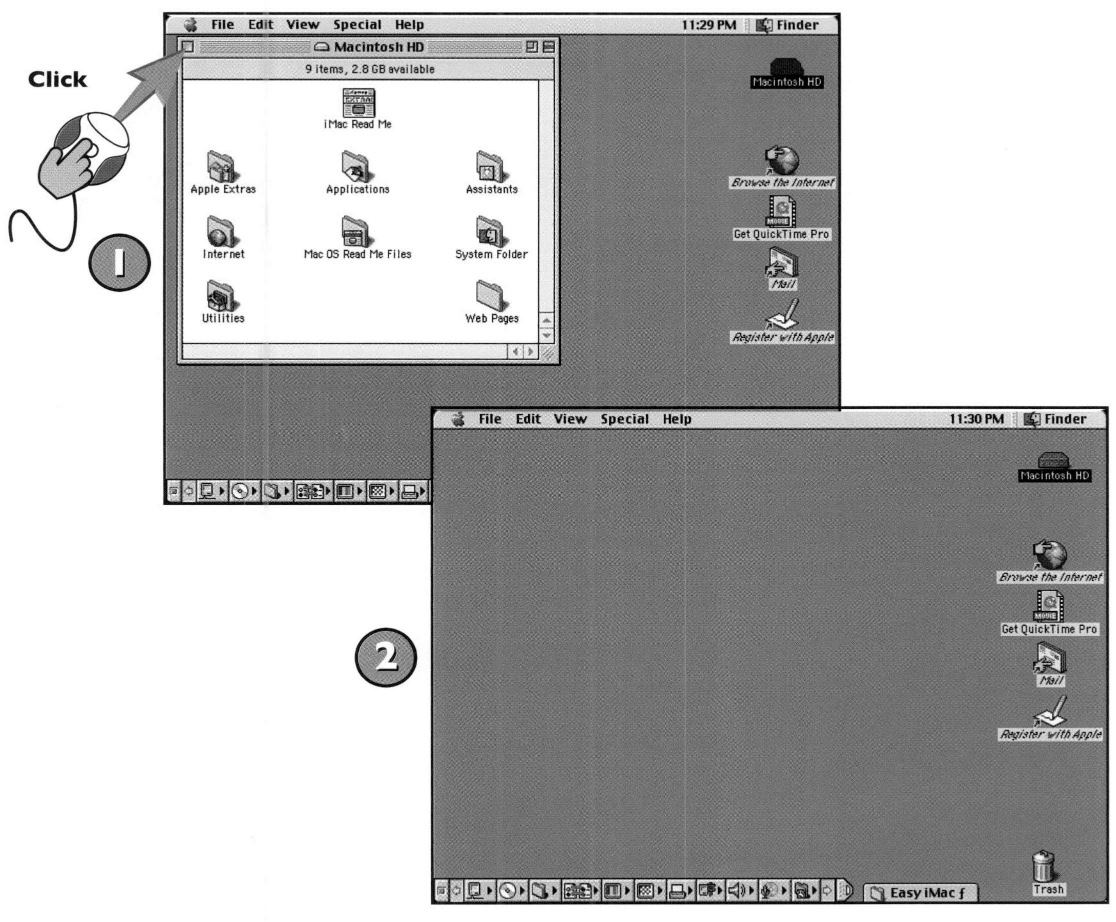

You close a window after you finish working with it and its contents. Too many open windows clutter the desktop as well as the **Applications** menu.

1. Click the **Close** button (the empty square in the top-left corner of the window).
2. The window is closed.

Hold down the **Control** key and click in the window to select a variety of options for viewing the contents in the window.

You can close all **Finder** windows by holding down the **Option** key while clicking the **Close** box of any window.

Task 6: Collapsing a Window

Start Here

You can reduce (collapse) a window so that it is still available, but not displayed on the desktop. You might want to minimize a window to temporarily move it out of your way, but keep it active for later use.

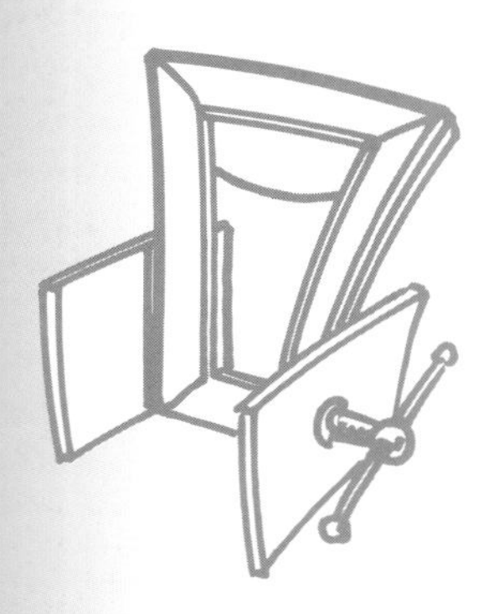

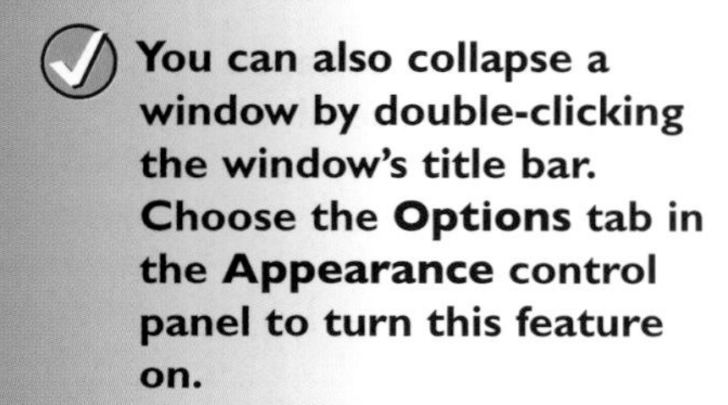
You can also collapse a window by double-clicking the window's title bar. Choose the **Options** tab in the **Appearance** control panel to turn this feature on.

1. Click the **Collapse** button in the window you want to minimize.

2. The bottom part of the window disappears, but the window's title bar remains visible.

End Task

Task 7: Uncollapsing a Window

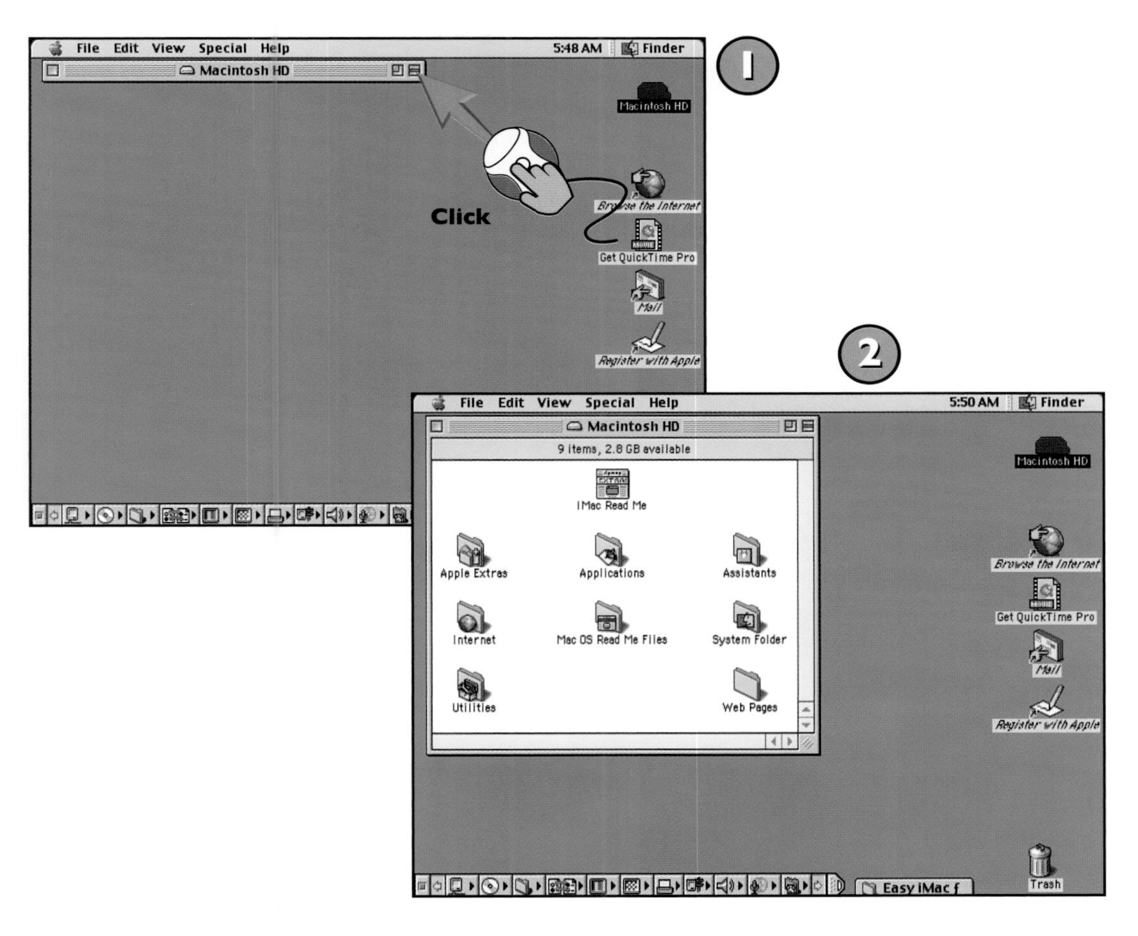

You can enlarge (uncollapse) a window so that it reopens to its original size.

1. Click the **Collapse** button.

2. The window enlarges to fill its original screen size.

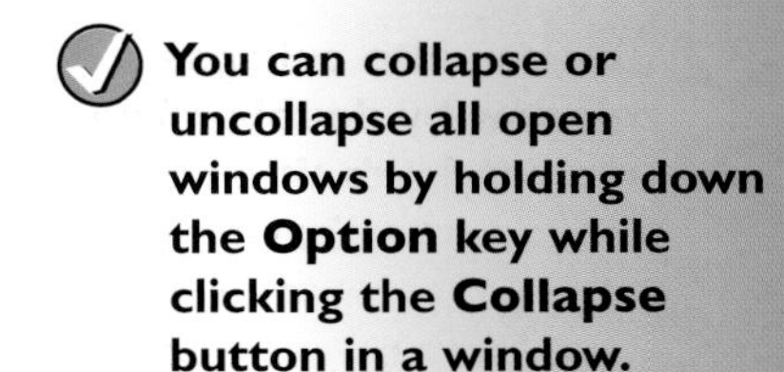

You can collapse or uncollapse all open windows by holding down the **Option** key while clicking the **Collapse** button in a window.

Task 8: Moving a Window

As you add more applications, folders, aliases, and so on to the desktop, you'll need more room to display these elements. You can easily move the windows around so you can view a full screen of window content.

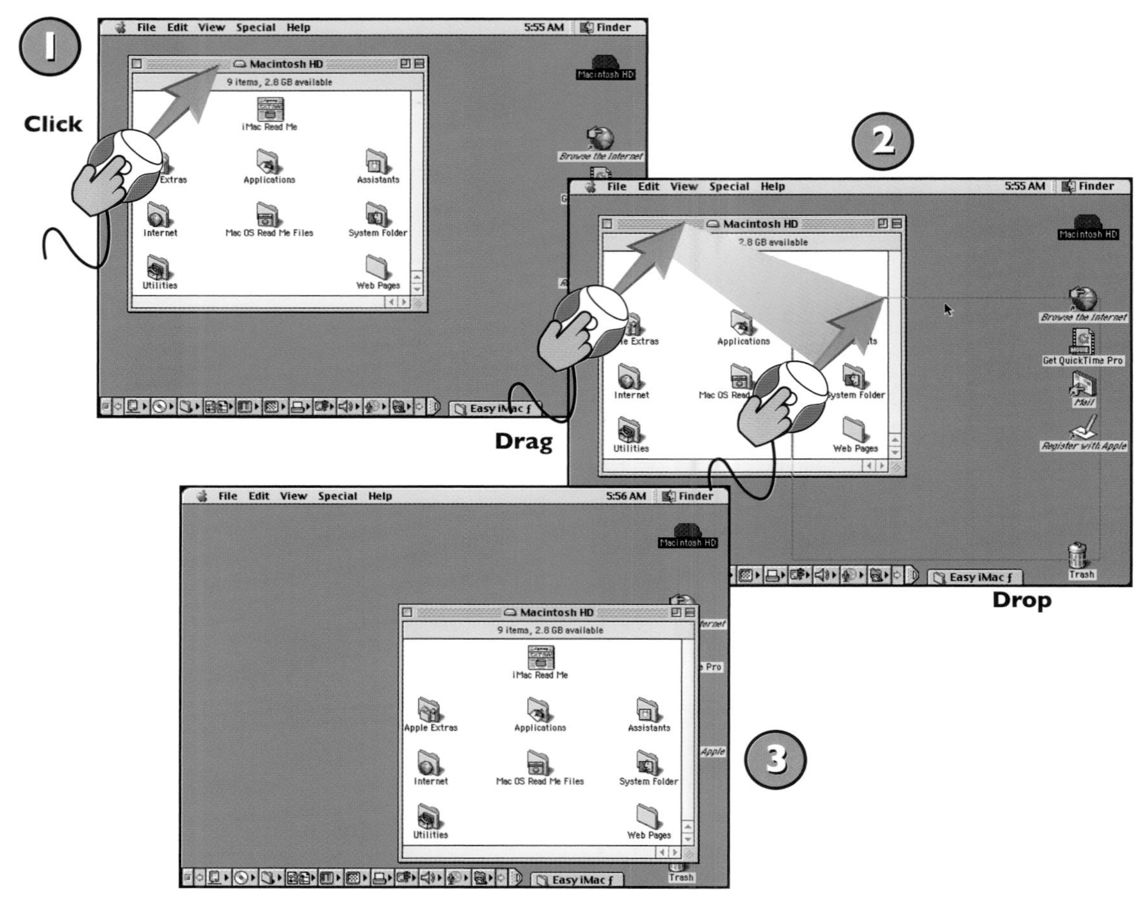

1. To move an open window, point to its title bar. Click and hold down the mouse button.
2. Drag the window to its new position. You can see the border of the window as you drag. Release the mouse button.
3. The window and its contents appear in the new location.

Be sure to point to the title bar when moving a window. If you point to any other area, you might resize the window instead of moving it.

Task 9: Resizing a Window

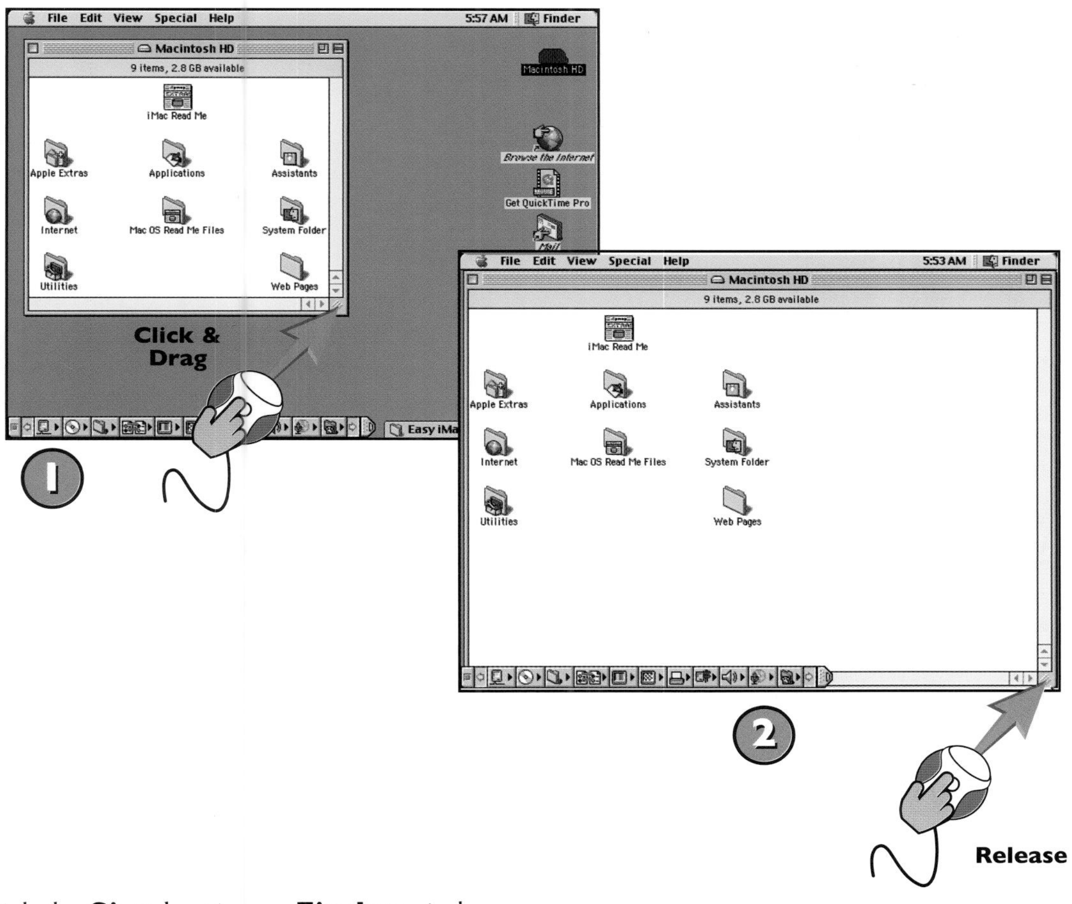

In addition to being able to move a window, you can resize a window to whatever size you want. Resizing windows is helpful if you want to view more than one window at the same time, or if you want to maximize a window to view as much of it as possible.

1. Click the **Size** box in any **Finder** window.

2. Drag the border to resize the window, and then release the mouse button. The window is resized.

Task 10: Restoring a Window

If you maximize a window, you can easily restore it to its original size. Restoring the window to a smaller size lets you view other windows in the background, or gain easy access to items on the desktop.

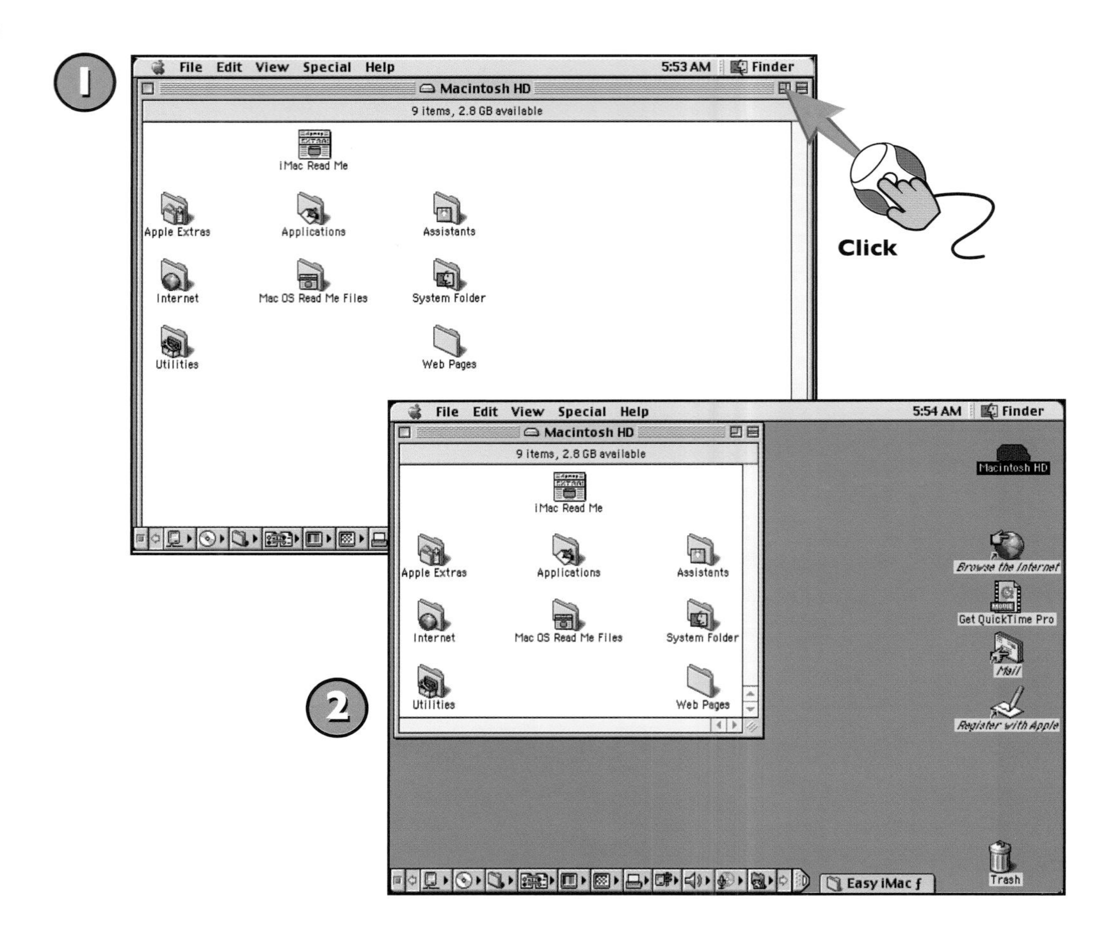

The first time you click the Zoom button, it will resize the window to show all window content at the smallest window size.

1. Click the **Zoom** button in a maximized window.
2. The window is restored.

Task 11: Scrolling a Window

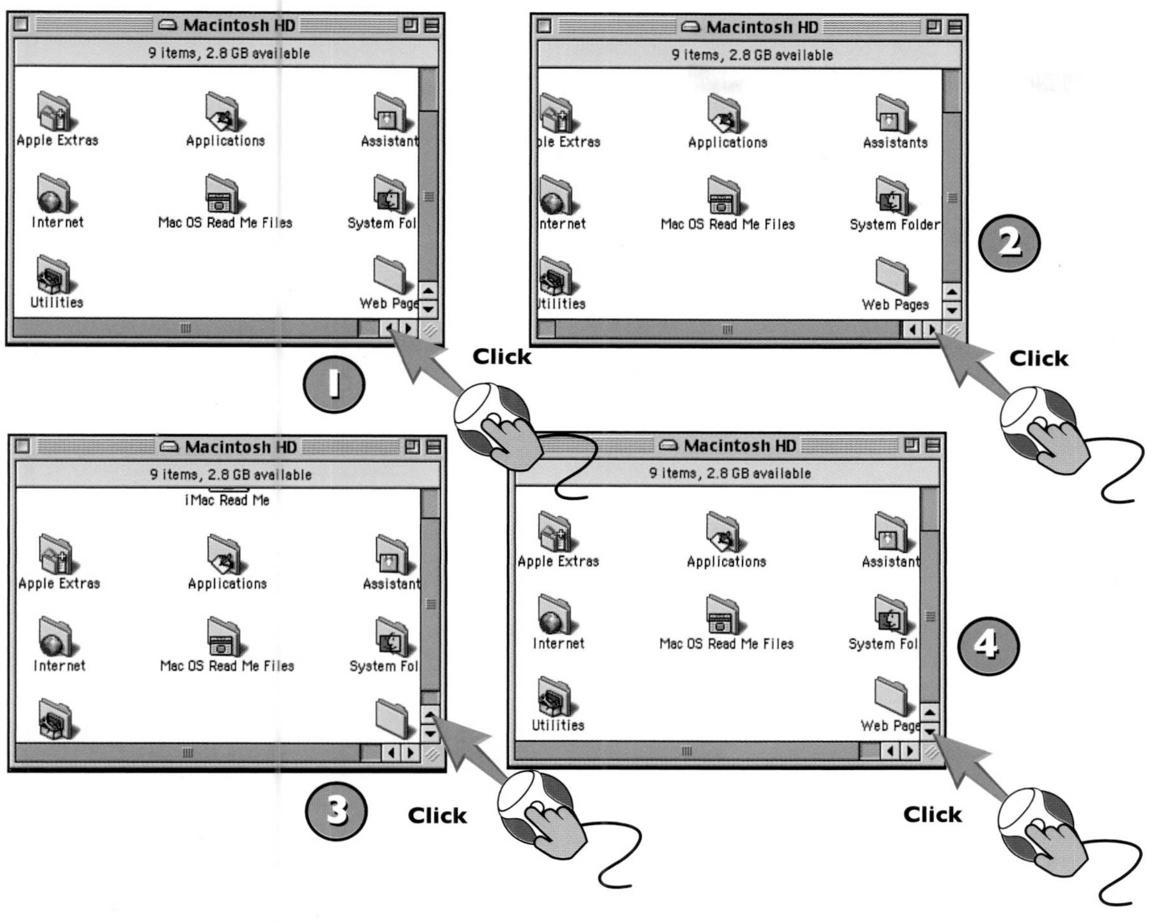

If a window is too small to show all its contents, horizontal and vertical scrollbars will appear along the edges of the window. You can use these bars to scroll through the window to see the other contents.

1. Click the left arrow to scroll left through the window.
2. Click the right arrow to scroll right through the window.
3. Click the up arrow to scroll up through the window.
4. Click the down arrow to scroll down through the window.

You can click anywhere in the scrollbar to jump in that direction to another part of the window. You can also click the scrollbar to scroll quickly through the window.

Task 12: Using Menus

Although you can perform many tasks by clicking the various onscreen objects, you must choose commands to perform the majority of Mac OS tasks. Commands are organized in menus to make them easy to find. Both Mac OS and its applications have a menu bar; each menu then contains a group of related commands.

The menu bar lets you customize Mac OS settings, get help, and more. The menu bar, located at the top of the screen, contains the **Apple**, **File**, **Edit**, **View**, **Special**, and **Help** menus.

✓ Selecting a command that is followed by an arrow displays a submenu. Clicking a command that is followed by an ellipsis will display a dialog box.

✓ To close a menu without making a selection, press the **Esc** key on your keyboard or click outside the menu.

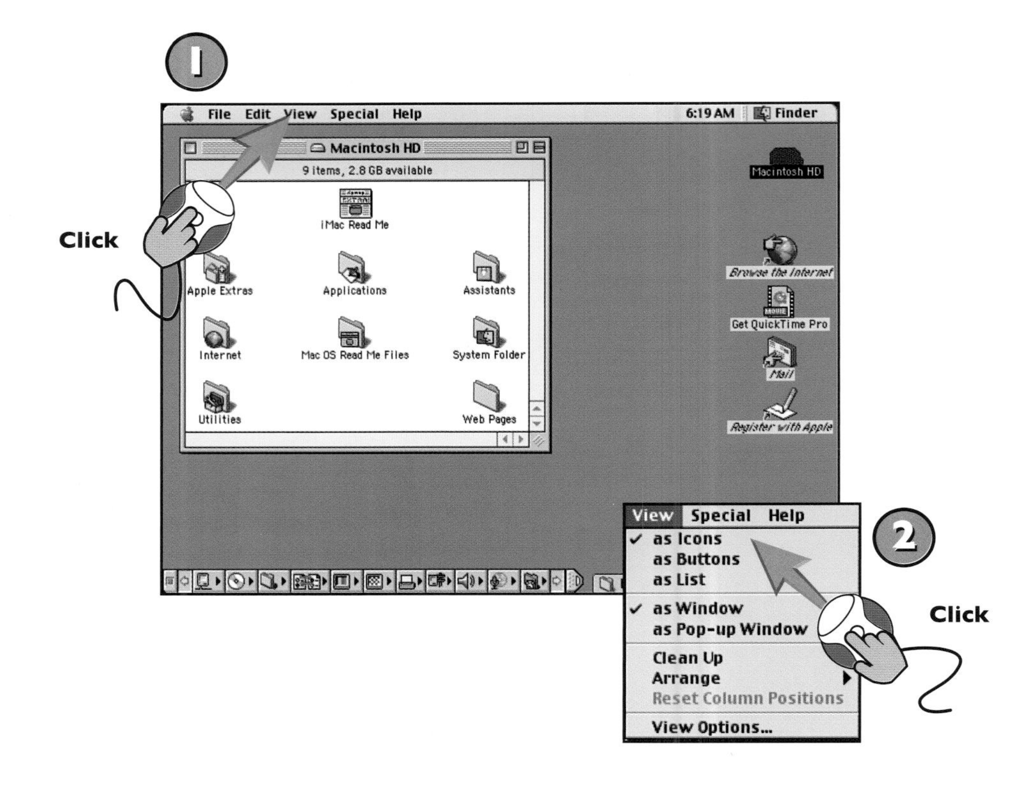

1. In the menu bar, click the menu name (in this case, the menu name is **View**).
2. Click the command you want.

Task 13: Using Context Menus

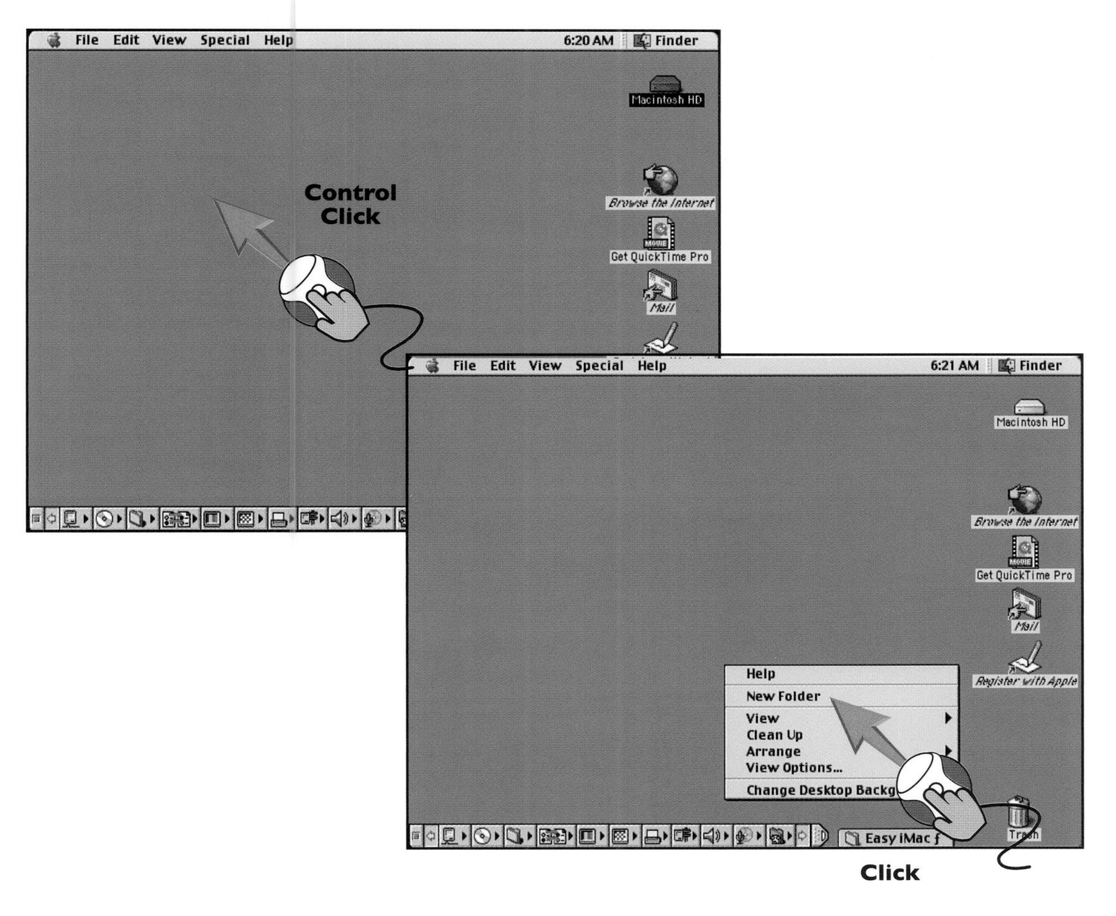

Contextual menus, also called context menus, shortcut menus, quick menus, and pop-up menus, provide common commands related to the selected item. You can, for example, quickly copy and paste, create a new folder, move a file, or rearrange icons using a contextual menu.

Hold down the **Ctrl** key and click the item for which you want to display a contextual menu. For instance, **Ctrl**+click any blank part of the desktop.

Click the command you want in the contextual menu.

Different context menus appear depending on what you're pointing to when you control-click the mouse.

Task 14: Arranging Windows on the Desktop

Start Here

As you work, you will often have several windows open on the desktop at one time. These windows will probably overlap, which can make it difficult to find what you want. To make your work easier and more efficient, Mac OS enables you to arrange the windows on the desktop in several different ways.

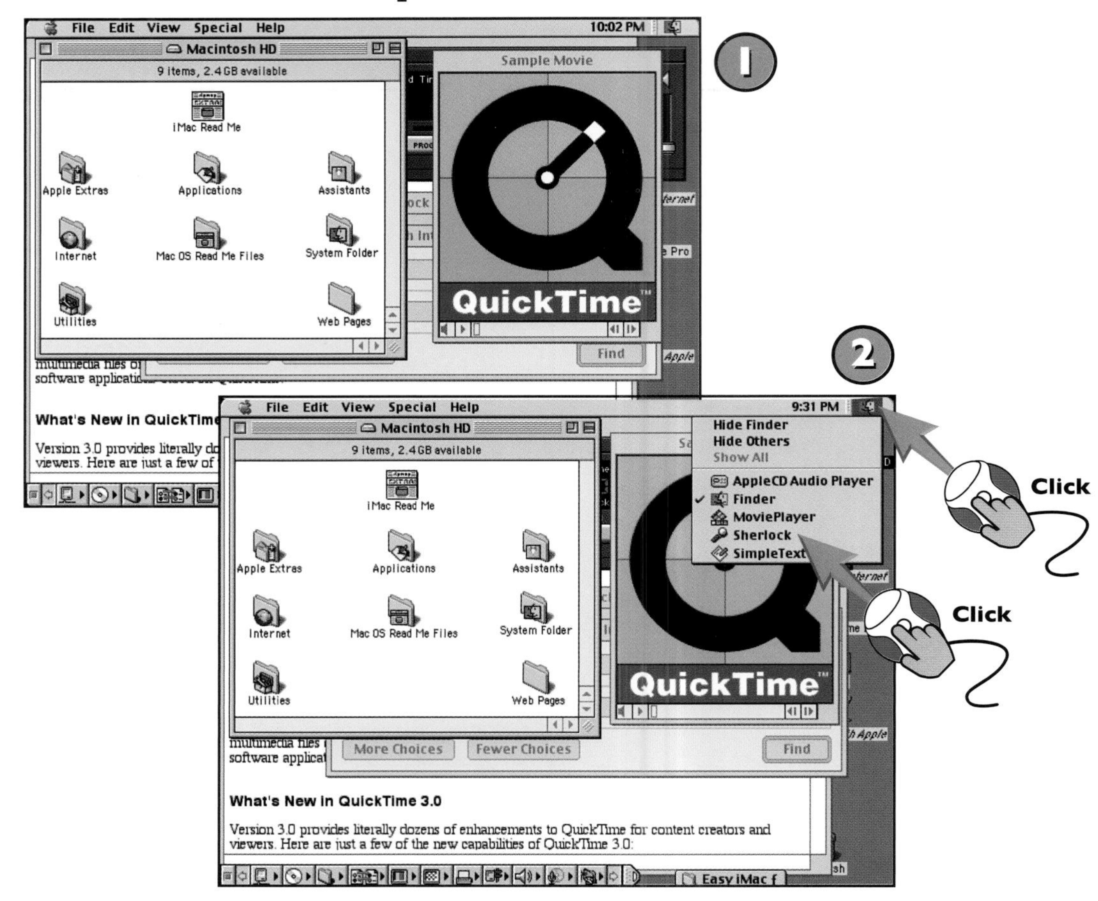

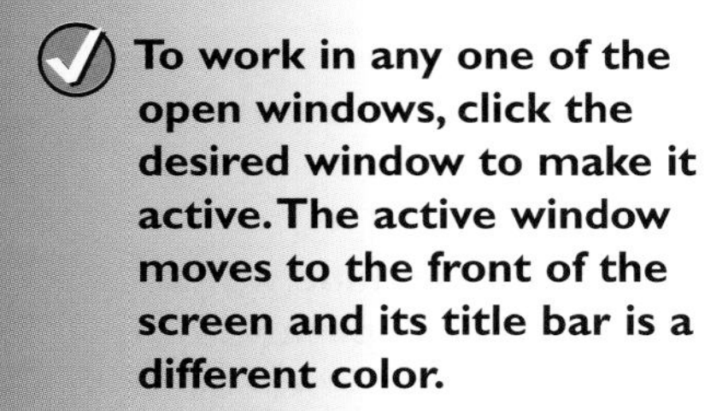

- **To work in any one of the open windows, click the desired window to make it active. The active window moves to the front of the screen and its title bar is a different color.**

- **Be sure to use the window's title bar to move a window.**

1. Open multiple windows on the desktop.

2. Open the **Applications** menu and select the application you want.

3

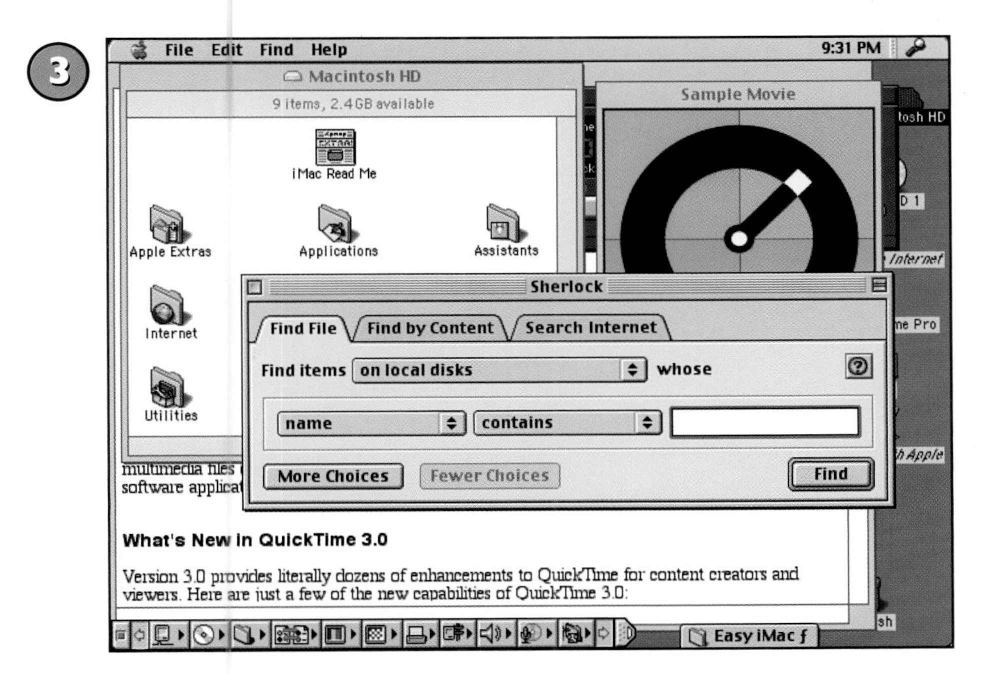

3 The window and the application you selected move to the front of the screen.

You can hide windows of other applications by selecting **Hide others** from the **Applications** menu.

Task 15: Using a Dialog Box or Control Panel

Start Here

When you choose certain commands, a dialog box prompts you for additional information about how to carry out the command. Dialog boxes are used throughout Mac OS; luckily all dialog boxes have common elements and all work in a similar way.

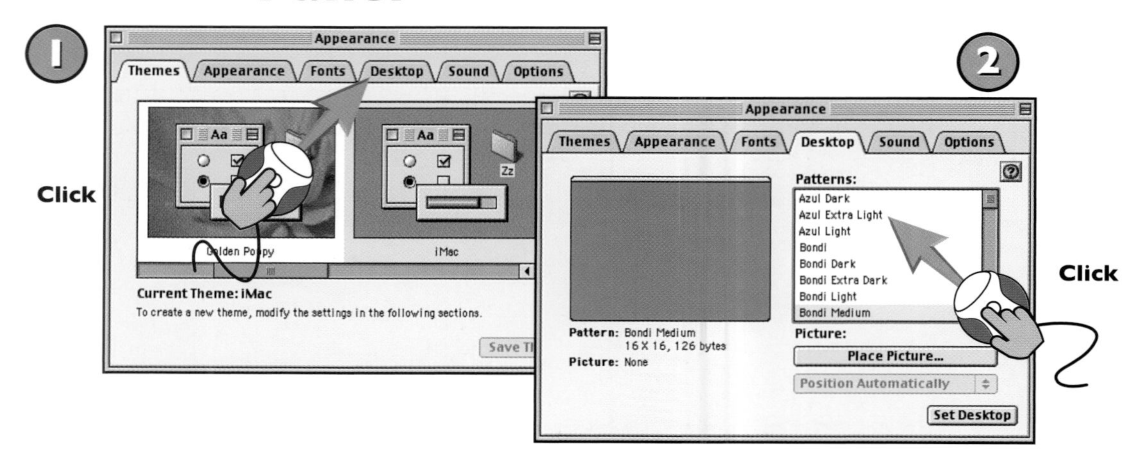

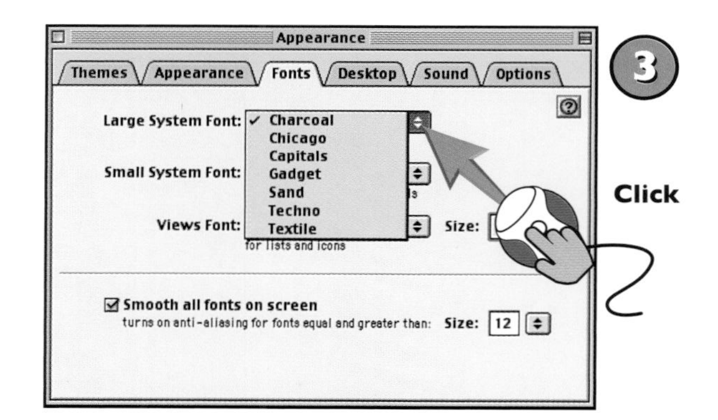

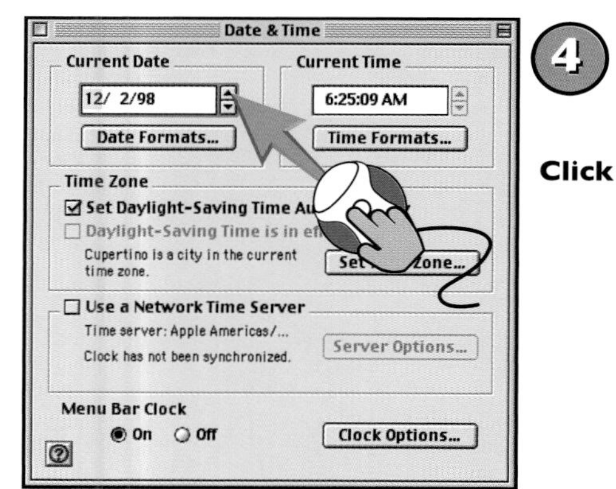

- Different dialog boxes will have different options. The figures in this section are meant to show the types of items you might find in a dialog box.
- Control panels differ from dialog boxes; settings are saved in control panels when the control panel window is closed.

1. To view a tab, click it.
2. To use a list box, scroll through the list and click the item you want to select.
3. To use a drop-down list box, click the arrow to the side of the box and then select the desired item from the list.
4. To use a spin box, click the arrows to increment or decrement the value or type a value in the text box.

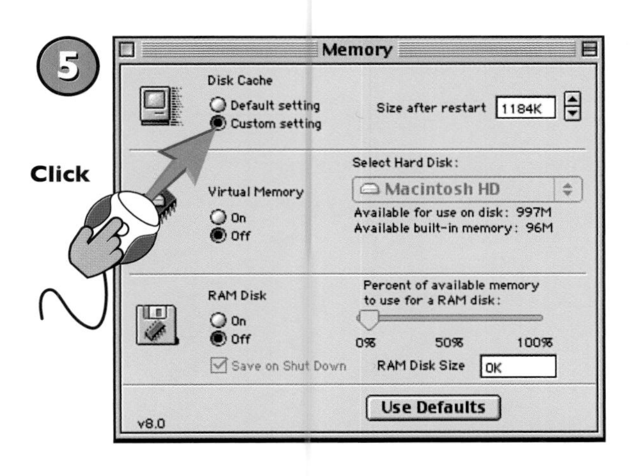

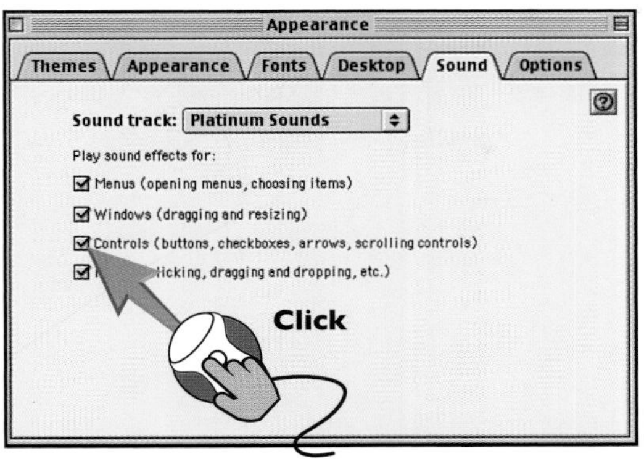

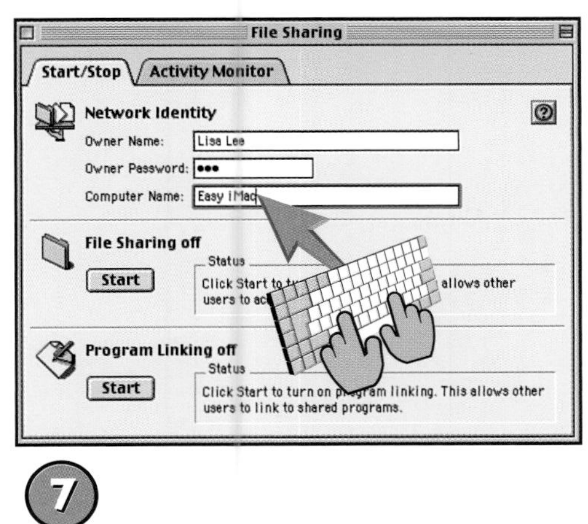

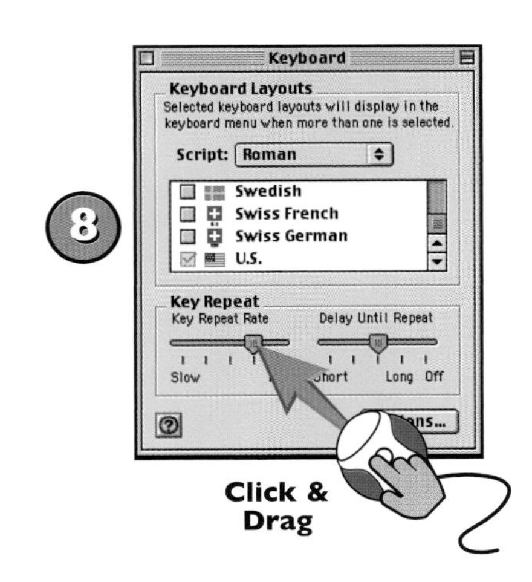

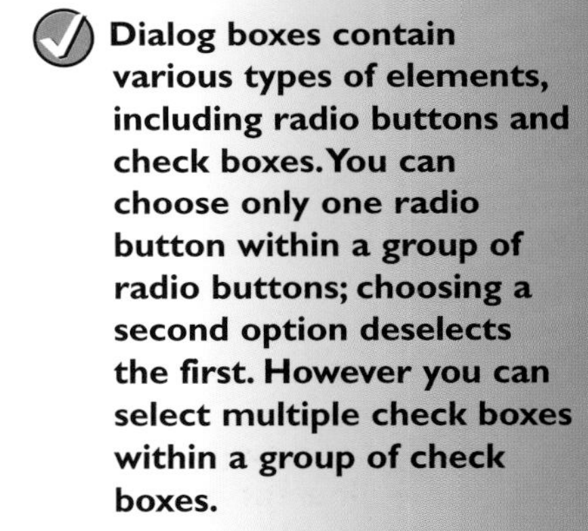

Dialog boxes contain various types of elements, including radio buttons and check boxes. You can choose only one radio button within a group of radio buttons; choosing a second option deselects the first. However you can select multiple check boxes within a group of check boxes.

When a dialog box is open, you cannot perform any other action until you accept any changes by clicking the OK button. To close the dialog box without making a selection, click the Cancel button.

5. Click a radio button to activate it.
6. Click a check box to select it (or to deselect a check box that is already checked).
7. Type an entry in a text box.
8. Click and drag a slider to select a different setting.

Task 16: Looking Up a Help Topic with Mac OS Help

Use the **Help** menu to locate help for performing specific procedures with your iMac, such as printing a document or playing QuickTime movies.

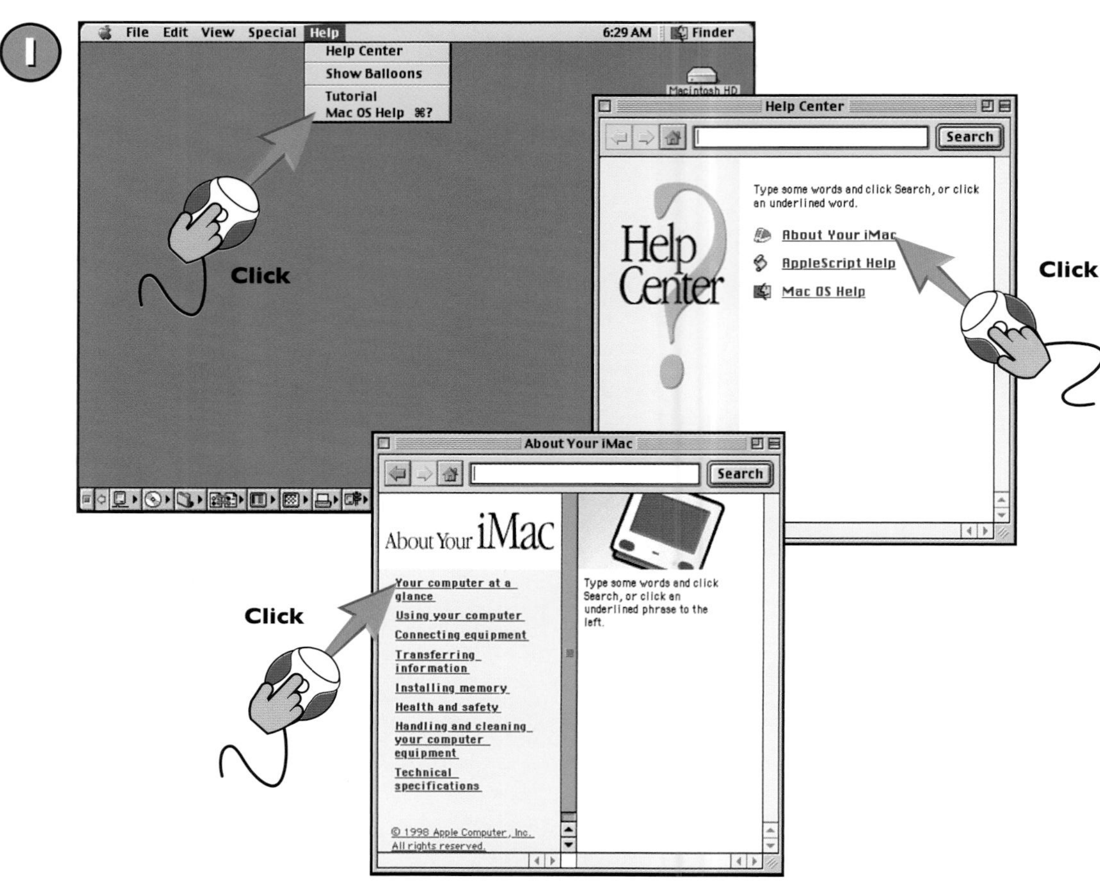

1. Open the **Help** menu and select **Mac OS Help**.
2. Select help category that seems most relevant to your needs (in this case, click **About Your iMac**).
3. Narrow your search by clicking an appropriate help topic (for now, click **Your computer at a glance**).

- Select **File | Print** to print a help topic.
- You can click any of the underlined text in the help area to display a definition of that term or to display related help information.

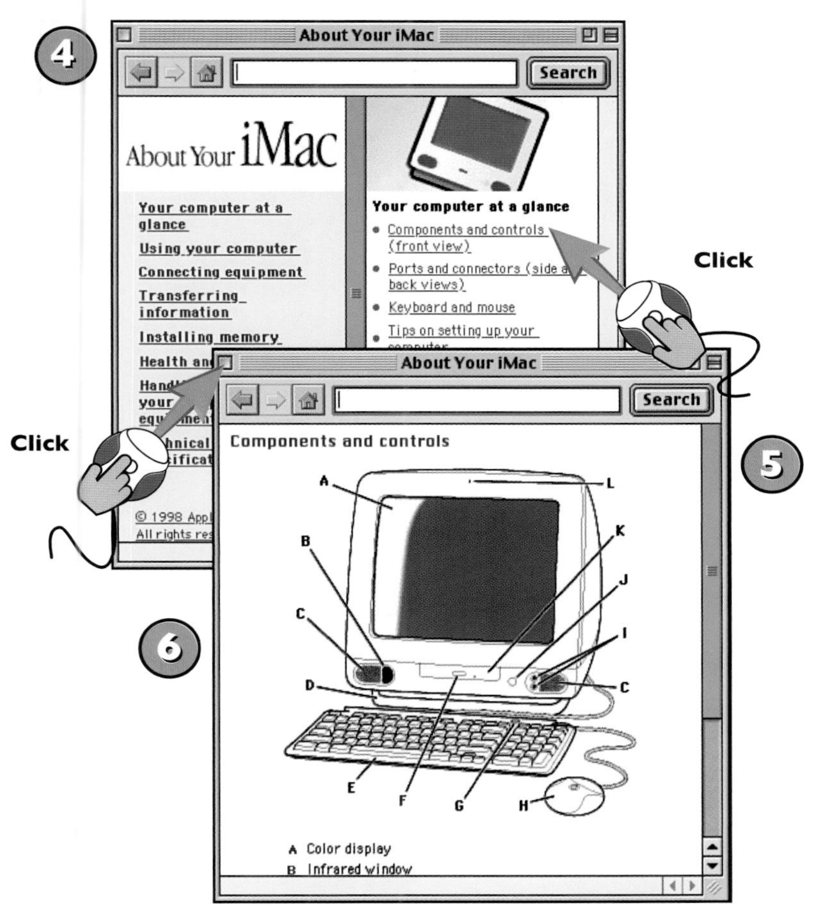

4. The pane on the right lists specific help articles; click the entry labeled **Components and controls (front view)**.

5. Review the help information.

6. Click the **Close** button to close the **Help** window.

Task 17: Searching for a Help Topic

If you don't find the topic in the main help window, try searching for it. The iMac will display a list of topics that contain what you are looking for; you can then select the one you want.

Start Here

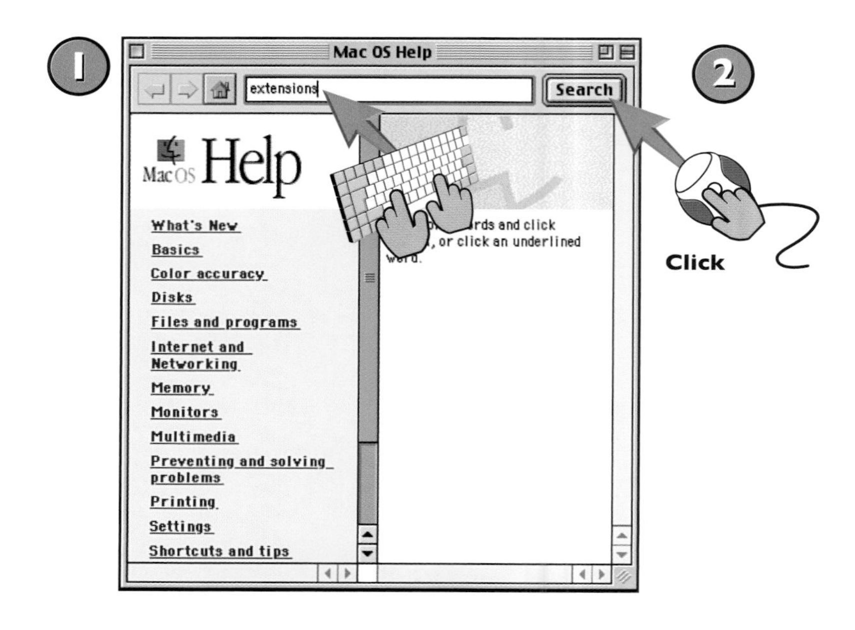

The iMac help function works in the same way throughout most applications. If you master help basics, you can apply these same skills to other applications.

1. Type one or more words that relate to the topic about which you want to find information.
2. Click the **Search** button in the **Help** window.

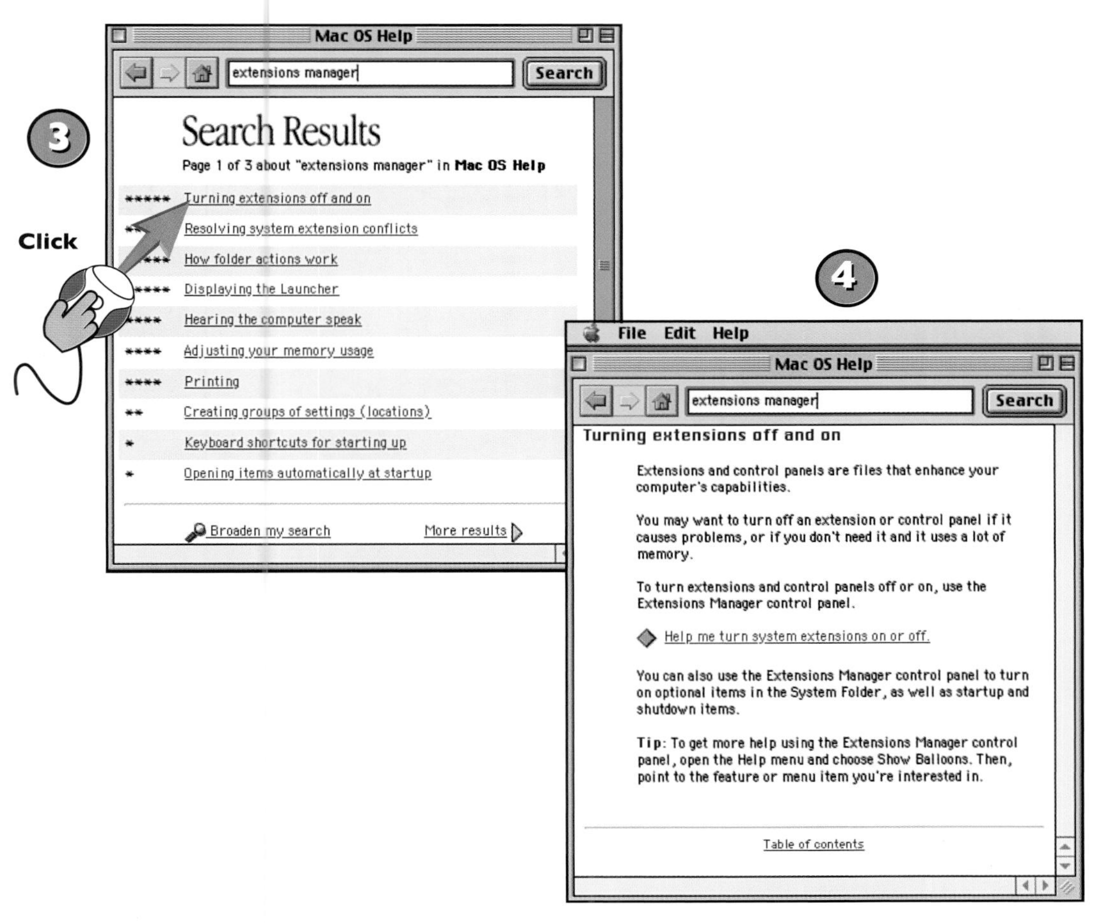

3. Click a promising-looking topic in the **Help** window

4. Review the information in the **Help** window

Task 18: Looking Up a Help Topic with Sherlock

If you want to find help on a topic via the Internet, such as the latest iMac troubleshooting tips, use Sherlock (of course, to use Sherlock to search the Internet, you must be connected to the Internet via a network connection or via an ISP).

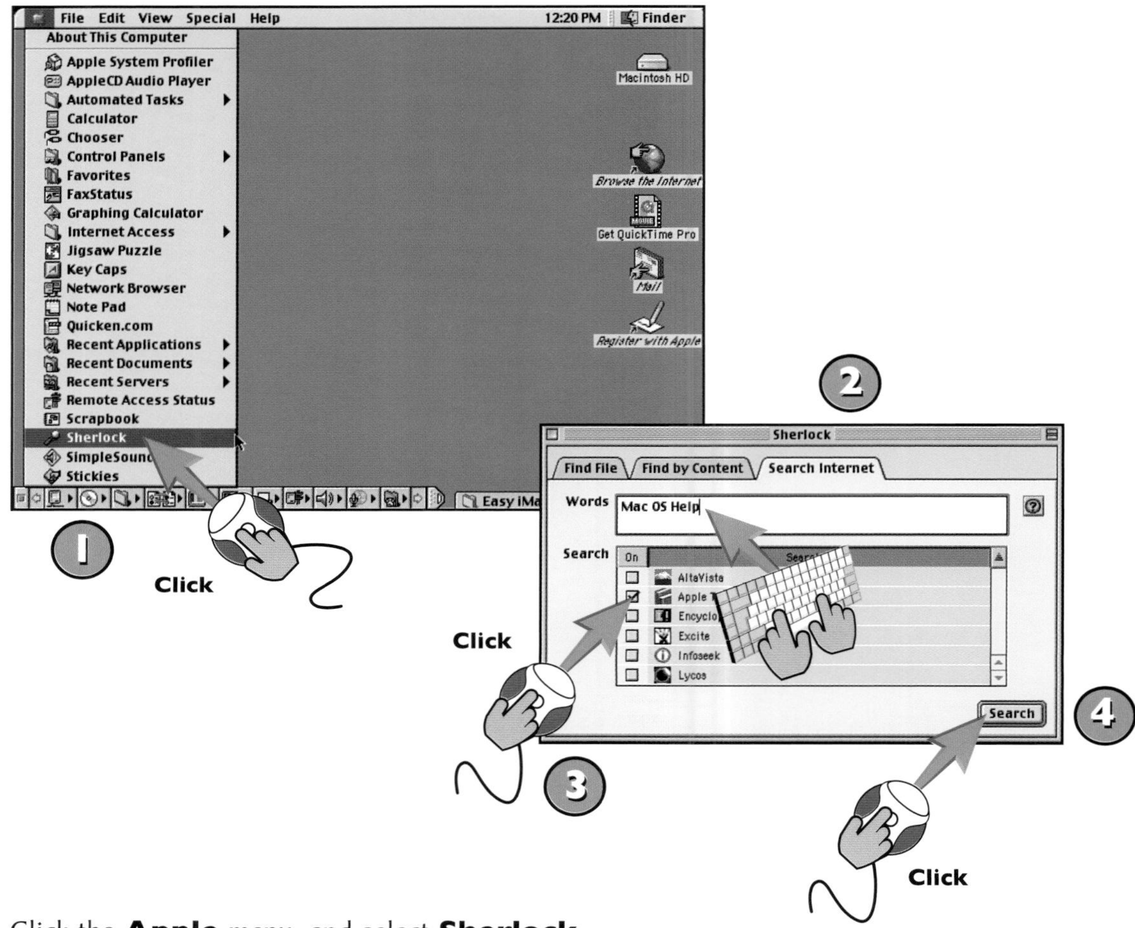

✓ **You can extend Sherlock's searching capabilities by adding plug-ins available at Apple's Web site (http://www.apple.com).**

! **You need to have Mac OS 8.5 to use Sherlock.**

1. Click the **Apple** menu, and select **Sherlock**.
2. Type one or more words that relate to the topic about which you want to find information (in this case, I've typed **Mac OS Help**).
3. Click the **Apple Tech Info Library** check box.
4. Click the **Search** button.

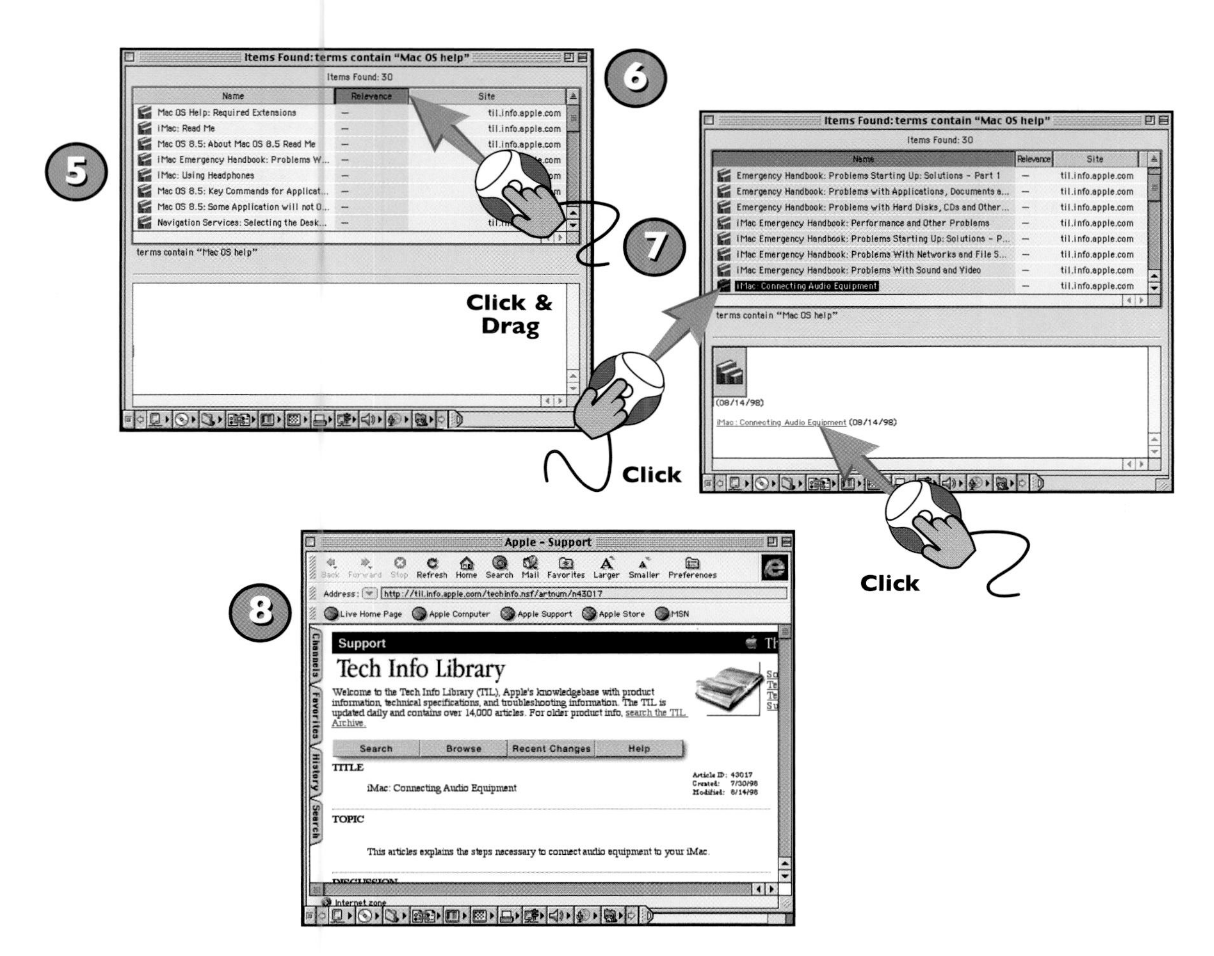

5 Review the results of the search.

6 Resize any column in the results window by dragging the edge of the column heading.

7 Click an entry in the list box (in this case, I've clicked the **iMac Connecting Audio Equipment** link), and then click a link in the bottom pane.

8 Review the selected information in Internet Explorer.

Task 19: Getting Context-Sensitive Help

When you open a window or control panel, you might not know what each of the options does. If you have questions about an option, you can view a description of that option by following the steps in this task.

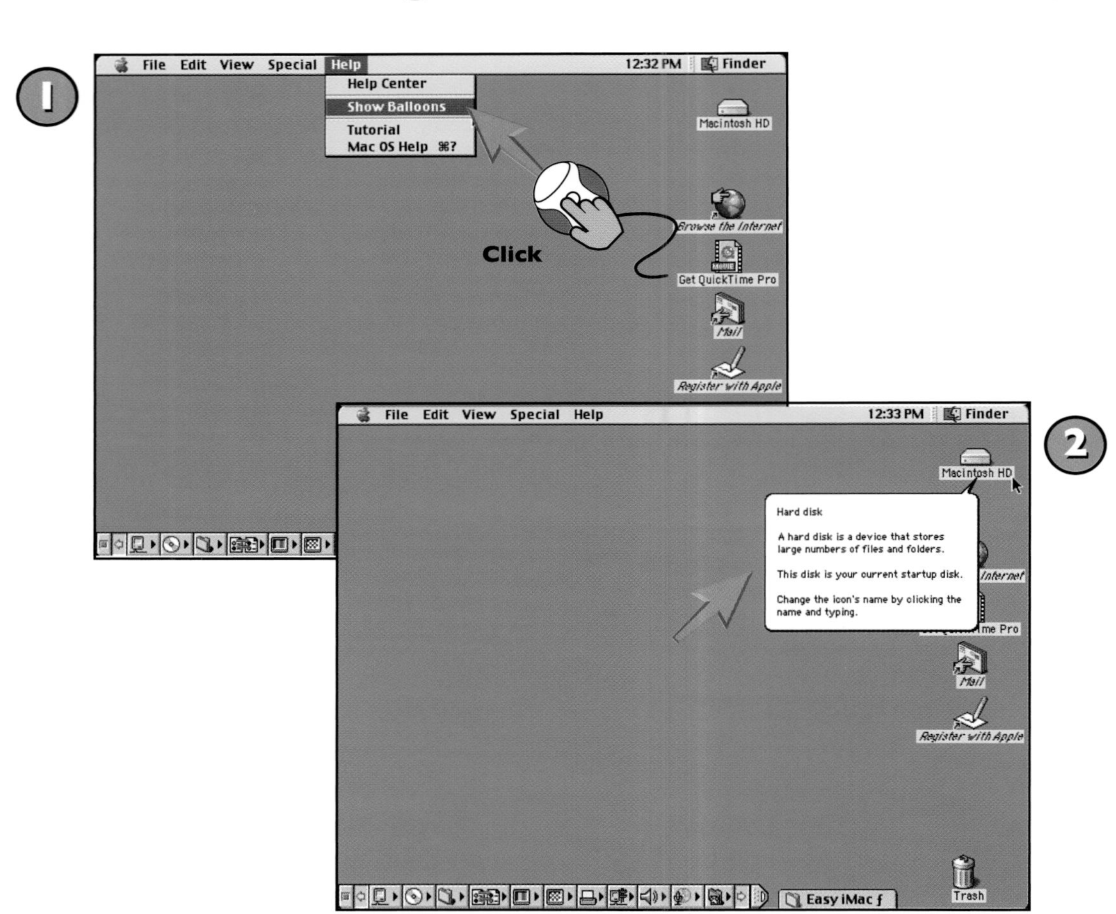

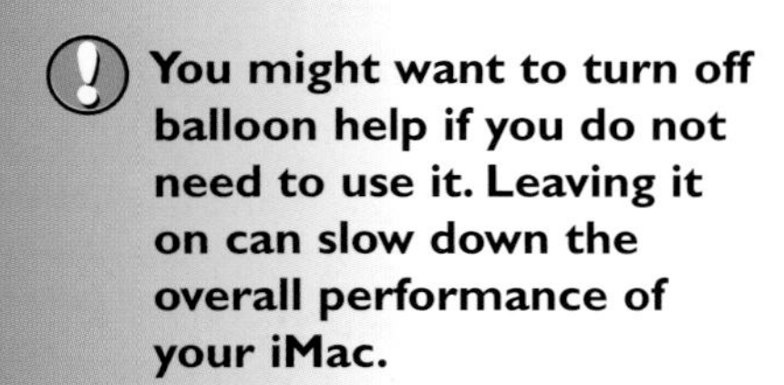

You might want to turn off balloon help if you do not need to use it. Leaving it on can slow down the overall performance of your iMac.

1. Select **Show Balloons** in the **Help** menu.

2. Move the mouse over an icon or window element (in this case, the hard drive icon). Review the information in the help balloon.

Task 20: Shutting Down the iMac

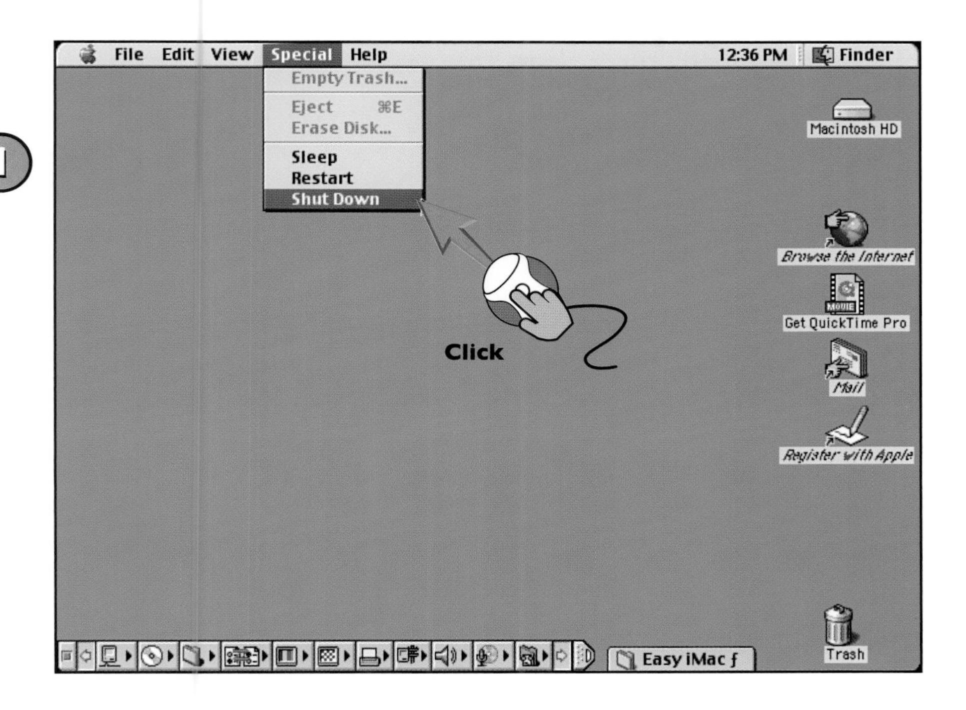

If you turn off the power to your computer before you properly shut the computer down, you could lose valuable data or damage an open file. Mac OS provides a safe shutdown feature that checks for open programs and files, and warns you to save unsaved files. You should always shut down before you turn off the power.

After you've closed down all open programs, click **Special**, then **Shut Down**.

- If you are installing software, or if you do not want to power off the computer completely, select **Restart** from the **Special** menu.
- You can also use the **Power** key to bring up a dialog to enable you to shut down or restart your iMac.

PART 2

Connecting to Online Services and the Internet

If you have an Internet connection and an account with an Internet service provider (ISP), you can venture beyond your iMac to resources available from online services, such as America Online, or from the Internet. America Online 4 is pre-installed in your iMac's Internet folder. Your iMac also provides Internet Explorer 4, a Web browser that offers you complete and convenient browsing for the Internet. As with any browser software, you can use Internet Explorer to view World Wide Web pages, to search for specific topics, and to download and upload files. In addition to browsing the Web, you can use Internet Explorer 4's mail application installed with Internet Explorer 4.01 and 4.5, Outlook Express, to exchange email messages with others who are connected to the Internet. You can also use Outlook Express to participate in newsgroups.

Tasks

Task 1: Connecting to AOL

Start Here

America Online (AOL) is the most popular online service company. AOL provides content, bulletin boards, email, and other services for subscribers. You can also access the Internet through AOL. iMac conveniently enables you to try out America Online; you'll find AOL in you iMac's **Internet** folder.

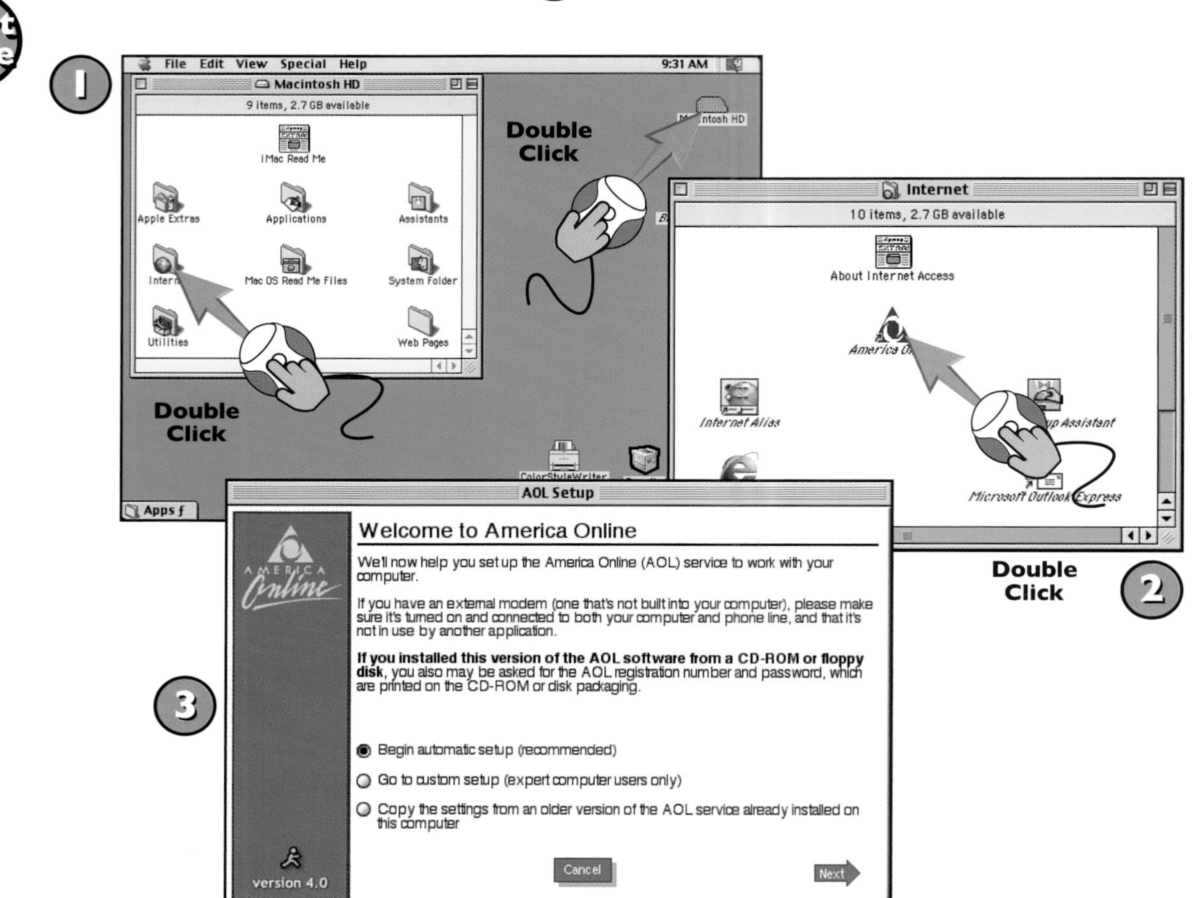

- You can cancel the setup at any time by clicking the **Cancel** button.
- AOL, like most online providers, offers a free trial subscription. After that subscription expires, you must pay for the service. Be sure you understand all the fees involved before you sign up.
- You can have up to five different login names with one AOL account.

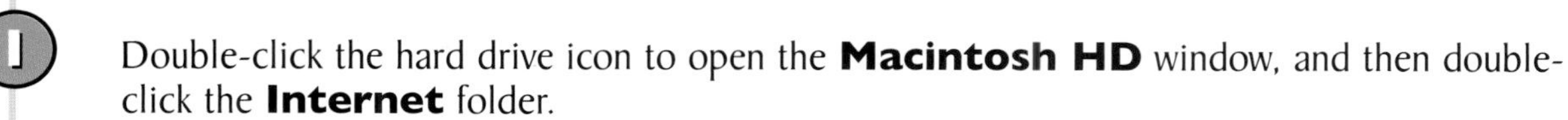

1. Double-click the hard drive icon to open the **Macintosh HD** window, and then double-click the **Internet** folder.
2. Double-click the **America Online** icon.
3. Follow the onscreen instructions to create a new account.

Task 2: Connecting to Apple's Web Site

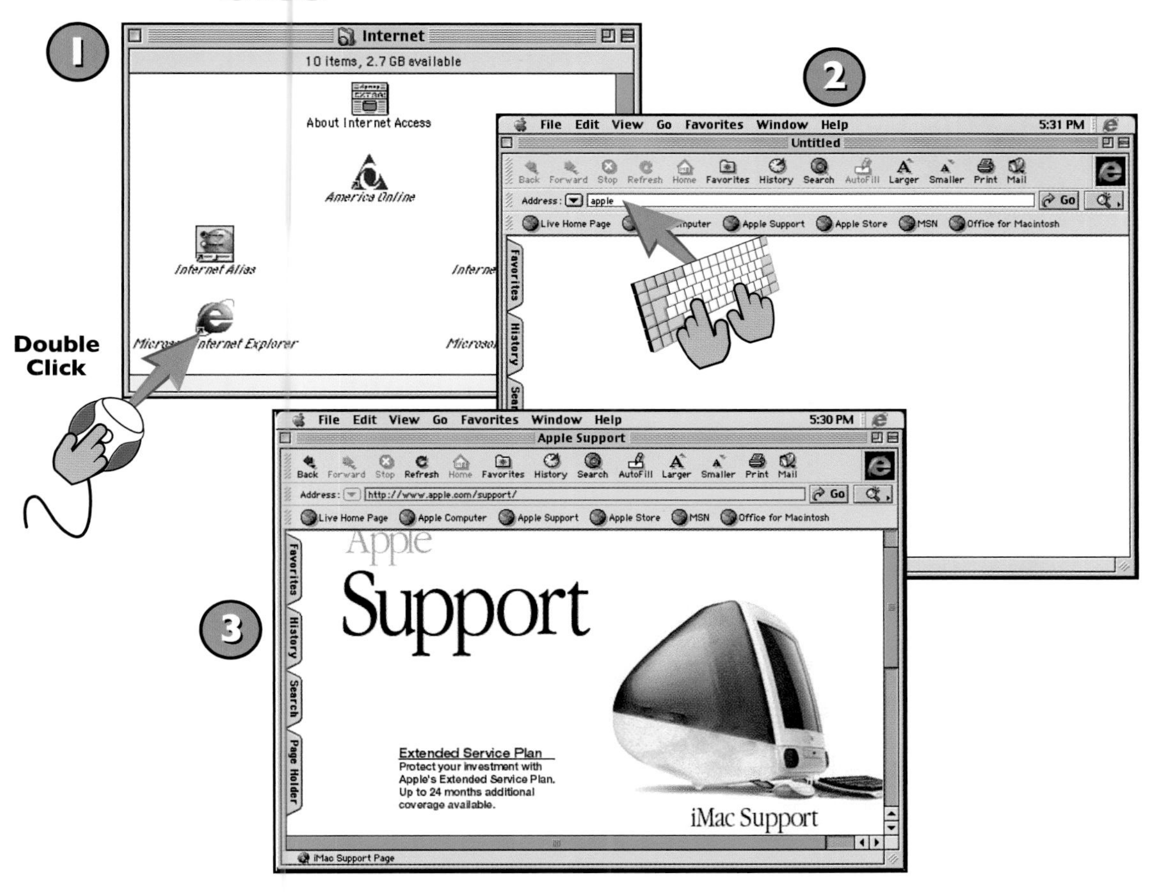

As you browse the Internet, you will probably need to visit Apple's Web site for support, new product information, developer information, or to download a software update for your iMac.

1. Double-click the **Microsoft Internet Explorer** icon in the **Internet** window (to access the **Internet** window, see the previous task).
2. Type **`apple`** in the **Address** field, and then press **Return**.
3. After Apple's Web page loads, click the **Support** link.

For support information about iMac, go to http://www.apple.com/support.

Task 3: Setting Up for the Internet

Start Here

To explore the Internet, you must have a modem and an Internet connection. You can get this connection through an online provider such as America Online, or you can get an account from an independent Internet service provider (ISP). Before you can take advantage of all the benefits of the Internet, you have to get your Internet connection set up.

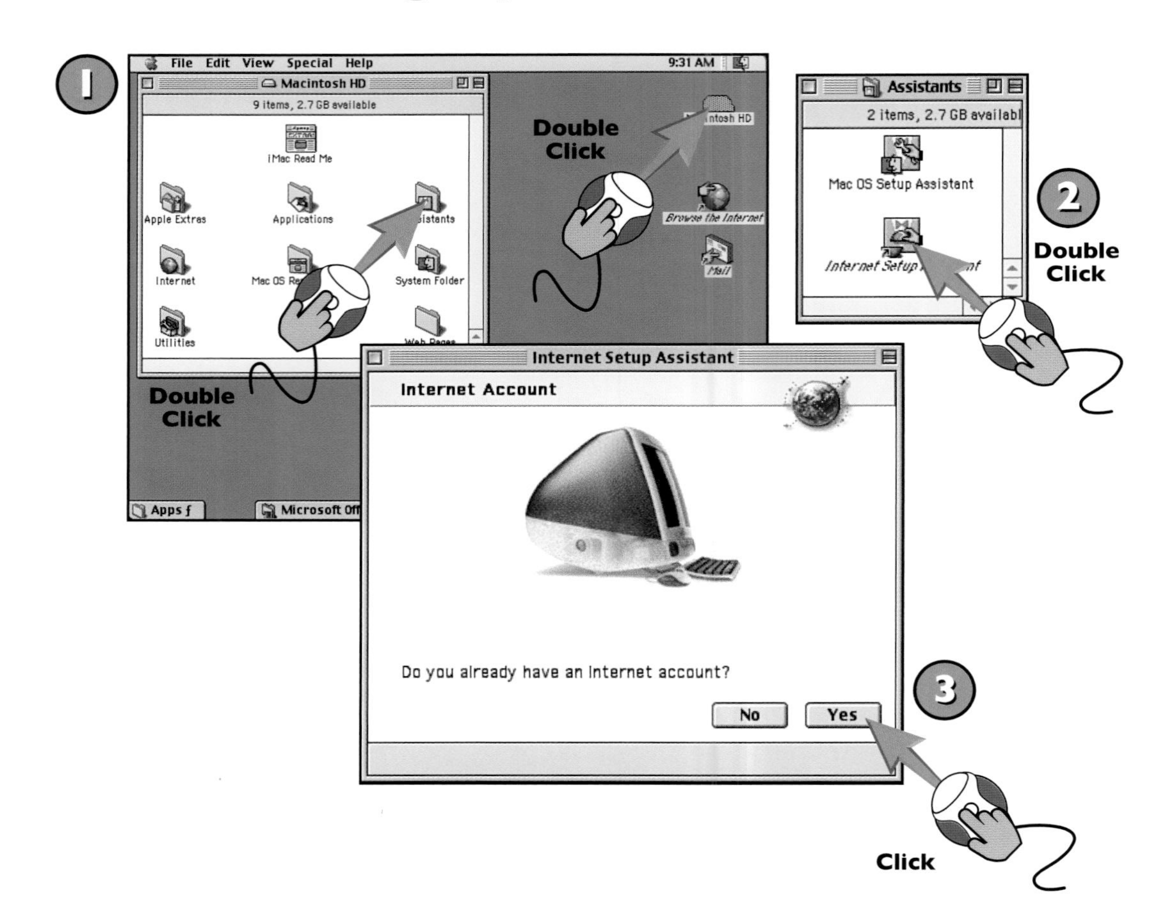

This task assumes that you already have an Internet account from an Internet service provider such as EarthLink, Netcom, Best, or AT&T. If you do not have an ISP and you want Mac OS to find one for you, choose **No** when asked **Do you already have an Internet account?** Apple recommends using EarthLink, which lets your iMac's 56Kbps modem connect to the Internet at the fastest possible rate.

1. Double-click the hard drive icon to open the **Macintosh HD** window, and then double-click the **Assistants** folder.
2. Double-click the **Internet Setup Assistant** icon.
3. Click **Yes** button on the first and second screens of the Assistant.

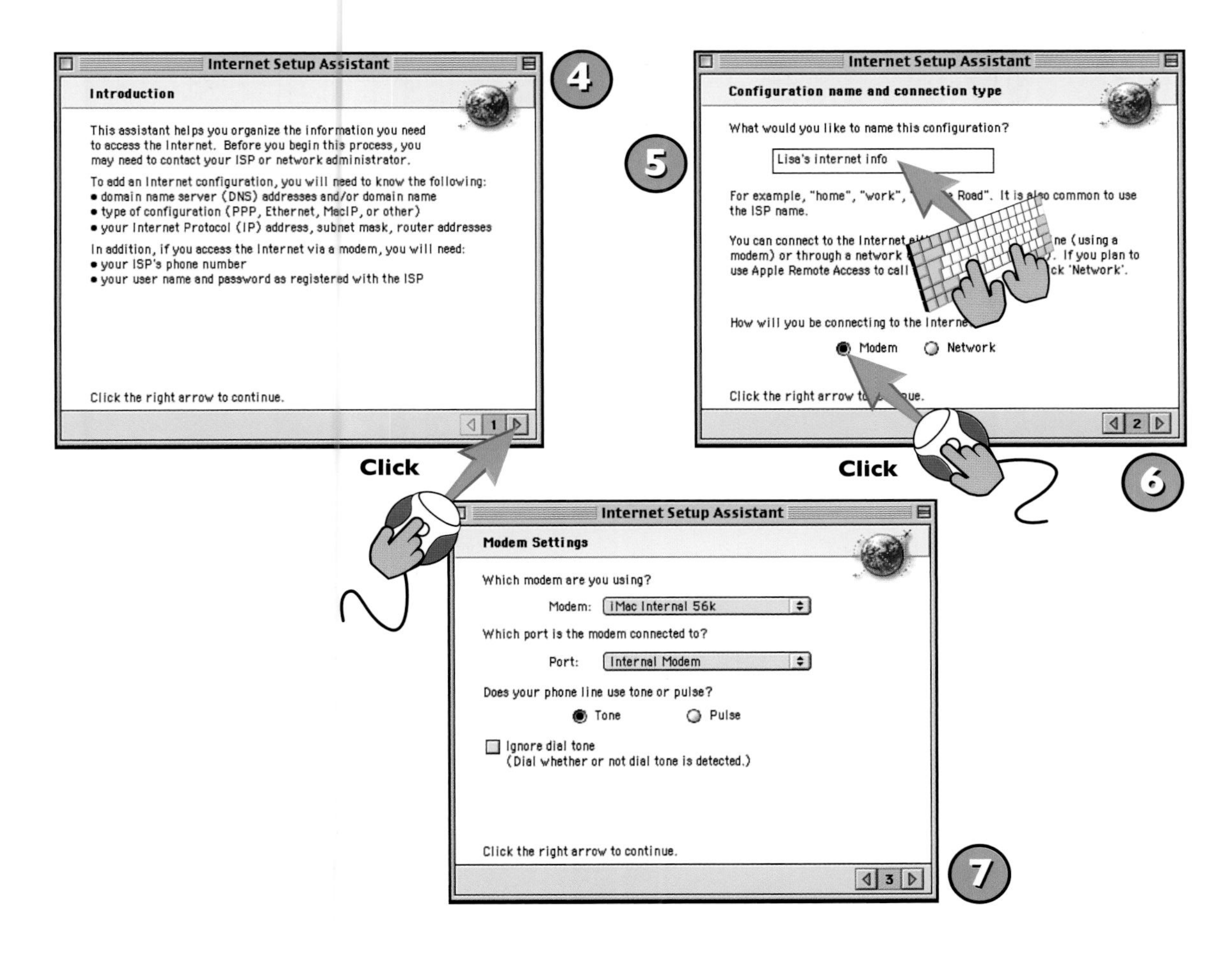

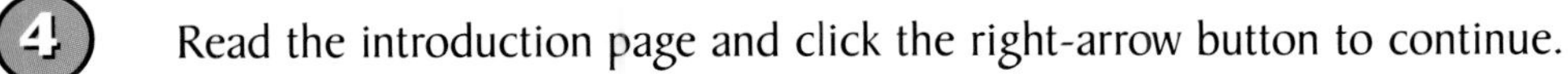

4. Read the introduction page and click the right-arrow button to continue.

5. Type a name for your Internet configuration (it can be anything you like).

6. Click the **Modem** radio button (unless you're connecting via a network), and then click the right-arrow button to continue.

7. Adjust the modem configuration by selecting the appropriate settings from the pop-up menus, and then click the right-arrow button to continue.

If you don't have an ISP, click No on the first screen of the Setup Assistant. Total Access will start automatically; see the next task for more information.

Be sure to compare pricing and services when selecting an ISP.

If you are trying to decide whether to use a particular ISP, consider the following:

- **Does it provide local phone number access?**
- **Does it provide 800 number access?**
- **Does it provide an email account?**
- **How reliable is its support?**
- **Does it provide free space for your own Web site?**
- **Does it provide any custom content or services on its Web site?**
- **Does it provide any software extras?**

Task 3: Continued

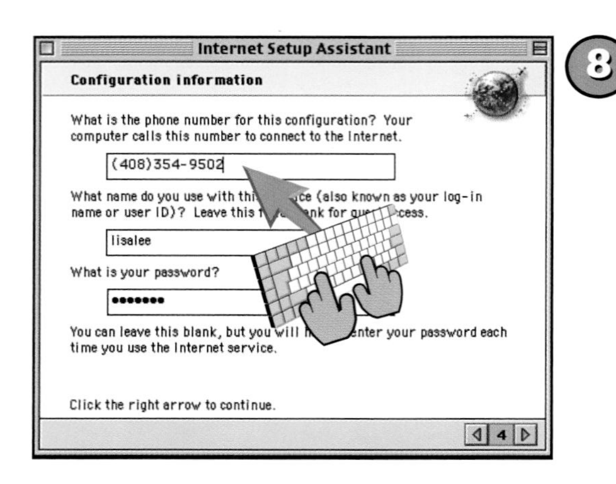

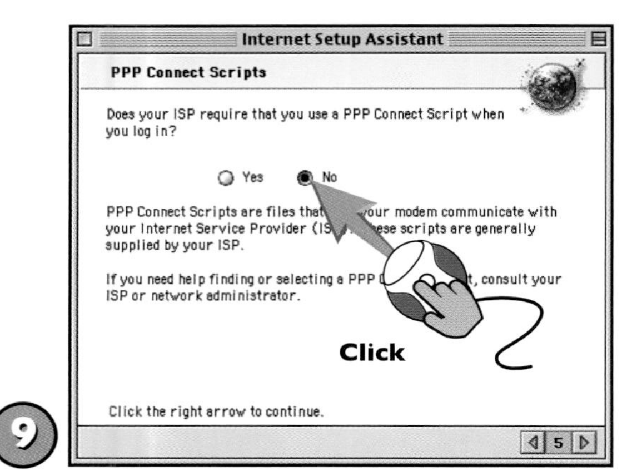

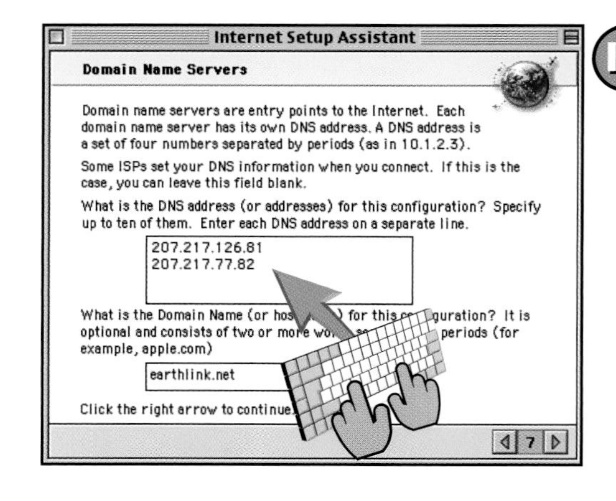

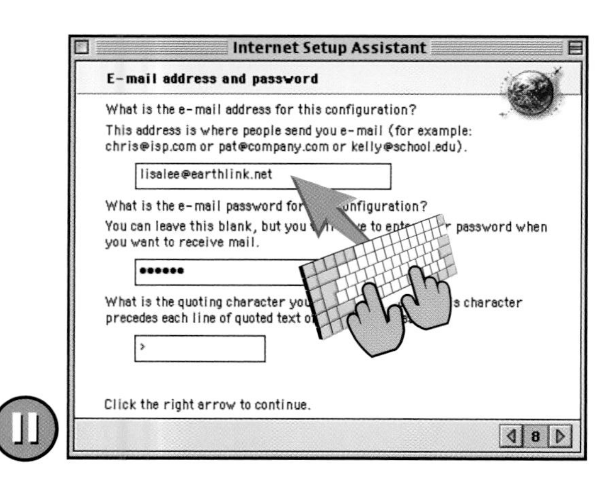

If your phone line requires a prefix (for instance, if you have to dial a 9 to reach an outside line), add the prefix to the phone number in the **Configuration Information** page of the Internet Setup Assistant.

You can quit the Internet Setup Assistant at any time by clicking **Cancel.** However, none of the data you entered will be saved unless you complete the Assistant. Luckily, you can go through the setup process more than once.

8. Type the phone number, user name, and password information for your ISP, and then click the right-arrow button to continue.

9. If your ISP requires a **PPP Connect Script** click **Yes**. (My ISP does not, so I have chosen **No**. Check with your ISP about this.) Click the right-arrow button to continue.

10. Type at least two DNS addresses and the domain name server name. (Get this information from your ISP.) Click the right-arrow button to continue.

11. If your ISP has provided you with an email account, type the appropriate information in the text fields. Click the right-arrow button to continue.

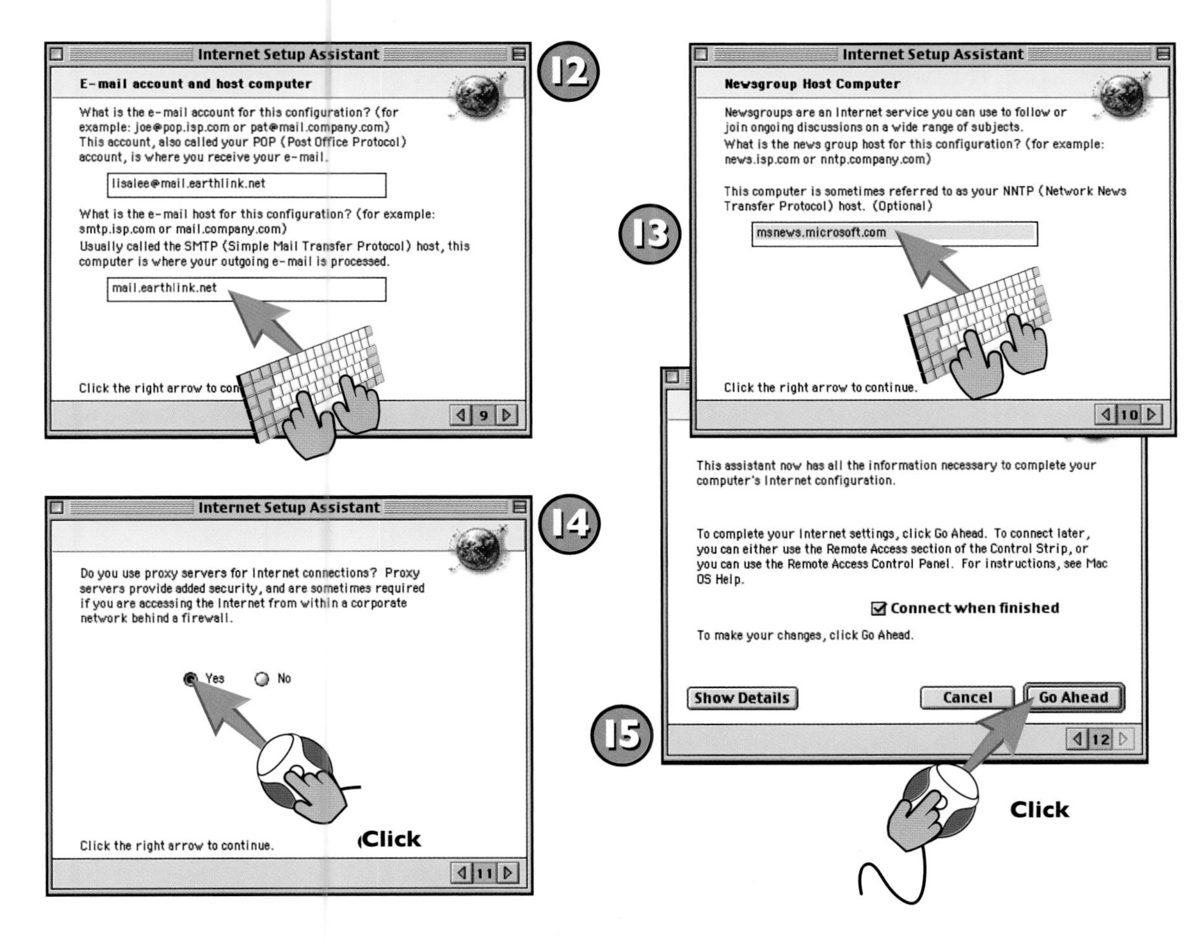

12 Type the email host information (in this case, **mail.earthlink.net**). Click the right-arrow button to continue.

13 Type the host name of the news server (or use the default news server), and then click the right-arrow button to continue.

14 If you need to use proxy servers with your Internet connection (you probably don't), click **Yes**, and then type the proxy server information in the next screen.

15 Click the **Go Ahead** button to save the information.

You can go back to a previous page at any time by clicking the left-arrow button.

iMac is set to disconnect after 10 minutes if there is no modem activity. You can turn off this feature in the Remote Access control panel. To adjust settings in the Remote Access control panel, click the Apple menu, choose Control Panels and then choose Remote Access. Click the Options button, then click a tab to view options settings for Remote Access.

You can open the Remote Access by clicking the Remote Access control strip module.

Task 4: Using EarthLink's Total Access

An alternative to using the Internet Setup Assistant is to use EarthLink's Total Access software. It works similarly to Internet Setup Assistant, but can only create an EarthLink Internet account for you.

Start Here

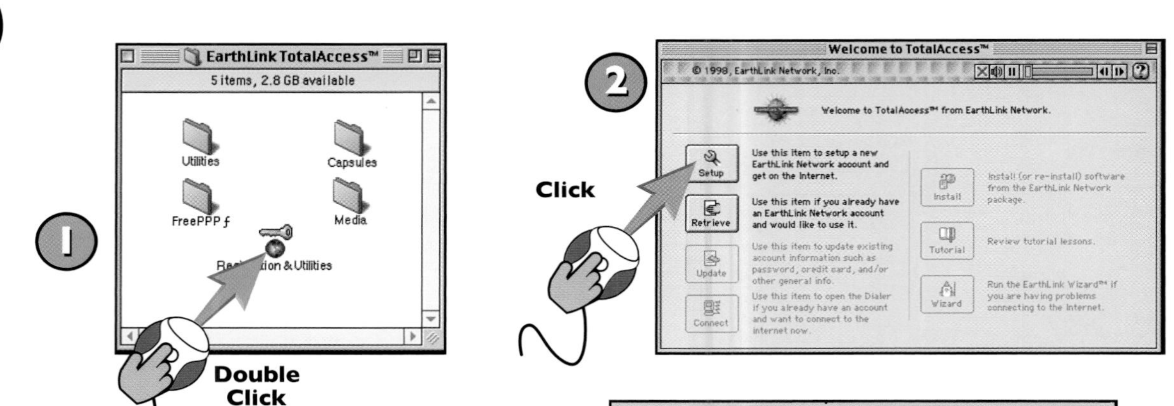

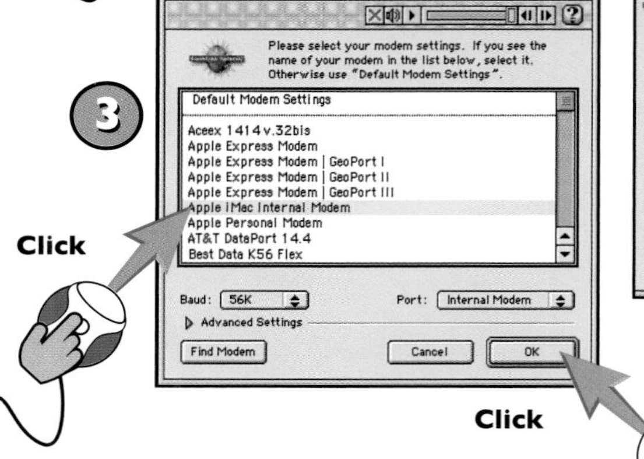

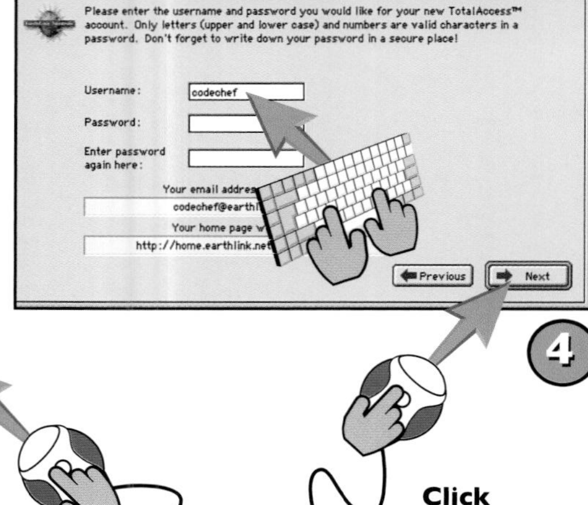

Double-click the hard drive icon, double-click the **Internet** folder, double-click the **EarthLink TotalAccess** folder, and then double-click the **Registration & Utilities** icon.

Click the **Setup** button.

Choose **Apple iMac Internal Modem** in the modem list window. Then click **OK**.

Type in a name and password, then click **Next**. Type in your billing information on the following screens to continue your registration.

EarthLink is one of the largest Internet service providers in the country.

If the Total Access software did not come preinstalled on your iMac, you can download it from the internet from EarthLink's Web site at http://www.earthlink.net.

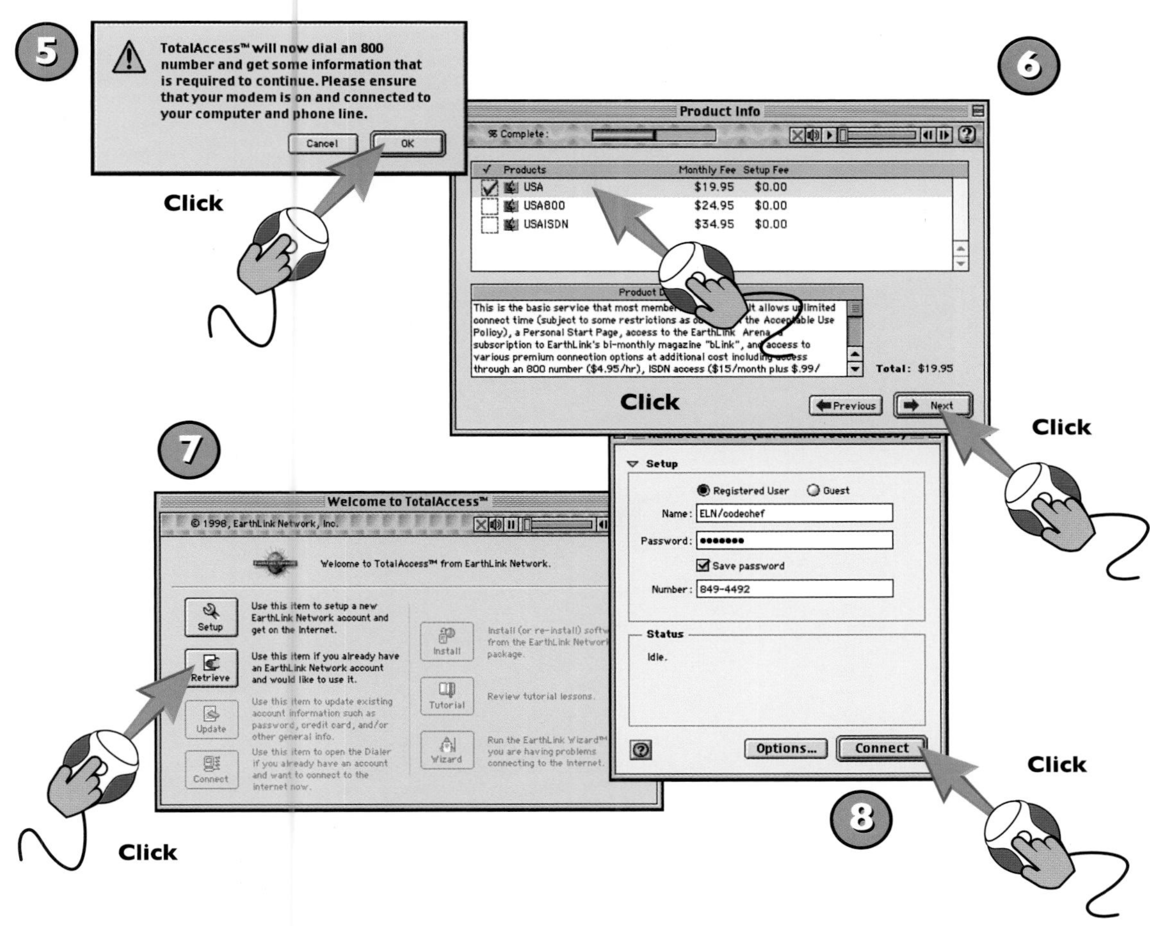

If you select a name that is not available, the EarthLink Setup software will let you choose a new name at the end of the account setup process.

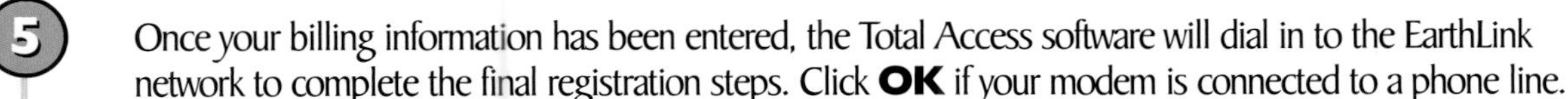

5. Once your billing information has been entered, the Total Access software will dial in to the EarthLink network to complete the final registration steps. Click **OK** if your modem is connected to a phone line.

6. Click on the EarthLink product or monthly fee you want to use. Then click **Next**. Continue through the remaining screens until you complete your account registration.

7. Once your account has been created, click the **Retrieve** button if you want Total Access to configure your iMac to dial in to the EarthLink network.

8. You can also add the EarthLink login, password, and dial-in phone number information manually into the **Remote Access** control panel. Click **Connect** to connect to the Internet.

Task 5: Starting Internet Explorer

Once you've got your Internet connection set up, you can start Internet Explorer and browse the Internet.

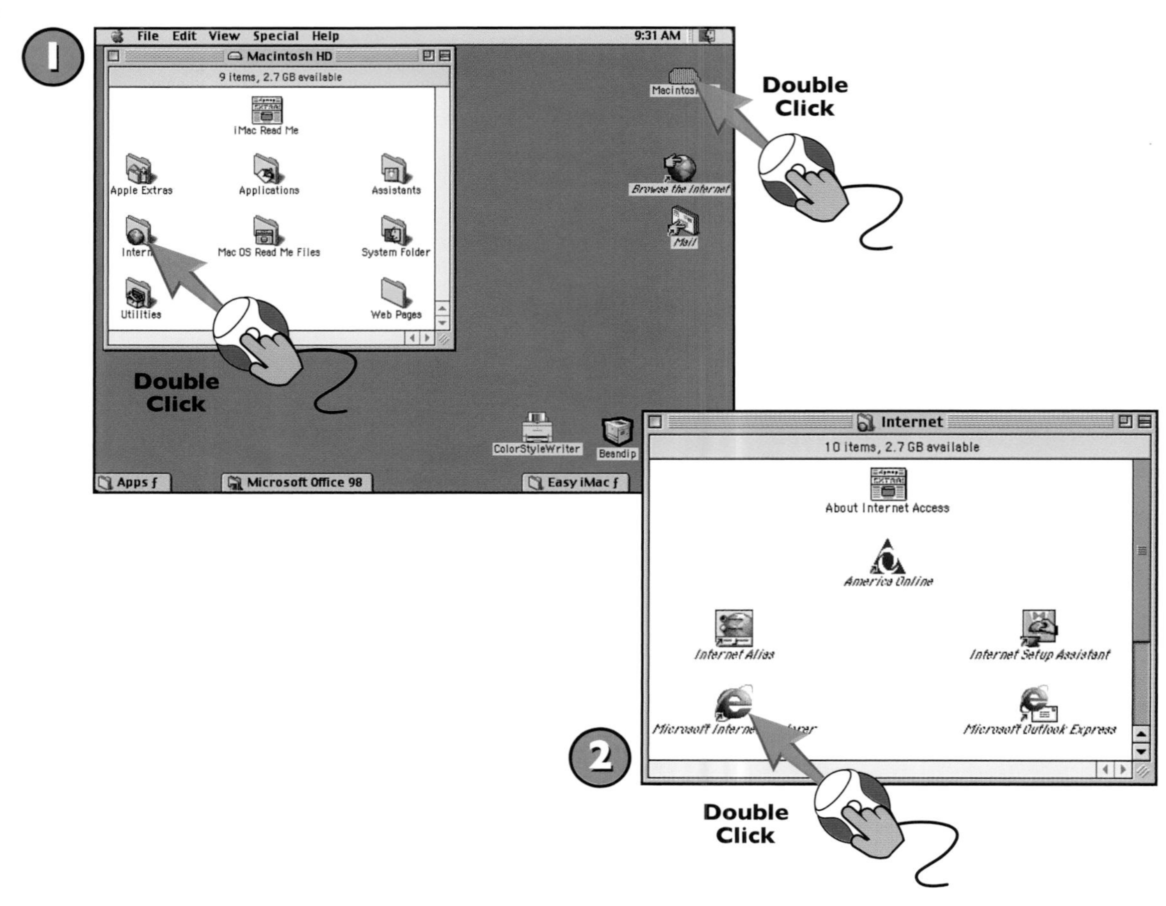

✓ If you have problems connecting—the line is busy, for instance—try again. If you continue to have problems, choose a different local number to dial in to, or check with your ISP.

✓ Your iMac is set up to disconnect after 10 minutes if there is no modem activity. If you need to use Outlook Express or Internet Explorer, you will automatically be reconnected when you launch either of these applications.

✓ To manually reconnect to your ISP, click the **Apple** menu, choose **Control Panels** and then choose **Remote Access**. Click the **Connect** button to reconnect.

1. Double-click the hard drive icon to open the **Macintosh HD** window, and then double-click the **Internet** folder.

2. Double-click the **Internet Explorer** icon.

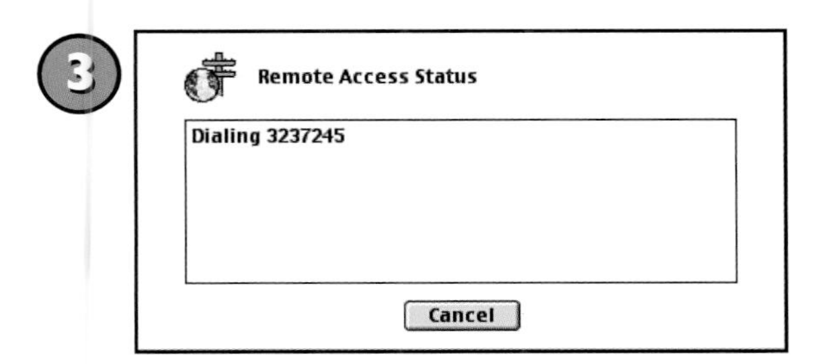

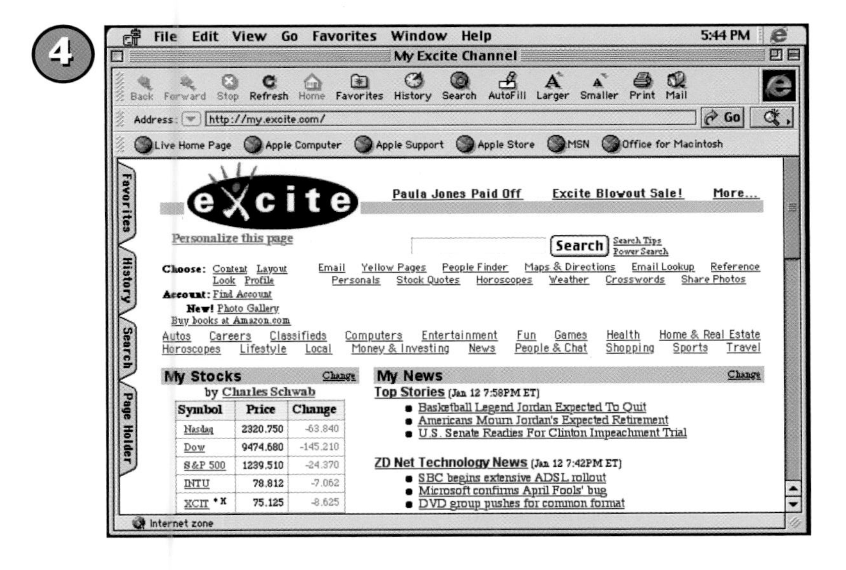

Your iMac is bundled with Internet Explorer 4.01. The tasks in this part use IE 4.5, which you can download from Microsoft's Web site (www.microsoft.com).

3. Wait for Remote Access to connect to your ISP.

4. Mac OS connects to your ISP. The **Internet Explorer** window appears and you see your start page (in this case, **http://my.excite.com**).

Task 6: Browsing with Links and Toolbar Buttons

Start Here

Information on the Internet is easy to browse because documents contain *links* to other pages, documents, and sites. Simply click a link to view the associated page. You can jump from link to link, exploring all types of topics and levels of information. Links are also called *hyperlinks*, and usually appear underlined and sometimes in a different color. You can also use the buttons in the toolbar to navigate from page to page.

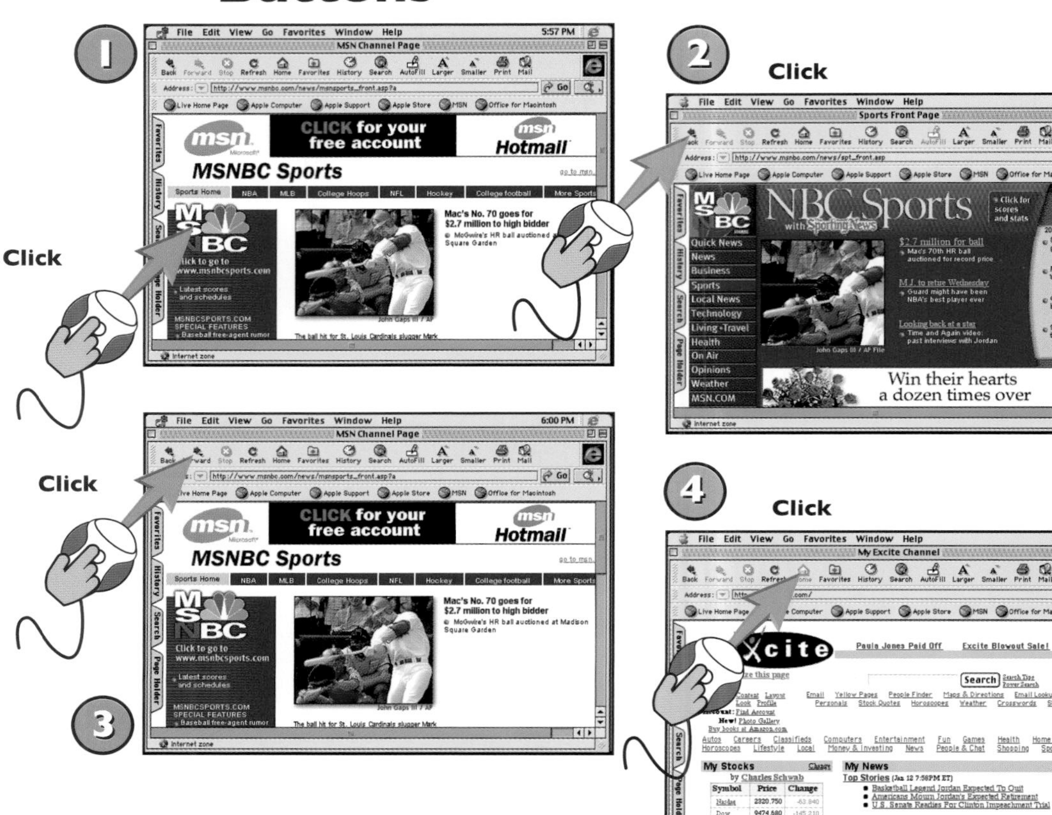

- If you see an error message when you click a link, it could indicate that the link is no longer valid, or that it is inaccurate. If the message indicates that the server is too busy, wait awhile then try again.

- Click any of the buttons in the **Links** toolbar to see some sites selected by Apple. You can select to view sites in several categories. The figures in this task show the links from the MSN sports page.

1. From the MSN sports page (**www.mnbc.com/news/msnsports_front.asp?a**), click a link (in this case, **msnbcsports.com**).
2. The page for that link appears (here, **www.msnbc.com/news/SPT-Front.asp**). Click the **Back** button in the toolbar to go to the last page you visited.
3. Click the **Forward** button to move forward through the pages you've already visited (you must have clicked the **Back** button before you can use the **Forward** button).
4. To return to your start page, click the **Home** button in the toolbar.

Task 7: Typing an Address

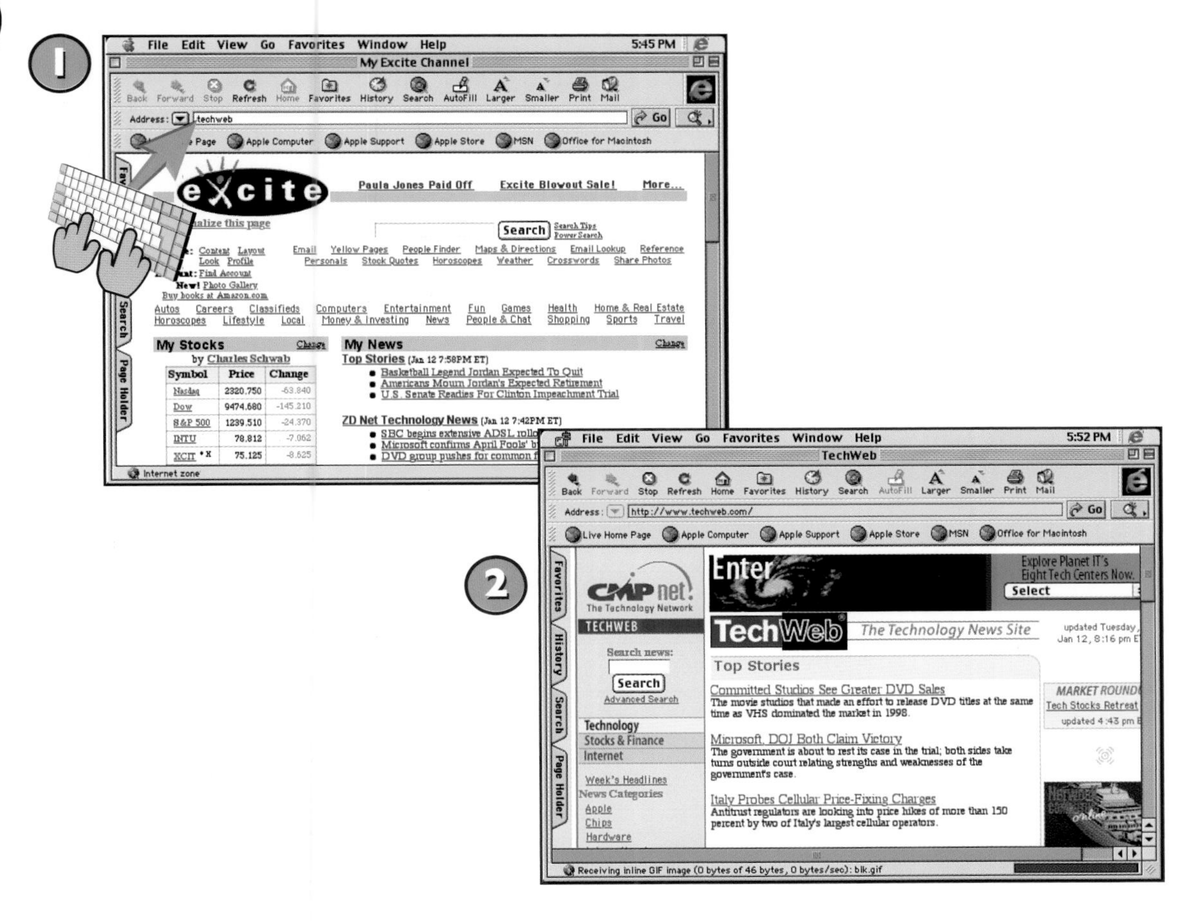

Typing a site's address is the fastest way to get to that site. An address, or *URL* (uniform resource locator), consists of the protocol (usually **http://**) and the domain name (something like **www.nba.com**). The domain name might also include a path (a list of folders) to the document. The extension (usually **.com**, **.net**, **.gov**, **.edu**, or **.mil**) indicates the type of site (commercial, network resources, government, educational, or military, respectively).

1. In the **Address** bar of the **Internet Explorer** window, type the address of the site you want to visit (in this case **techweb**), and then press **Return**.
2. Internet Explorer displays the page associated with the URL you typed.

New with Internet Explorer 4 is a feature called *AutoComplete*. If you have typed an address before, you can simply type its first few letters; Internet Explorer will display the rest.

A chat room is a kind of Web site that lets you type text to another person, or chat, in real-time over the Internet. One of the more popular chat sites to visit is **http://www.talkcity.com**.

Start Here

Task 8: Adding a Site to Your Favorites List

When you find a site that you especially like, you might want a quick way to return to it without having to browse from link to link or having to remember the address. Fortunately, Internet Explorer 4 enables you to build a list of favorite sites and to access those sites by clicking them in the list.

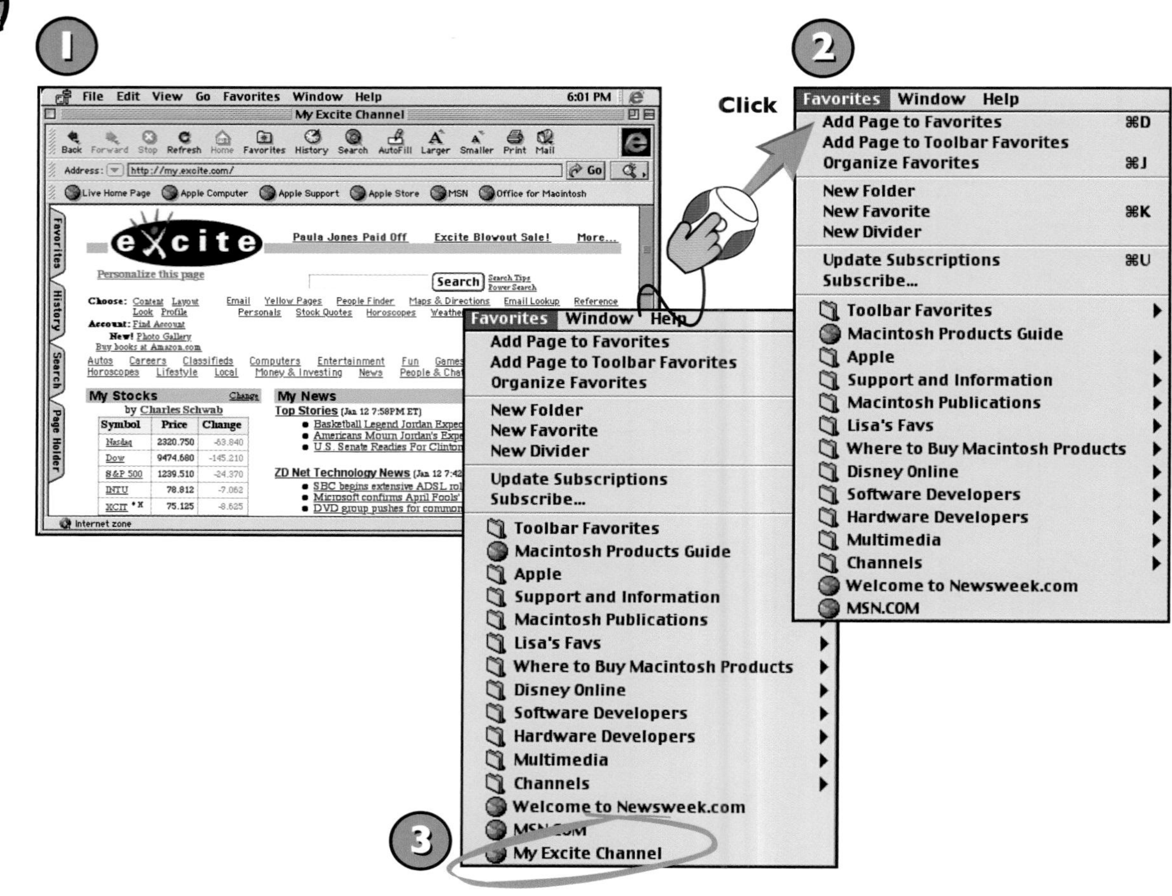

✓ You can subscribe to certain sites, and set up Internet Explorer to update the sites regularly.

✓ To remove a site from your Favorites list, choose **Favorites**, and then click **Organize Favorites**. Select the site you want to delete, then click the **Delete** key on the keyboard.

1. In Internet Explorer, open the Web site that you want to add to your Favorites list.
2. Click the **Favorites** menu (do not click the **Favorites** toolbar button), and then click the **Add Page to Favorites** command.
3. Click the **Favorites** menu. The name of the Web page appears at the bottom of the **Favorites** menu.

Task 9: Going to a Site in Your Favorites List

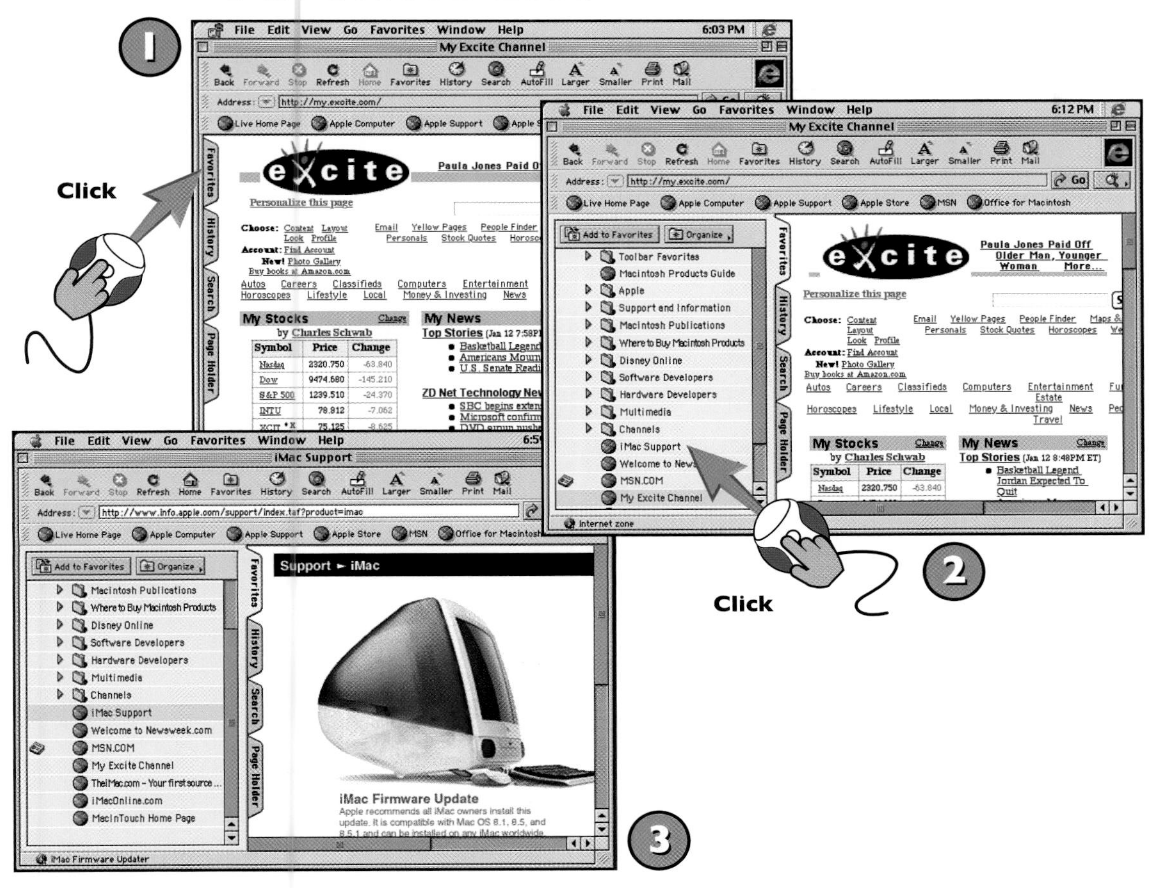

After you have added a site to your Favorites list, you can easily reach that site by displaying the list and selecting the site.

1. Click the **Favorites** tab in the **Internet Explorer** window.

2. The pane on the left side of the screen contains your Favorites list, while the right-side pane contains the current page. Click the site you want to visit.

3. Internet Explorer displays the site you selected from the Favorites List.

- To close the **Favorites** pane, click its tab.
- You can also reach a site by opening the **Favorites** menu.
- You can set up folders to group sites together. For more information on adding folders, see the next task.

Task 10: Rearranging Your Favorites List

Start Here

If you add several sites to your Favorites list, it might become difficult to use. You can organize the list by grouping similar sites together in a folder. You can add new folders and move sites from one folder to another.

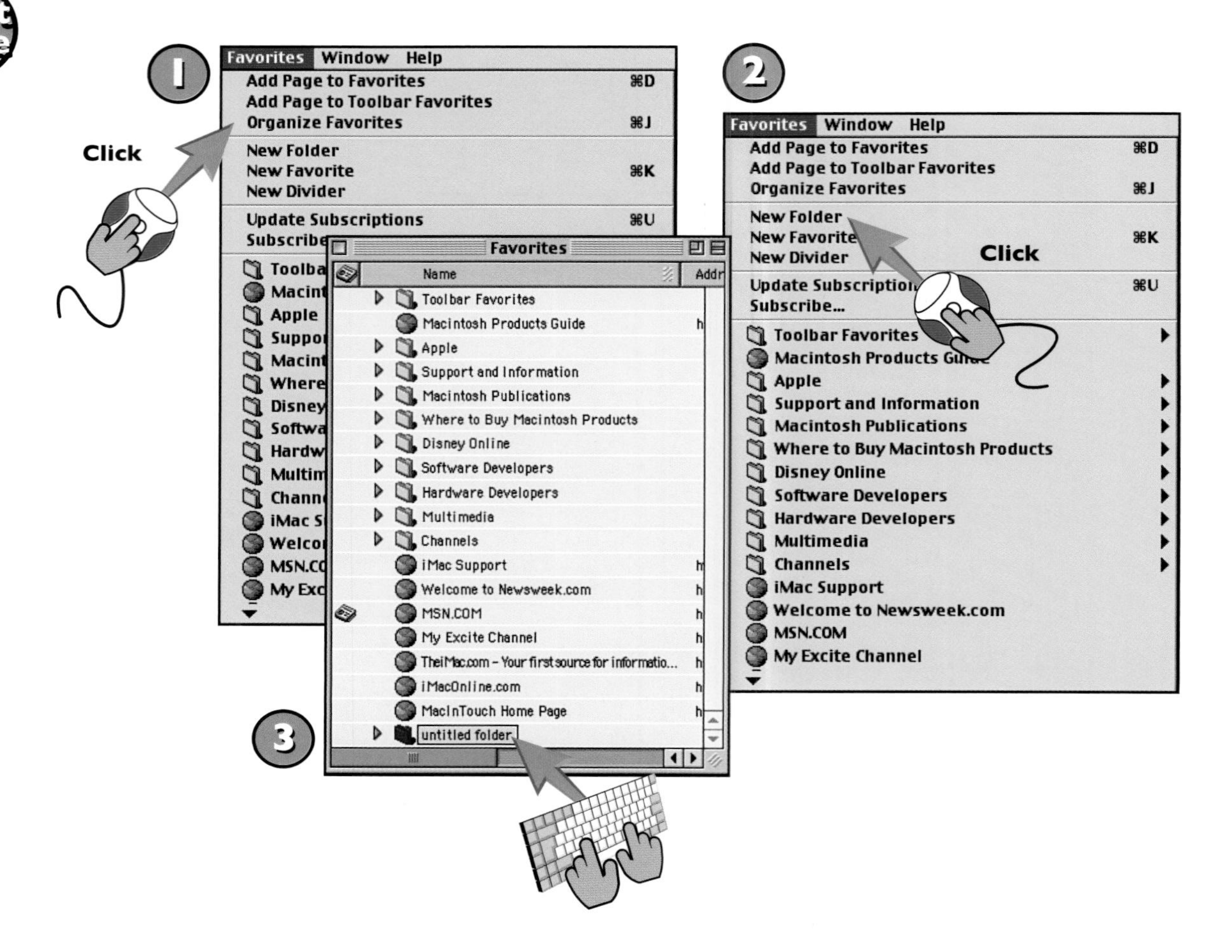

1. Click the **Favorites** option in the menu bar, and then choose **Organize Favorites**.
2. To create a new folder, click **Favorites** and choose the **New Folder** command.
3. The default name is **untitled folder**. Type the folder name and press **Return.**

- You can drag a site from the list to a folder where you want to place the site.
- To rename a site or folder in your Favorites list, click the name of the site or folder and wait about one second. Type a new name, and press **Return**.

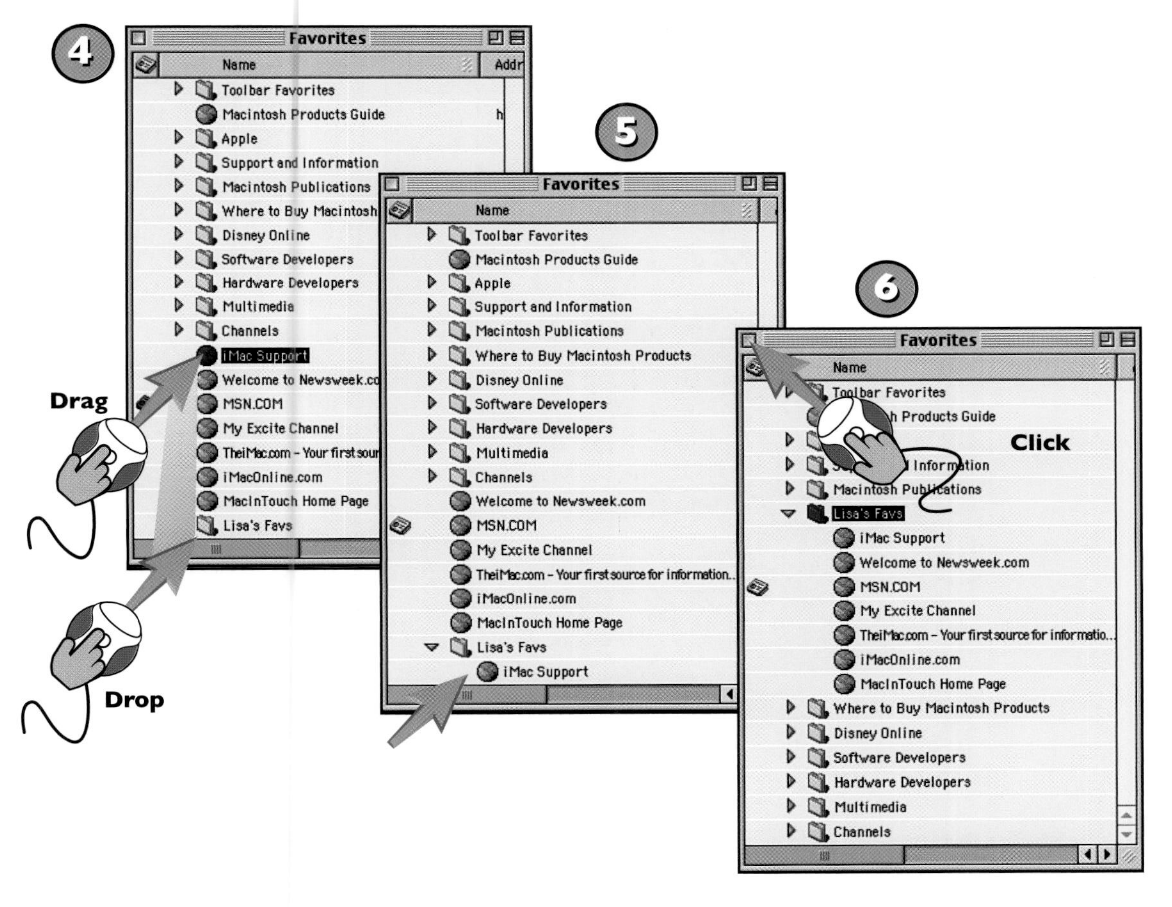

4. To move a site to the new folder (named **Lisa's Favs**), select the site, and drag it to the folder you want.
5. The site appears under the folder where you placed it.
6. When you are finished moving all the sites you want to rearrange, click the **Close** box.

To delete a site, select it and click the Delete key or drag the site to the Trash.

You can also add a favorite URL, file, or folder to the Favorites folder located in the Apple menu.

Task 11: Working with Page Holder

Start Here

If you have been surfing the Web and have grown tired of clicking the **Back** button, a new feature in Internet Explorer 4.5 called Page Holder is a great alternative. Page Holder lets you keep a Web page in the pop-up window of Internet Explorer, allowing you to store two Web pages in one Internet Explorer window.

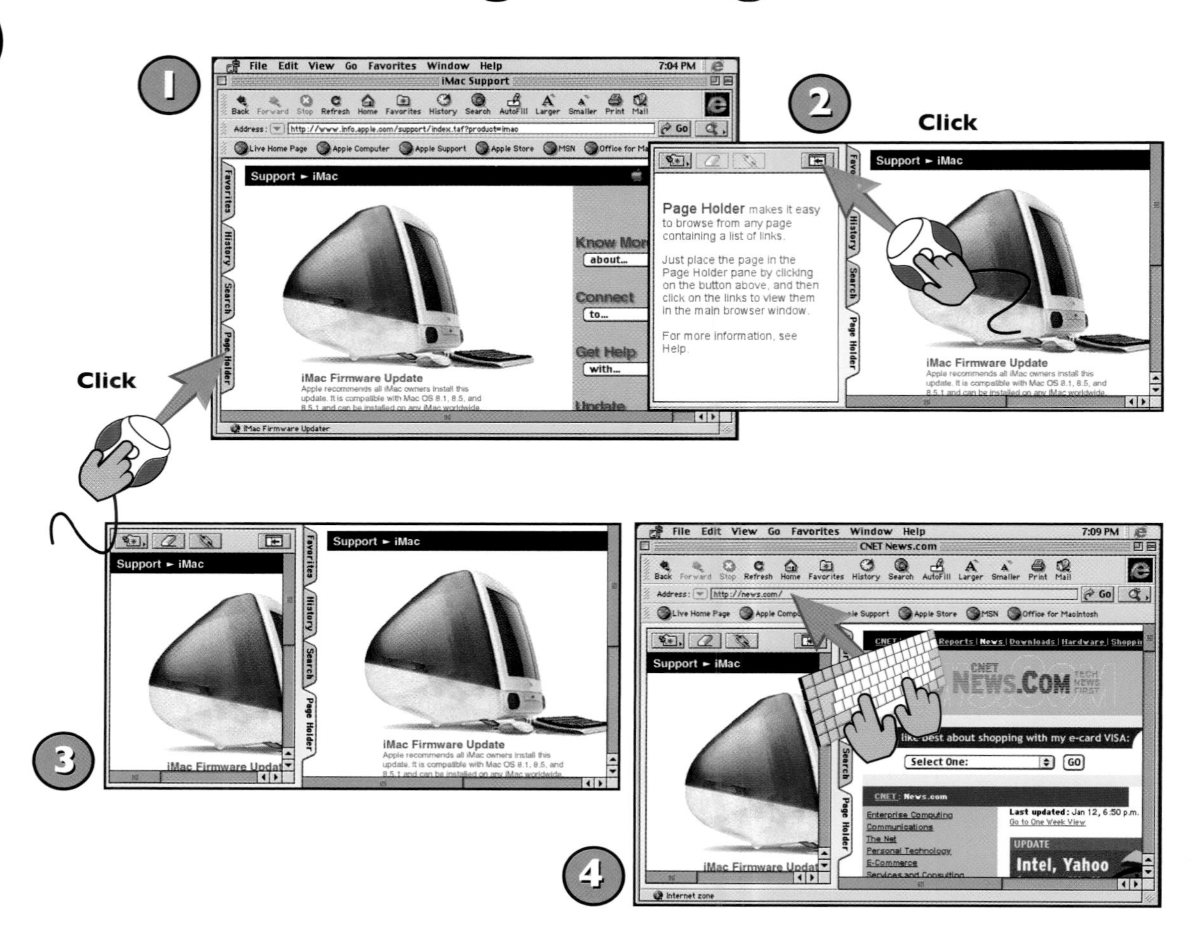

Page Holder is a feature of Internet Explorer 4.5, but not Internet Explorer 4.01, which ships with the iMac. To upgrade to IE 4.5, visit Microsoft's web site at www.microsoft.com.

You can add a URL in the **Page Holder** window to your **Favorites** menu by clicking on the **Favorites** folder icon in the **Page Holder** toolbar.

1. Load a Web page, then click the **Page Holder** tab in the **Internet Explorer** window.
2. Click the left arrow icon in the **Page Holder** window to move the page in the main window into the **Page Holder** window.
3. The page from the main window appears in the **Page Holder** window.
4. Type a different URL into the same window (in this case **http://www.news.com**). Press **Return**.

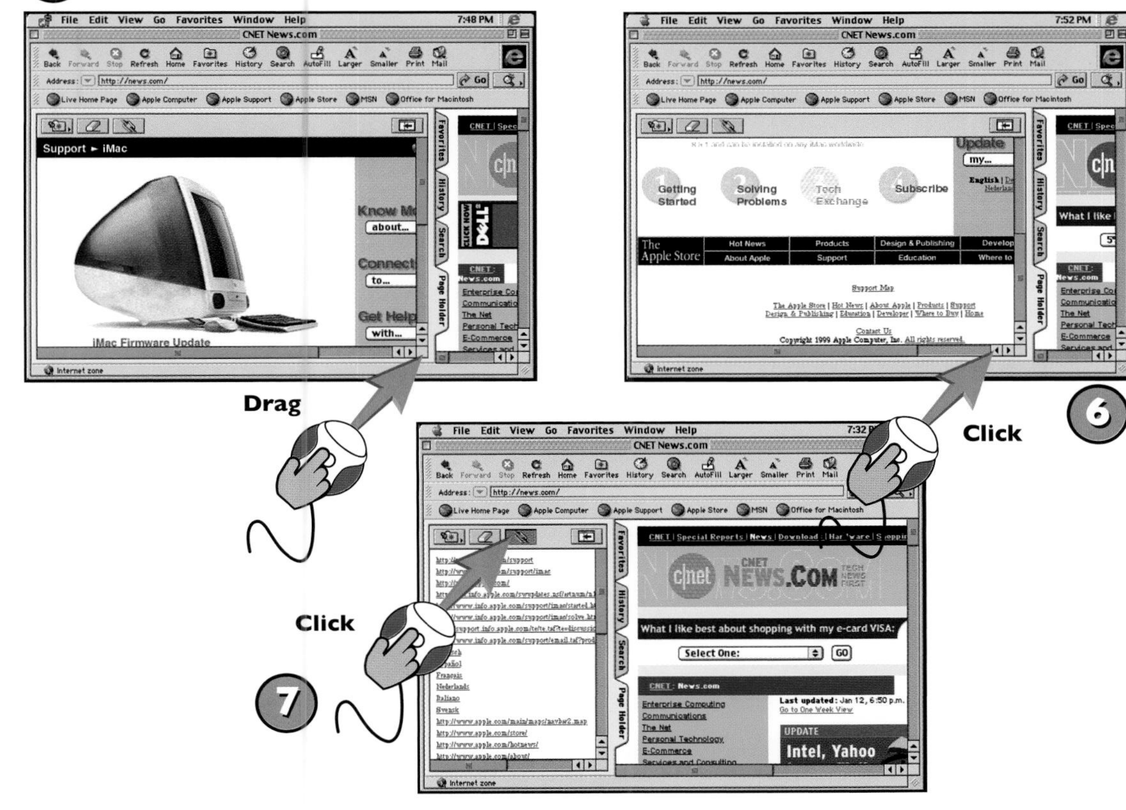

5. Drag the lower edge of the **Page Holder** window to the right to access the previous web page.

6. Click on the scrollbar controls to view or select any links in the **Page Holder** window.

7. Click the **Links** button to only view the links available in the **Page Holder** window.

You can clear the Page Holder window by clicking on the Erase button in the Page Holder toolbar.

Hide the Page Holder window by clicking the Page Holder tab.

Another new feature of Internet Explorer 4.5 is AutoFill. Click the AutoFill button on the toolbar to add your personal information to Internet Explorer. When you go to any web site to fill out a form, AutoFill automatically fills in your personal information for you.

Task 12: Searching the Internet with Sherlock

The Internet includes far too many kinds of computers and even more Web sites and Web pages to be counted. Looking for the site you want by browsing can be like looking for a needle in a haystack. Instead, you can search for a topic, and find all sites related to that topic. To search, you can use a search engine on the Internet or one on your iMac. The basic procedure is the same, but the results of the search can vary. Sherlock is the search engine built into Mac OS 8.5.

Start Here

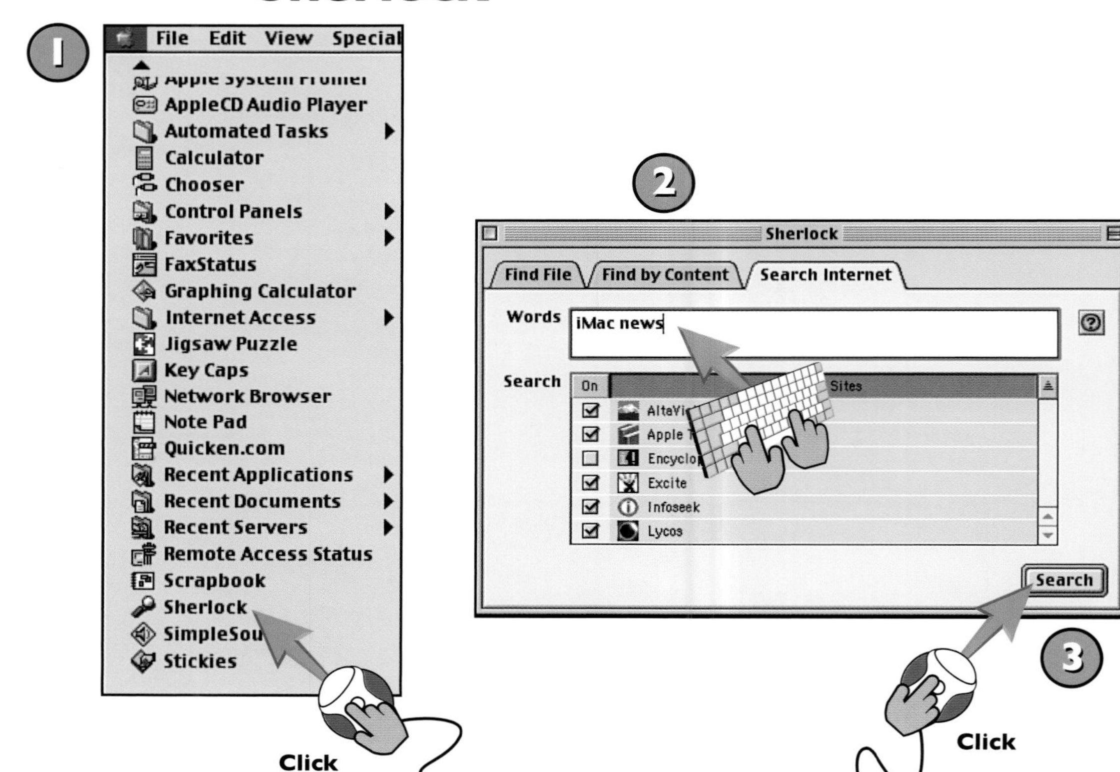

1. Click the **Apple** menu and choose **Sherlock**.
2. In the **Search Internet** tab, type the word or phrase you want to find.
3. Click the **Search** button.

If you don't find the topic you want, try a different search engine. The result may be different.

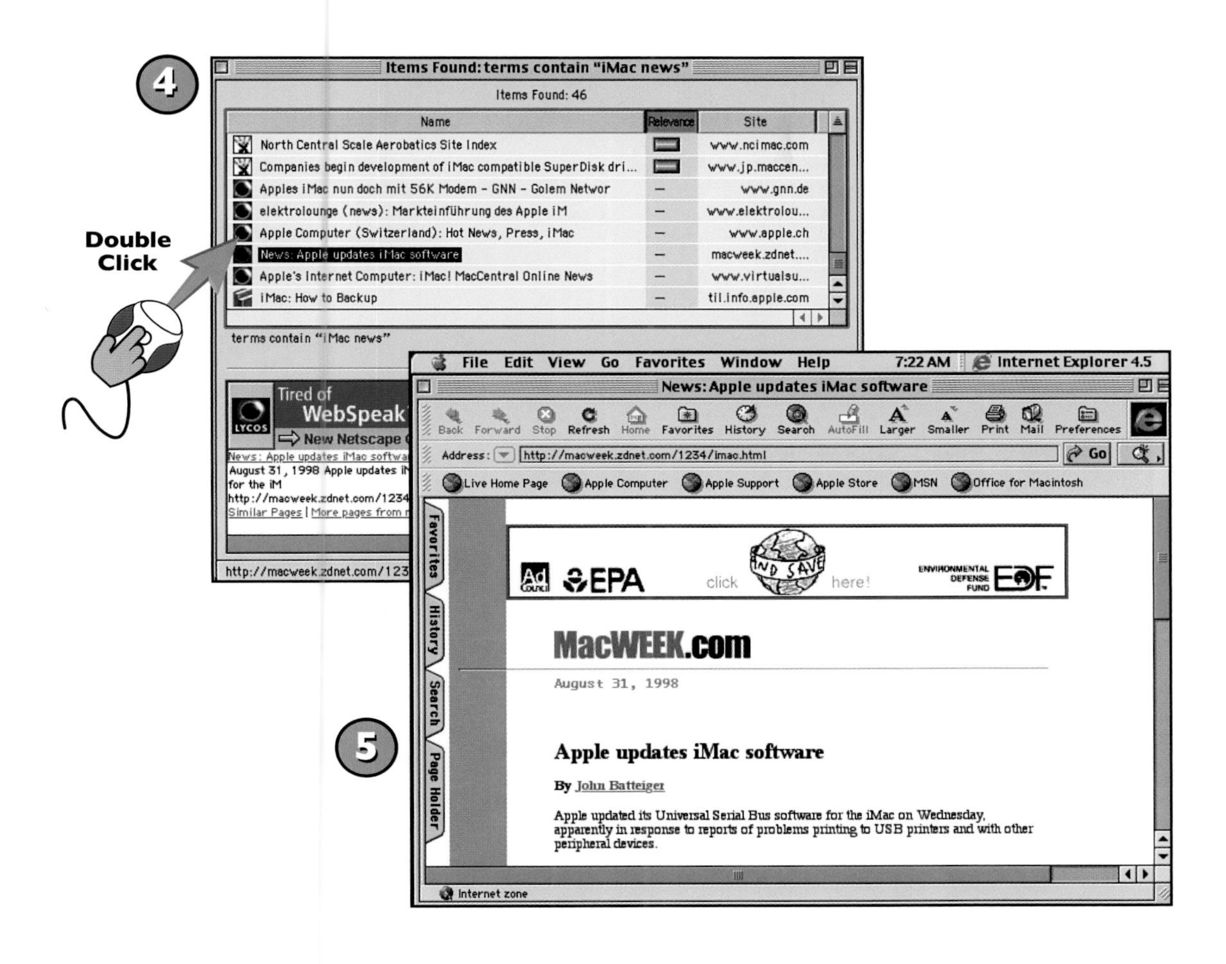

The results of the search are displayed in link format. Scroll down until you find the link you want, and then double-click it.

The page you selected appears.

If you're using Mac OS 8.1, you need to upgrade to Mac OS 8.5 to use Sherlock.

You can scroll through the search results to see all the results. To close the Search Results window, click its Close box.

You can have more than one search result window open at the same time.

Task 13: Setting Internet Security Levels

With Internet Explorer 4, you can assign different zones to various sites, and assign a security level to each zone. Assign the **Local** zone to sites on your intranet; assign the **Trusted** zone to any sites from which it is safe to download and run files; assign the **Restricted** zone to sites from which it is not safe to download and run files. The **Internet** zone is assigned to all other sites by default. A site's assigned zone is displayed in the status bar.

Start Here

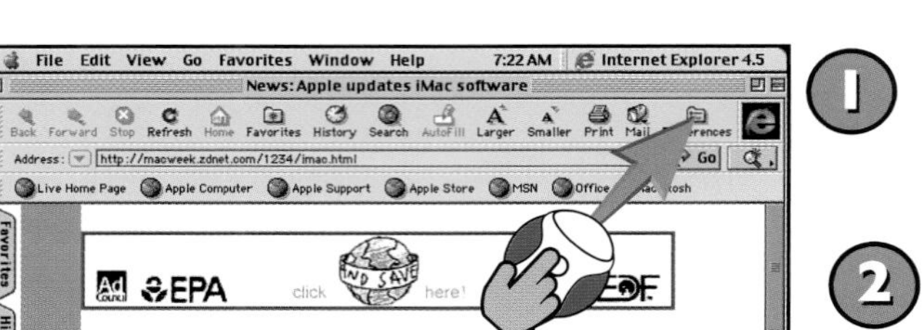

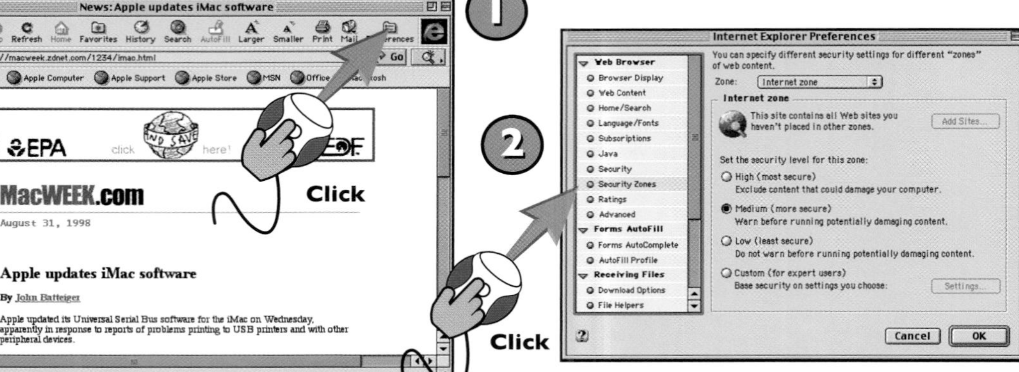

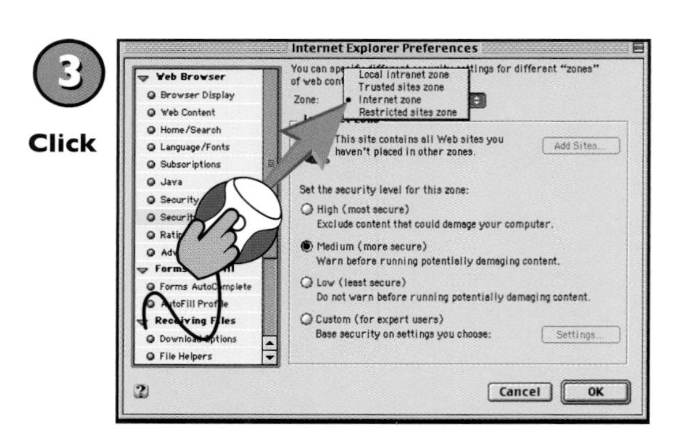

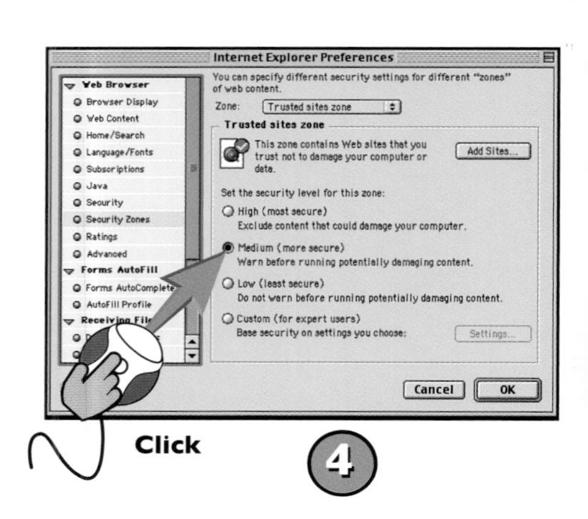

You may need to resize the toolbar to access the **Preferences** button. Alternatively, open the **Edit** menu and choose **Preferences.**

If you're not sure which sites are secure, look for the lock icon in the lower-left corner of the browser window. The lock icon indicates that the page is secure.

1. To view information about zones or to alter the settings of a zone, click the **Preferences** button.
2. Click **Security Zones** under **Web Browser**.
3. To set the security level for a zone, select the zone from the **Zones** pop-up list.
4. Click the **High**, **Medium**, **Low**, or **Custom** radio button in the **Set the security level for this zone** section.

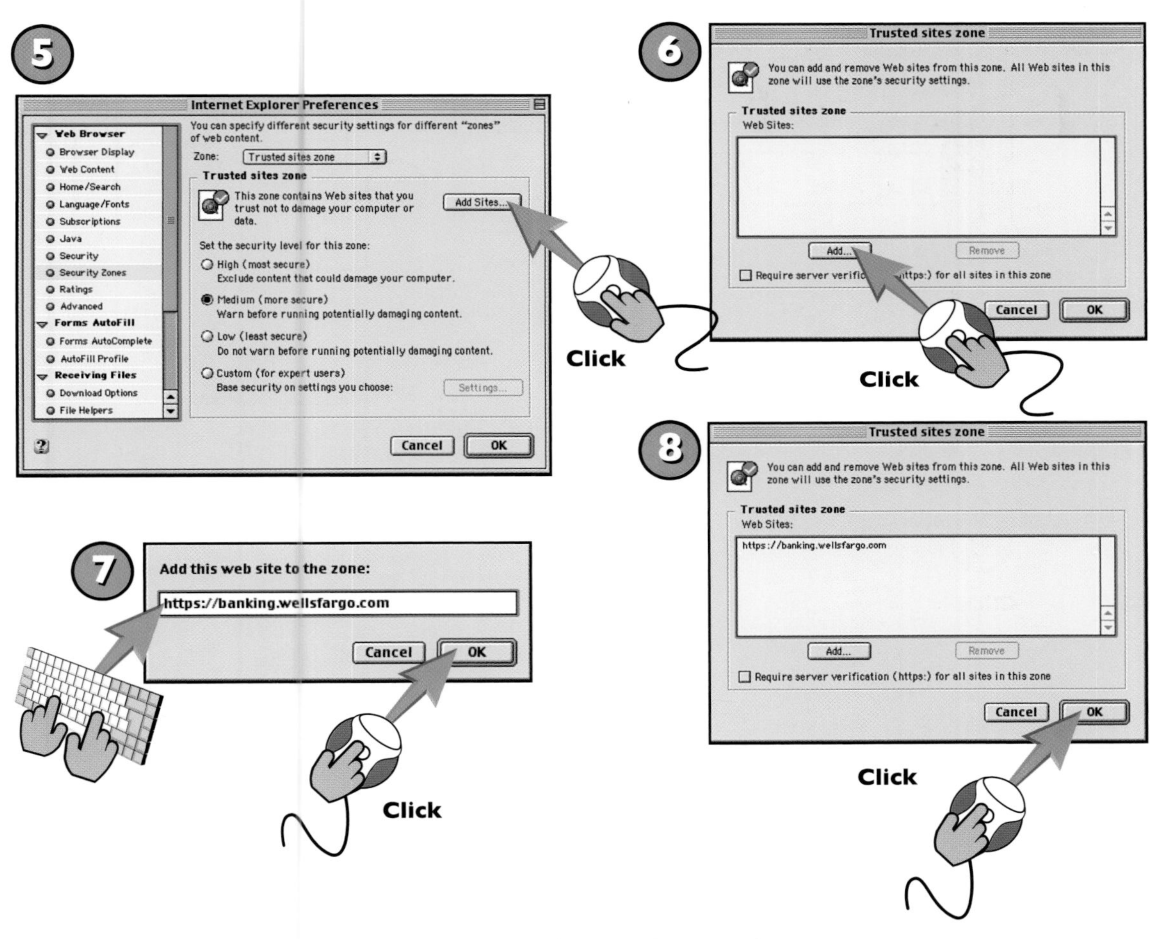

5. To add Web sites to a particular zone, click the **Add Sites** button.

6. Click the **Add** button.

7. Type the address of the site you want to add, and click **OK**.

8. The site is added. Repeat steps 6 and 7 to add more sites, and then click **OK** to confirm.

To remove a site from a zone, click Preferences and then select Security Zones. Click the Zone tab, and select a zone. Click the Add Sites button, then choose a site. Click the Remove button, then click OK three times to exit the Preferences dialog box.

Task 14: Using the History List

Start Here

As you browse from link to link, you might remember a site that you like, but not remember that site's name or address. You can easily return to sites you have visited by displaying the History list. From this list, you can select the week you want to review, and then the site you want to visit.

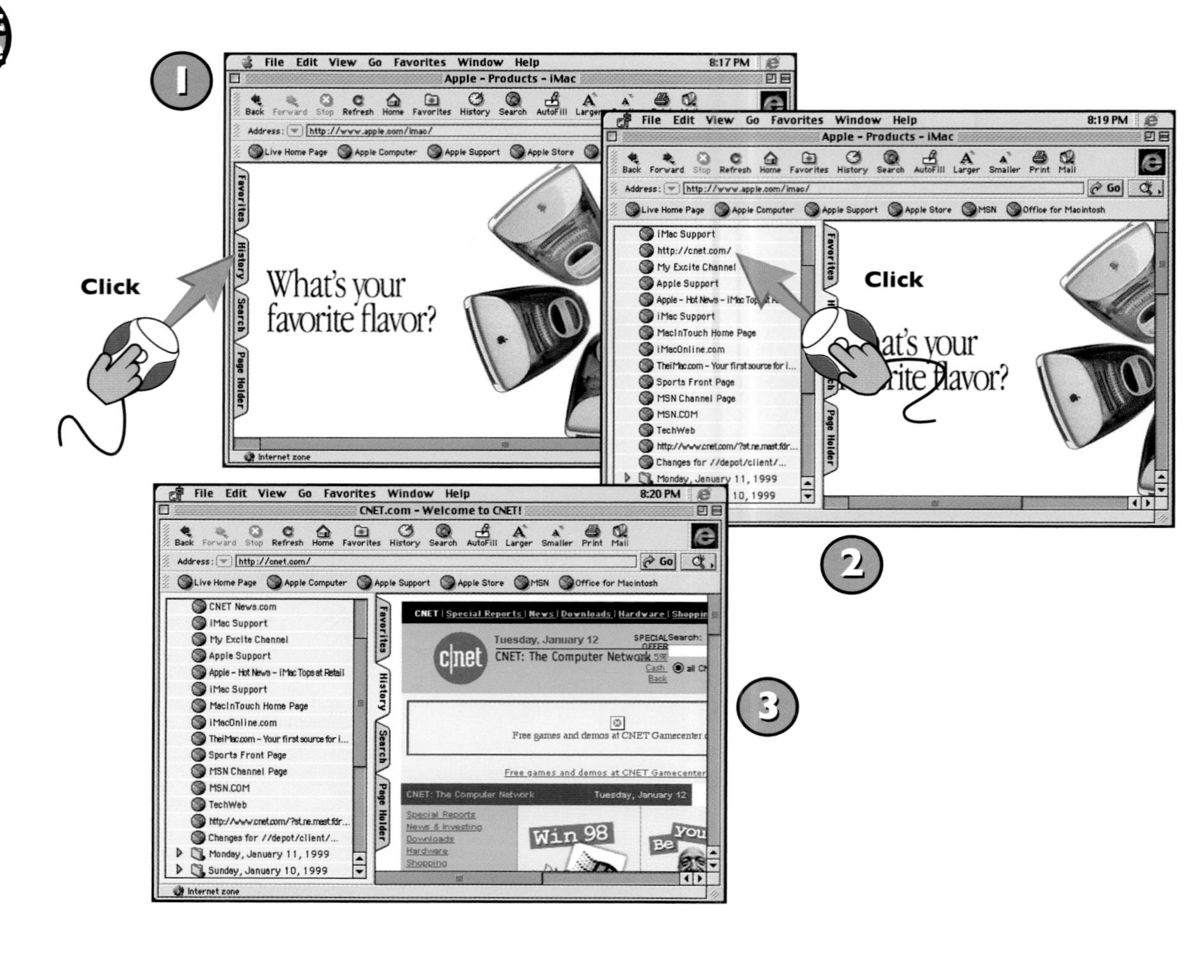

To close the History list, click the tab in the **History** pane.

You can select how many days the history is kept, and you can clear the History list. Choose **Go** and click **Open History**, and then select the folder representing the day you want to remove. To clean the history, select all items in the window and move them to the Trash.

1. Click the **History** tab.
2. Internet Explorer displays the **History** list in a pane on the left side of the window. If necessary, select the day whose list you want to review, and then click the site you want.
3. Internet Explorer displays site you selected.

End Task

Task 15: Quitting Internet Explorer

When you are finished browsing the Internet, you need to quit Internet Explorer and also end your connection to your Internet service provider.

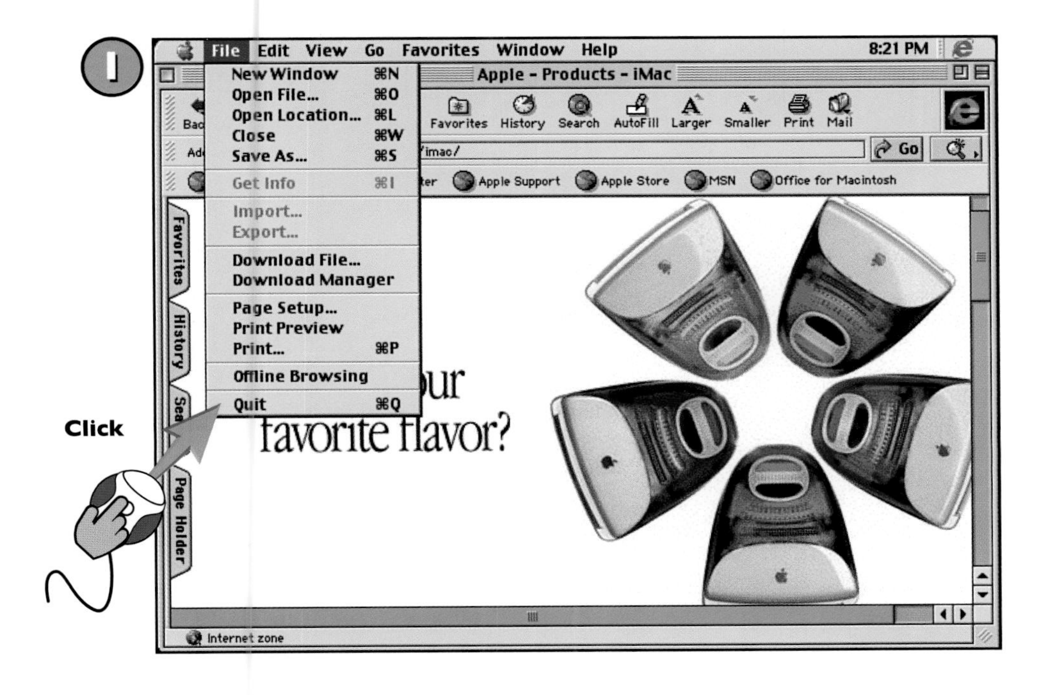

To quit Internet Explorer, click the **File** menu and choose the **Quit** command.

Click **OK** if you are prompted to log off your ISP connection.

Task 16: Starting Outlook Express

Start Here

You can use Outlook Express to create, send, and receive email over the Internet. You can also send files by attaching them to your messages.

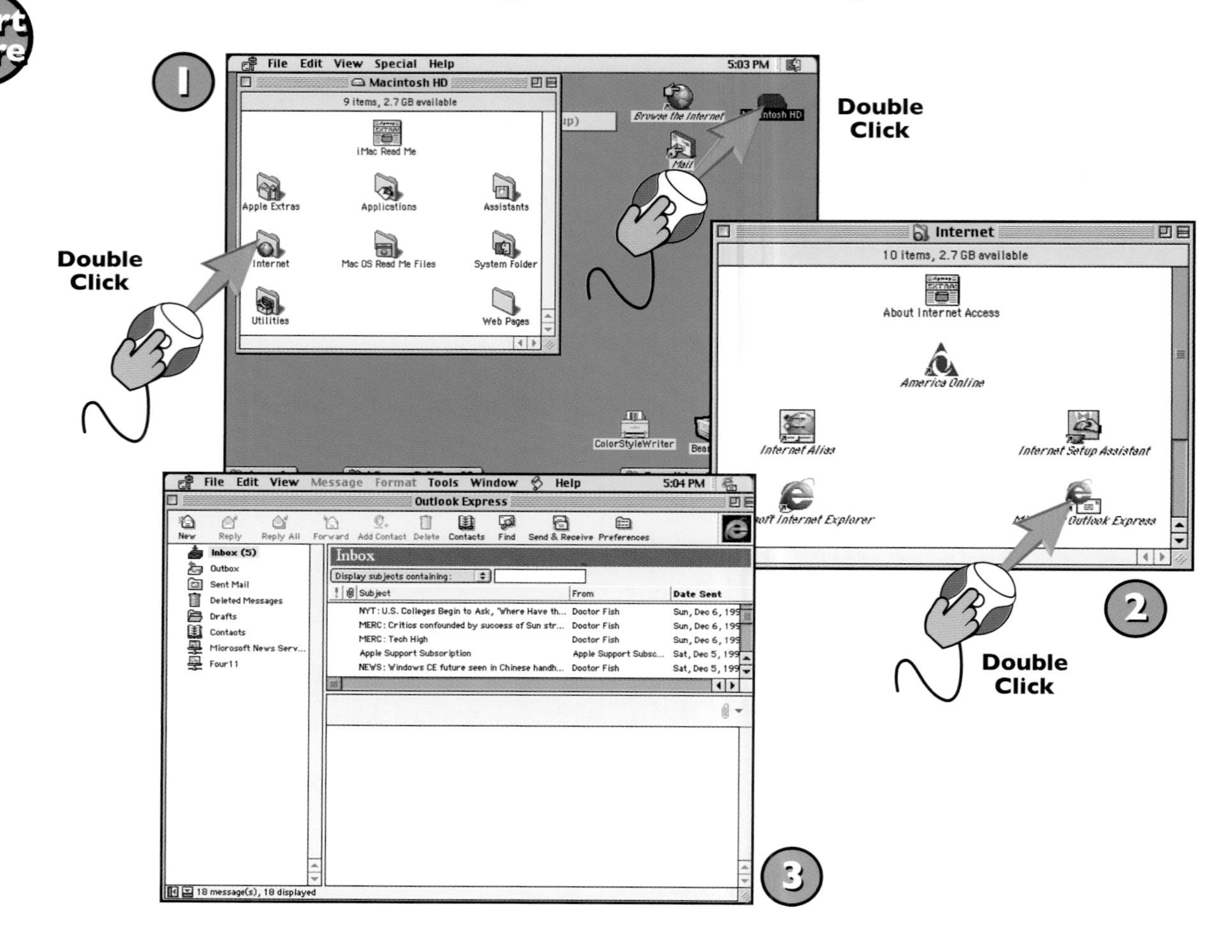

1. Double-click the **Macintosh HD** icon, then double-click the **Internet** folder.
2. Double-click the **Microsoft Outlook Express** icon.
3. Outlook Express is started.

✓ To use Outlook, your iMac must be configured for use over the Internet.

✓ iMac is set to disconnect after 10 minutes if there is no modem activity. If you need to use Outlook Express or Internet Explorer, you will automatically be reconnected when you launch either of these applications.

✓ To manually reconnect to your ISP, click the Remote Access control strip module and choose the **Connect** command.

✓ To start Outlook Express from Internet Explorer 4, click the **Mail** button in the toolbar.

Task 17: Reading Mail

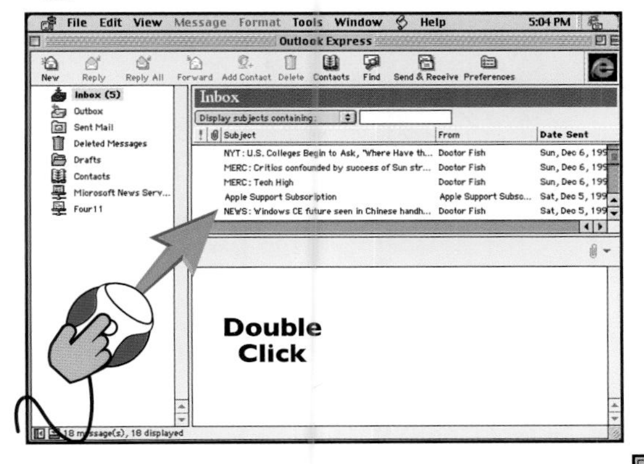

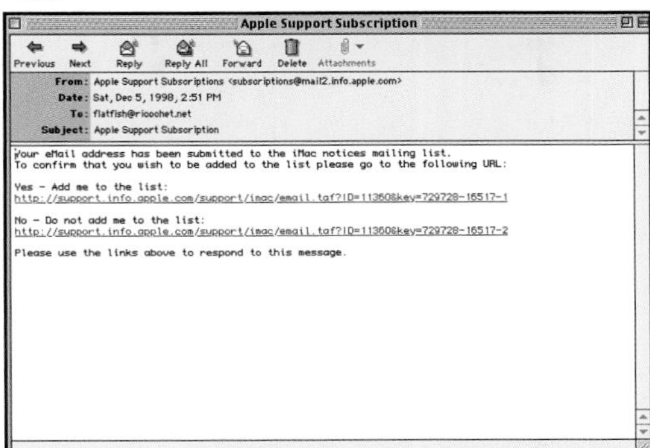

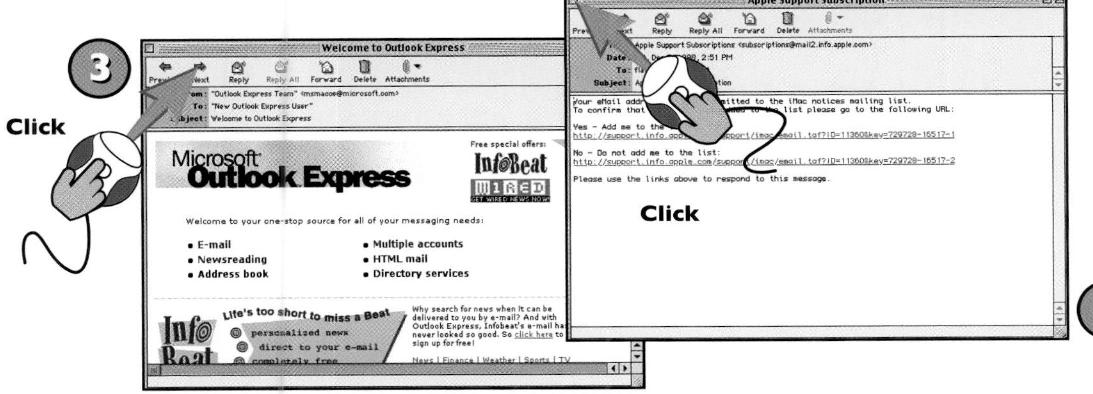

When you start Outlook Express and get connected to your ISP, click the Send & Receive button. Your messages are downloaded from your Internet mail server to your iMac. The number of messages in your inbox appears in parentheses next to the **Inbox** link in the folder list (the pane on the left side of the screen). The message list (the upper-right page) lists all messages. Messages appearing in bold have not yet been read; you can open and read any message in the message list (whether it's bold or not).

1. In the message list of the **Outlook Express** window, double-click the message you want to read.
2. The message you selected is displayed in its own window. You can scroll through the contents to read the message.
3. To display the next message in the message list, click the **Next** arrow; to display the previous message in the message list, click the **Previous** arrow.
4. To close the message, click the **Close** box.

✓ To print an open message, choose **File**, select **Print**, and then click **Print** in the **Print** dialog box.

✓ To delete a message, select the message, then choose **Edit** and click the **Delete Message** command, or click the **Delete** button in the toolbar.

Task 18: Responding to Mail

Start Here

You can easily respond to a message you've received. Outlook Express completes the address and subject lines for you; you can then simply type the response.

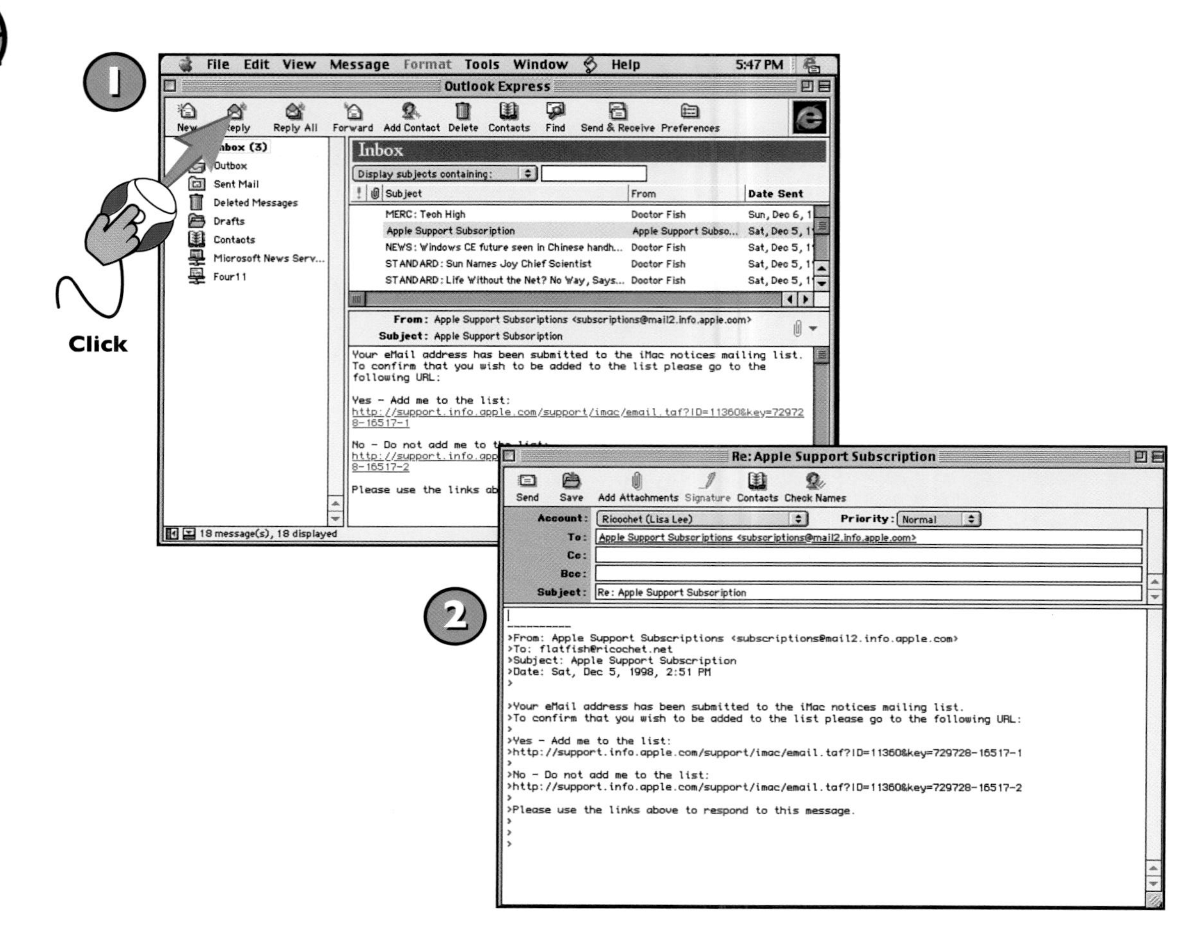

1. Click on the message to which you want to reply, and click the **Reply** button in the toolbar.

2. The address and subject lines are completed, and the text of the original message is appended to the bottom of the reply message.

✓ To forward a message, click the **Forward** command in the **Message** menu or click the **Forward** button in the toolbar. Type the address of the recipient, and then click in the message area and type any message you want to include. Finally, click the **Send** button.

✓ You can also choose the **Reply to Sender** command in the **Message** menu.

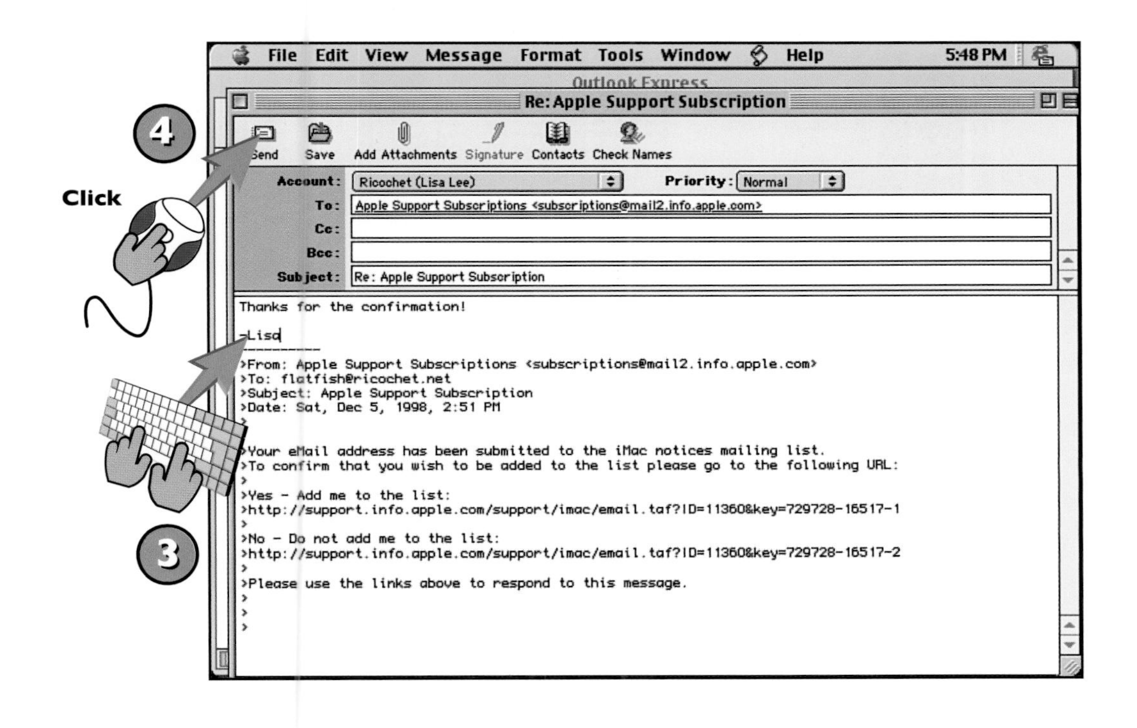

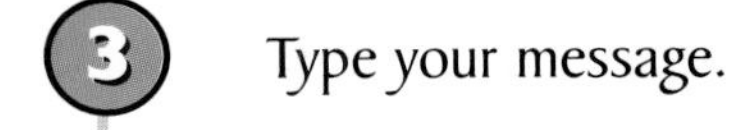

3. Type your message.

4. Click the **Send** button.

Task 19: Creating and Sending Mail

Start Here

You can send a message to anyone with an Internet email address. Simply type the recipient's email address, a subject, and the message. You can also send carbon copies (Cc) and blind carbon copies (Bcc) of messages, as well as attach files to your messages.

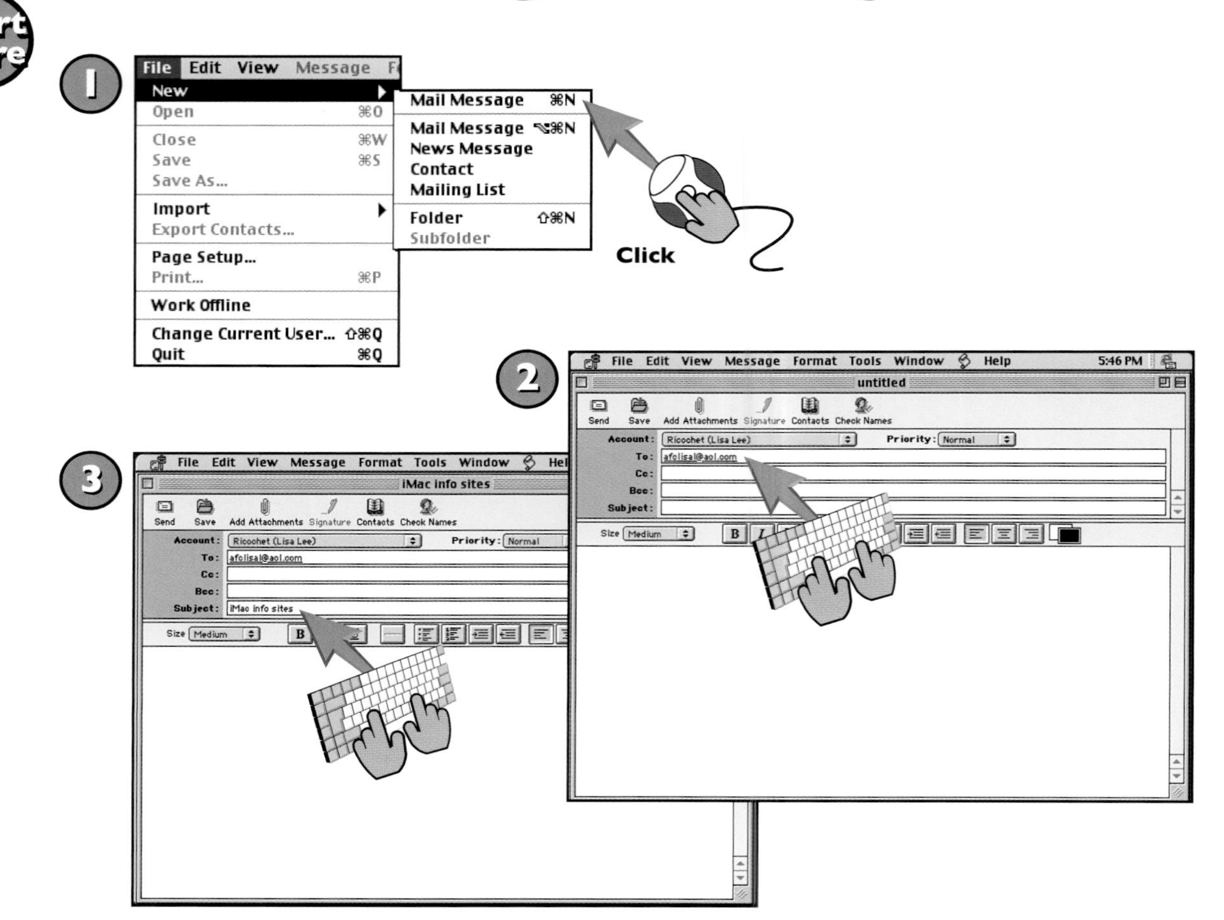

- You can also click the **Compose a mail message** button in the toolbar to create a new message.
- If you enter an incorrect address and the message is not received by the recipient(s), you most likely will receive a **Failure to deliver** notice. Be sure to type the address in its proper format.
- To attach a file—such as a spreadsheet or word-processing document—to your message, simply drag and drop the file to the open message window in Outlook Express.

1. In the **Outlook Express** window, click **File**, choose **New,** and then click **Mail Message**.
2. Type the recipient's address (as well as any Cc and Bcc addresses). Addresses are in the format ***username@domainname.ext*** (for example, **afclisa@aol.com**).
3. Type a subject in the **Subject** text box, and then press **Tab**.

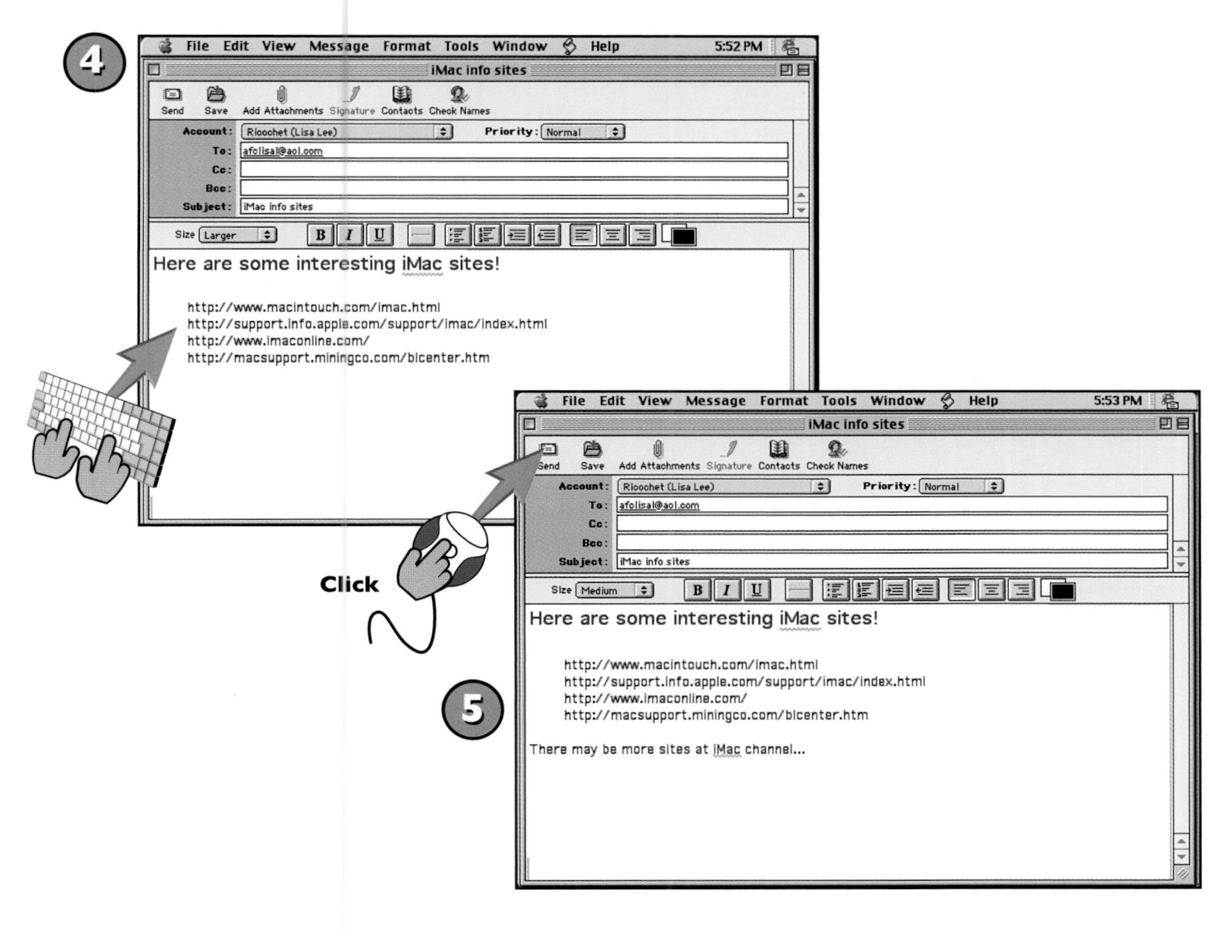

4. Type your message.

5. When you've completed the message, click the **Send** button.

If you are sending one large file or several files with an email, they will be easier to send and download if you compress them before attaching them to an email. Use Stuffit Lite (available over the Internet at www.download.com and other Internet sites) to compress one or several files or a folder, then attach the compressed archive file to an email.

If you are connected to the Internet, the message is sent when the Send button is clicked. If you're not connected to the Internet, Outlook Express places the message in the Outbox, where it remains until the next time you connect to your ISP. You can connect and send the message by clicking the Send and Receive button.

Task 20: Subscribing to Newsgroups

A *newsgroup* is a collection of messages relating to a particular topic. Anyone can post a message, and anyone who subscribes to the newsgroup can view and respond to posted messages. You can join any of the hundreds of thousands of newsgroups on the Internet to exchange information and learn about hobbies, businesses, pets, computers, people of different walks of life, and more. You use Outlook Express for both email and newsgroups.

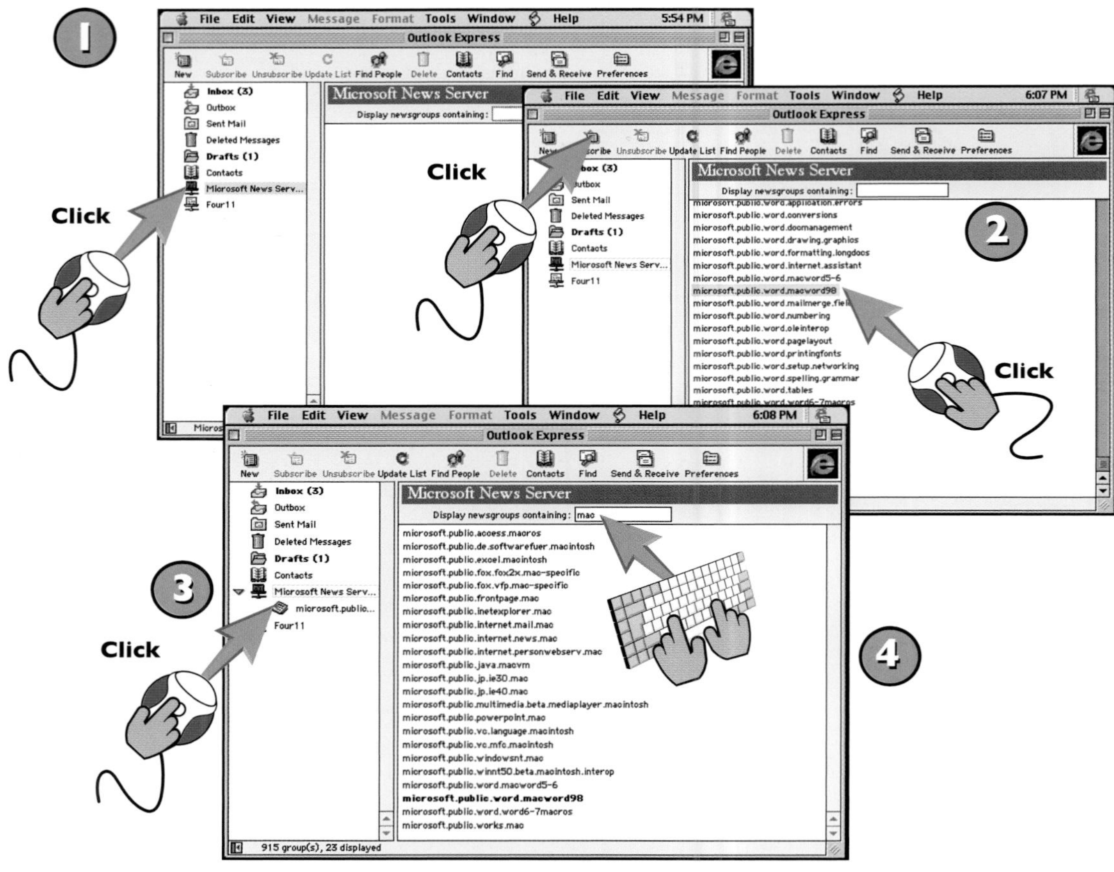

✓ You can search for a specific word—for example, **chocolate** or **saxophone**—by entering the word in the **Display Newsgroups Containing** text box.

1. In the **Outlook Express** folder list, click the news server icon (in this case, **Microsoft News Server**).
2. After the list of newsgroups loads, click a newsgroup, then click the **Subscribe** button in the toolbar.
3. An icon for the newsgroup you subscribed to (in this case, **microsoft.public.word.macword98**) will be added to the folder list below the **Microsoft News Server** entry.
4. To find other newsgroups that interest you, type the name of a topic area in the **Display newsgroups containing** text box (I've typed `mac`).

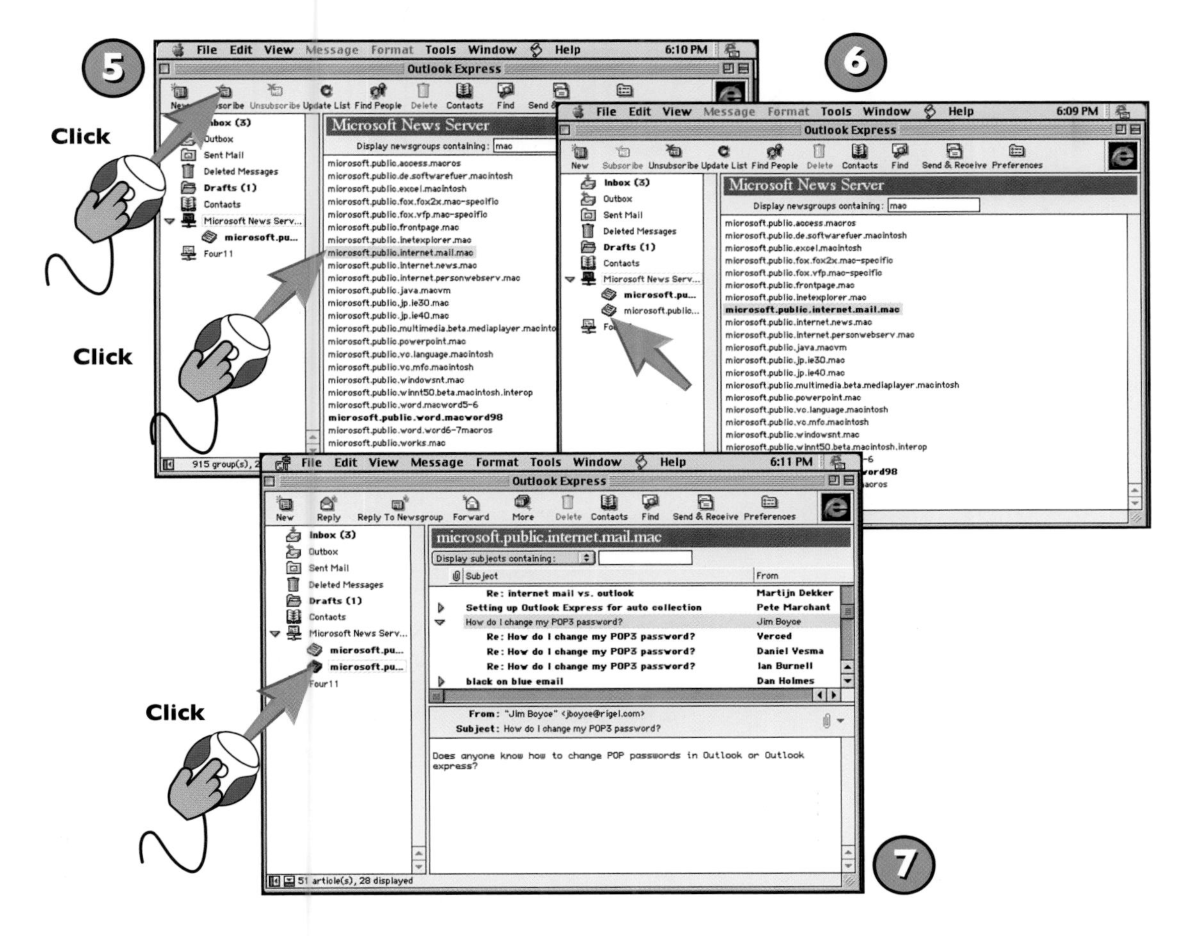

5 Select a newsgroup from the **Newsgroups** list (in this case, **microsoft.public.internet.mail.mac**) and click the **Subscribe** button.

6 The newsgroup icon is added below the **Microsoft News Server** icon in the Outlook Express folder list.

7 Click on a newsgroup icon in the folder list to view the messages for that newsgroup; double-click one of the messages to view it.

To view more newsgroups, type the news server for your ISP into the Outlook Express News Server Preferences.

To unsubscribe to a newsgroup, click the Microsoft News Server icon. Select the newsgroup to which you want to unsubscribe, and then click the Unsubscribe button.

To update a newsgroup list, select a news server and click the Update List button in the toolbar.

Task 21: Reading Newsgroup Messages

After you have subscribed to a newsgroup, you can review any of the messages in that group. When a new message is posted, it starts a *thread*, and all responses are part of this thread. You can review all the current messages in the thread.

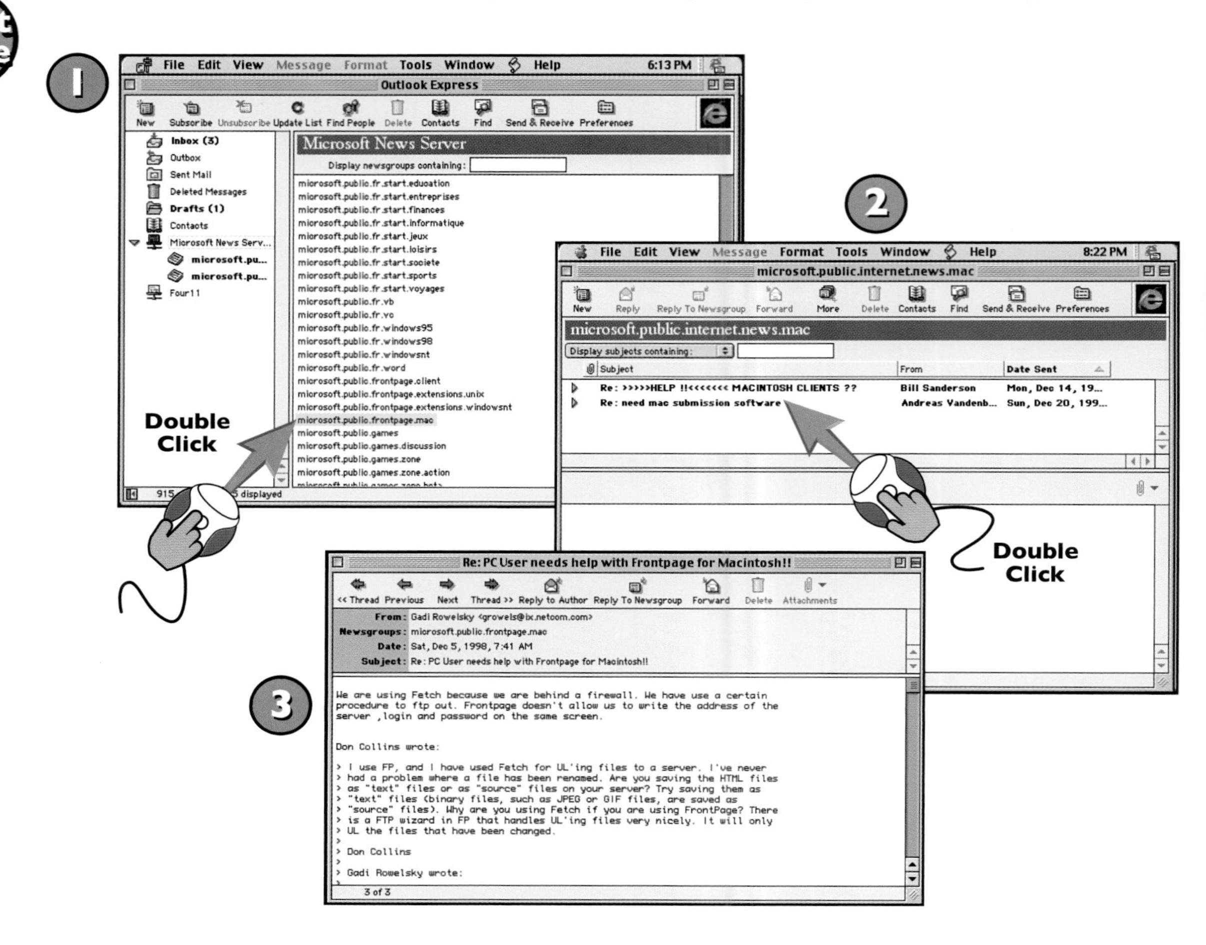

Keep in mind that newsgroups are not usually monitored. You might come across messages that you find offensive. If so, it's best to just unsubscribe from that newsgroup.

1. In the folder list of the **Outlook Express** window, double-click the newsgroup you want to review.
2. A list of that newsgroup's messages appears in the message list. Double-click the message you want to read.
3. The message is displayed in its own window.

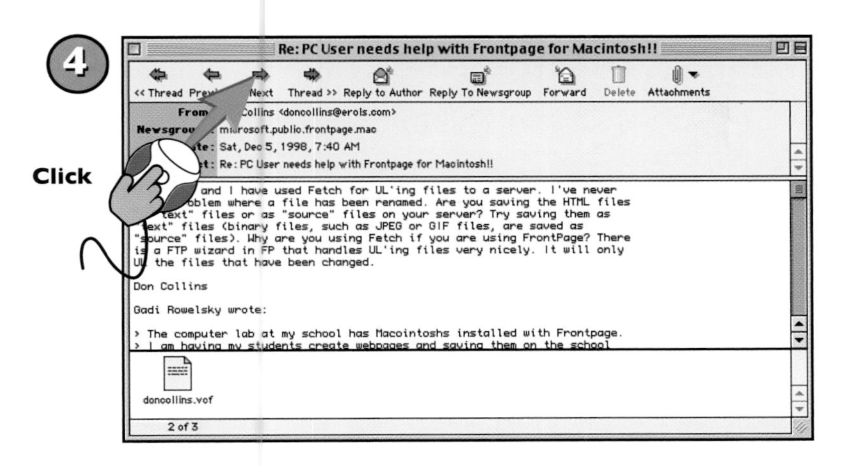

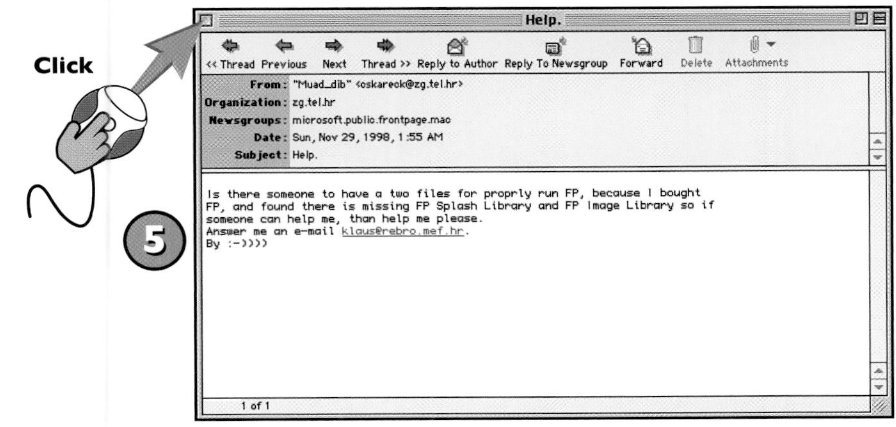

4. To display the next message, click the **Next** arrow; to display the previous message, click the **Previous** arrow in the toolbar.
5. To close the message, click the **Close** box.

To print a message, select it in the window, click **File**, and choose **Print**. To save a message, select it, click **File**, and then choose **Save As**. Then assign the message a location on your hard drive and click the **Save** button.

Messages in bold have not yet been read; messages with a collapsible arrow next to them have responses.

Task 22: Posting New Messages

Start Here

After you review messages, you might want to post your own opinion or ask a new question. One way to do this is to post a new message, or start a new thread.

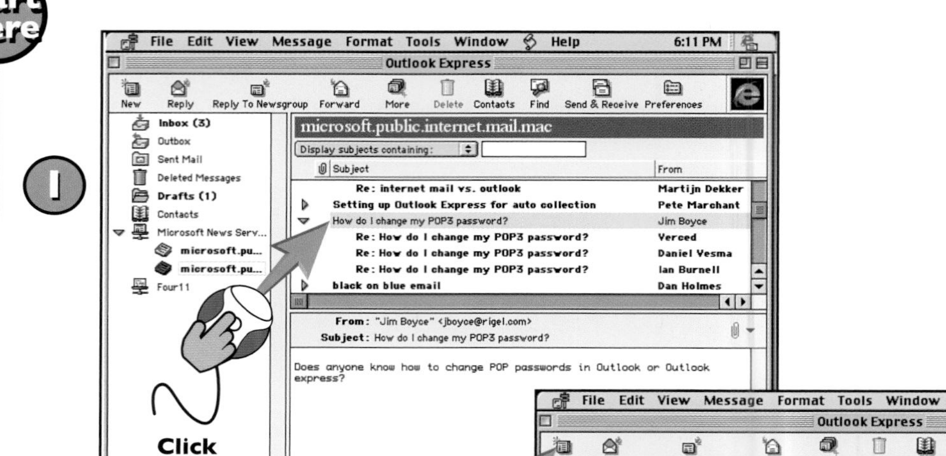

Click

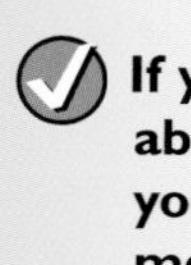

If you change your mind about posting a message, you can cancel the message if you have not already clicked **Post**. Simply click the message's **Close** button and, when prompted, click the **Don't Save** button to confirm that you don't want to save the message.

In the list of folders, select the newsgroup to which you want to post a new message.

Click the **New** button.

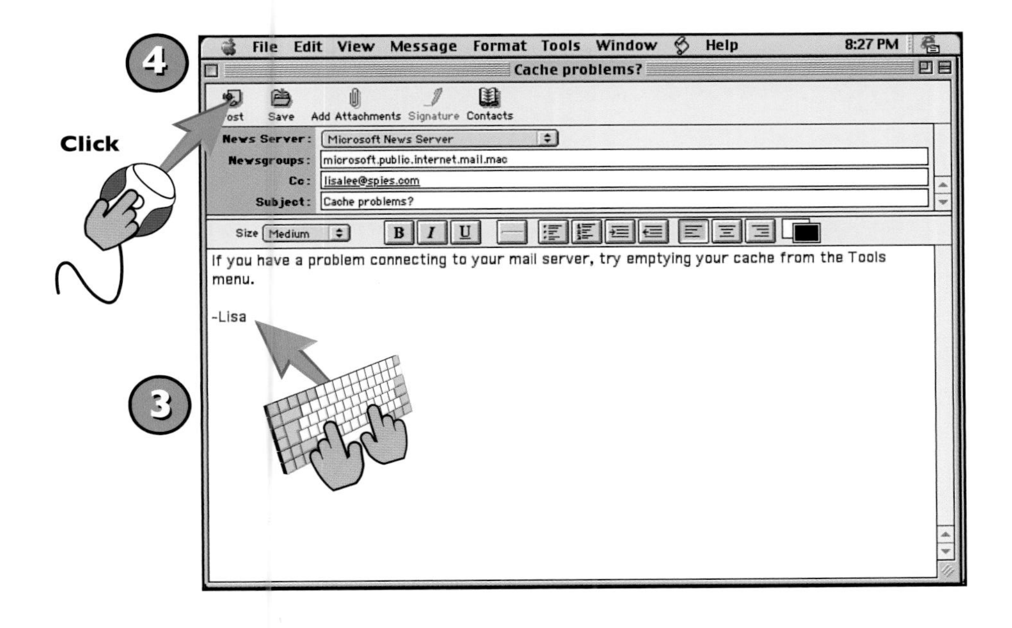

3. Enter subject line, review the addressee, and type your message.

4. Click the **Post** button on the toolbar.

Start Here

Task 23: Replying to an Existing Newsgroup Message

If you come across a newsgroup message to which you want to respond, you can post a reply to that message.

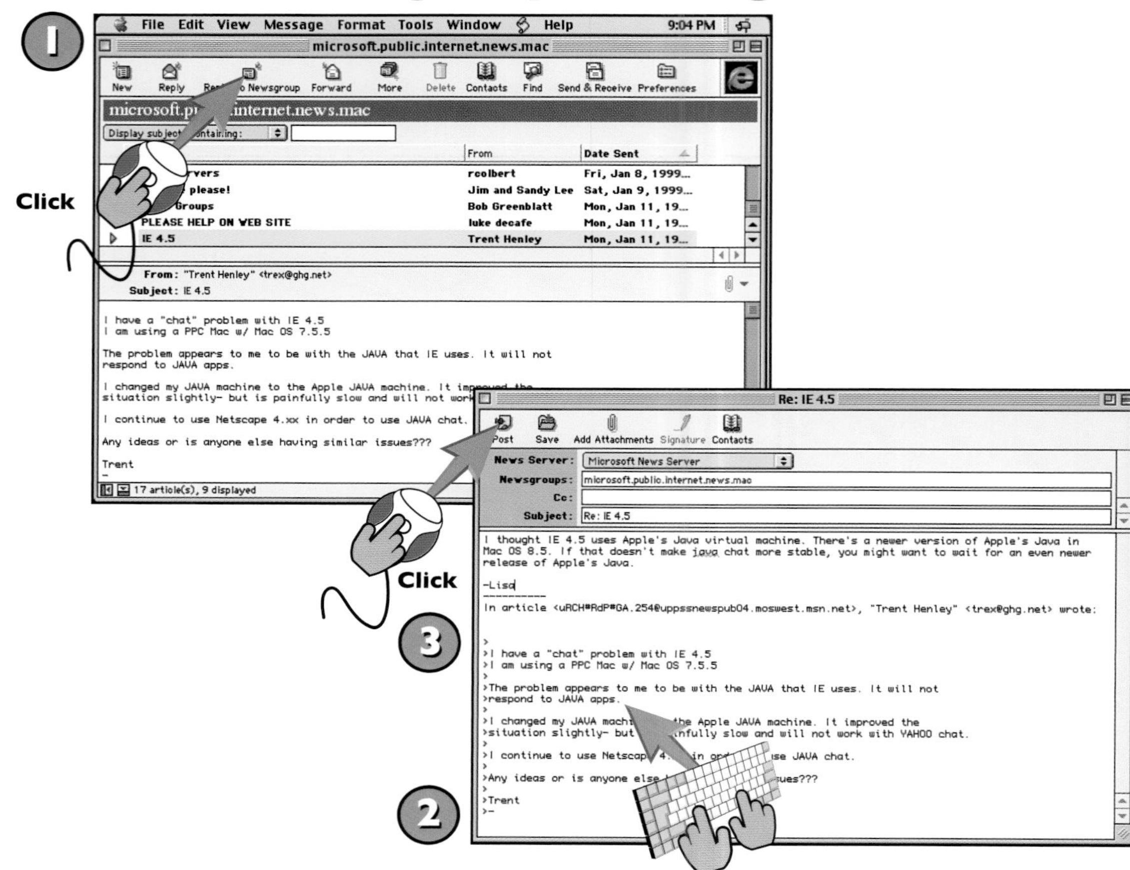

If you reply to an email, the text from the original email will automatically be included in your reply, but formatted with quotes.

You can also reply to messages privately by emailing the author as opposed to the entire group. To send such an email message, click the **Reply to Sender** button. Type your message, and click the **Send** button.

1. Display the message to which you want to reply, and then click the **Reply to Newsgroup** button.
2. Type your message.
3. Click the **Post** button.

Task 24: Quitting Outlook Express

When you have finished reading, writing, and sending email or posting to newsgroups, you can quit Outlook Express. Click the **OK** button if you are prompted to disconnect from your ISP when you quit Outlook Express.

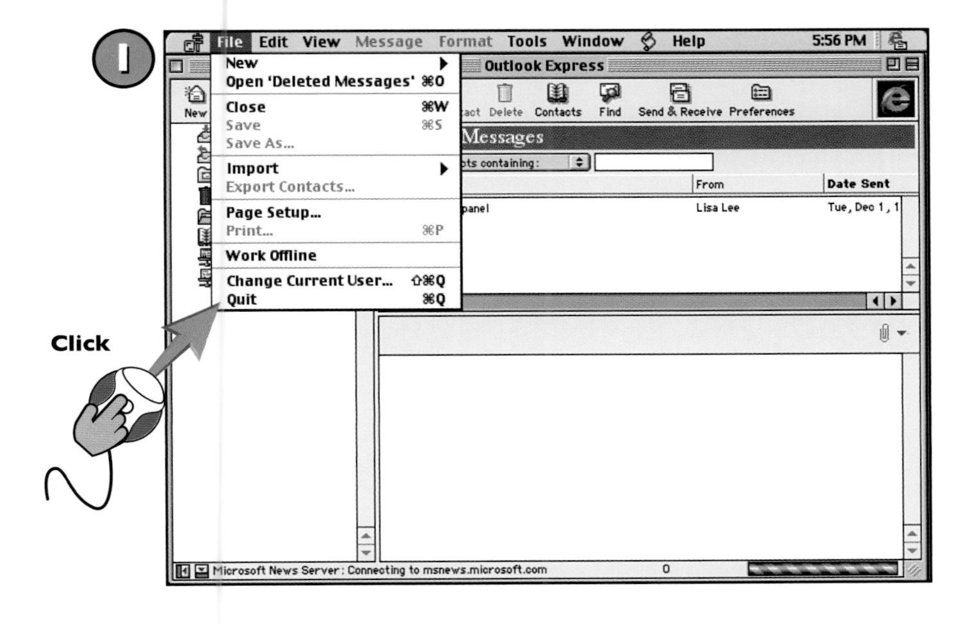

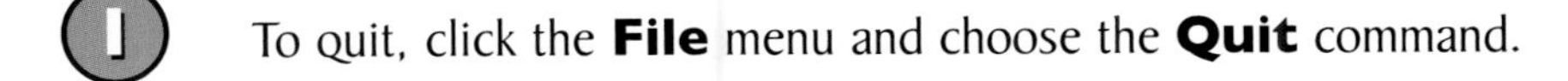

1. To quit, click the **File** menu and choose the **Quit** command.

3

PART

Part 3

iMac Hardware

More and more people are replacing their old PCs and Macs with an iMac. Its slim and colorful design not only weighs less than most desktop computers, but also outperforms them. iMac hardware consists of a 15-inch monitor, a CD-ROM drive, a 2D/3D ATI graphics card with 6MB of VRAM (2MB of VRAM on RevA iMacs), two USB ports, a built-in microphone, an external microphone port, three sound output ports, stereo speakers with SRS surround sound, and one modem and 10/100 Ethernet port—plus, of course, the USB keyboard and mouse.

iMacs do not include a floppy drive, nor do they have traditional SCSI, serial, or ADB ports for connecting hard drives, keyboards, or a mouse. The best and the worst thing about iMacs is its use of USB; each iMac has two USB ports. The best part is that one USB port can support as many as 127 devices. The worst part is that if you have older Macintosh hard drives or a scanner, you can't use them with your iMac. However, you can purchase an adapter for ADB or serial devices, and iMac developers are introducing more and more new USB products as more iMacs are taken home. In this part, you will learn how to use these new iMac hardware features, and harness the power of your iMac.

Tasks

Task 1: Adding a USB Device

USB (Universal Serial Bus) is a relatively new hardware and software technology that enables you to connect mice, keyboards, printers, joysticks, hubs, scanners, cameras, and hard drives to your iMac. You can swap USB devices without having to power off your iMac, and you can plug several USB devices into hubs to extend the number of devices attached to your iMac. To use most USB devices, you must install software—such as extensions, control panels, and drivers—in order to access the USB hardware. This task will explain how to connect an Iomega USB Zip drive to your iMac.

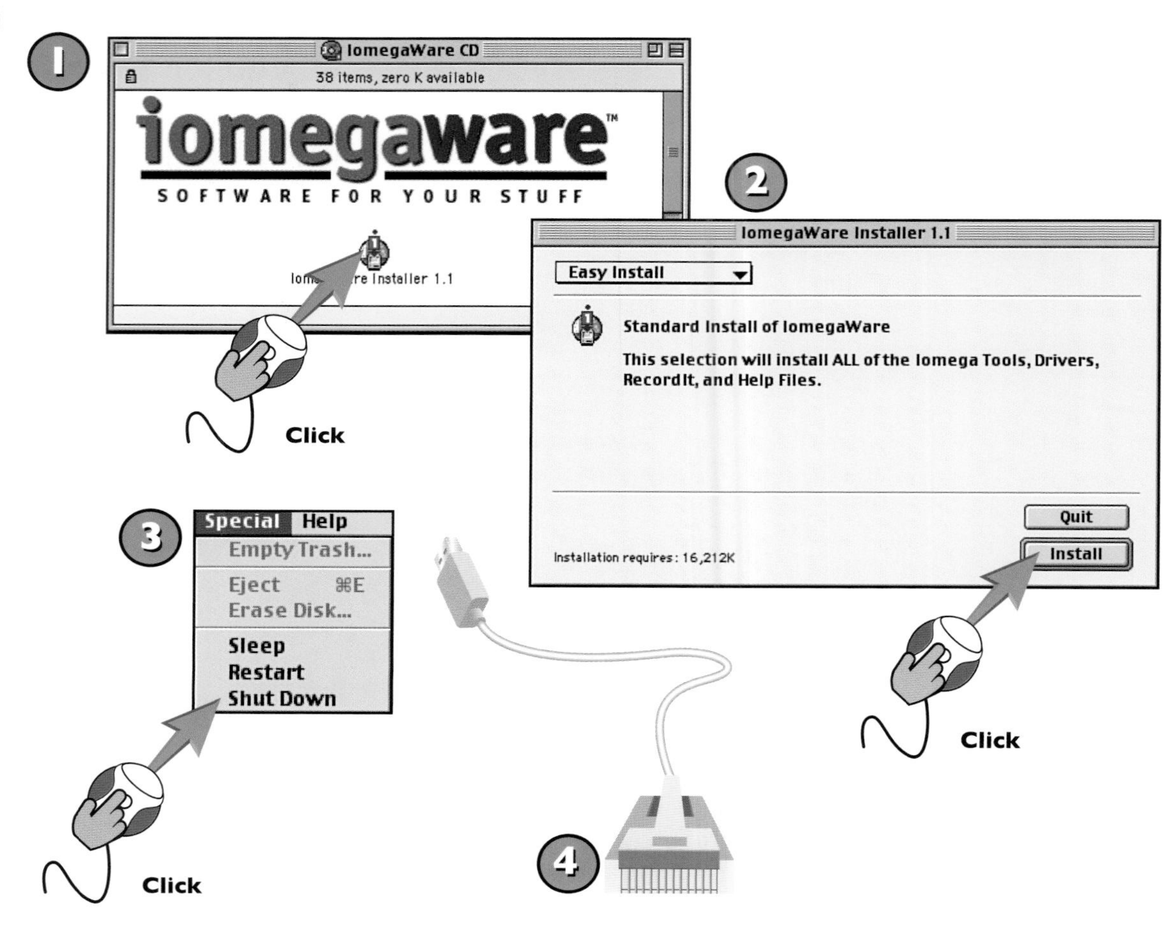

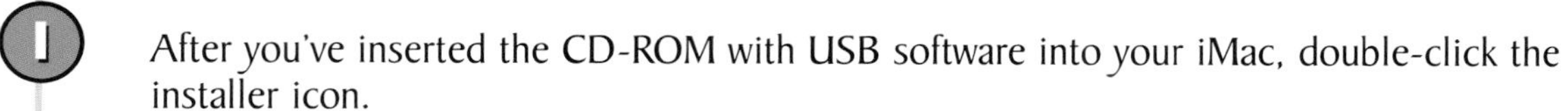

1. After you've inserted the CD-ROM with USB software into your iMac, double-click the installer icon.
2. Follow the prompts to install the USB software for your USB device.
3. Power off your iMac.
4. Connect the USB and power cables to the USB device.

For best results, click **Special** and choose **Sleep** before adding, removing, or swapping **USB** devices.

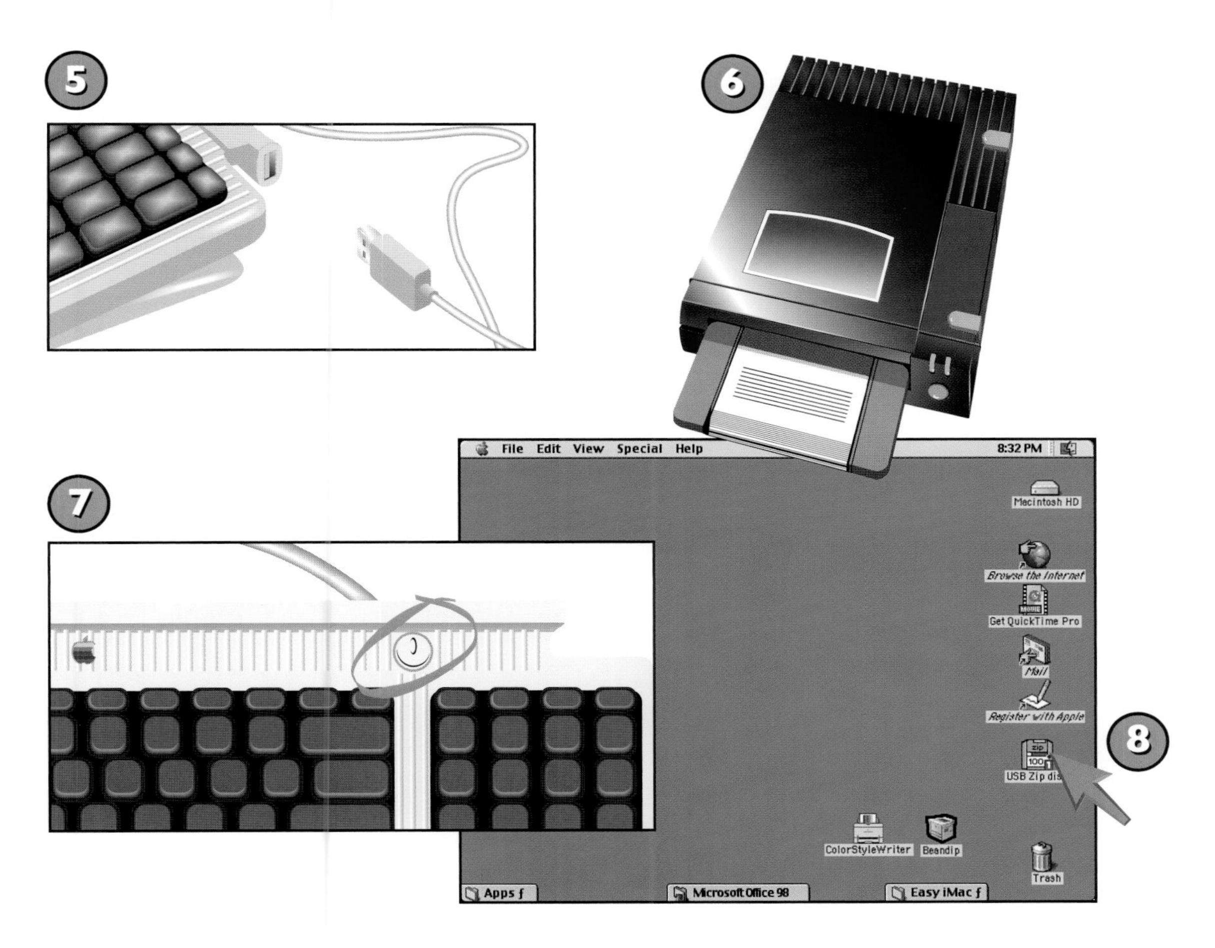

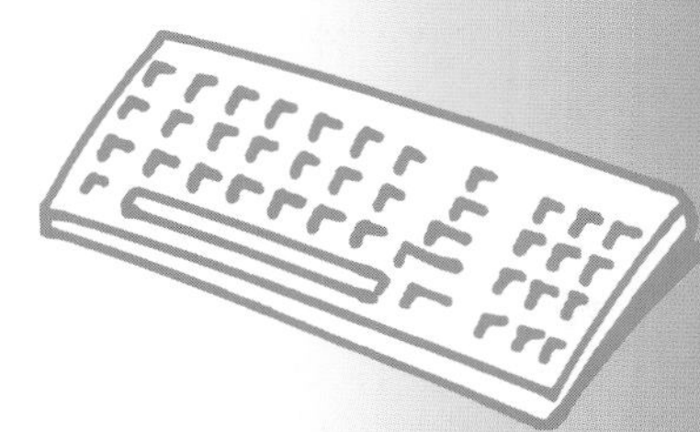

5. Connect the USB device to your iMac or its keyboard (in this case, insert the USB Type A connector end of the Zip drive cable in your keyboard).

6. Insert a Zip cartridge into the drive.

7. Power on your iMac.

8. Use the Zip disk in the same way you use your Macintosh hard drive to store files and folder.

If you decide you no longer want to use a certain USB device on your iMac, uninstall the USB software, then disconnect the cable and the USB device from your iMac.

Task 2: Adding Adapter Devices

If you do not have a USB device, you can purchase a variety of adapters for printers, keyboard, mice, and many others. There are USB-to-parallel, USB-to-serial, and USB-to-ADB port adapters and converters on the market ranging in price from $30 to $100.

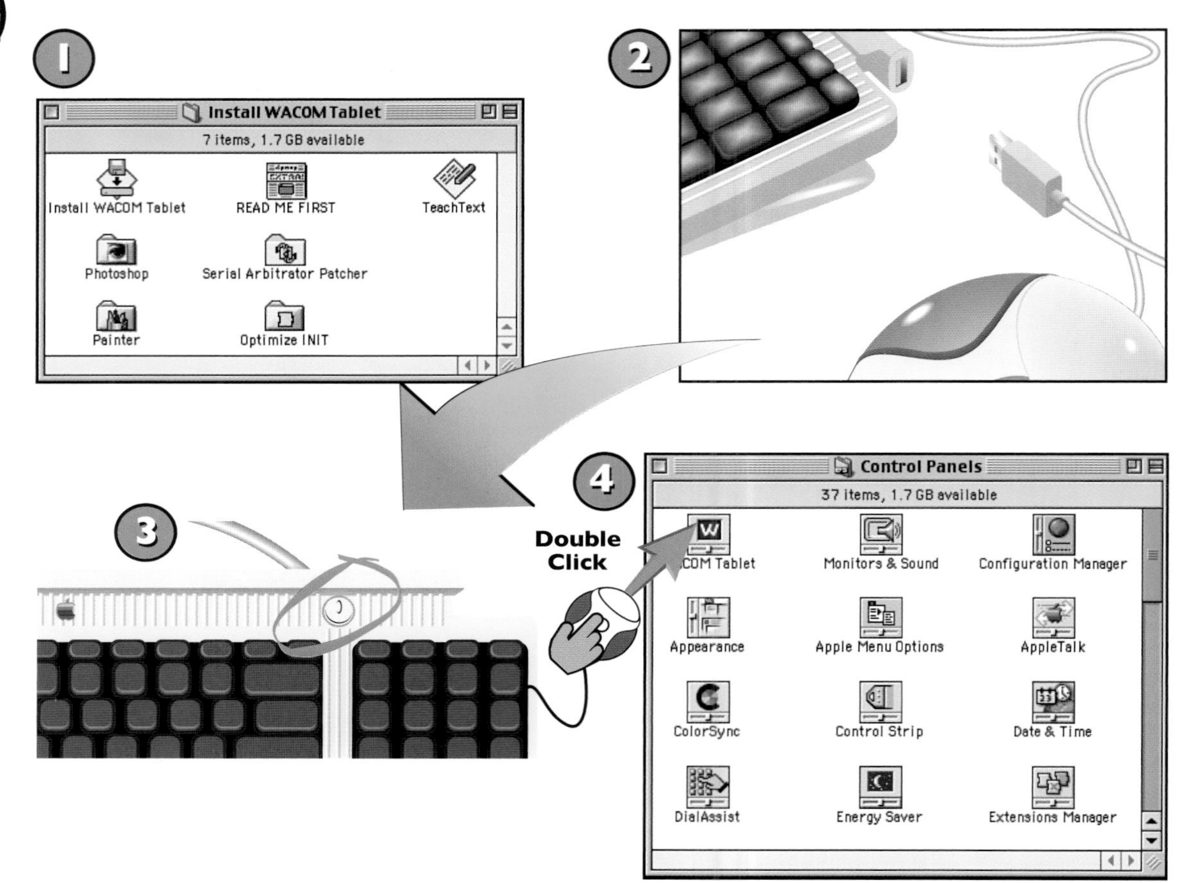

Be sure to install any software for the ADB device before connecting it to a USB adapter. Make sure the software is compatible with Mac OS 8.5, too.

If your ADB device also requires a serial port to operate, it will not work with the USB-to-ADB adapter since it will not be able to connect to a serial port.

Install any software for the ADB device (in this case the software is for a WACOM ArtZ tablet).

Connect the USB adapter and ADB device to your iMac (in this case, connect the WACOM tablet to the USB adapter).

Power on your iMac.

Use the ADB device. For example, move the mouse or press some keys to confirm that the newly added device works.

Task 3: Connecting a Printer

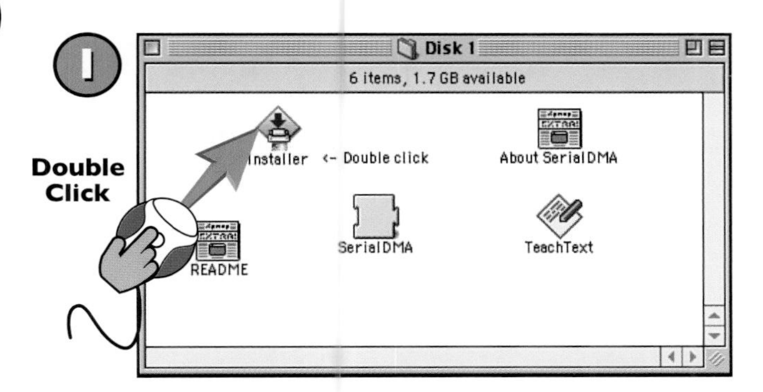

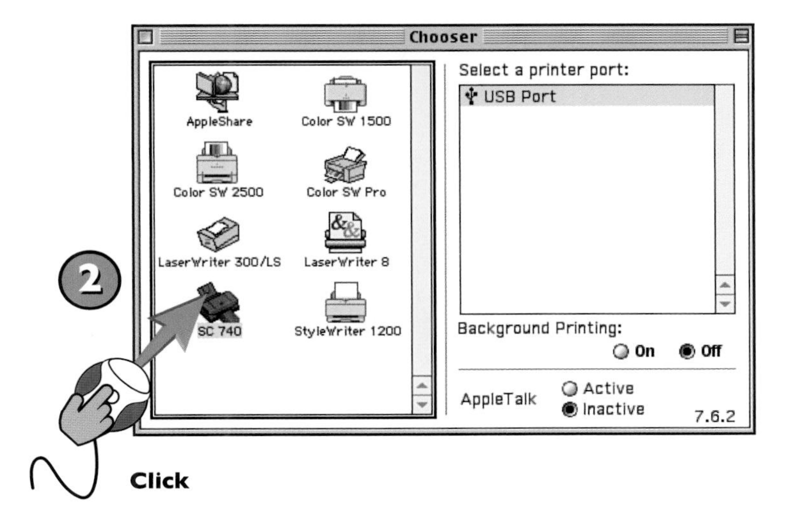

There are several ways to connect a printer to your iMac—the easiest is over an Ethernet network. You can also purchase a printer that has a USB port. If you have a printer with a parallel connector, you can use a USB-to-parallel port adapter with a parallel printer as long as you also have Macintosh printer software that works with your printer.

1. Connect the printer to your iMac and then install the printer software on your iMac (in this case, the software is for the Epson Stylus Color 740 printer).

2. Open the Chooser and select the printer (in this case the Epson 740 printer driver). Then print a document to the printer to ensure that it works.

You can connect printers that use the serial port if you use a USB-to-serial port adapter.

To remove a printer, remove the printer software, then disconnect the printer cables from the other USB devices connected to your iMac.

Task 4: Using an Infrared (Wireless) Connection

PowerBook 3400, 2400, and G3 models have an infrared hardware port that supports irDA, the same infrared protocol supported by your iMac. The wireless connection on your iMac enables you to transfer files between your iMac and a PowerBook, laptop, portable, or computer peripheral, such as a printer, that has a compatible infrared port.

Start Here

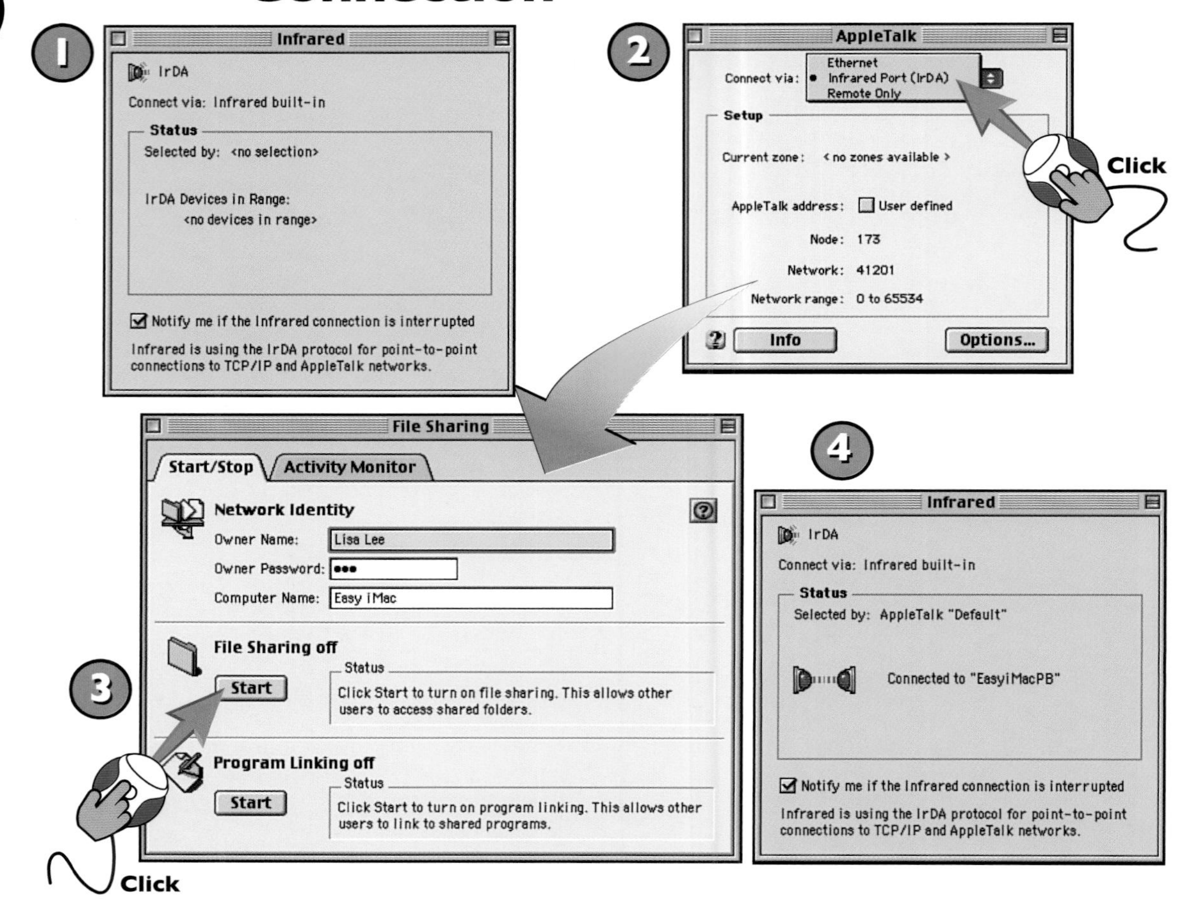

- Your PowerBook needs to be within 30 feet of your iMac to communicate with it reliably.
- iMac will talk to any other device that uses the irDA protocol, including PCs and peripherals.
- RevC iMacs—grape, blueberry, lime, strawberry, and tangerine iMacs— do not have an irDA port.

1. Open the **Infrared** control panel on both Macs (open the **Apple** menu, choose **Control Panels**, and select **Infrared**). Leave the window open to view the status of your IR session.
2. On the iMac, open the **AppleTalk** control panel. Click the **Connect Via** pop-up menu and choose **Infrared Port (irDA).**
3. Open the **File Sharing** control panel on your iMac and click the **Start** button in the **File Sharing off** area.
4. The **Infrared** control panel status will show that you are connected to the other irDA device.

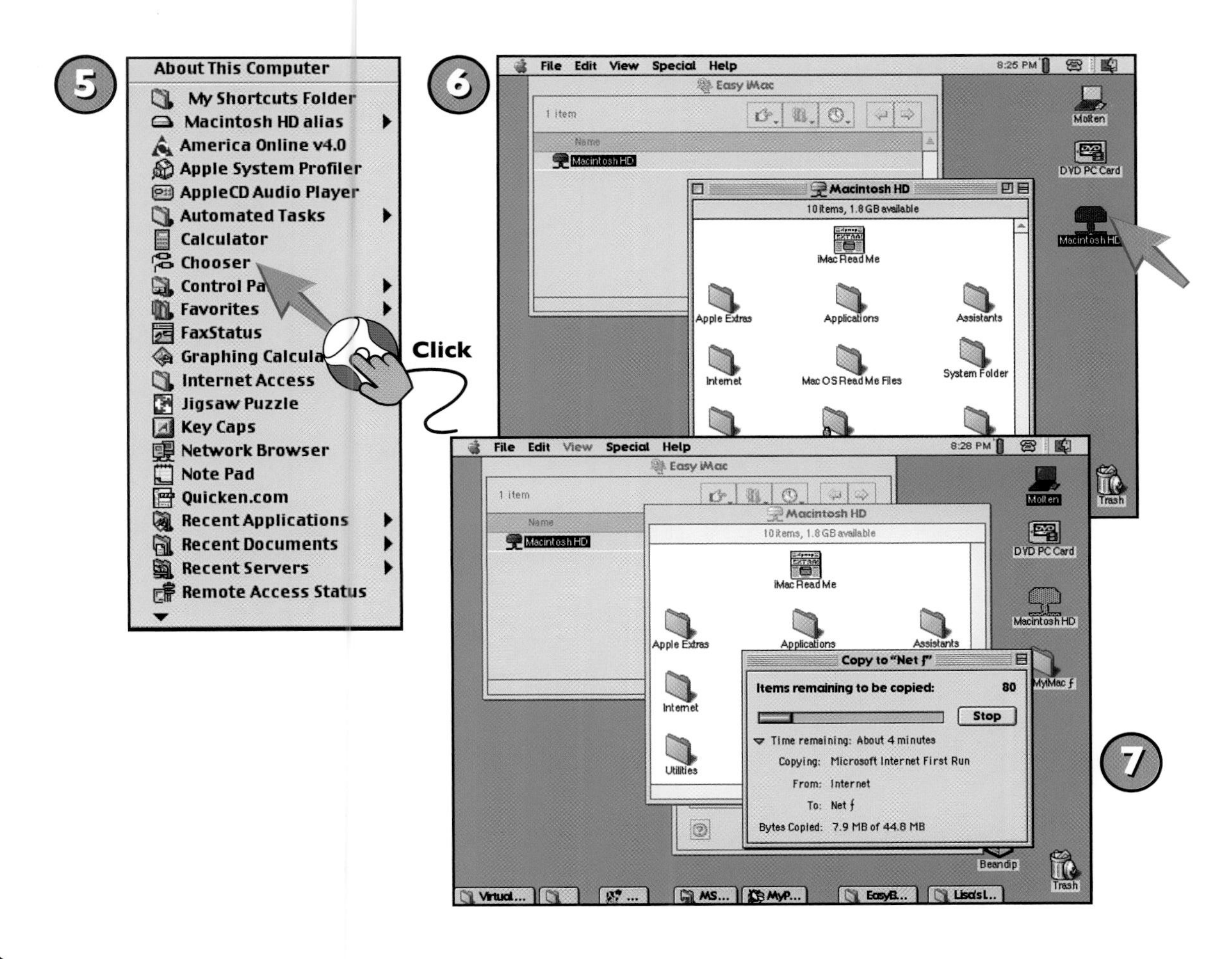

5. Click the **Apple** menu and select **Chooser** or **Network Browser** on your PowerBook.

6. Click the **AppleShare** icon in **Newwork Browser** and double-click the iMac's name. Enter login and password information, and click **OK** to mount the iMac's hard drive on the PowerBook's desktop.

7. Transfer files to the iMac as you would to a network server.

- **Infrared connections work like TV remote controls. For the connection to work, there must be a direct line of sight between the two devices.**

- **Transferring files over an infrared connection is slower than transferring them over Ethernet. If you have more than 1MB or 2MB of data to send between your iMac and a PowerBook, you should use an Ethernet connection instead of an infrared connection to transfer the data.**

- **To disconnect, move the iMac hard disk icon to the PowerBook's Trash icon.**

- **For more information about copying folders and files from your iMac to a network server, see Part 5, Task 13, "Copying Folders and Files."**

Task 5: Adding Memory

DRAM (dynamic random-access memory) and SGRAM (synchronous graphic RAM) are the two key kinds of memory in your iMac. DRAM is used to run Mac OS and any Mac OS applications. SGRAM also works with Mac OS and applications in order to bring more colors—at a fast rate—to your screen. Your iMac comes with 6MB of SGRAM (RevA iMacs only have 2MB of VRAM), and with 32MB of DRAM.

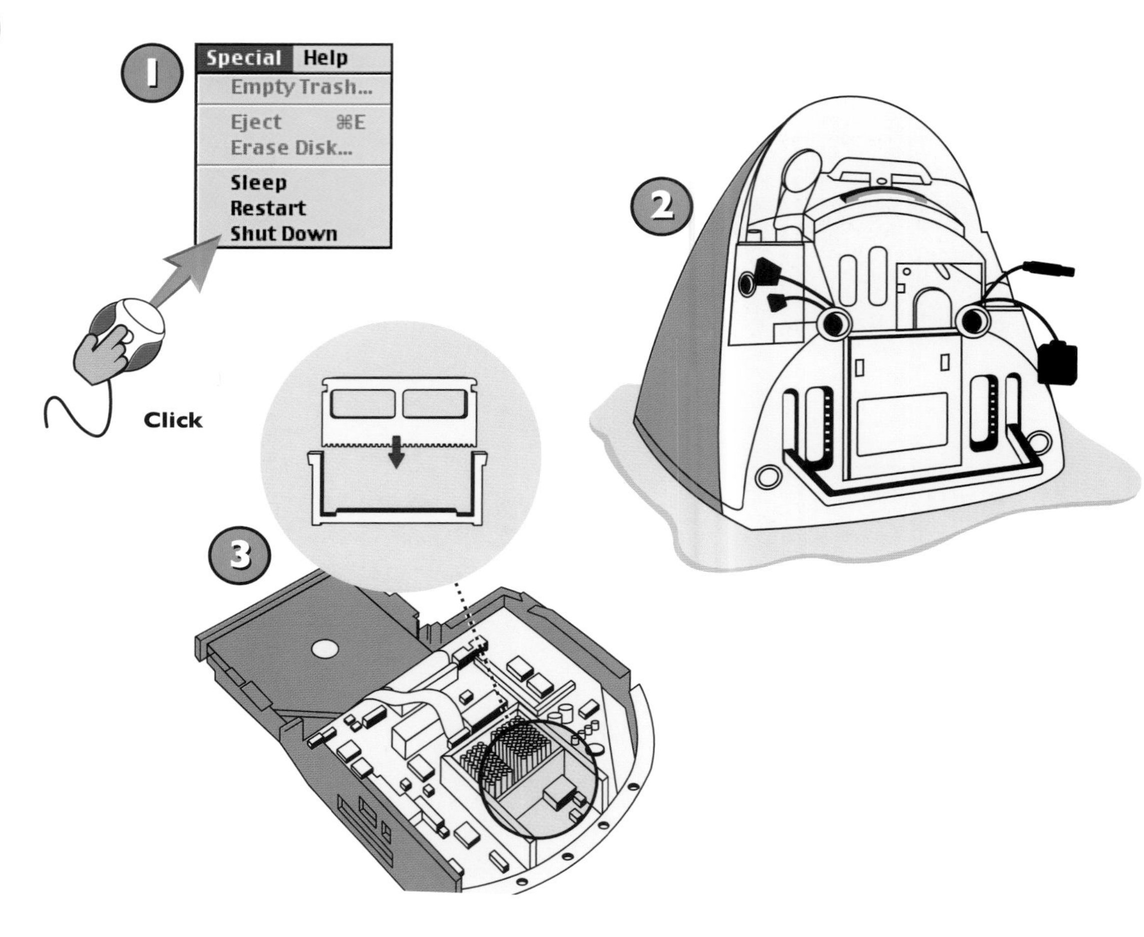

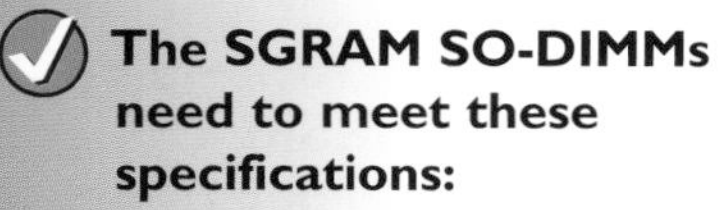

The SGRAM SO-DIMMs need to meet these specifications:

16, 32, 64 or 128MB of SDRAM-based memory

3.3 volt unbuffered, 64-bit wide, 144-pin with serial presence detect

100 MHz/10 nano-second (ns) cycle time or faster

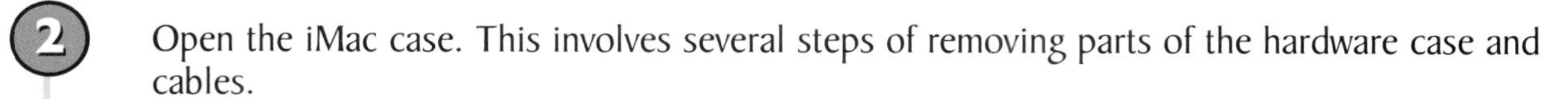

1. Power off your iMac.
2. Open the iMac case. This involves several steps of removing parts of the hardware case and cables.
3. Install the memory into the empty socket on the logic board, and then close the iMac case.

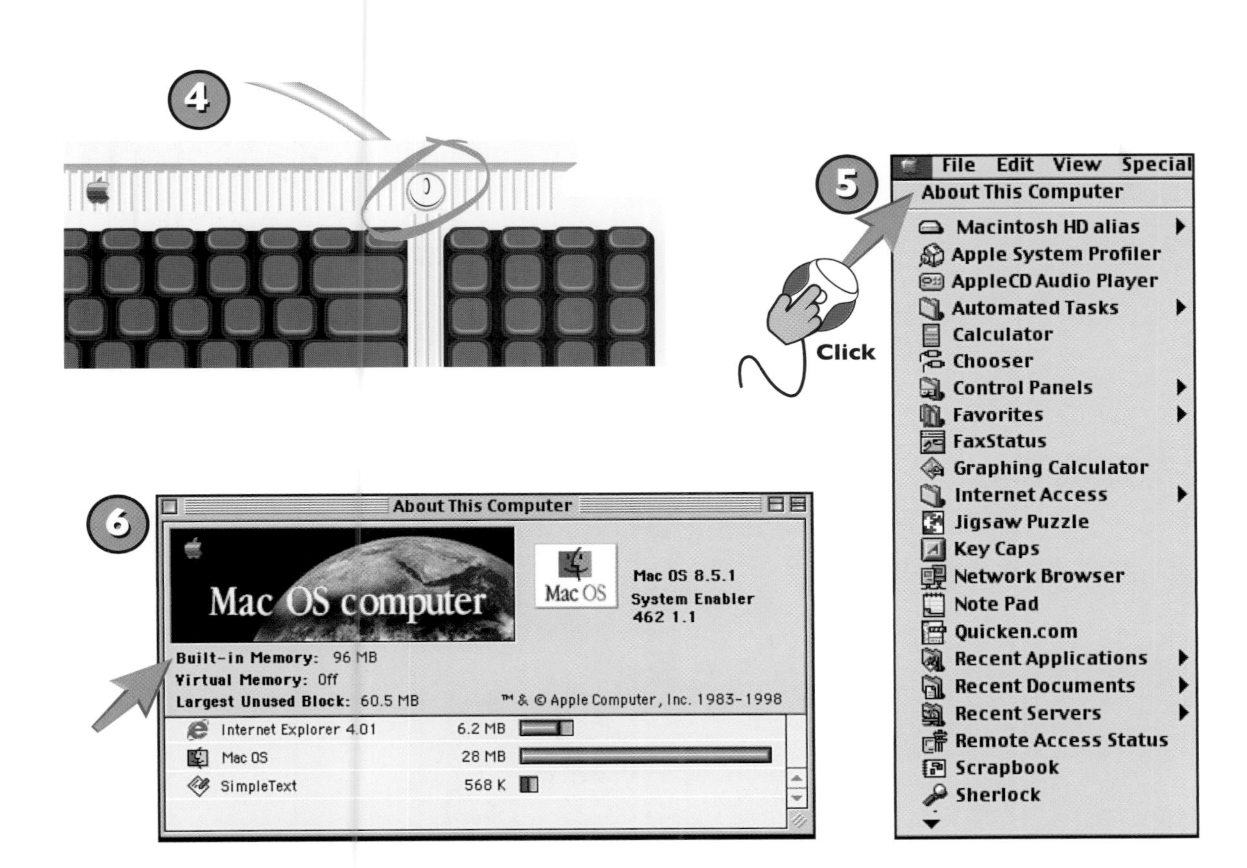

Your iMac uses synchronous dynamic random-access memory modules supplied in small outline dual inline memory modules (SO-DIMMs). There are two slots for memory on the iMac logic board. One slot consists of a 32MB memory chip, and the second can be used to add more memory.

Your iMac includes step-by-step instructions to install memory (including opening the case); you can find these instructions in Apple's Help Center. To use Apple's Help Center, open the **Help** menu and choose **Help Center**. Click **About Your iMac**, then click **Installing Memory**. If you haven't ordered your memory, read the **Memory Technical Specifications**. Otherwise, click **Installing memory in your computer** and follow the instructions to open your iMac's case so you can install the memory module.

4. Power on your iMac.

5. Click the **Apple** menu and choose **About This Computer**.

6. The amount of built-in memory should reflect the amount of memory you have just installed.

Task 6: Connecting to a Network

Start Here

To add your iMac to a 10/100BaseT Ethernet network, simply plug in the 10BaseT connector into the iMac's 10/100BaseT port. If you are setting up an Ethernet network, you will need a 10BaseT or 100BaseT Ethernet hub to connect with each computer on the network.

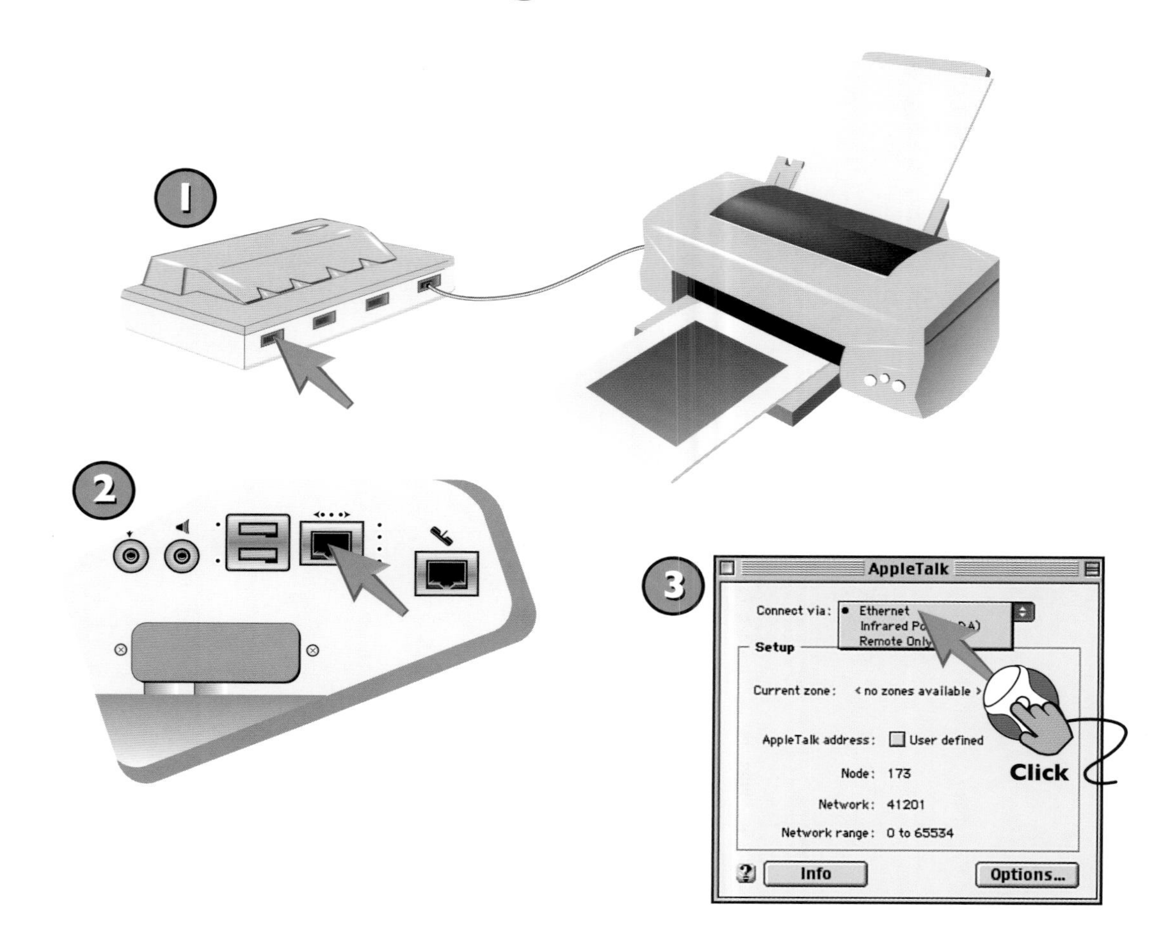

✓ The 10BaseT connector looks similar to a telephone or modem connector, but is slightly larger.

✓ It is possible to use a 10BaseT cable to connect two computers to create a network between them. However, you need to purchase a special patch cable—called a *crossover cable*—that twists one of the wires inside the Ethernet jack so you can bypass using an Ethernet hub. A traditional 10BaseT cable will not work.

1. Plug one end of the 10BaseT connector into an Ethernet hub.
2. Connect the other end into your iMac's Ethernet port.
3. Open the **AppleTalk** control panel (click the **Apple** menu, choose **Control Panels**, then choose **AppleTalk**), click the **Connect via** pop-up menu, and choose **Ethernet**.

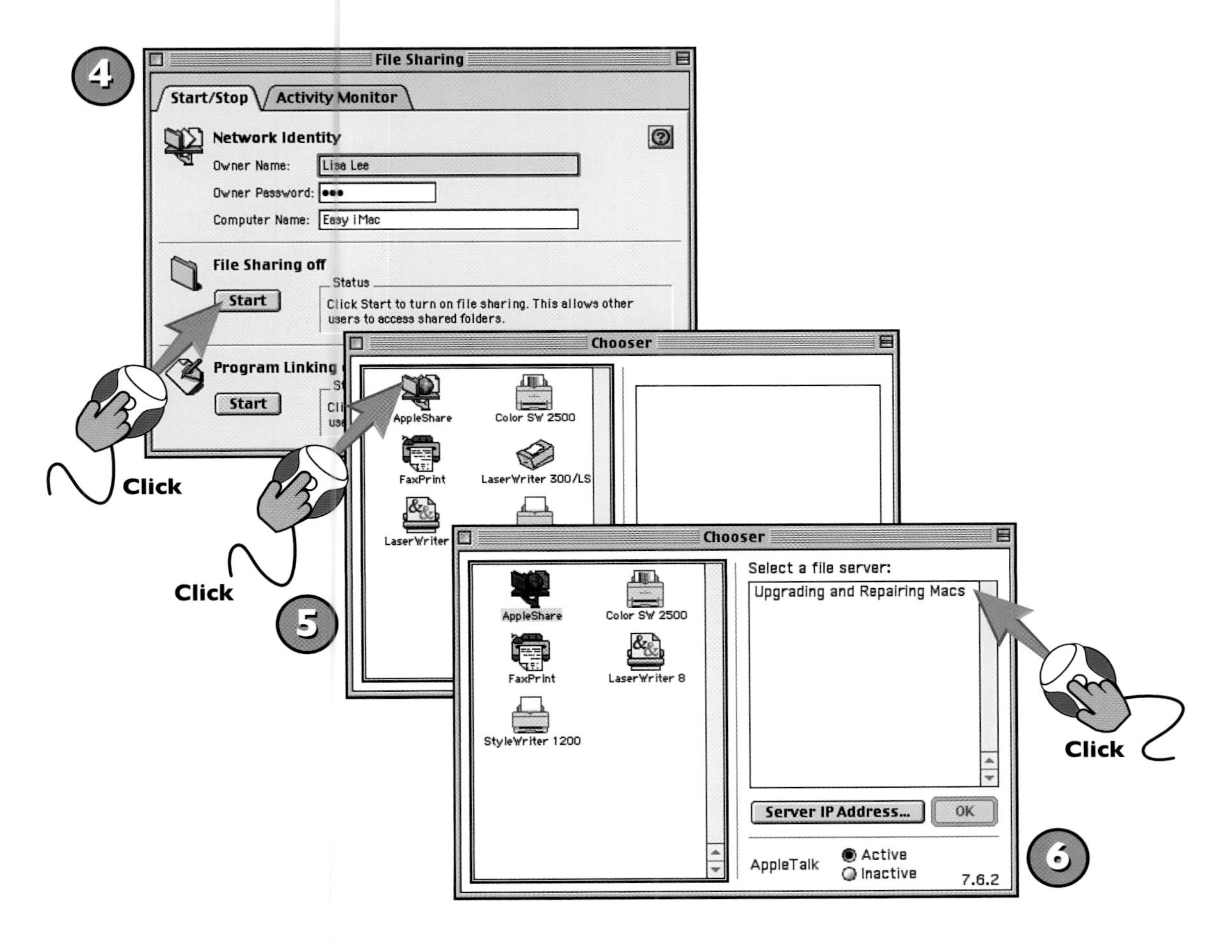

4. Repeat steps 2 and 3 on the second computer on the network, and then open the **File Sharing** control panel. Click the **Start** button under **File Sharing off**.

5. Click the **Apple** menu, select **Chooser**, and then click the **AppleShare** icon.

6. Once file sharing is started on the second computer, its name appears in the **Chooser** window on your iMac.

You can also use your modem to connect to another printer. However, 10/100BaseT is a more efficient and faster network connection.

If you are unable to select Ethernet in the AppleTalk control panel, check the Ethernet cables and make sure the light on the Ethernet port is lit (indicating that it senses a connection). Try unplugging and replugging in the 10BaseT connector to make sure it is connected correctly.

Task 7: Using USB Hubs

One of the best things about USB is that you can add a hub to centralize the USB device connections. Most hubs are either four- or seven-port hubs. You can plug one end of the hub into your iMac, and add four additional devices to the other side of the hub. A hub not only reduces cable clutter, but improves the performance of several USB devices connected to one iMac.

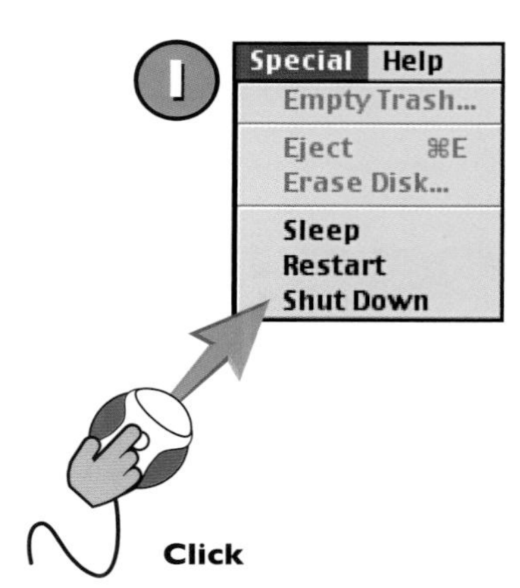

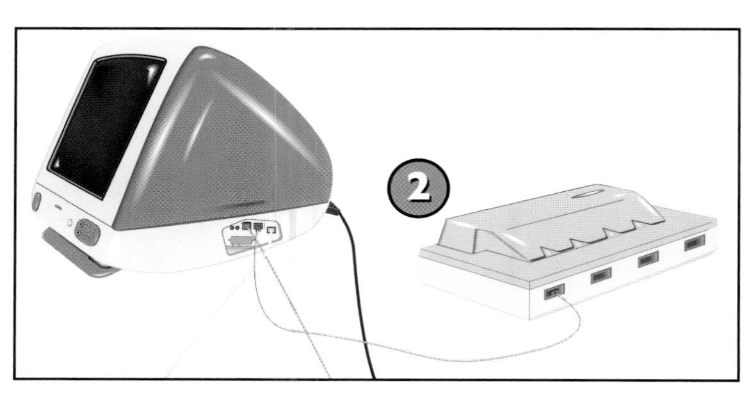

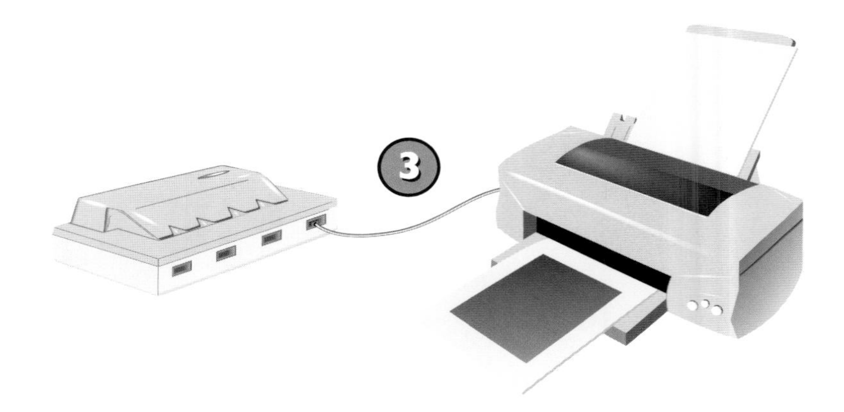

✓ Four-port hubs cost approximately $100. Seven-port hubs range in price from $130 to $200.

✓ Your iMac comes with two USB ports, so if you do not plan to purchase any additional USB products, you probably won't need to purchase a USB hub.

1. Power off your iMac.
2. Connect the hub to your iMac.
3. Connect any USB devices to the hub.

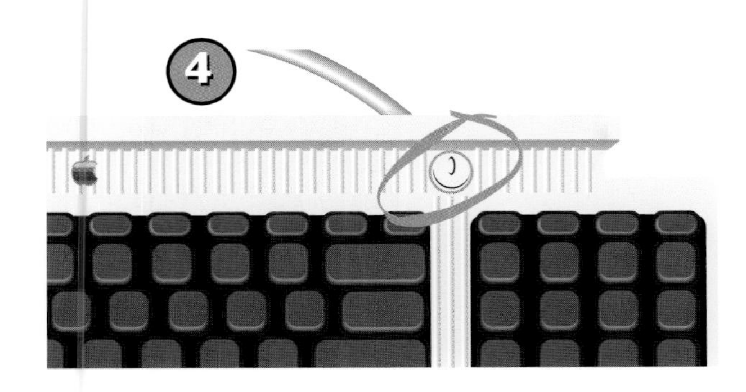

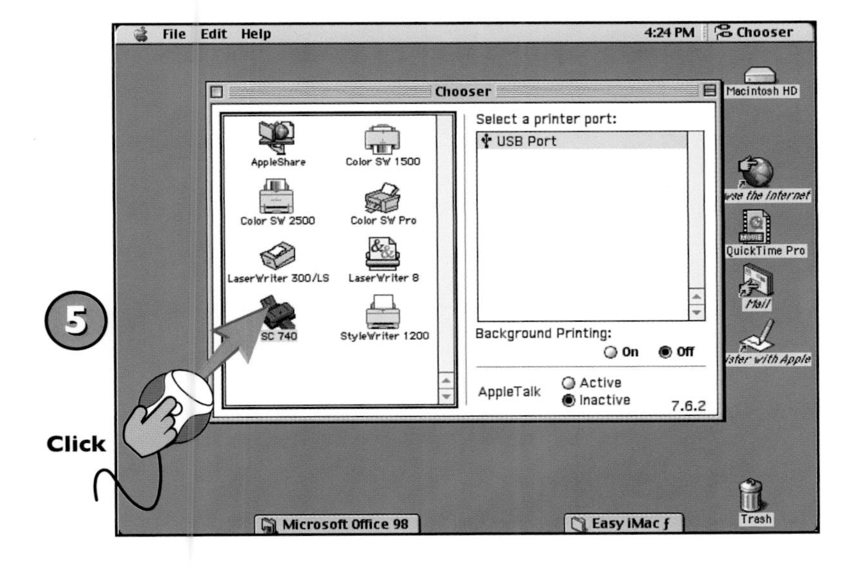

4. Power on your iMac.

5. Use the devices to make sure they work. To test a USB printer, open the **Apple** menu, select **Chooser**, click the printer driver, click **File**, and choose **Print One Copy**.

If you are considering buying a hub, try to approximate the number of USB devices you currently have as well as the number you plan to purchase, then add one or two additional ports to that number.

If you have several USB devices, with a lot of cabling between them, you may notice a decrease in performance of your USB devices. Adding a USB hub may improve USB performance with your iMac.

Task 8: Troubleshooting iMac Hardware

Start Here

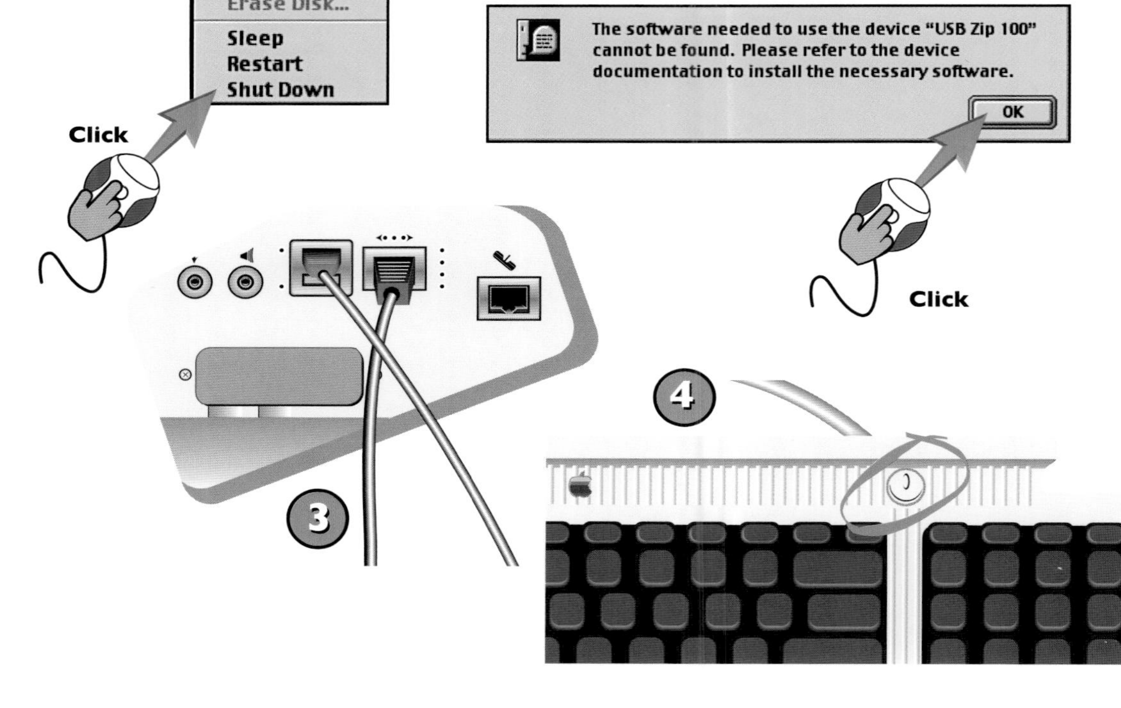

In general, adding software and hardware to iMac is easy and trouble-free. When a problem does occur on your iMac, don't panic. There are some easy steps you can take to isolate the cause of the problem. The first thing to try (if the problem does not involve data loss) is to reproduce the problem.

1. Power off your iMac. Connect a USB device to your iMac.
2. Power on your iMac. If you do not have USB software installed, you will see a dialog asking you to install the software for the USB device (in this case the software for the USB Zip drive).
3. If you have installed all software to use a USB device with your iMac, disconnect any additional USB devices from your iMac. (You do not need to disconnect your mouse or keyboard.)
4. Power on your iMac and try to reproduce the problem. If it is no longer reproducible, check to see if each USB cable works correctly.

The Internet is a great resource for troubleshooting hardware and software problems. Newsgroups, message boards, and Web pages have a wealth of information that you can use to get your iMac working again. Sites I visit regularly are www.imacintouch.com, www.imacworld.com, www.theimac.com, and the imacchannel.

You should periodically check Apple's Web site (www.apple.com) for software updates for your iMac.

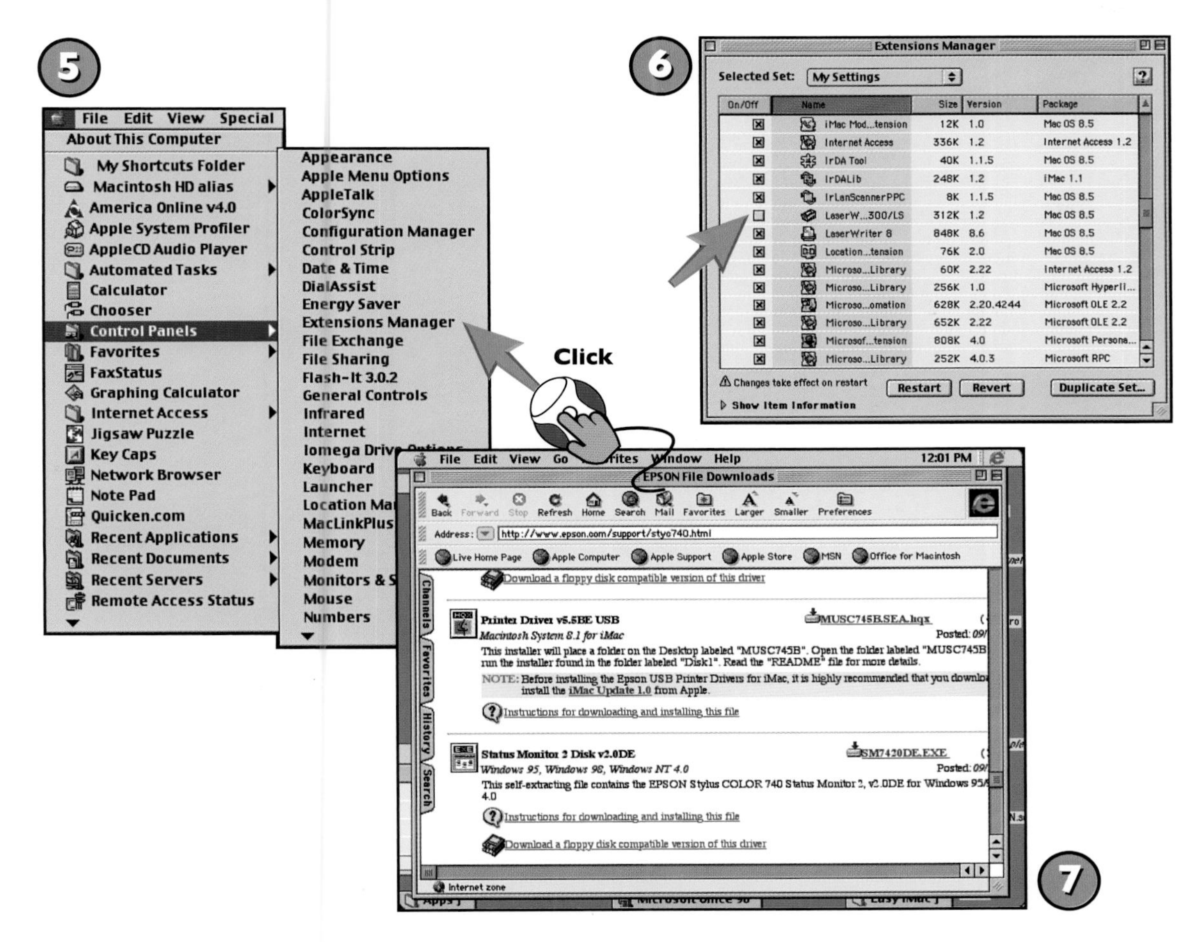

5 If the problem still occurs, click the **Apple** menu, choose **Control Panels**, then choose **Extensions Manager**.

6 Turn off any USB-related software, including software for any ADB, serial, or network devices, by unchecking the boxes next to their names.

7 Restart your iMac and see if the problem goes away. If not, check for a software update from the manufacturer's Web site (in this case, **www.epson.com**).

You might want to use a cable from a working computer to make sure you are not using a cable that does not work correctly.

If the problem continues to occur after you have removed any additional hardware on your iMac, try starting up your iMac with the Shift key pressed down to disable extensions to see if the problem goes away. If it does, you may have an extensions conflict in your System folder.

Using Applications in iMac

One advantage of using the iMac is the enormous number of available applications. You can use many word-processing, database, spreadsheet, drawing, and other applications in Mac OS. This variety of applications provides you with all the tools you need to perform your everyday tasks.

iMac applications are easy to open and use, and enable you to save data in files of different names and in various locations on your hard disk or a floppy disk. You can open a file at any time to view, edit, or print it. This part covers starting and working with applications. Several applications come bundled with your iMac. For more information about how to use these applications, see Part II, "iMac Software."

Tasks

Task 1: Starting an Application from the Apple Menu

Start Here

Most of the time you spend using your computer will be with an application. You can start an application in any number of ways, including from the **Apple** menu. After the application has run at least once, you can also select it from the **Recent Applications** folder in the **Apple** menu.

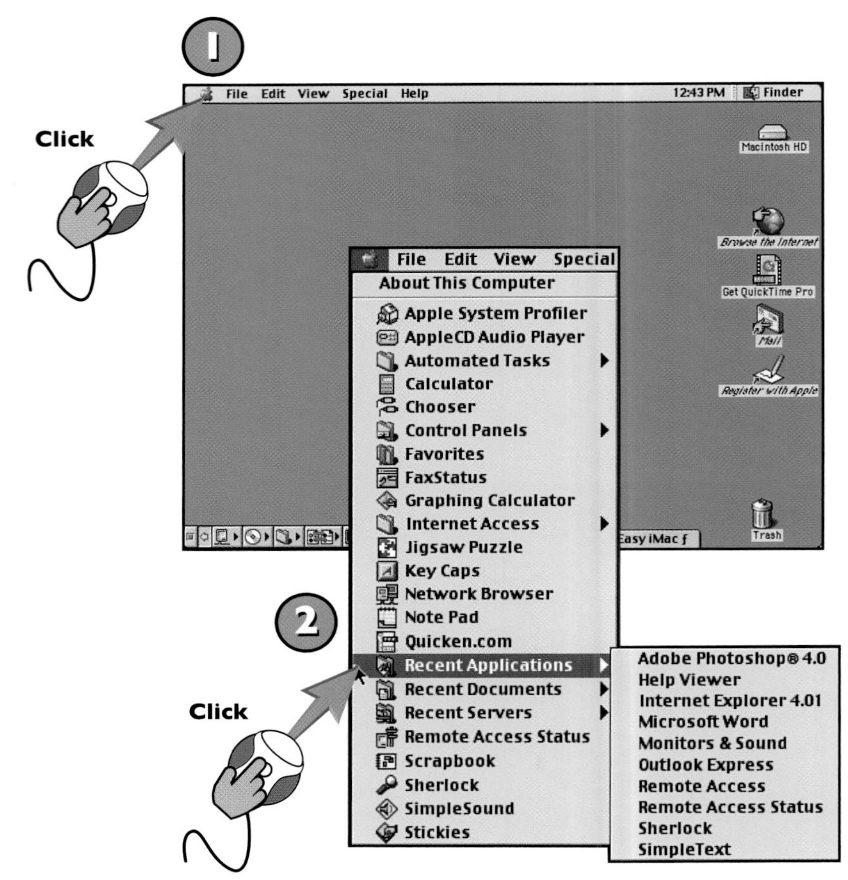

1. Click the **Apple** menu.

2. Select the **Recent Applications** menu item.

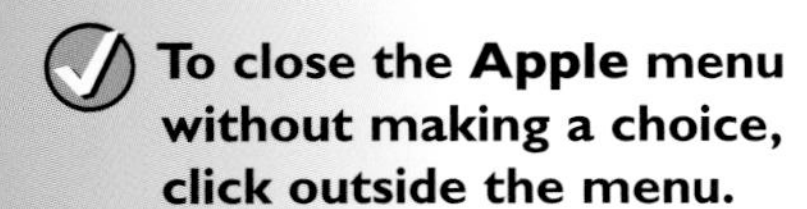

To close the **Apple** menu without making a choice, click outside the menu.

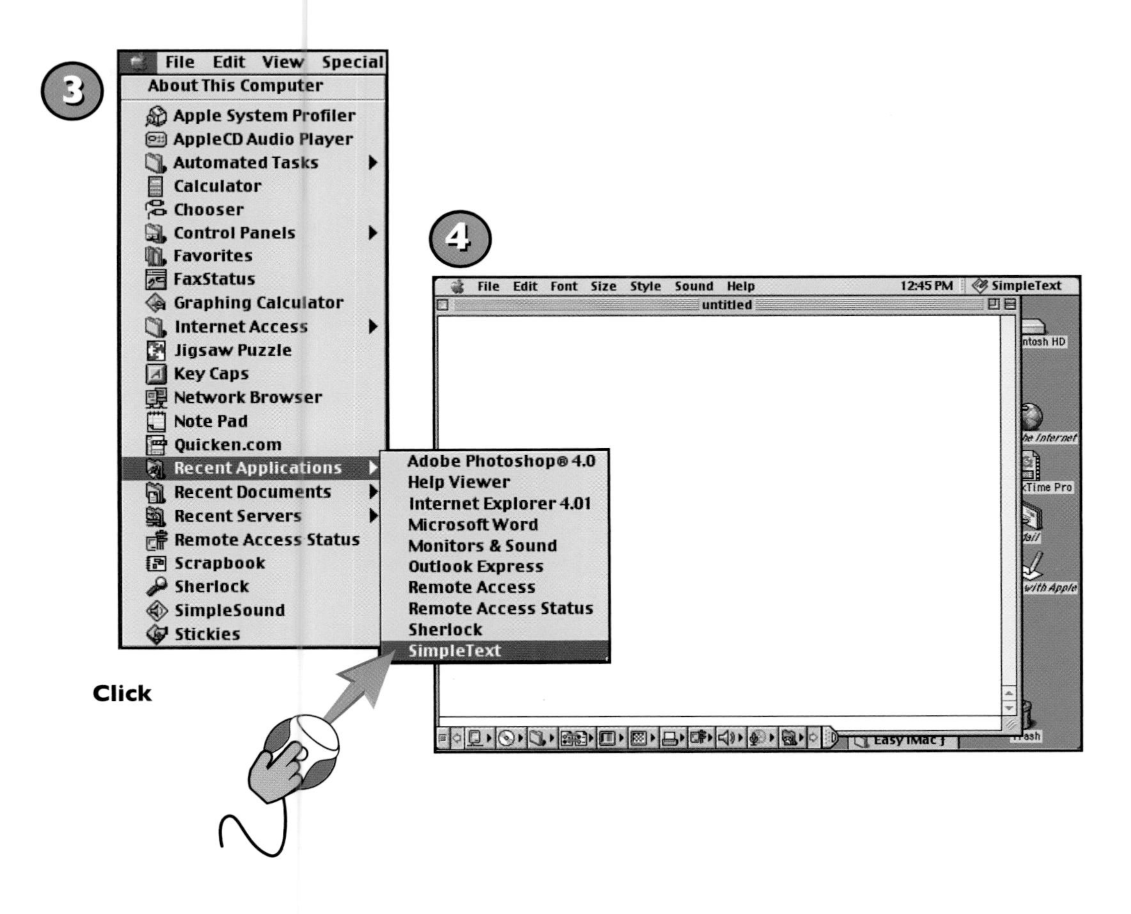

Select the application you want to start.

The application opens in its own window.

Task 2: Starting an Application from an Alias

If you frequently use an application, you might want to be able to access it right from the desktop. To do so, you can set up a shortcut, or alias, icon and then start the application by double-clicking that icon.

Start Here

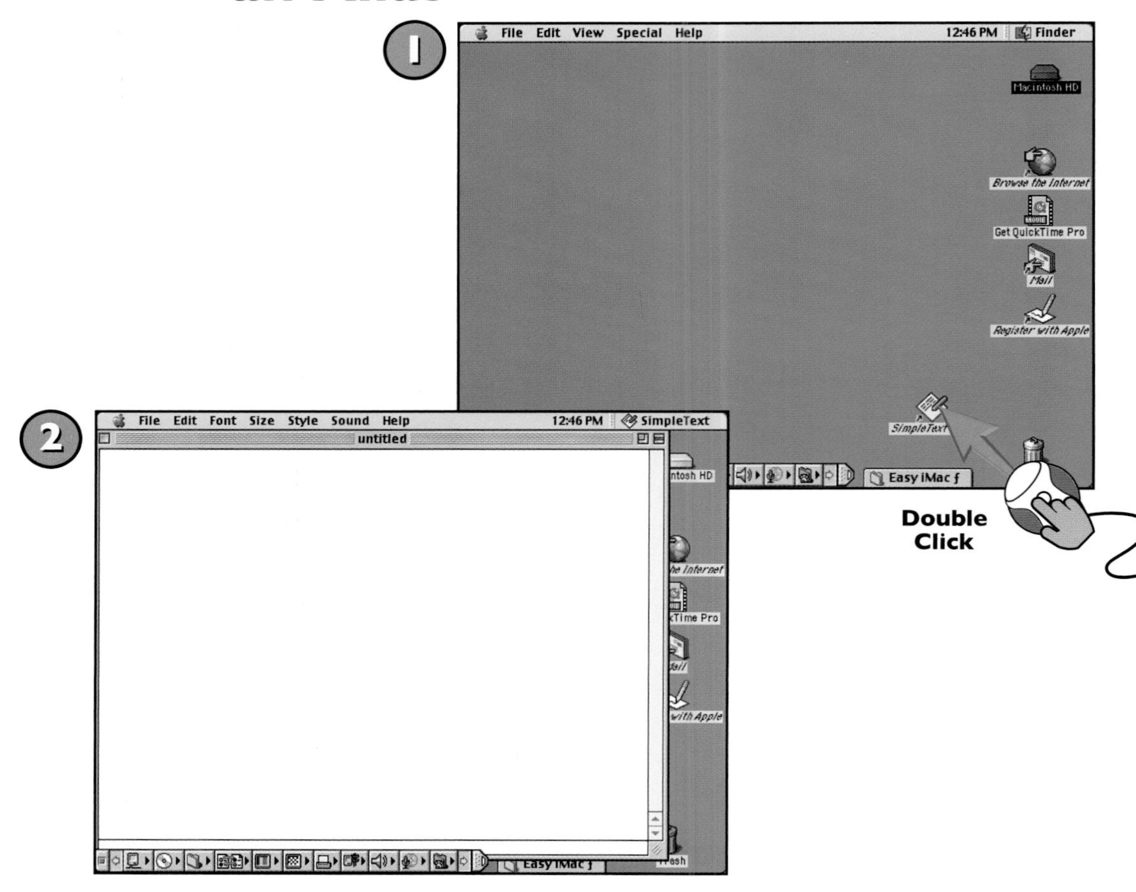

If nothing happens when you double-click the icon, or if the icon moves, it might be because you haven't clicked quickly enough or because you clicked and dragged by accident. Be sure to press the mouse button twice quickly to open an application.

To find out how to create an alias to an application, see Task 1, "Adding Aliases," of Part 8, "Setting Up Applications."

1. Double-click the **SimpleText** application alias icon on the desktop.

2. The application starts and displays its own menu bar and window.

End Task

Task 3: Starting an Application and Opening a Document

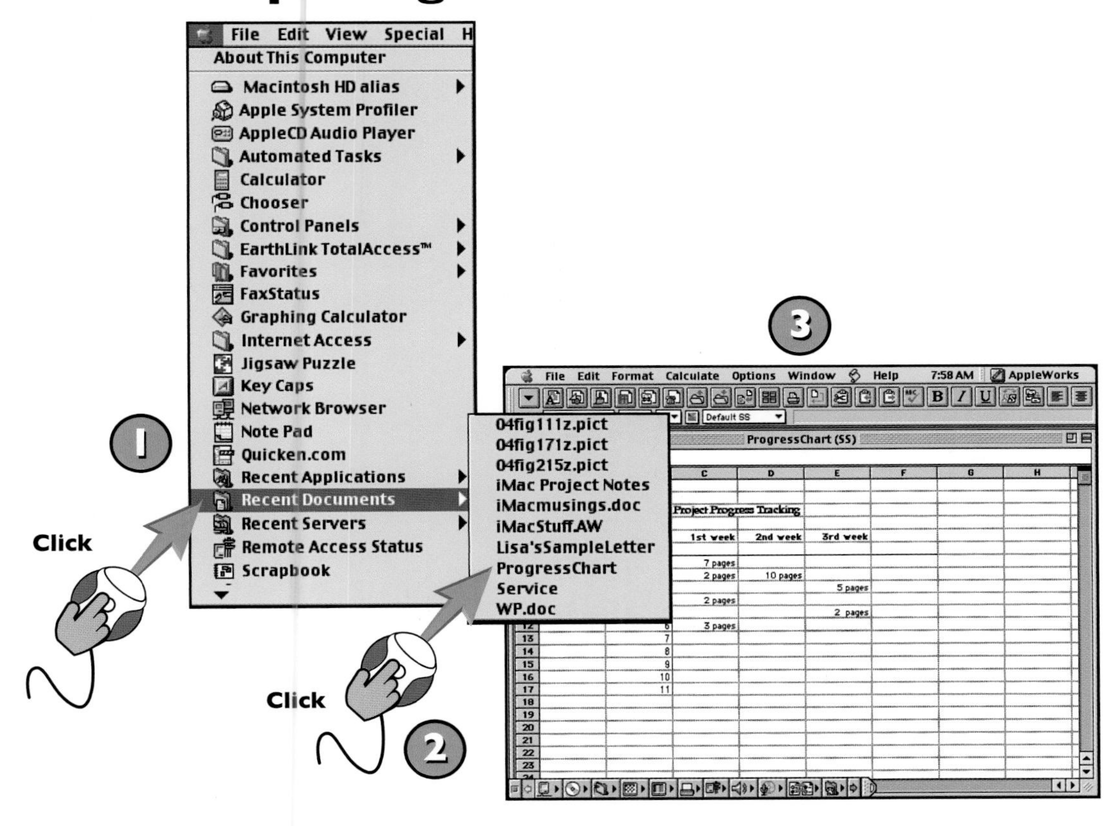

If you want to work on a document that you recently had open (in AppleWorks, for example), you can use an alias to both start AppleWorks and open the document. Mac OS's **Recent Documents** folder lists from 0 to 9999 documents that you have opened most recently.

1. Open the **Apple** Menu and choose **Recent Documents**.
2. Click the document file that you want to work on (in this case, **Progress Chart**).
3. The application for that document starts, and the document is opened.

Task 4: Switching Between Applications

Start Here

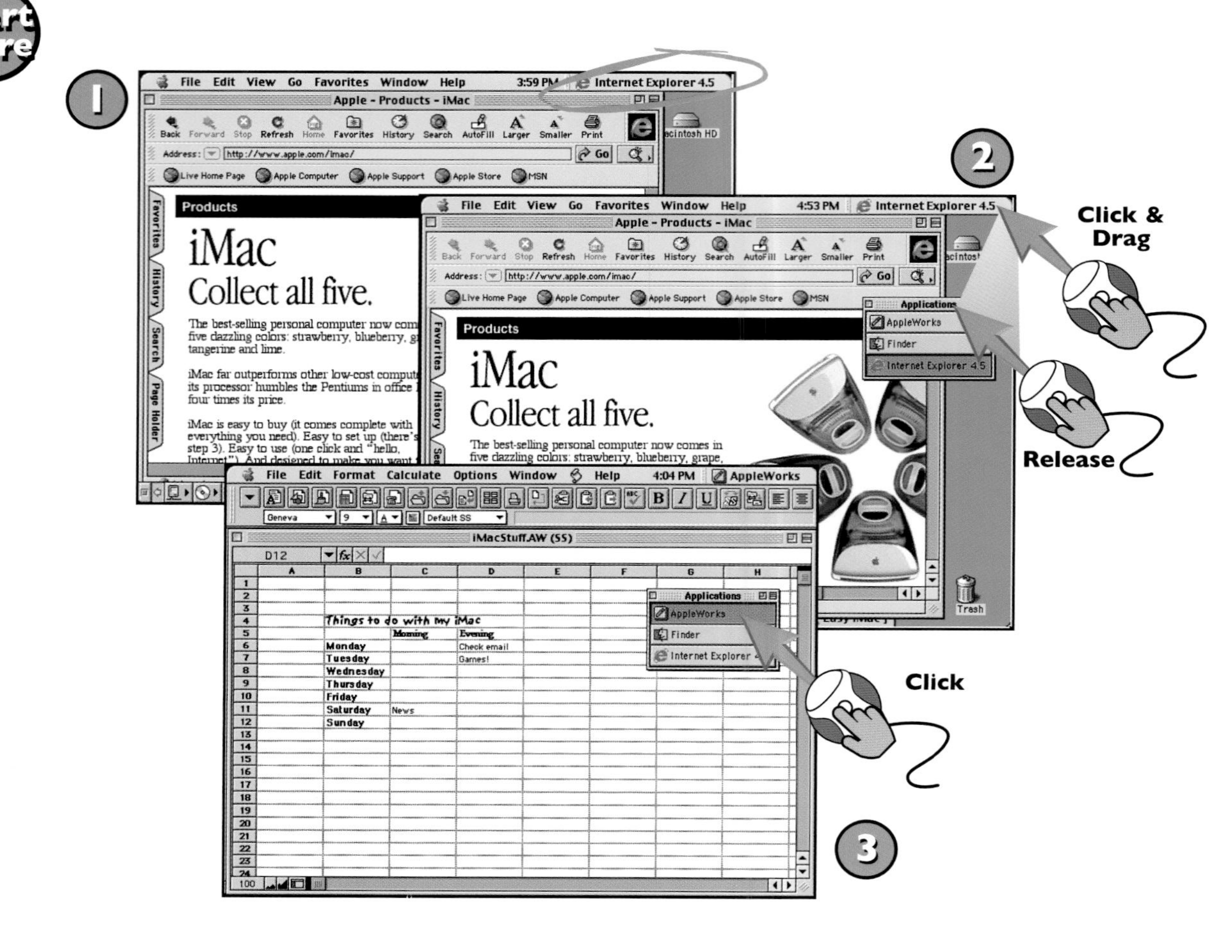

Start multiple applications. You'll see the name of the active application (in this case, Internet Explorer 4.5) on the **Applications** menu button.

Click the **Applications** menu button to see the other open applications listed in the menu. Drag the **Applications** menu away from the menu bar to turn it into a floating window.

Click **AppleWorks**. AppleWorks becomes the active application.

End Task

Most likely, you will work with more than one type of document and more than one type of application. For example, you might want to work on a spreadsheet while reading a Web page in your browser. Switching between applications enables you to share and compare data.

The number of programs you can have open at any one time depends on the amount of RAM (random access memory) in your system.

You can tell what programs are open by viewing the Applications menu. Each menu item is an application currently running on your iMac. The amount of hard drive space can also affect how many applications you can run at the same time.

You can make the Applications menu a floating window by clicking and dragging it to the desktop.

Task 5: Closing an Application

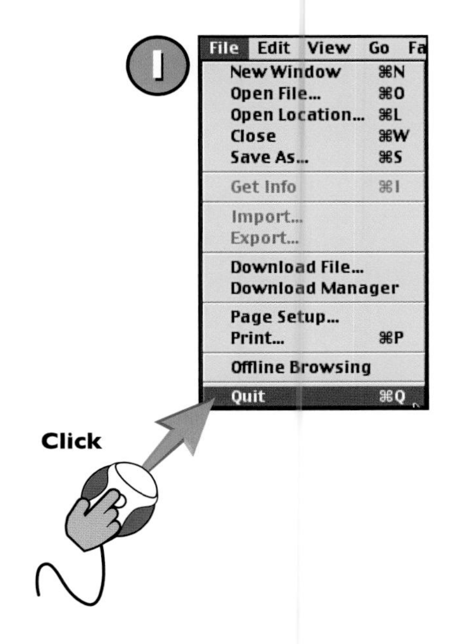

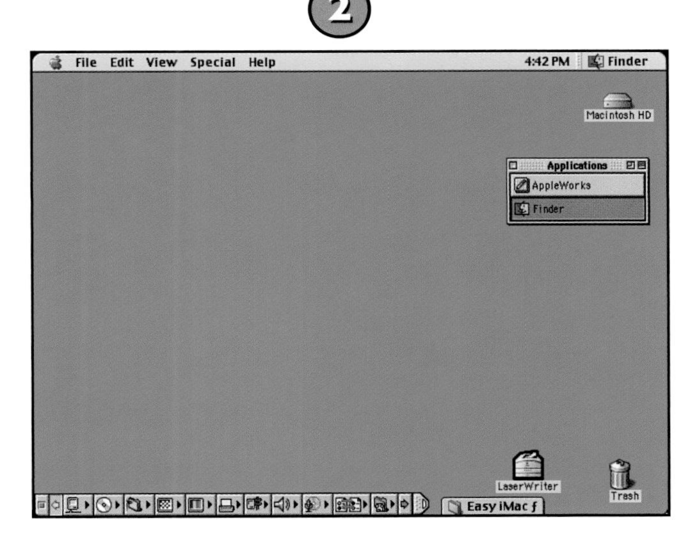

When you finish working in an application, you should close it to free system memory. Too many open applications can tax your system's memory and slow the computer's processes, such as saving, printing, switching between applications, and so on.

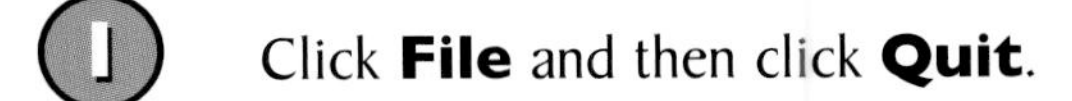

1. Click **File** and then click **Quit**.

2. The application (in this case, Internet Explorer) is closed. Notice that the entry for Internet Explorer has disappeared from the **Applications** menu.

To close an application, you can also press Command+Q.

If you have not saved a file and choose to close that file's application, a message box appears asking if you want to save the file. If you do, click Yes; if not, click No. If you want to return to the document, click Cancel. For more information, see the next task.

Task 6: Saving a Document

You can save documents and files so that you can refer to them later for printing, editing, copying, and so on. The first time you save a file, you must assign that file a name and folder (or location). You save documents pretty much the same way in all applications; this task shows you how to save a document in AppleWorks.

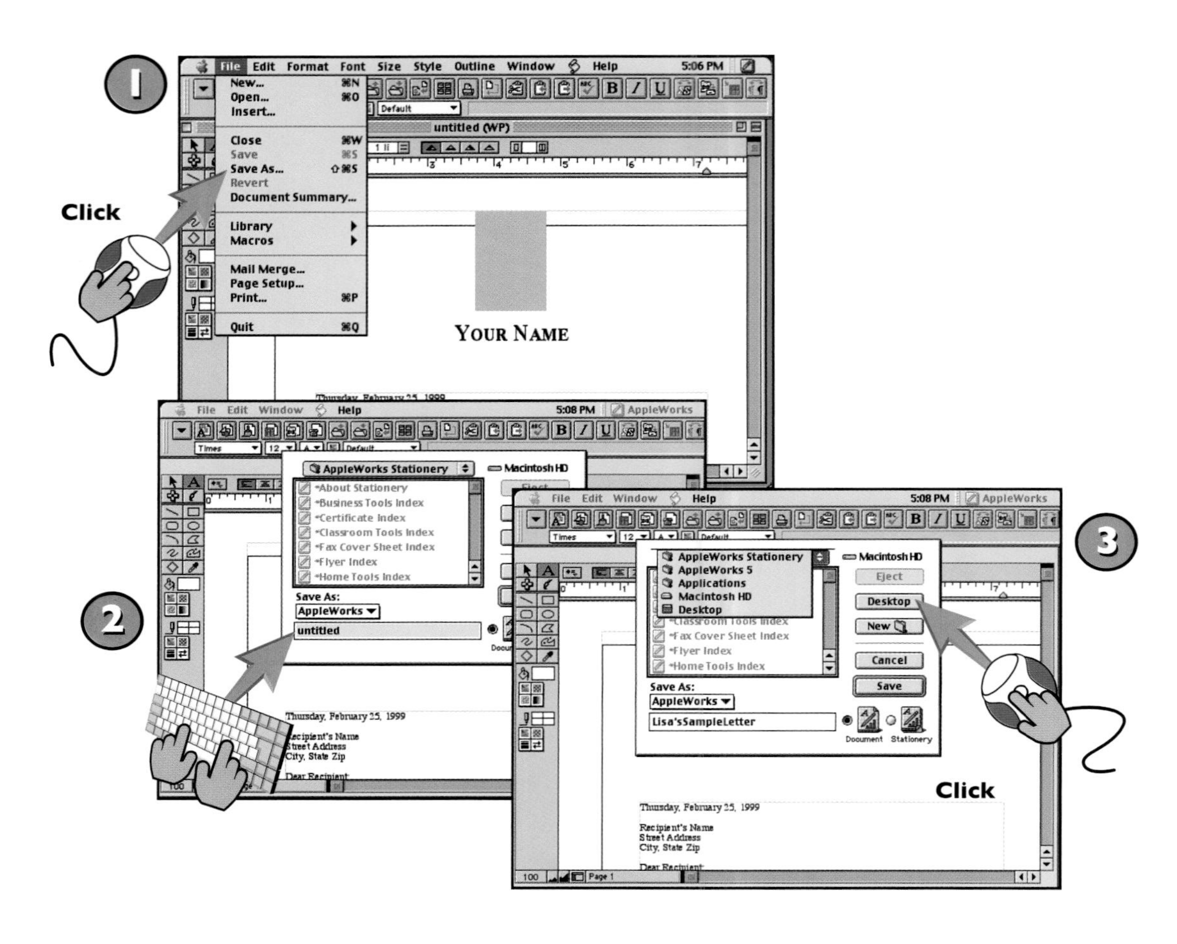

After you've saved and named a file, you can simply click **File** and select **Save** to resave that file to the same location with the same name. Any changes you have made since the last save are reflected in the file.

To save the file with a different name or in a different location, use the **Save As** command in the **File** menu and enter a different filename or folder.

1. Click **File**, and then click **Save As**.
2. The program might propose a name for the file. You can either accept this name or type a new one.
3. To save the document in another drive, click on the **Desktop** button and select the drive you want.

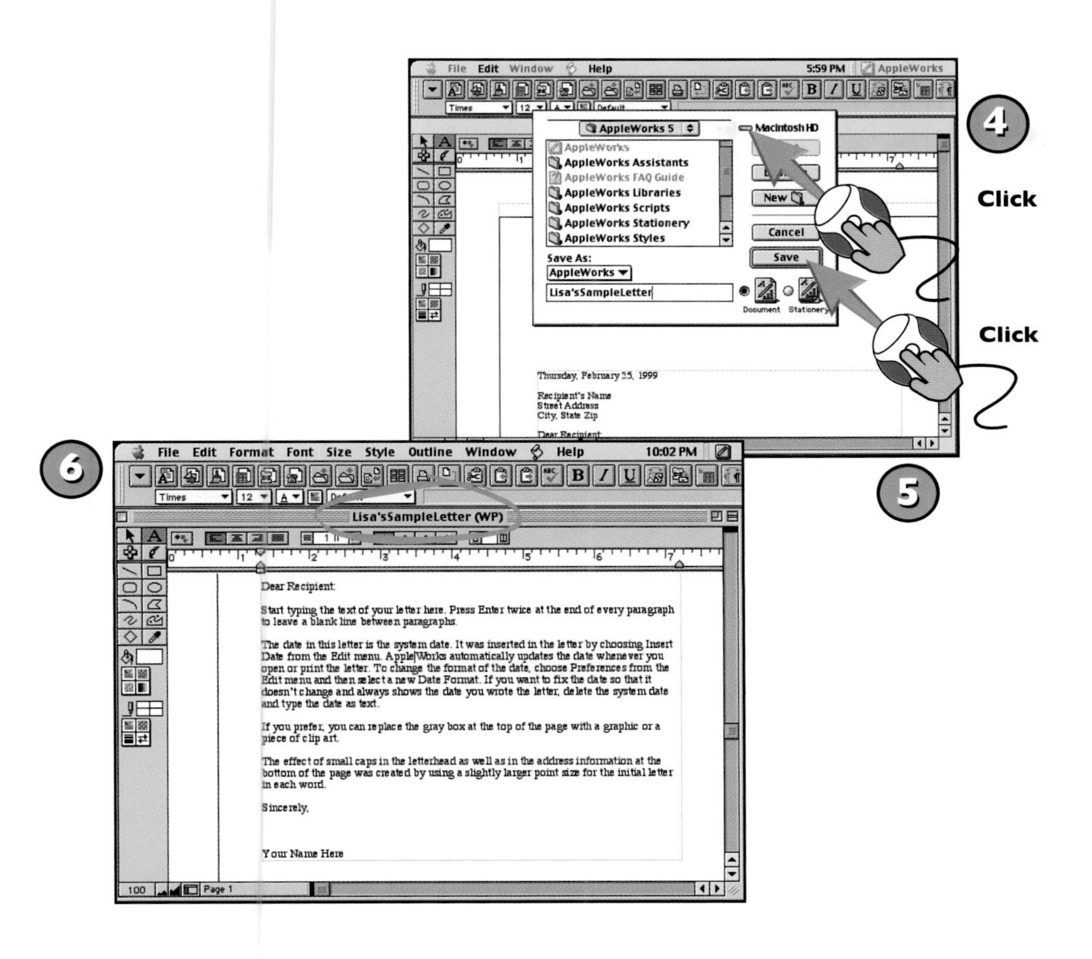

4. To save the document in another folder, double-click the desired folder in the list. To move up through the folder structure, click the hard disk icon.

5. Click the **Save** button.

6. The application saves the file and returns to the document window. The document name is listed in the title bar.

Task 7: Opening a Document

The purpose of saving a document is to make it available for later use. You can open any of the documents you have saved by selecting **File** and choosing **Open**.

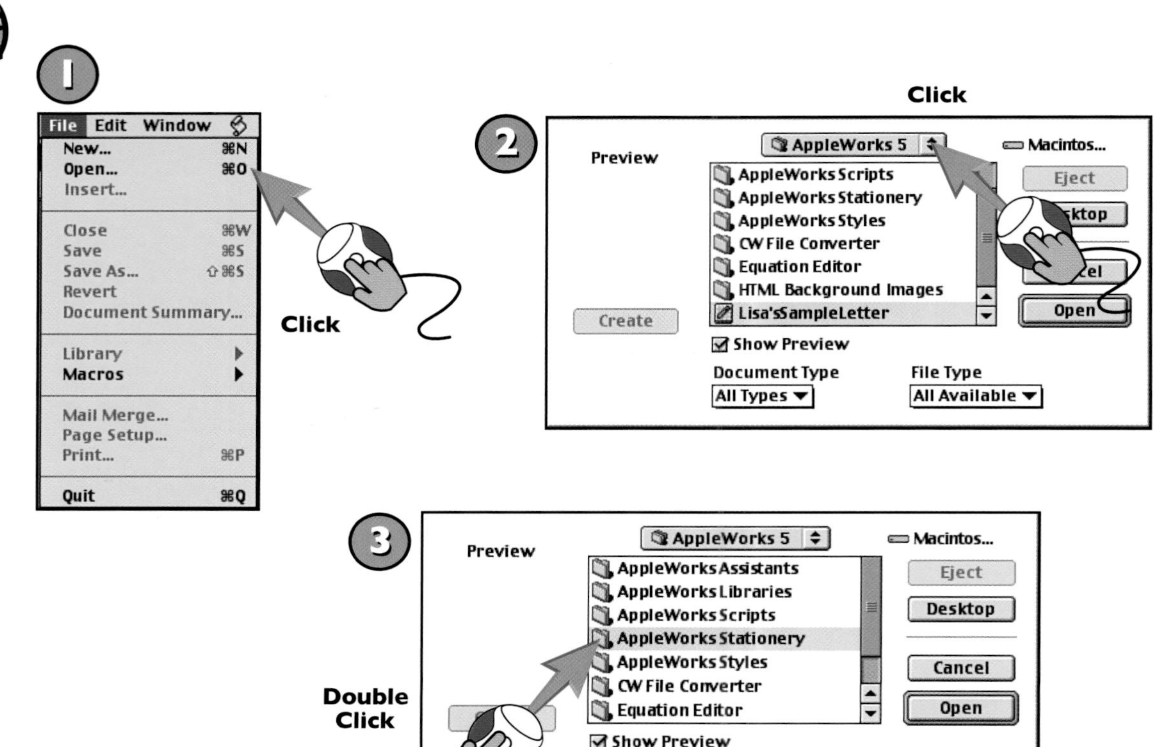

If you can't find the file you want to work with, it could be because you did not save it where you thought you did. Try looking in a different drive or folder. If you still can't find it, try searching for the file (for more information about searching for files, see Part 5, "Working with Disks, Folders, and Files").

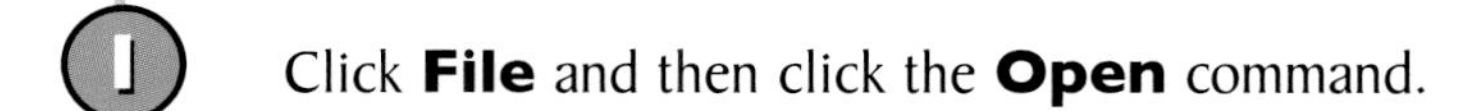

1. Click **File** and then click the **Open** command.
2. If the file you need is listed in the dialog box, double-click it and skip the remaining steps. If the file is not listed, click the drop-down list and select another folder to view.
3. Double-click the folder name where you placed the file.

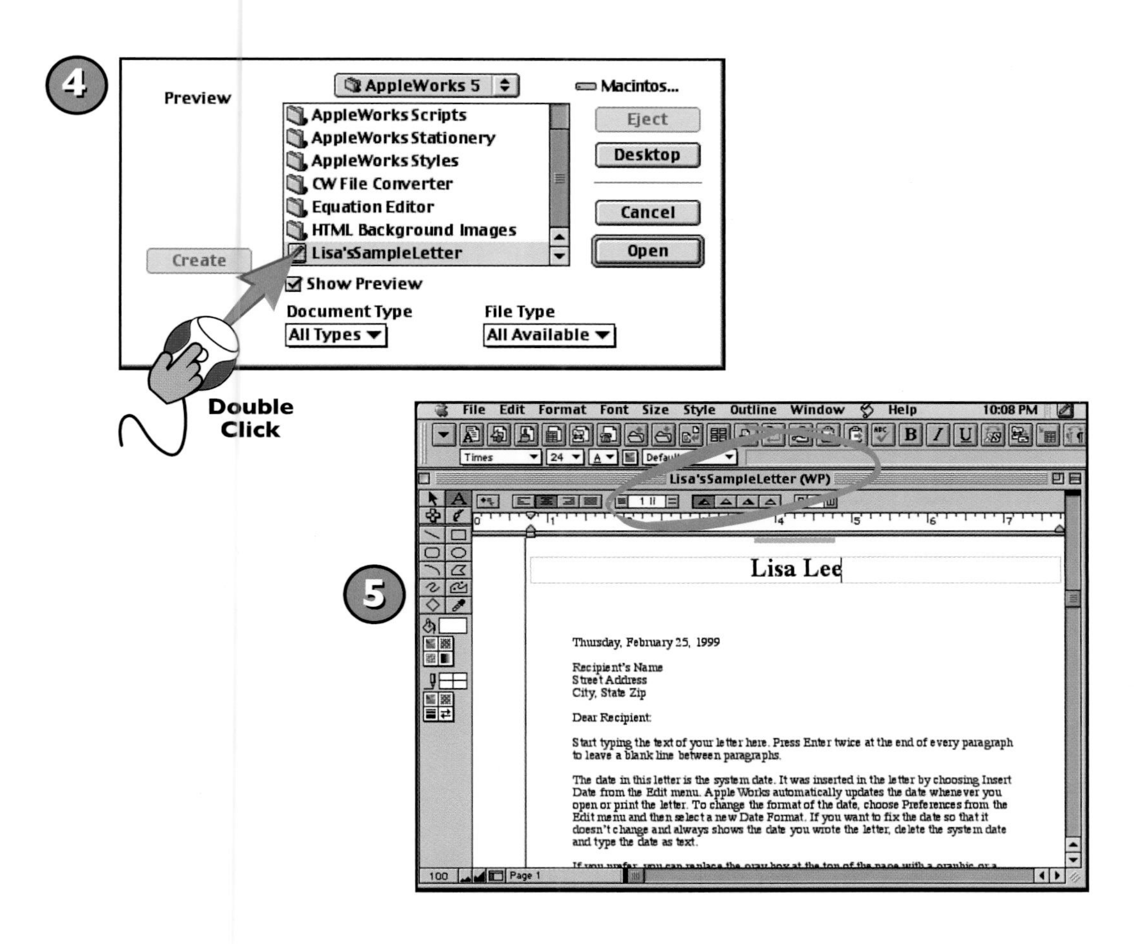

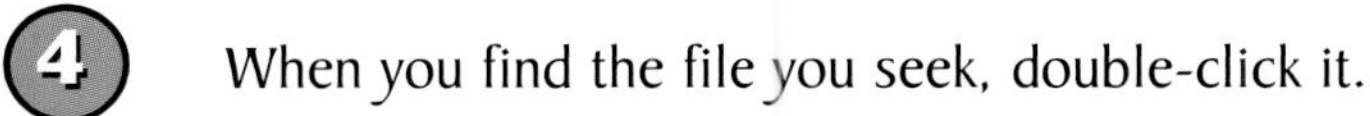

4 When you find the file you seek, double-click it.

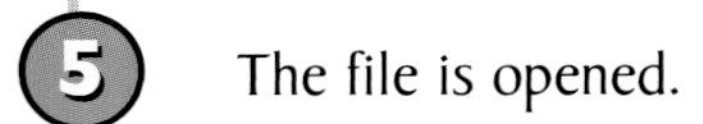

5 The file is opened.

As a shortcut, you can double-click a document to open it. If the application that created it is on your hard disk, the application will automatically start and open the document.

Task 8: Switching Between Open Documents

Start Here

You can work with several documents in your application, opening as many documents as it allows. Simply click **File** and select the **Open** command to open the files you want to work with. Then you can easily switch between any of the open documents.

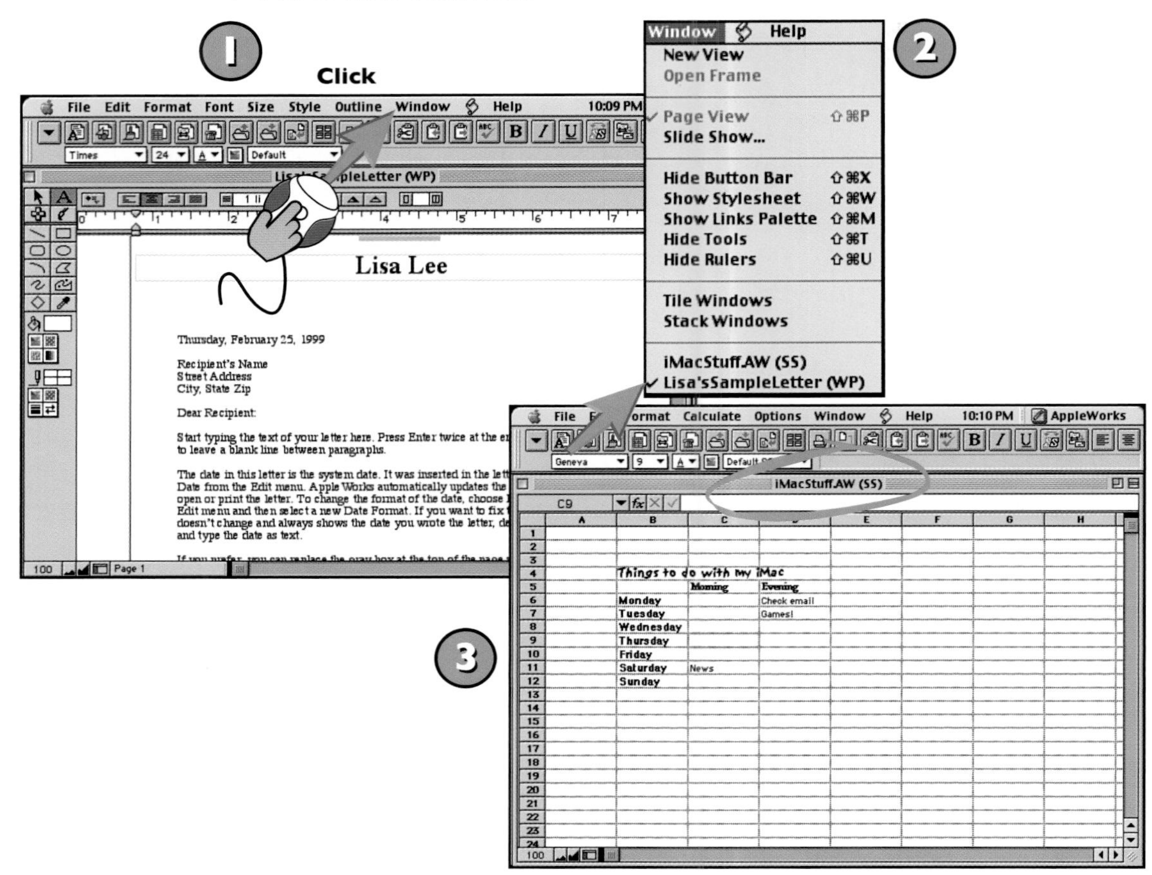

Don't confuse switching between documents with switching between applications. For more information, refer to Task 4, "Switching Between Applications."

You can arrange all open documents in the window to make your desktop easier to manage. Click **Window**, select the **Arrange All** command, and then choose the arrangement you want.

The active window's title bar shows the Platinum window theme; other windows have dimmed title bars.

1. Click **Window**.
2. Notice that the active document has a check mark next to its name. Click the document that you want to switch to (in this case, the document called **iMacStuff.AW**).
3. The document you just clicked in the **Window** menu becomes the active document.

End Task

Task 9: Creating a New Document

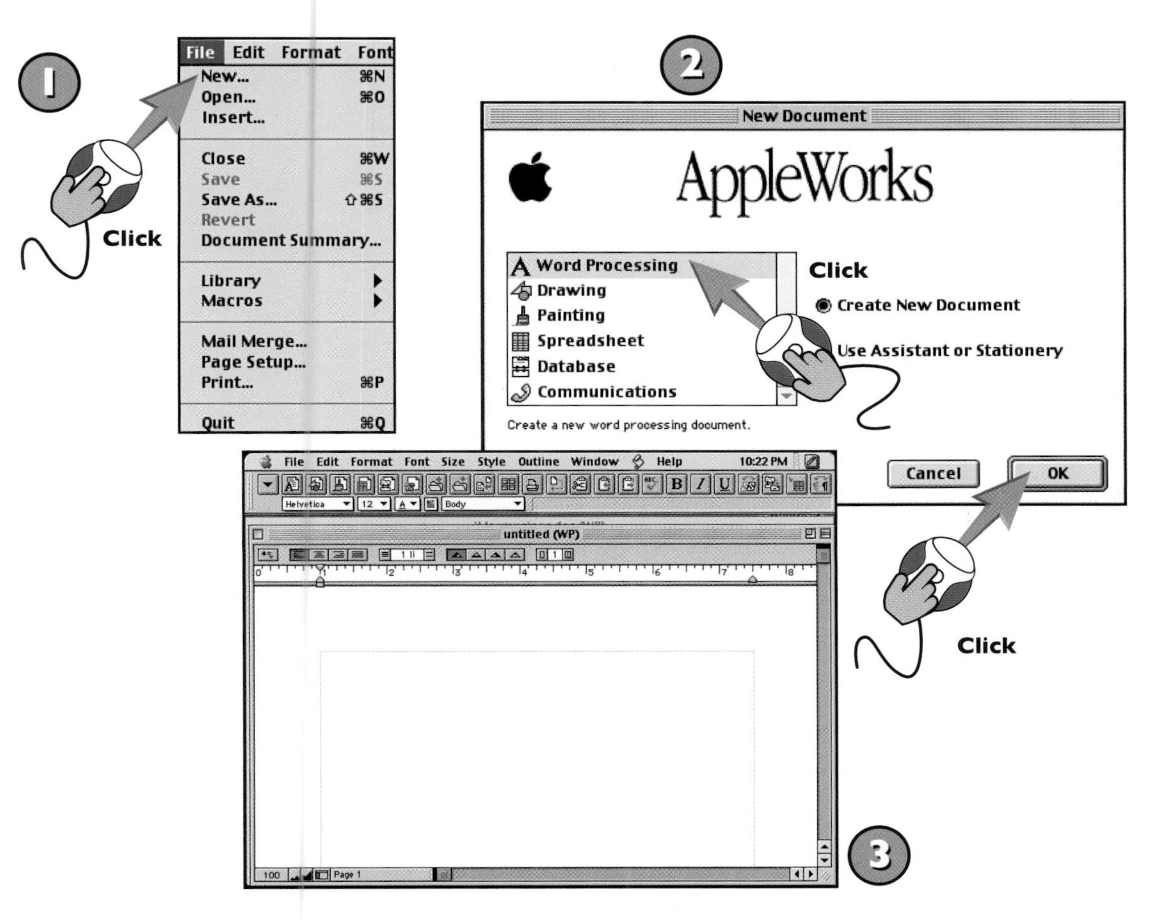

When you want a new "sheet" of paper, you can create a new document. For complex programs such as PowerPoint (a presentation application) and FileMaker Pro (a database application), you might be prompted to make some selections before the new document is created. For others, you simply select the template you want. (A *template* is a predesigned document.)

1. Click **File**, and then click the **New** command.
2. In the **AppleWorks** window, select the application you want to use, and make sure the **Create New Document** radio button is selected. Click the **OK** button.
3. A new document is displayed.

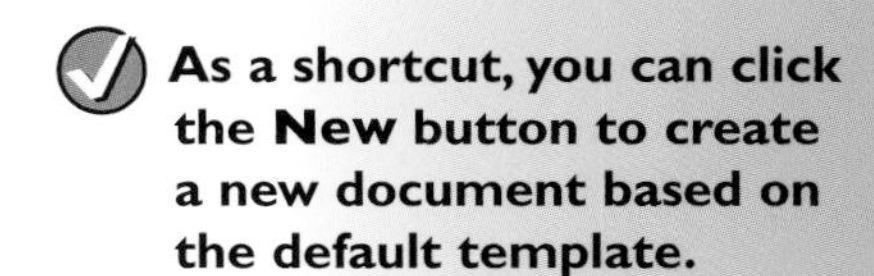

As a shortcut, you can click the **New** button to create a new document based on the default template.

Task 10: Closing a Document

When you save a document, it remains open so that you can continue working. If you want to close the document, you can easily do so. You should close documents that you are no longer using in order to free up memory.

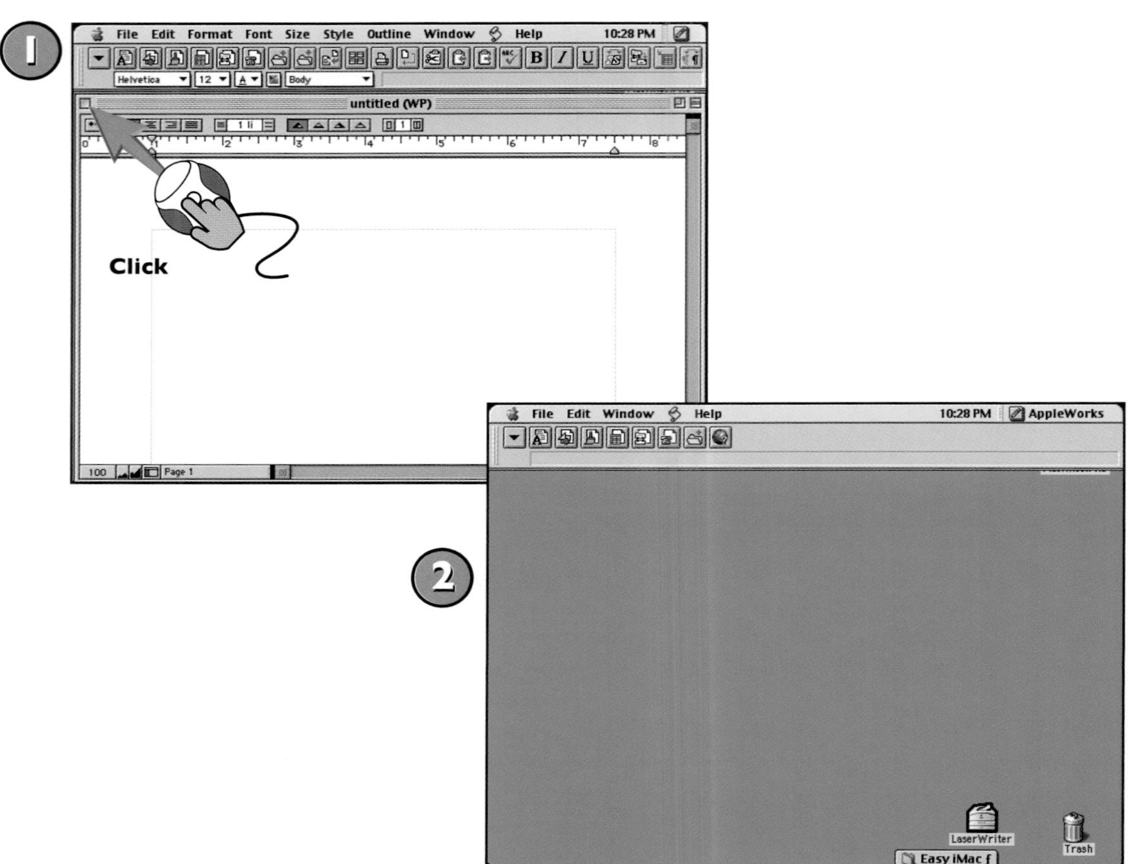

1. Click the **Close** button.
2. The document is closed, but the application remains open. You can create a new document or open an existing document, or you can close the application by selecting **File** and then **Quit**.

If you click the **Close** button on the document window, the application menu bar remains visible and the application is still open. To quit the application, press **Command+Q**.

In most programs, the document window has its own set of controls—separate from the controls for the application window. You can move, resize, restore, collapse, and close the document window using the skills you learned in Part 1, "Getting Started."

Task 11: Selecting Text

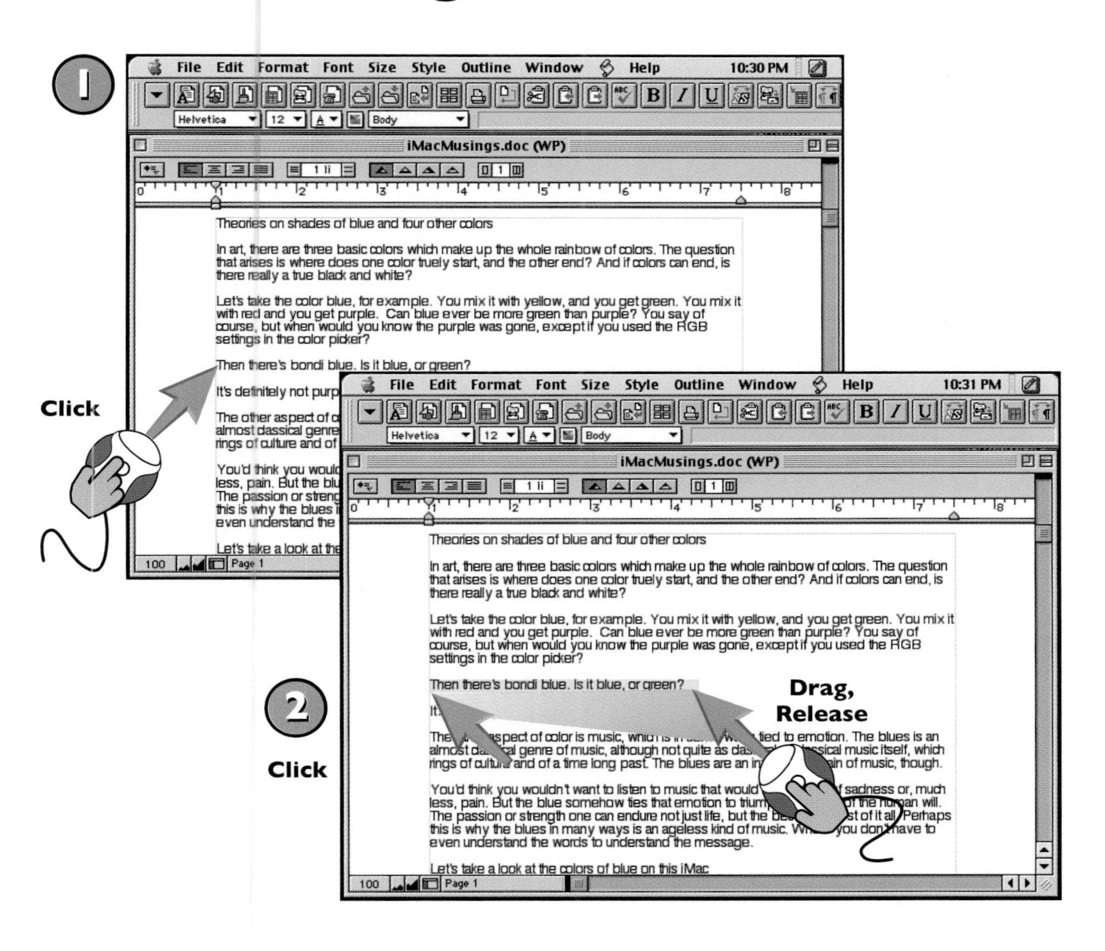

One of the primary skills you need for working with data is knowing how to select what you want to work on. For instance, you can select text and then delete it, move it, copy it, change its appearance, and more.

1. Click at the start of the text you want to select.

2. Hold down the mouse button and drag across the text, then release the mouse button. The selected text appears highlighted.

If you prefer to use the keyboard to select text, hold down the **Shift** key and use the arrow keys to highlight the text you want to select.

To deselect text, click outside the text.

Task 12: Copying Text

One of the most common editing tasks is to copy text. You can copy text and paste it in the current document or in another document.

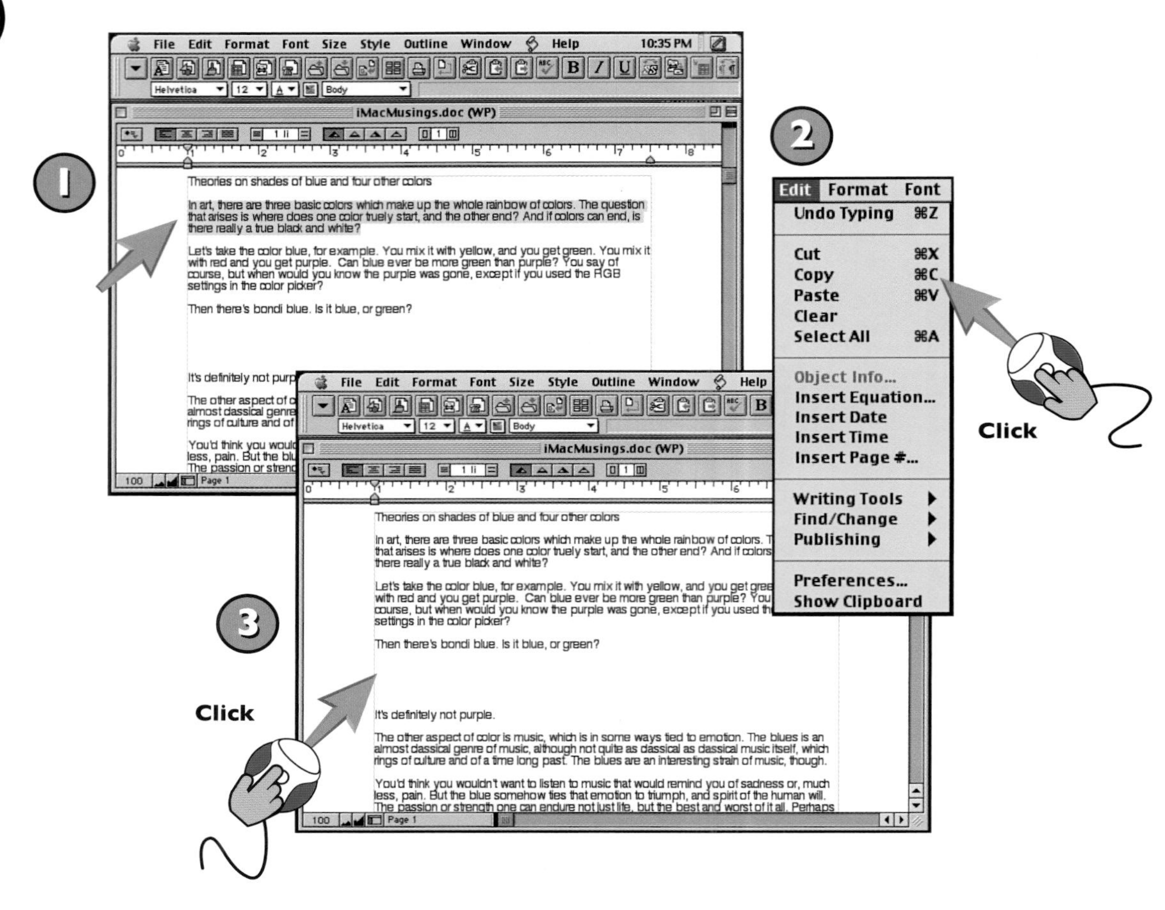

1. Select the text you want to copy.
2. Click **Edit**, and then select the **Copy** command. iMac copies the text and places it on the Clipboard, a temporary holding place.
3. Click the spot in the document where you want to put the copied data.

To copy data from one open document to another, select the text and then move to the document where you want to paste the text using the Window menu.

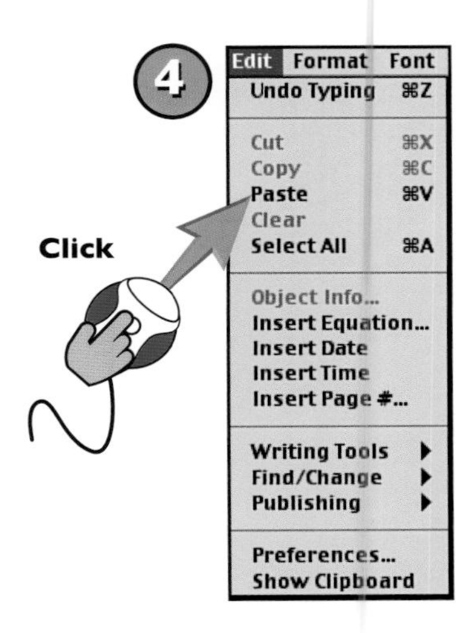

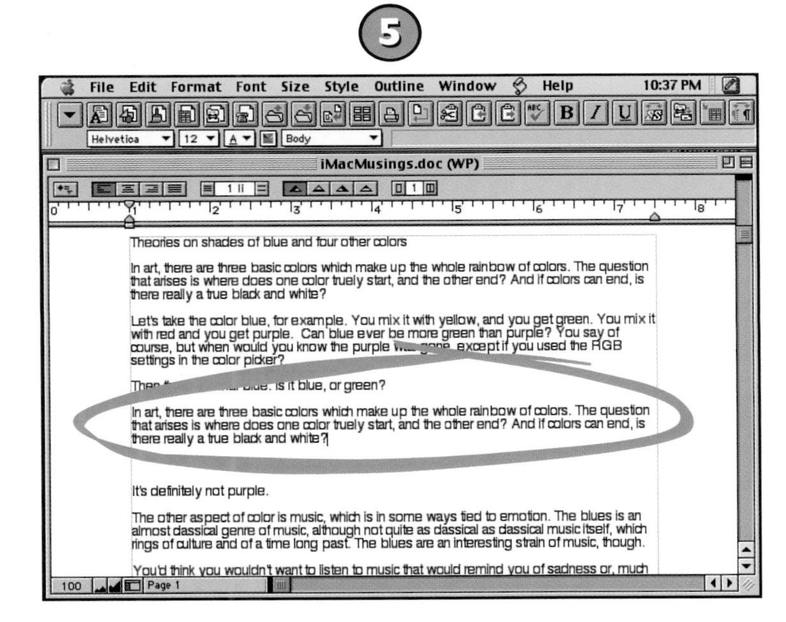

4. Click **Edit**, and then select the **Paste** command.

5. The data is pasted into the document.

For information about copying data from one application to another, see Task 14, "Copying Data Between Documents."

End Task

Task 13: Moving Text

Start Here

Just as you can copy text, you can move text from one location in a document to another location in the same document. Moving text is similar to copying text, except that when you move something it is deleted from its original location.

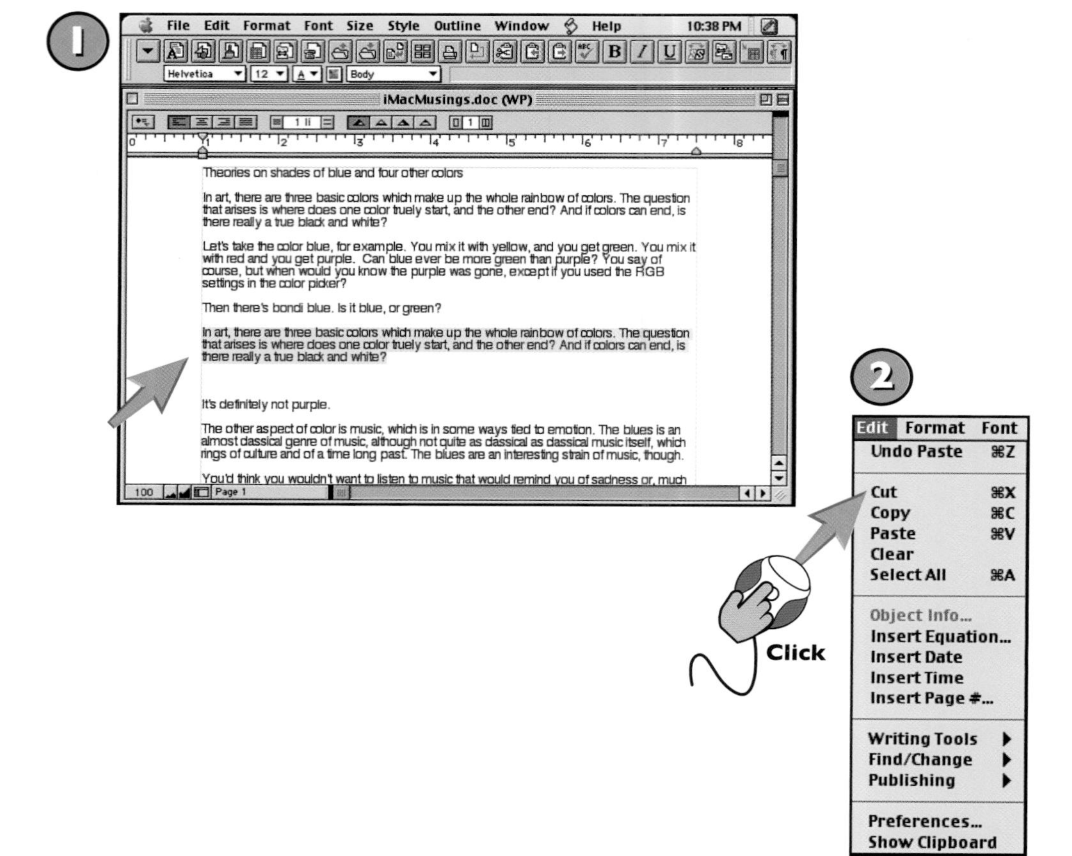

✓ For help on moving data from one document to another, see Task 15, "Moving Data Between Documents."

✓ You can undo a paste operation if you change your mind after performing the action. Simply click **Edit** and then select the **Undo Paste** command to remove the text you just pasted.

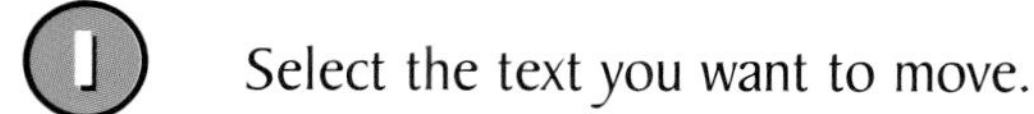

1. Select the text you want to move.

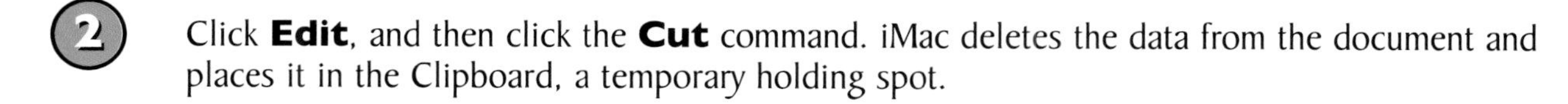

2. Click **Edit**, and then click the **Cut** command. iMac deletes the data from the document and places it in the Clipboard, a temporary holding spot.

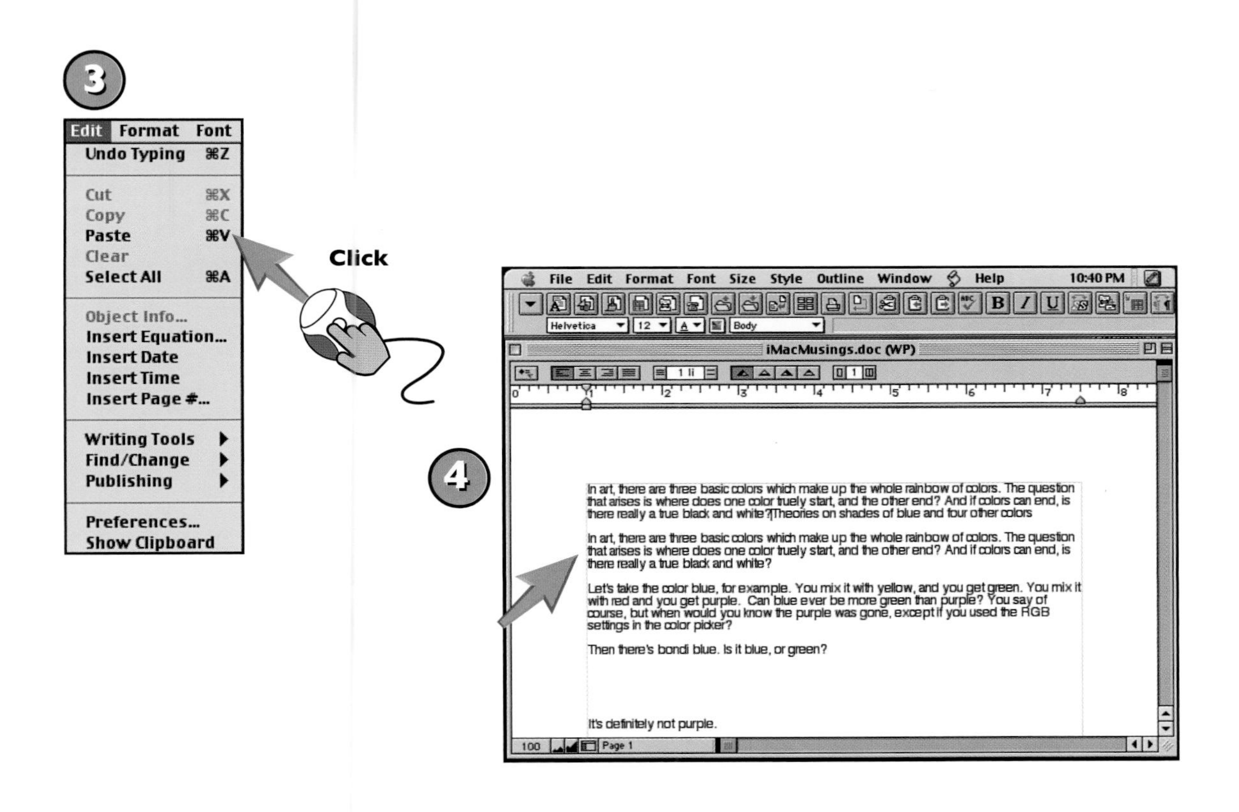

Click in the document where you want to place the text. Open the **Edit** menu and then select the **Paste** command.

The text is pasted into the new location.

You can also move text by selecting any text, then dragging it to another document, or to the desktop. This is called "Drag and Drop."

Task 14: Copying Data Between Documents

Start Here

You can copy data from a document in one application and paste it into another document in another application to save time typing. In addition to being able to copy text, you can copy spreadsheets, figures, charts, clip art, and so on. Using copied text and graphics saves you time in your work.

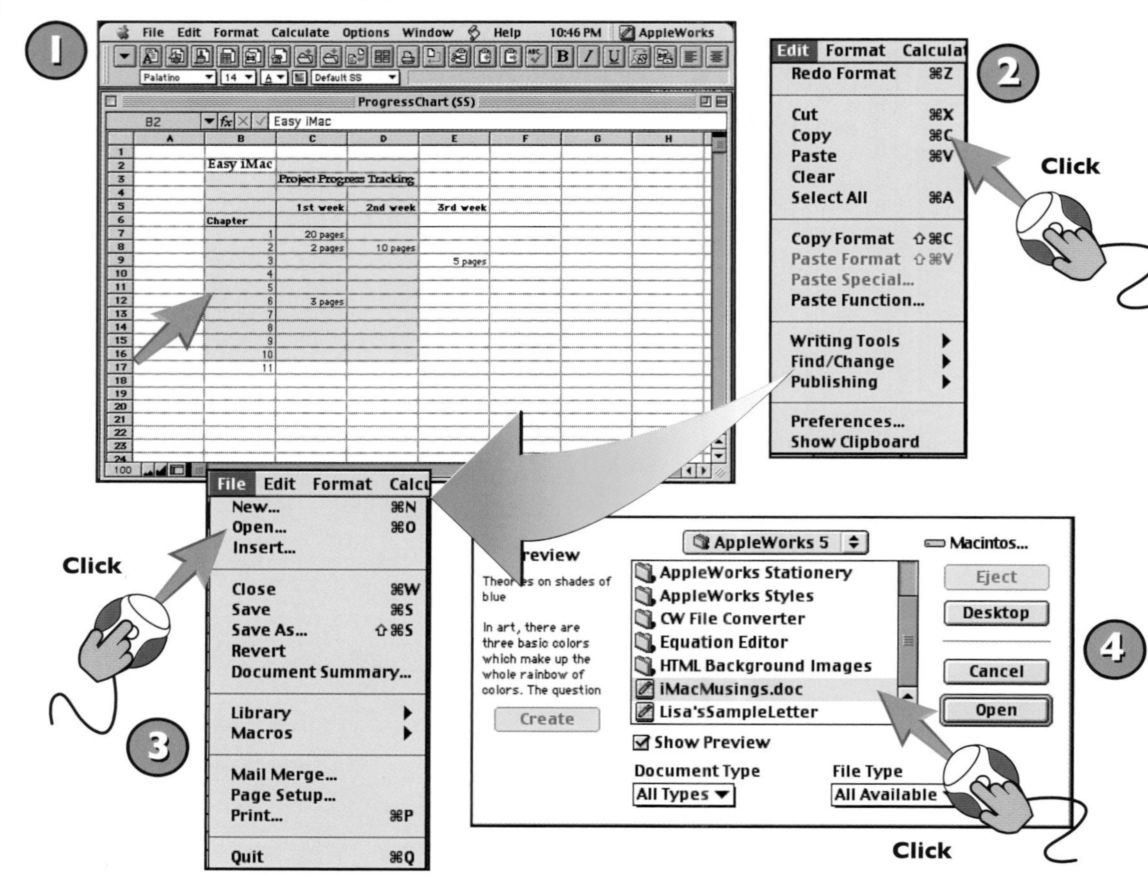

You can also use the keyboard shortcut **Command+C** to copy and the keyboard shortcut **Command+V** to paste. Also look for toolbar buttons for **Copy** and **Paste** buttons.

1. Select the data you want to copy.
2. Click **Edit**, and then click the **Copy** command.
3. Click **File**, and then click the **Open** command.
4. Choose an AppleWorks document you want to switch to (in this case, a word-processing document).

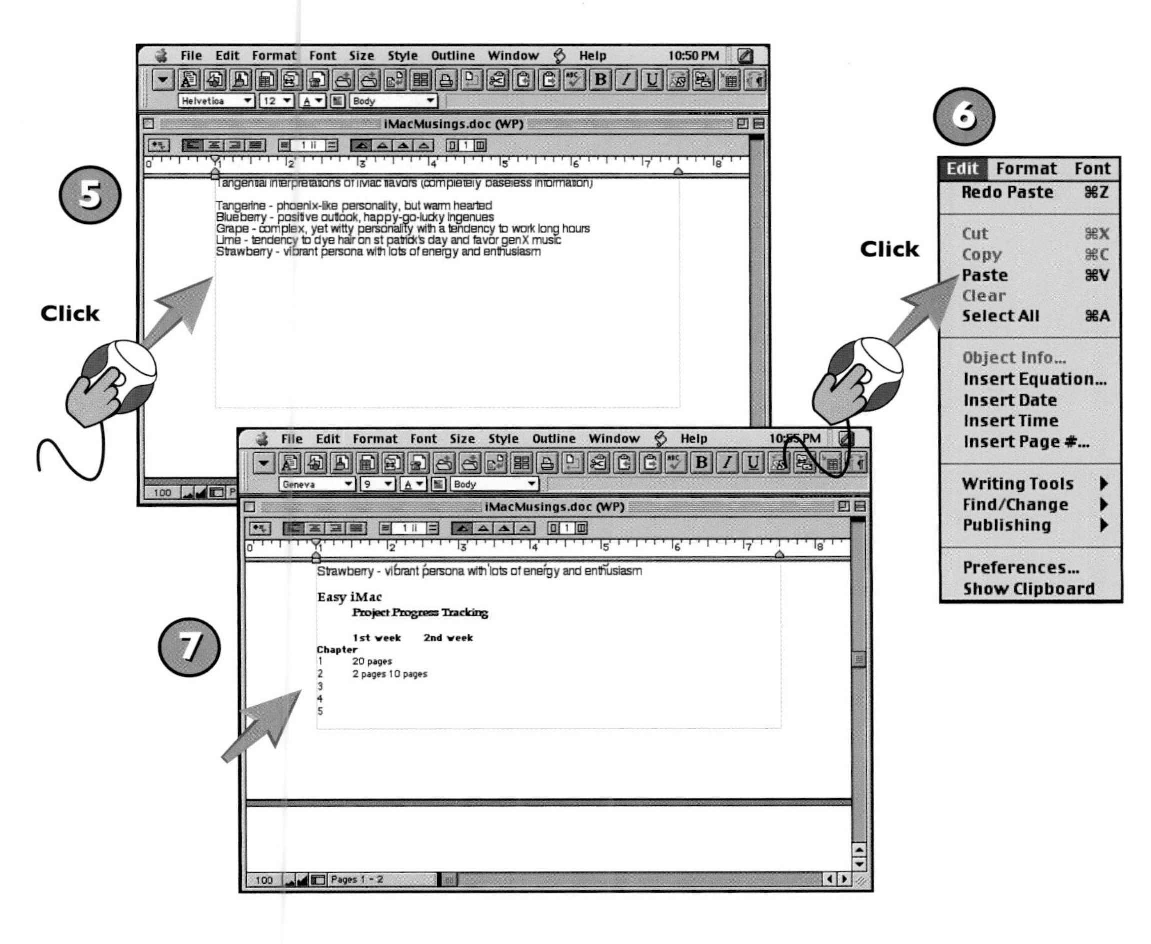

5. In the word-processing document, click the location where you want to paste the copied data.

6. Click **Edit**, and then click the **Paste** command.

7. The data is pasted into the document.

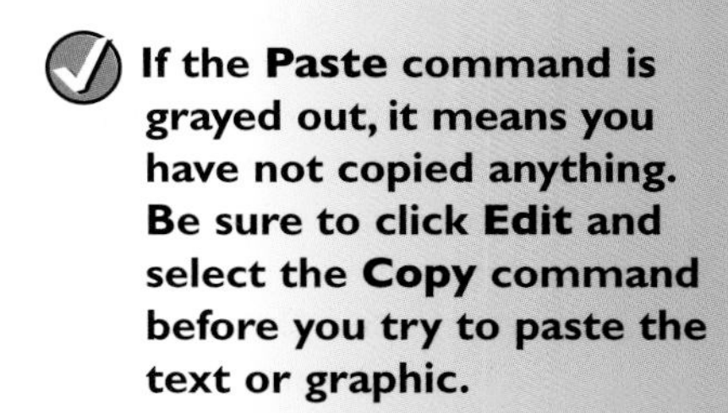

If the Paste command is grayed out, it means you have not copied anything. Be sure to click Edit and select the Copy command before you try to paste the text or graphic.

Task 15: Moving Data Between Documents

Start Here

You can also move information from one document to another. For instance, you can cut a table of numerical data from a spreadsheet and paste it into a report in the word processor in AppleWorks.

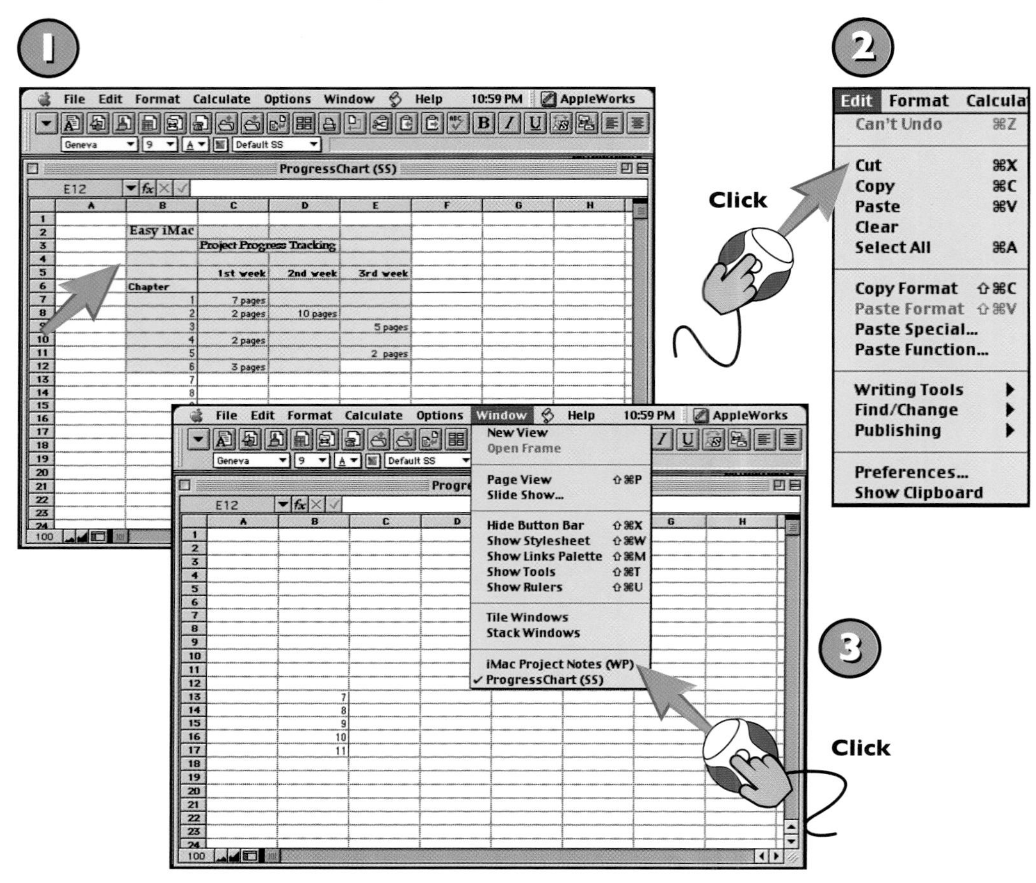

You can also use the keyboard shortcut **Command+X** to cut, and use the keyboard command **Command+V** to paste. Look also for toolbar buttons for **Cut**, **Copy**, and **Paste**.

1. Select the data you want to move.

2. Click **Edit**, and then click the **Cut** command. iMac deletes the data from the document and places it in the Clipboard, a temporary holding spot.

3. Open the **Window** menu and choose the document you want to switch to (in this case, **iMac Project Notes**).

Next Step

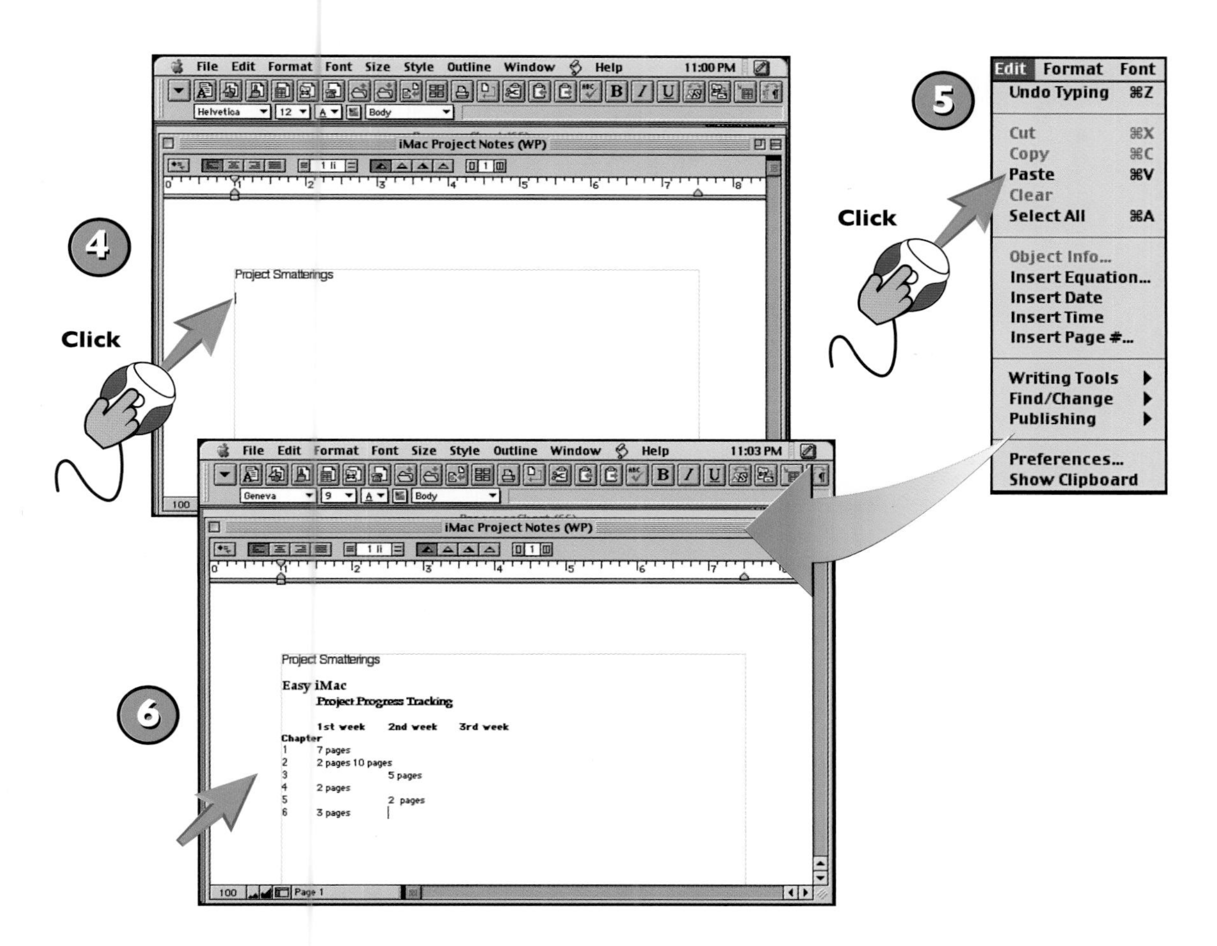

1. Click in the document where you want to place the data.
2. Click **Edit**, and then click the **Paste** command.
3. The data is pasted into the document.

PART 5

Working with Disks, Folders, and Files

One part of working with your iMac is learning how to work with the documents you save and store on your system. Think of your computer's hard drive as a filing cabinet. To keep your files organized, you can set up folders. Folders on the hard drive represent drawers in the filing cabinet, and each folder can hold files or other folders. You can open and close folders, view a folder's contents, copy and move folders, and create or delete folders.

The more you work on your computer, the more files and folders you add. After a while, your computer will become cluttered, and you'll need a way to keep these files organized. Mac OS provides features that can help you find, organize, and manage your files. You can copy files, move files, delete unnecessary files, and more.

Tasks

Task 1: Navigating Your Hard Disk with the Mouse

You can view the contents of your hard disk in a variety of ways. The easiest way is to use what Apple calls a click-and-a-half on your hard disk icon. This changes the arrow cursor into a magnifying glass, and then opens any hard disk icon or folder over which you hold the magnifying glass. Using a click-and-a-half, you can navigate your hard disk without having to open and close windows to get to what you want.

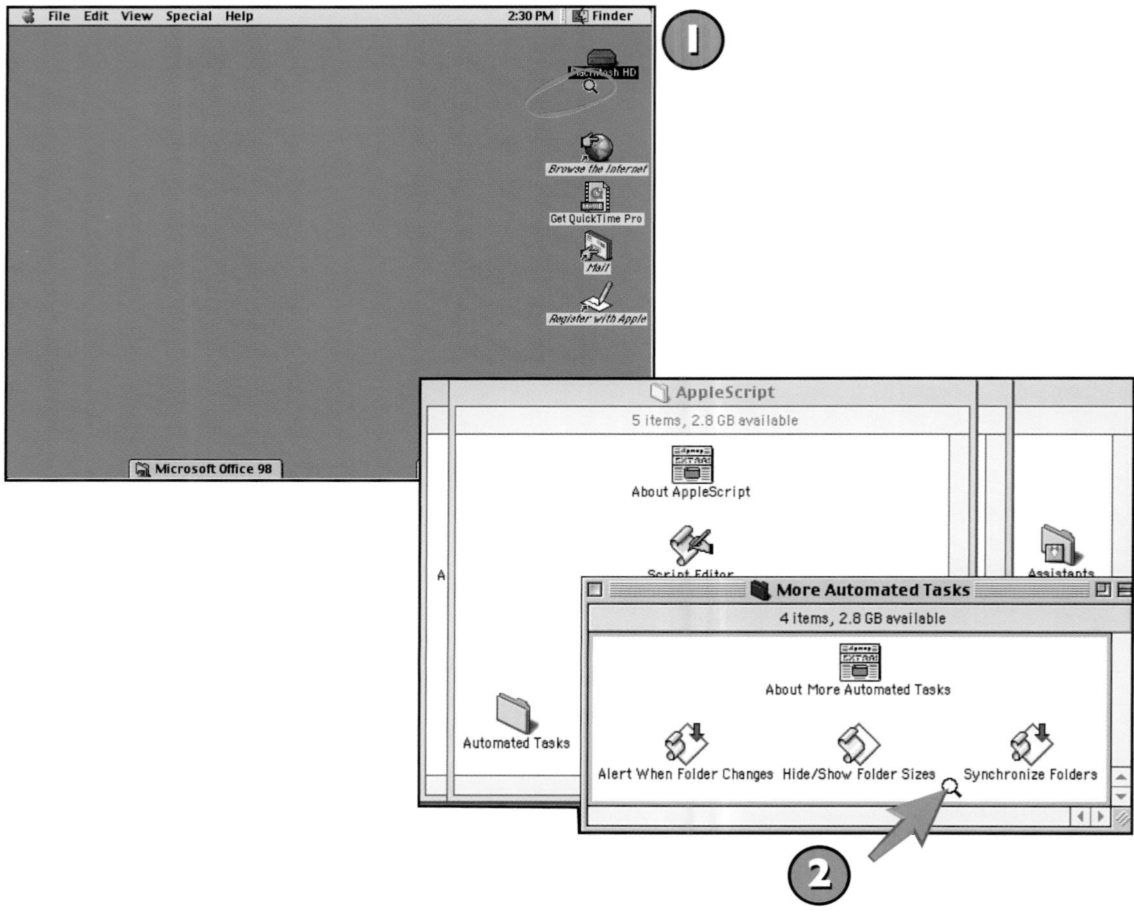

1. Click once on the hard drive icon on your desktop, then click again and hold down the mouse button. The pointer changes to resemble a magnifying glass.
2. The hard drive's window will automatically open.Open any folders in the window by moving the magnifying glass cursor over the folder icon.

If you want to stop using the magnifying glass, simply move it over to the desktop. Any windows opened by your previous navigation will automatically close.

Task 2: Opening Folders

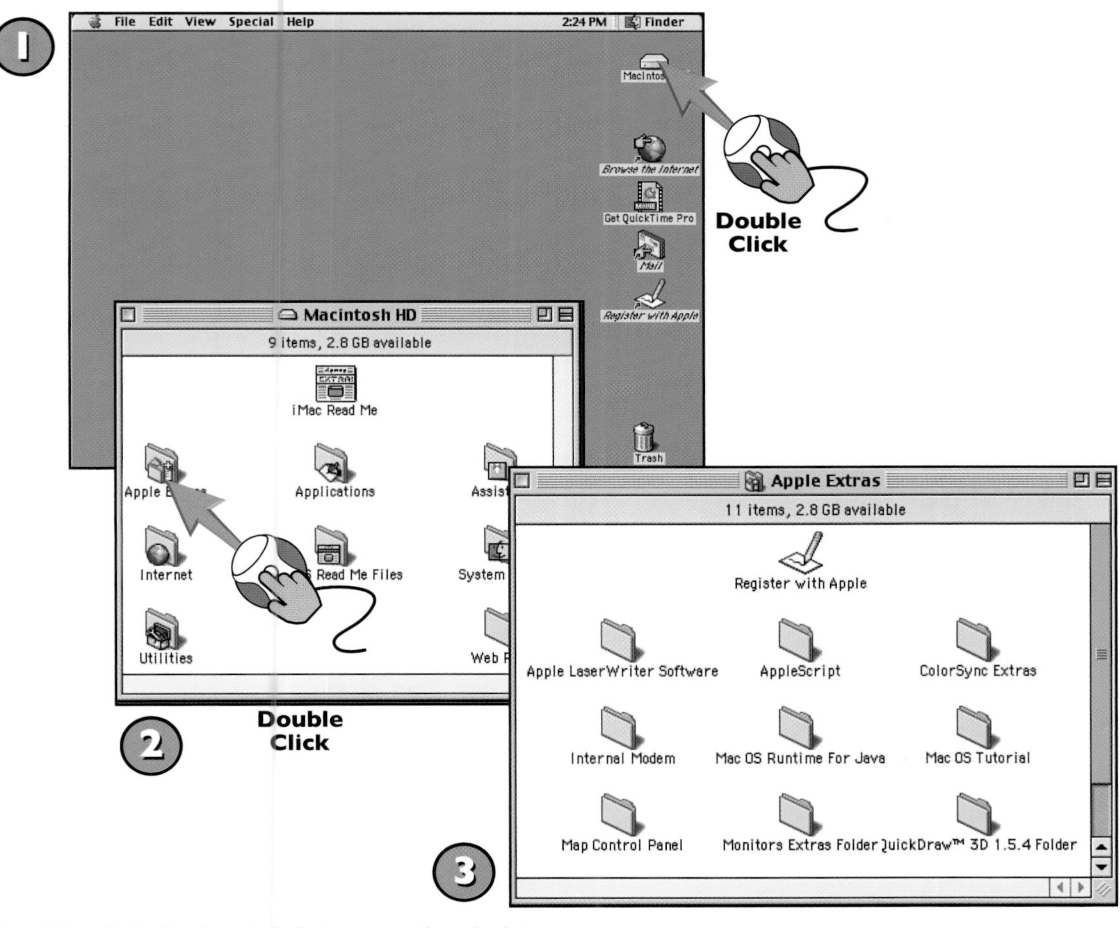

Folders contain files, applications, or other items that you can use to do work in Mac OS. You can display the contents of a folder to work with the files—move a file, create a shortcut icon, start a program, and so on.

1. Double-click the hard disk icon on the desktop.
2. Each icon you see represents a folder on your hard drive. Double-click any of the folders.
3. Each file folder icon represents groups of files and folders. Each page icon represents a document.

Remember that you can use the scrollbars to scroll through the window. Also, you can move and resize the window as needed.

You can select how the contents of a folder are displayed in Task 3, "Customizing a Folder's Window View," and Task 5, "Changing View Options," later in this part.

To close a window and all its associated windows, hold down the **Shift** key and click the **Close** button.

Task 3: Selecting a Folder's Window View

Start Here

There are several ways you can view the contents of a window; the default view is **as Icons**. The **as List** view provides the most information and the most flexibility for displaying file and folder information. The **as Buttons** view is another way you can view files and folders on your hard drive.

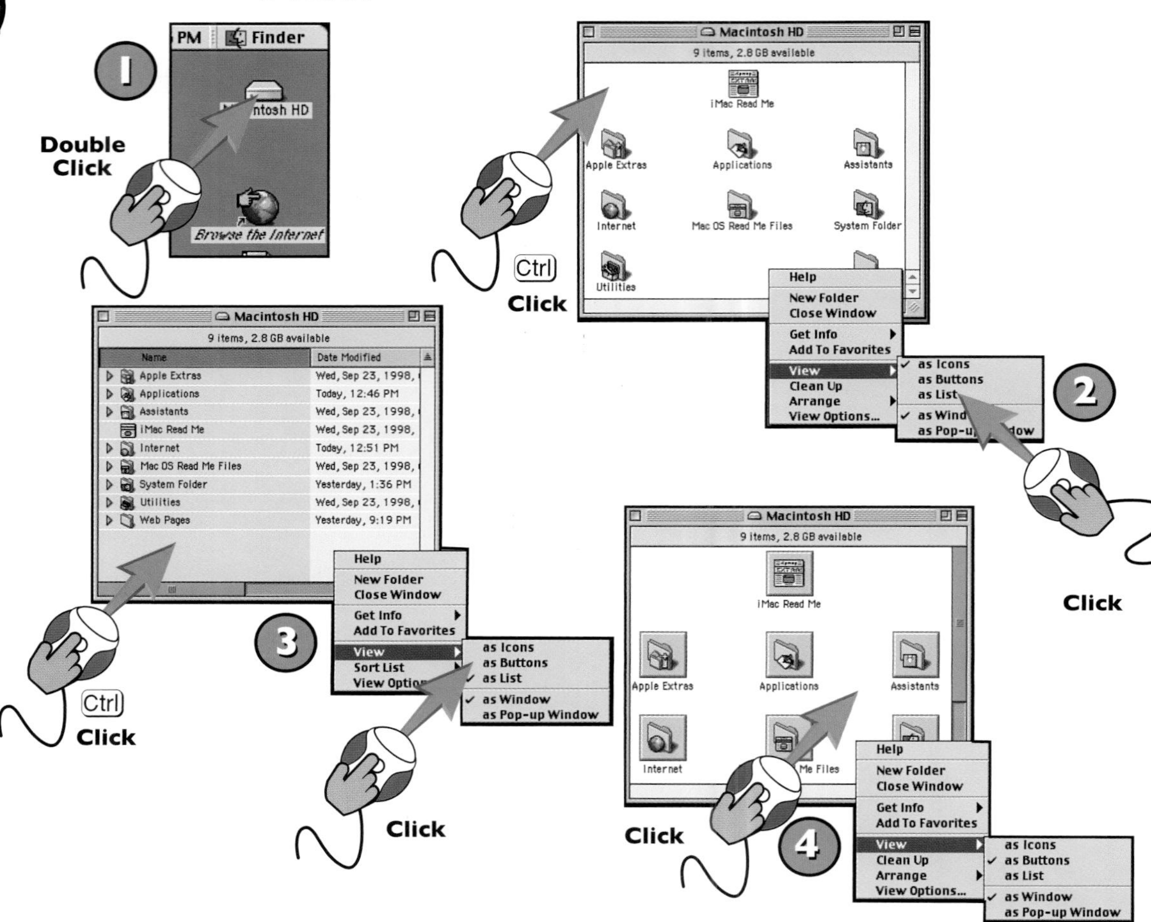

✓ If nothing happens when you double-click an icon, it might be because you did not click quickly enough or because you single-clicked, moved the mouse, and single-clicked again. You have to click twice in rapid succession. A good way to practice using the mouse is to play Jigsaw Puzzle.

✓ Any folder window can be viewed in **as Icon, as List,** or **as Button** mode. However, you can only view icons on the desktop as icons or as buttons.

1. Double-click the hard disk icon on the desktop.

2. All files and folders in the window are represented by icons. Press and hold the **Ctrl** key on your keyboard, click an empty spot on the window, and select **View | as List** from the context menu.

3. Hold down the **Ctrl** key, click an empty spot on the window, and select **View | as Buttons** from the context menu.

4. All files and folders in the window are represented by buttons.

End Task

Task 4: Sorting Window Contents

1

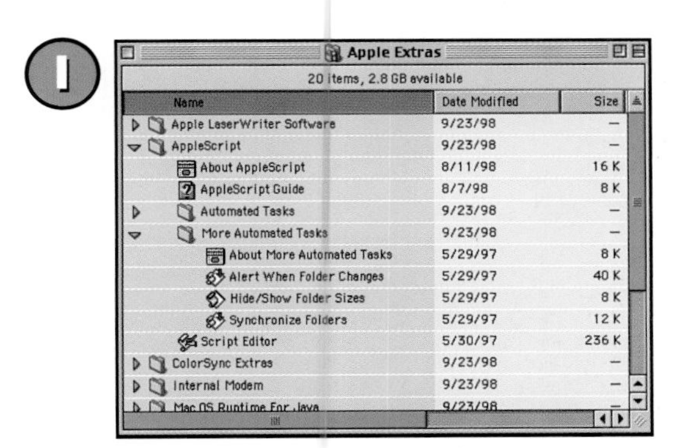

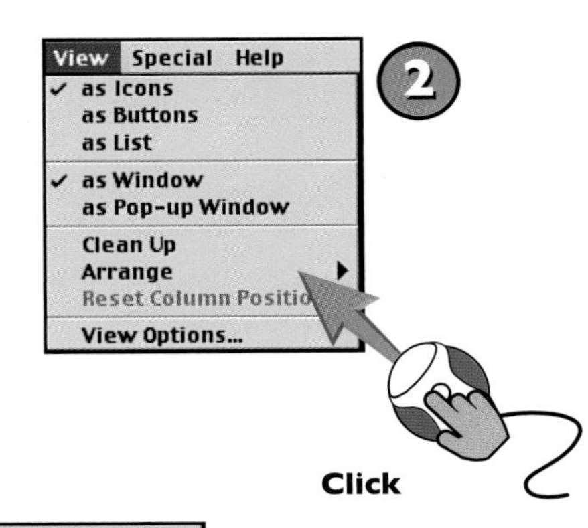

2

Click

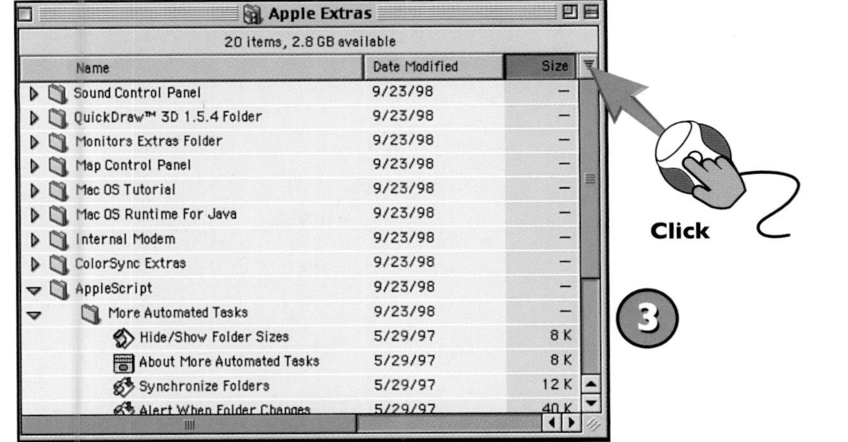

Click

3

1. Open the window you want to sort and change to the view you want. In this case, the window is displayed in **List** view so that you can see the results of sorting by different columns.

2. Click **View**, select the **Arrange** command, and choose the sort order you want (in this case, **by Size**). Mac OS sorts the files in the selected order.

3. To change the ascending or descending sort order in a window in **as List** view, click the arrow icon above the top of the right scrollbar.

You sort the contents of a window in as List view so that you can more easily find the files you want. Mac OS enables you to arrange the files in a folder by name, kind, label, comments, version, type, date, and size. You can move the columns to the left or right of each other and view the items in ascending or descending order. You can sort files viewed as large, medium, or small icons.

You can sort icons in View as Icons or View as Buttons mode, too. Choose the View | Arrange to sort the items in the onscreen window.

You can move any columns in as List view by clicking the top of the column and dragging it to the desired location.

You cannot sort items on the desktop.

Task 5: Changing View Options

You can customize the way folders and files appear in a window by changing the window's view options. Each window can have a different view. For example, a folder with two files might be easier to navigate in as **Icons** view, while a folder with 30 files and folders might be easier to view in as **List** view.

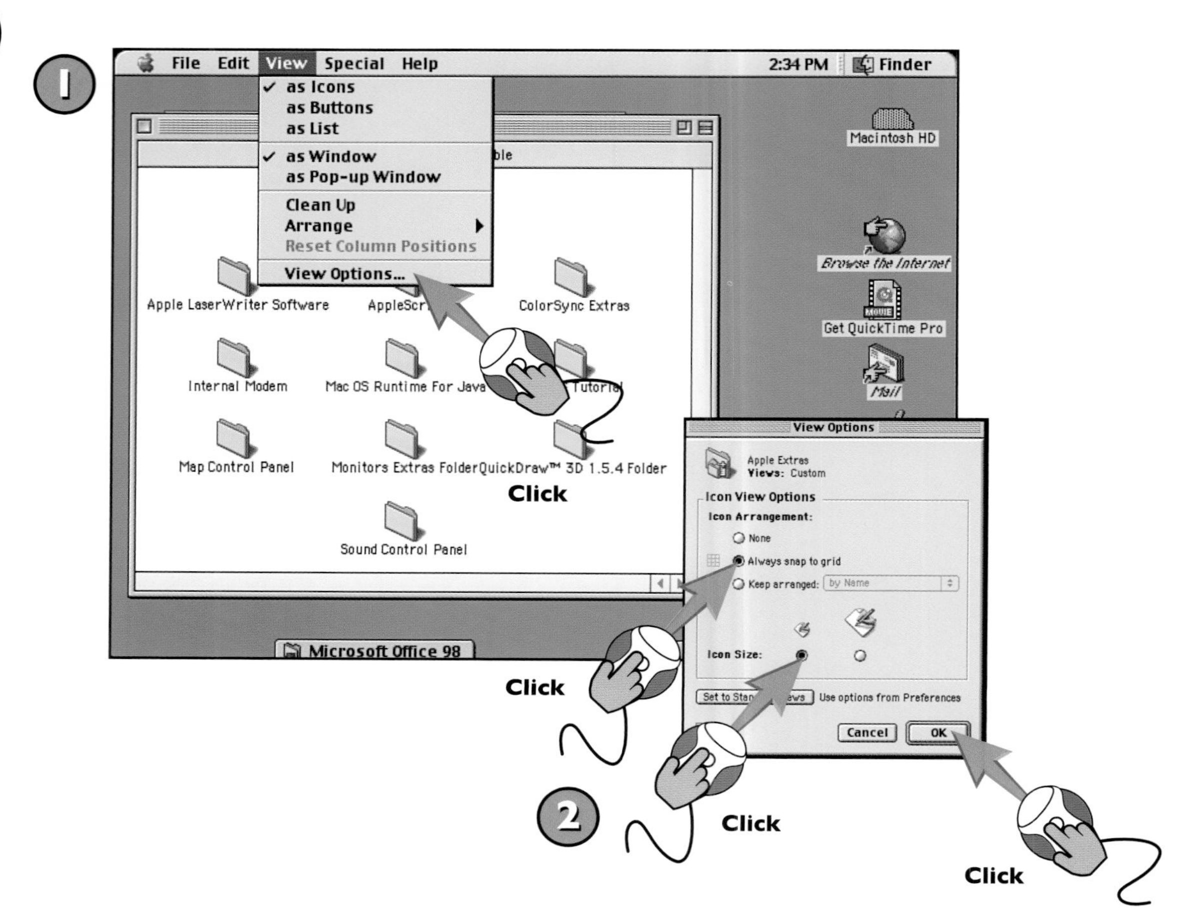

1 Click **View**, and then select the **View Options** command.

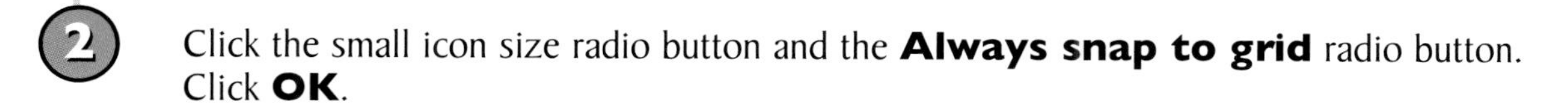
2 Click the small icon size radio button and the **Always snap to grid** radio button. Click **OK**.

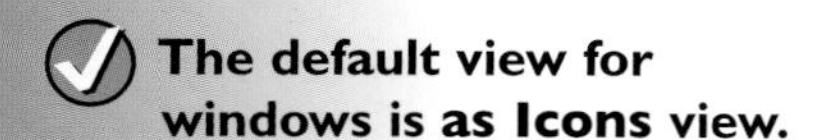
The default view for windows is as **Icons** view.

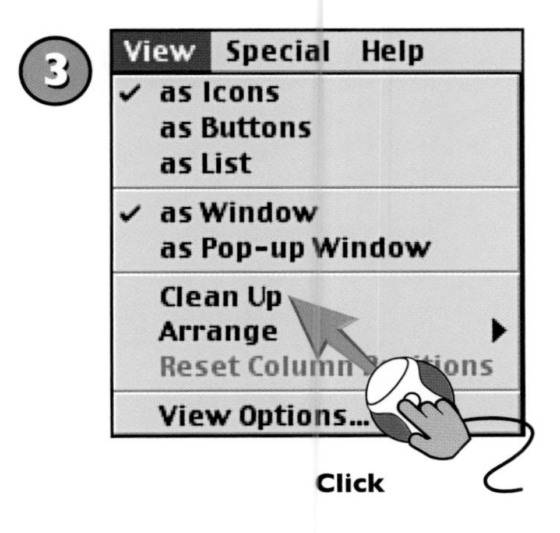

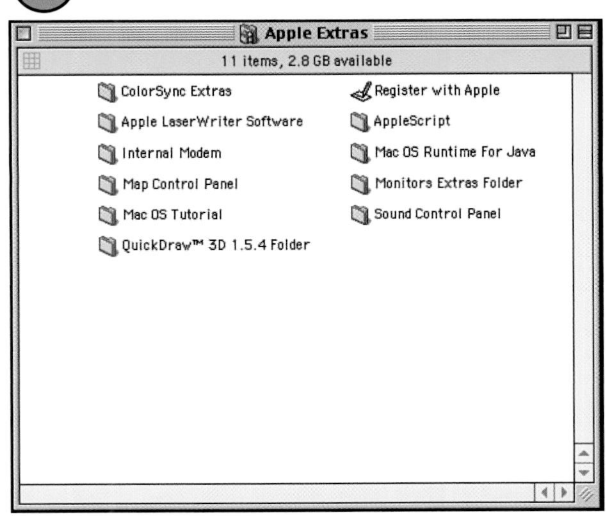

3. Click **View**, and then select the **Clean up** command.

4. The contents of the window are displayed in small icon view and are mapped to the grid. You may need to resize the window.

Task 6: Finding Files and Folders with Sherlock

After you've worked for months with your applications, your computer will become filled with various folders and files, which can make it nearly impossible for you to know where everything is. Luckily, Mac OS includes Sherlock, which helps you locate specific files or folders by name, file type, size, location, and so on.

Start Here

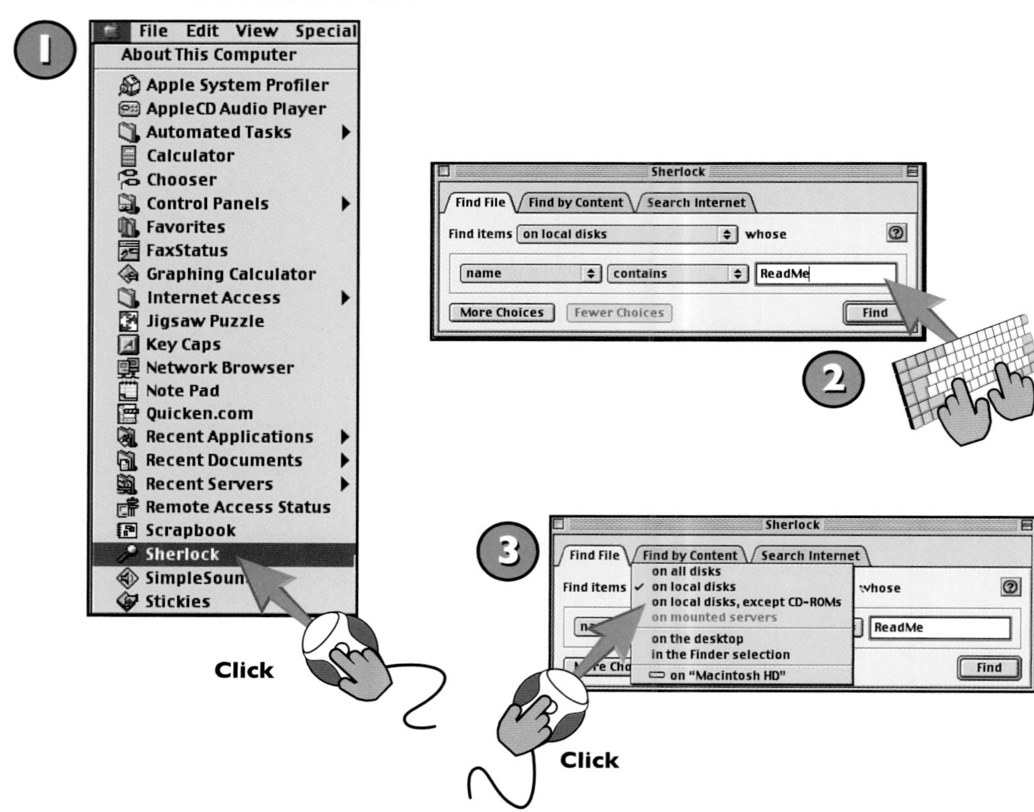

1. Click the **Apple** Menu and select the **Sherlock** command.
2. Enter the name of the file you want to search for.
3. To change the drive on which Sherlock will conduct the search, display the **Find Items** pop-up menu and select the drive you want to search.

Sherlock is not a feature of Mac OS 8.1. You must upgrade to Mac OS 8.5 in order to use Sherlock. Apple offers an upgrade from 8.1 to 8.5 for a nominal fee.

A shortcut to start Sherlock is **Command+F**.

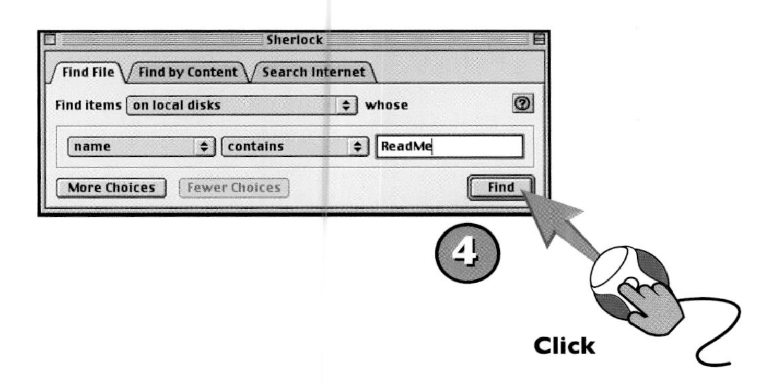

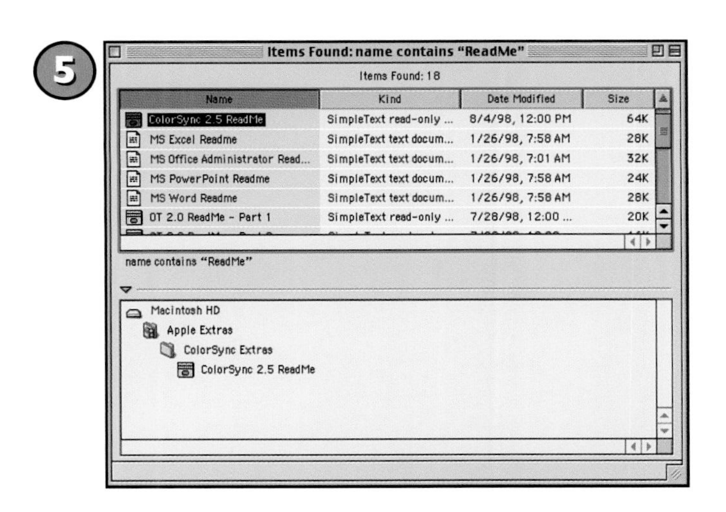

4 Click the **Find** button.

5 Mac OS searches the hard drive and displays a list of found files in the **Items Found** window. You can double-click any of the listed files or folders to go to that file or folder.

If you do not know the name of the file but you know what type of file it is, click the Name pop-up menu and select Kind or File type.

Task 7: Using Sherlock to Search by Category

You can use Sherlock to search your hard drive or the Internet for files using a variety of search categories.

Start Here

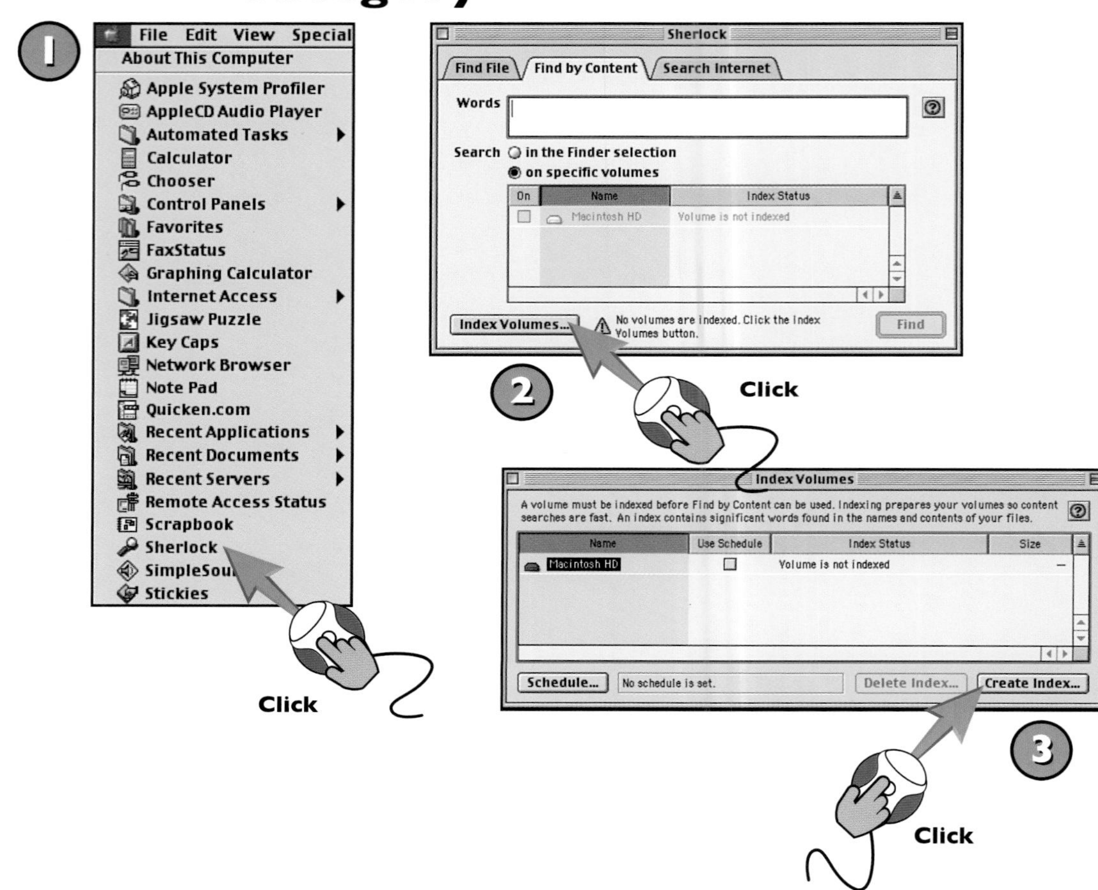

1. Click the **Apple** menu and select the **Sherlock** command.

2. Click the **Find by Content** tab, then click the **Index Volumes** button.

3. Select a volume and click **Create Index** button. Then click the **Create** button to create an index of your hard drive. Creating the index may take a while (1-3 hours).

Close Sherlock just like you do any other application: Select the **Quit** command from the **File** menu. You can also close Sherlock by clicking the **Close** button.

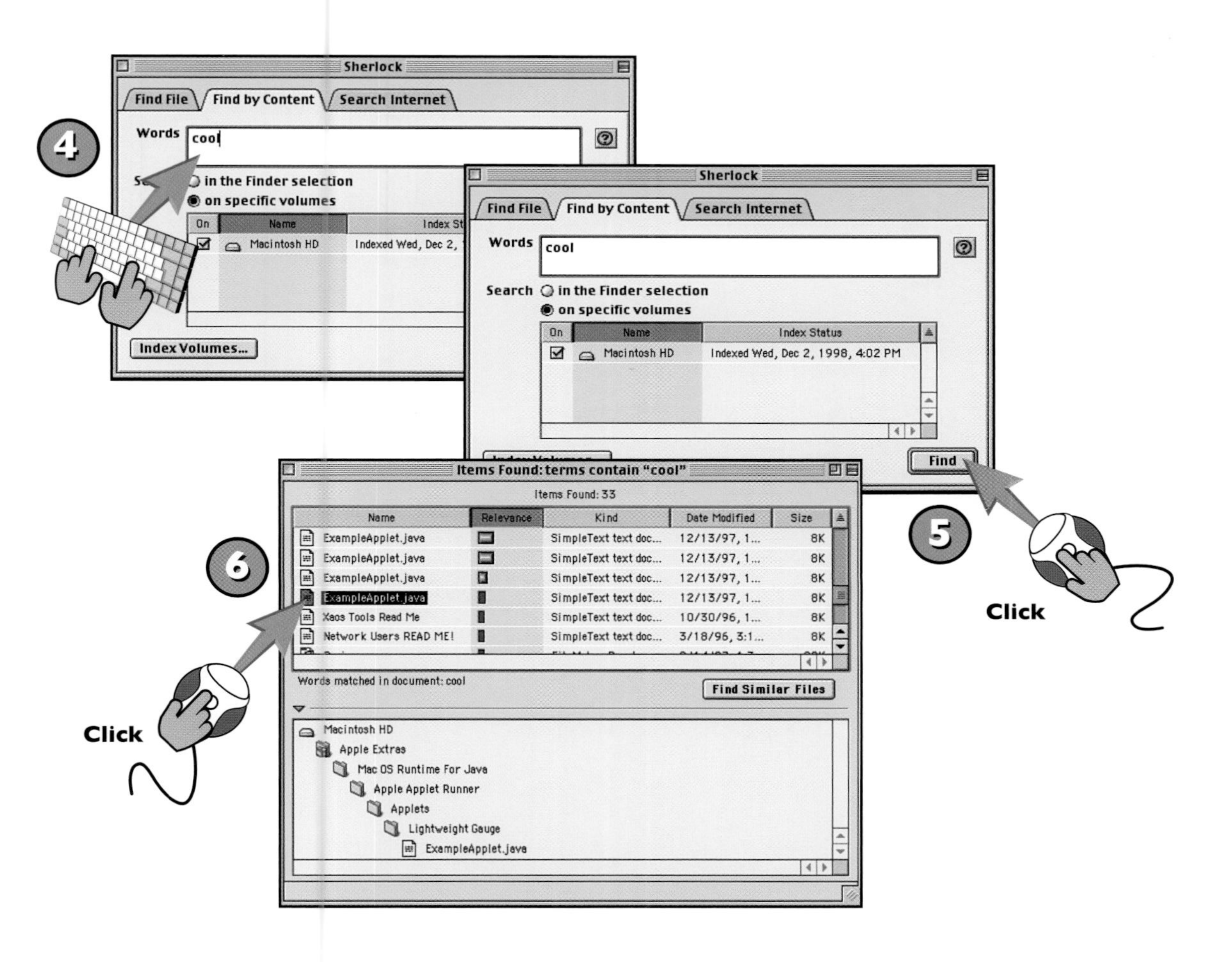

4. Type the name or words you want to search for.

5. Click the **Find** button.

6. Select the file you searched for from the search results window.

You can double-click to open any of the folders shown in the results window to view any items within the folder.

You can drag any item out of the results window to move it to the desktop or a new location.

Task 8: Selecting a Single Folder or File

When you want to work on folders or files (copy, move, print, delete, and so on), you start by selecting the folders or files you want. Selecting a single folder file is simple.

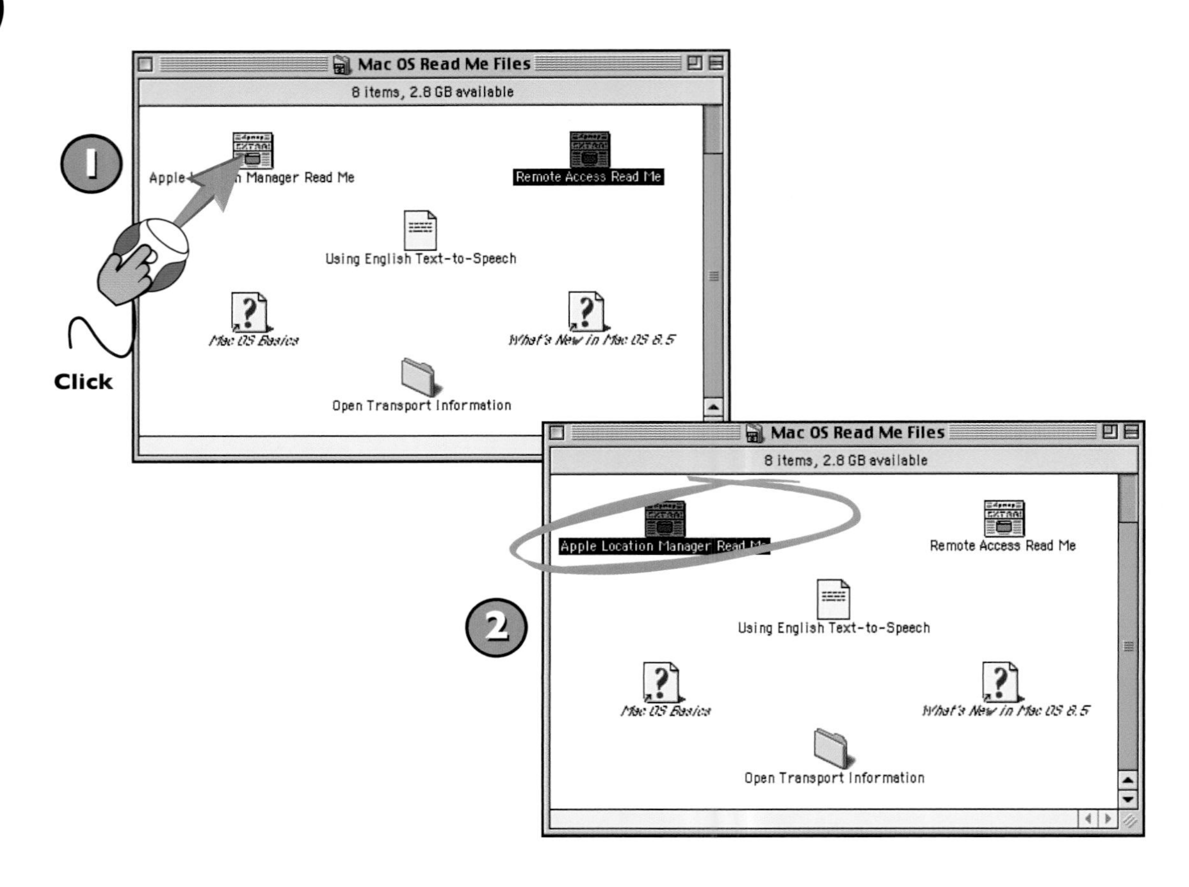

1. Click the folder or file you want to work with.
2. That folder or file is selected.

✓ To deselect a folder or file, click outside the file list.

✓ You can select a single file in a window by typing one or several characters of the file name.

Task 9: Selecting Adjacent Folders or Files

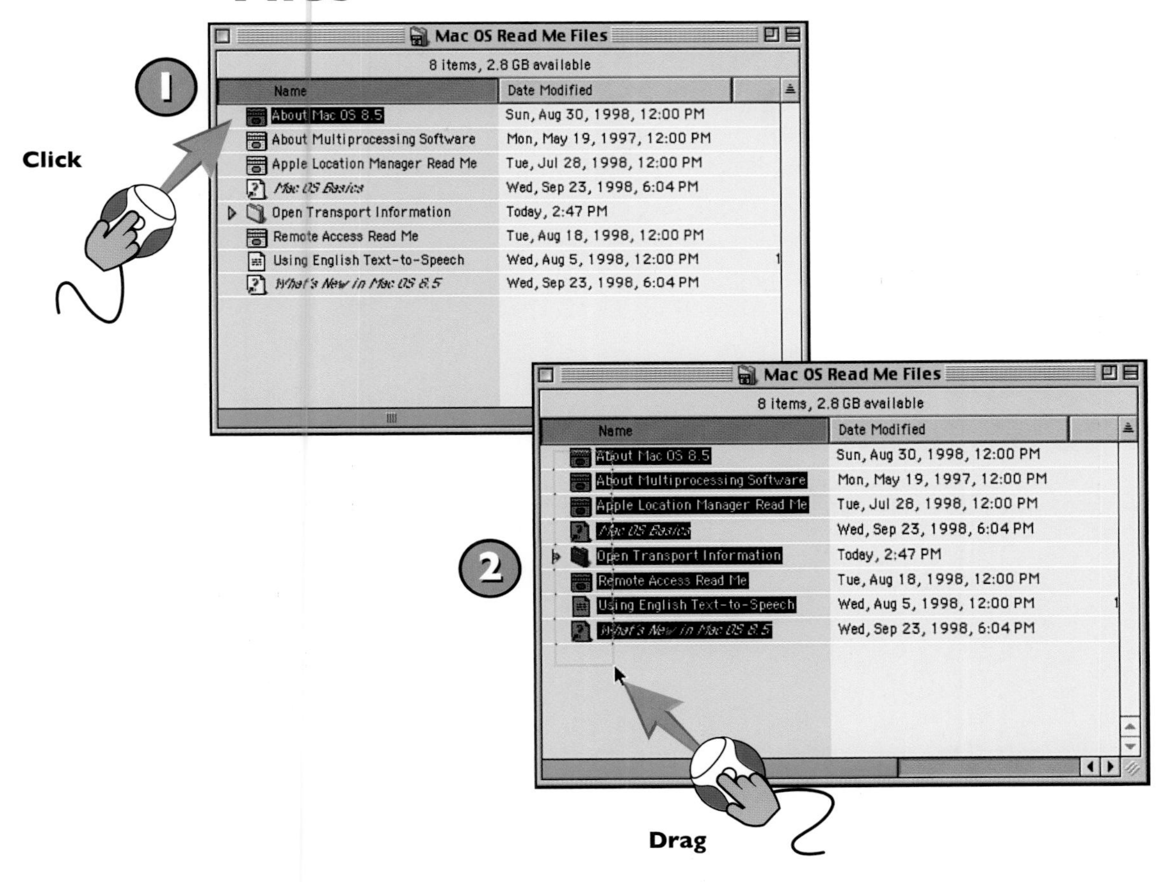

Mac OS 8.5 enables you to easily select multiple files or folders that are grouped together.

Click next to the first folder or file of the group that you want to select, and then drag the mouse around the items you want to select.

Release the mouse once you've highlighted all the items in the window; the first and last folder or file—as well as all the folders and files in between—are selected.

Task 10: Selecting Nonadjacent Folders or Files

Even if the folders or files that you want to select are not grouped together, you can still select them using Mac OS 8.5.

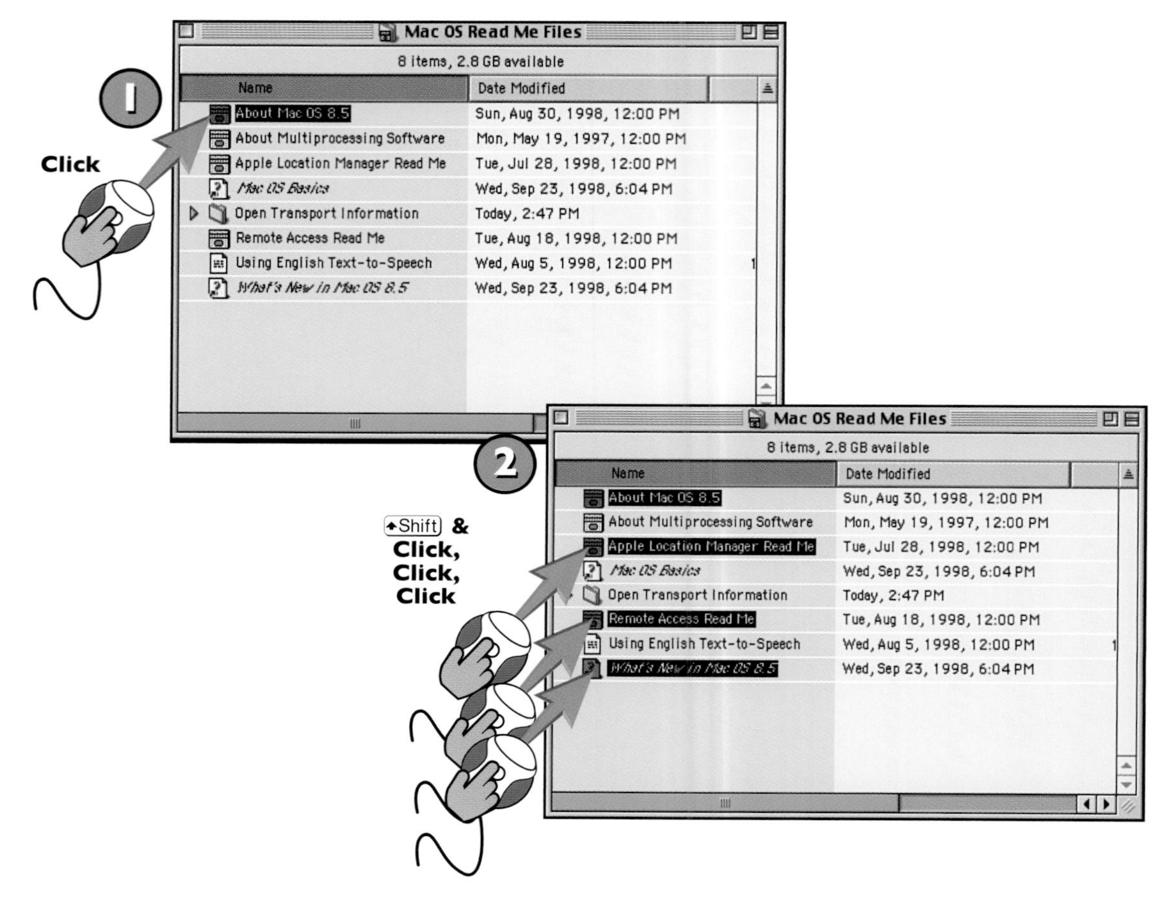

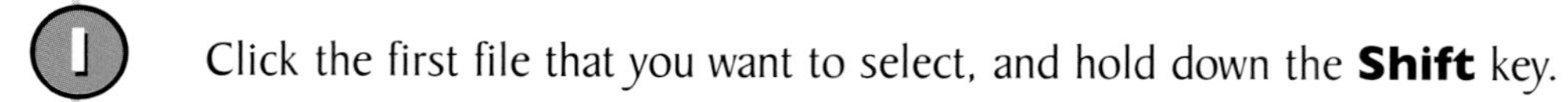

1. Click the first file that you want to select, and hold down the **Shift** key.

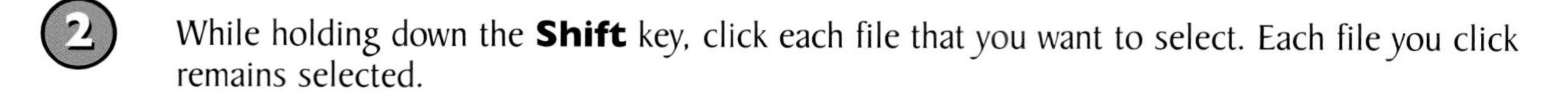

2. While holding down the **Shift** key, click each file that you want to select. Each file you click remains selected.

Task 11: Selecting All Folders or Files

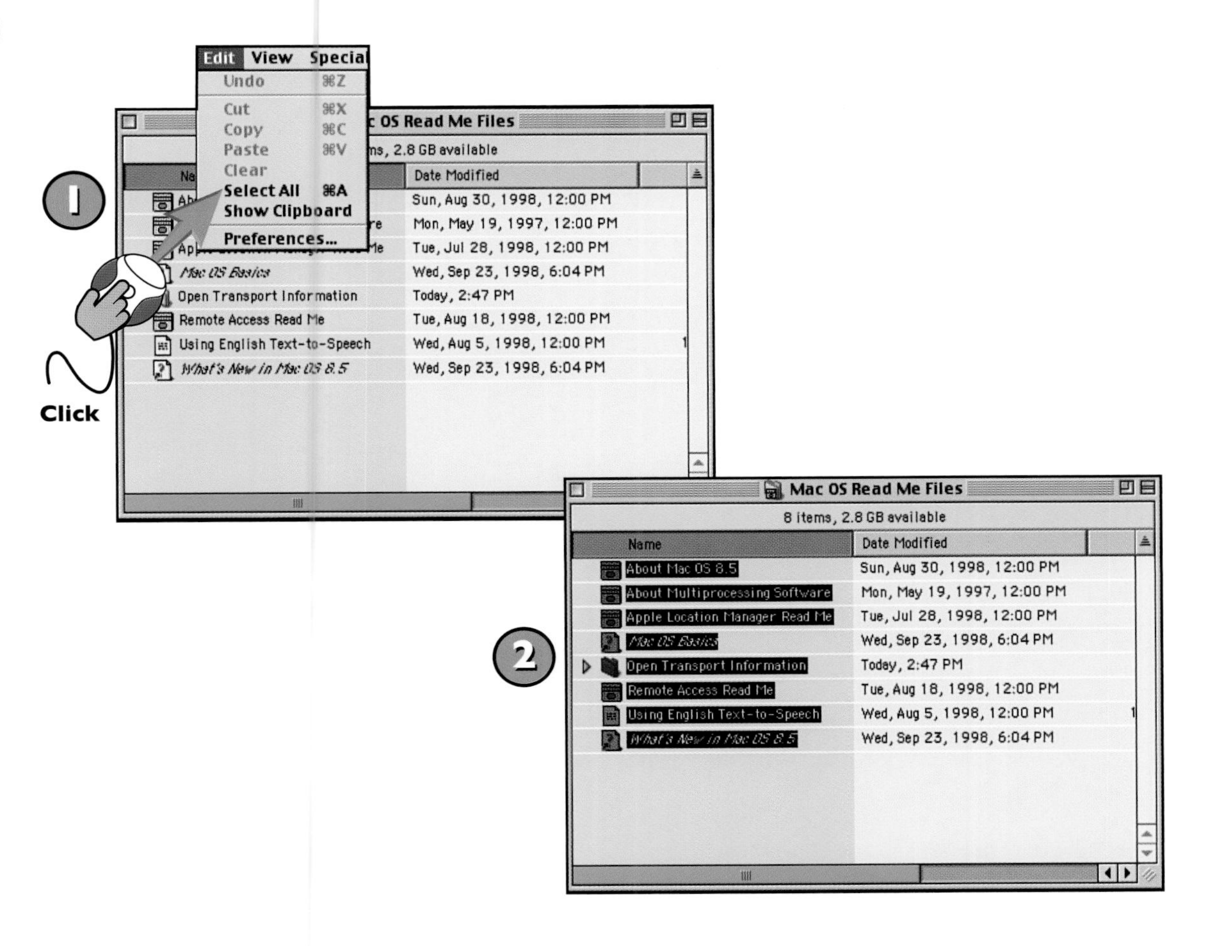

Mac OS 8.5 enables you to easily select all the folders and files in a window.

1. Click **Edit** and then click the **Select All** command.

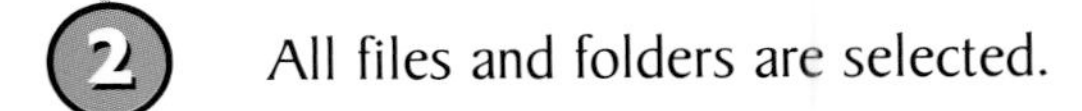

2. All files and folders are selected.

Task 12: Creating a Folder

Working with your files is easier if you group related files into folders. For example, you might want to create a folder in your word-processing program's folder to hold all the documents you create with that program. Creating a folder enables you to keep your documents separated from the program's files so you can easily find your document files.

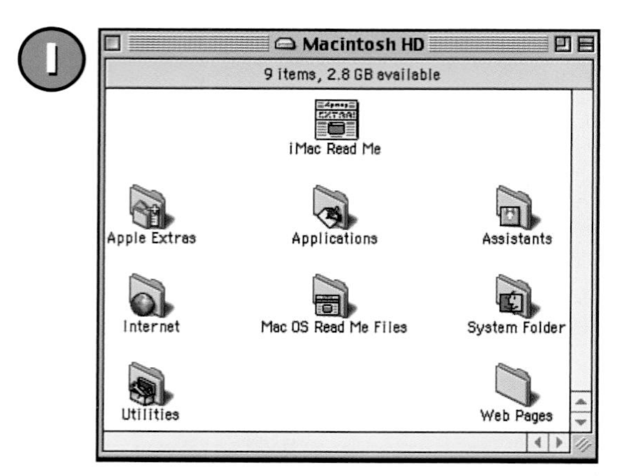

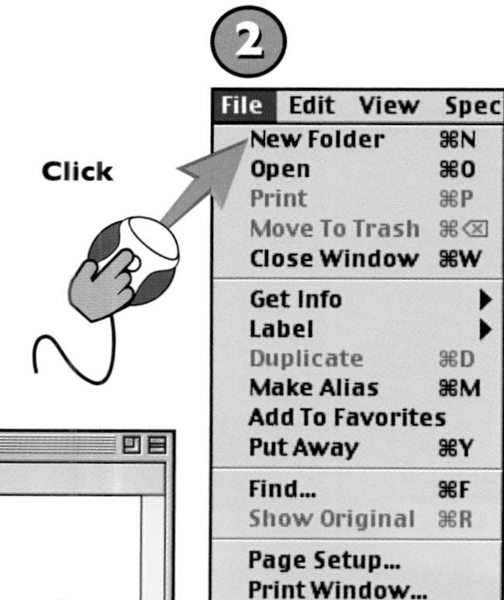

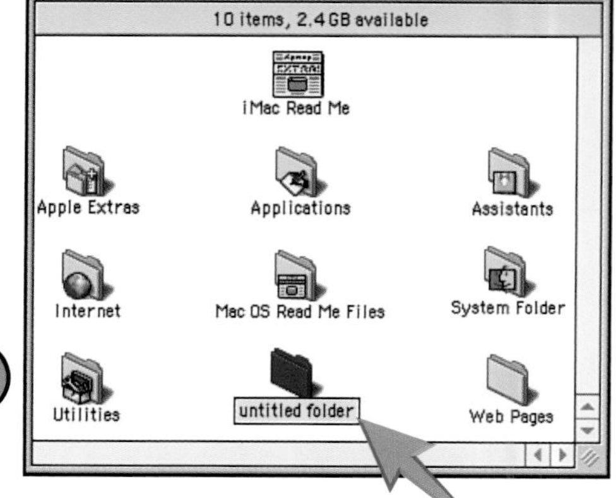

If you change your mind about the new folder, you can always delete it. To delete the folder, select it and then move it to the trash icon.

1. Open the window for the folder or disk where you want to create the folder.
2. Click **File**, select the **New Folder** command.
3. The new folder appears in the drive window, and the name is highlighted.

Next Step

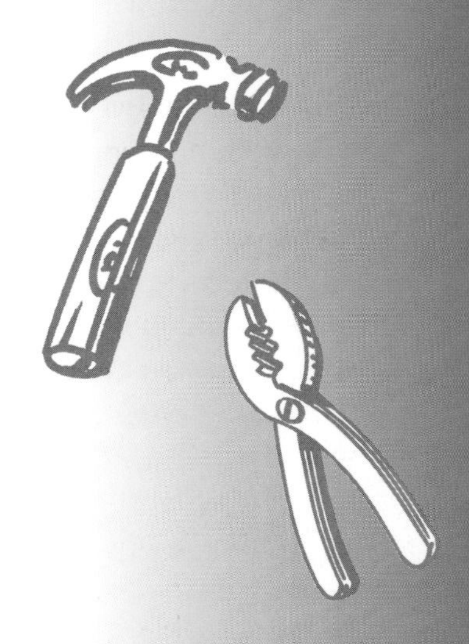

4 To change the name of the folder, type a new name and press **Return**.

5 The folder is added.

The folder name can contain as many as 31 characters, and can include spaces.

Task 13: Copying Folders and Files

The iMac makes it easy for you to copy a file or folder to a new location. You can, for example, copy a file or folder to another location on the hard drive if you want to revise the original file or folder for a different use.

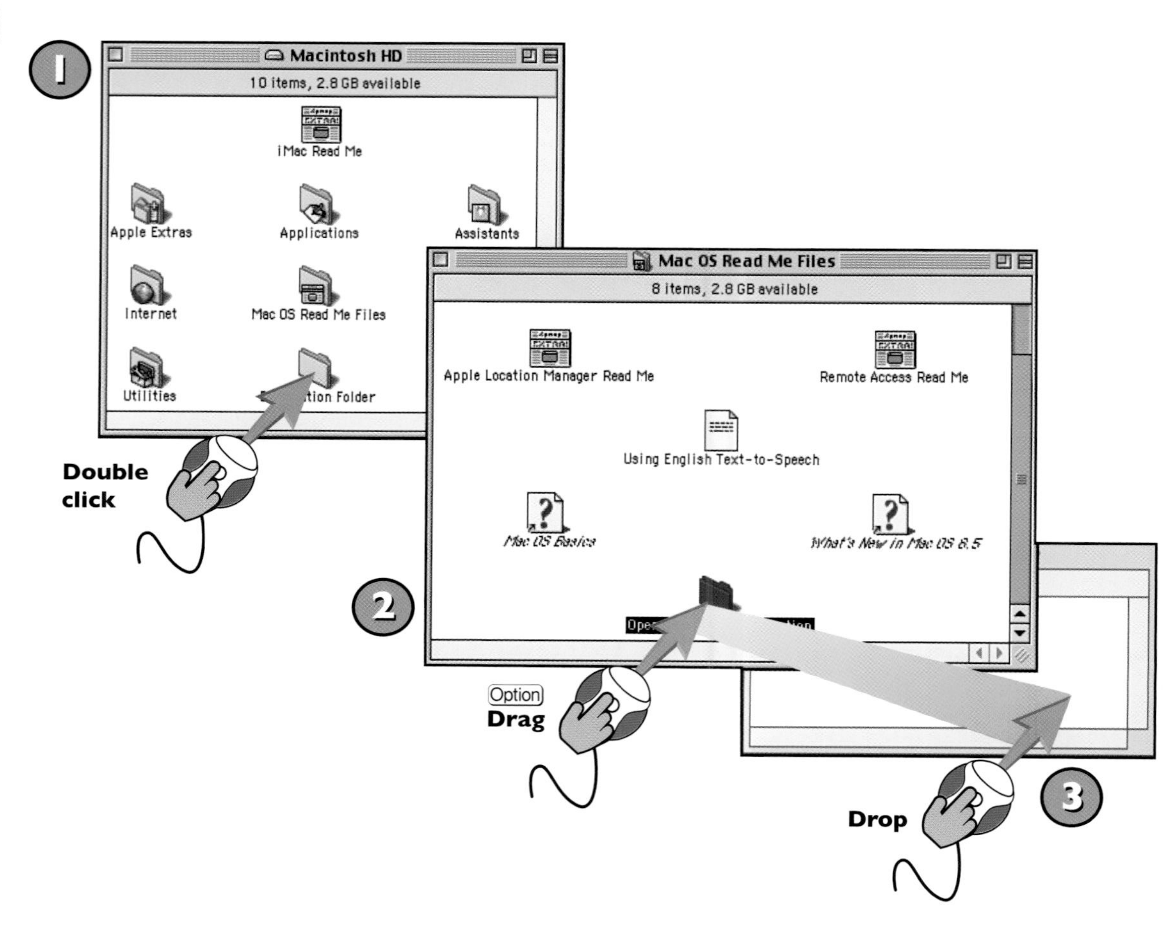

- You can copy a file or folder by first opening both the window that contains the file or folder (the source) and the window to which you want to copy the file or folder (the destination). Click the file or folder in the source window and drag it to the destination window.
- You can also use the **Duplicate** command or **Option+click+drag** the file or folder to create a copy.
- You can select specific files or folders by holding down the **Shift** key then clicking on the files or folders you want to choose.

1. Open the folder you want to copy files or folders to.
2. Go to the source folder and select the folder or file you want to copy.
3. Press the **Option** key and drag the folder or file to the destination folder.

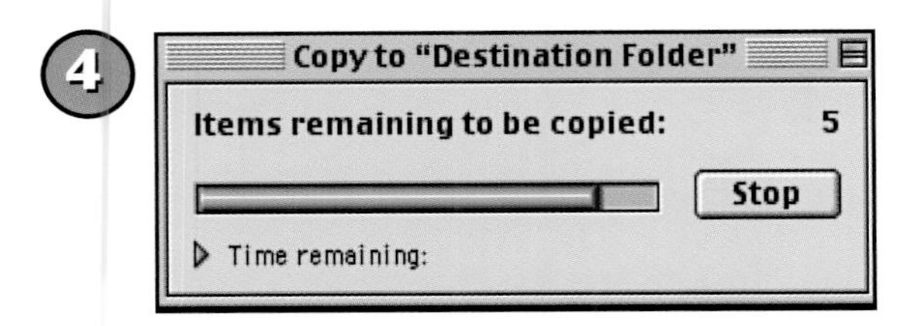

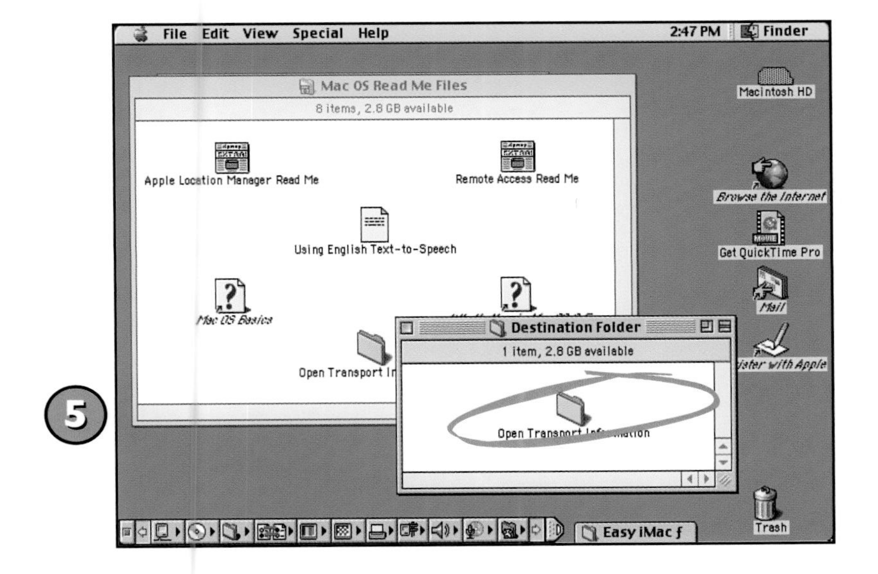

4. Observe the copy dialog as it copies your file or folder to the new folder.

5. The copy of the file or folder appears in the destination window.

Task 14: Moving Folders and Files

You can move files or folders to another folder so that you can reorganize your hard drive. For example, you might want to move all related files and folders to the same place on your hard drive so you can find them quickly and easily.

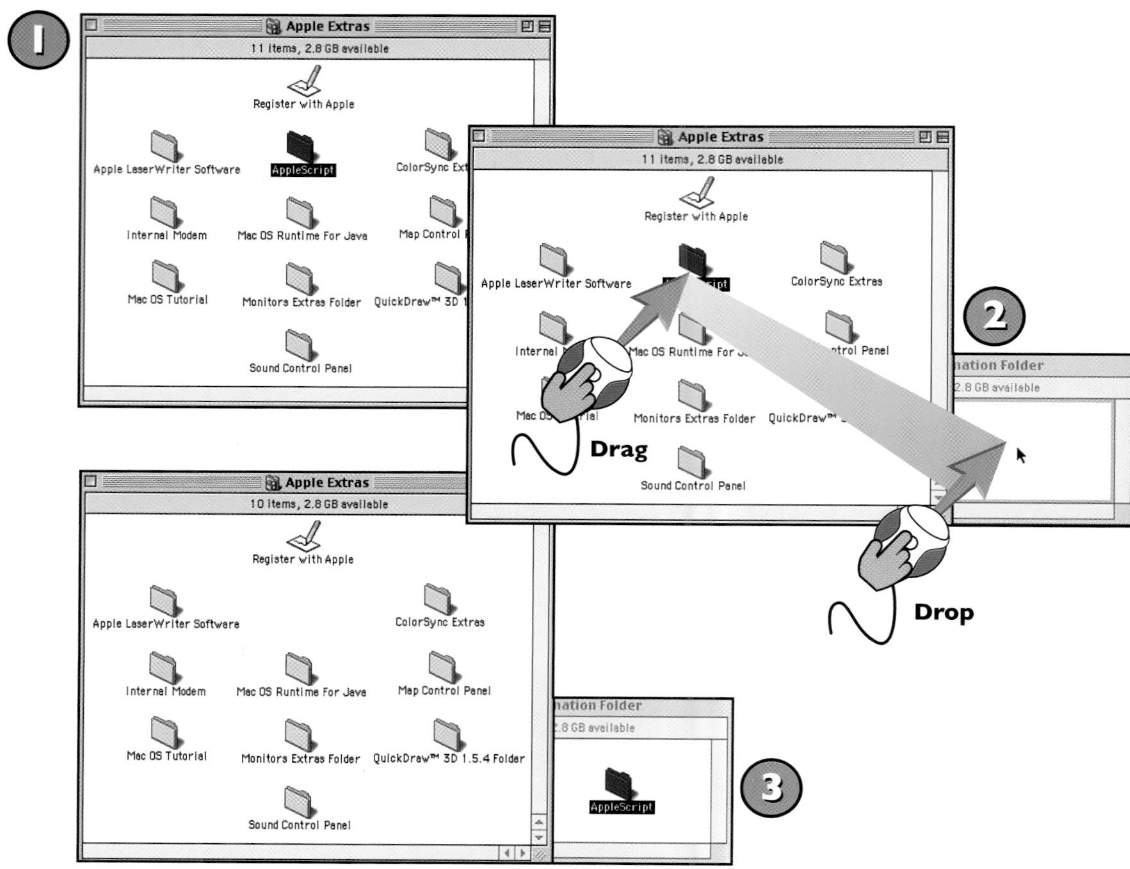

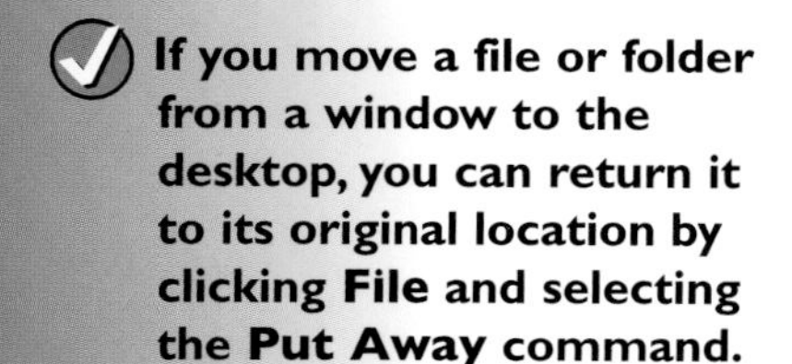

✓ If you move a file or folder from a window to the desktop, you can return it to its original location by clicking **File** and selecting the **Put Away** command.

1. Select a folder or file that you want to move.
2. Click and drag the folder to the destination window or folder icon, and then release the mouse button.
3. Mac OS moves the folder to the new location.

Task 15: Renaming Folders and Files

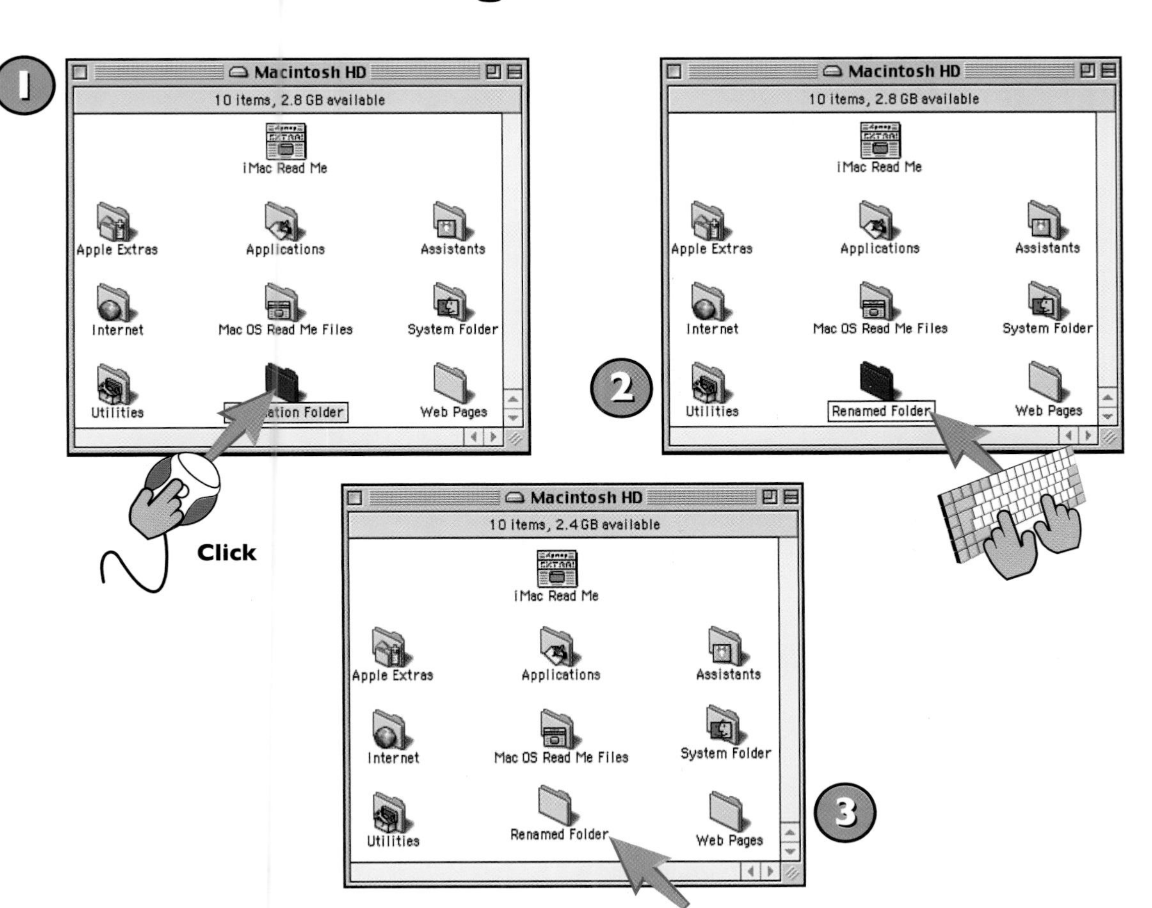

As you add more and more folders and files to your computer, you will eventually need to rearrange and reorganize them. In addition to needing to know how to copy and move folders and files, you'll need to know how to rename them (for instance, in case you want to give a folder a more descriptive name). Fortunately, iMac lets you easily rename files and folders.

1. Click the folder or file that you want to rename.
2. Wait for about one second or press the **Return** key. Type a new name for the folder, and press **Return**.
3. The folder is renamed.

As a shortcut, click the folder or file once to select it, and then single-click within the name to edit the name.

Task 16: Creating a Pop-Up Folder Window

If you use a folder frequently, you can move it to the bottom of the desktop window to turn it into a pop-up folder. You can access a pop-up folder from Finder or any application.

Start Here

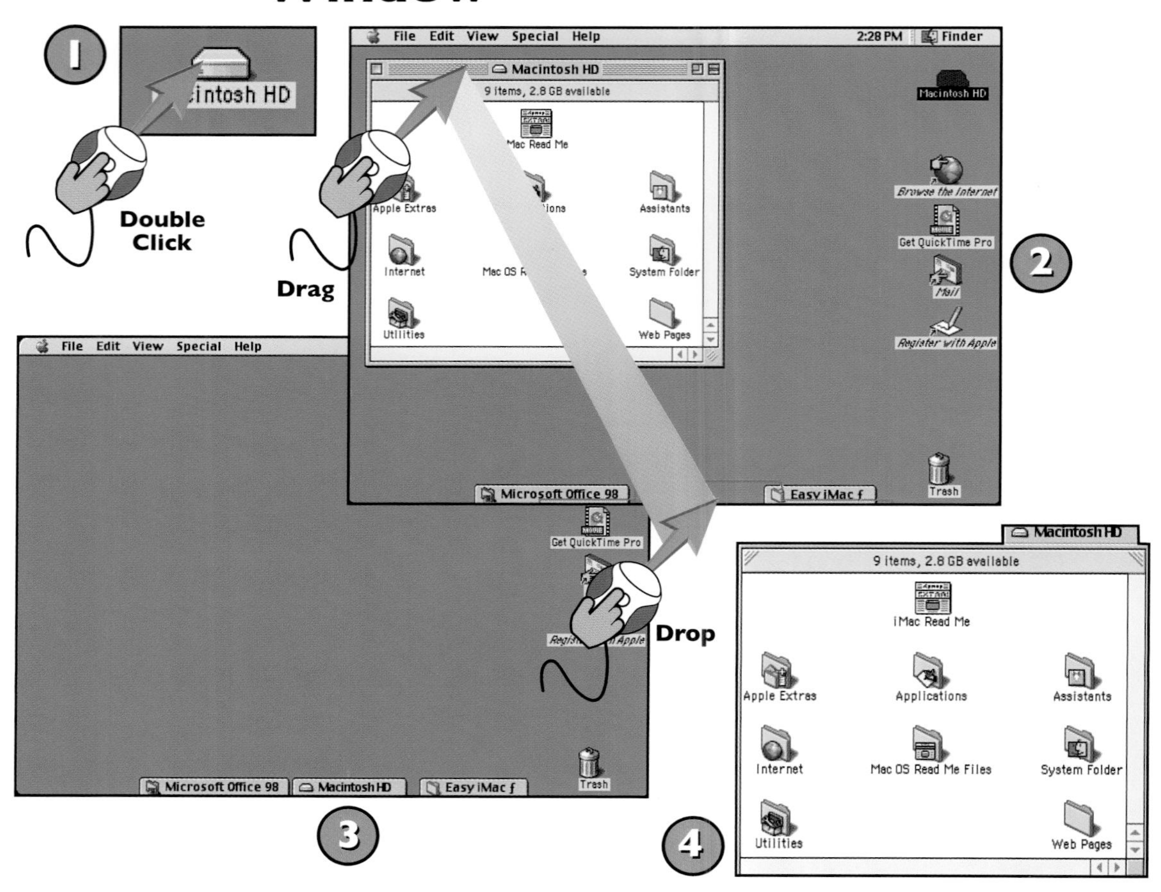

1. Double-click the hard disk icon on the desktop.
2. Move the window to the bottom of the desktop by clicking the window title bar and dragging.
3. The window title bar turns into a tab.
4. Click the pop-up window tab to view window contents.

If you forget where a pop-up folder resides on your hard disk, you can Command+click the title bar of the pop-up window to view the path of the folder on your hard disk.

Task 17: Creating an Alias to a File or Folder

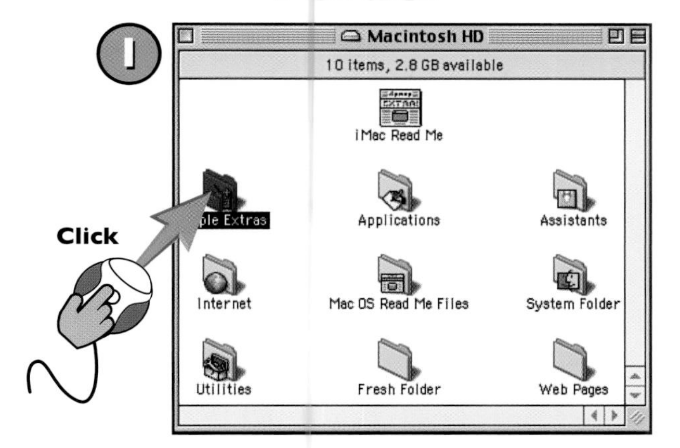

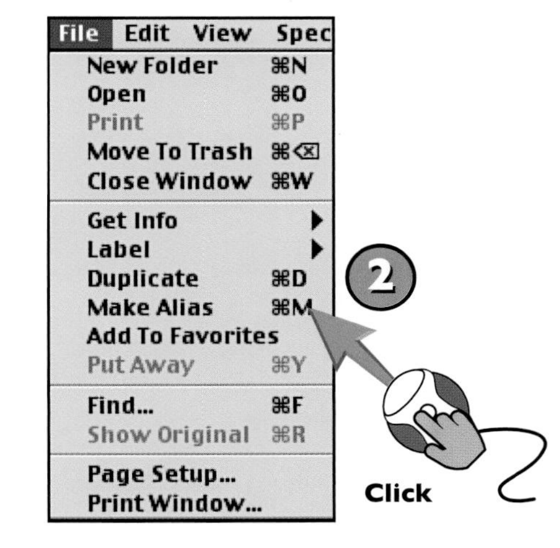

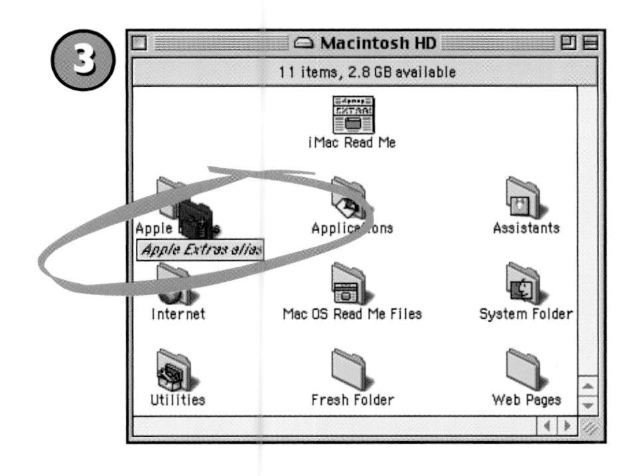

If you often use the same file or folder, you might want fast access to it. If so, you can create a shortcut, or alias icon, for the file or folder on the desktop. Double-clicking a file's alias icon opens the file in the application you used to create the file. Double-clicking a folder displays the contents of the folder in a window.

1. Select a folder or file you want to create an alias for.

2. Click **File** and select the **Make Alias** command.

3. Mac OS creates an alias to the folder or file.

To delete an alias icon, move it to the Trash.

You can find the original file of the alias by Ctrl+clicking the alias and selecting Show Original.

To rename an alias icon, click it, then wait for the text to highlight. Type a new name and press Return.

Task 18: Changing a Folder or File Label

You can group or label files or folders with a color. Color labels can help you more easily identify a particular file or folder in a window or on the desktop.

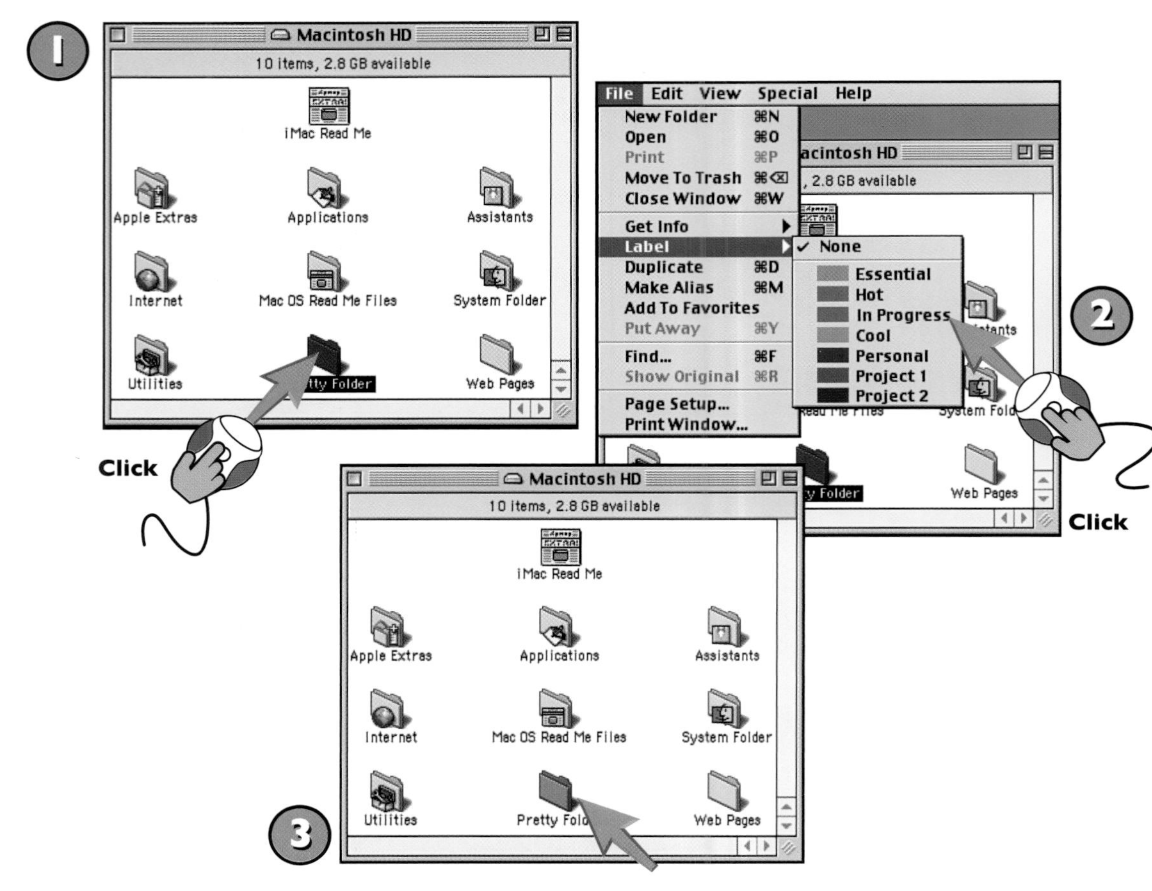

1. Click on a folder in a window.
2. Click **File** and select a color from the **Label** submenu.
3. Mac OS adds the label to the folder.

✓ You can change the label colors by clicking **Edit** and selecting the **Preferences** command. In the **Preferences** window, select the **Labels** tab and click on a color you want to change. To change the color, select a different color from the color picker wheel.

Task 19: Deleting Folders and Files

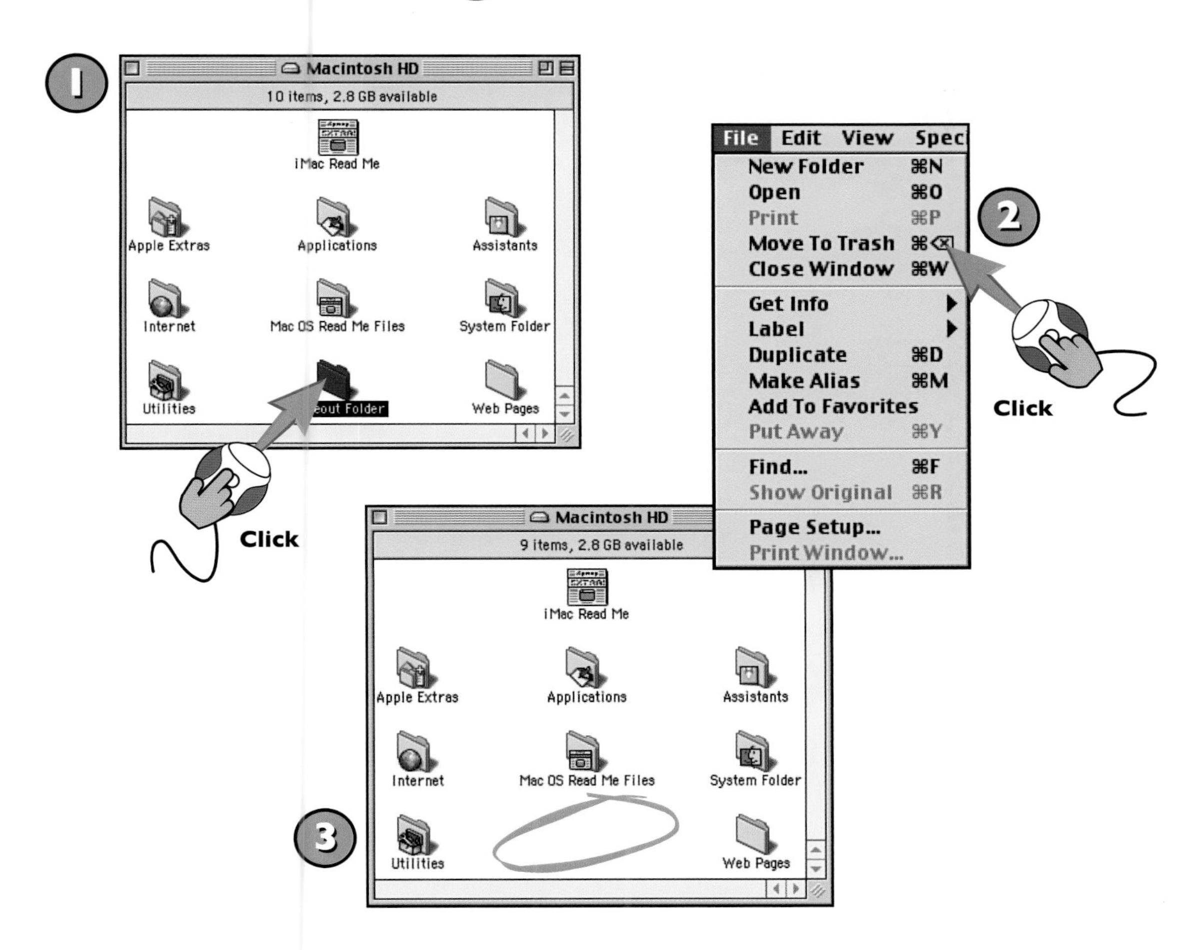

Eventually, your computer will become full of files and folders, and you'll have a hard time organizing and storing them all. You may need to clean house by deleting files and folders you no longer need. Mac OS 8.5 keeps folders and files that you want to delete in the Trash.

1. Click the folder or file that you want to delete.
2. Click **File** and then select the **Move to Trash** command.
3. The folder or file is moved to the Trash.

Files placed in the Trash are not deleted until you empty the trash. See Task 21, "Emptying the Trash," for information about permanently deleting files and folders from your system.

You can move any item to the Trash by Ctrl+clicking an icon and selecting the Move to Trash command.

Task 20: Undeleting a File or Folder

Sometimes you move a file or folder to the Trash by mistake. You can retrieve the file or folder from the Trash (as long as the Trash has not been emptied) and return it to its original (or a new) location.

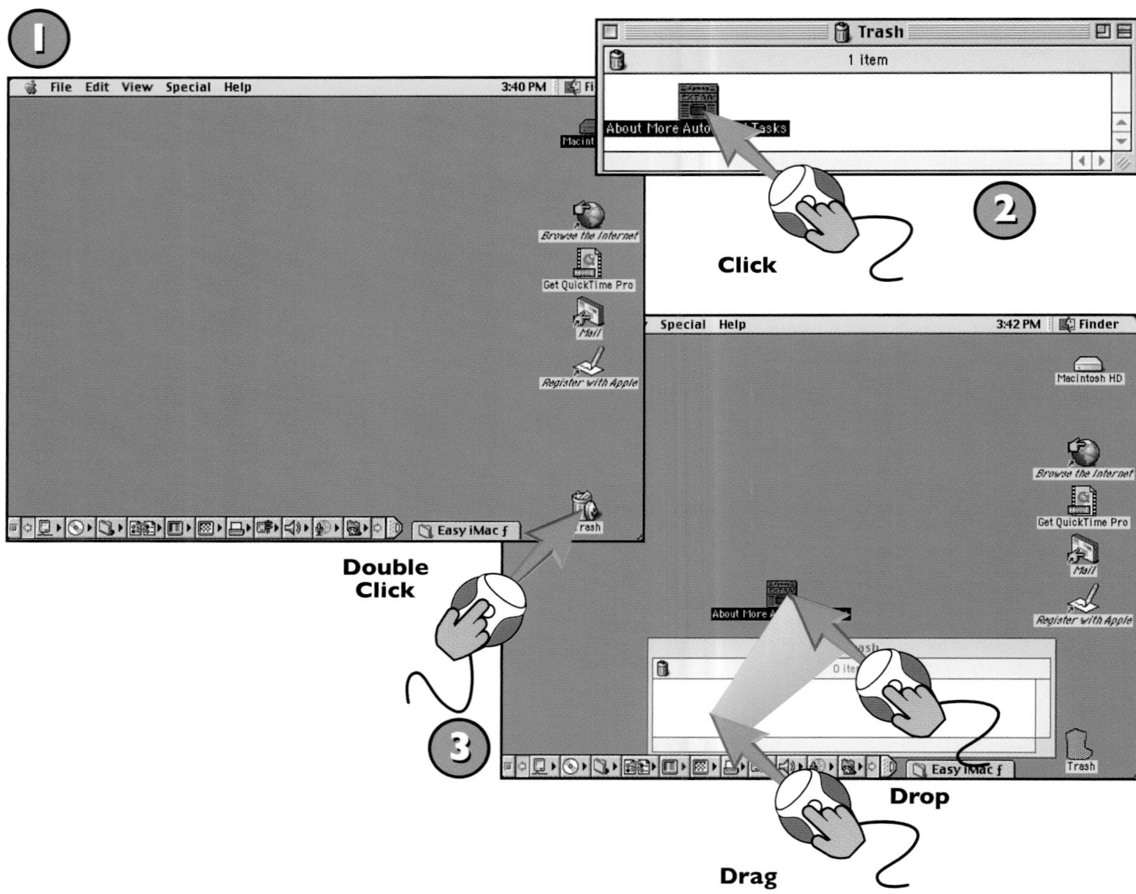

1. Double-click the **Trash** icon.
2. Select a file in the **Trash** window.
3. Move the file to the desktop.

Task 21: Emptying the Trash

If you want to permanently remove from your system the files in the Trash, you can empty it.

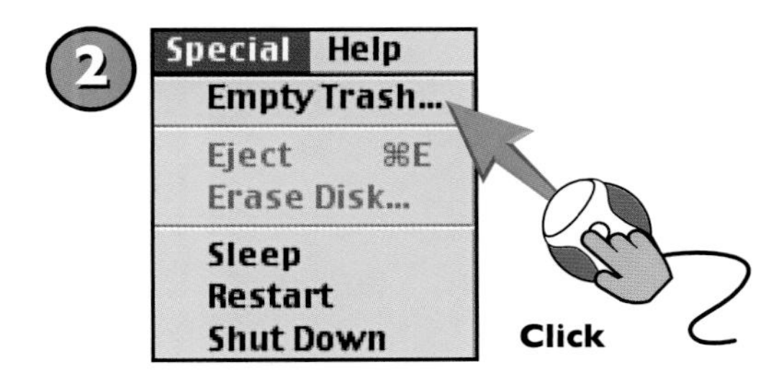

The Trash contains 3 items, which use 72 K of disk space. Are you sure you want to remove these items permanently?

Cancel OK

Click

1. When the **Trash** icon appears to be brimming with garbage, it means that there is at least one file or folder in the Trash.
2. To empty the trash, click **Special** and select the **Empty Trash** command.
3. Mac OS displays an alert asking you to confirm whether you want to delete all the files in the Trash; click **OK**.
4. The Trash is emptied; notice that the **Trash** icon no longer appears to overflow with garbage.

✓ An alternative way to empty the Trash is to press the **Ctrl** key and select **Empty Trash**.

✓ If you change your mind about deleting the folder, click the **Cancel** button in the **Confirmation Alert** dialog after selecting **Empty Trash** from the **Special** menu.

✓ If you have Norton Utilities 4.0 (or newer), you can use the Norton FileSaver Control Panel and Norton's UnErase feature to recover many files after you've emptied the Trash.

✓ If you select **Get Info on the Trash**, you can turn off the warning message that appears whenever you empty the Trash.

PART 6

Printing with Mac OS

Your iMac uses Mac OS as its operating system, which in turn enables you to use any Mac OS application on your iMac. All Mac OS applications use the same setup for your printer, which saves time and ensures that you can print from any Mac OS application without resetting for each program. Mac OS 8.5 includes printer software for PostScript and non-PostScript printers made by Apple and other vendors. If needed, you can install additional printer software, or set up more than one printer. In addition, you can easily manage printing for all of your applications.

You print a document from the application in which you created it. When you send a file to the printer, the file first goes to a ***print queue***, or holding area. The print queue can contain one or many files at any time, and you can make changes to this print queue. While a file is in the print queue, you can pause, restart, and even cancel the printing. This part shows you how to control and manage printing in Mac OS.

Tasks

Task 1: Setting the Default Printer

If you have more than one printer connected, you must select one as the default. The default printer you set in Mac OS is the printer your applications automatically use when you choose to print.

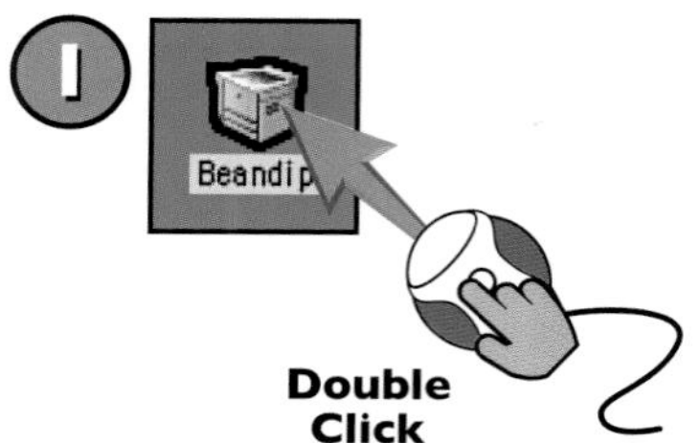

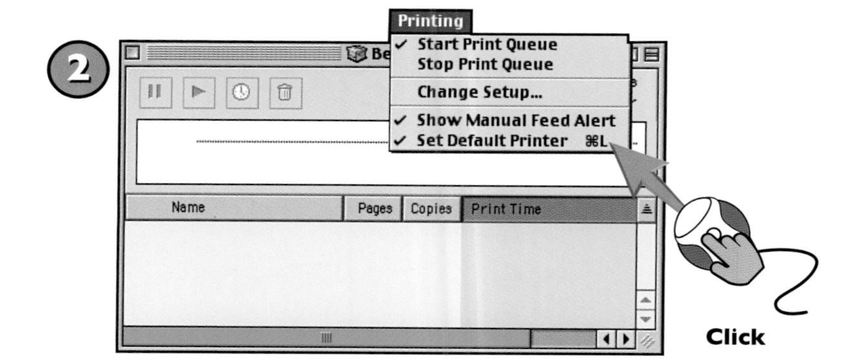

1. Double-click a desktop printer icon on the desktop.

2. Click **Printing** and click the **Set Default Printer** command.

To use a different printer, you can select and drag a document to any other desktop printer icon.

You can change the default printer by double-clicking any desktop printer icon, or selecting any desktop printer icon and pressing Command+L.

Task 2: Printing a Document

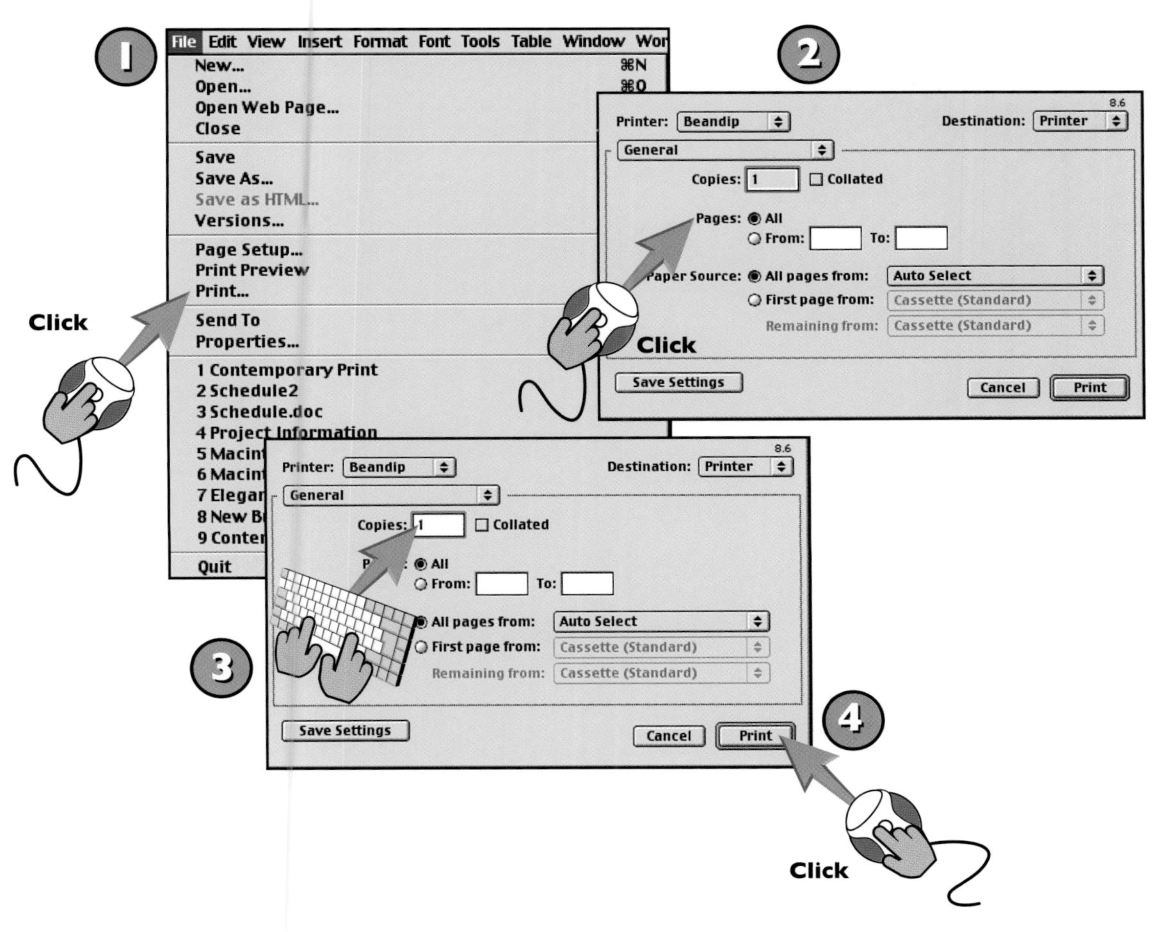

Once you've set a default printer, you can print from any application using this printer. Printing your documents gives you a paper copy you can proofread, use in reports, give to co-workers, and so on.

1. Click **File**, and then click the **Print** command.
2. In the **Print** dialog, specify a page range.
3. Enter the number of copies you want printed.
4. Click the **Print** button.

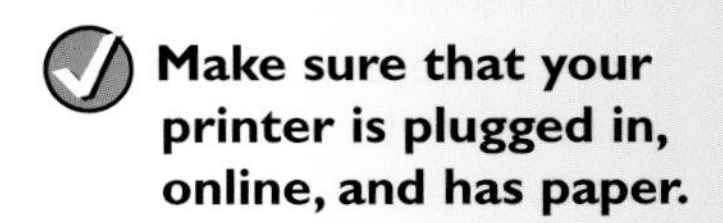

Make sure that your printer is plugged in, online, and has paper.

If you want to use a printer other than the default, choose the printer you want to use from the **Printer** pop-up menu list in the **Print** dialog box.

Task 3: Viewing the Print Queue

You can print directly to the printer, or you can print in the background. The default setting for the iMac is to print to the background, which enables you to spool several documents to a print queue. The print queue lists the documents that have been sent to a printer, and shows how far along the printing is.

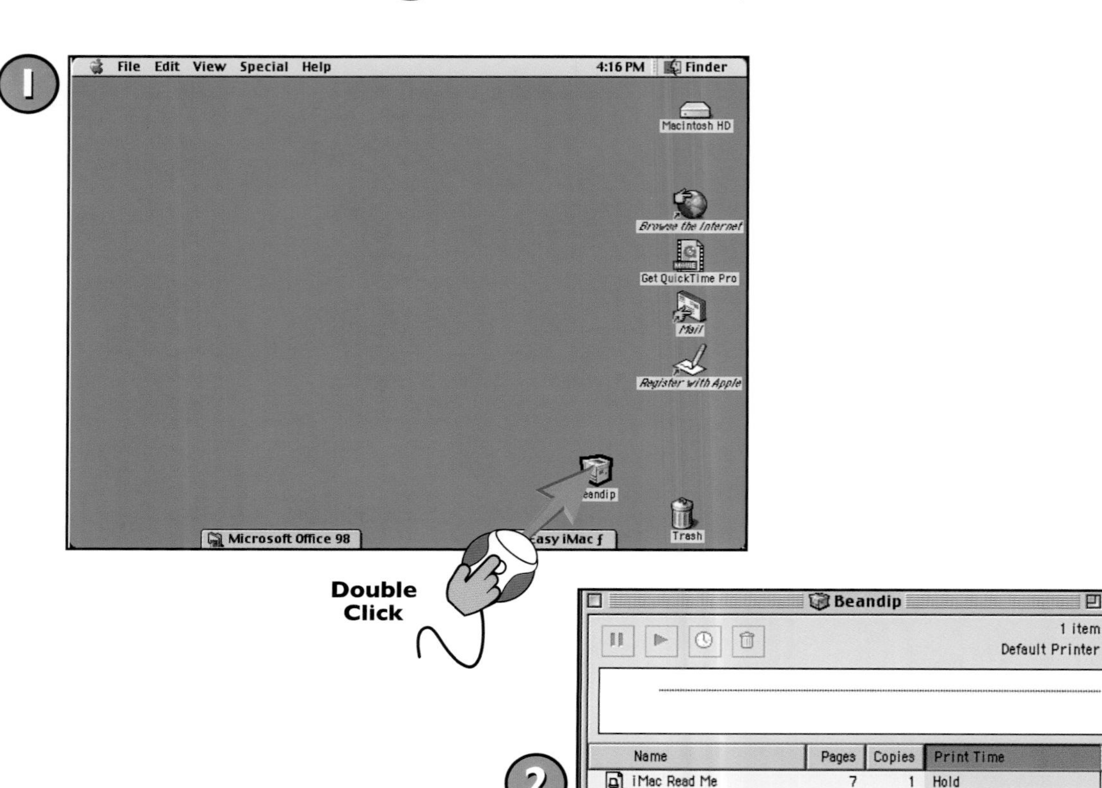

The controls for choosing foreground or background printing vary, depending on the kind of printer you are using. For example, if you are using the LaserWriter 8 printer driver, you can choose foreground or background printing in the **Print** dialog. If you are using a **USB** printer, you can turn off background printing from the **Chooser**.

You can display the print queue by double-clicking the **Printer** icon on the desktop. This icon appears whenever you select a printer from the **Chooser** application.

Double-click the printer icon on the desktop (in this case, **Beandip** is the name of the desktop printer icon for my LaserWriter 12/640 PS printer, which uses the LaserWriter 8 printer driver software).

The printer window displays a list of the documents in the queue as well as statistics about the document being printed.

Task 4: Pausing and Restarting a Print Job

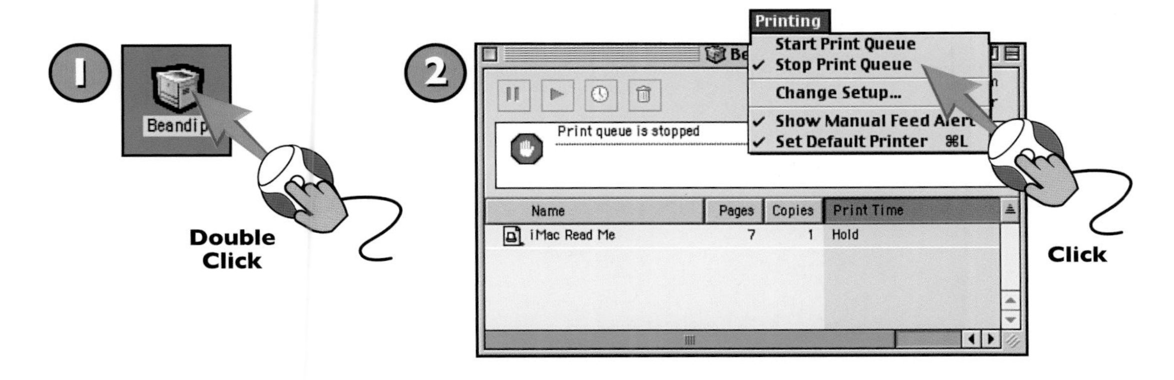

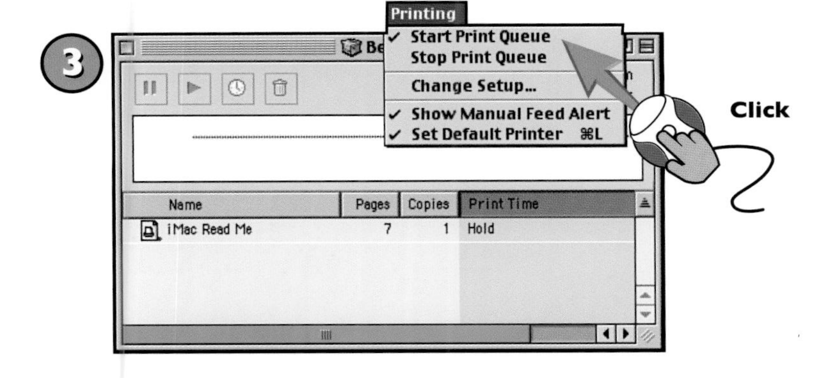

1. Double-click the desktop printer icon.
2. Click **Printing** and then choose the **Stop Print Queue** command.
3. Click **Printing** and then click the **Start Print Queue** command to resume printing.

You might want to pause printing when you have to make a change in the text or when you want to load a different paper type.

- **You have to be quick to pause or stop a short print job. If nothing appears in the print queue, it probably means that the entire print job has already been sent to the printer.**
- **You can use the button controls in the print queue window to pause printing on a specific job (if, for example, you have sent several jobs to the printer but want to pause and change paper for a particular job). Select the job you want to pause, and click the Pause button at the top of the print queue window.**
- **To restart the printer after you have paused it, click the Play arrow icon in the print queue window.**

Task 5: Canceling Printing

If you discover an error in the job you are printing or if you decide that you need to add something to it, you can cancel the print job. Canceling the print job prevents you from wasting time and paper.

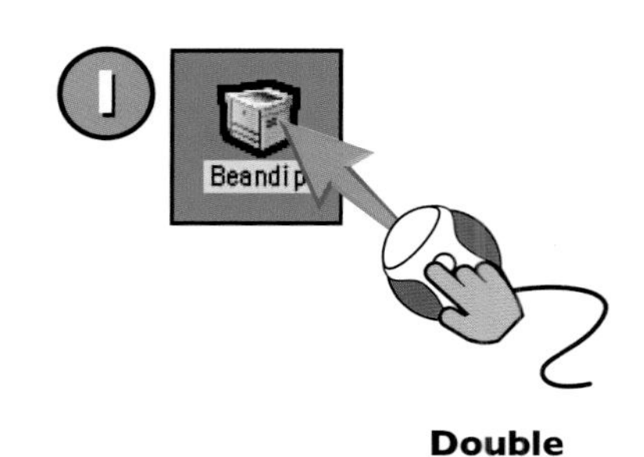

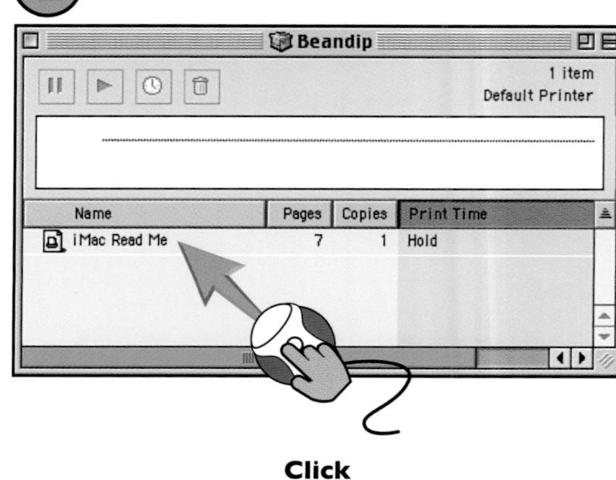

Depending on your computer and your printer, the print job might be listed in the print queue for only a few seconds before it is sent to the printer. You might not be able to cancel it in time.

1. Double-click the desktop printer icon to open the print queue window.
2. Select the document you want to cancel.

Next Step

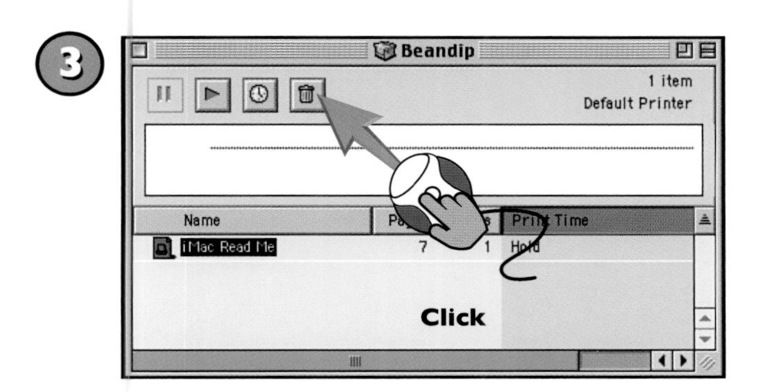

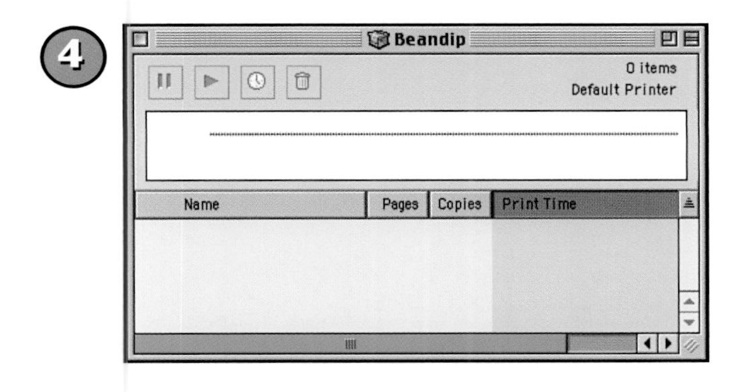

3. Click the **Trash** icon in the toolbar.

4. The item is removed from the print queue and placed in the Trash.

Task 6: Changing Printer Settings

You can easily change printer settings. You might, for example, switch to a different printer driver so that your printer works better with your applications; alternatively, you might change the paper tray, the printer description file, or specify whether you want double or single-sided printing (whether these types of options are available depends on the printer you use).

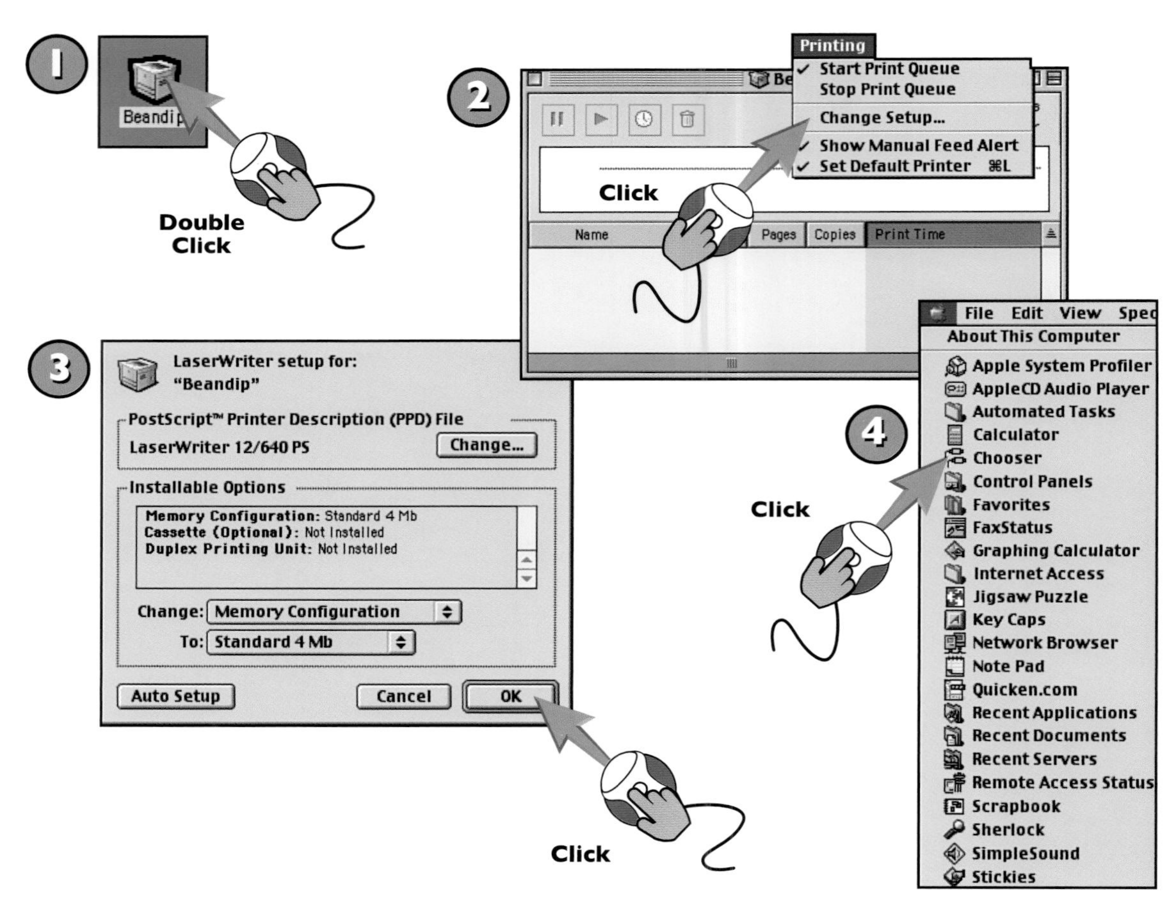

1. Double-click a desktop printer icon.
2. Open the **Printing** menu and choose the **Change Setup** command.
3. Adjust printer settings as desired. When finished, click **OK**.
4. Open the **Apple** menu and then click **Chooser**.

Use the Chooser to select a printer driver. Choose which driver to use from the left-side window.

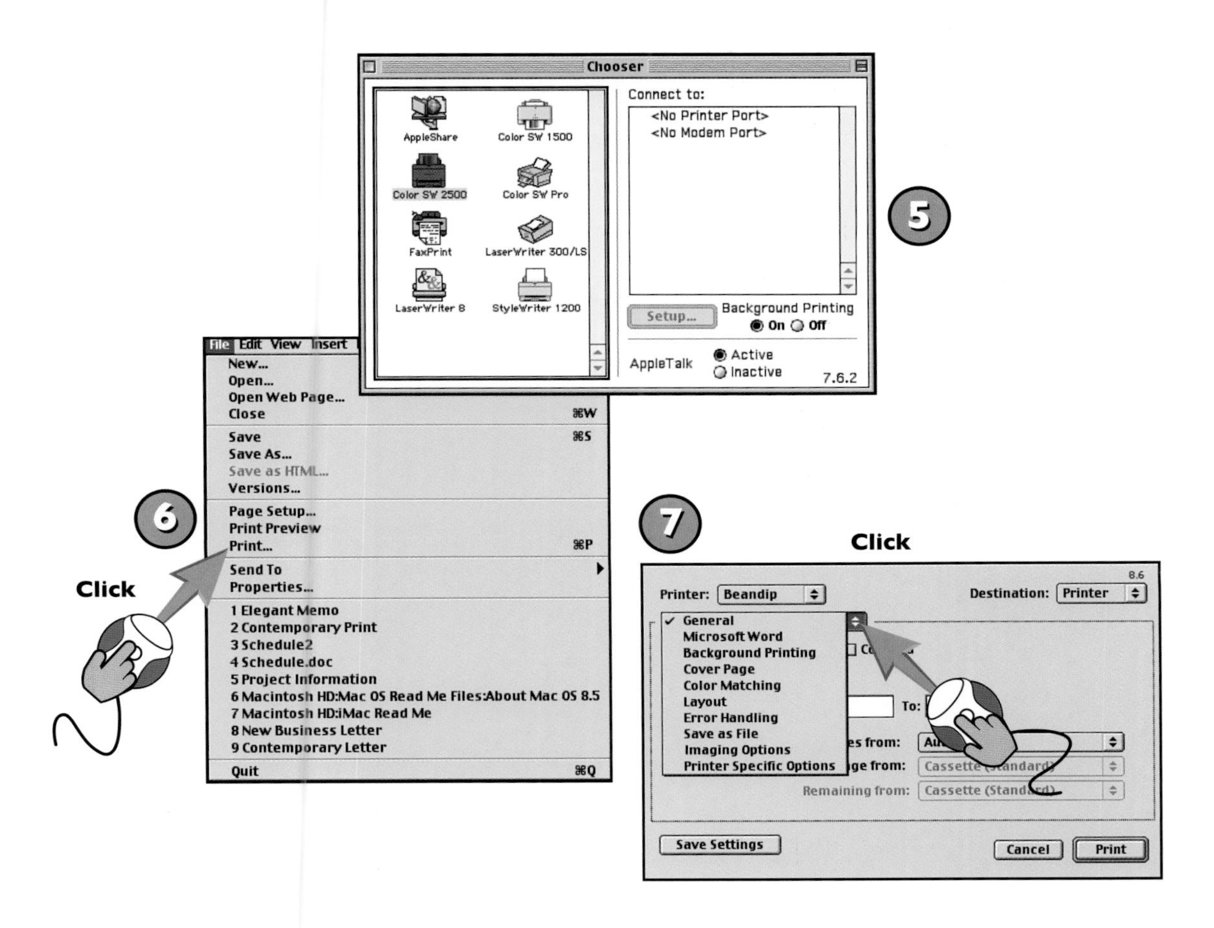

5. Here you can specify whether background printing is enabled, and you can select the printer port (in this case, no ports are available for the selected printer because the iMac has only USB ports).

6. Close the Chooser by clicking the **Close** button. Then open the **File** menu and choose **Print**.

7. The **Print** dialog options vary from printer to printer (in this case, the **LaserWriter 8 Print** dialog has many options to choose from).

Task 7: Adding a Printer

Start Here

If you buy a new printer, you can easily configure your iMac to use it by using the Chooser application.

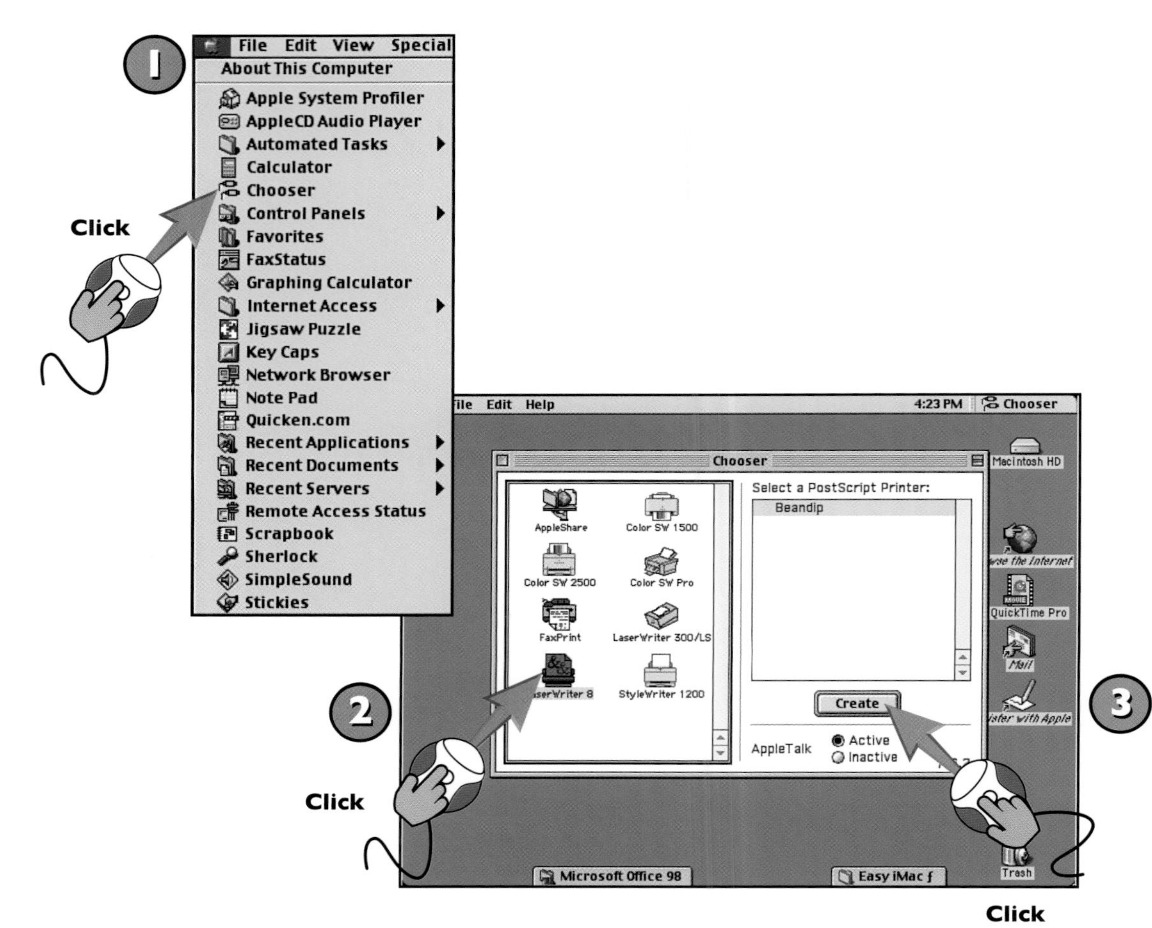

1. Click the **Apple** menu and click **Chooser**.
2. Click on a printer icon in the **Chooser** window (in this case, the **LaserWriter 8** icon).
3. Click the **Create** button.

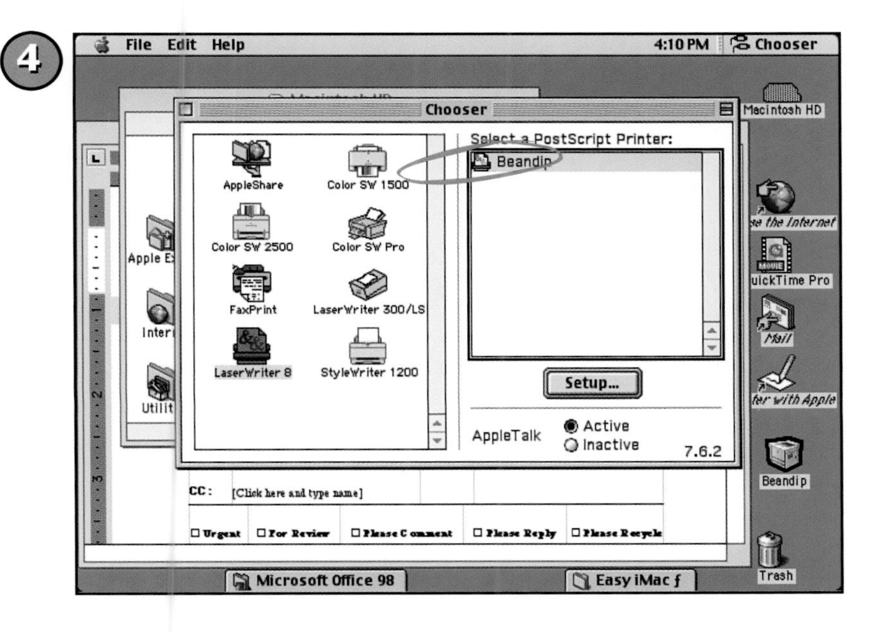

Mac OS automatically creates a desktop printer icon on your desktop. The printer, with a LaserWriter icon, appears in the printer list in the **Chooser** window.

Task 8: Adding a Printer Icon to the Desktop

Start Here

Your iMac gives you fast access to your printer by enabling you to add a printer icon to your desktop. You can then double-click this icon to view the print queue. You can also drag documents from a file window to the desktop printer icon to print the documents.
If you disable the desktop printing extensions by moving them out of the system folder, you can only print to the printer selected in Chooser.

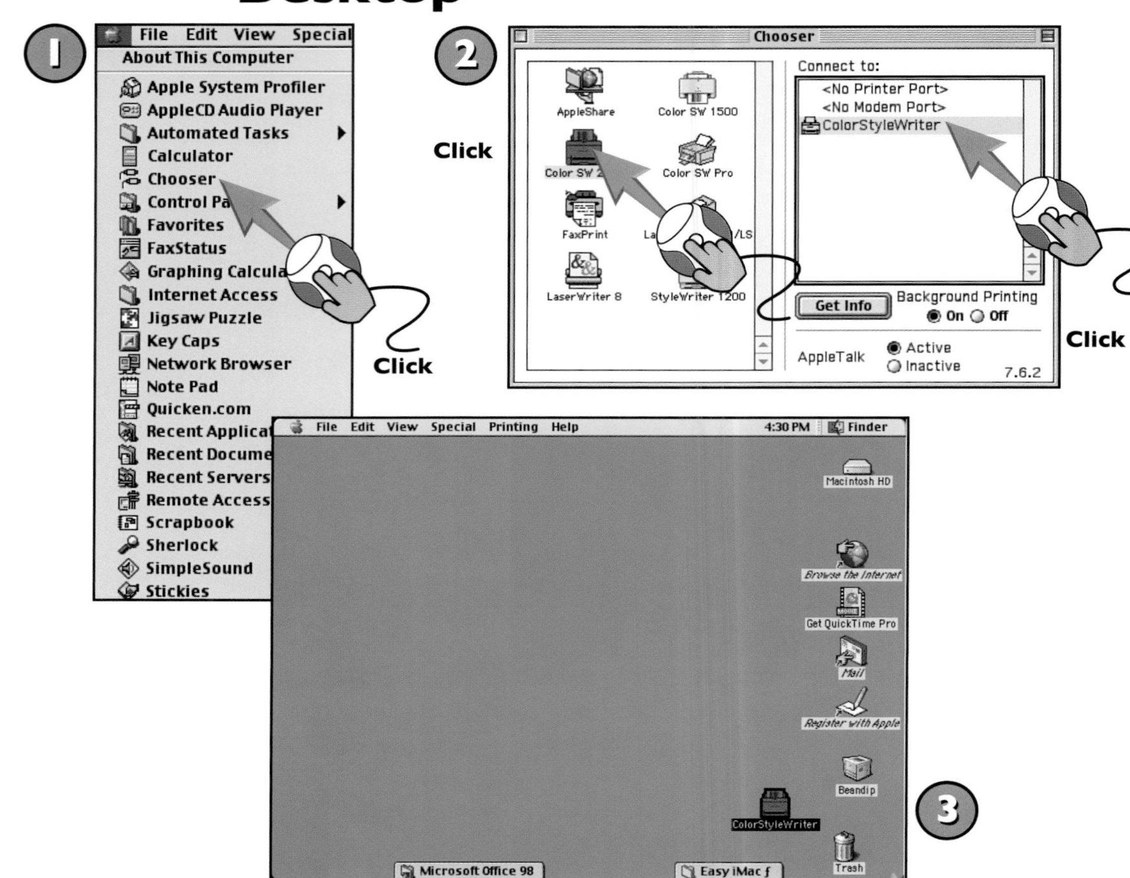

If you have more than one desktop printer, you can move a desktop printer you might not use very often to a different folder to reduce desktop clutter.

You automatically create a desktop printer when you configure a printer in **Chooser**. For more information on creating a new printer, see Task 7, "Adding a Printer."

1. Click the **Apple** menu and click **Chooser**.
2. Click the printer icon and then the printer name. If you are adding another LaserWriter printer (not the case here), choose the **Create** button.
3. The desktop printer icon appears on the desktop. You can access desktop printers from the control strip.

Task 9: Deleting a Printer Icon from the Desktop

If you get a new printer, you can delete the setup for the old printer so that you don't get confused about which printer is which. Deleting a printer removes it from the desktop.

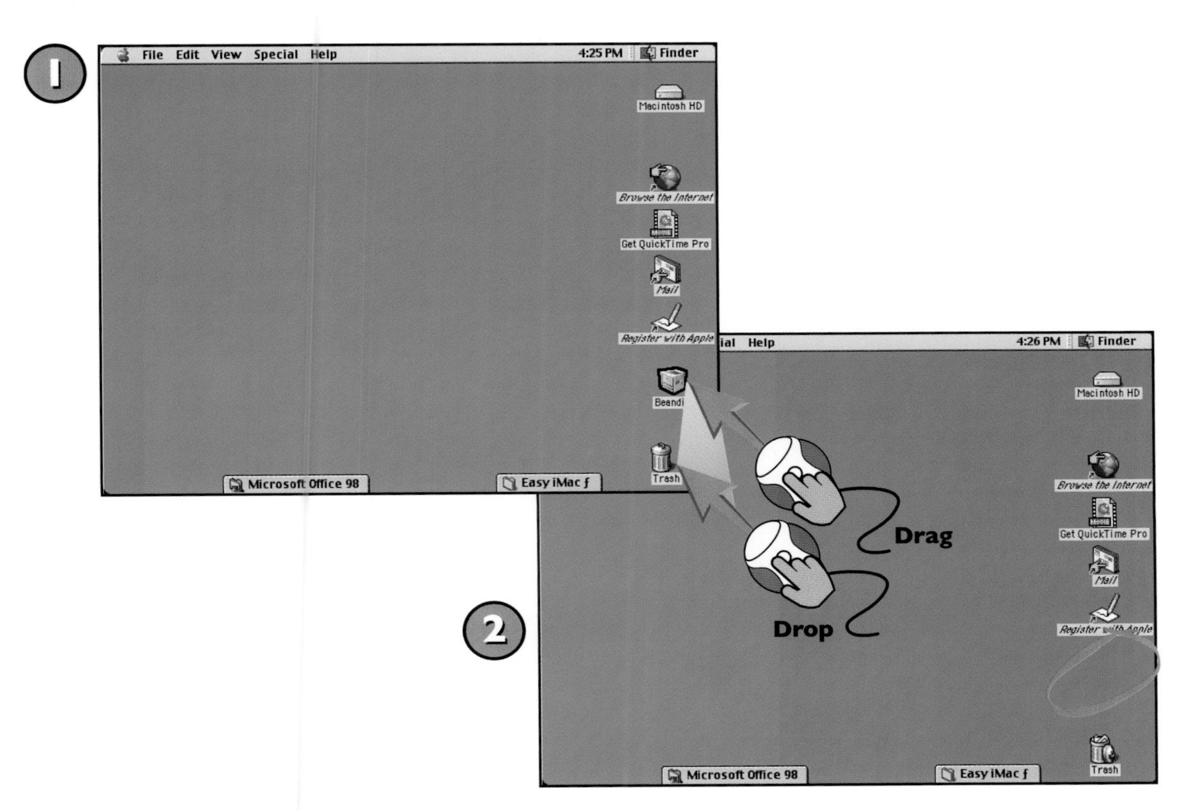

1. Click a desktop printer icon that you would like to delete and drag it to the **Trash** icon.

2. Release the mouse button. The printer is deleted.

If you delete a printer by mistake, you can always add it back using the Chooser (refer to the preceding task).

7

PART

Personalizing Mac OS

To make Mac OS most suited to your work, Apple has made it easy for you to customize it. You can change many elements in Mac OS, such as the scrolling controls on windows, the font used to display file and folder names, and the general appearance of Mac OS. You can adjust colors used for onscreen elements such as sliders, progress bars, and labels. You can change how the mouse works, when and what sounds are played, and more. Mac OS 8.5 includes many options for setting up your work environment just the way you want. This part shows you how to customize Mac OS.

Tasks

Task 1: Showing and Hiding Applications

Mac OS shows the application icon and name in the menu bar at all times as a default setting. To view another application running under Mac OS, open the **Applications** menu and click the application you want. The name of the previous application disappears from the menu bar, and the current, newly selected application icon and name appears.

Finder is one application that is always open with Mac OS 8.5. When you select it in the **Applications** menu, you can view the desktop and any open windows.

Most, but not all, control panels will appear in the **Applications** menu when opened. For example, Color Sync, General Controls, Mouse, Numbers, QuickTime Settings, Speech, and Text will not appear on the **Applications** menu.

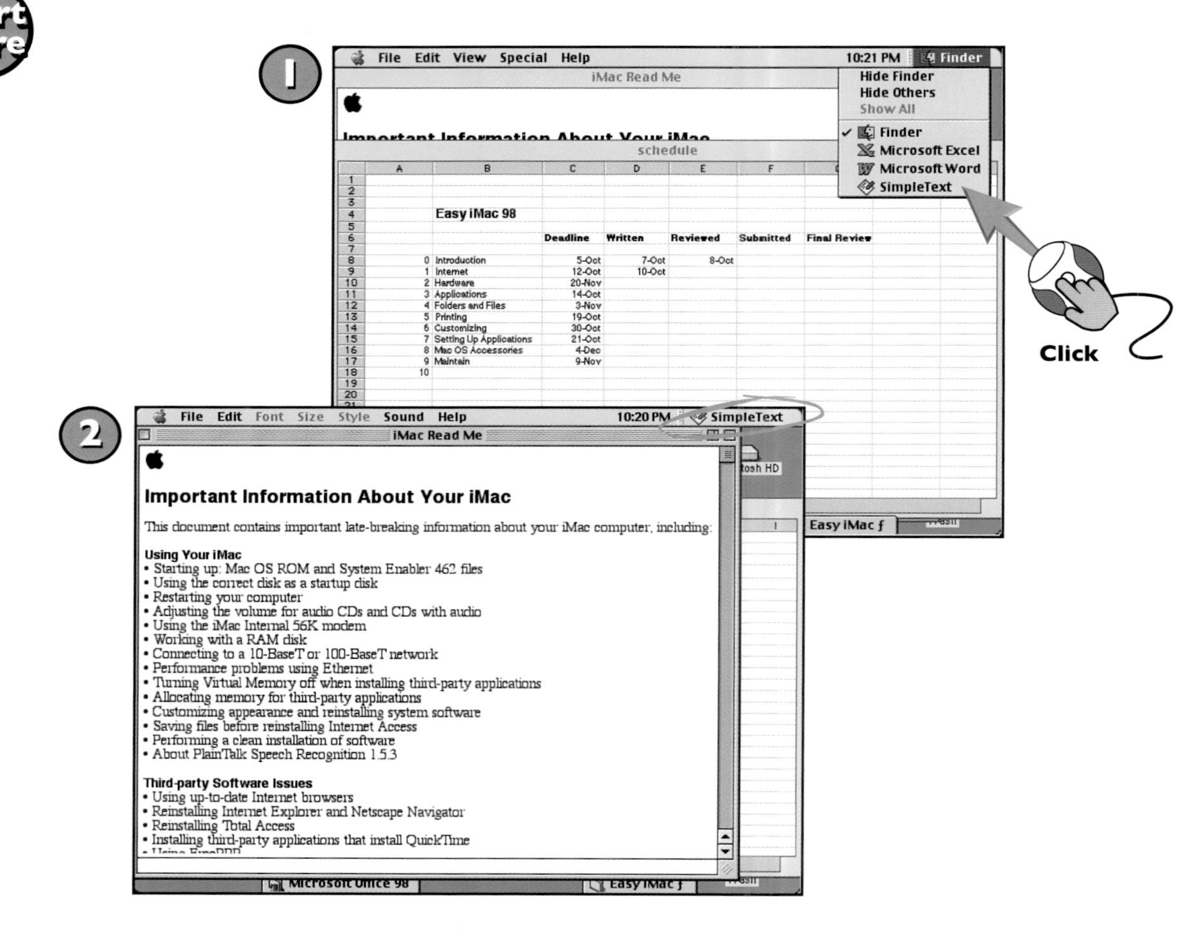

1. With several applications open, click the **Applications** menu and choose a different application.

2. Mac OS switches to the application you chose. The name of the application appears in the **Applications** menu area.

Task 2: Moving the Applications Menu

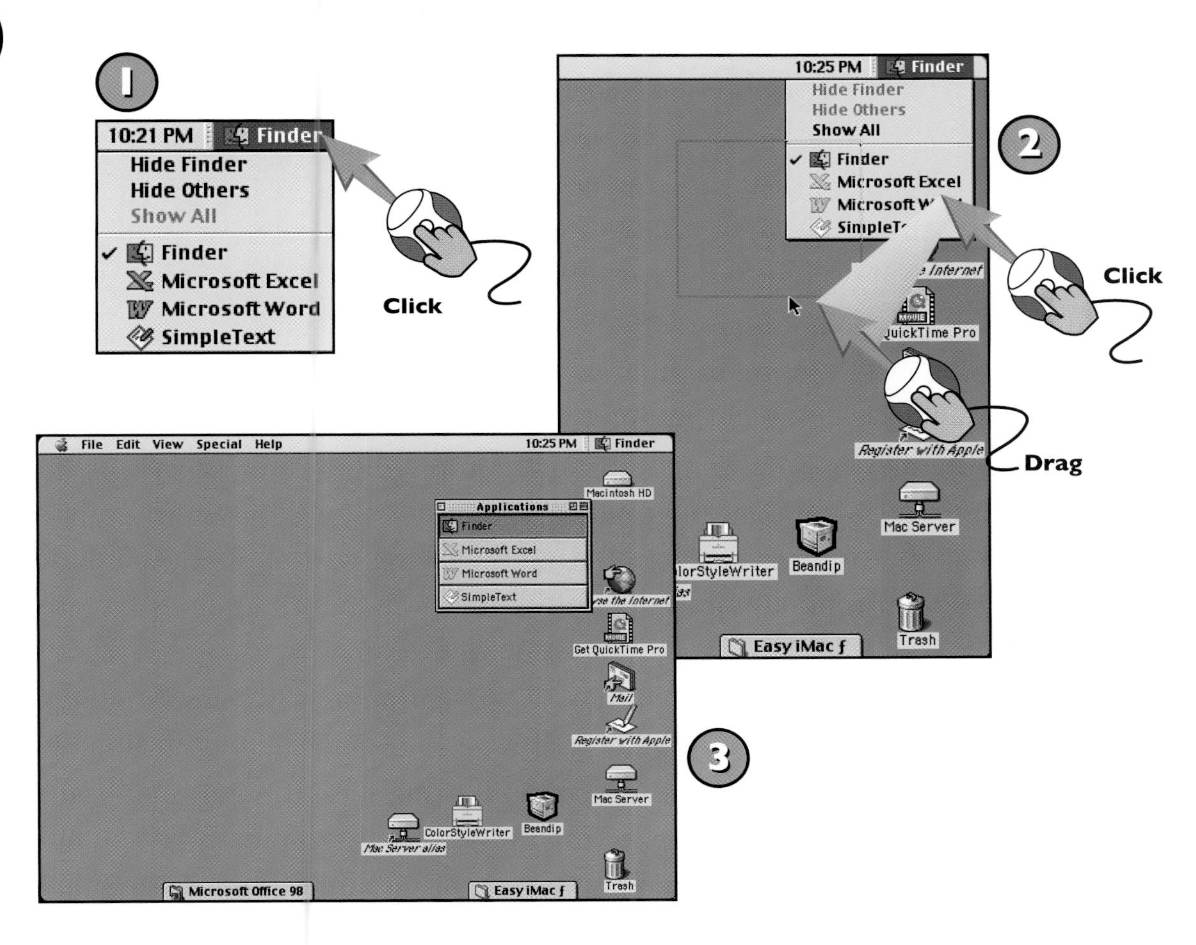

1. Open the **Applications** menu.

2. Drag the **Applications** menu away from the menu bar.

3. The **Applications** menu becomes a floating window, showing all open applications.

You can configure the Applications menu to "float" over your desktop so that you can switch to any other application with a single click of the mouse. You can also collapse the floating Applications menu to maximize the amount of screen space available to another document window.

You can resize the Applications menu button so that the application name does not appear by dragging the left edge of the Applications menu button to the right.

You can enable or disable the clock in the menu bar by opening the Date and Time control panel and clicking the On or Off radio button for the menu bar clock.

If an application is displaying an alert message, the application's icon may blink to indicate that you need to go to that application to read the message.

Task 3: Choosing a Desktop Picture

You can personalize your desktop in Mac OS by adding a desktop picture. Mac OS 8.5 offers many colorful desktop picture options, including photos of landscapes, flowers, and buildings; 3D art; convergent colors; and many more.

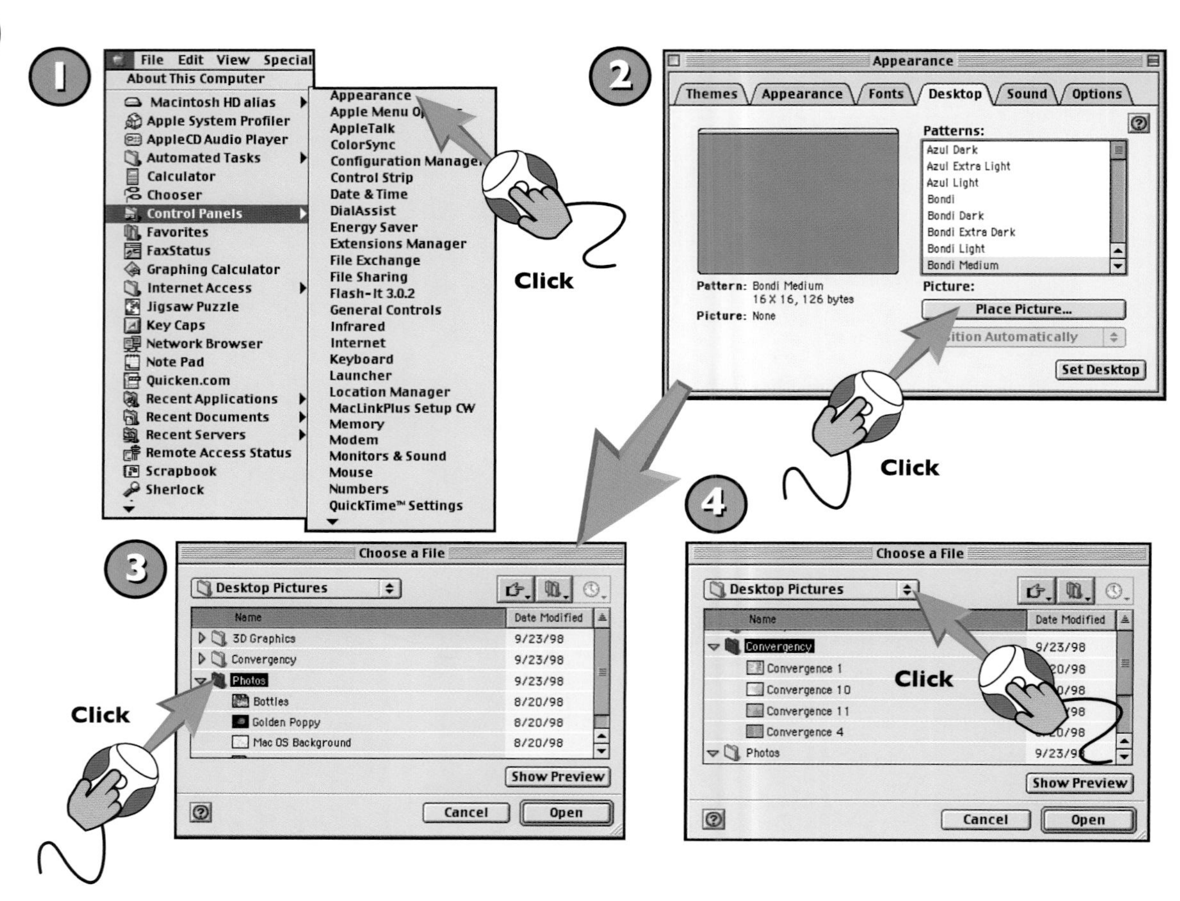

✓ You can also add a pattern to the desktop as covered in the next task.

✓ If the image you selected is blurry, it might be because Mac OS has scaled a smaller image to fit the size of your screen. Deselect **Scale to Screen** to view the image at its original size on the desktop.

✓ If your desktop picture doesn't fit your entire screen, you might want to choose **Tile on Screen** to turn a desktop picture into a large pattern.

1. Click the **Apple** menu, choose **Control Panels**, and then choose the **Appearance** control panel.
2. Choose the **Desktop** tab and click the **Place Picture** button.
3. In the **Choose a File** window, click on a picture file.
4. To choose a picture in a different folder, navigate to it using the pop-up menu, or use the **Shortcuts**, **Favorites**, or **Recent** button.

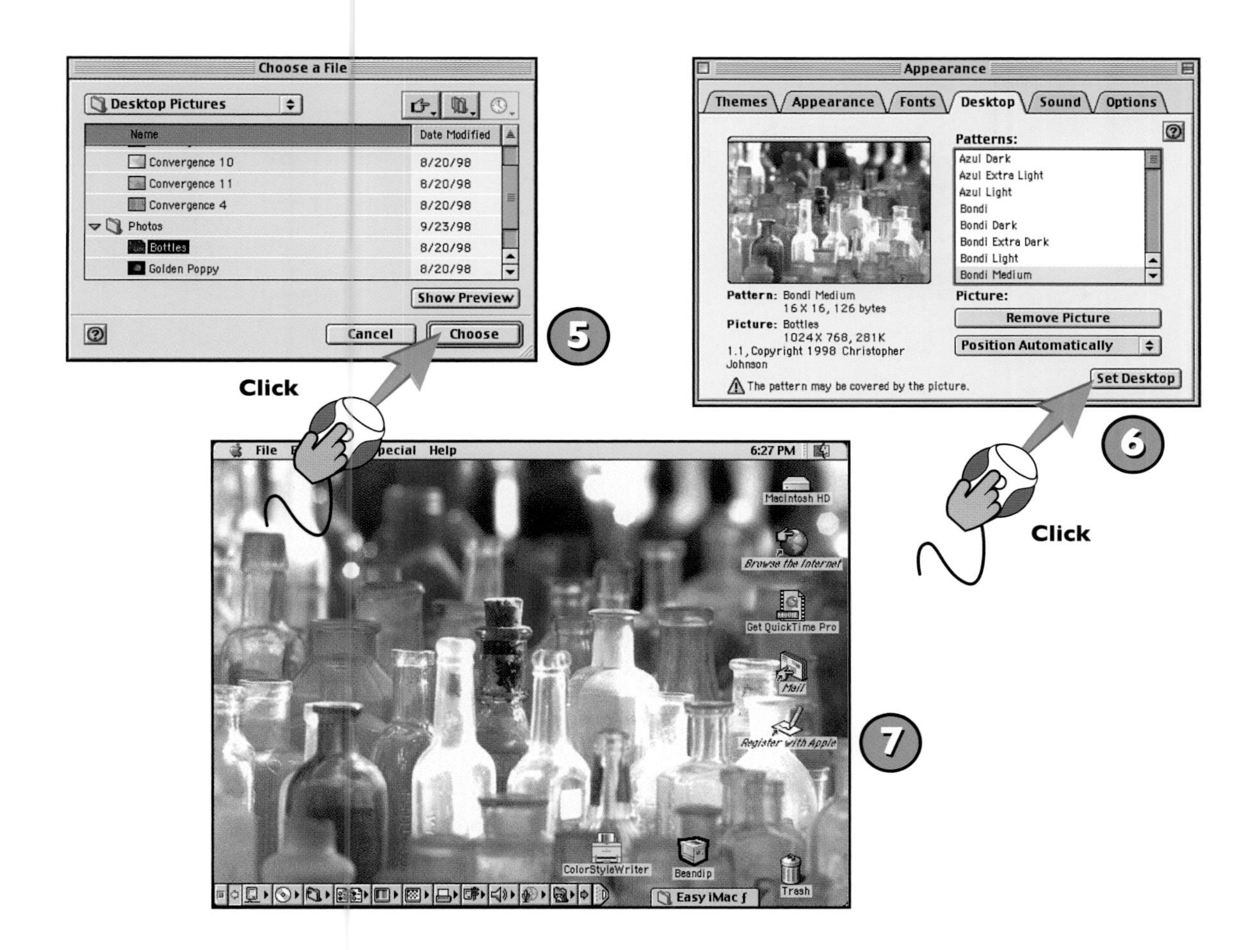

5 After you have selected a file, click the **Choose** button.

6 Click the **Set Desktop** button.

7 The picture you selected is displayed on the desktop.

Click **Show Preview** to preview images in the **Choose a File** window. The preview will show you a snapshot image of the picture and can help you choose the picture you want.

To exit the **Choose a File** window, click **Cancel.**

More desktop pictures are available on the iMac Software Install CD-ROM. You can preview the pictures by inserting the iMac Software Install CD-ROM while the **Appearance** control panel is open. Open the **Choose a File** window, go to the **Additional Desktop Pictures** folder, and preview any image in that folder.

Task 4: Choosing a Desktop Pattern

Start Here

If you don't like the selections for desktop pictures, you might want to experiment with a pattern. A pattern can range in size from an 8x8-pixel to a 128x128-pixel image, and is repeated across the entire desktop.

- To remove a pattern from the **Pattern** list, select the pattern you want to remove and press **Command+X**.

- To add a desktop pattern to the list of patterns in the **Desktop** tab of the **Appearance** control panel, click the pattern in the **Scrapbook** file and drag it to the desktop. Mac OS will convert that pattern into a picture clipping file. Drag the picture clipping file over the **Pattern** window.

  To add a desktop pattern on the CD-ROM to the list of patterns in the **Desktop** tab of the **Appearance** control panel, copy the **Additional Desktop Pattern** file to your hard disk.

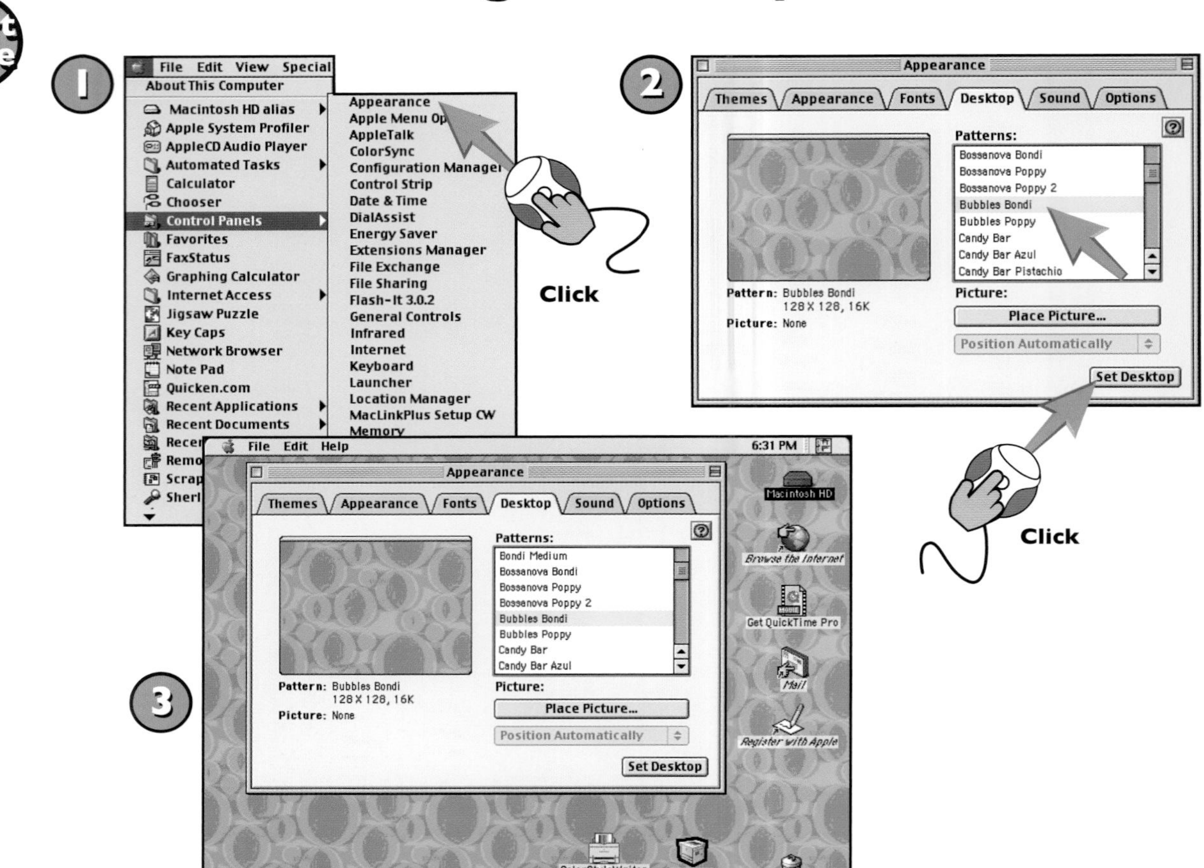

1. Click the **Apple** menu, choose **Control Panels**, and then choose the **Appearance** control panel.

2. In the **Desktop** tab, choose a pattern from the **Patterns** list. The pattern appears on the left side of the window. When you find a pattern you like, click **Set Desktop**.

3. Mac OS uses the desktop pattern on your desktop.

Task 5: Using Themes

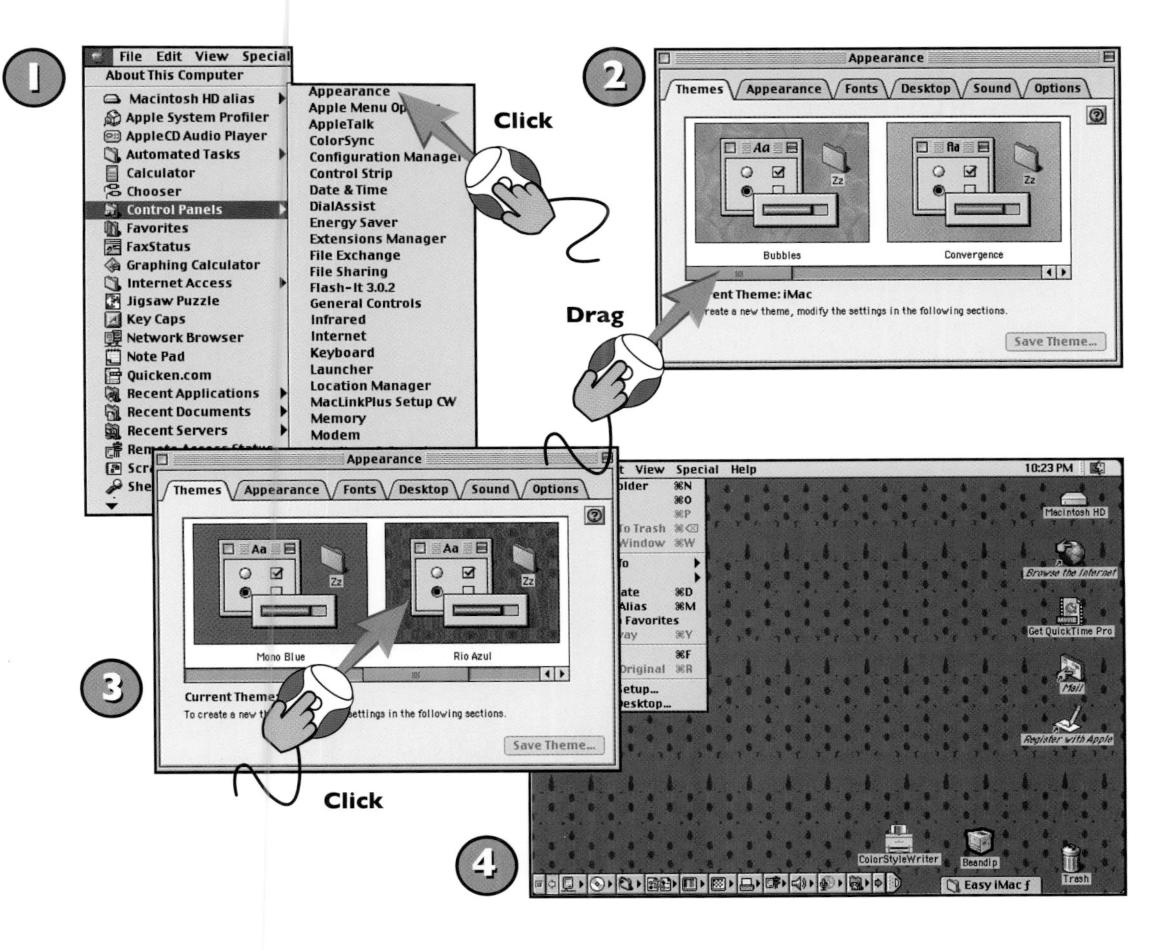

You can change one or many appearance settings in the **Appearance** control panel. Any combination of appearance settings can be saved as a theme. A *theme* consists of the colors, font, desktop image, sound settings, and window settings chosen in the **Appearance** control panel. A theme lets you quickly switch from one set of custom settings to another.

1. Click the **Apple** menu, choose **Control Panels**, and then click **Appearance**.
2. Click the **Themes** tab, and view the various available themes by clicking and dragging the scrollbar.
3. Click on a theme.
4. Mac OS changes the fonts, colors, desktop picture, and window and sound settings for the theme (in this case Rio Azul is the name of the theme I selected).

You can create your own theme by choosing your settings in the **Appearance** control panel, selecting the **Themes** tab, and clicking **Save Theme**.

Task 6: Changing Highlight Colors on Your iMac

There are two different color-related control panels in Mac OS 8.5: **Appearance** and **ColorSync.** The **Appearance** control panel lets you choose the highlight color you see when you select text in Mac OS and its applications.

- The highlight color is the color of a highlighted item, such as text or graphics in an application. You can easily view the highlight color by typing in a SimpleText application window and then selecting some text.

- To recover the original colors or settings, click **Cancel** instead of **OK.** If you have already closed the dialog box, you can revert to one of the themes in the **Themes** tab of the **Appearance** control panel.

- You can also use the **Appearance** control panel to customize the highlight color of a menu. Click the **Variation** pop-up menu, and select a color you want for highlighting any menus and controls.

Start Here

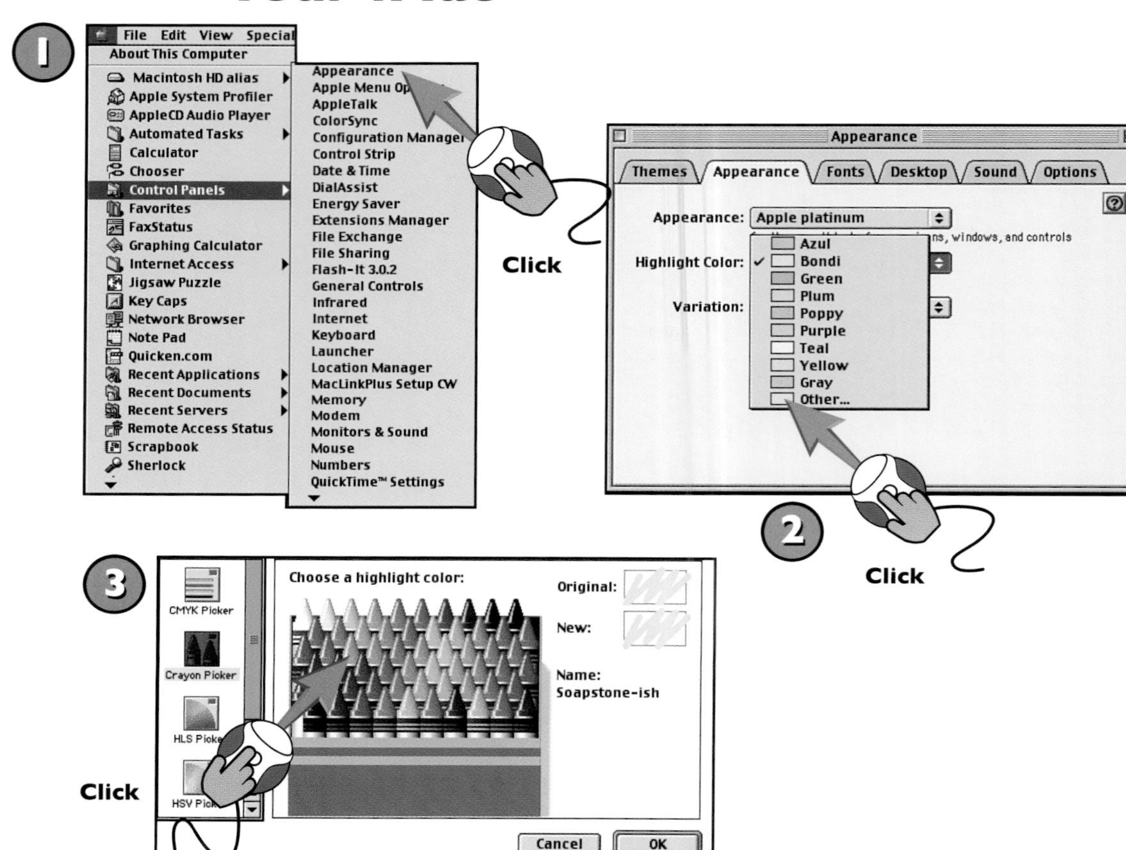

1. Click the **Apple** menu, then choose **Control Panels** and click the **Appearance** control panel.
2. Click the **Appearance** tab and choose **Other** from the **Highlight Color** pop-up menu.
3. Select a color from the **Color Picker** window, and click **OK**. If you can't decide on a color, click the **Crayon Picker** in the **Color Picker** window and select a crayon color.

Start Here

Task 7: Synchronizing Colors on Your iMac

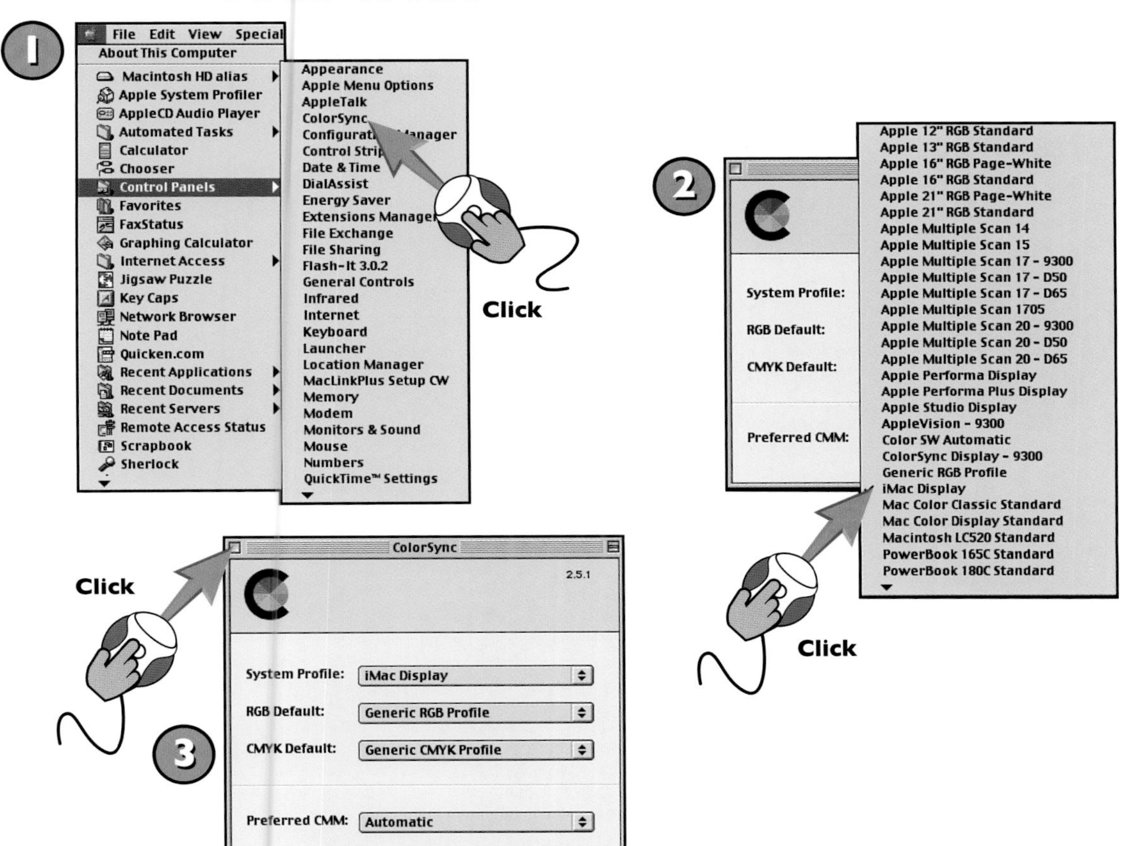

ColorSync is Apple's color-management technology, which enables color synchronization between the iMac's screen, printers, scanners, and cameras. Color Sync lets your iMac use the correct color on paper as well as on your screen.

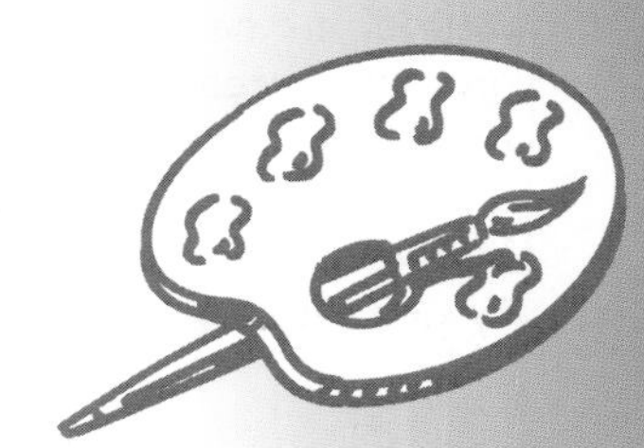

1 Click the **Apple** menu and choose **Control Panels** and then click **ColorSync**.

2 Choose **iMac display** for the **System Profile** and **RGB Default** pop-up menus.

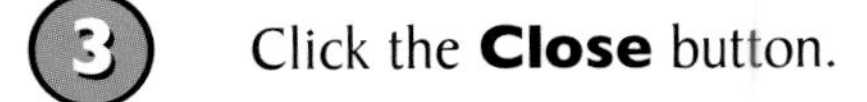

3 Click the **Close** button.

Task 8: Tweaking Your Monitor

The iMac monitor allows you to select certain options about how it operates, such as the number of colors it displays or its *resolution*. (Resolution measures the number of pixels or picture elements displayed. An example of a common resolution is 800x600. The larger the resolution, the larger the desktop size; desktop elements, such as icons, appear smaller.) You might need to change your monitor's display properties if you want to use a different size desktop with a particular application, or if you want to change how the monitor looks.

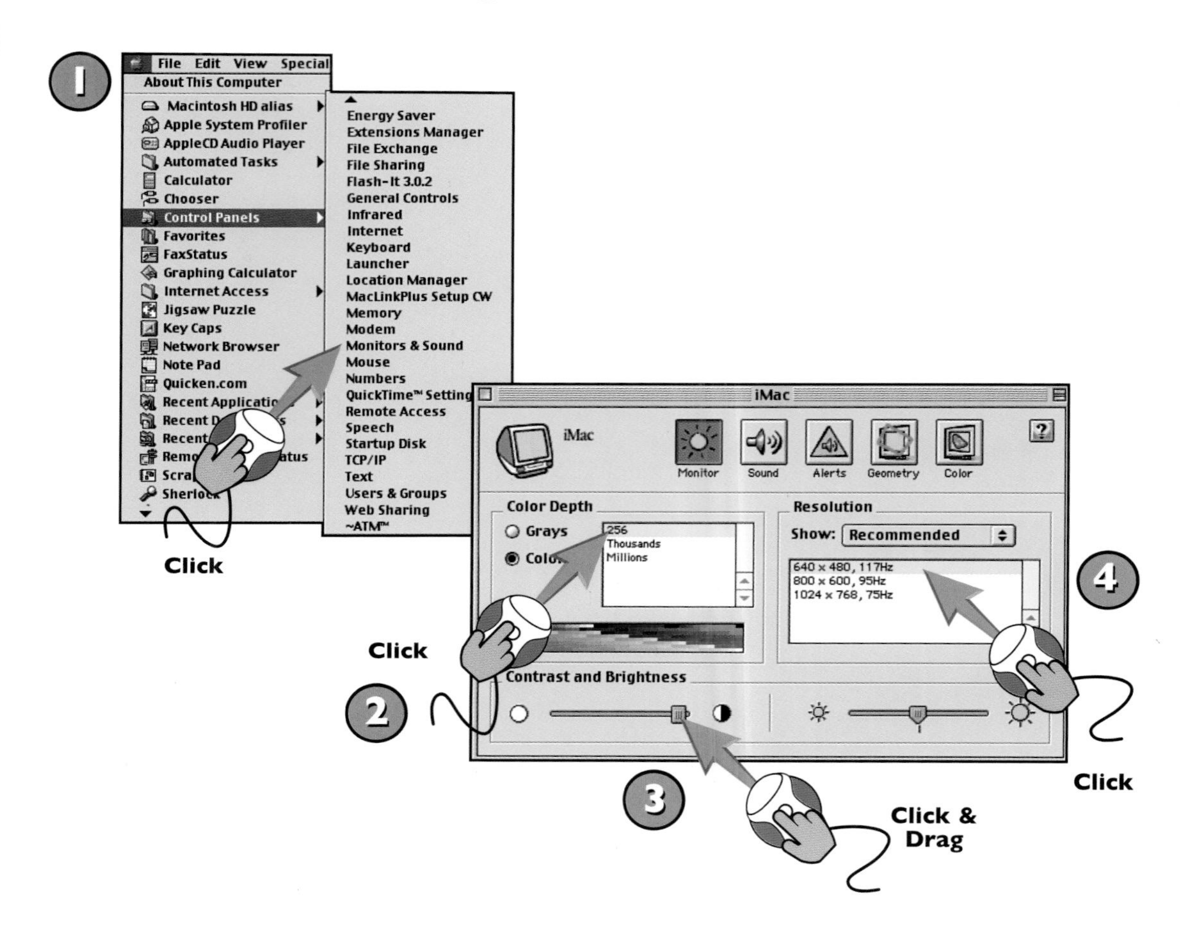

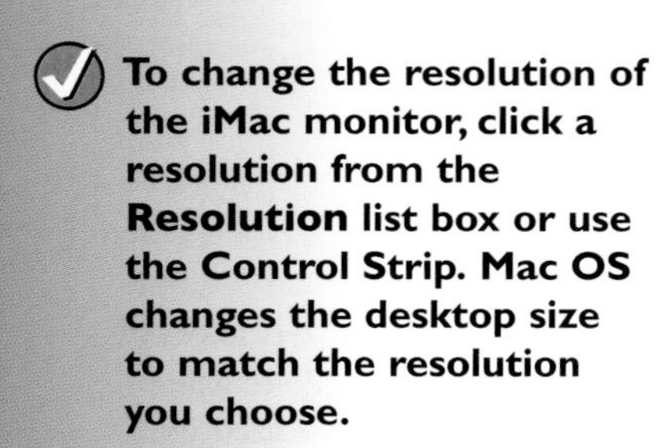

To change the resolution of the iMac monitor, click a resolution from the **Resolution** list box or use the Control Strip. Mac OS changes the desktop size to match the resolution you choose.

1. Click the **Apple** menu, choose **Control Panels**, and click **Monitors & Sound**.
2. Select the color depth you want from the list box on the left.
3. Adjust the contrast and brightness by clicking the slider and dragging it to the setting you want.
4. Click the resolution you want in the list box on the right.

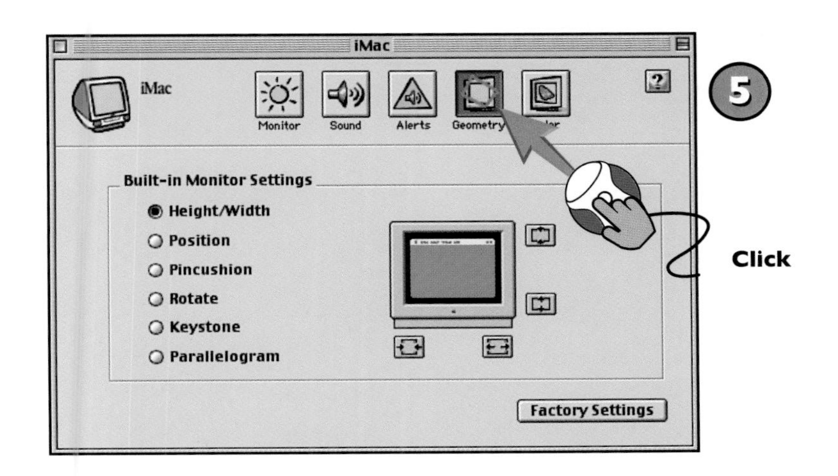

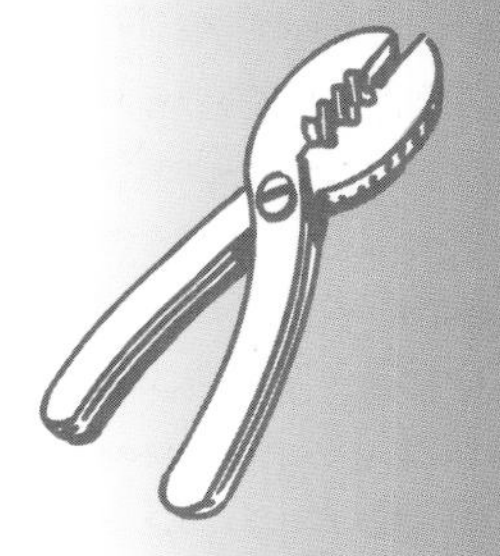

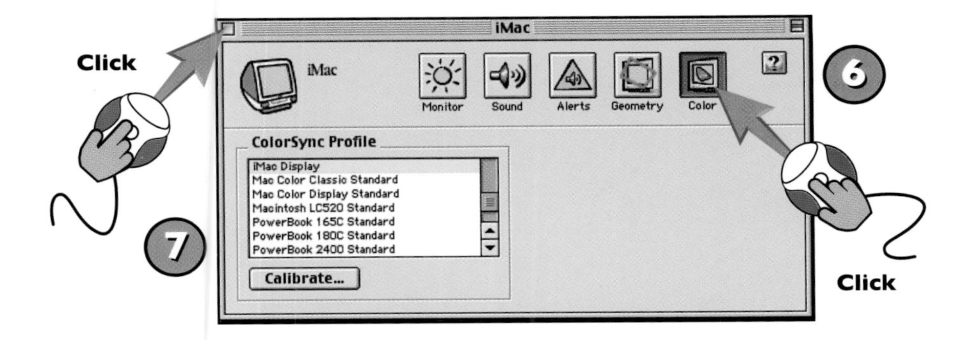

Click the **Geometry** button to adjust the built-in monitor settings. Click **Factory Settings** to restore the monitor to its original settings.

Click the **Color** button to choose and calibrate the ColorSync profile for your monitor.

Click the **Close** box when you have finished adjusting your monitor settings.

Click Help and choose Mac OS Help to view more information about how to adjust your monitor's settings.

Task 9: Changing How Your Sound Works

Another way to customize how your iMac looks and feels is to change the sound your iMac makes when it issues an alert. Other sound settings you can adjust include the sound-monitoring source, the quality of sound output, sound balance, and the sound volume of your iMac. You can also choose 3D sound if you have external speakers set up with your iMac.

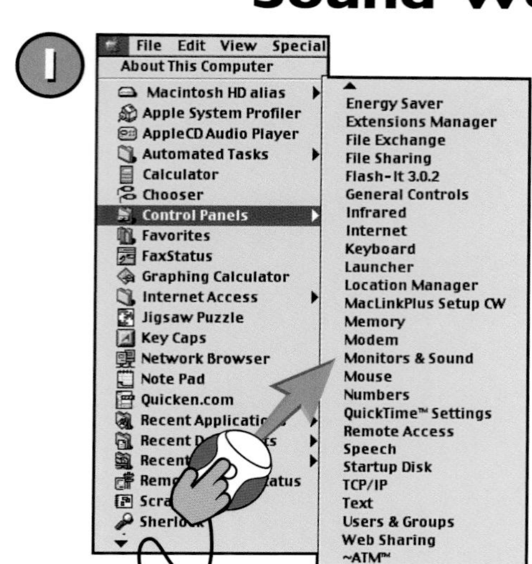

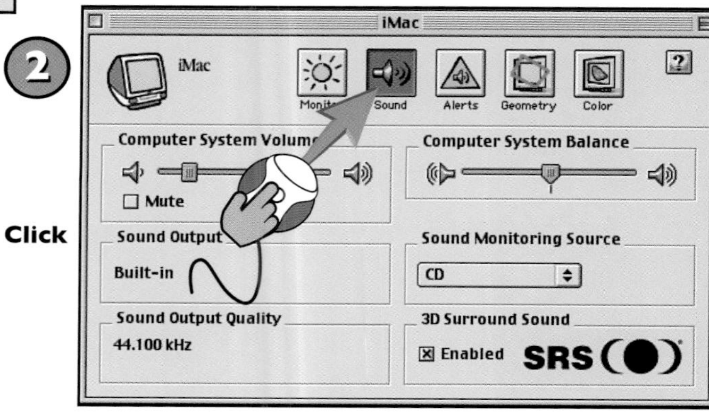

1. Click the **Apple** menu, choose **Control Panels**, and click **Monitors & Sound**.

2. Click the **Sound** button. Adjust the sound system balance between the left and right speakers by dragging the slider.

You probably won't need to adjust most sound settings on your iMac.

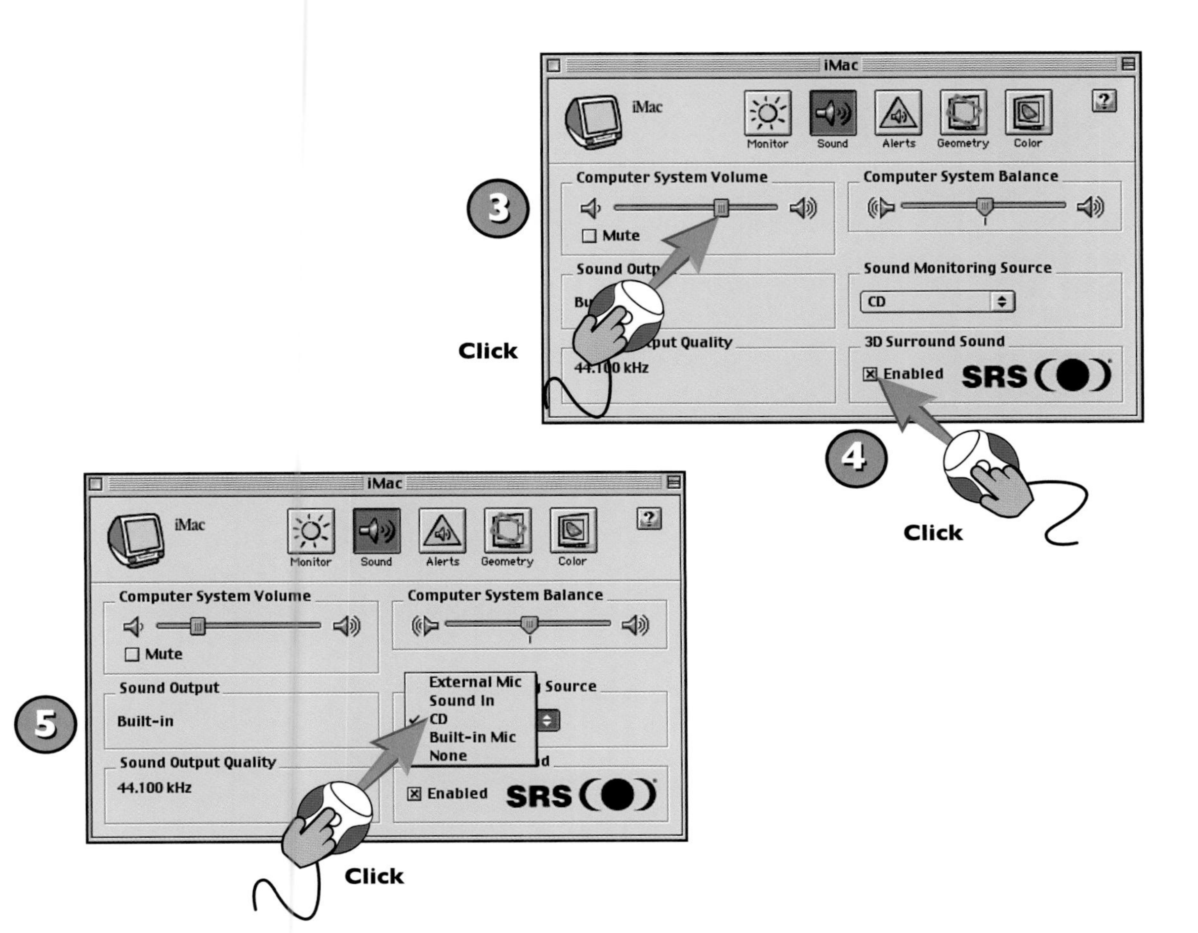

3. Adjust the iMac's volume by dragging the **Computer System Volume** slider to the left or right.

4. Click the **3D Surround Sound** check box to enable 3D surround sound with your iMac or external speakers.

5. Click the **Sound Monitoring Source** pop-up menu to choose a recording source (in this case, the CD-ROM drive).

If the overall system volume is muted or set to zero in the slider, iMac flashes the menu bar instead of playing a sound to issue an alert.

Task 10: Changing the System Alert Sound

When you perform certain actions in Mac OS 8.5, you might hear a sound. You might hear a sound when you receive an email, or as an alert. You can use the default simple beep as your alert sound, or you can select a different sound.

- You can download sounds from the Internet and drop them on the **System** file to add them to the list of alert sounds available to your iMac.

- Although the iMac comes with several alert sounds from which to choose, you can create your own alert sounds by using the built-in microphone or an audio CD. For more information about recording sound, see Part 9, Task 11, "Using SimpleSound."

- Alert sounds have a separate volume setting than the overall iMac volume setting. You can adjust this volume setting in the **Monitors & Sound** control panel.

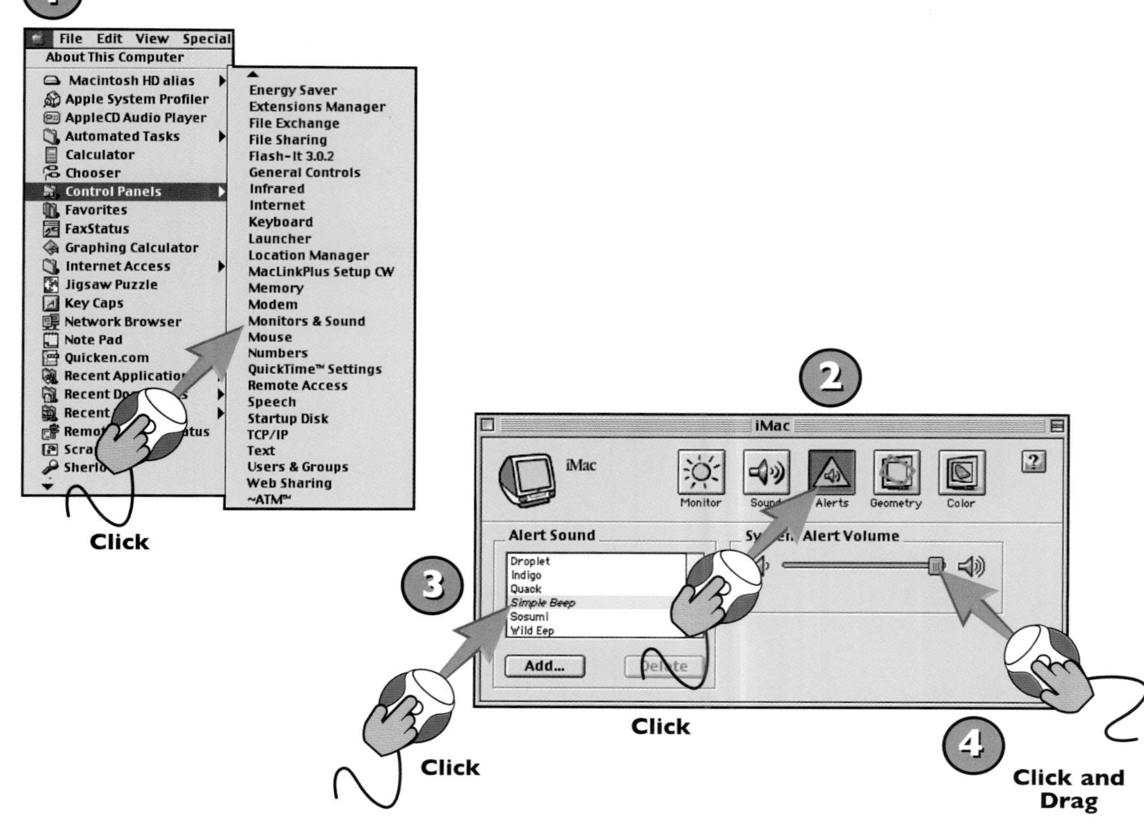

1. Click the **Apple** menu, choose **Control Panels**, and click **Monitors & Sound**.
2. Click the **Alerts** button in the **Monitors & Sound** control panel.
3. Click on a sound in the list. The sound plays.
4. Click and drag the slider to adjust the volume of the alert sound.

Task 11: Changing How the Mouse Works

Start Here

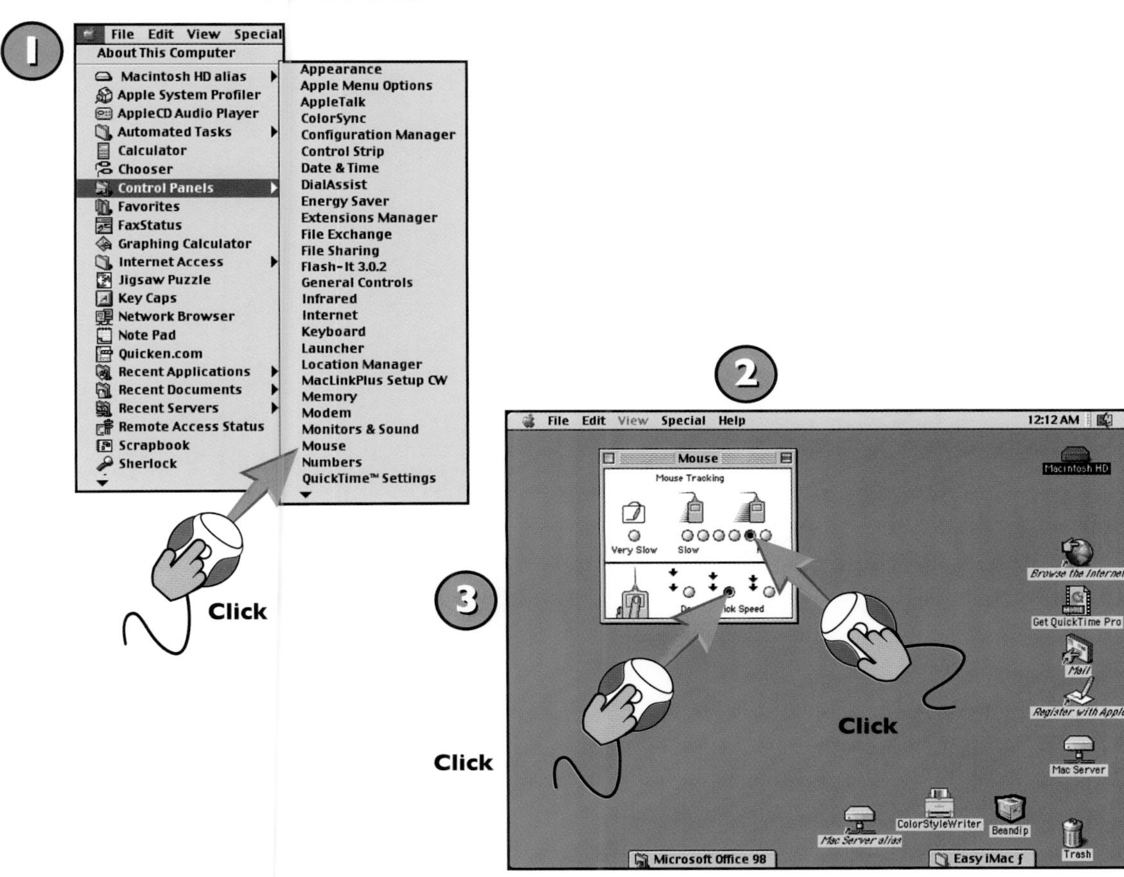

You can adjust the mouse tracking and double-click speed to make using the mouse more comfortable for you. In addition, you can decrease your pointer speed so that you can easily find your mouse onscreen when you move it quickly.

- You can test the double-click speed by double-clicking a folder icon.
- If you would like to cross the entire desktop with minimal mouse movement, select a faster mouse tracking speed.
- If you double-click while on a network and the iMac does not appear to respond, Mac OS might be busy loading a Web page or downloading email. Wait a moment to see if the double-click occurs. If not, wait for the network activity to complete, then try double-clicking again.

1. Click the **Apple** menu, choose **Control Panels**, then click **Mouse**.
2. Click the appropriate radio button to choose the mouse tracking speed you want.
3. Click the appropriate radio button to choose the double-click speed you want.

Task 12: Changing the System Date and Time

If your iMac's clock (or date) is wrong, you should correct it because Mac OS stamps the time and date on every file you save, including email files.

Start Here

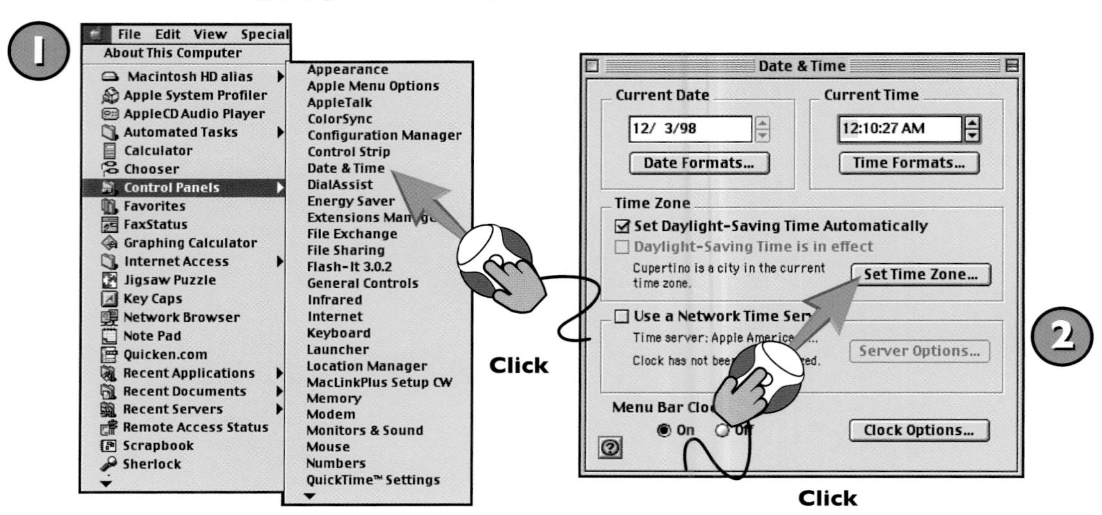

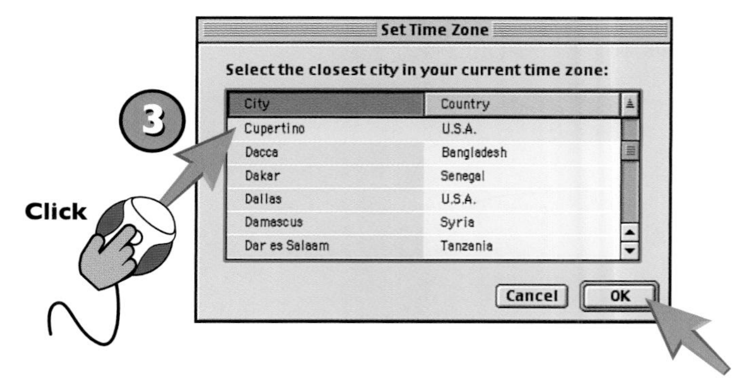

- You can click the time in the menu bar to display the current date.
- If the date is wrong, it could indicate that you need to replace the battery on the iMac's logic board. Apple included instructions for replacing the battery with the iMac documentation.
- Some email applications use the **Time Zone** setting to determine what time to stamp on your email.

1. Click the **Apple** menu, choose **Control Panels**, then click **Date & Time**.
2. Click the **Set Time Zone** button in the **Date & Time** control panel.
3. In the **Set Time Zone** dialog, choose the city and country representing the time zone where you live, and click **OK**.

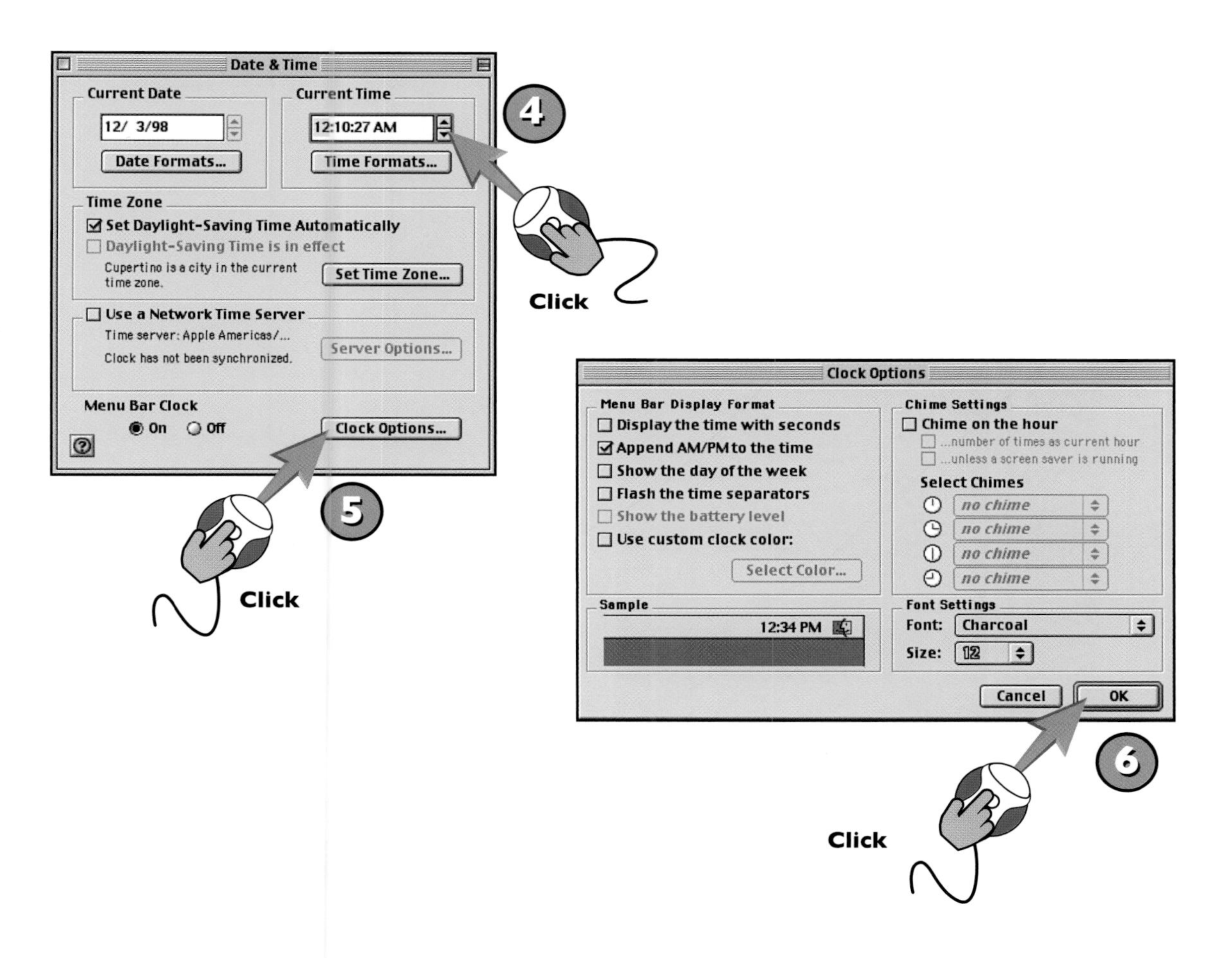

4. Use the spin controls or type the correct numbers into the date and time fields.

5. Click the **Clock Options** button.

6. Customize the clock under **Menu Bar Display Format**, **Chime Settings**, and **Font**. Click **OK**, and then click the **Close** button in the **Date & Time** control panel.

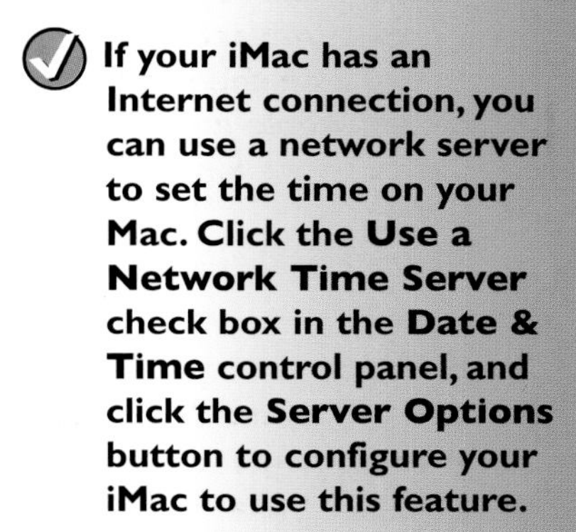

If your iMac has an Internet connection, you can use a network server to set the time on your Mac. Click the **Use a Network Time Server** check box in the **Date & Time** control panel, and click the **Server Options** button to configure your iMac to use this feature.

Task 13: Using Energy Saver

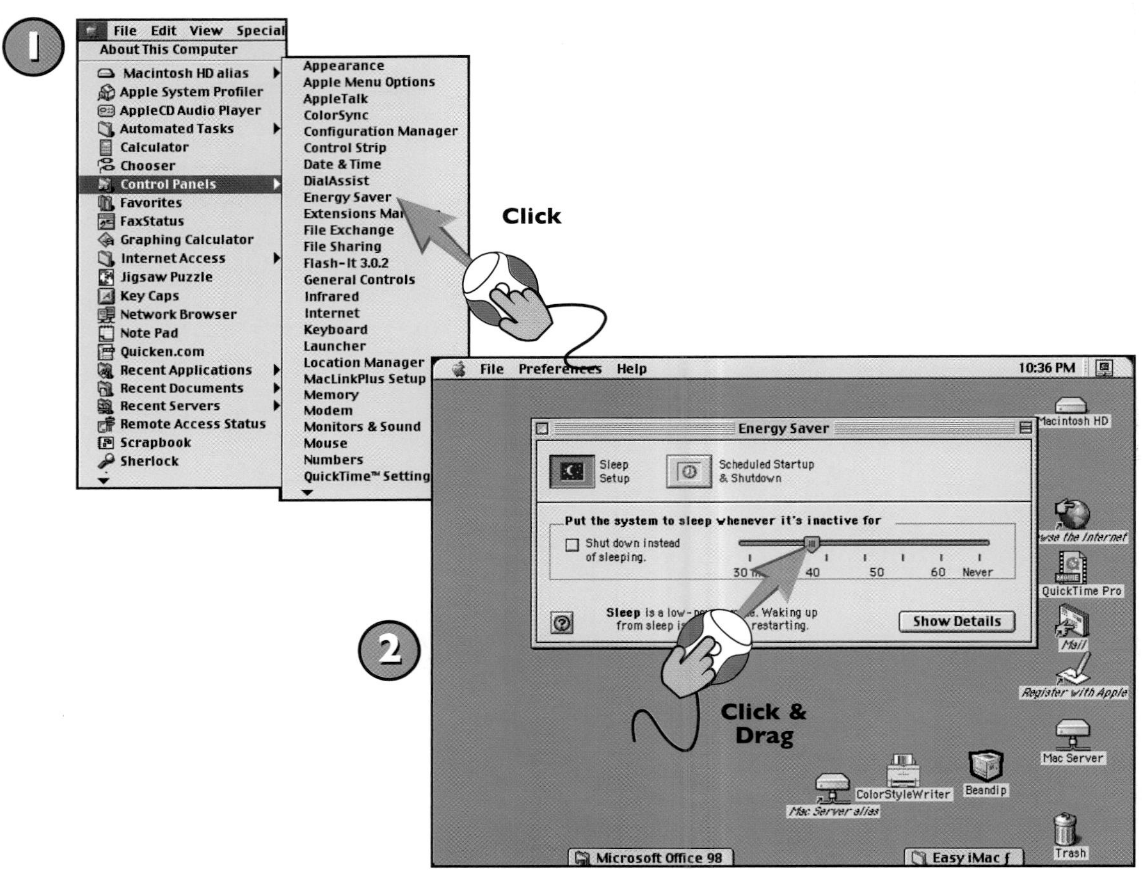

You can specify when your iMac sleeps—that is, when the iMac dims the display and puts the hard drive into low power mode (also known as *spinning down the hard disk*). These energy-saving features help your iMac reduce wear on the monitor, hard disk, and computer.

- To use additional features in the **Energy Saver** control panel, click the **Show Details** button.
- If your iMac has **File Sharing** turned on, you can access it while it is sleeping.
- The iMac's sleep feature acts similarly to a screen saver. However, instead of saving your screen, your iMac goes into a low-power mode, dimming the screen and spinning down the hard disk.
- A good setting for activating sleep is 15 or 20 minutes.

1. Click the **Apple** menu, then choose **Control Panels** and **Energy Saver**.

2. Slide the energy saver setting to the time you want.

Task 14: Protecting Your System and Applications Folders

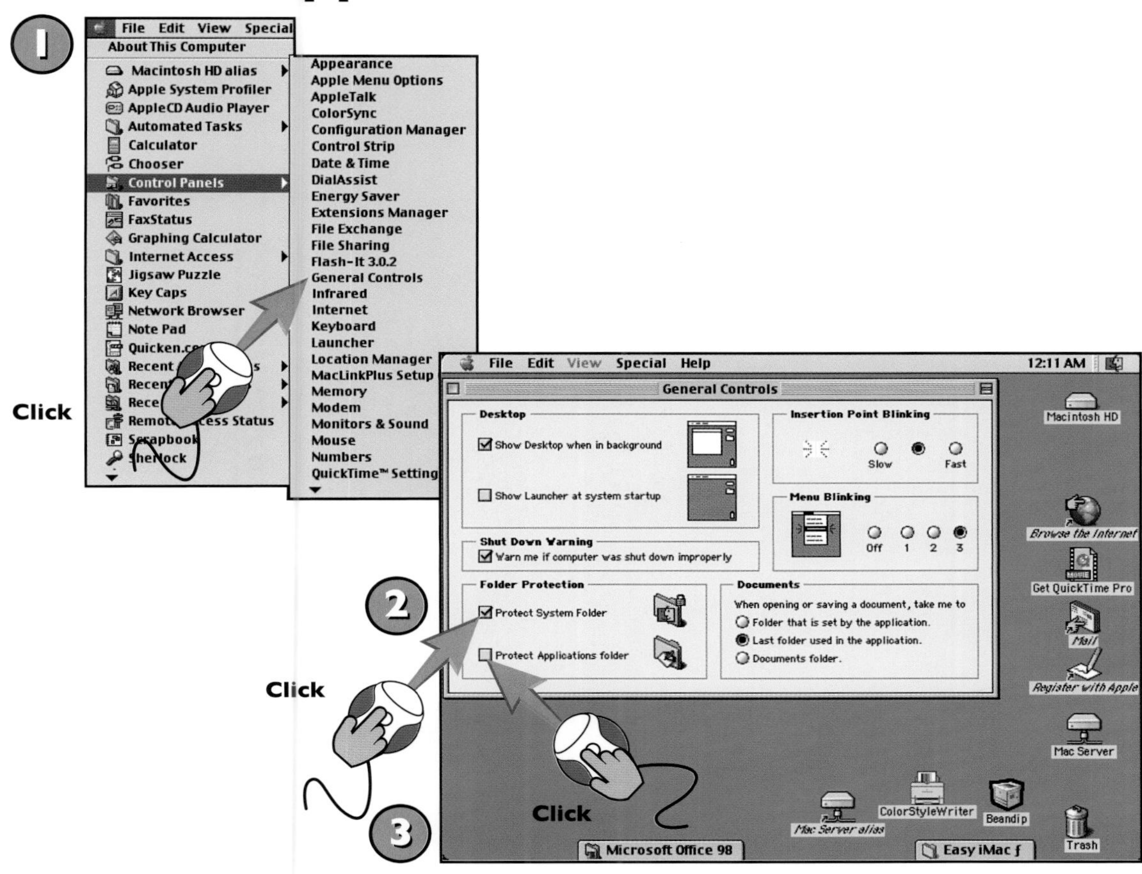

If you're not the only one using your iMac, you might want to protect the files and folders installed in the **System** and **Applications** folders. You do this through the **General Controls** control panel. Other features you can choose from in the **General Controls** control panel include the insertion point blinking speed, the menu blinking speed, whether to show the desktop when its in the background, and where an application should save a document.

1. Click the **Apple** menu, choose **Control Panels**, then click **General Controls**.
2. Click the **Protect System Folder** check box.
3. Click the **Protect Applications Folder** check box.

If you choose not to use this feature on your iMac, you might want to make more frequent backups of your hard drive instead.

Protecting your system and applications folders can slow down the overall performance of your iMac. If you notice your software slowing down, you might choose to leave this feature off.

Task 15: Setting Up Mac OS for Multiple Users

If more than one person uses your iMac, you might want to purchase and install At Ease 3.0, and then update it to At Ease 3.03. With At Ease, you can customize access to your iMac for up to 30 different people. Each person can use a fixed or custom setup of Mac OS with a login account. Each time that person logs on, all those settings will be used.

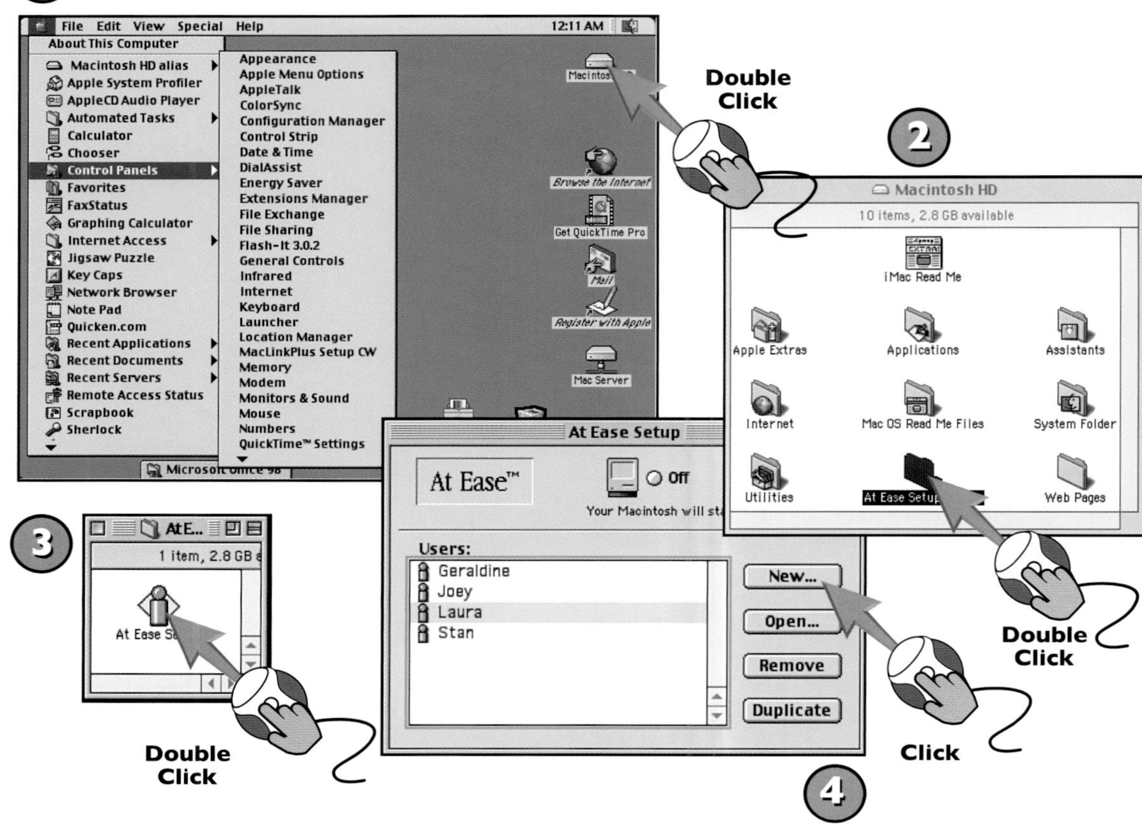

1. Double-click the **Macintosh HD** icon on your desktop.
2. Double-click the **At Ease Setup Folder** icon in the **Macintosh HD** window.
3. Double-click the **At Ease Setup** icon.
4. Click the **New** button to create a new user.

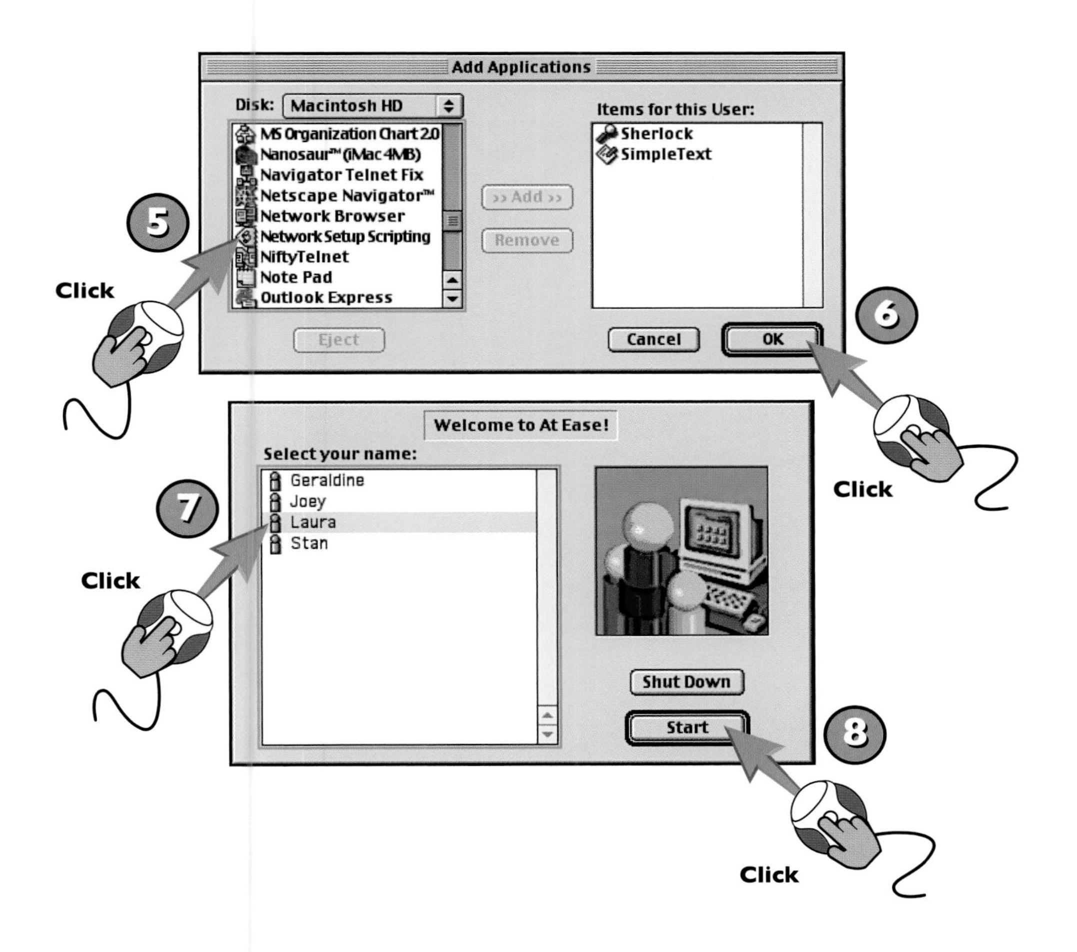

5. In the **Add Applications** dialog, choose the applications you want the user to be able to access, and click **Add**.

6. Click **OK**, and add any additional requested information to complete the At Ease user setup. Click the **On** radio button, then click **File** and choose **Quit** to exit **At Ease Setup**.

7. Restart the iMac to activate At Ease, and then click on a login name in the **Welcome to At Ease** window.

8. Click **Start**.

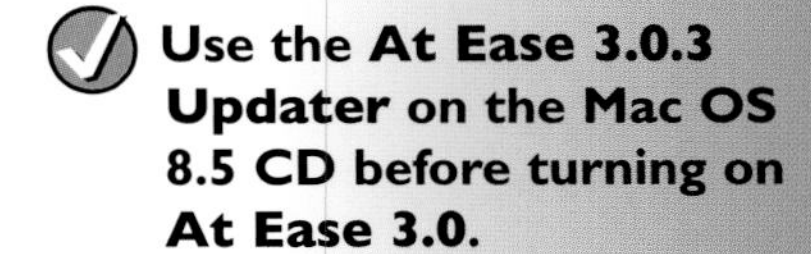

Task 16: Setting Up Mac OS for the Impaired

Start Here

You can employ various settings for the keyboard, sounds, display, and mouse to make your iMac easier to use. For example, you can use the features in the **Easy Access** control panel to provide audio feedback when you use your iMac keyboard; you can use **Sticky Keys** to press one key at a time for key combinations; you can use **Mouse Keys** to use the keyboard to control the cursor instead of a mouse; and you can use **Slow Keys** to set the delay time between keys pressed on the keyboard.

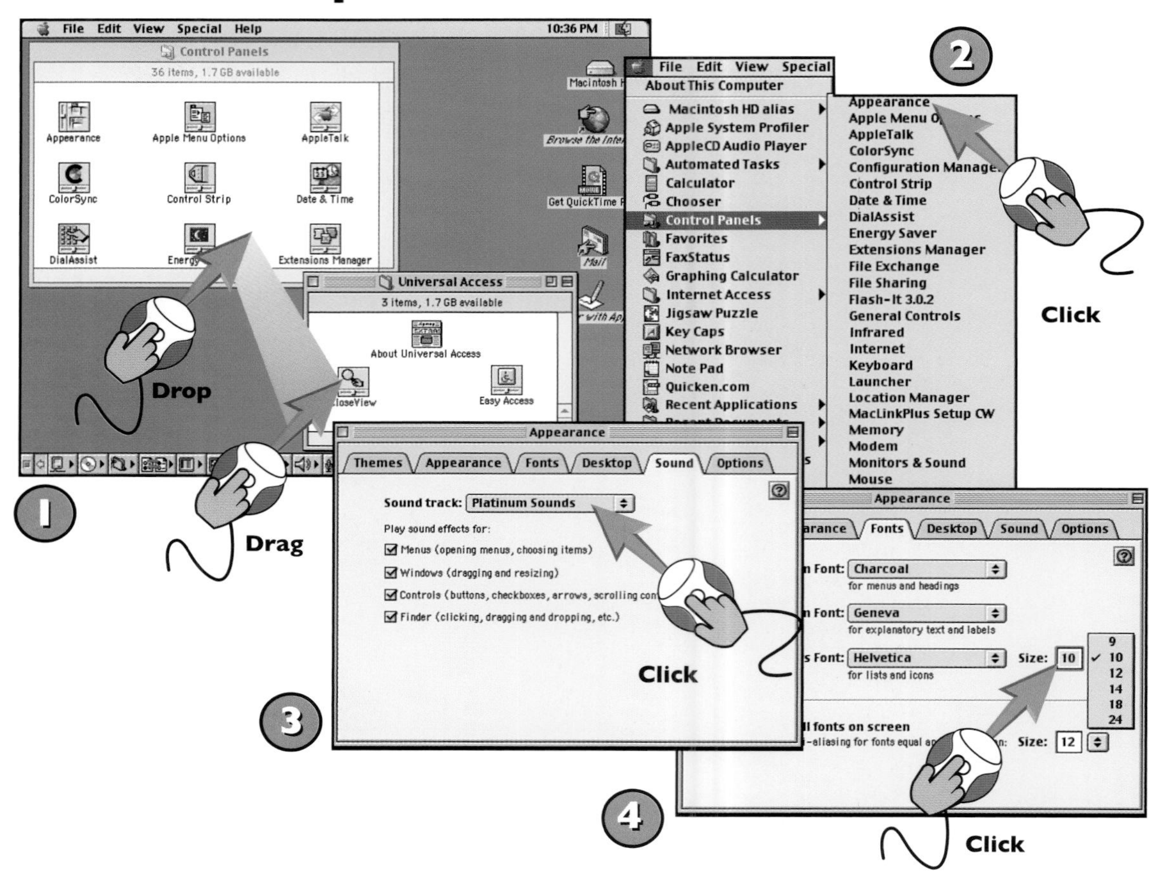

1. Copy the **Easy Access** and **CloseView** control panels to the **Control Panel** folder, and then restart your iMac.

2. Click the **Apple** menu, choose **Control Panels**, then click **Appearance**.

3. In the **Sound** tab of the **Appearance** control panel, click the **Soundtrack** pop-up menu and select **Platinum Sounds**.

4. In the **Fonts** tab of the Appearances control panel, click the **Views Font** pop-up menu, select a font, and then adjust its size as desired.

The **Easy Access** and **CloseView** control panels can be found on the **iMac Software Install CD-ROM** in the **Universal Access** folder located inside the **CD Extras** folder.

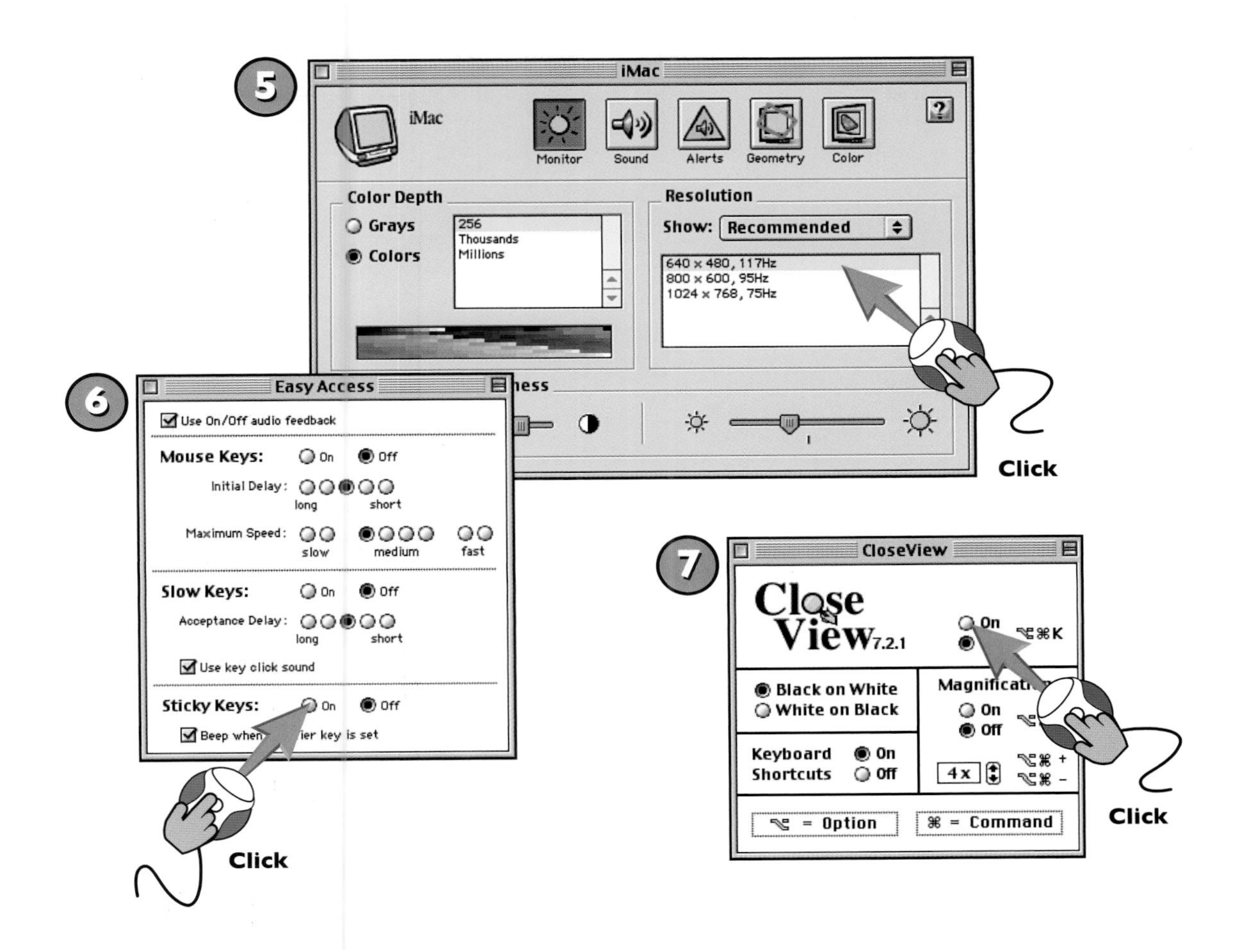

5. Click the **Apple** menu, choose **Control Panels**, then click **Monitors & Sound**. Select **640x480** to enlarge the desktop so that icons and text are the largest possible size.

6. In the **Control Panels** window, double-click the **Easy Access** icon. Click the appropriate **On** radio button to enable any of the Easy Access features.

7. In the **Control Panels** window, double-click the **CloseView** icon. Change the settings as desired, and then select the **On** radio button to activate the **CloseView** settings.

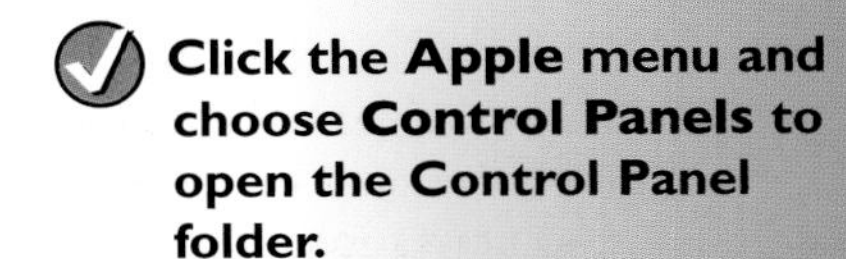

Click the Apple menu and choose Control Panels to open the Control Panel folder.

PART

Setting Up Applications

Most of the time you spend using your iMac will be spent using some application. To make it as easy as possible, Mac OS enables you to set up several ways for starting programs. You can create shortcuts, or ***aliases***, to an application and place the alias on the desktop to make it more accessible. You can install new applications and remove applications you no longer use. This part shows you how to accomplish all of these setup tasks and more.

Tasks

Task #		Part #
1	Adding Aliases	180
2	Renaming Aliases	181
3	Deleting Aliases	182
4	Adding Applications to the Apple Menu	183
5	Deleting Applications from the Apple Menu	184
6	Adding Folders to the Apple Menu	185
7	Rearranging the Apple Menu	186
8	Starting an Application When You Start Mac OS	188
9	Installing Applications	190
10	Uninstalling Applications	191
11	Using AppleScript	192
12	Using File Sharing	194

Task 1: Adding Aliases

You can create aliases and place them on the desktop or in the Apple menu to provide quick access to applications. You then double-click an alias to quickly start that program—without having to open menus and folders.

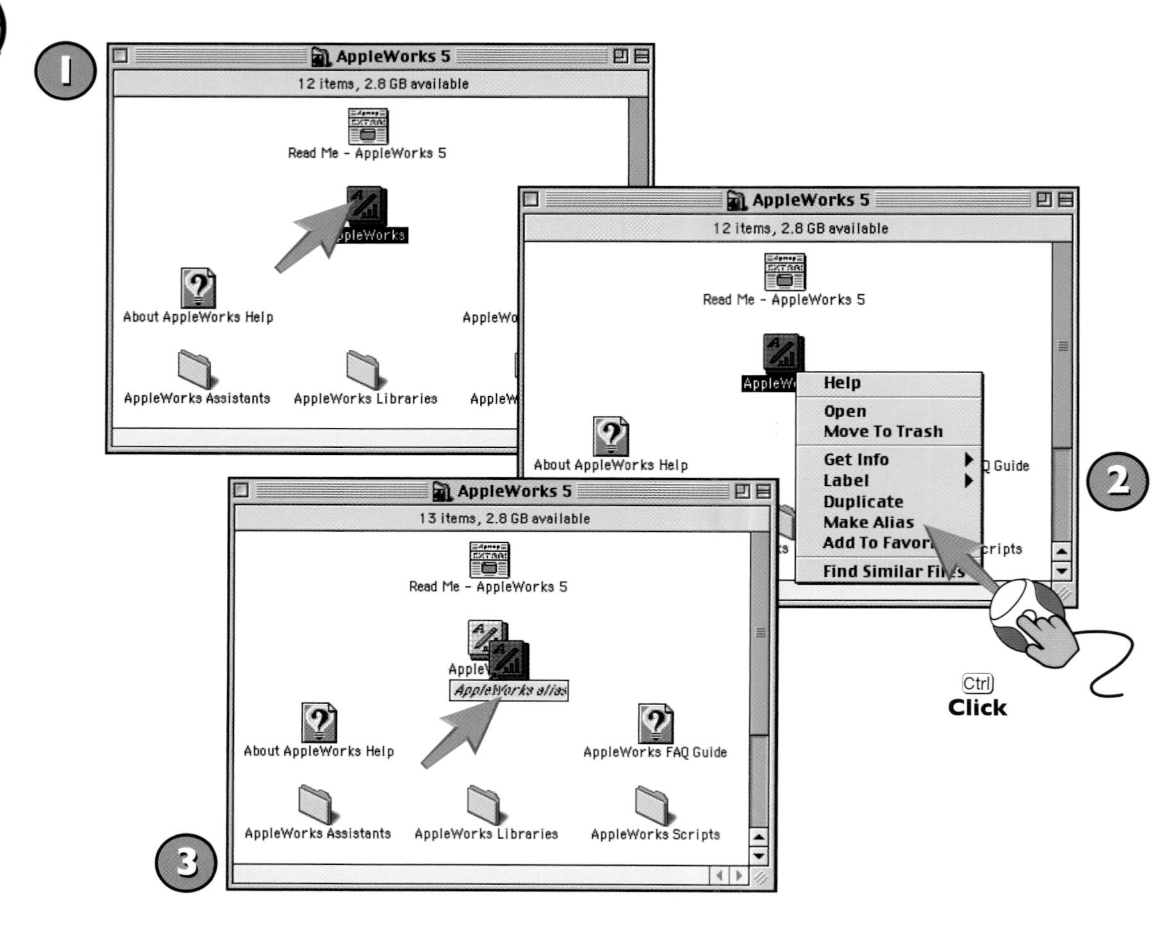

If an alias cannot find its original application, you can search for it. Click **Fix Alias** to use the **Fix Alias** window to locate the application corresponding to the alias.

You can create an alias to files or folders (covered in Part 5, "Working with Disks, Folders, and Files") or to your printer (covered in Part 6, "Printing with Mac OS").

You can't replace an application with an alias. Do not delete the application after creating an alias to it.

1. In an open window, display the application file for which you want to create an alias icon.
2. Holding down the **Ctrl** key, click the icon and choose **Make Alias**.
3. Mac OS adds the alias to your desktop.

Task 2: Renaming Aliases

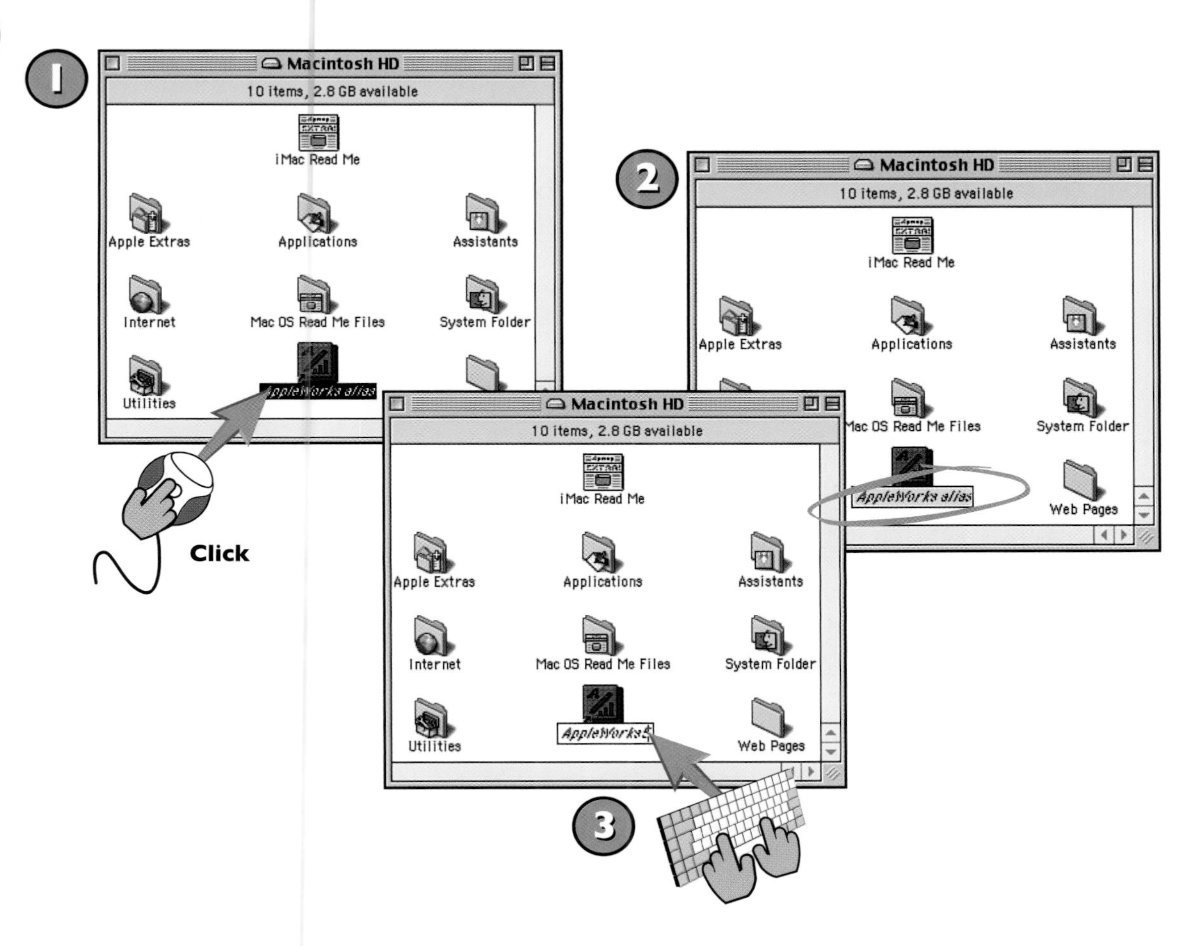

When you create an alias, Mac OS 8.5 assigns a name to the icon. Nonetheless, you might want to use a different name. For instance, rather than the name **System Folder alias**, you might prefer **Mac OS Folder.** You can rename any of the alias icons anywhere on your hard drive.

1. Click the name area of the alias icon you want to rename.
2. Wait about one second; the text becomes highlighted.
3. Type a new name for the alias and press **Enter**.

Alias icons are always named with text formatted in *italics*.

Task 3: Deleting Aliases

You can use aliases to quickly open the program you need. But as time passes, your needs for programs might change, and your desktop might become cluttered with application icons you no longer need. Just as you can create new aliases as you add new applications, you can delete aliases you no longer use.

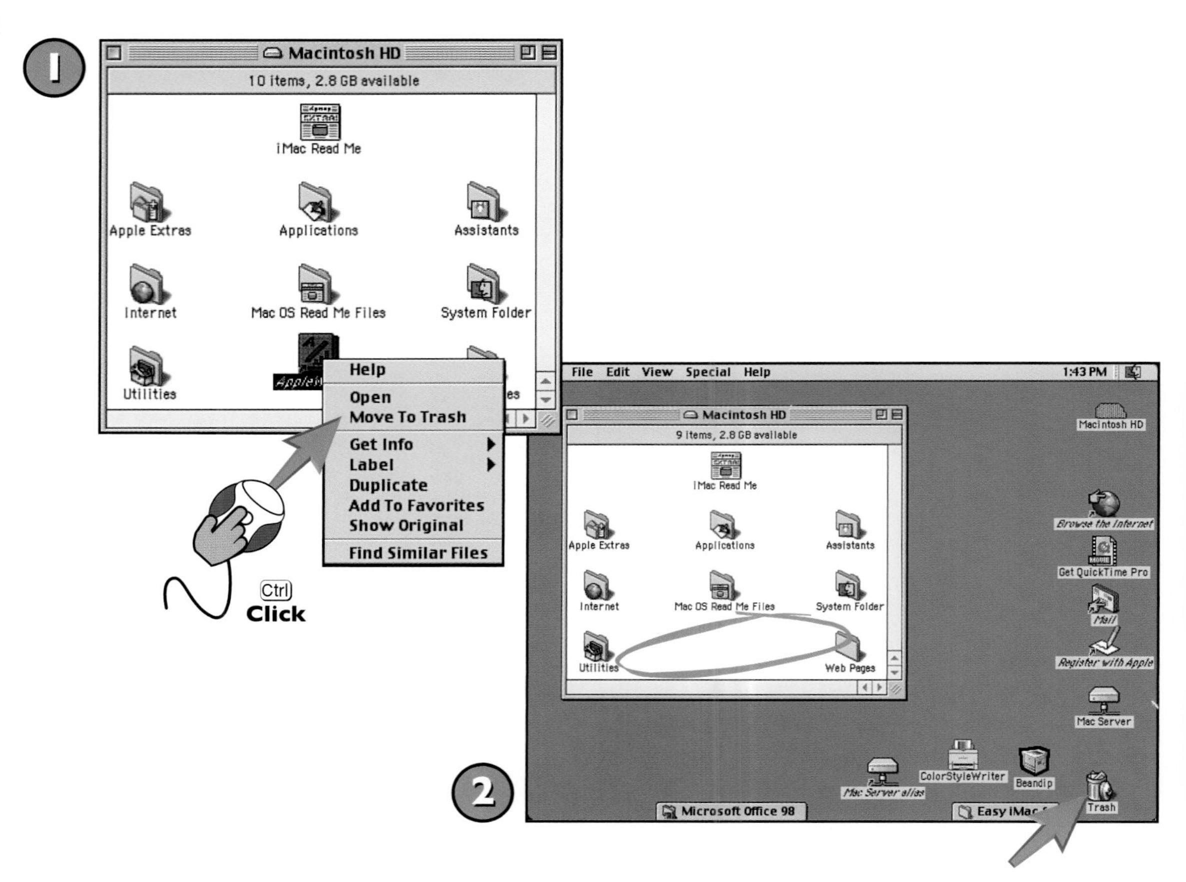

1. Holding down the **Ctrl** key, click the alias icon you want to delete and choose **Move To Trash**.
2. Mac OS moves the alias to the Trash. The alias will be deleted from the hard drive the next time **Empty Trash** is chosen from the **Special** menu.

Deleting an alias does not delete that application from your hard drive. To delete the application, you must uninstall it. Uninstalling applications is covered in Task 10, "Uninstalling Applications."

If you change your mind about deleting an item, you can move the alias out of the Trash. To do so, double-click the Trash icon and click and drag the alias to the desktop.

Task 4: Adding Applications to the Apple Menu

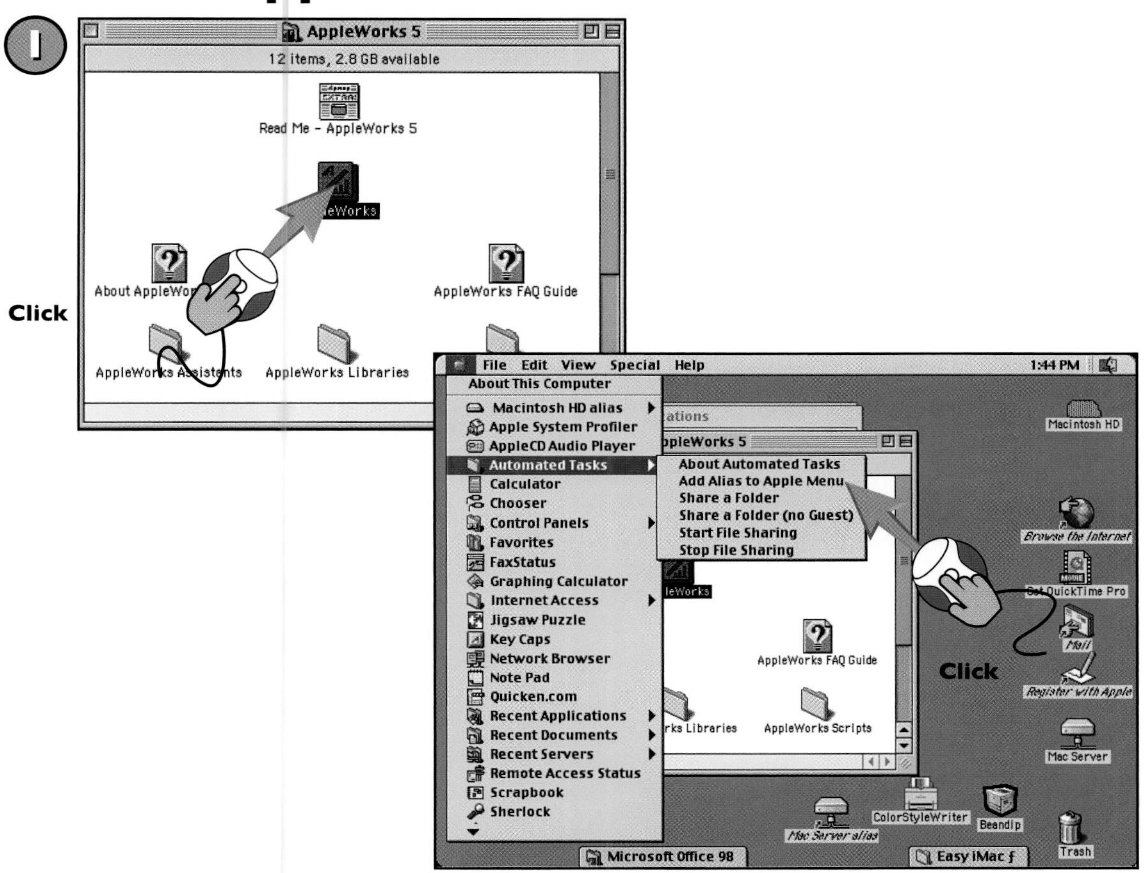

With most applications, you need to tunnel through several folders in order to open the application. You can add an alias to an application to the Apple menu to enable quick, easy access.

1. Select the application icon (in this case, the **AppleWorks** icon).

2. Click the **Apple** menu, choose **Automated Tasks**, and select **Add Alias to Apple Menu**. Mac OS adds the application alias to the **Apple** menu.

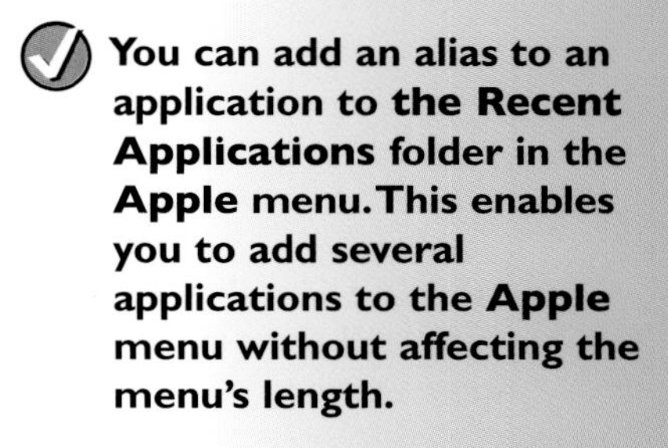

You can add an alias to an application to the Recent Applications folder in the Apple menu. This enables you to add several applications to the Apple menu without affecting the menu's length.

Task 5: Deleting Applications from the Apple Menu

Start Here

At first, you might add all kinds of icons to the **Apple** menu. But after you use the iMac more and more, you might want to streamline the **Apple** menu and weed out programs that you don't use. If your **Apple** menu becomes cluttered, you might want to delete icons for applications that you don't use.

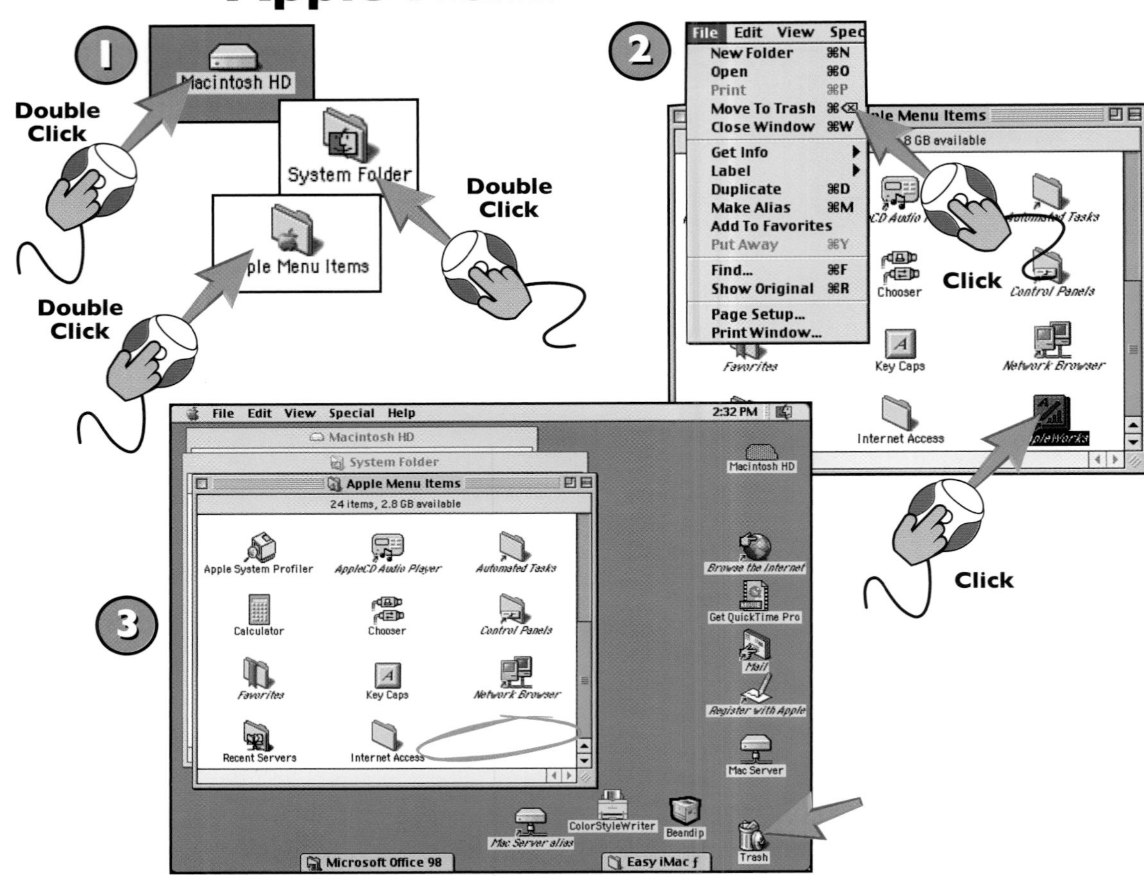

You can also follow this procedure to remove a folder from the **Apple** menu. Simply select the folder and select **Move To Trash** from the **File** menu.

1. Double-click the hard drive icon, the **System** folder, and the **Apple Menu Items** folder.
2. In the **Apple Menu Items** window, click the application icon you want to delete (in this case, **AppleWorks**), click **File**, and then choose **Move To Trash**.
3. Mac OS moves the file from the **Apple Menu Items** folder to the Trash.

End Task

Task 6: Adding Folders to the Apple Menu

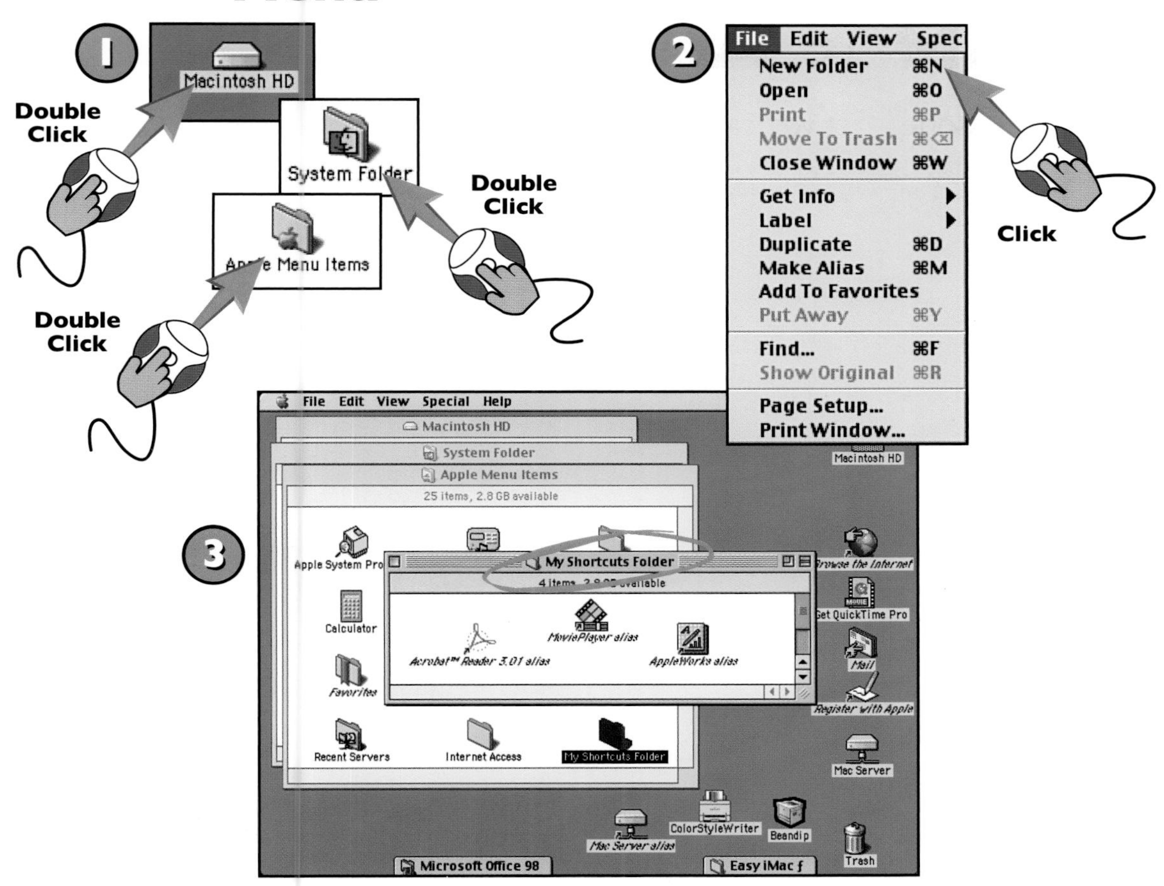

When you install a new application, that application's installation sets up application folders and icons for itself. If you don't like the arrangement of the folder and icons, you can change it. For instance, if more than one person uses your iMac, you might set up folders for each person and then add the applications that a certain person uses to his or her folder.

Double-click the hard drive icon, the **System** folder, and the **Apple Menu Items** folder.

Click **File** and choose **New Folder** to create a new folder in the **Apple** menu.

Use drag and drop to add any aliases to applications to this folder, and then name the folder according to its contents (in this case, **My Shortcuts Folder**).

You can delete folders. To do so, simply hold down the **Ctrl** key and click the folder you want to delete. Then choose the **Move To Trash** command.

Task 7: Rearranging the Apple Menu

After you set up folders, you can organize your **Apple** menu, putting the program icons in the folder and order you want.

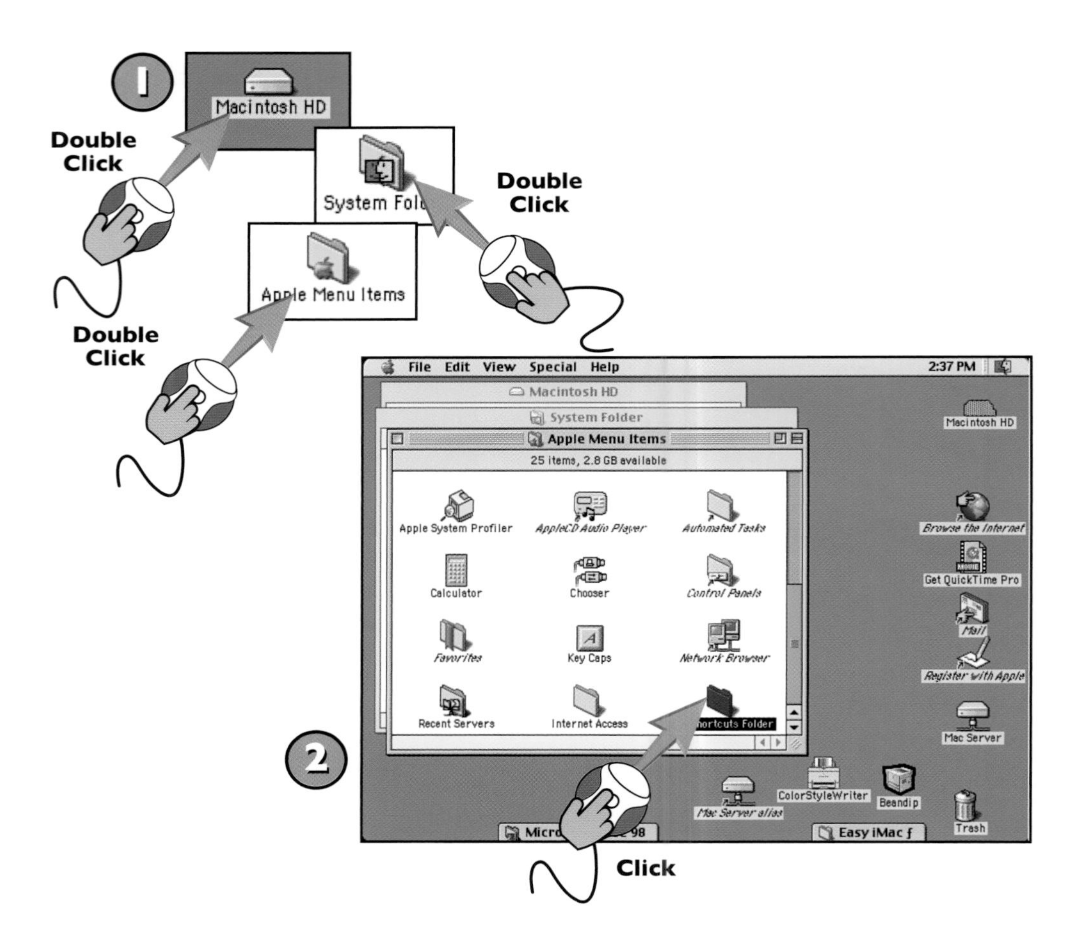

If the **Apple** menu becomes cluttered with too many icons, create a folder and place any group of icons in it. Placing several icons in one folder makes it easier for you to find items in the **Apple** menu.

1. Double-click the hard drive icon, the **System** folder, and the **Apple Menu Items** folder.

2. Click on the name of the icon that you want to appear at (or near) the top of the **Apple** menu (in this case, **My Shortcuts Folder**).

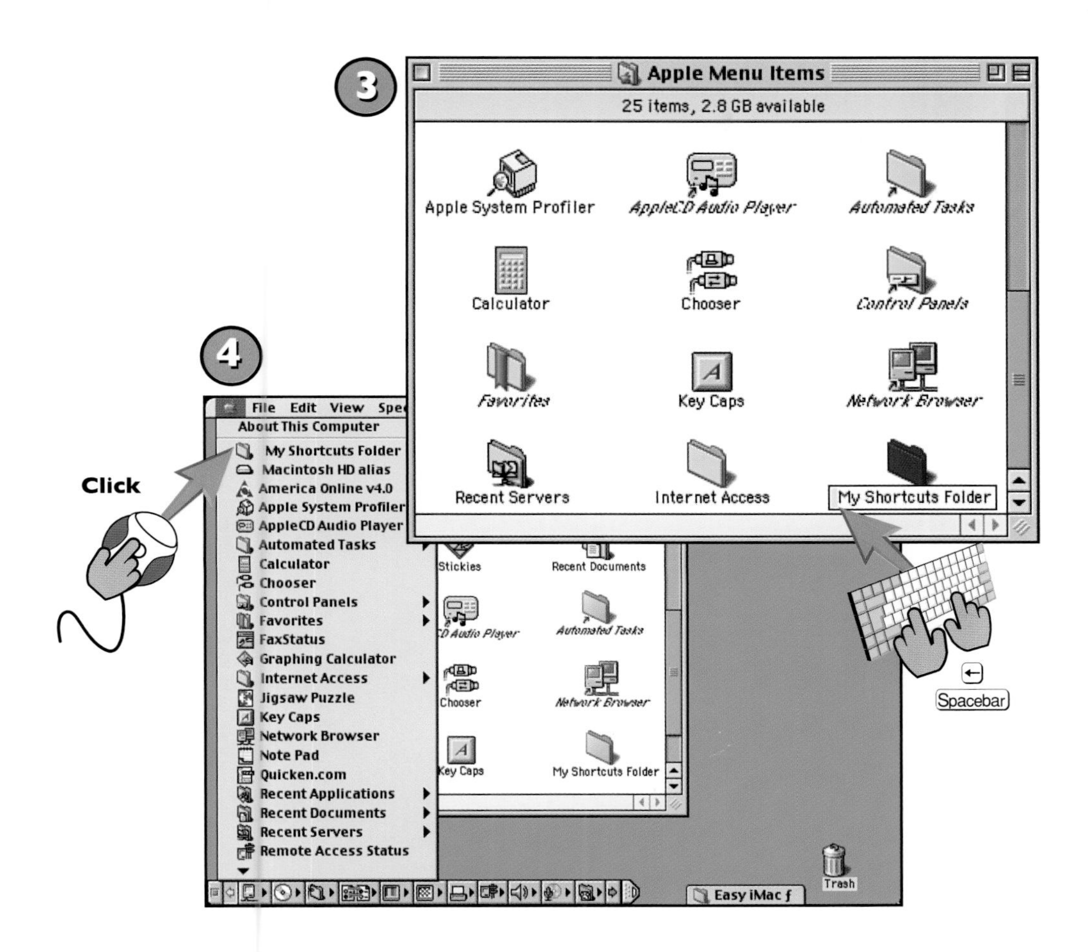

3 Press the **left arrow** key once, then press the **spacebar** once.

4 Click the **Apple** menu. Note that the **My Shortcuts Folder** icon appears at the top of the menu.

Task 8: Starting an Application When You Start Mac OS

Mac OS enables you to start one or more applications at the same time that you start Mac OS by turning your iMac on. Applications you might want to open automatically include those that you use everyday or those that you use first thing every morning.

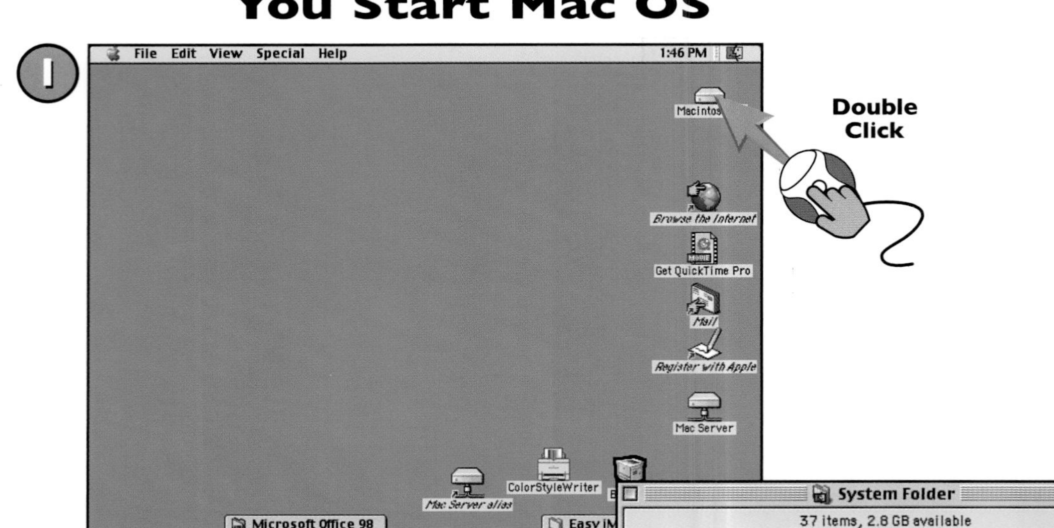

If you don't shut down your iMac at night, these applications will not be started each morning. They are started only when you start Mac OS.

You can also run applications when you shut down Mac OS. Instead of placing an alias in the **Startup Items** folder, place the alias in the **Shutdown Items** folder.

1. Double-click the hard drive icon, and then double-click the **System** folder.
2. Double-click the **Startup Items** folder.

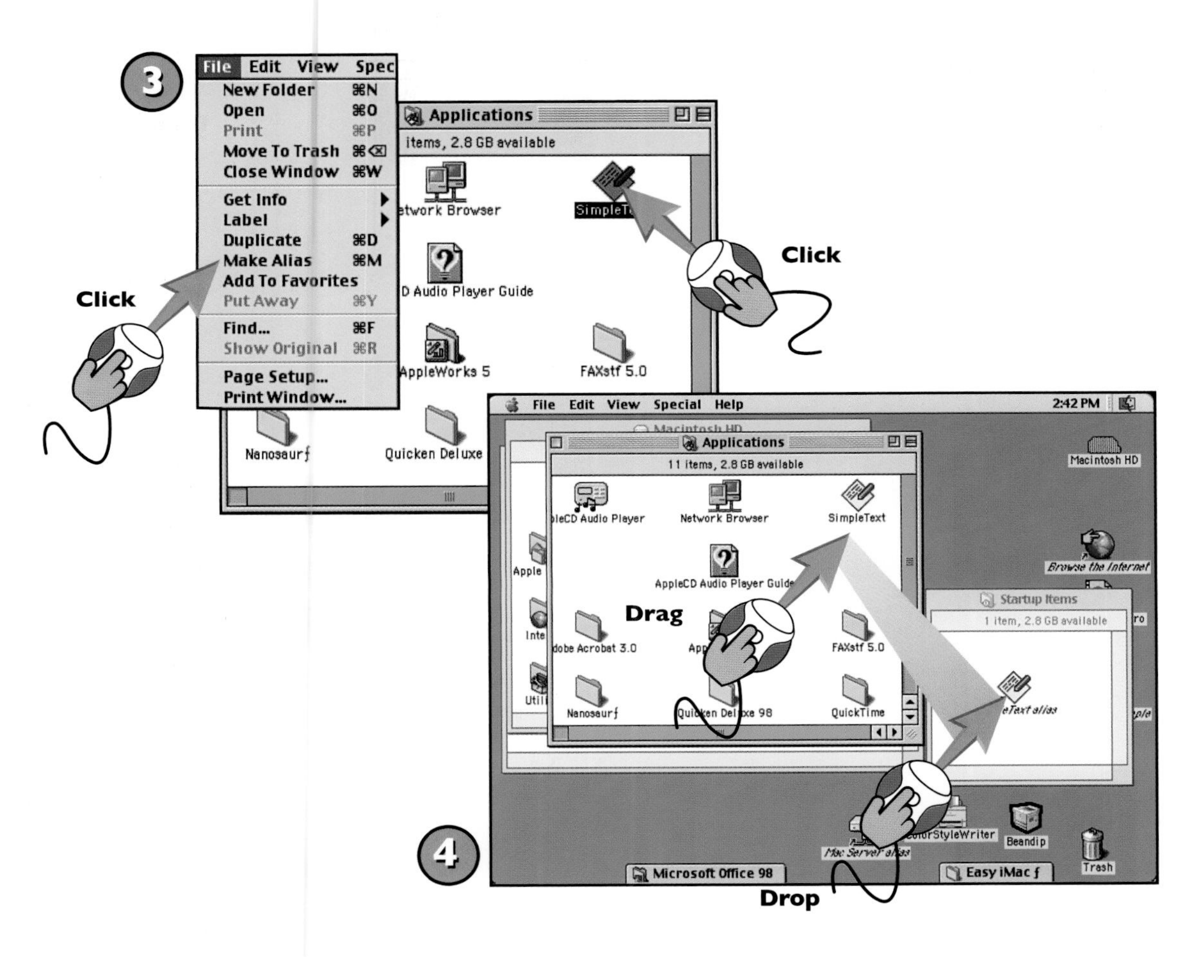

3. Find and select the application you want to run at startup, and then create an alias by selecting **Make Alias** from the **File** menu.

4. Drag the alias to the **Startup Items** folder. Restart Mac OS, and the application will open after Mac OS starts up.

Task 9: Installing Applications

When you bought your iMac, it came with certain applications already installed. If you want to add to these, you can purchase additional programs and then add them to your systems. Installing a new program basically copies the program files to a folder on your hard drive and, in some cases, may add an alias icon to the Apple menu for starting the application.

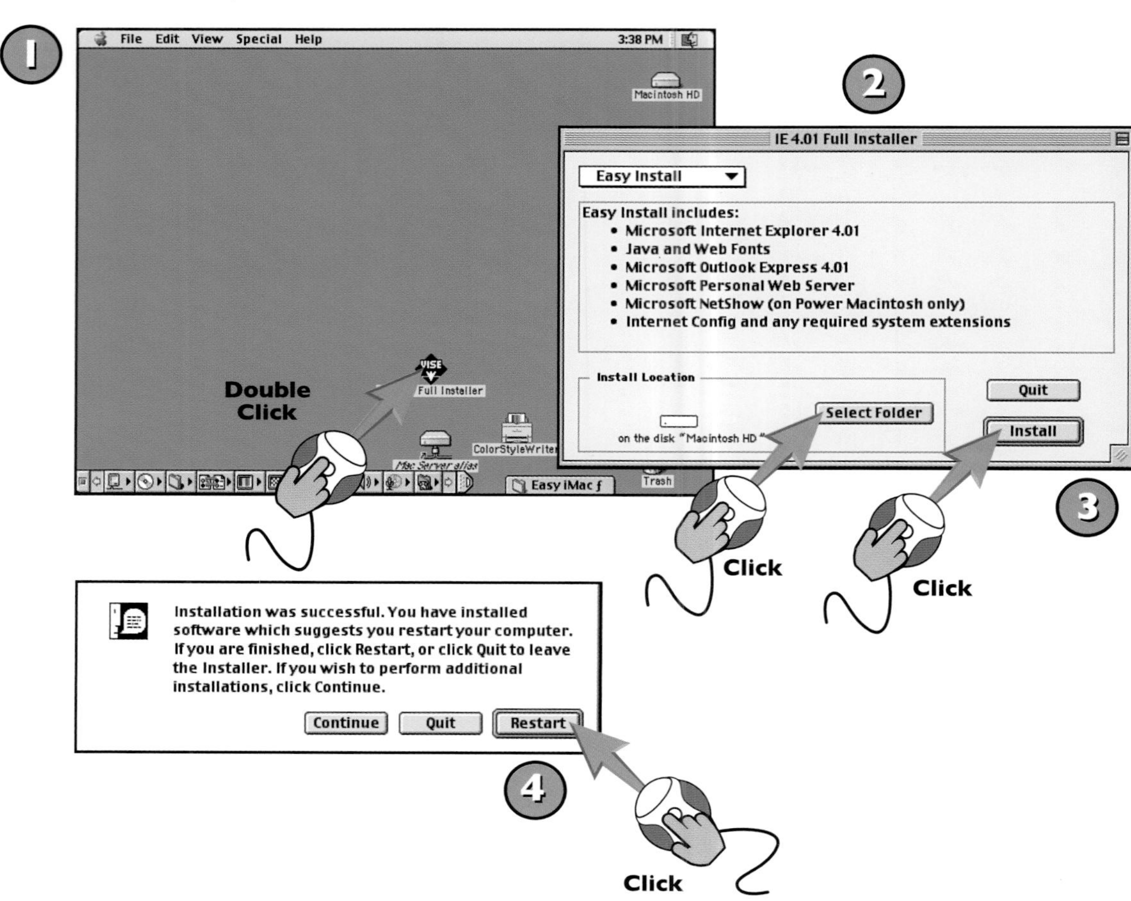

✓ **Some installation applications may vary from the steps in this procedure. If an easy installation of the software is not available, choose the typical or default installation for the software.**

✓ **If the installer has a 68K or Power PC installation option, choose the PowerPC installation for your iMac.**

1. Double-click the installer application icon. Click **Accept** if you agree with the licensing agreement for the software you are installing.
2. Click the **Select Folder** button (or pop-up menu) to choose where you want the application installed on your hard drive.
3. Click the **Install** button and follow any instructions presented in the installer application.
4. Click the **Continue** button if you need to install additional applications. If prompted, click **Restart**. Otherwise, click **Quit**.

Task 10: Uninstalling Applications

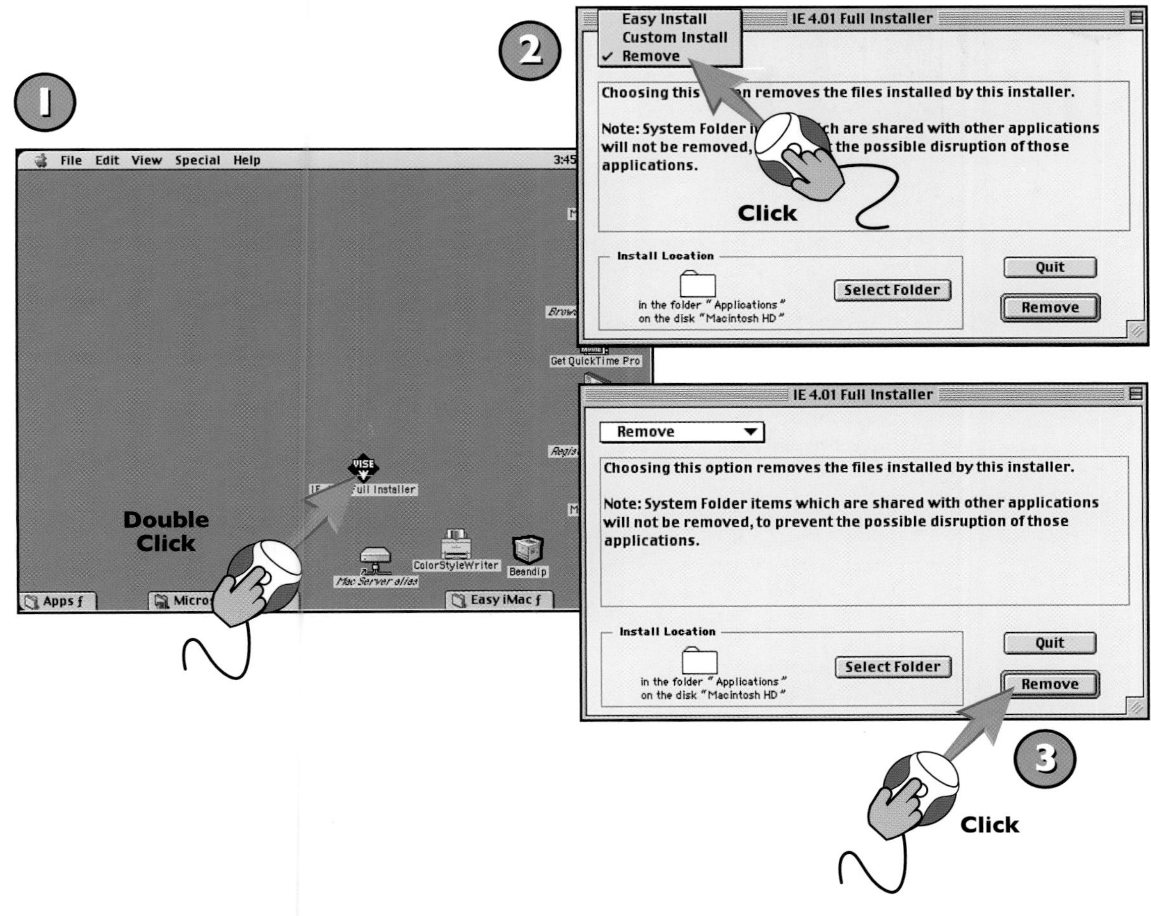

1. Double-click the installer application icon.
2. Click the pop-up menu and choose **Remove**.
3. Click the **Remove** button. The installer application uninstalls the files and returns you to the installer application window.

You can remove an alias icon from the Apple menu, but doing so leaves that application on your hard drive. When you want to get rid of the application and its files entirely, you can uninstall it. This removes the application and all its related files and folders from your hard drive. You should move any data files from your application's folders if, for example, you plan to use them with another application.

Some programs do not include an uninstall option in their installer applications. In most cases, you can move the application folder to the Trash to uninstall it.

Before you uninstall an application from your iMac, you might want to create a backup of the application. It is possible the files created by that application may not be 100 percent compatible with a different application.

Task 11: Using AppleScript

Mac OS includes a scripting language, AppleScript. If you have applications that support AppleScript, you can automate tasks in those applications by creating an AppleScript script. The Script Editor application is located in the AppleScript folder, which is installed by Mac OS in the Apple Extras folder.

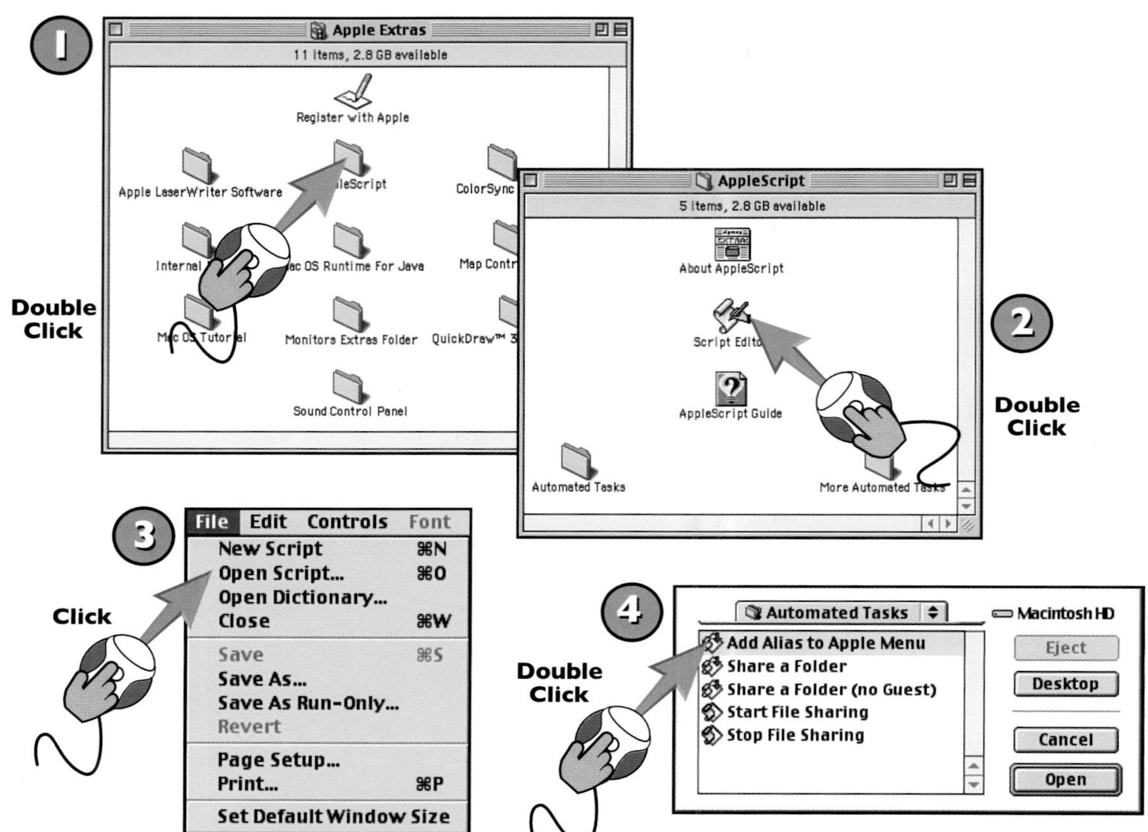

- Most applications support a core set of AppleScript commands such as opening and quitting an application.
- Mac OS comes with several AppleScripts, which are located in the Automated Tasks folder in the Apple menu.

1. Double-click the hard drive icon, then the **Apple Extras** folder, and finally the **AppleScript** folder.
2. Double-click the **Script Editor** application icon.
3. Click **File** and choose the **Open Script** command.
4. Double-click the **Automated Tasks** folder, and then double-click an **AppleScript** file (in this case, the **Add Alias to Apple Menu** script).

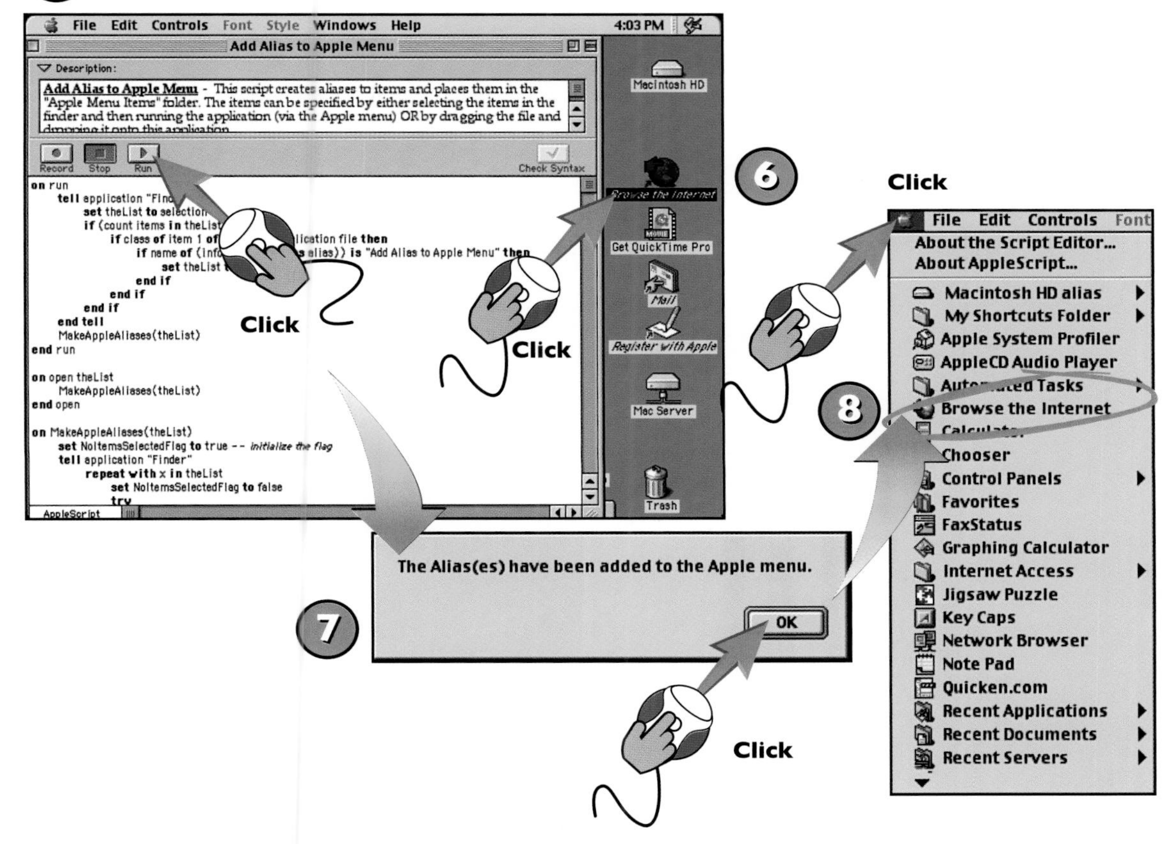

5. View the contents of the **Add Alias to Apple Menu** file in the **Script Editor** window.

6. Select an icon you want to add to the **Apple** menu (in this case, the **Browse the Internet** alias on the desktop). Click the **Run** button.

7. Mac OS runs the AppleScript. Click the **OK** button to close the dialog.

8. Click the **Apple** menu. Note that the item has been added to the **Apple** menu.

- **You can modify the AppleScript in the Script Editor. The Script Editor can help you use the AppleScript programming language to complete your AppleScript scripts.**

- **You can use an existing AppleScript script to create your own. Once you are able to successfully run your own AppleScript, you can add it to the Automated Tasks folder in the Apple menu.**

- **You can change the AppleScript dictionary to create scripts for different applications. Click the File menu and choose Open Dictionary to choose a dictionary you want to use with your AppleScript script.**

Task 12: Using File Sharing

If your iMac is on a network, you can share files with other computers on the network. If another Macintosh is on the network, the other Mac can directly access the iMac on the network using File Sharing.

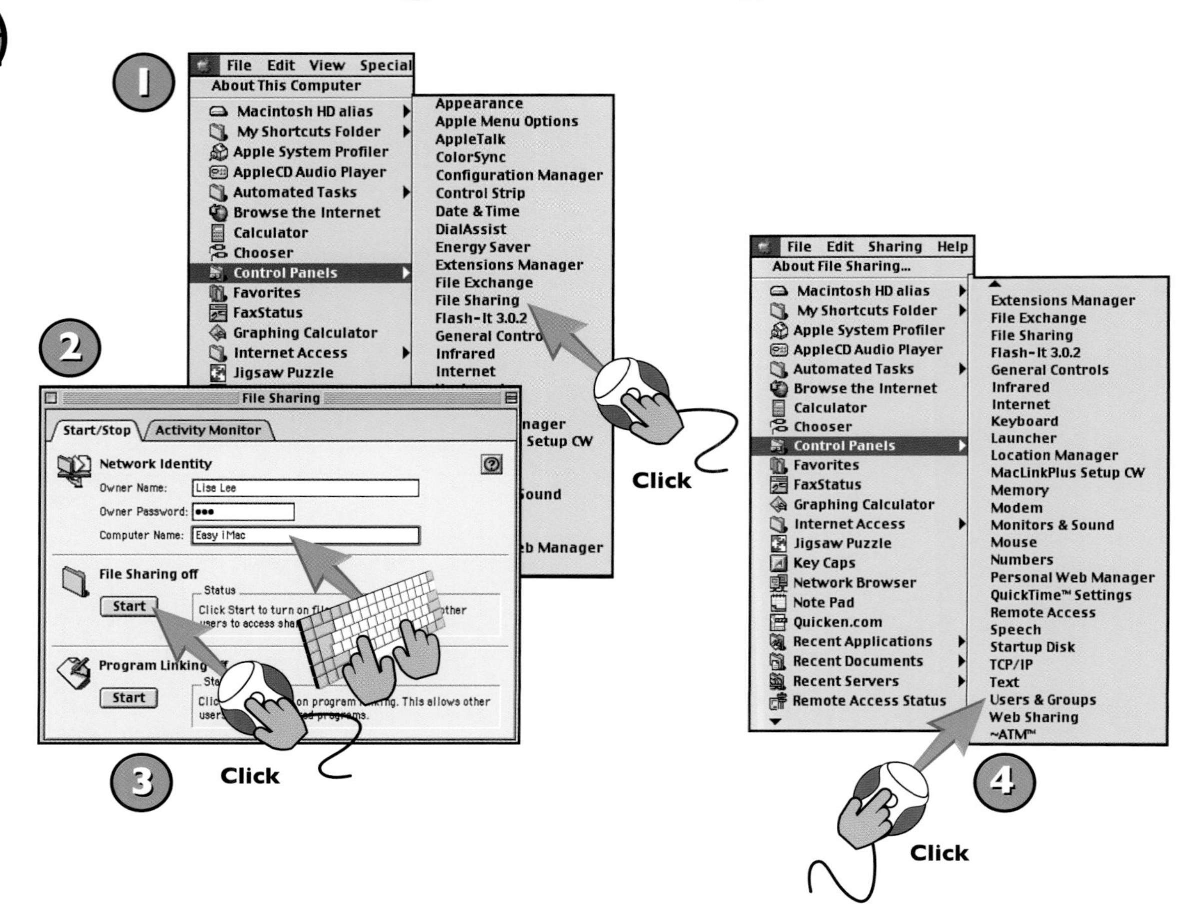

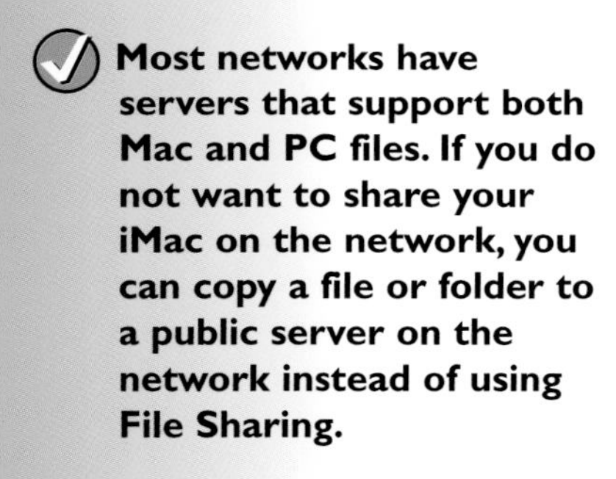

Most networks have servers that support both Mac and PC files. If you do not want to share your iMac on the network, you can copy a file or folder to a public server on the network instead of using File Sharing.

1. Click the **Apple** menu, choose **Control Panels**, and choose **File Sharing**.

2. Type in the owner name, the owner password, and the computer name in the appropriate fields.

3. Click on the **Start** button under **File Sharing off**.

4. Click the **Apple** menu, choose **Control Panels**, and then choose **Users & Groups**.

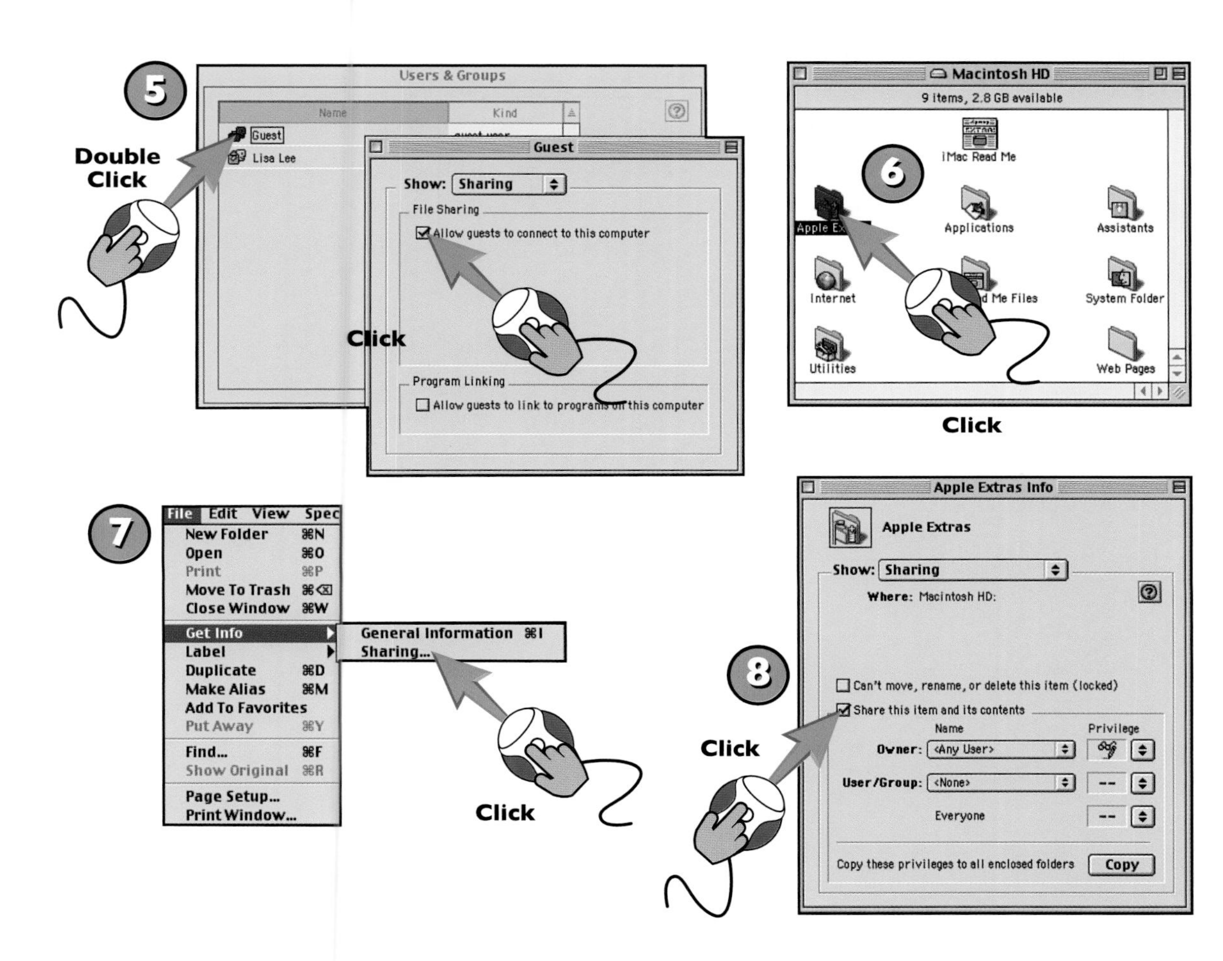

5 Double-click **Guest**, then click **Sharing** in the **Show** pop-up menu. Click the **Allow guests to connect to this computer** check box.

6 Find and select the folder you want to share.

7 Click the **File** menu, choose **Get Info**, and then choose **Sharing**.

8 Click the **Share this item and its contents** check box. The folder is now shared on the network to any Mac that logs on to your computer with guest access.

If you leave File Sharing on, it will use additional memory and will have a considerable performance impact on your iMac whenever another Macintosh accesses your iMac over the network. For optimal performance, only turn on File Sharing when you need to share a file on your iMac.

Guest access to your iMac is not a security issue if you know everyone else on your network. However, granting guest access to your iMac is generally not recommended. Anyone who connects to your iMac can copy your files, folders, or applications to their computer without you knowing about it.

PART 9

Using iMac Accessories

iMac provides several accessories that you can use to help you in your work. Many of these accessories—such as Key Caps—are not full-blown applications, but they are useful for specific jobs on your iMac. Accessories include a calculator, a graphing calculator, and a jigsaw puzzle game, as well as applications such as SimpleText, Movie Player, Note Pad, Stickies, and various Internet applications. (The Internet applications are discussed in Part 2, "Connecting to Online Services and the Internet.") iMac also includes some multimedia tools for playing CDs and for recording and playing back sounds. This part covers the basic applications included with your iMac.

Tasks

Task 1: Playing Games

Start Here

Apple provides several games that you can play to break up your workday with a little entertainment. Use any of the games to fill a lunch hour or coffee break and to ease the tensions of the day. Playing games is also a good way to help you get the hang of using the mouse. For instance, playing Jigsaw Puzzle can help you practice such mouse skills as clicking, dragging, and so on.

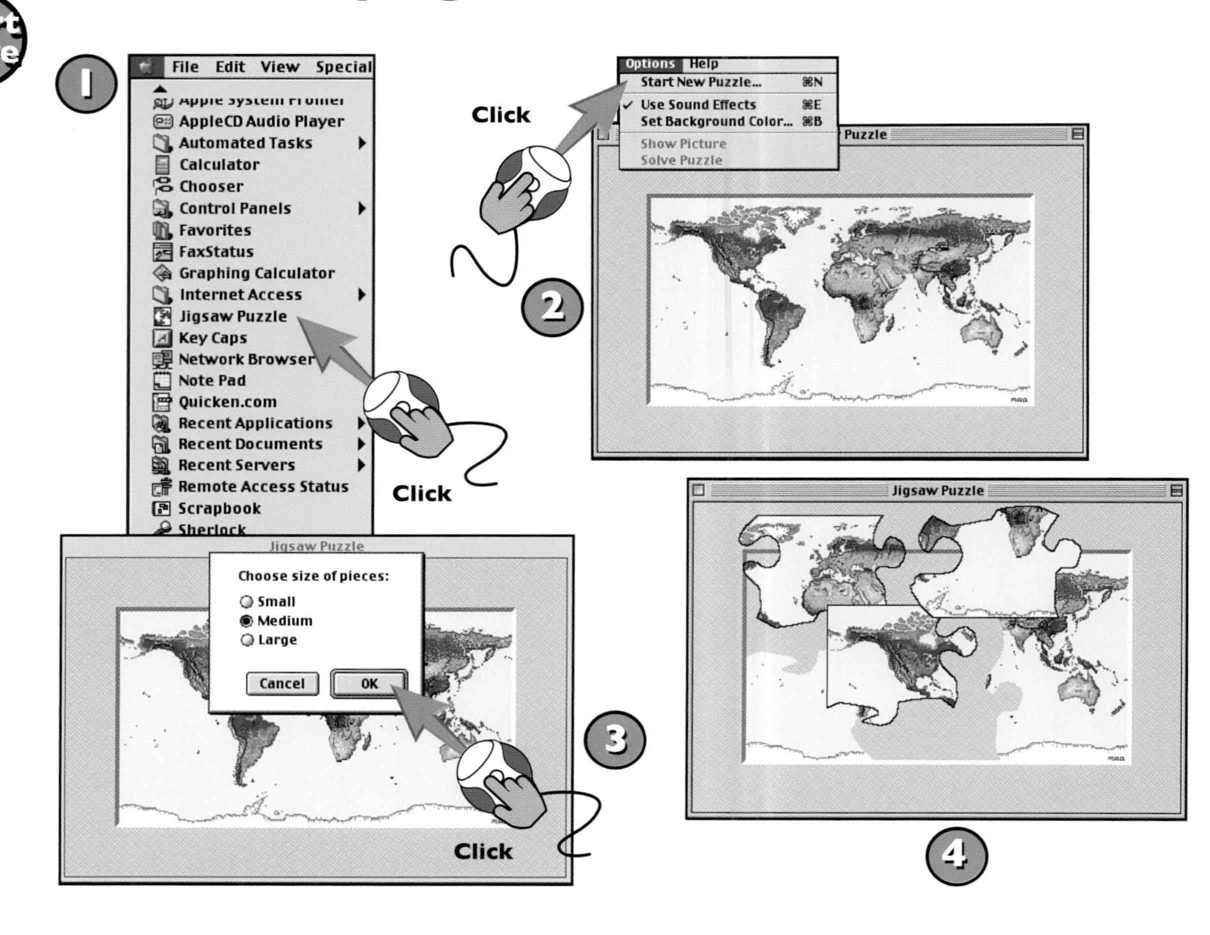

1. Click the **Apple** menu and choose **Jigsaw Puzzle**.
2. Click the **Options** menu and choose **Start New Puzzle**.
3. Choose a small, medium, or large puzzle, and then click **OK**.
4. Click and drag the puzzle pieces into their proper places. A sound plays when the puzzle is completed.

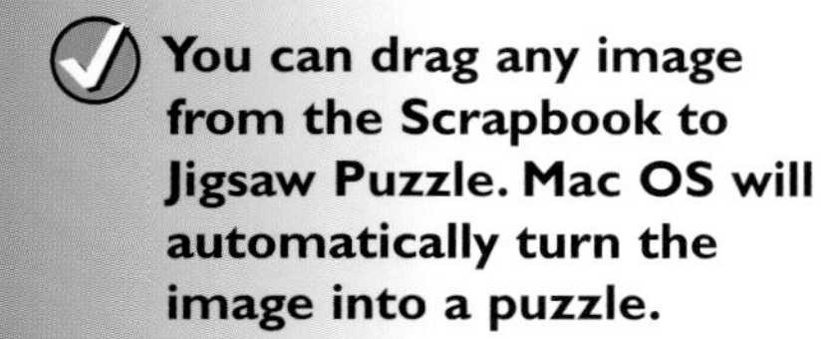
You can drag any image from the Scrapbook to Jigsaw Puzzle. Mac OS will automatically turn the image into a puzzle.

End Task

Task 2: Using Stickies

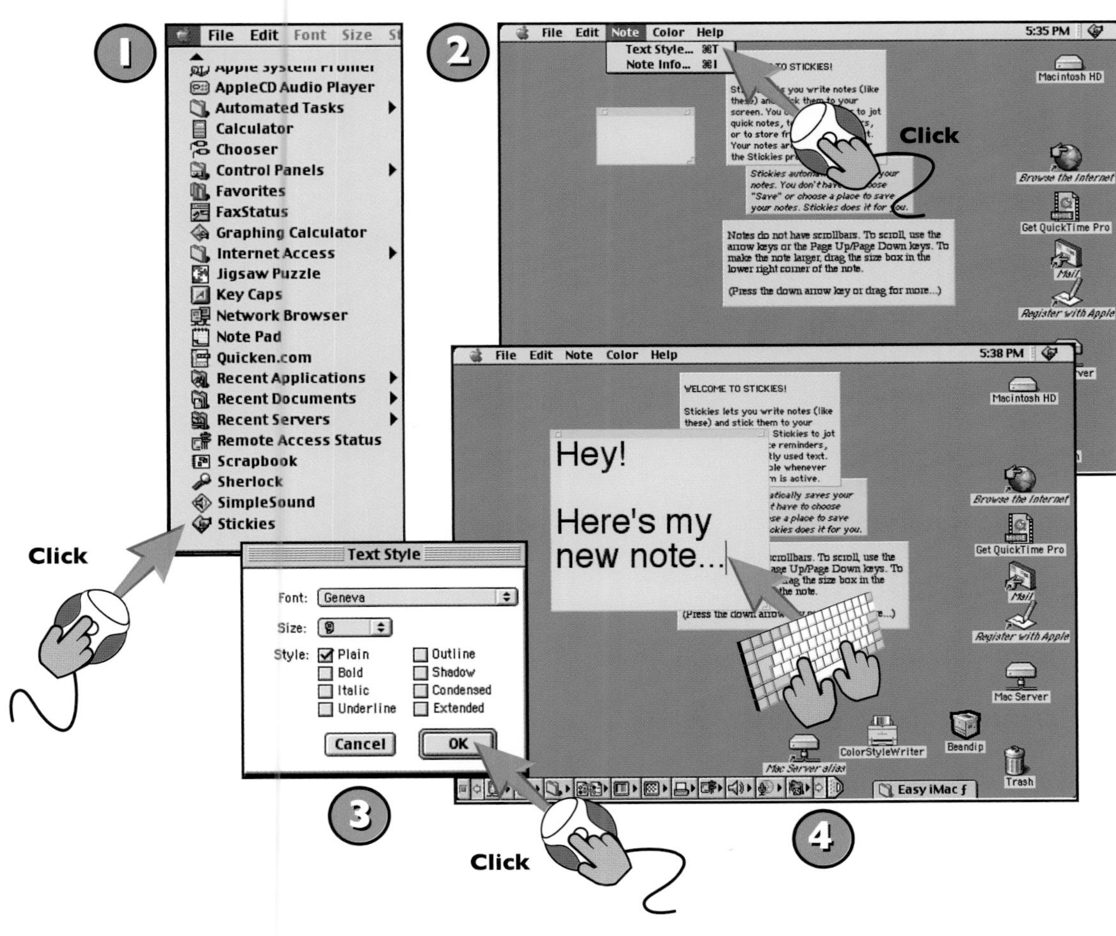

As you browse the Internet or work on a document, you may want to save small sections of text to another window for future use. iMac provides Stickies and Note Pad as applications that can be used to store text.

1. Click the **Apple** menu and choose **Stickies**.
2. To change text styles, click the **Note** menu and choose **Text Style**.
3. Choose a font, size, and style, and then click **OK**.
4. Type text into any **Stickies** window. Any changes you make to a Stickies note are saved automatically.

✓ Change the color of a sticky note by clicking the **Color** menu and choosing the color you want.

✓ Click the **File** menu and choose **Quit** to exit the Stickies application. The first time you quit Stickies, you will be asked if you want Stickies to open whenever you start your iMac. If you choose yes, an alias to Stickies is placed in the **Startup Items** folder of your **System** folder. If you do not want Stickies to open at startup, move its alias out of the **Startup Items** folder.

Task 3: Using Note Pad

You can keep text snippets in the Note Pad application. The main difference between Note Pad and Stickies is color and size. Note Pad stores all its pages on one note pad, whereas Stickies opens a separate window for each note.

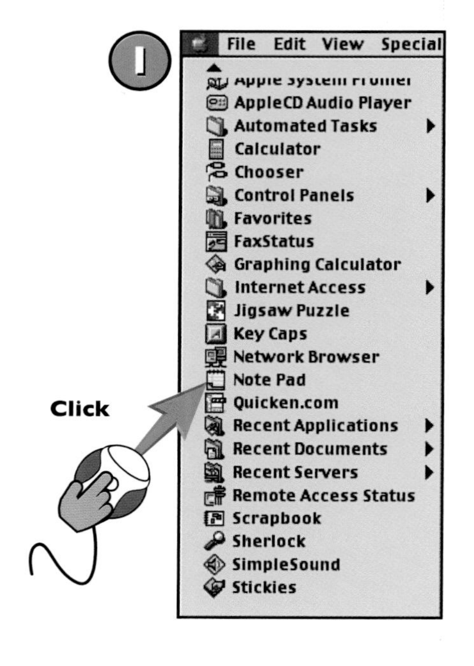

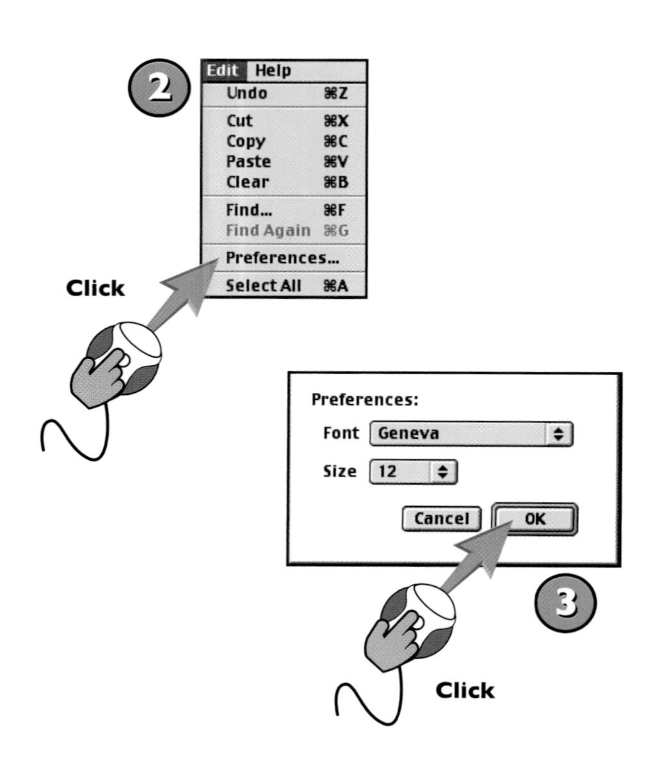

You can rename the Note Pad file in the System folder. This file contains the text stored in Note Pad. If you double-click the renamed Note Pad file, it will open and show its contents within Note Pad.

1. Click the **Apple** menu, and choose **Note Pad**.
2. Click the **Edit** menu and choose **Preferences**.
3. To change the font style in the **Note Pad** window, select a font and font size, and then click **OK**.

Next Step

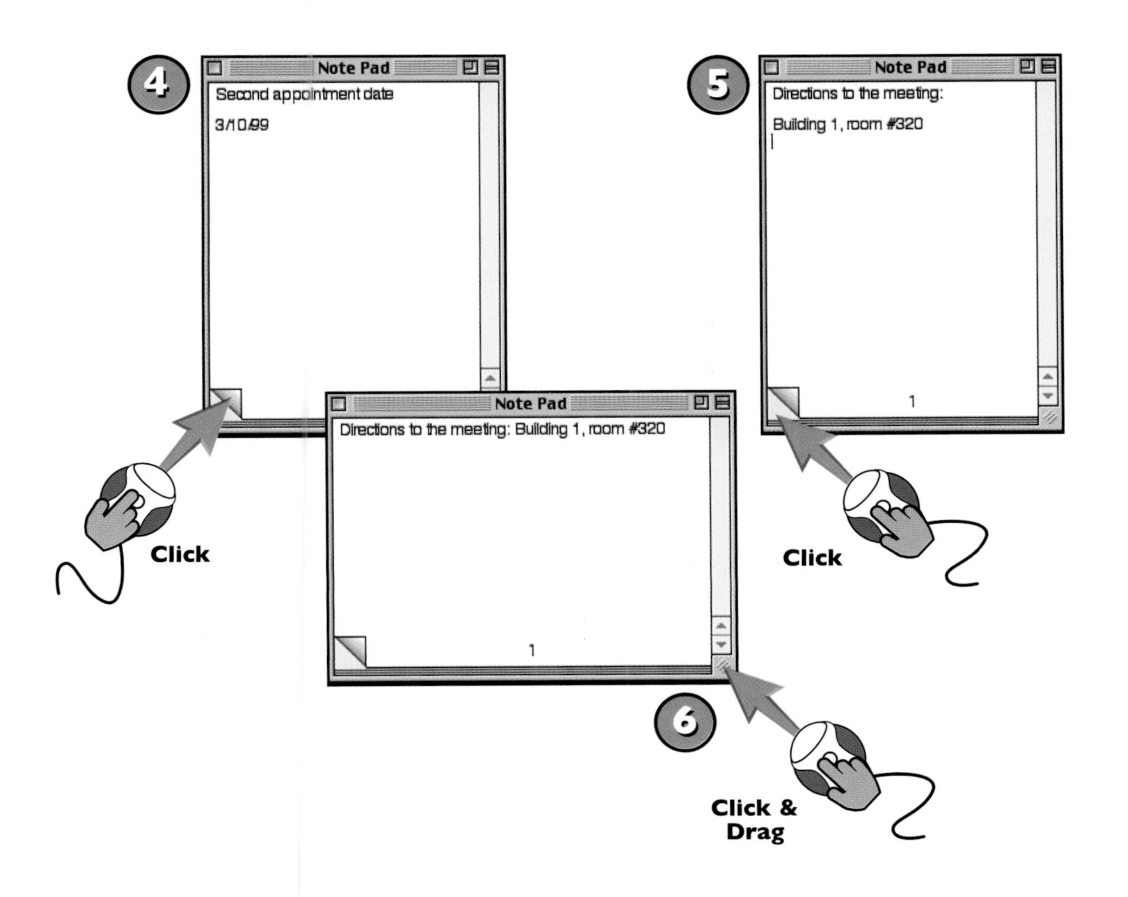

4. Click on the top triangle area in the bottom-left corner of Note Pad to turn one page forward.
5. Click the bottom triangle area of the bottom-left corner of Note Pad to turn one page backward.
6. Click and drag the grow box to grow or shrink the **Note Pad** window.

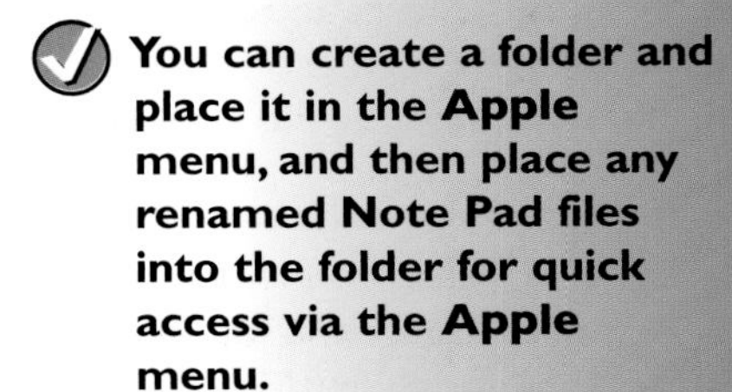
You can create a folder and place it in the Apple menu, and then place any renamed Note Pad files into the folder for quick access via the Apple menu.

Task 4: Typing Text in Note Pad

You can add or delete text anywhere on a Note Pad page. To do this, you use the arrow keys and the alphanumeric keys in combination with the mouse.

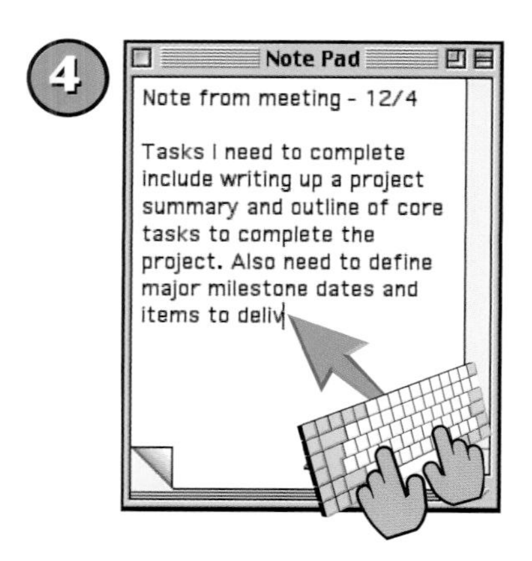

- **If you make a mistake while typing, press the Delete key to backspace and remove one character at a time. Then retype the text.**
- **Although Stickies and Note Pad automatically save your documents, most applications, such as SimpleText, only save a document when you select the Save command. Be sure to periodically save your document. See Task 6, "Saving a Document," in Part 4, "Using Applications."**
- **If you're not sure how to select text, refer Part 4, Task 11, "Selecting Text."**

1. Type the text. You don't need to press **Return** at the end of each line; Note Pad automatically wraps the lines within a paragraph.
2. To end a paragraph and start a new one, press **Return**. The insertion point moves to the next line.
3. To move to a different location in the document, click the spot where you want to place the insertion point.
4. To add text, start typing. To remove text, press the **Delete** key on your keyboard.

Task 5: Using SimpleText

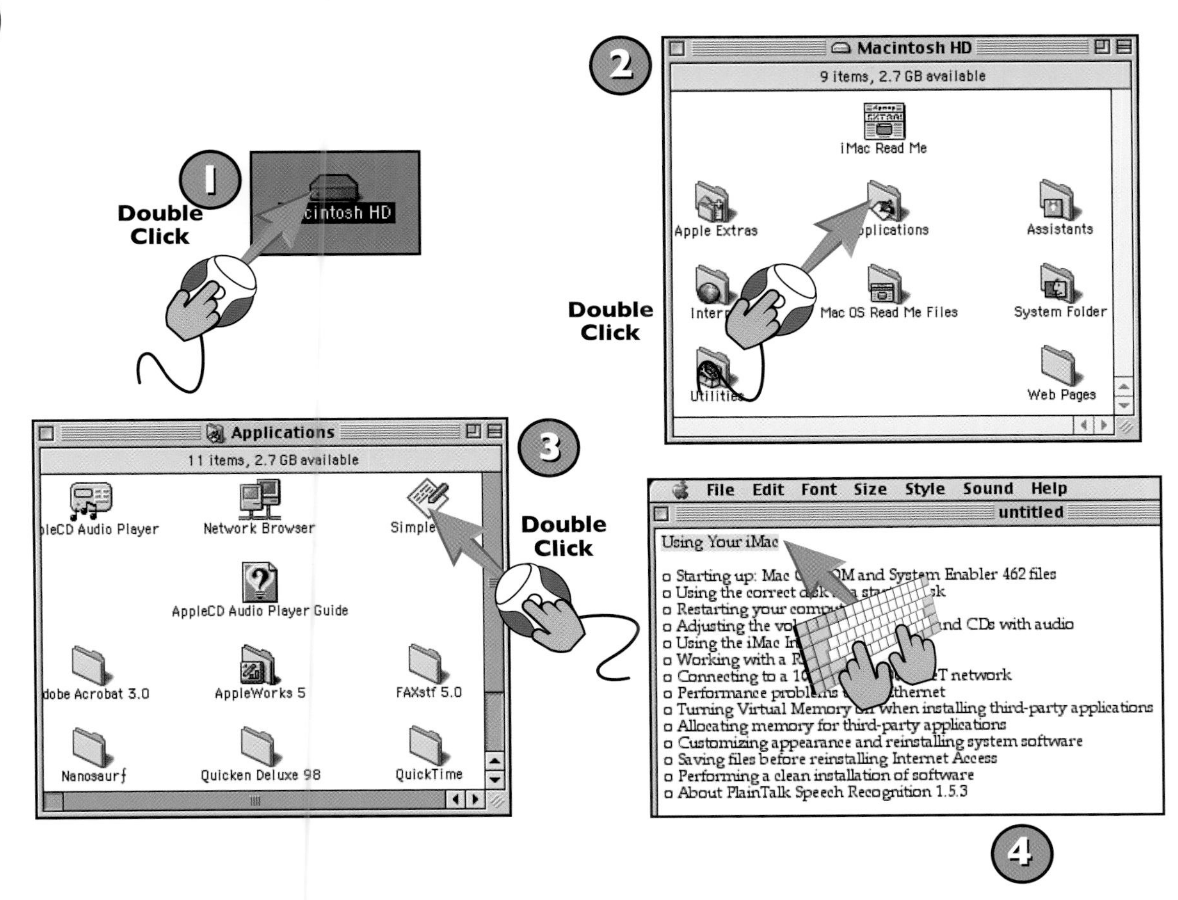

The most common type of simple file is the text file. You can find instructions on how to install an application and other information in text files; some configuration files are also text files. To edit and work with this type of file, you can use SimpleText, which has text-editing features similar to Note Pad and Stickies. However, SimpleText saves each text file as an individual file on your hard drive. Plus, it has the capability to find and replace text in a document. SimpleText can also read many more types of files, such as QuickTime movies, sound files, QuickDraw 3D files, and Read Me files, which are included with most Macintosh application products.

1. Double-click the hard drive icon.
2. Double-click the **Applications** folder.
3. Double-click the **SimpleText** icon.
4. The **SimpleText** window opens; type whatever text you want.

✓ You can view many kinds of documents with SimpleText. However, you can edit only text documents with this program.

Task 6: Using Key Caps

Start Here

Several fonts are installed in your **System** folder on your iMac. A *font* consists of a core set of characters, usually consisting of the alphabet. Additional characters can be viewed using the Key Caps application. These additional characters can be typed by holding down the **Option** or **Ctrl** keys while typing on the alphanumeric keys on the keyboard.

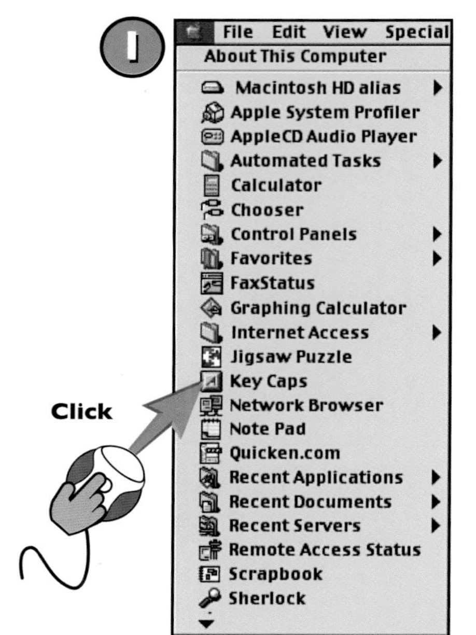

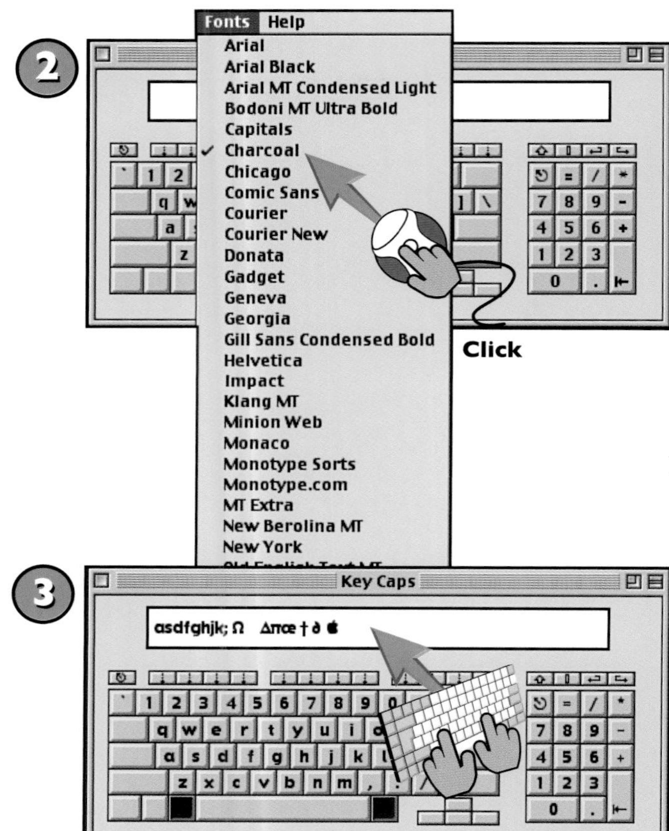

1. Click the **Apple** menu and choose **Key Caps**.
2. Click the **Font** menu and choose a font.
3. Type text in the **Key Caps** window to view the font style.

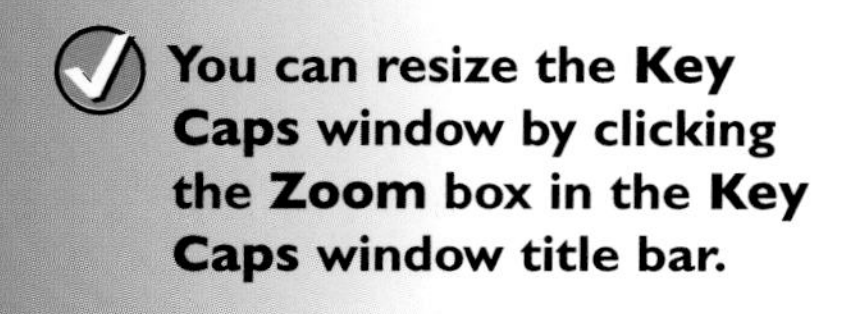

You can resize the **Key Caps** window by clicking the **Zoom** box in the **Key Caps** window title bar.

End Task

Task 7: Viewing an Image with SimpleText

Start Here

SimpleText can open several kinds of image documents, including those in PICT, JPEG, 3DMF, and GIF file formats.

1. Double-click the image document you want to view.
2. A file translation window opens. Click the **Open** button.
3. The image opens in SimpleText.

You can create a screenshot of your iMac screen by pressing **Command+Shift+3.** Mac OS names the screenshot **Picture 1** and saves it to your hard drive folder.

You can create a custom screenshot and choose only part of the screen to capture by dragging your mouse. Press **Command+Shift+4**, then select the part of the screen you want to capture. Mac OS names the screenshot **Picture 1** and saves it to your hard drive folder. If you hold down the **Ctrl** key, you can save the screen shot to the clipboard and paste it into an application such as Scrapbook or use it as a desktop pattern.

Task 8: Formatting Text in SimpleText

You can easily make simple changes to the appearance of the text using the SimpleText application. For example, you can change the font or font size, and you can make text bold, italic, or underlined. This task touches on just a few of the formatting changes you can make. Experiment to try out some of the other available formatting features.

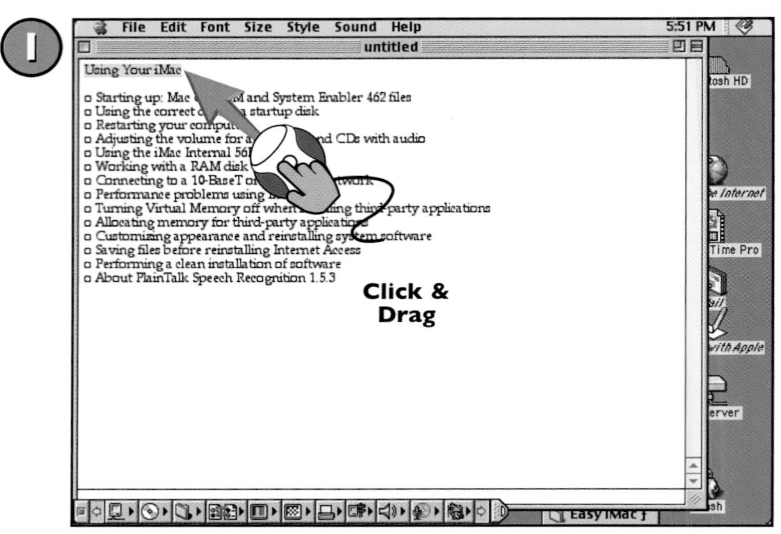

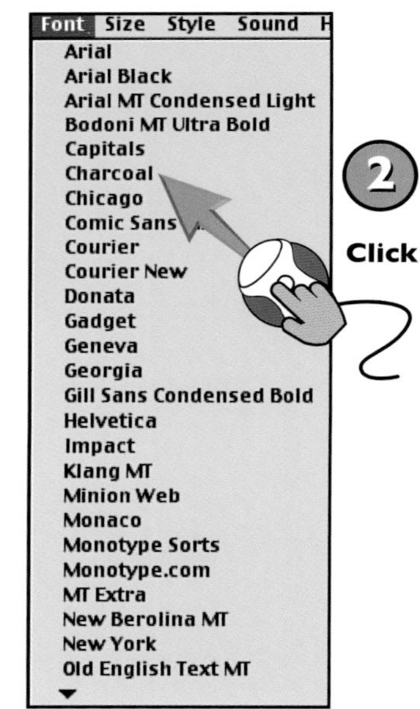

1. Select the text you want to change. (If you need help selecting text, refer to Task 11 in Part 4.)
2. To use a different font, click the **Font** menu and choose the font you want.

✓ Formatting text can make it easier for people reading your document to comprehend what they are reading.

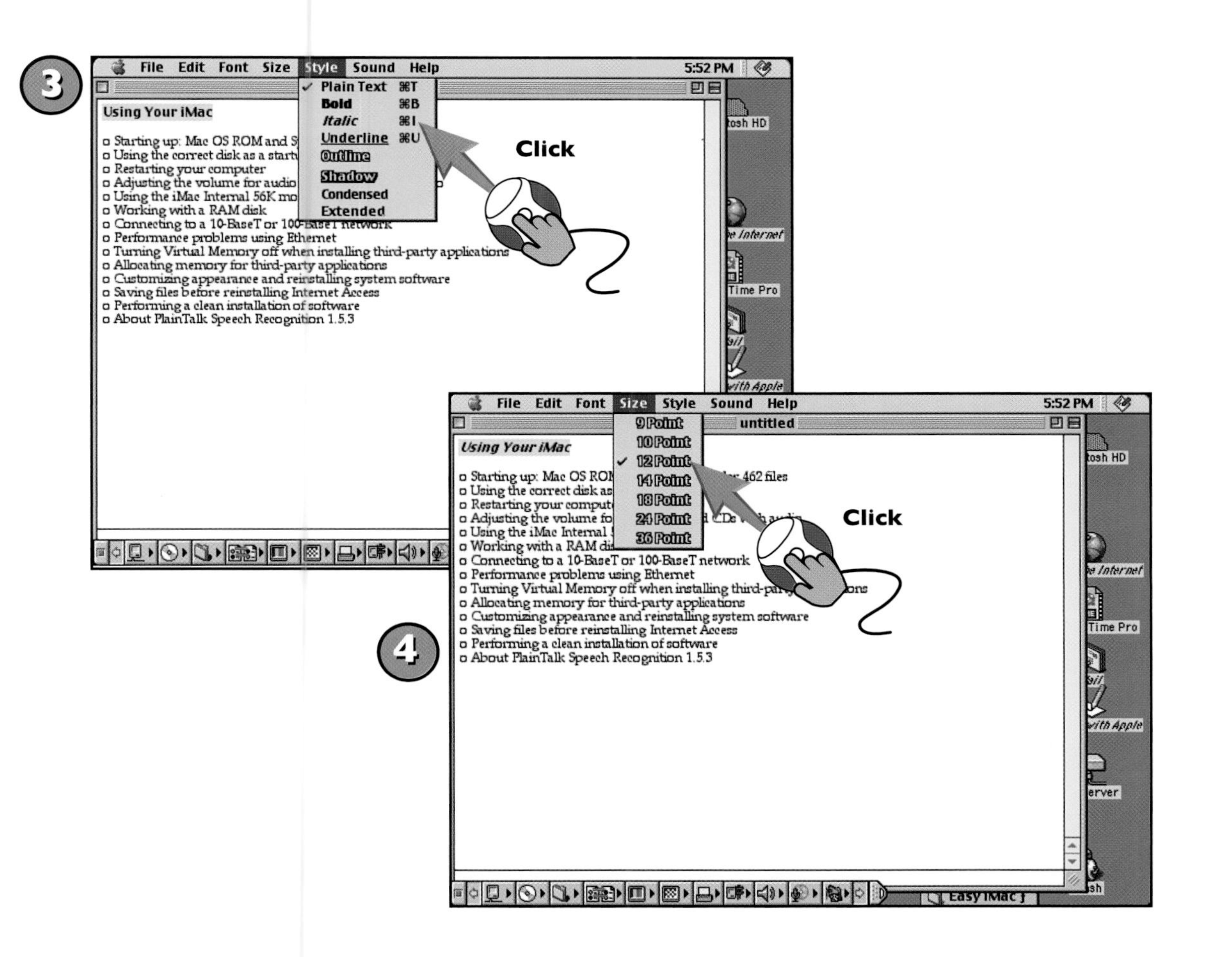

To make text bold, italic, underline, and so on, select the text you want to change, click the **Style** menu, and choose the desired font style. In this case, I selected **Italic**.

To change the font size, select the text you want to change, click the **Size** menu, and choose the font size you want.

Task 9: Using Scrapbook

You can use Scrapbook to store snippets of text, art, or sounds. Scrapbook is an application that stores several kinds of data.

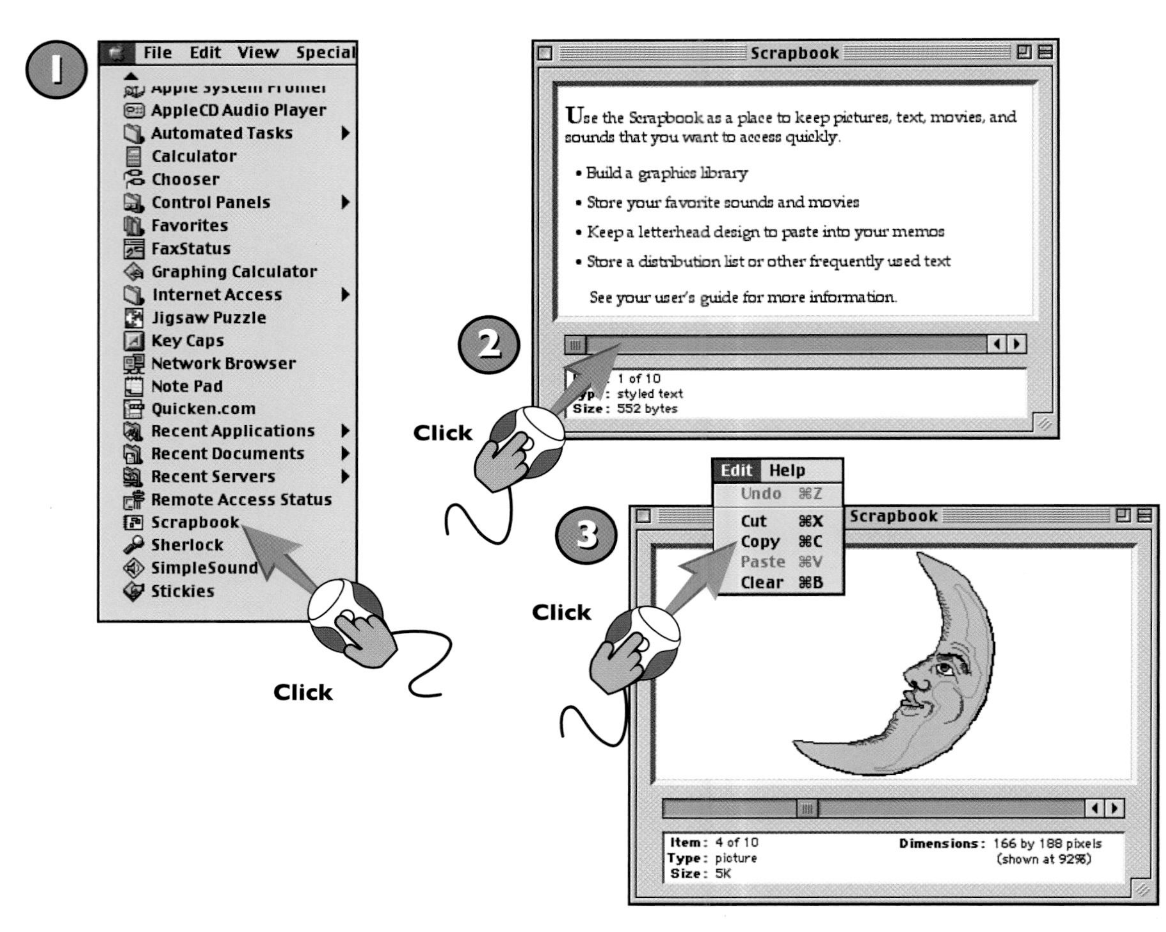

1. Click the **Apple** menu and choose **Scrapbook**.
2. Click to the right or the left of the scrollbar thumb to view each piece of data stored in the Scrapbook.
3. To copy an item from Scrapbook, click **Edit** and choose **Copy**. Mac OS will convert the item to a clipping file. Double-click the clipping to view it.

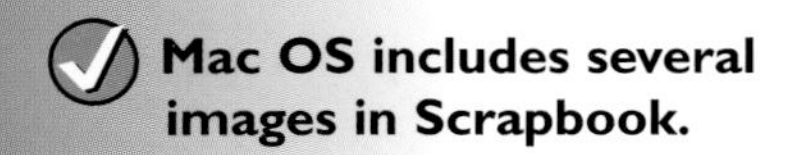

Mac OS includes several images in Scrapbook.

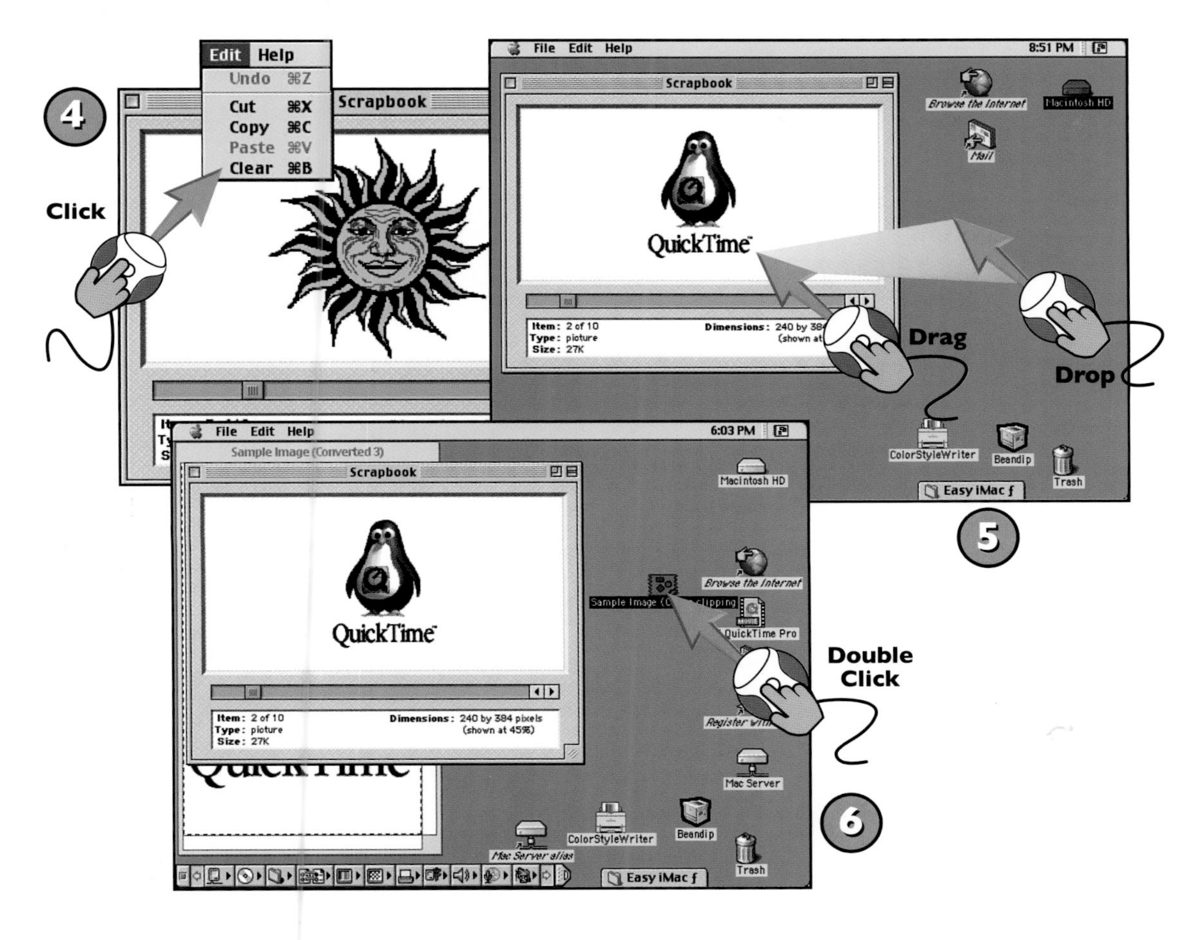

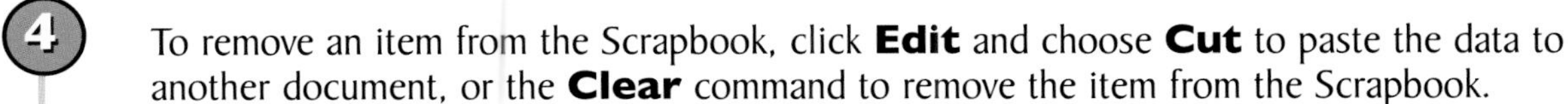

4. To remove an item from the Scrapbook, click **Edit** and choose **Cut** to paste the data to another document, or the **Clear** command to remove the item from the Scrapbook.

5. To move an item from the Scrapbook to another application (in this case, SimpleText), select the item and drag it to the desktop.

6. Mac OS converts the image into a clipping file—in this case, the name of the file is **Sample Image (Converted Clipping)**. Double-click the clipping to view it.

If you use Scrapbook to store a lot of data, you may eventually need to increase the amount of memory allocated to the Scrapbook application as the Scrapbook file grows larger. For more information about how to increase application memory, see Part 10, "Maintaining Your iMac," Task 12, "Increasing Application Memory."

Task 10: Using Sherlock

Using Sherlock, you can find files on any hard drive or network server, or you can index your hard drive so that you can search it (Sherlock can search a 4GB hard drive in about 90 seconds). If you have Internet access, you can download Sherlock plug-ins for several Internet sites so that you can search the Internet quickly before you actually log on to it.

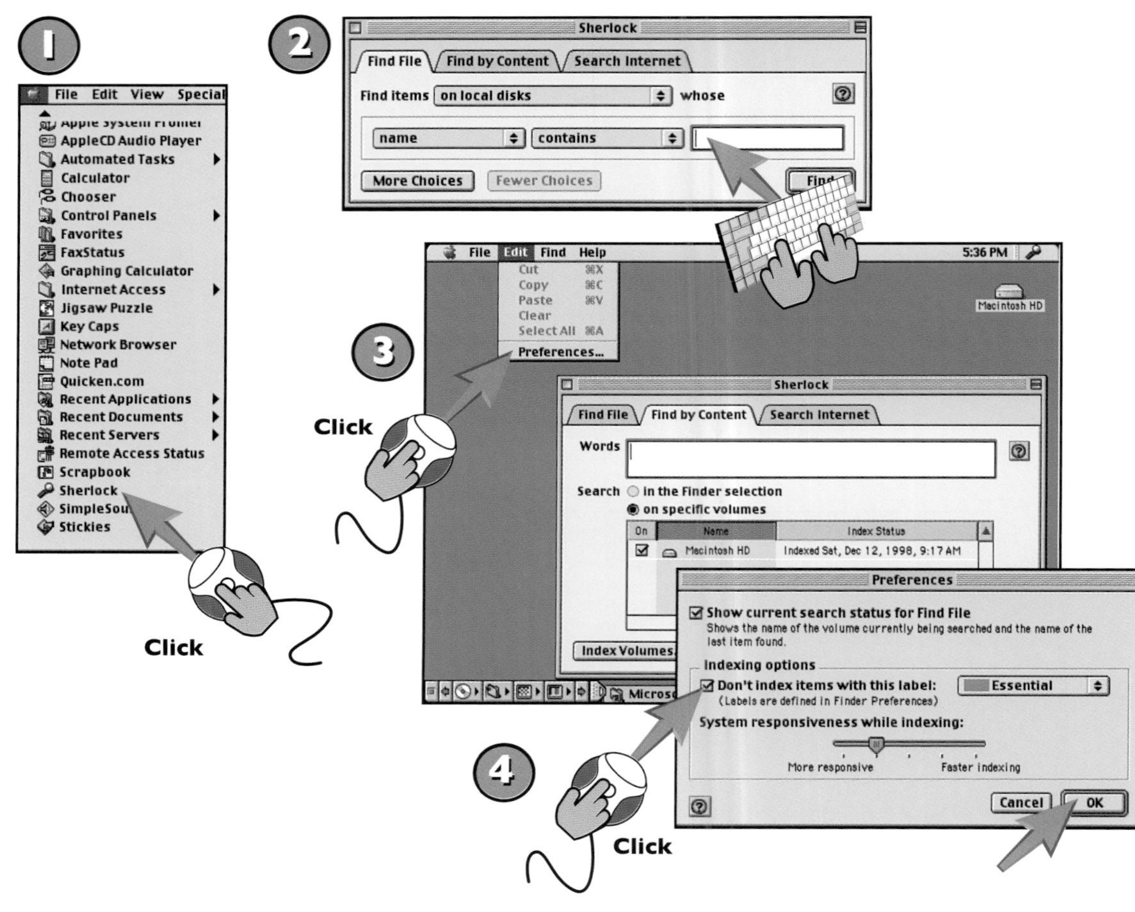

✓ You can save and open search criteria with Sherlock. Click **File** and choose **Open Search Criteria** to open any previously saved search criteria.

✓ You can adjust the speed of Sherlock's search. To do so, open Sherlock, click the **Edit** menu, and choose **Preferences**. Adjust the **System responsiveness while indexing** slider to allow for more speed or more accuracy when Sherlock is searching.

1. Click the **Apple** menu and choose **Sherlock**.

2. To look for a file or folder, type one or two words found in the file or folder's name into the text field in the **Find File** tab.

3. Click the **Find by Content** tab. Click **Edit**, and choose **Preferences**.

4. Click the **Don't index items with this label** check box, and choose the label you want excluded from the index. Click **OK**.

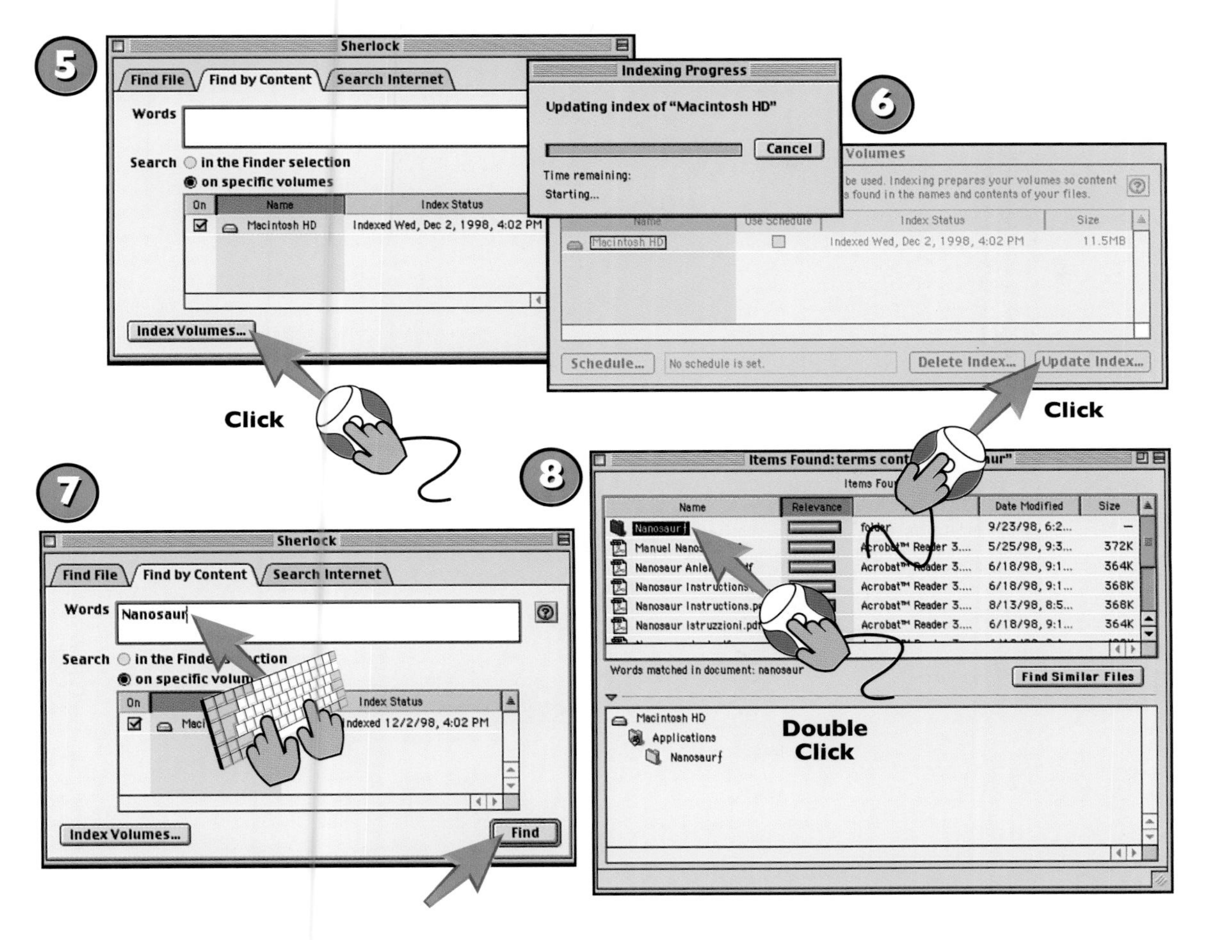

Click the **Index Volumes** button, then click either **Create** or **Update** depending on your needs (I've clicked **Update**).

Click the **Update Index** (or **Create Index**) button. A dialog will keep you apprised of the progress.

Once the indexing is complete, type the word (or words) you want to search for in the **Words** text field, and click **Find**.

View the search results in the **Items Found** window. Double-click any item to open it.

You can display the status of your search in the Find File window. Click the check box for Show current search status for Find File in the Sherlock Preferences window to activate this feature.

For more information about searching for a file or folder, see Task 6, "Finding Files and Folders with Sherlock" in Part 5, "Working with Disks, Folders, and Files."

Task 11: Using SimpleSound

Your iMac provides a variety of multimedia software, such as SimpleSound and SimpleText, which enable you to add sound to presentations or documents you create on your iMac. This task shows you how to use SimpleSound to record your own sounds and add them to your **System** file to use as an alert sound. (You can follow these steps with SimpleText, too.)

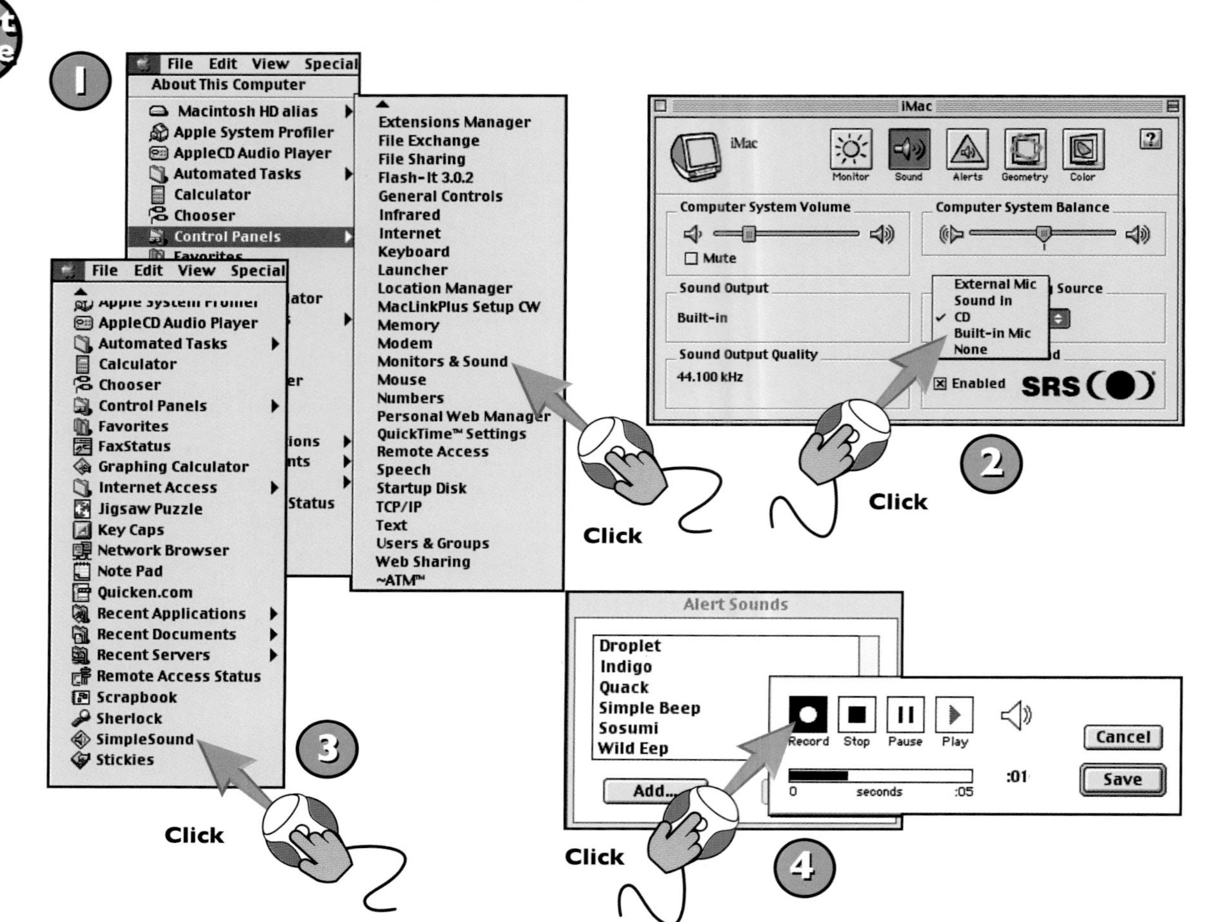

1. Click the **Apple** menu, choose **Control Panels,** then select **Monitors & Sound**.
2. Open the pop-up menu in the **Sound Monitoring Source** area and choose **Built-in Mic**.
3. Click the **Apple** menu and choose **SimpleSound**.
4. Click the **Add** button, then click the **Record** button to record a sound.

Your iMac has a built-in microphone, located above the iMac screen, that you can use to record sounds.

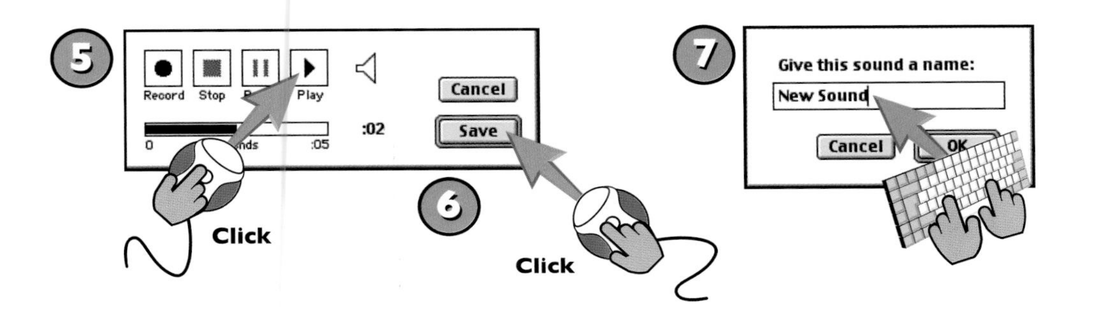

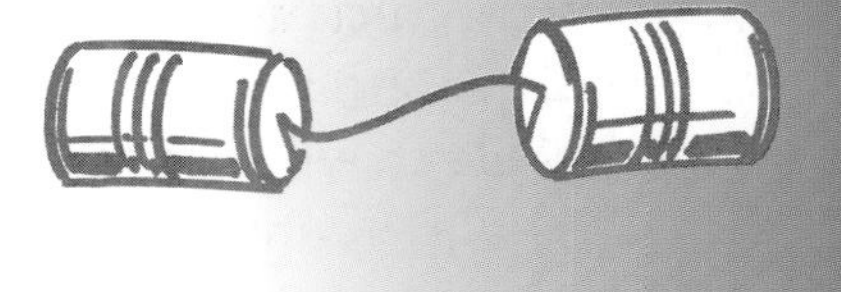

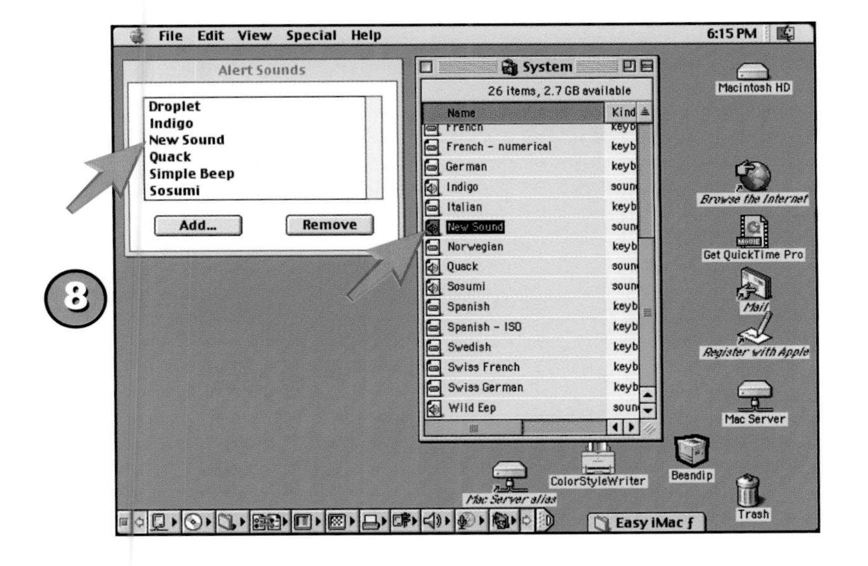

5. Click the **Play** button to listen to your recording.

6. Click the **Save** button if you want to save the sound.

7. Name the sound.

8. The new sound appears in the list of alert sounds.

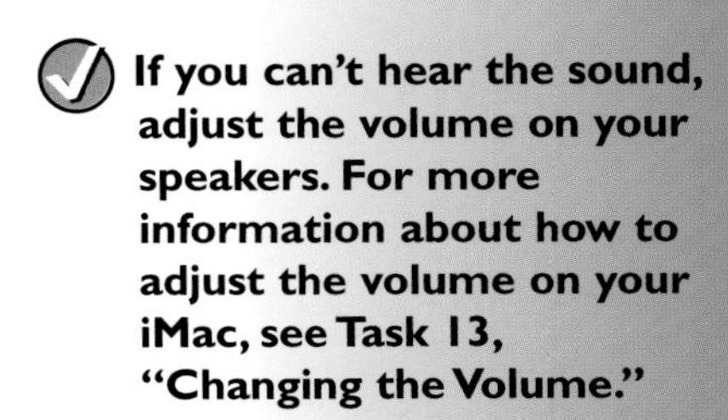

If you can't hear the sound, adjust the volume on your speakers. For more information about how to adjust the volume on your iMac, see Task 13, "Changing the Volume."

Open the System file to move or copy the sound for use with an application or document.

Task 12: Playing an Audio CD

Start Here

In addition to being able to play back sound files, you can play audio CDs using the Apple CD Audio player. This means you can listen to the background music of your choice as you work.

- If you insert a CD, it will start automatically. Settings for this feature are located in the **QuickTime Settings** control panel.
- You can also control the Audio CD Player controls from the CD strip module in the control strip.
- If you want to continuously play an audio CD, click the **Repeat** button.
- You can add song titles to each audio CD by clicking the green arrow at the bottom left of the **Apple CD Audio Player** window. Select any track, and type its title. iMac will remember the track information the next time you play the audio CD.

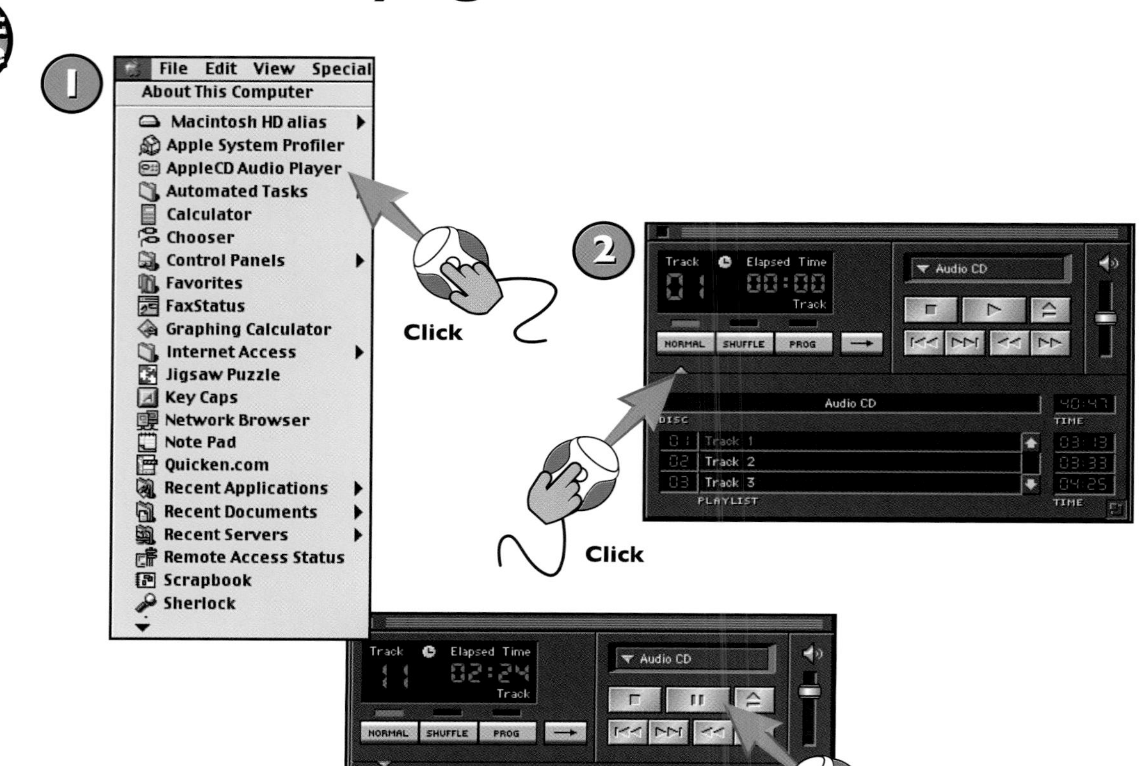

1. Click the **Apple** menu and choose **Apple CD Audio Player**, and then insert an audio CD into your iMac's CD-ROM drive.
2. Click the arrow at the bottom of the **Apple CD Audio Player** window to view the audio tracks on the audio CD.
3. Click **Play** to start the audio CD. Click **Pause** if you want to pause the audio CD.

Task 13: Changing the Volume

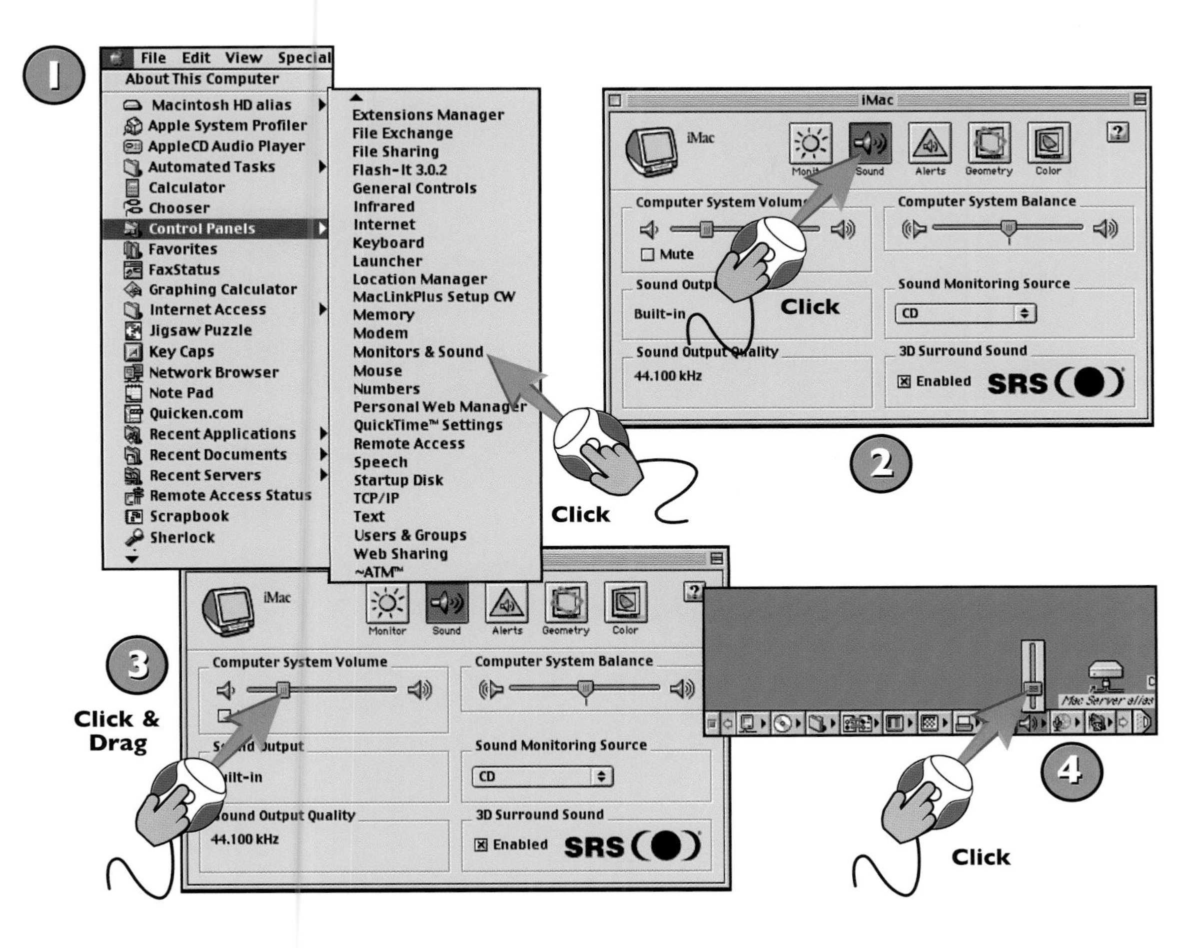

1. Click the **Apple** menu, choose **Control Panels**, then select **Monitors & Sound**.
2. Click the **Sound** button in the **Monitors & Sound** control panel.
3. Click and drag the volume slider to set the volume level on your iMac.
4. Click the **Volume** module in the control strip then choose the volume level you want.

To adjust the volume of your iMac, you can choose from several different software controls. You can control the sound volume with the sound module in the control strip or the **Volume** slider in the **Monitors & Sound** control panel.

- You can move the control strip to the left or right side of your screen by holding down the **Option** key and clicking and dragging the right end of the control strip.
- If you are playing an audio CD, you can adjust the volume control in the Apple Audio CD Player application in addition to the volume controls in the control strip and **Monitors & Sound** control panel.
- Click the **Mute** check box in the Sound section of the **Monitors & Sound** control panel to turn off sound output on your iMac.

Task 14: Playing a Media File

Media files are a combination of text, graphics, sounds, video, and animations. As computers take more and more advantage of the multimedia features of your iMac, you will find more media files for your use. For instance, your iMac provides some sample media files. To play these presentations, you can use Movie Player.

The Internet includes many types of media files you can use with your iMac. For information on browsing the Internet, see Part 2, "Connecting to Online Services and the Internet."

Be sure file sharing and virtual memory are turned off when playing a movie with Movie Player. Movie playback performance will be slower with either turned on.

You can create your own media files with Movie Player by paying a nominal registration fee to Apple.

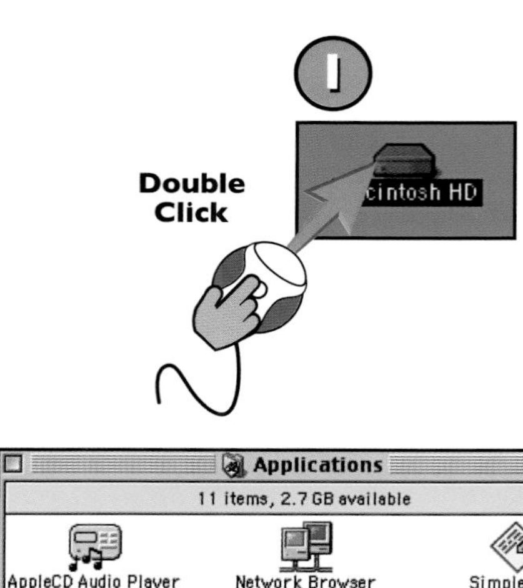

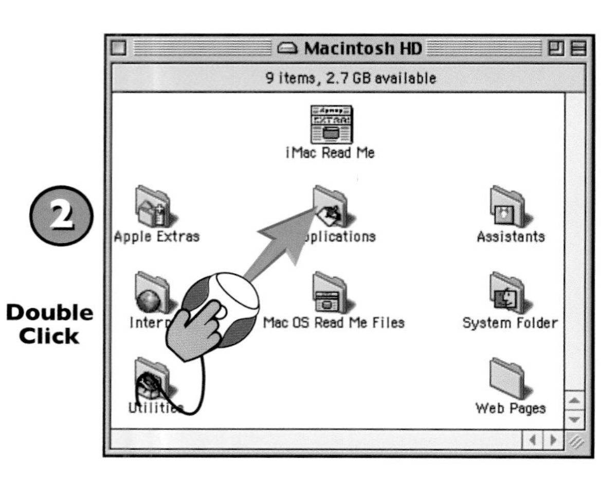

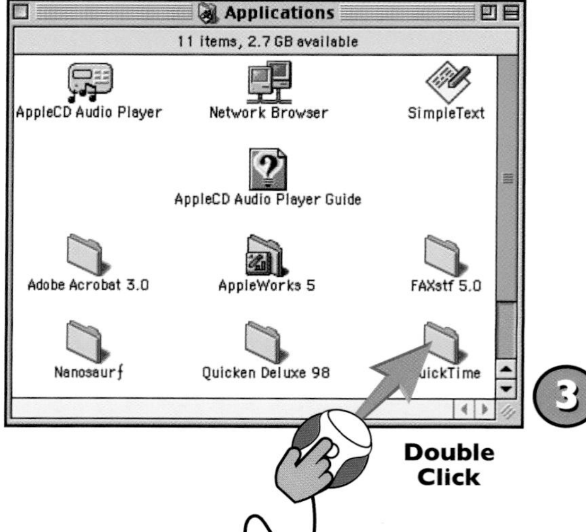

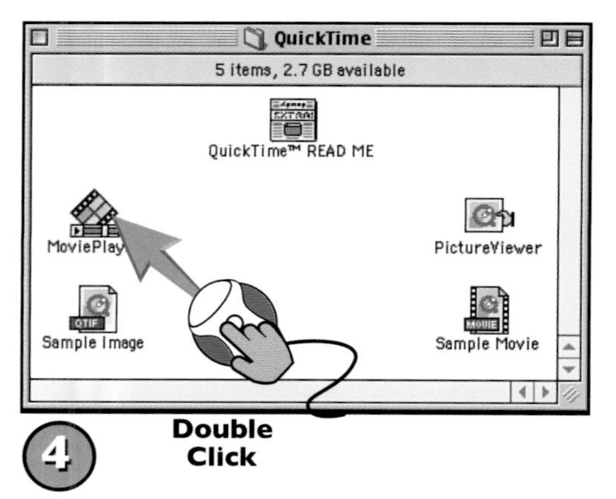

1. Double-click the hard drive icon.
2. Double-click the **Applications** folder.
3. Double-click the **QuickTime** folder.
4. Double-click the **Movie Player** icon.

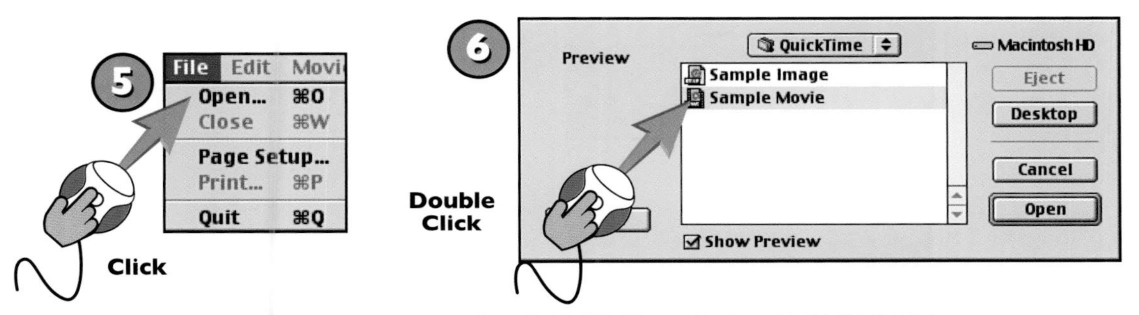

5. Click **File** and choose **Open**.

6. Double-click the **Sample Movie** file.

7. Click on the **Play** button in MoviePlayer.

- Click the **Speaker** icon to set the volume level of the movie.
- Click the **Pause** button to pause the movie.
- Click the **Step Forward** or **Step Backward** buttons to move a single frame forward or backward in the movie.
- Resize the movie by dragging the **Grow** box of the movie window.

Task 15: Editing a QuickTime Movie Using Movie Player

Movie Player is one of several media players Apple includes with Mac OS. Movie Player, which works with QuickTime (Apple's multimedia technology), enables your iMac to open, view, and edit virtually any kind of media file created by computers today.

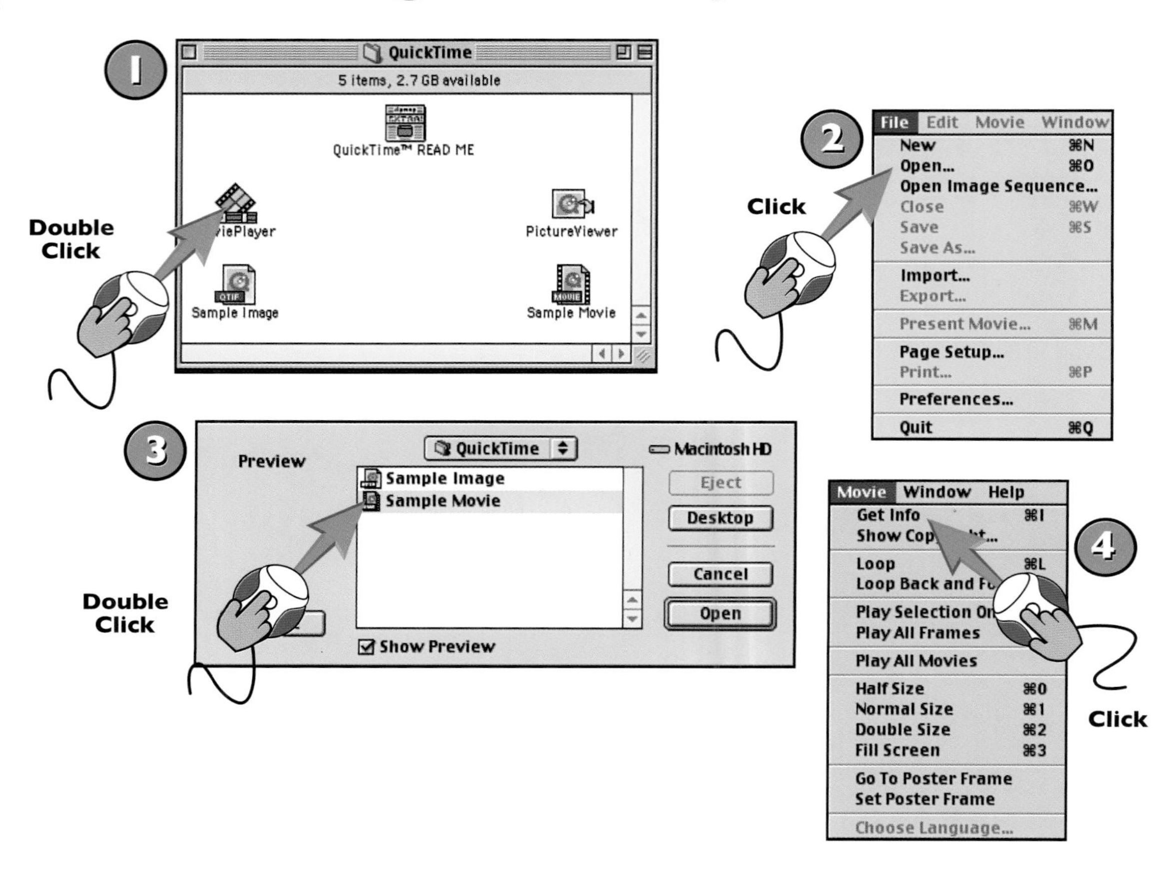

- You need to have a registered copy of Movie Player in order to use the editing features covered in this task. You can see whether Movie Player is registered by opening the **QuickTime Settings** control panel. Click the pop-up menu and choose Registration. If Movie Player is not registered, click the **Register Online** button to register Movie Player with Apple.

- You can edit audio and video tracks with Movie Player.

1. Double-click the **Movie Player** icon in the **QuickTime** window (see the last task if you need help reaching this window).
2. Click the **File** menu and choose **Open**.
3. Double-click the **Sample Movie** file.
4. Click the **Movie** menu and choose **Get Info.**

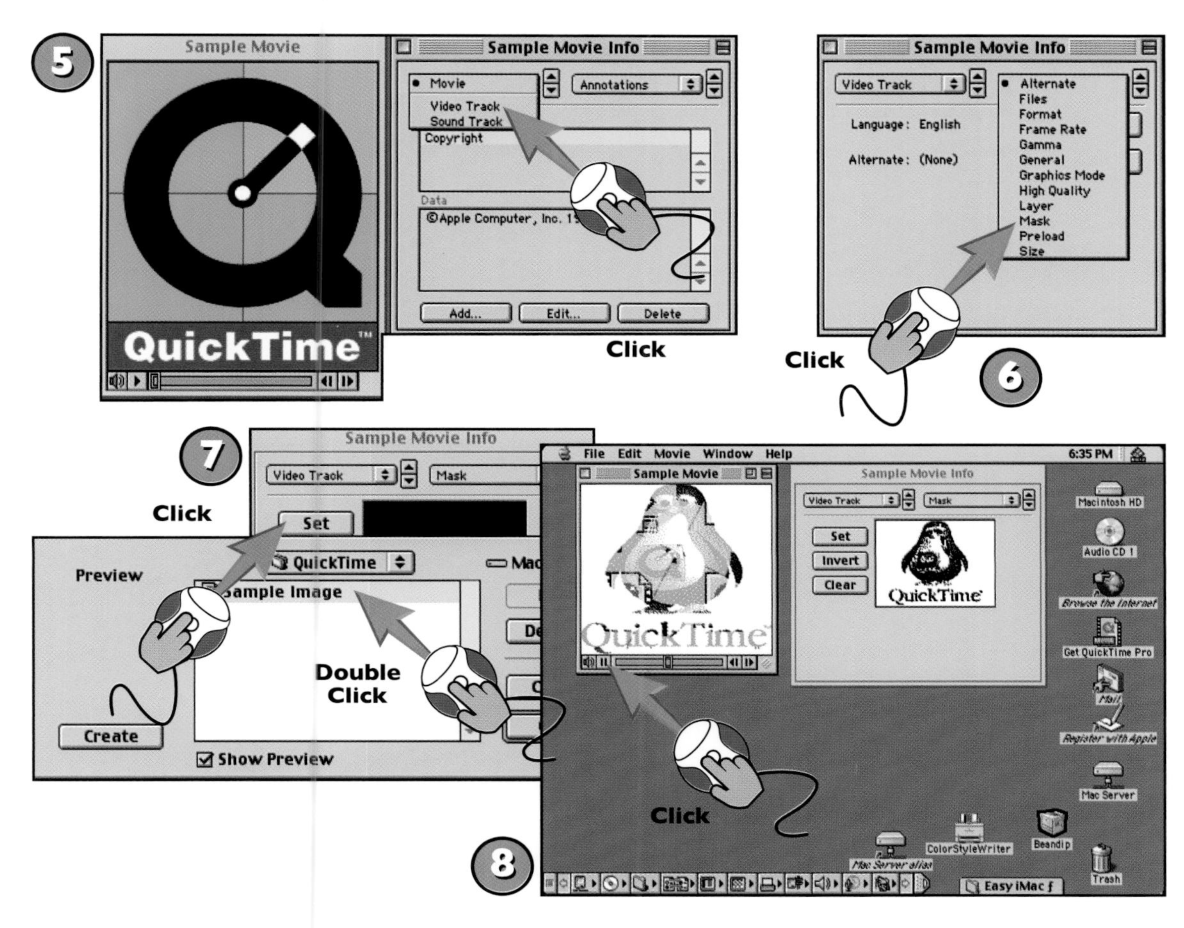

5. Click the left pop-up menu and choose **Video Track**.

6. Click the right pop-up menu and choose **Mask**.

7. Click the **Set** button and double-click the **Sample Image** file.

8. Click the **Play** button. Notice that the penguin image is now a part of each frame of the QuickTime sample movie.

Movie Player can convert most media files to its own QuickTime file format. It can also compress a file to optimize playback performance over the Internet.

If you are editing large video or movie files, be sure you have enough hard disk space available to work with the file.

Task 16: Using Calculator and Graphic Calculator

Start Here

If you need to perform a quick calculation, use the calculator application included with your iMac. You can add, subtract, multiply, divide, and more with this tool. If you want to graph more complex mathematical equations, you can use the graphing calculator.

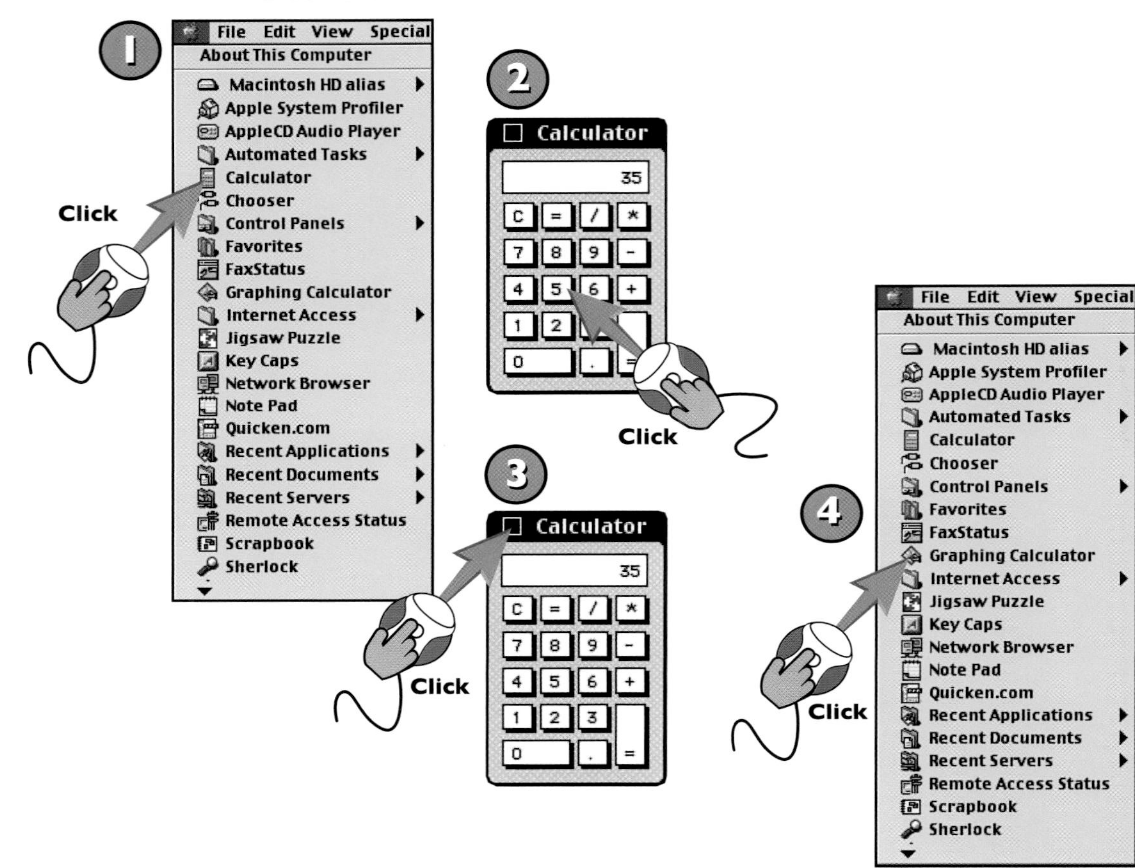

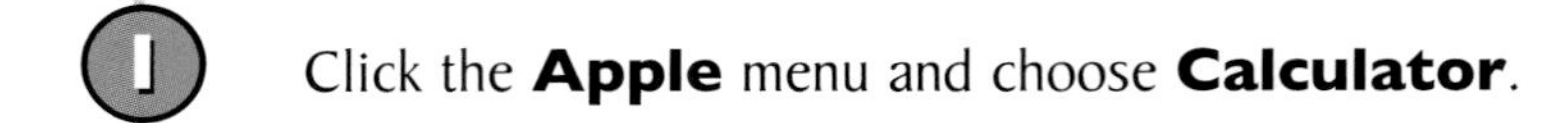

1. Click the **Apple** menu and choose **Calculator**.
2. Click the buttons on the calculator to enter an equation. (You can also use the keyboard to enter an equation.)
3. When you are finished, click the **Close** button.
4. Click the **Apple** menu and choose **Graphing Calculator**.

✓ **The graphing calculator has a built-in demo. To run the demo, click the Demo menu and choose Full Demo. Run the demo to review features such as 2D and 3D graphing and animation.**

✓ **You can cut and paste or drag and drop images onto the 3D graphing window of the graphing calculator.**

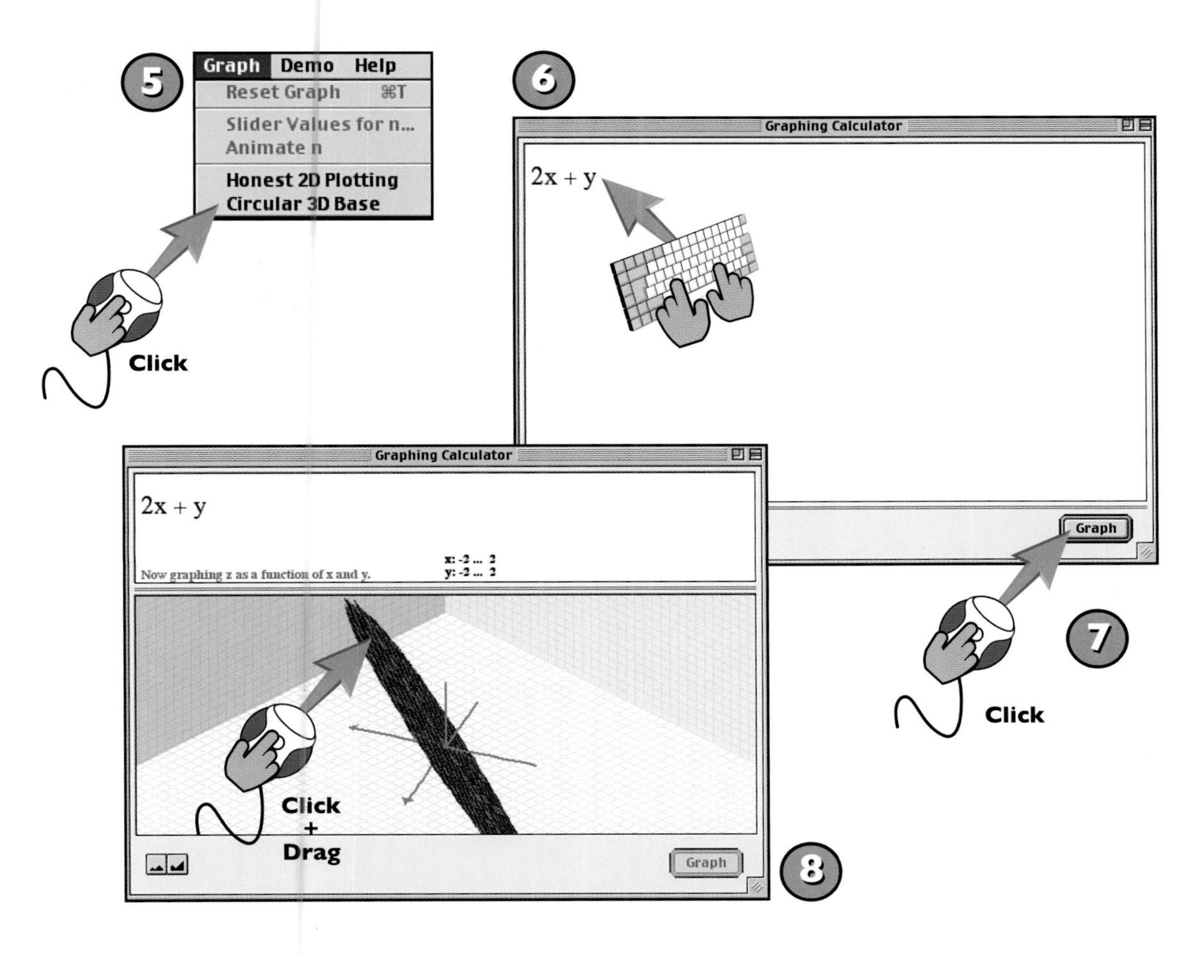

5 Click the **Graph** menu and choose **Circular 3D Base**.

6 Type a mathematical equation.

7 Click the **Graph** button.

8 Click the 3D animation to speed up or slow down the rotation speed of the 3D image.

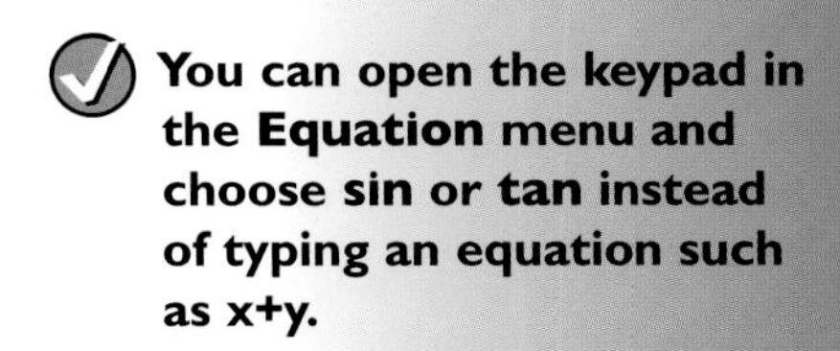

You can open the keypad in the Equation menu and choose sin or tan instead of typing an equation such as x+y.

Press the Option key while dragging the 3D animation to move the 3D grid.

Task 17: Using Chooser

If your iMac is on a network, or if you have a printer connected to your iMac, you will need to use the Chooser application. Chooser enables you to select a network server or printer to work with your iMac. You can also use the Network Browser in Task 18, "Using the Network Browser," to work with network servers connected to your iMac.

✓ For more information about printing with Chooser, see Part 6, "Printing with Mac OS."

✓ You can activate AppleTalk from Chooser, or from the **AppleTalk** control panel. Click the **Apple** menu and choose **Control Panels**, and then choose **AppleTalk** to open the **AppleTalk** control panel. If AppleTalk is inactive, click the **Yes** button when you are asked if you want to make AppleTalk active when closing the control panel.

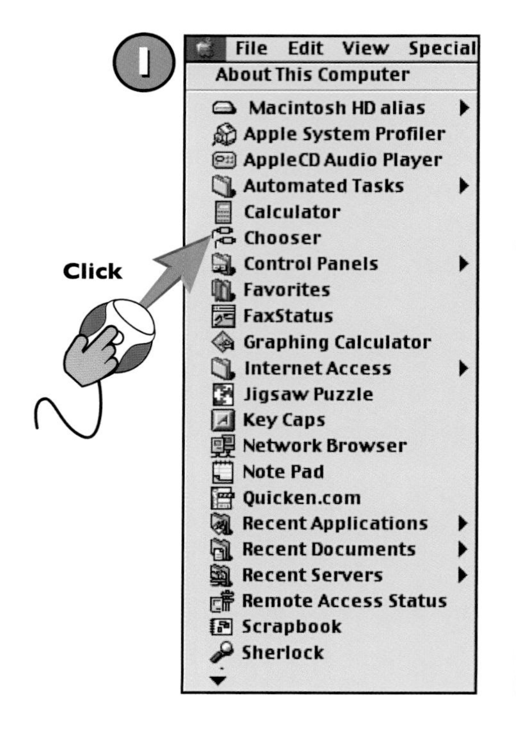

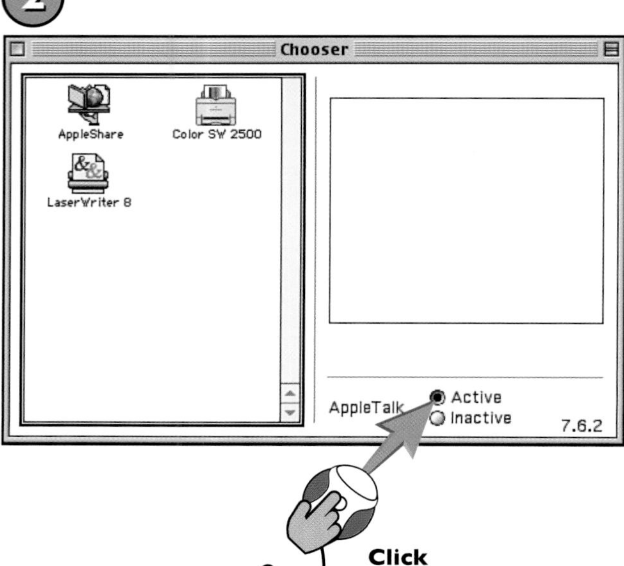

1. Click the **Apple** menu, then choose **Chooser**.

2. Click the **Active** radio button to turn AppleTalk on.

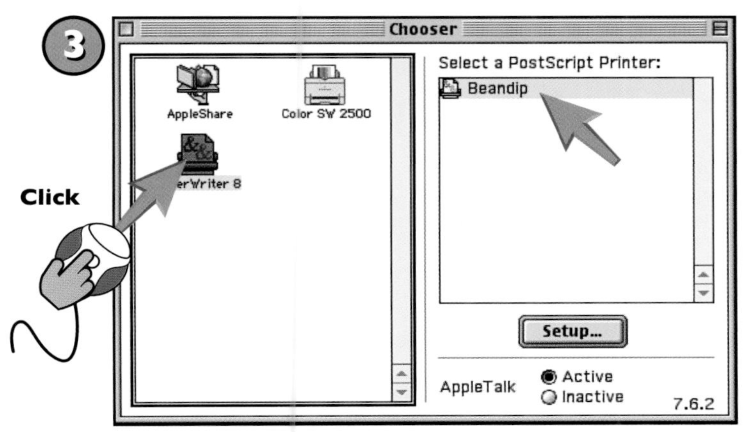

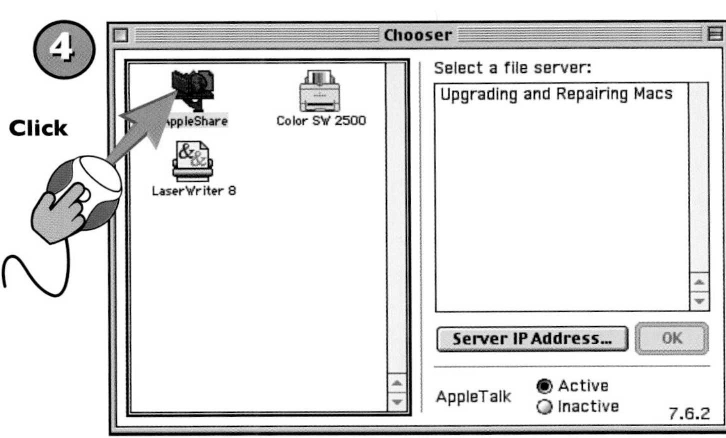

Click a printer driver to choose the default printer device you want to use. (If your network has only one printer, that printer will automatically be selected when you click the printer driver.)

Click the **AppleShare** icon to view any network servers available on your local network.

Task 18: Using the Network Browser

The network browser is a newer version of the network server feature in the Chooser application in Mac OS. The main window of the network browser shows any AppleShare servers on your network, including any Macintoshes that may have file sharing turned on. The network browser lets you view your network servers in a resizable window, and access any of your favorite or recent servers with a click of a button.

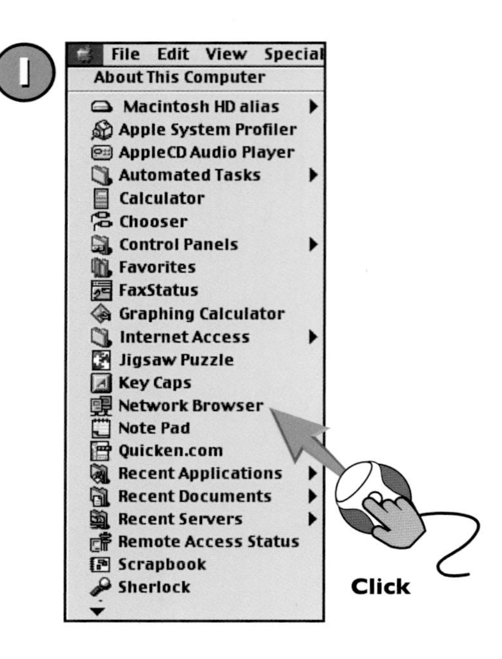

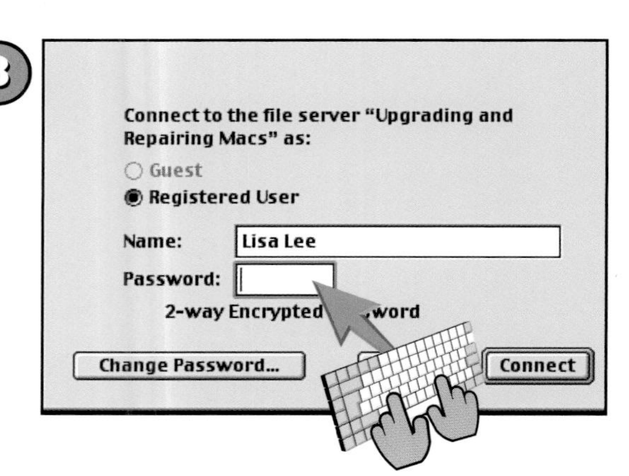

Mac OS 8.1 does not include the Network Browser application.

You can select a favorite network server by clicking the **Favorites** folder button.

Click the **Shortcuts** button to choose a previously selected network server.

1. Click the **Apple** menu and choose **Network Browser**.
2. Double-click the network server you want to use.
3. Enter your password to the server.

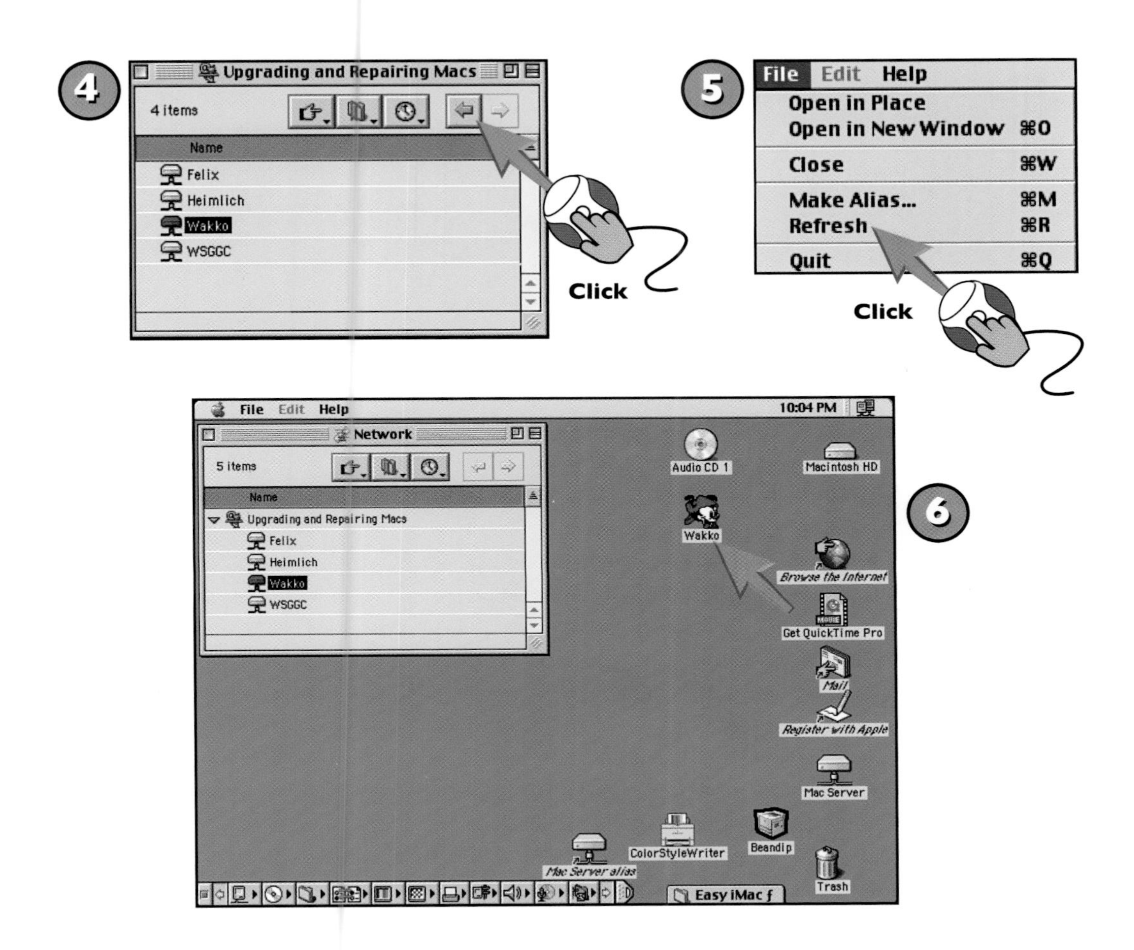

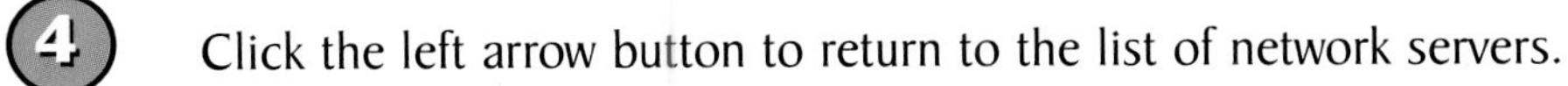

4 Click the left arrow button to return to the list of network servers.

5 Click **File** and choose **Refresh** to view any computers added to your local network. Double-click a network server to log in to it, and enter any login information.

6 After you enter the login and password information, the server icon will appear on your desktop. You can work with this icon as you would the **Macintosh HD** icon.

Use the Recents button to view and choose a network server you previously used.

To remove the network server from your desktop, select the network server icon and press Command + Y, or press the Ctrl key and choose Put Away, or drag the server icon to the Trash.

Task 19: Using the Control Strip

The fastest way to access some of the major Mac OS features on your iMac is to use one of the control strip modules. The control strip appears at the bottom left of your iMac's desktop, and is always the foremost window on your screen. Control strip modules let you control your audio CD player, turn file sharing on or off, or change the resolution of your monitor with a click of a button.

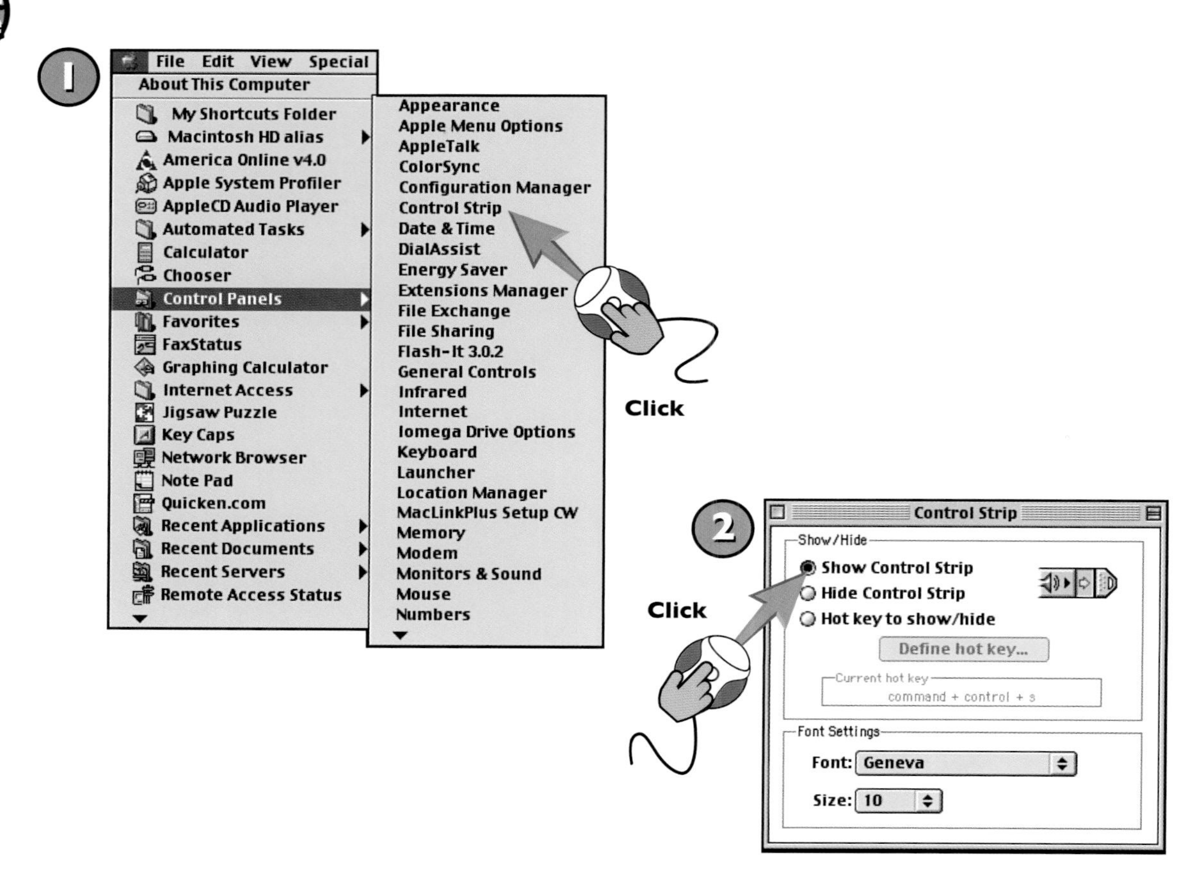

You can show or hide control strip modules by clicking the right tab of the **Control Strip** window.

You can adjust the viewable area of the Control Strip window by clicking and dragging the right tab to the left or right.

1. Click the **Apple** menu, choose **Control Panels**, and choose **Control Strip**.
2. Click the **Show Control Strip** radio button.

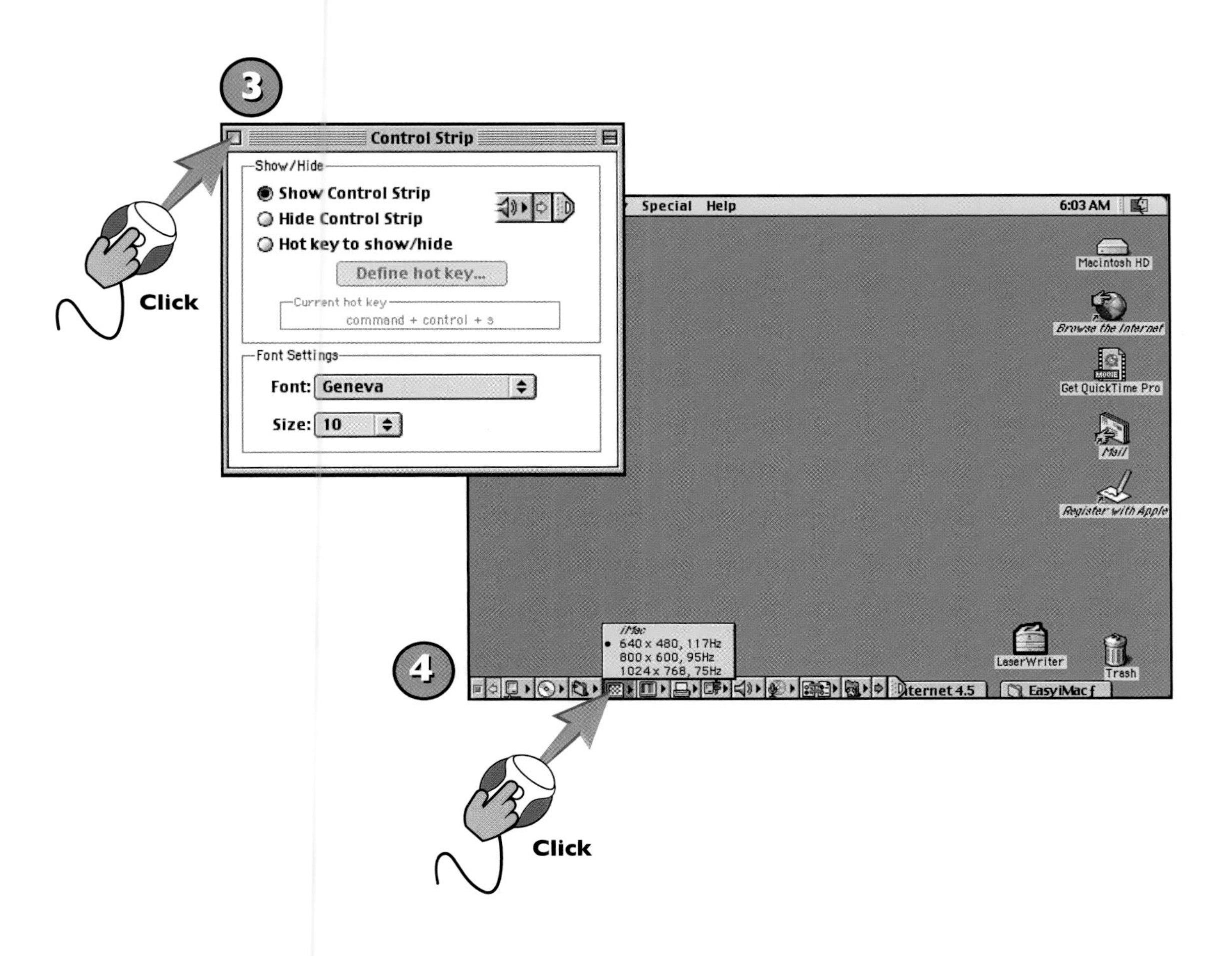

3. Close the **Control Strip** window.

4. Click any control strip module to change a setting (in this case, the resolution of your monitor).

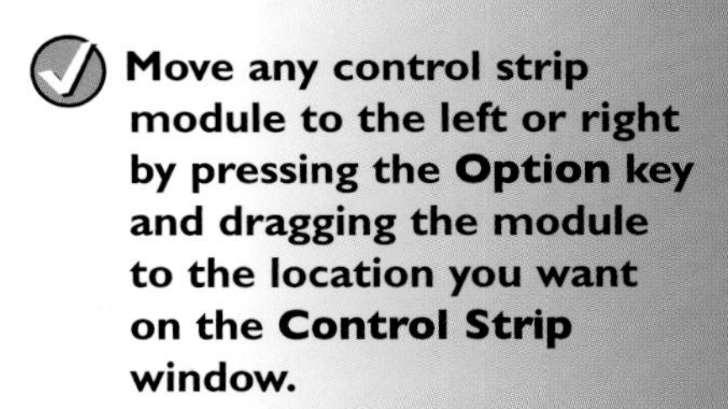

Move any control strip module to the left or right by pressing the Option key and dragging the module to the location you want on the Control Strip window.

You can position the control strip to the left or right of your screen by pressing the Option key and dragging the Control Strip window to either side of your screen.

PART 10

Maintaining Your iMac

This part introduces three general concepts that are useful for maintaining your iMac: identifying your iMac's System information, regular maintenance, and troubleshooting.

Tasks involved in identifying your system information include using Apple's System Profiler application, About This Computer, and the Get Info window. Backups, Disk First Aid, and Norton Utilities' Speed Disk are all tools you can use for regularly maintaining your iMac. Finally, troubleshooting tasks include using the Reset button, Extensions Manager, and how to perform a clean install of Mac OS.

To safeguard your data files, you should periodically make an extra copy, called a ***backup***. Although your iMac includes two CD-ROMs with a backup of the original software installed on your iMac, be sure to create at least one copy of any important folders or files just in case a digital disaster strikes.

Tasks

Task 1: Displaying Disk Information

You can display information about your disks, such as the size, the amount of space used, and the amount of free space. You can also choose a label for the hard drive icon; the label is used in the hard drive window's title bar to identify the disk.

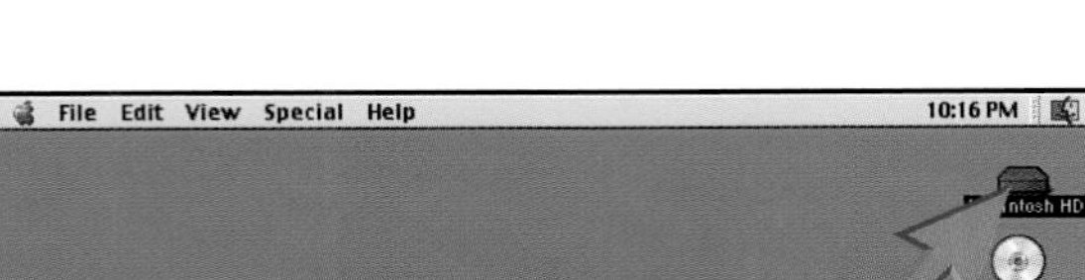

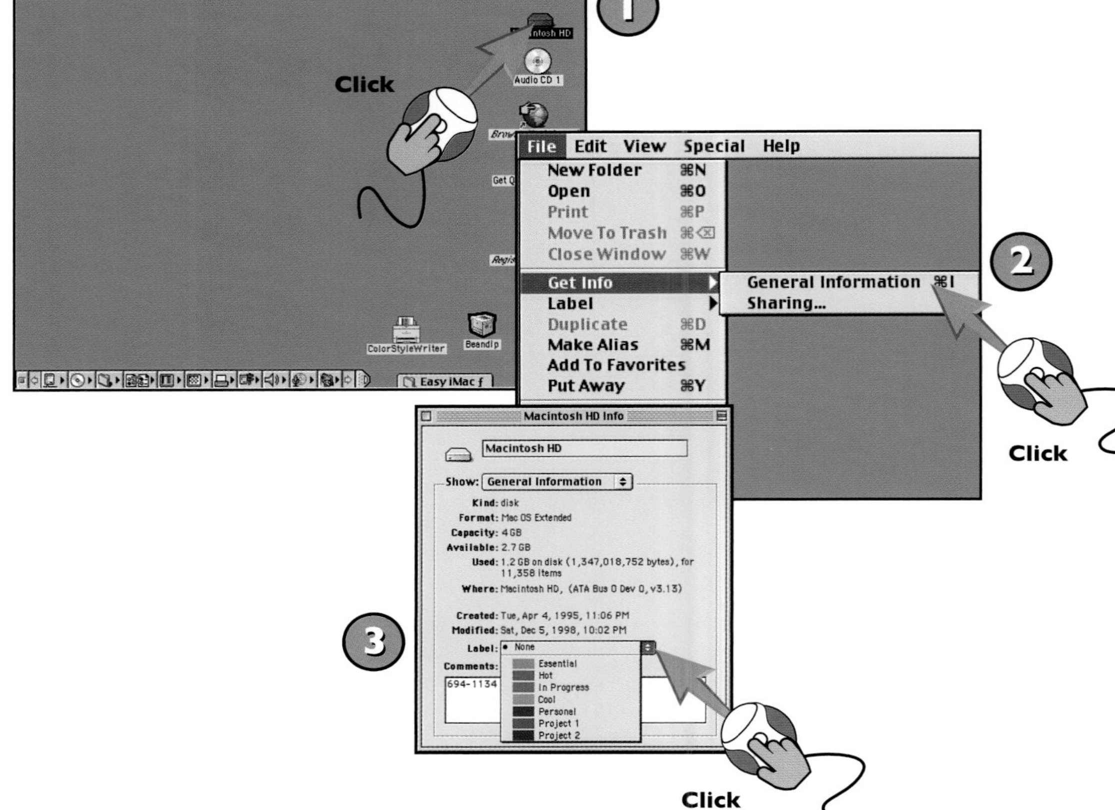

You can view the amount of free disk space in any **Finder** window title bar.

Your iMac is formatted with the Mac OS Extended File format. Although you can reformat the disk with the Mac OS Standard File format, sticking with the Extended File format is recommended.

1. Click the **Macintosh HD** icon.
2. Open the **File** menu, choose the **Get Info** command, and select **General Information**.
3. View the disk information in the **General Information** window. Click the **Label** pop-up menu to choose a label for the **Macintosh HD** icon.

End Task

Task 2: Scanning Your Disk for Errors

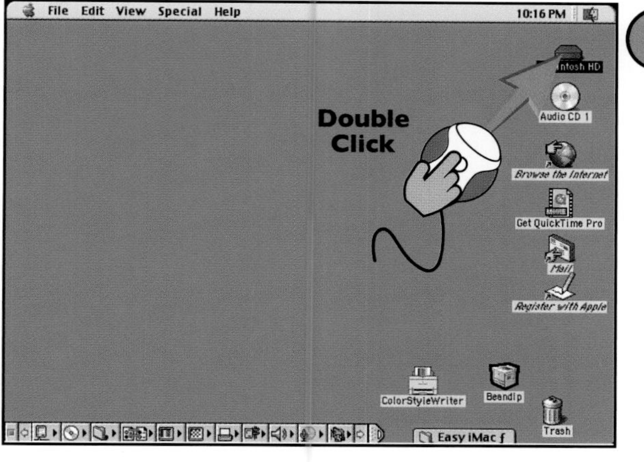

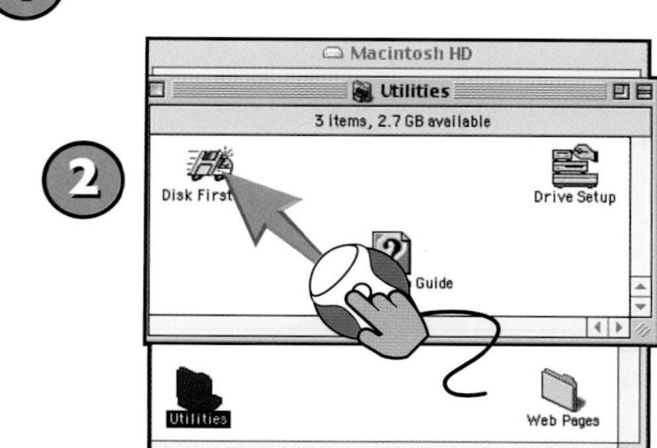

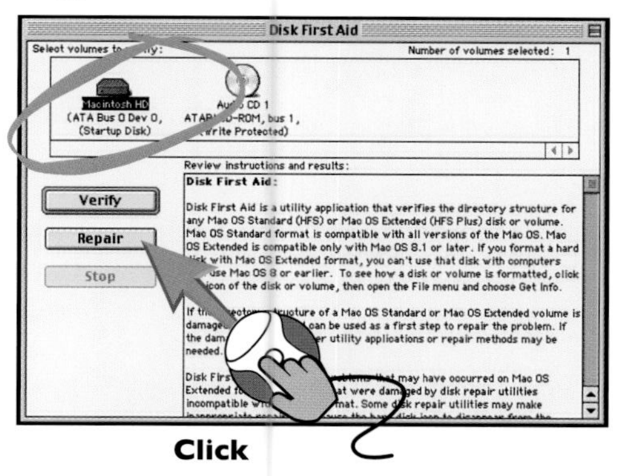

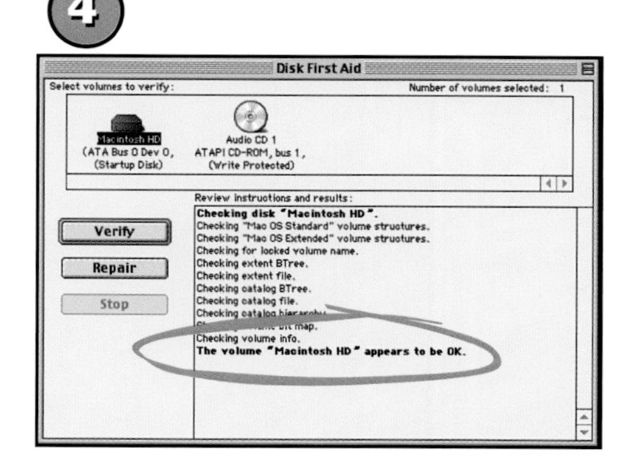

Sometimes parts of your hard disk get damaged, and you might see an error message when you try to open or save a file. Alternatively, you might notice lost or disarrayed data in some of your files. You can scan and repair the disk for damage using Apple's Disk First Aid application.

1. Double-click the **Macintosh HD** icon.
2. In the **Macintosh HD** window, double-click the **Utilities** folder. Then, in the **Utilities** window, double-click the **Disk First Aid** icon.
3. Click the icon representing your hard drive in the **Disk First Aid** window (in this case, **Macintosh HD**), and then click the **Repair** button.
4. If Disk First Aid says your hard disk appears to be OK, as is the case here, you're in the clear. If a problem is found, Disk First Aid will try to repair it.

If your iMac crashes, Mac OS will automatically run Disk First Aid when you start up your iMac. Any damage found will be repaired.

Better tools for scanning and repairing your hard disk include Symantec's Norton Utilities for Macintosh, version 4.0 or higher, TechTool Pro from Micromat, or Disk Warrior from Alsoft.

Task 3: Using the Reset Button

Start Here

As you use your iMac, you may encounter hardware or software incompatibilities that result in a crash. A *crash* is when your iMac unexpectedly stops working normally. It may freeze, or show a blank error message. Alternatively, you might be able to move the mouse, but not click anything onscreen.

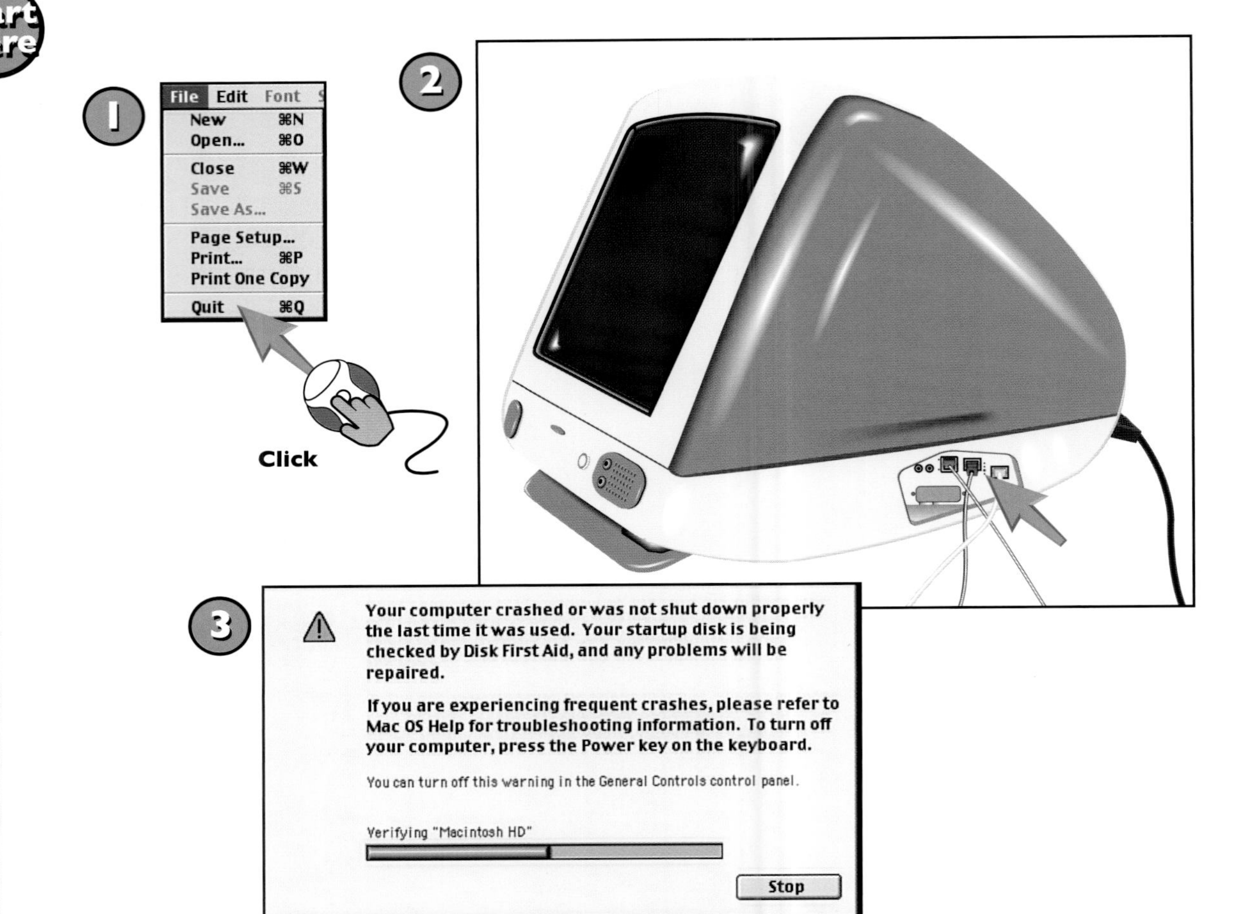

The **Reset** button is located inside the side panel of your iMac. If you do not want to use a paper clip, you can purchase a plastic button that you press to access the **Reset** button. It's called the iMac button from Joe Lee, available at http://www.imacbutton.com

Use the **Shut down** command in the **Special** menu whenever you can to power off your iMac. The **Reset** button should be used only if there is no other way to turn off your iMac.

1. If you can, quit any applications and save any open documents.
2. Use the tip of a paper clip to press the **Reset** button on the side of your iMac.
3. Your iMac will restart, and automatically run Apple's Disk First Aid software to verify there are no errors on the startup disk.

Task 4: Cleaning up Unnecessary Files

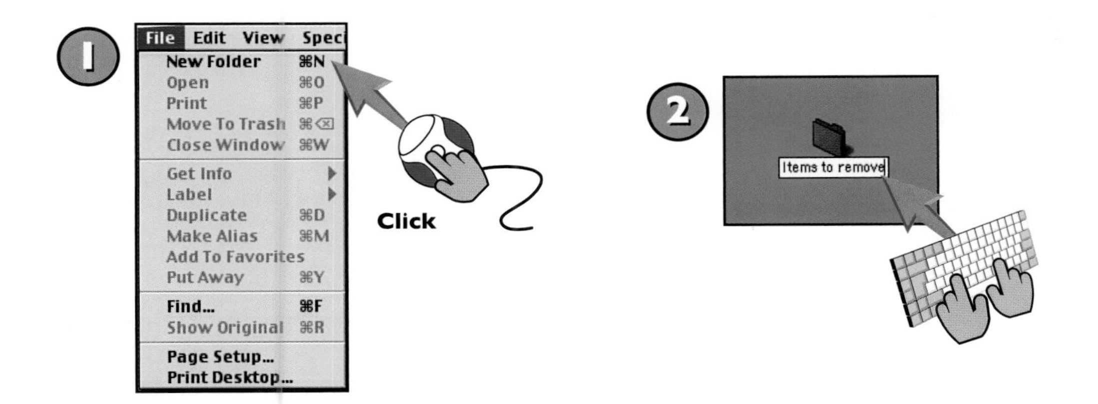

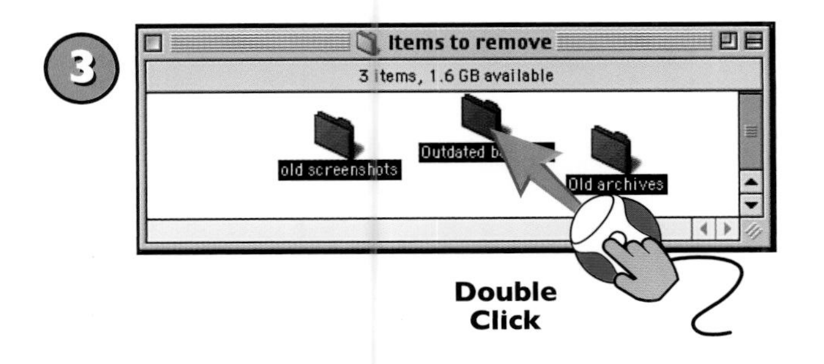

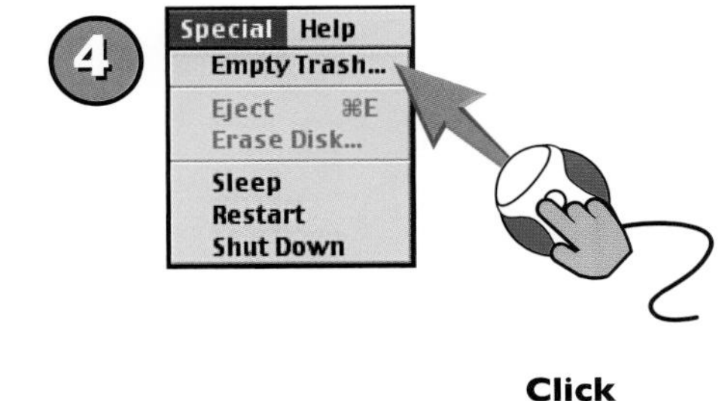

On your iMac, unnecessary files may be hogging your disk space. Applications such as Internet Explorer store temporary files that you can delete in the MS Internet Cache folder and America Online folder located in the System folder on your hard disk. The **Trash** also houses files that you have deleted, but are still kept in case you need them. You can easily get rid of these files and gain some disk space.

1. Click **File** and choose the **New Folder** command.
2. Name the folder **Items to remove**. For more information about naming folders, see Task 15 of Part 5.
3. Double-click the **Items to remove** icon to open its window, then drag any defunct files or folders on your hard disk to the **Items to remove** window.
4. Drag the **Items to remove** folder to the Trash, then open the **Special** menu and choose **Empty Trash**.

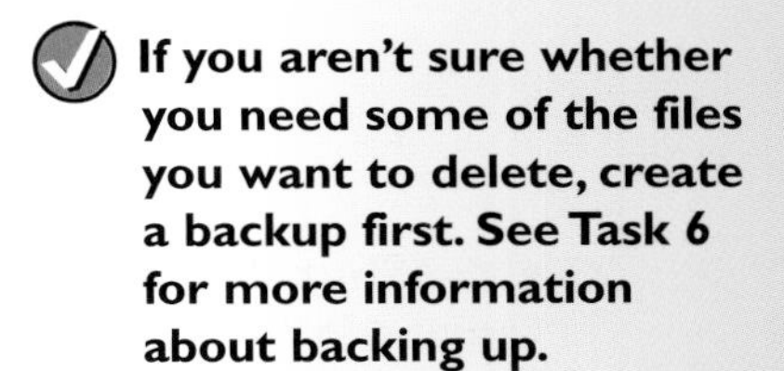

If you aren't sure whether you need some of the files you want to delete, create a backup first. See Task 6 for more information about backing up.

Be sure you don't need any of these files. Once they are deleted, you cannot get them back.

Task 5: Defragmenting a Disk

Start Here

When a file is stored on your hard drive Mac OS places as much of the file as possible in the first available space (called a *cluster*) on the hard drive, moves to the next cluster to store the next part of the file, and so on until the whole file is stored. Because this storage method fragments your disk files, you might find that, after a while, it takes a long time to open a file or start a program. To speed access to files and to help prevent problems with fragmented files, you can *defragment* your disk, putting files in clusters as close to each other as possible.

This task uses Norton Utilities 4.0 because Mac OS does not provide any software for defragmenting your hard disk.

Be careful when defragmenting. You might want to back up first. See Task 6 for information about backing up.

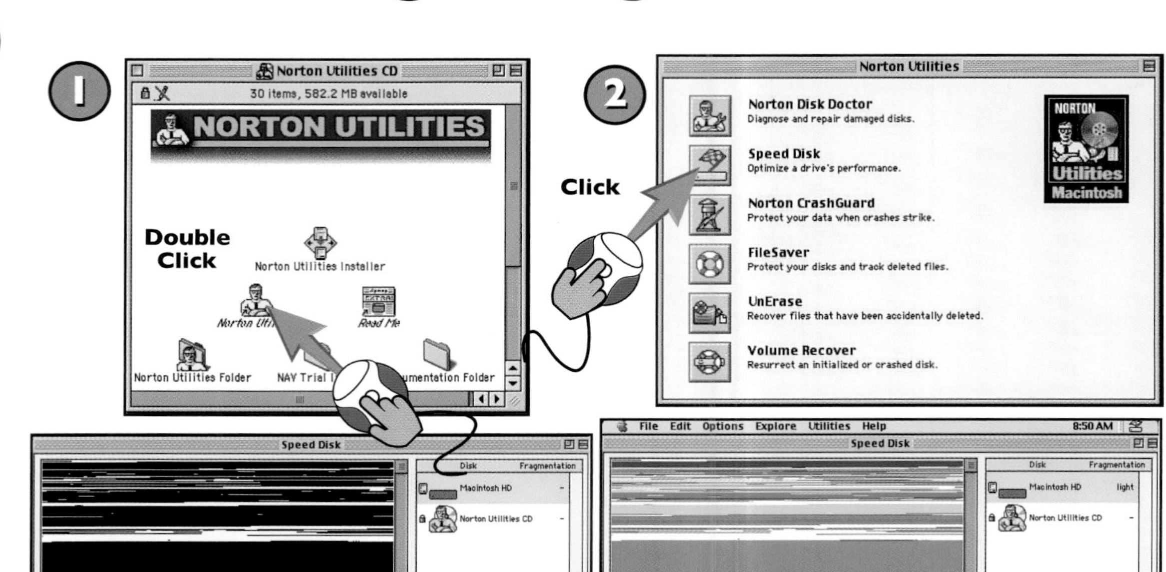

Insert the Norton Utilities CD, and double-click its icon on your desktop. Then double-click the **Norton Utilities** icon.

Click the **Speed Disk** icon in the **Norton Utilities** window.

After you click **OK** in the alert dialog, click the **Check** button to determine how fragmented your drive is.

Information about your hard disk, including fragmentation, appears in the lower portion of the window. Click **Optimize** to defragment your hard drive.

Task 6: Backing Up Files on Your iMac

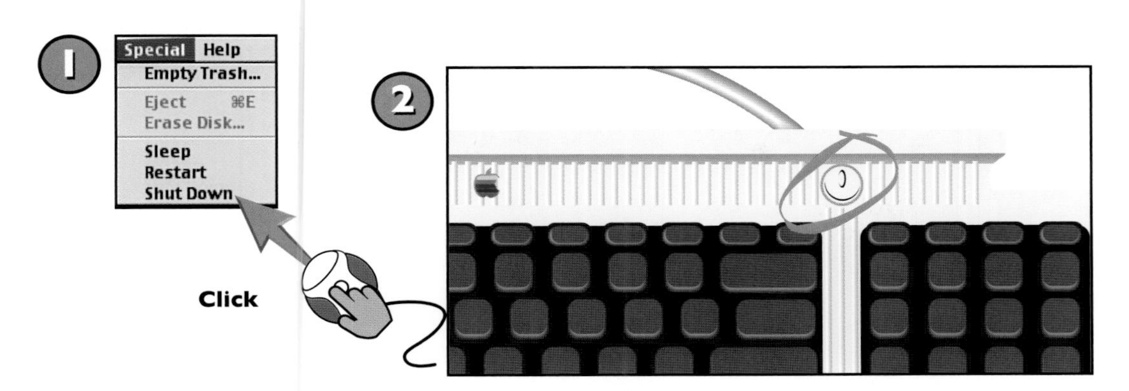

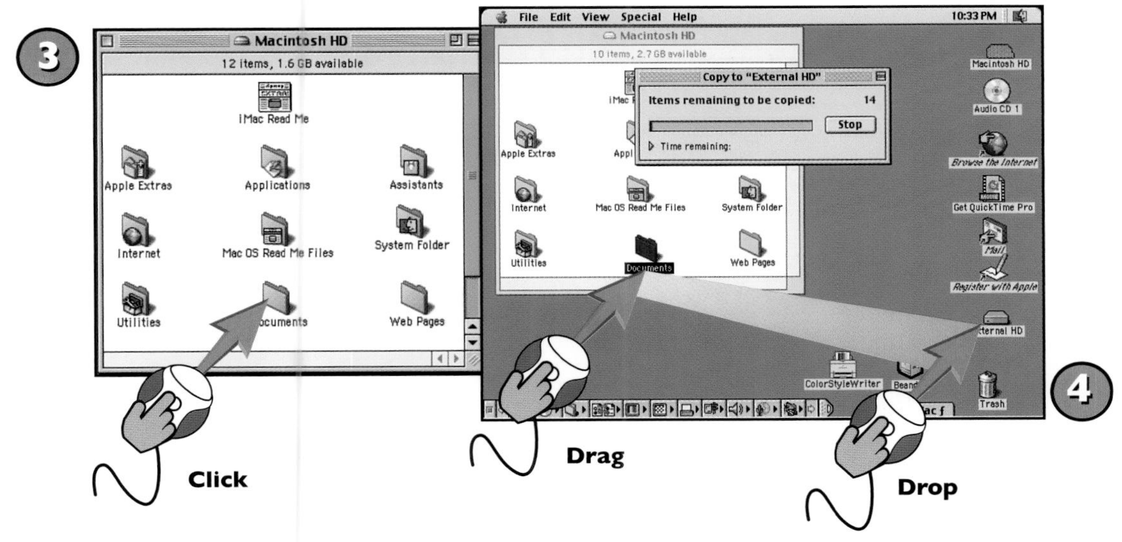

To safeguard your data, you should back up the files on your iMac. That way, if something happens to the original files, you can restore them with this extra copy.

It's a good idea to purchase an external drive, such as an Iomega Zip drive, to store backups of your files and folders. Zip disks store up to 100MB of files, almost ten times more than a floppy disk. Alternatively, if you plan on frequently backing up tons of information, you might want to purchase a tape backup system. This method is faster and more convenient than backing up to floppy disks or to a disk file.

1. Power off the iMac.
2. Connect an external hard drive to your iMac. Then power on the iMac.
3. Double-click the **Macintosh HD** icon and select any folders or files you want to back up.
4. Drag the folders or files to the external hard drive icon on your desktop. Mac OS copies the folders and files to the external disk drive.

If you are working on an important file—one you don't want to lose—you should make at least three backup copies of the file with at least one copy on an external disk such as a floppy, Zip disk, or a second hard drive.

Task 7: Restoring Backed-Up Files

If you ever face some cataclysmic digital disaster with your iMac, you'll be glad you took the time to back up your important files. This task shows you how to restore those files from the external drive on which the backup has been stored to your iMac's hard drive. However, you can similarly restore your backup from a floppy disk, network server, or removable medium.

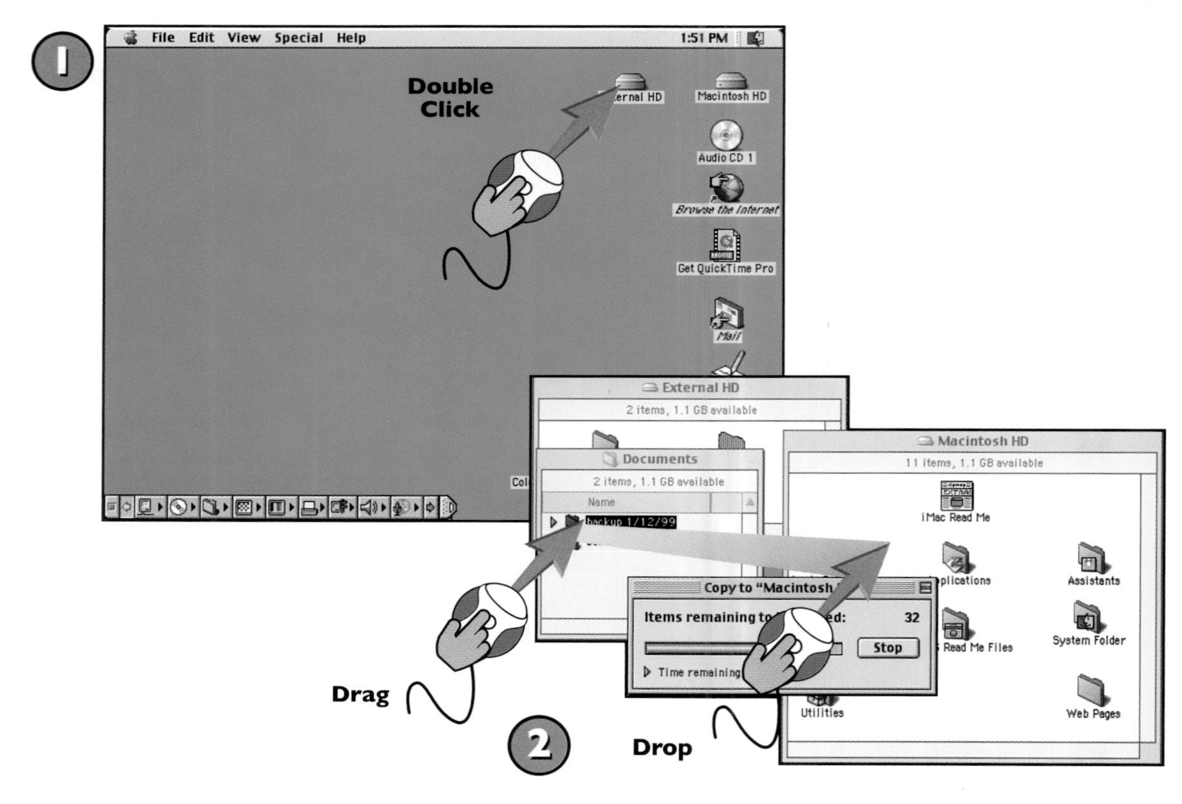

Even though you can access and work with the backed-up files on the second hard disk just as you would the internal disk on your iMac, it's still a good idea to go ahead and restore them to your system.

1. Double-click the icon representing your external drive to open its window.

2. Locate and select the files or folders that you want to restore in the external drive's window, and then drag them to the **Macintosh HD** icon.

Task 8: Restoring Your iMac's Software

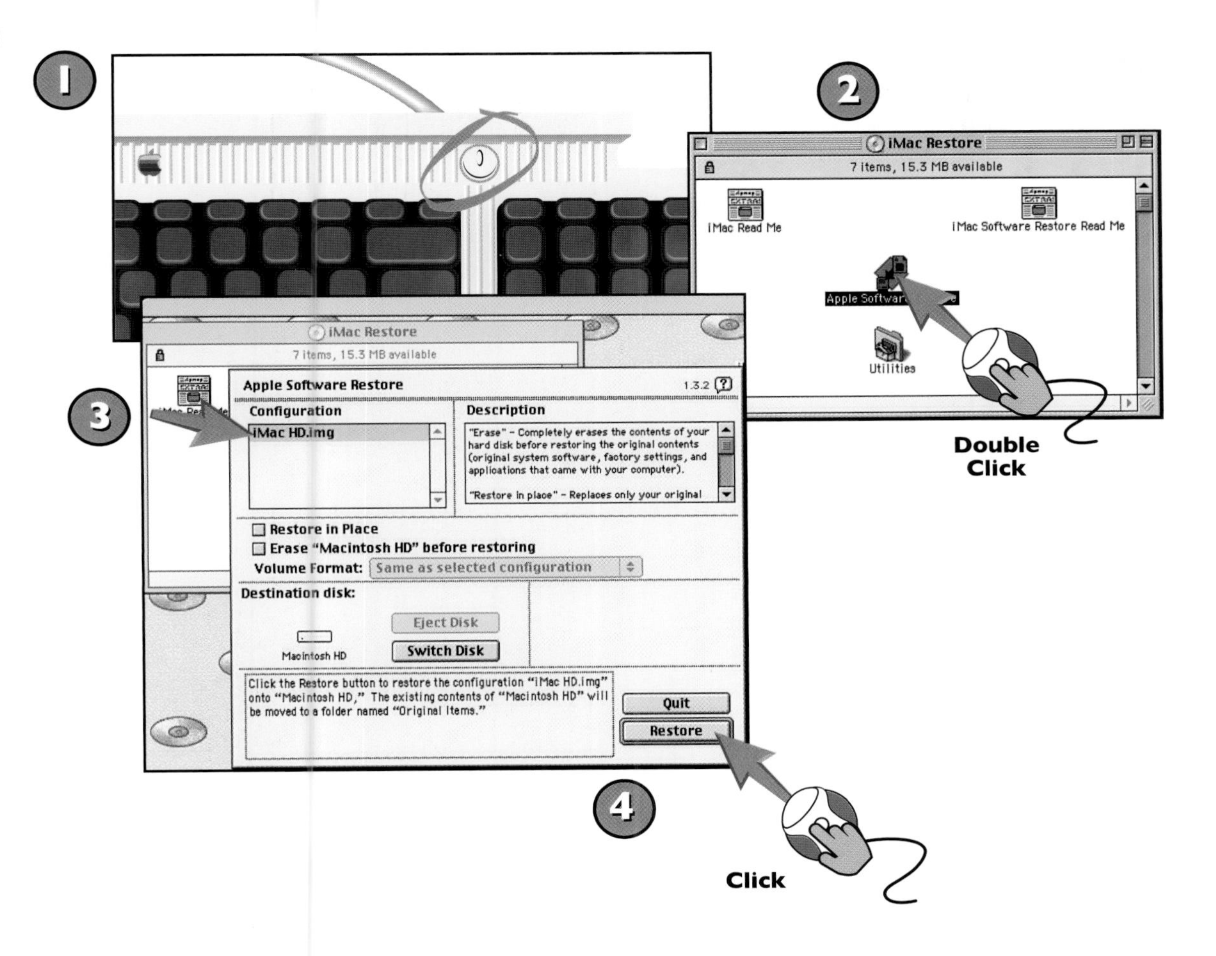

Along with your iMac comes a CD-ROM, called iMac Software Restore, that can restore the original software installed on your iMac in the event some disaster wipes your system clean (you'll find this CD in the book of CD-ROMs that came with your iMac).

✓ You can restore selected files from the iMac Software Restore CD. Simply double-click the iMac HD.img file in the Configuration list in the Apple Software Restore window (see step 2). Once the image mounts on your desktop, you can drag-copy any files or folders from the image file to your iMac's hard disk.

✓ If you use an application such as Retrospect Remote to back up your files, you also need to use the Retrospect application to restore a file.

1. Insert the iMac Software Restore CD-ROM, and then restart your iMac. Press and hold the **C** key during startup.
2. Double-click the **iMac Restore** icon on the desktop, and then double-click the **Apple Software Restore** icon in the **iMac Restore** window.
3. Click the **OK** button in the **Apple Software Restore** welcome dialog, and then review the settings in the **Apple Software Restore** main window.
4. Click the **Restore** button. Apple Software Restore will restore the files from the CD onto your hard drive.

Task 9: Formatting a Hard Disk

Formatting a hard disk is not a task you would perform for regular maintenance of your iMac. However, if you have an external drive, you may want to reformat it to erase all previous data. Be sure to create a backup of any hard drive before you format it. Formatting a hard disk permanently removes any data on the disk.

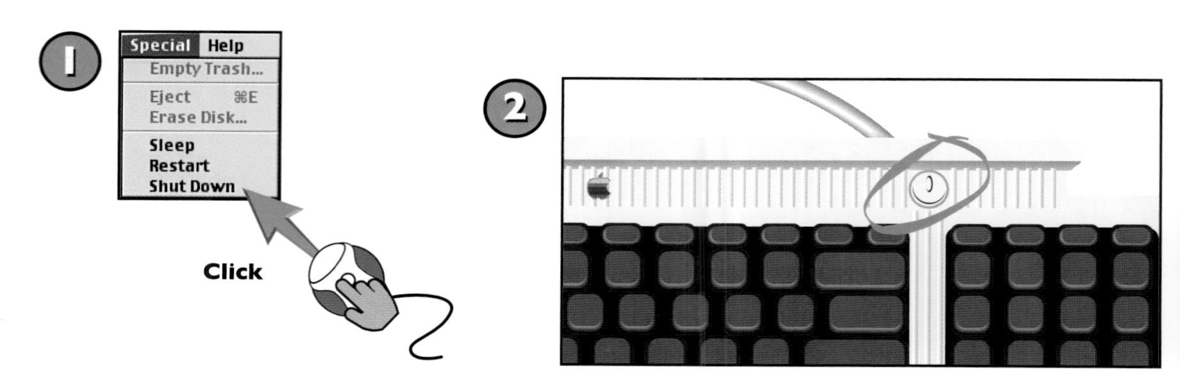

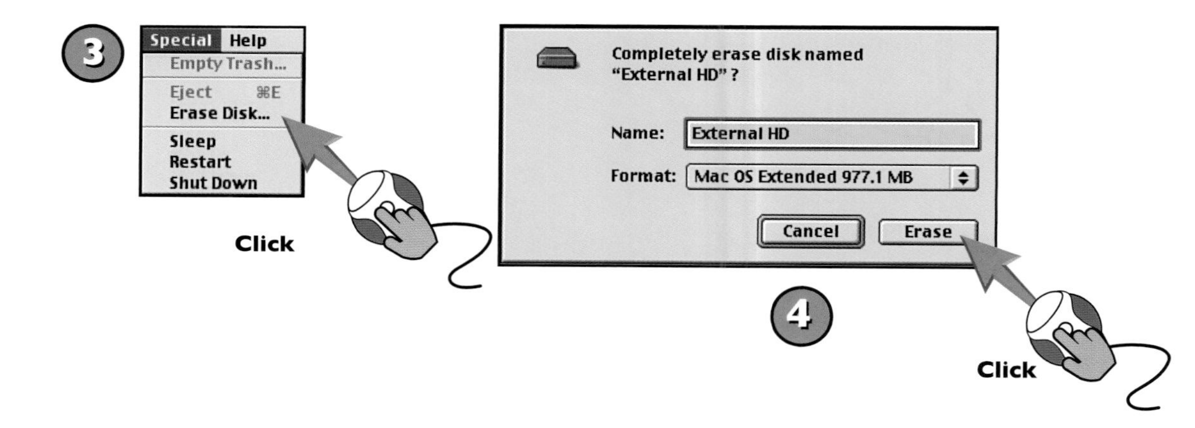

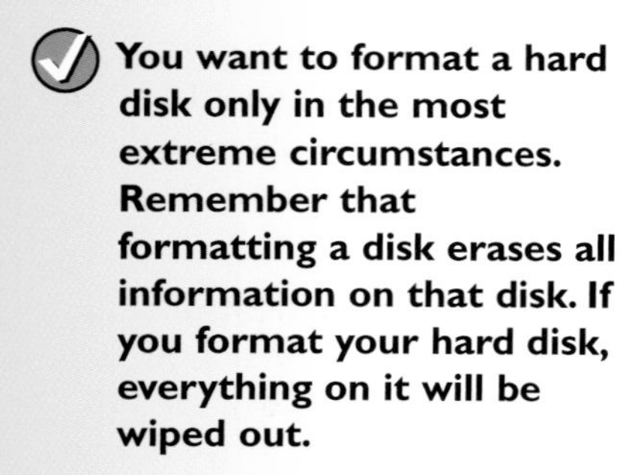

You want to format a hard disk only in the most extreme circumstances. Remember that formatting a disk erases all information on that disk. If you format your hard disk, everything on it will be wiped out.

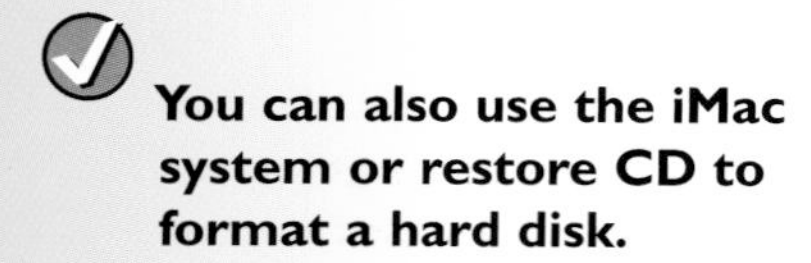

You can also use the iMac system or restore CD to format a hard disk.

1. Click **Special** and choose the **Shut Down** command to power off the iMac.
2. Once you've connected the external drive that you want to format to your iMac, power on your iMac.
3. The external hard drive icon appears on the desktop. Click its icon, and then open the **Special** menu and choose **Erase Disk**.
4. You can enter a name for the formatted disk and choose what format you want to use (Standard or Extended). Click **Erase** to erase the disk, or **Cancel** to return to the desktop.

Task 10: Using Apple System Profiler

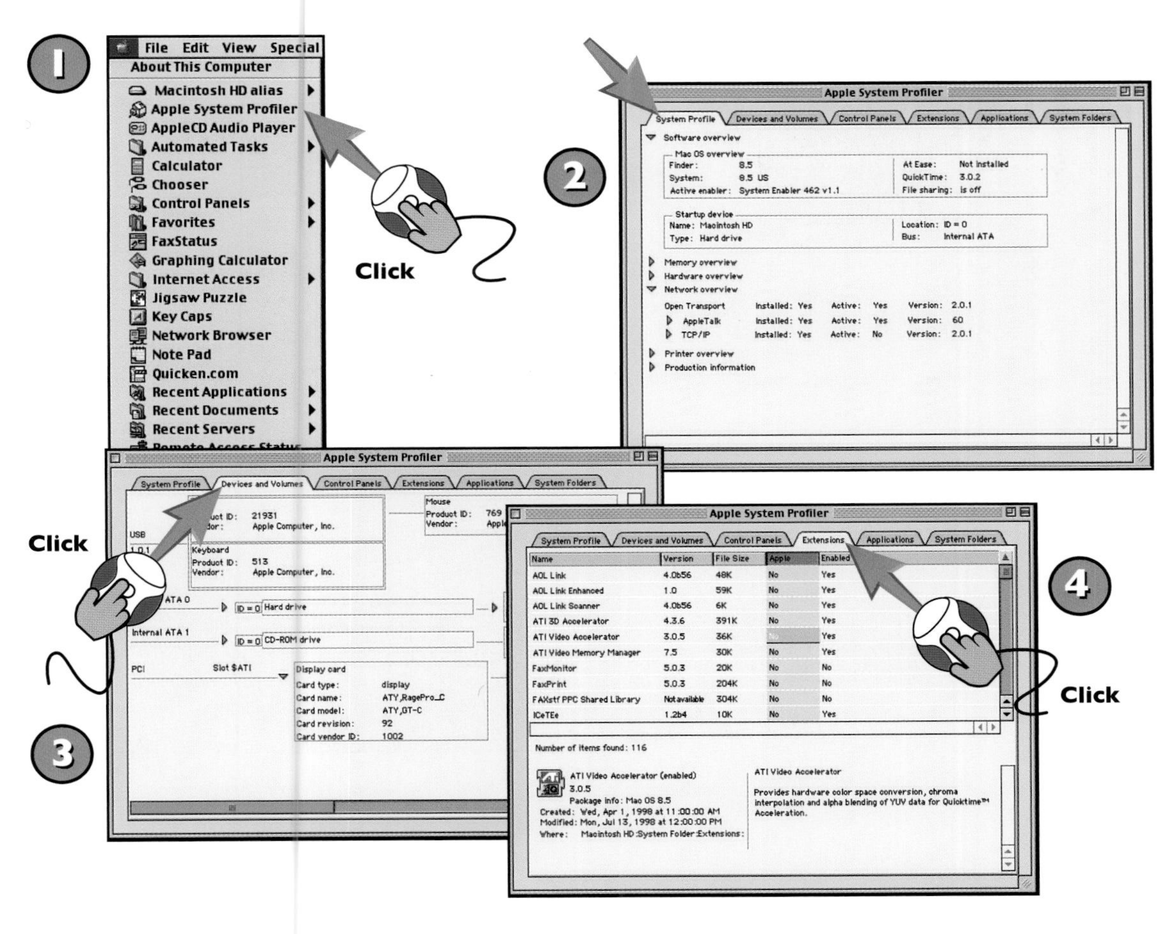

When you are troubleshooting, you sometimes need to display information about your system. You can find this information in the Apple System Profiler. You can use the information in Apple System Profiler to help isolate what may or may not be working correctly with your iMac or to save a log of your iMac's configuration.

1. Click the **Apple** menu and choose **Apple System Profiler**.
2. View the hardware, software, memory, network, and production information in the **System Profile** tab.
3. Click the **Devices and Volumes** tab to view the internal and external devices connected to your iMac.
4. Click the **Control Panels, Extensions,** and **Applications** tabs to view the software currently installed and running on your iMac.

✓ You can view memory usage information by selecting the **About This Computer** command in the **Apple** menu.

✓ Some applications, such as Microsoft Word 98 and Internet Explorer 4.01 and 4.5, have a system information window built into the **About** box. Click the **System Info** or **Support** button in the **About** box for these applications.

Task 11: Rebuilding Your Desktop

All the icons for your folders and files are stored in two database files on your hard drive collectively called the *desktop database*. If your application or document icons lose their custom icon, try rebuilding your desktop.

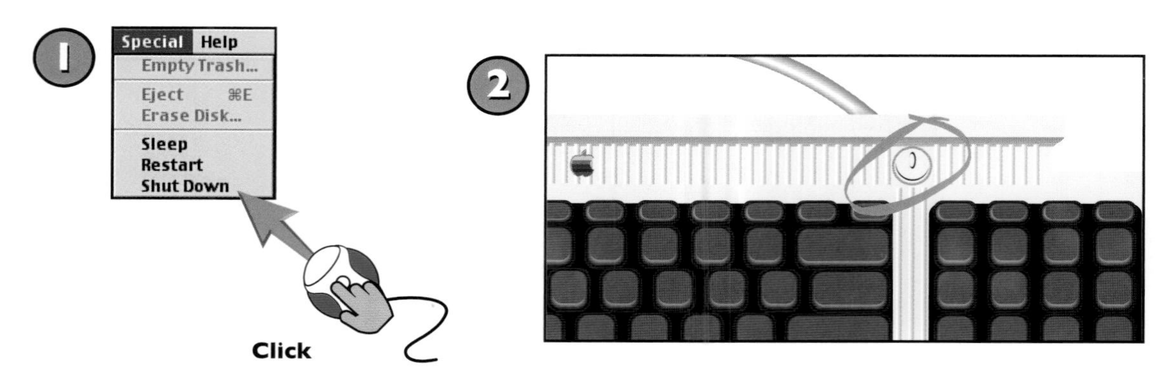

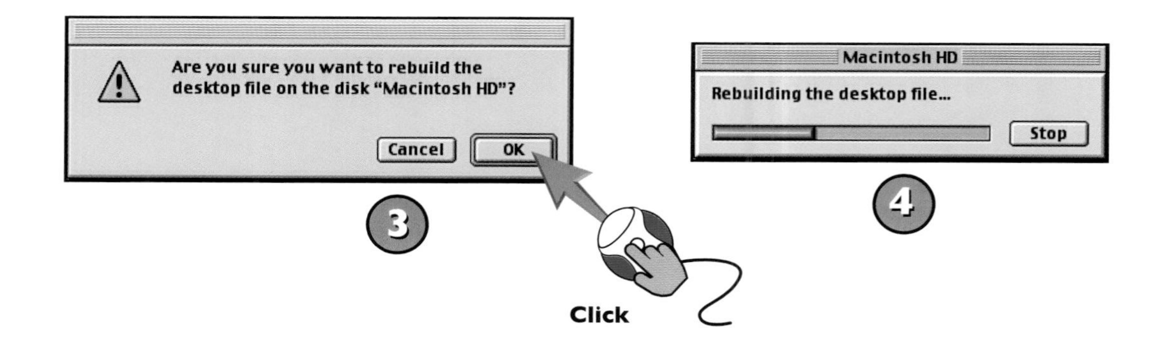

- If you crash while shutting down your iMac, press the **Command+Option** and **Escape** keys. This forces the active application to quit. You must restart after you use this key combination.

- If you hold down the **Command+Option+P+R** keys right after powering on your iMac, you will clear (or zap) the **PRAM**. Several control panel settings, such as your monitor colors and printer settings will be changed back to their default settings when **PRAM** is cleared. **PRAM**, also known as parameter **RAM**, is where **Mac OS** stores many of its software settings.

1. Power off your iMac.
2. Power on the iMac, and hold down the **Command+Option** keys.
3. Click **OK** when Mac OS asks you if you want to rebuild your desktop.
4. Wait for the progress bar to indicate that your iMac has finished rebuilding the desktop. Once the desktop appears, you can use your iMac.

Task 12: Increasing Application Memory

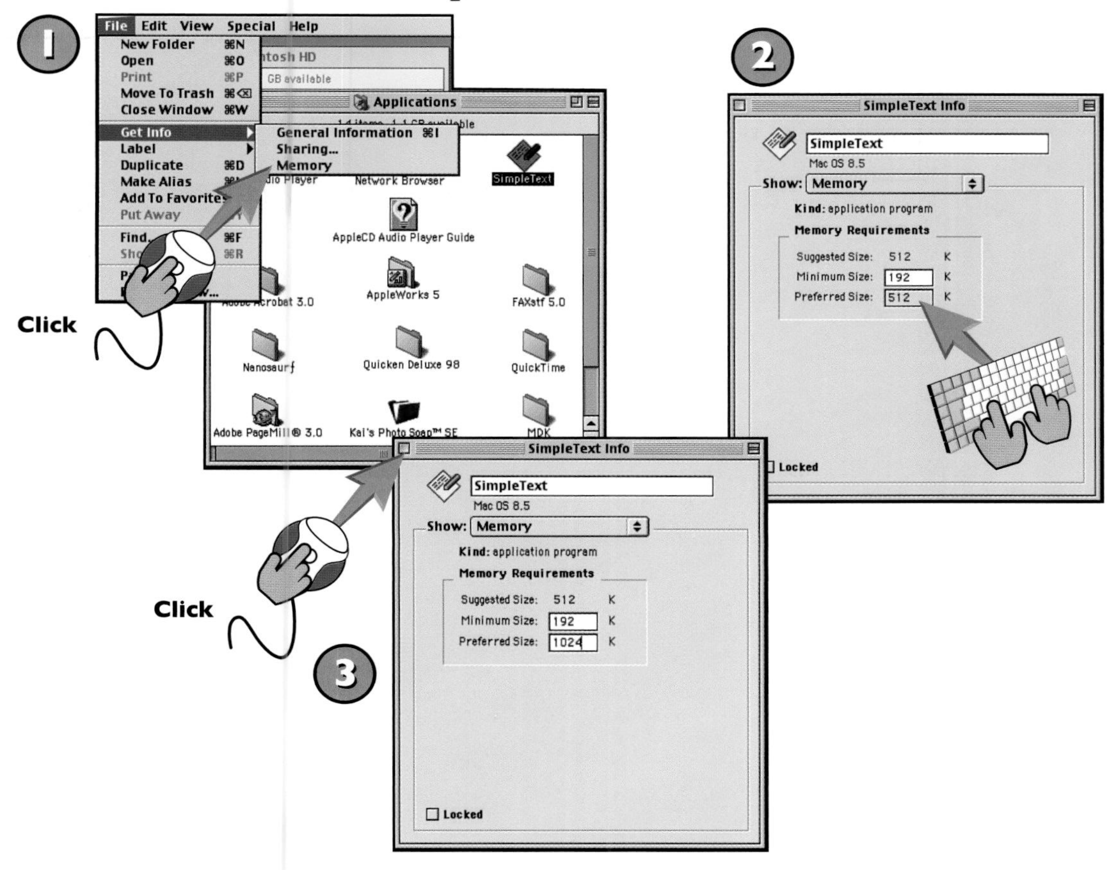

When you use an application, Mac OS sets aside a specific amount of memory for that application to consume. (The publisher of an application determines the minimal and suggested amount of memory the application uses as a default setting.) As you use an application, you may observe slower performance when you are working on a large document, or you may see an error message indicating that the application is running low on memory as you open more than one window. This task will show you how you can increase the amount of memory an application uses.

1. Select an application icon, and then click **File**, choose **Get Info**, and select **Memory**. You must quit the application before you can change its memory settings.
2. In the **Preferred size** text field, type a larger number.
3. Click the **Close** box. The next time you start the application, it will use the preferred size.

✓ **You can view and monitor how much memory an application is using. To do so, start the application, click the Apple menu and choose the About This Computer command.**

Task 13: Displaying System Information

As you are using applications, you might want to know how much memory is being used and how much is available. This information is always available in Mac OS in the **About This Computer** window. For the most detailed information about what hardware and software settings are on your iMac, use the **Apple System Profiler** application.

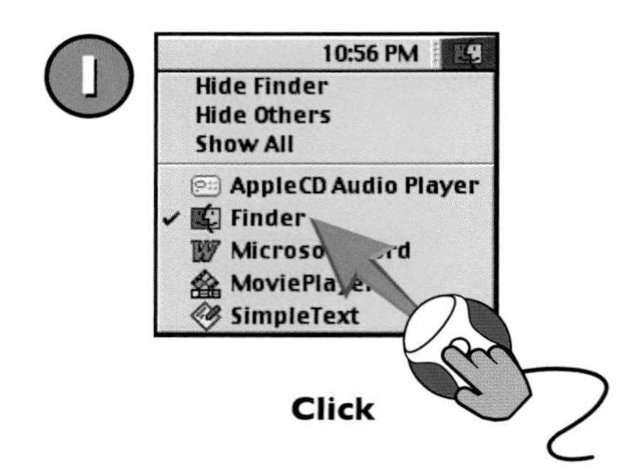

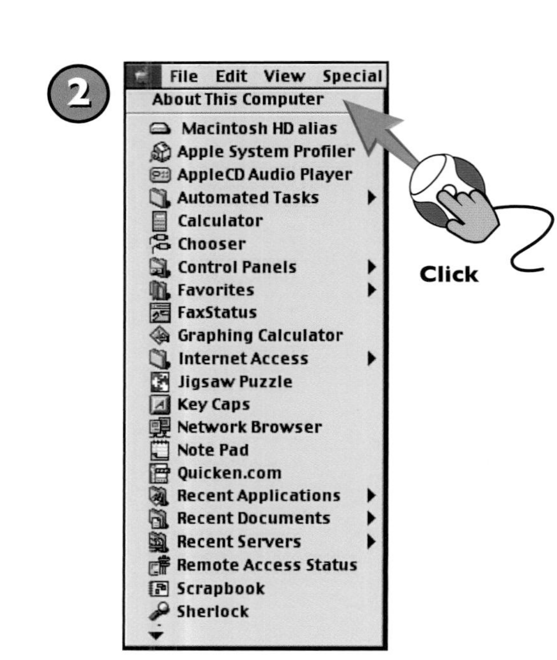

1. If an application other than Finder is active, click the **Applications** menu and choose **Finder**.
2. Click the **Apple** menu, then choose the **About This Computer** command.

You can use the **About This Computer** window to monitor the amount of memory in use by any open application running on your iMac.

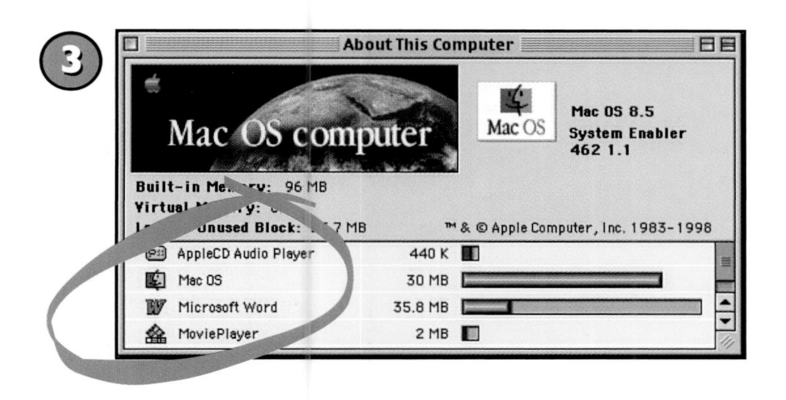

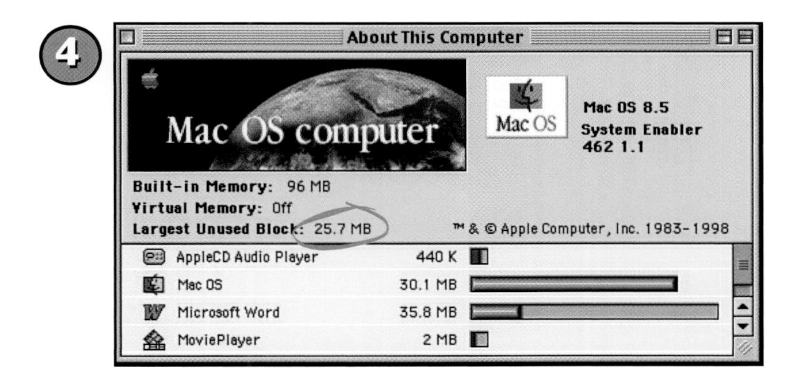

3. Each open application, including Mac OS, is listed in this window, along with the amount of memory each has been allocated and how much of it is being used.

4. The largest unused block is the amount of free memory available to your applications.

If you add up all memory allocated for open applications along with the largest unused block, it should approximately add up to the amount of virtual memory (if virtual memory is on in your Memory control panel) or built-in memory. If the numbers don't match, it's time to restart your iMac.

Task 14: Checking System Performance

Start Here

Over time, the software and hardware on your iMac may slow down and need to be upgraded or replaced. One way to objectively measure your iMac's hardware and software performance is to run performance software. This task uses the MacBench 5.0 performance tests to measure processor and disk performance on an iMac. You can purchase MacBench from ZDLabs on the Internet.

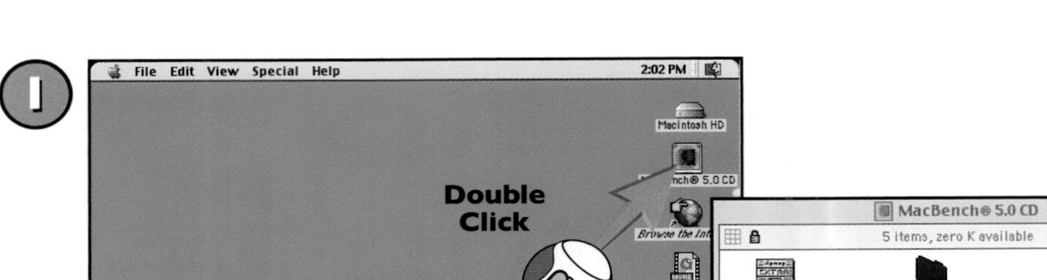

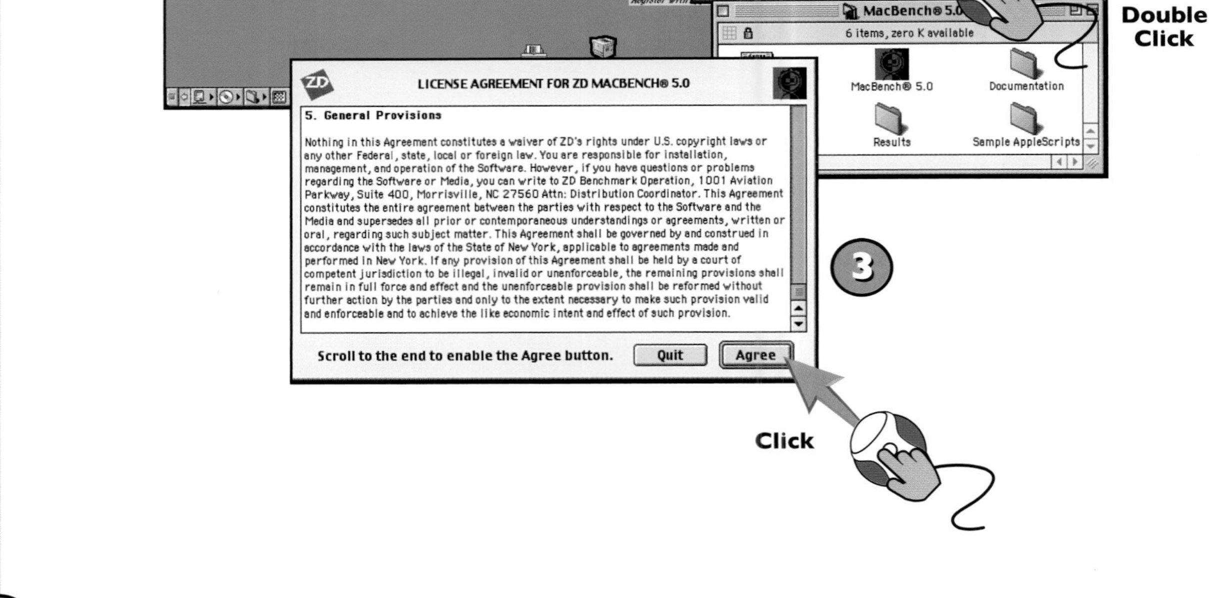

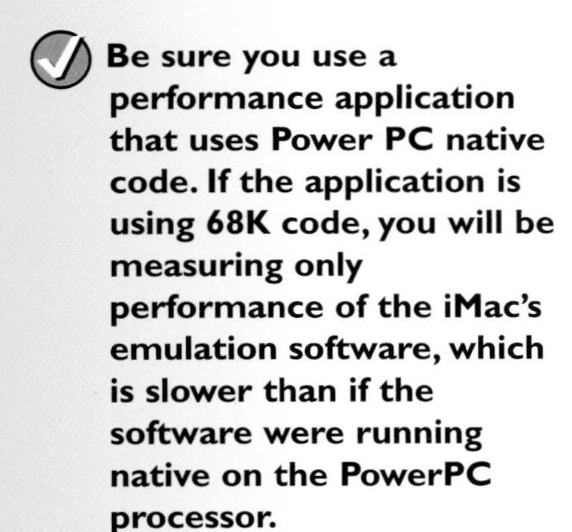

Be sure you use a performance application that uses Power PC native code. If the application is using 68K code, you will be measuring only performance of the iMac's emulation software, which is slower than if the software were running native on the PowerPC processor.

1. Insert the MacBench CD into the CD-ROM drive, and double-click the **MacBench 5.0 CD** icon on the desktop.
2. Double-click the **MacBench 5.0** icon in the **MacBench 5.0 CD** window, and again in the **MacBench 5.0** window.
3. Click **Agree** in the licensee agreement window.

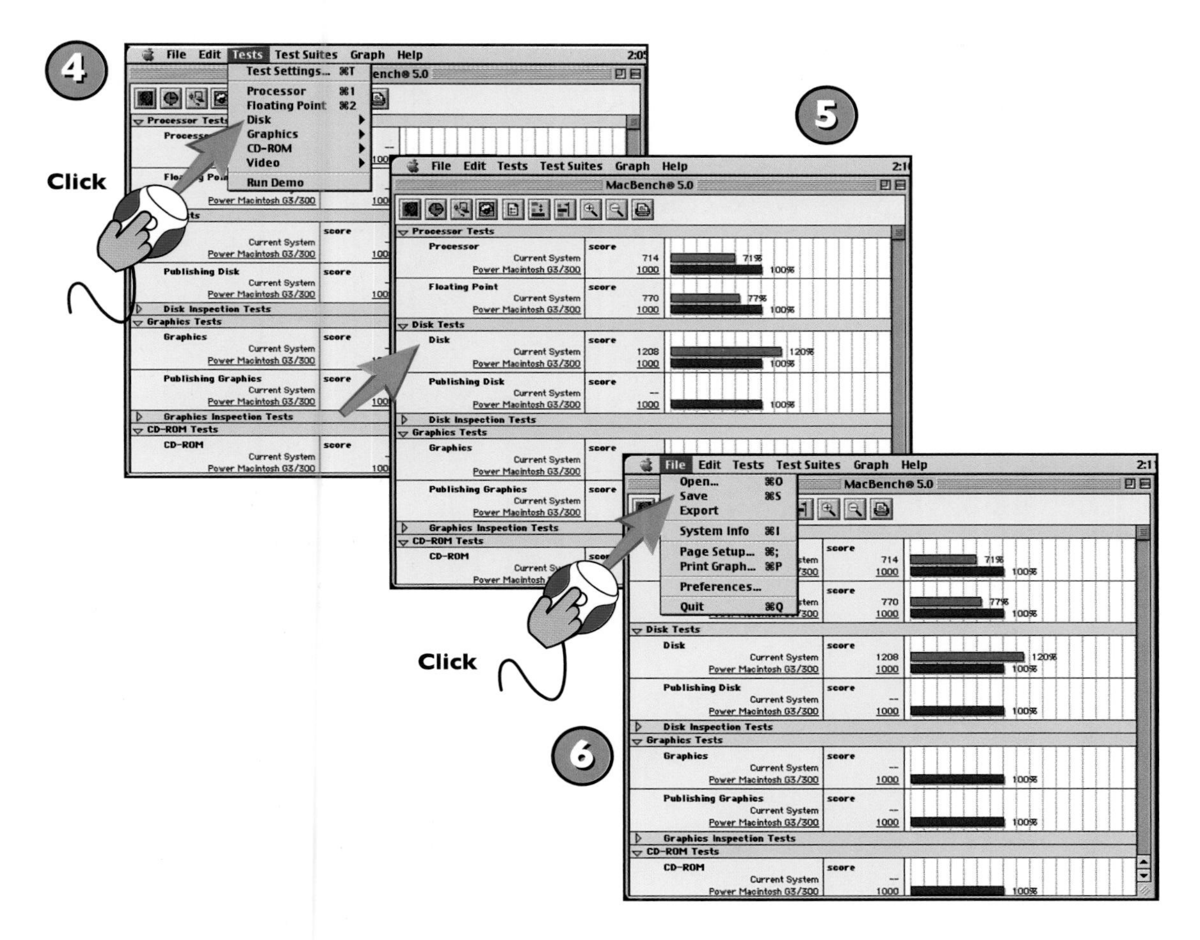

1. Open the **Test** menu and choose **Processor** or **Disk**, depending on what type of test you want to run. (I've chosen **Disk**.)

2. Compare the results with those of a previous test for your iMac. (This is the first test I've run so my machine's performance is being compared with a Power Macintosh G3/300's performance.)

3. Click **File** and choose **Save** to save the results to your hard drive to compare at a later date.

If you do not want to purchase performance software, you can compare a task such as copying files over a network or from one hard disk to another with a second iMac. If the second iMac is faster than yours, it is possible you may have a fragmented hard drive, or you may just need to adjust some of your Mac OS settings.

Task 15: Using Extensions Manager

Start Here

Mac OS contains a core set of *extensions*, which enable features such as networking and printing, external devices such as DVD-ROM drives, and technologies such as AppleScript, QuickTime, and QuickDraw 3D. Many more extensions are available as shareware on the Internet; it is usually with these non-commercial software products that software problems arise. You can use Extensions Manager to keep track of the different control panels and extensions you add to your system folder.

Most software conflicts are caused by extensions or control panels added to the system folder. If you have added software to your system folder and notice that Mac OS is crashing more frequently, hold down the spacebar when your Mac starts up and choose **Mac OS 8.5 Base set** from the **Selected Set** pop-up menu in Extensions Manager.

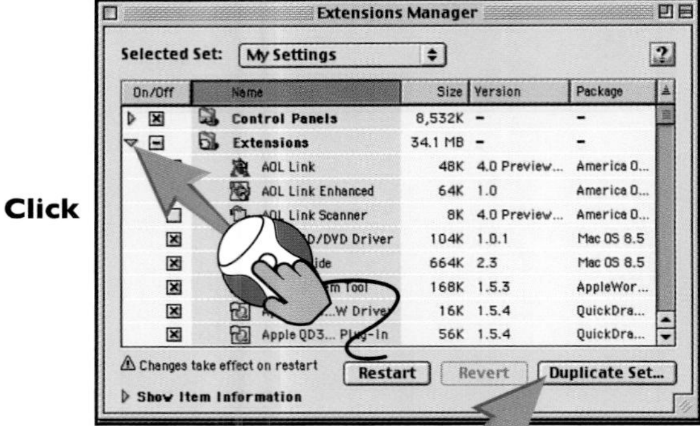

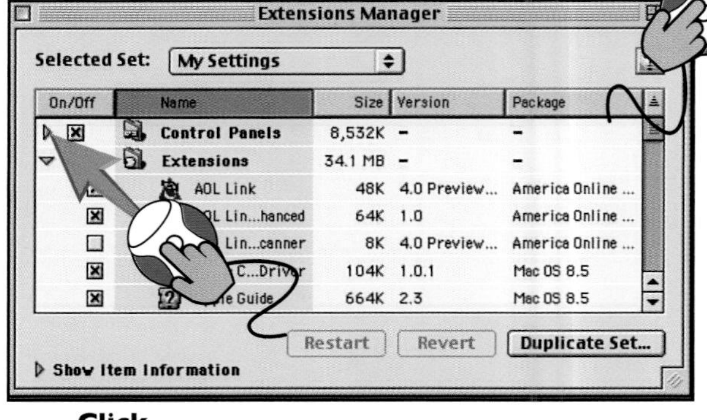

1. Click the **Apple** menu and choose **Control Panels**, then choose **Extensions Manager**.
2. Click the arrow next to the **Control Panels** or **Extensions** folder to view the control panels and extensions installed in the system folder.
3. Click the **Duplicate Set** button and type some text to name the new set.
4. Click the arrow to the left of the **Control Panels** folder icon.

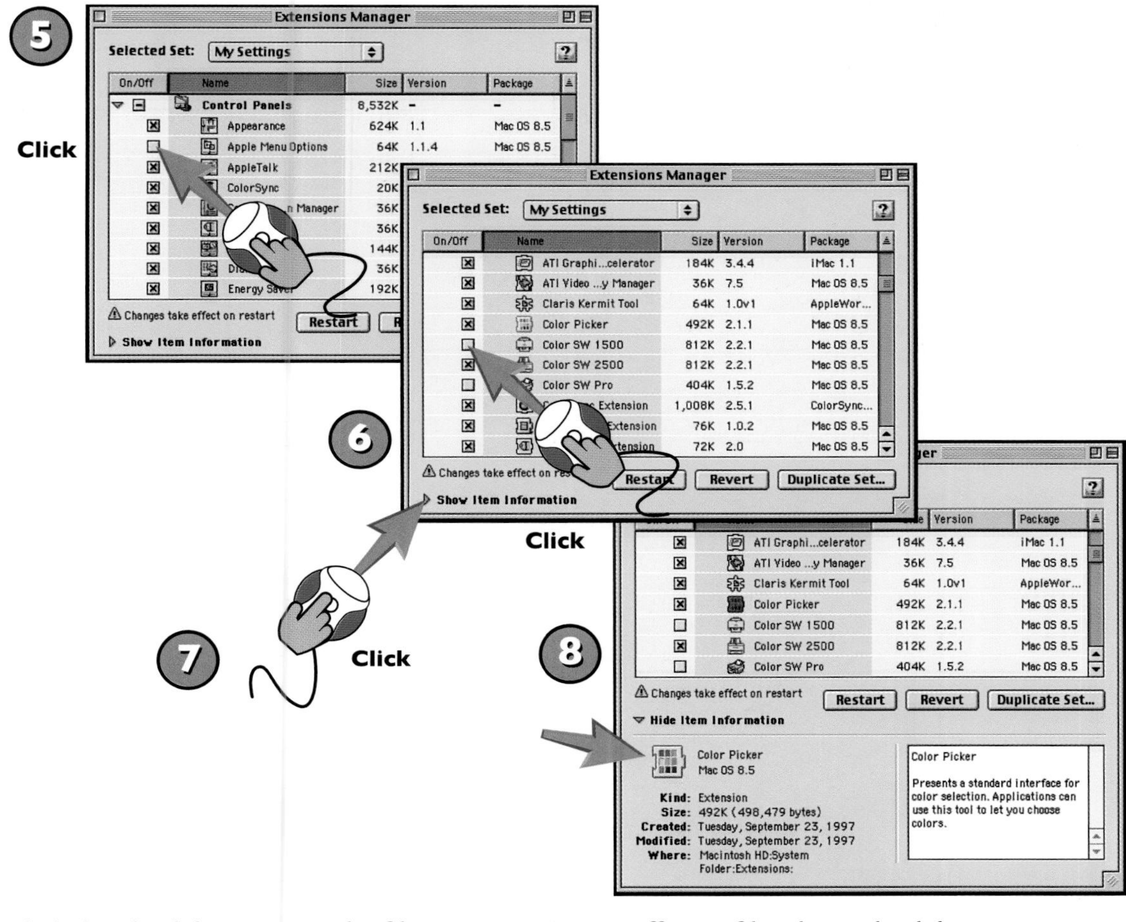

Extensions Manager saves a group of extensions as a *set*. The information in a set is saved to a file in the Extensions Manager Preferences folder, which is in the Preferences folder of your system folder. Extensions Manager automatically saves changes made to a set.

If you are trying to isolate an extension conflict, turn off any non-Apple extensions as a starting point, then restart. Turn any new extensions on, one at a time, and restart until you find the one which reproduces the software problem.

If you see a lock icon next to a set name, you cannot modify the set. Click File and choose Duplicate Set to create a modifiable set.

5. Click the check box next to the file you want to turn off. Any file whose check box is empty will not load when your iMac starts up.

6. If you know which printer you will use, you can turn off any extraneous printer extensions in the Extensions Manager set.

7. To view more information about an item, click it, then click the **Show Item Information** arrow.

8. The item information is displayed.

Task 16: Performing a Clean Install of Mac OS

There are two ways to install Mac OS software onto your hard drive. The default setting is to update an existing system folder. When a system folder is updated, the installer application tries to replace as many of the older system resources as possible with new ones, and is usually successful. A clean install of Mac OS, however, creates a new system folder on your hard drive. This task uses the iMac Software Install CD to install Mac OS 8.5.

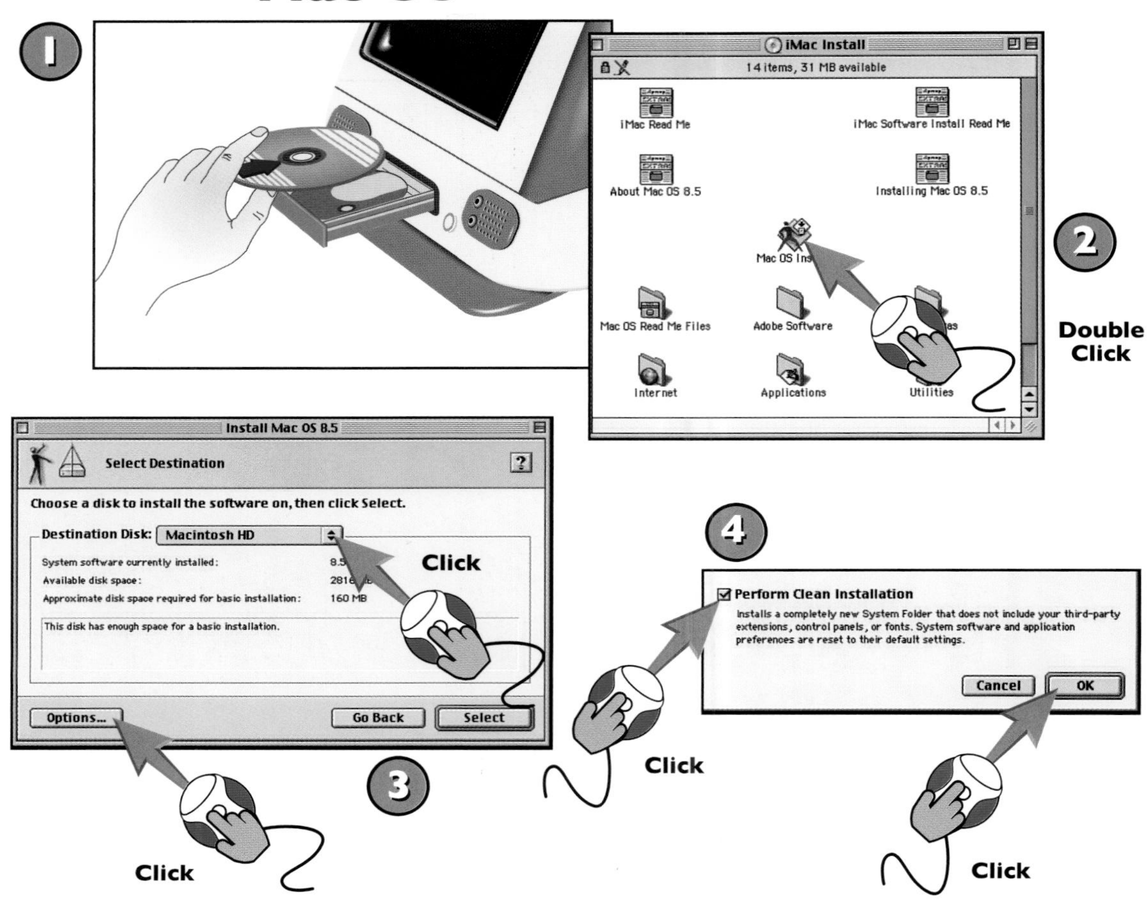

You should only need to perform a clean install if you must replace the system folder on your iMac.

After you complete the clean installation of Mac OS, create a backup copy of the system folder.

1. Insert the iMac Software Install CD-ROM in the iMac and hold down the **C** key as the iMac starts up.
2. Double-click the **iMac Install** icon on the desktop, and then double-click the **Install Mac OS** icon in the **iMac Install** window.
3. Select the hard drive you want to use from the **Destination Disk** drop-down list, and then click the **Options** button.
4. Click the **Perform Clean Installation** check box, and then click **OK**.

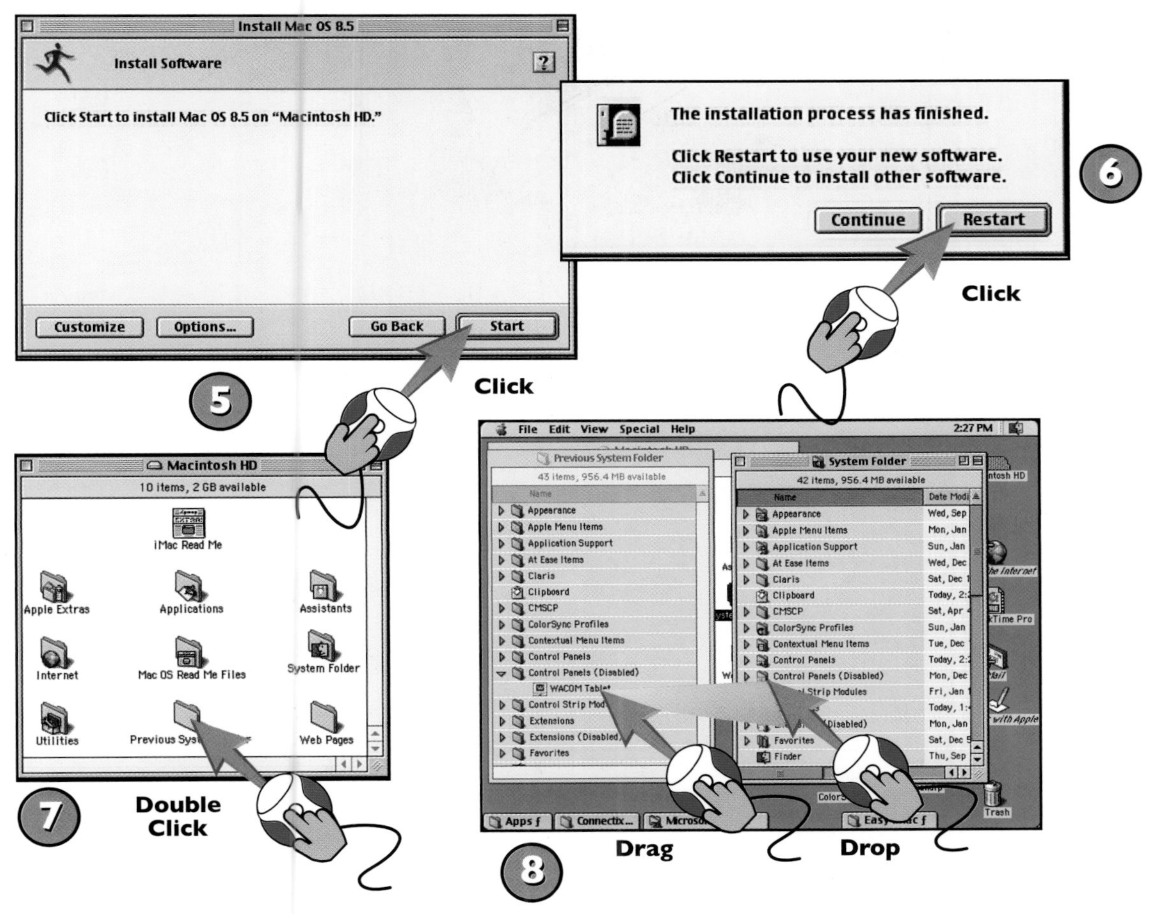

5. Continue through the Install Mac OS application windows. Finally, click the **Start** button to install Mac OS.

6. Once the installation is complete, click the **Restart** button.

7. After your iMac restarts, double-click the **Macintosh HD** icon. Notice that the previous system folder still appears on the hard disk.

8. Move any files or folders you might need from the previous system folder to the new system folder.

After you complete a clean install, the new system folder will have only Mac OS software. Any third-party control panel, extensions, or applications you had installed with your previous system folder may need to be moved or reinstalled into the new system folder.

iMac Software

Your iMac is bundled with several applications that are preinstalled onto your hard disk. A backup of these applications is available on the iMac Software Restore CD-ROM, as well as the iMac Software Install CD-ROM. The most recent addition to the iMac bundle is Adobe PageMill 3.0. AppleWorks 5, Quicken 98, Adobe Acrobat 3, and Nanosaur are also provided with your iMac. Also included is Kai's Photo Soap.

Some of the software bundled with your iMac may not be installed, such as PageMill 3.0, and Kai's Photo Soap. Install these software applications from their respective CD-ROM included with your iMac.

Tasks

Task 1: Viewing Files with Adobe Acrobat

Many of the instruction manuals included with the software on your iMac can be viewed with Adobe Acrobat. Adobe Acrobat can open files, but the files themselves cannot be modified or edited. You cannot create any files with Adobe Acrobat.

Start Here

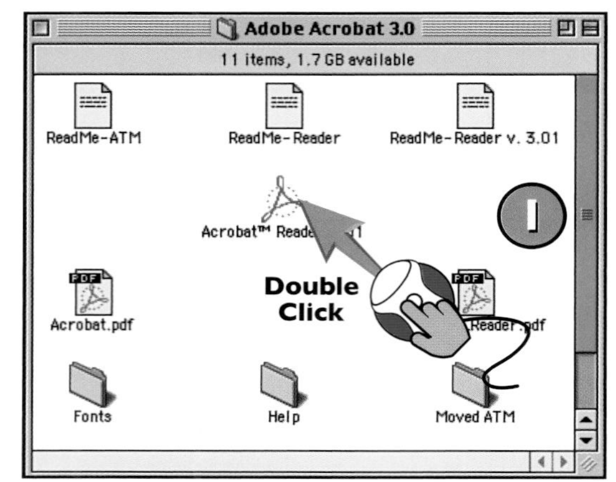

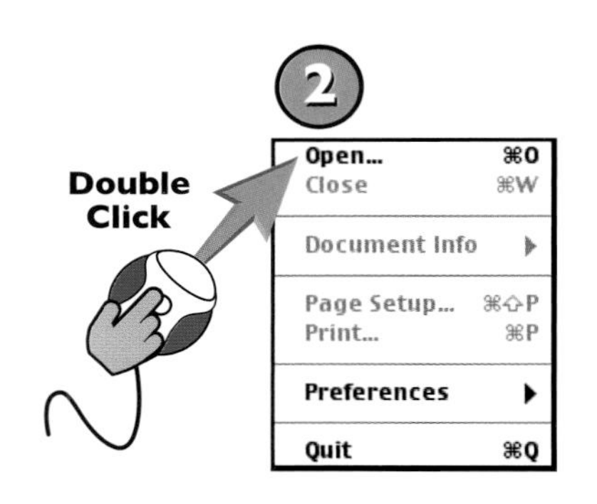

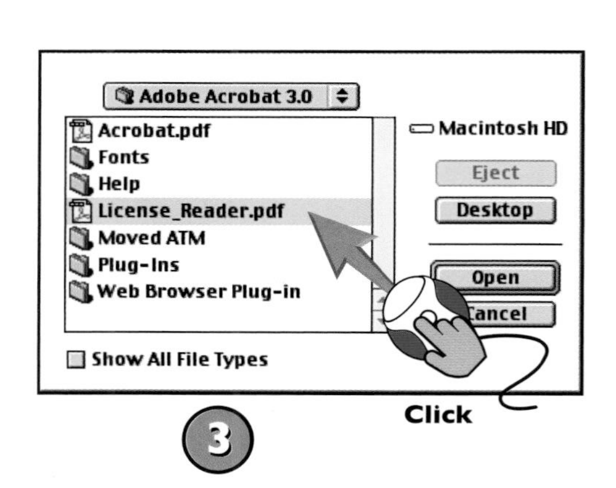

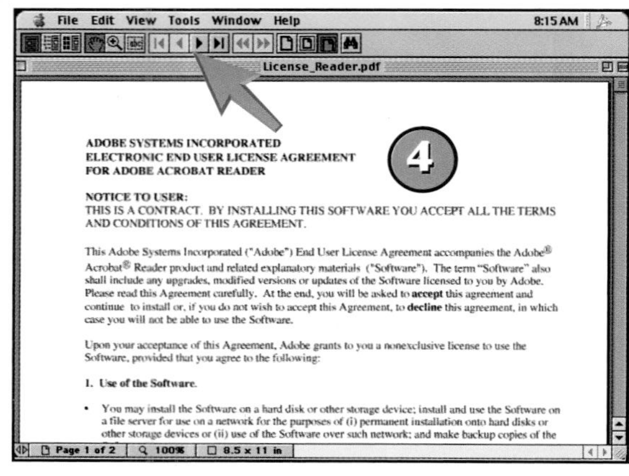

- Any Adobe Acrobat file will have an icon similar to the Adobe Acrobat symbol. Acrobat file names usually end in **.pdf**.
- If an Acrobat document is more than a few pages long, you might want to print it.
- Click the page number information at the bottom left of the document window to bring up a dialog window. Type the page number you want to go to, and press **Enter** to go to the page you want.

1. Double-click the **Macintosh HD** icon, open the **Applications** window, and then open the **Adobe Acrobat** window. Finally, double-click the **Adobe Acrobat** icon.
2. Click **File**, then choose **Open**.
3. Select a file to view (in this case **License_Reader.pdf**).
4. Use the **Page Up** and **Page Down** keys on your keyboard to view the pages of the document; use the toolbar buttons to turn pages in the document.

Task 2: Starting AppleWorks's Word Processor

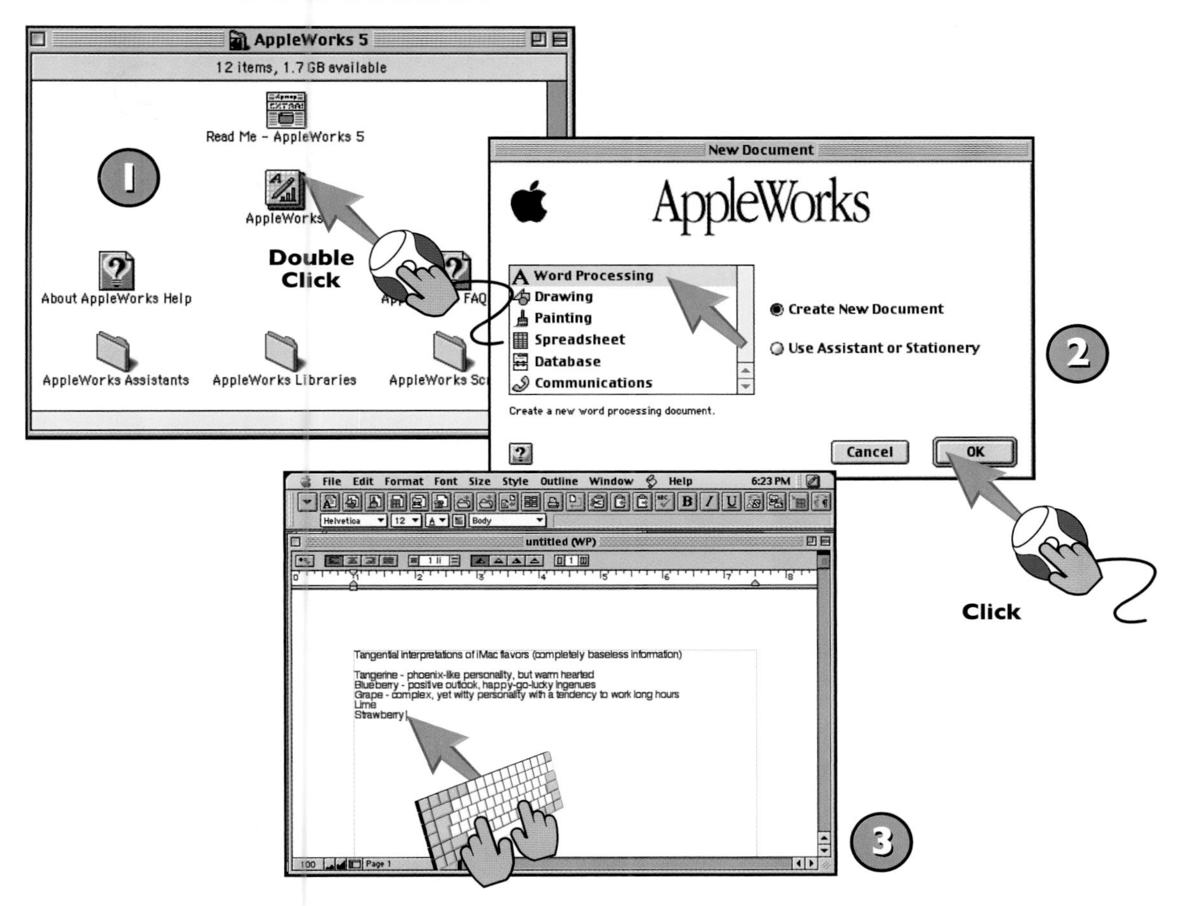

AppleWorks 5, formerly known as ClarisWorks 5, is a multi-featured application that contains a word processor; spreadsheet application; a paint, drawing, and communications application; and a database application. The word processor in AppleWorks can open large documents, which is one of the main limitations of SimpleText and other text viewers. In addition, you can use AppleWorks to create and edit your own documents. This task shows you how to start the AppleWorks word processor.

1. Open the **Macintosh HD** window, double-click **Applications**, double-click **AppleWorks 5**, and double-click **AppleWorks**.
2. Click **Word Processing**, and then click **OK**.
3. The AppleWorks word processor opens; simply click in the window and type to start working on your new document.

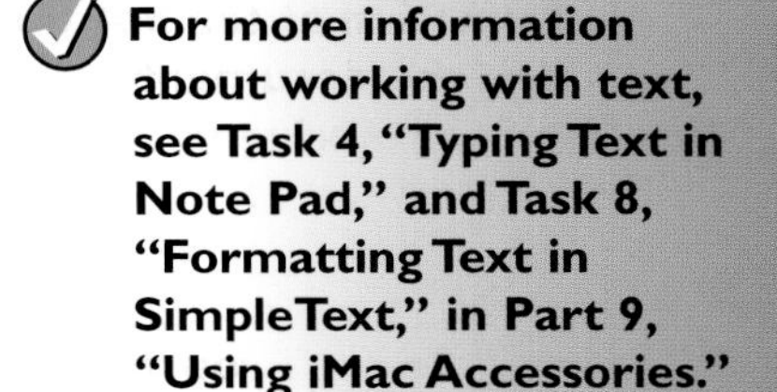

For more information about working with text, see Task 4, "Typing Text in Note Pad," and Task 8, "Formatting Text in SimpleText," in Part 9, "Using iMac Accessories."

Task 3: Formatting Your Word-Processed Documents

Start Here

Once you've typed a bit of text in your AppleWorks word-processed document, you may want to pep it up a bit. Formatting text makes it easier for you and others to read. It can also help emphasize key elements of your message.

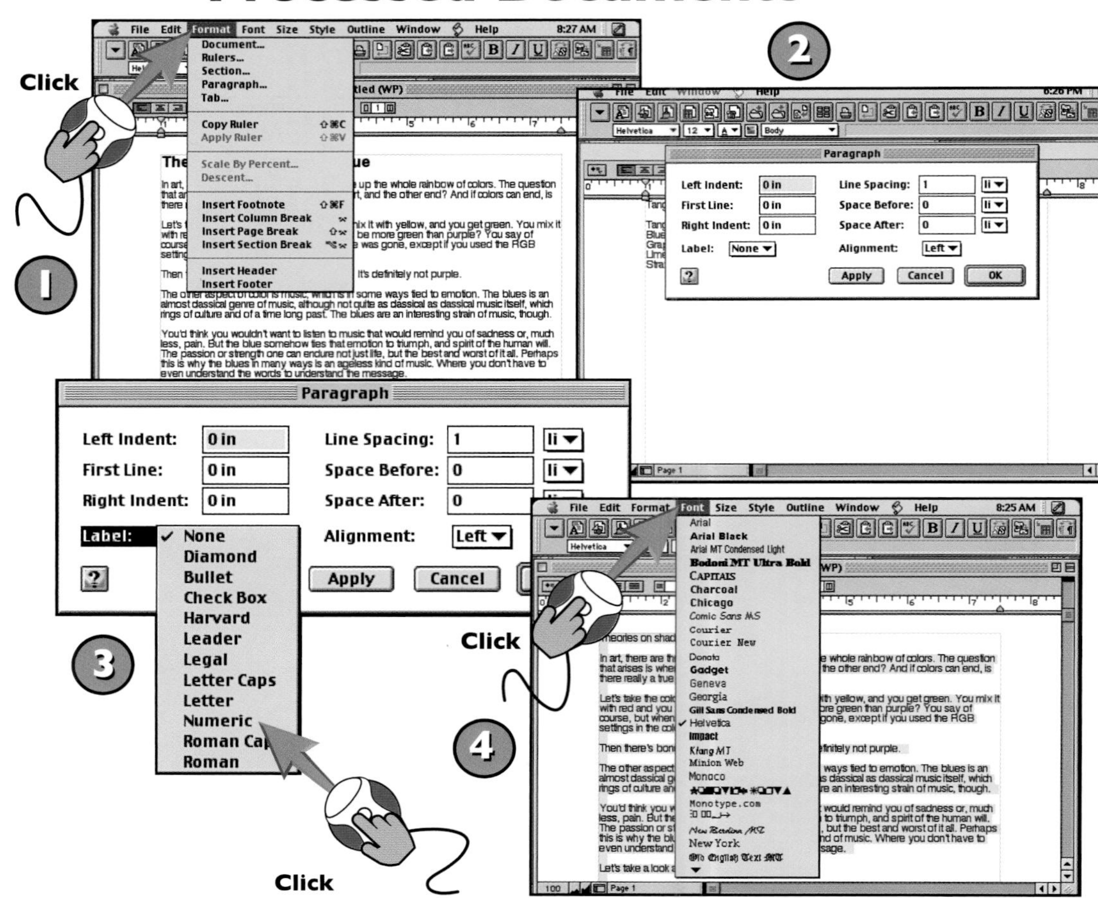

✓ The default view for the word processor is to show the margin settings in addition to the text area of the file. The layout of the window matches the way it will print. The term *WYSIWYG*, which stands for *what you see is what you get*, is used to describe this kind of feature in an application.

✓ If you'd rather convert your text to a bulleted list, series of check boxes, or any of a number other options, simply select it from the **Label** drop-down menu shown in step 3.

Click **Format** to view the formatting options available to you.

To set the indents and spacing in your document, specify them in the **Paragraph** window. Open it by selecting **Paragraph** from the **Format** menu.

To convert a set of paragraphs into a numbered list, select the paragraphs, choose **Paragraph** from the **Format** menu, and select **Numeric** from the **Label** drop-down menu. Click **Apply**.

To change the font in your document, select the text you want to change, and choose the font you want from the **Font** menu.

Task 4: Creating a Spreadsheet with AppleWorks

Start Here

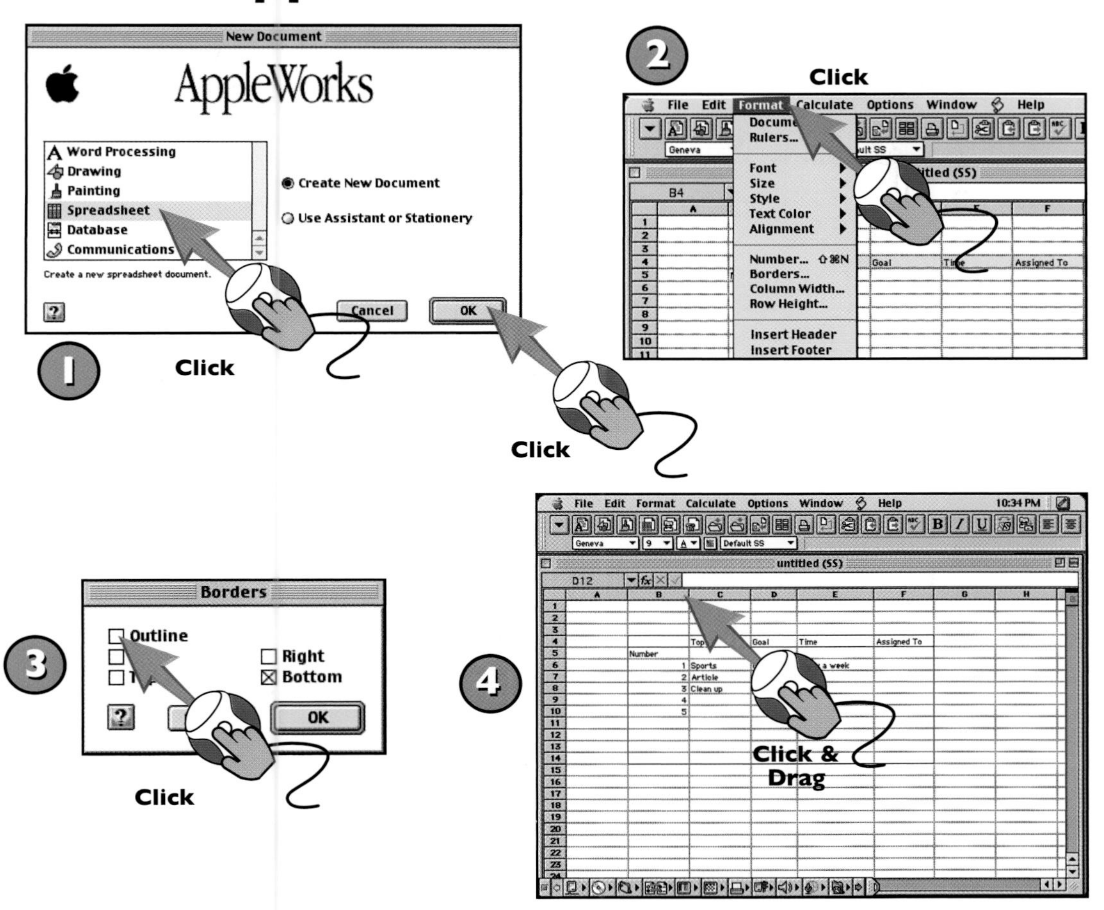

Another kind of document used on your iMac is a spreadsheet. Spreadsheets are commonly used to track both scheduling and accounting-related tasks. You can create long lists with an expandable way to track information, or you can automate AppleWorks to update information in another document, such as a database, whenever the spreadsheet changes.

1. In AppleWorks' **New Document** window, click **Spreadsheet**, and then click **OK**. (Refer to step 1 of Task 2 if you need help opening this window.)
2. Type some information into several cells, then open the **Format** menu and choose **Font**, **Style**, or **Size** to change the text format in one or several cells.
3. Add a border to a series of selected cells by choosing **Borders** from the **Format** menu. Select the type of border you want from the dialog that appears.
4. Click and drag a column's edge to adjust the width of the cells in that column.

You can use equations in addition to text in each cell of the spreadsheet.

You can format text in a spreadsheet in the same way you format text in a word processor.

Task 5: Creating Diagrams and Charts with AppleWorks

The drawing tools in AppleWorks are great for creating charts for presentations, or diagrams that you can add to documents or Web sites. A diagram could show the process flow of a work task, such as how a chapter is edited for a book, or how to create a Web page.

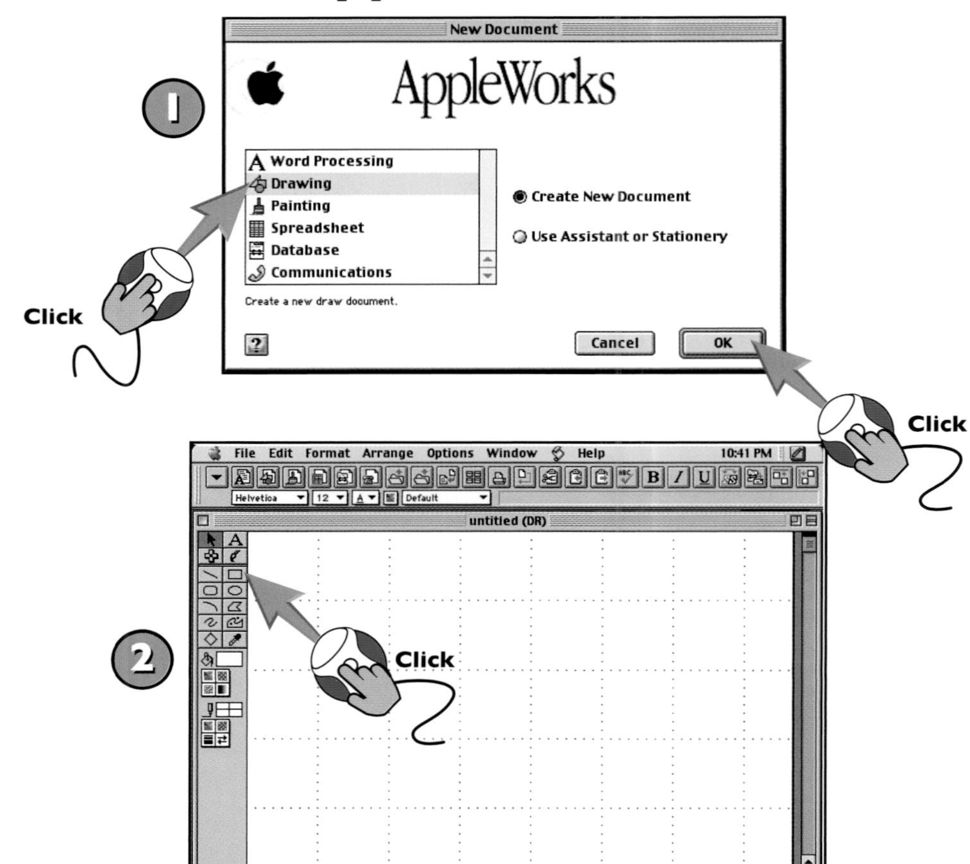

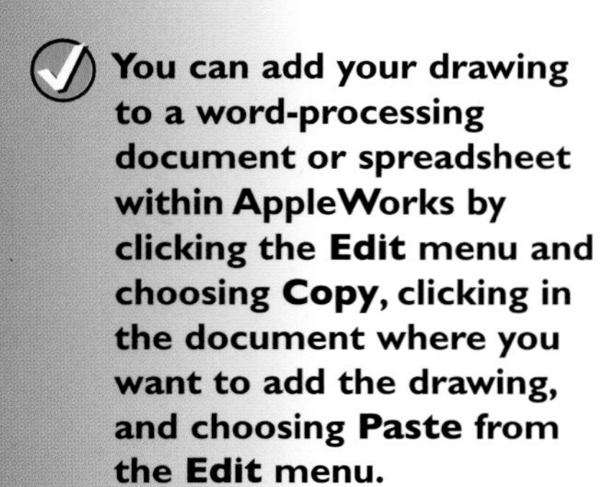

You can add your drawing to a word-processing document or spreadsheet within AppleWorks by clicking the **Edit** menu and choosing **Copy**, clicking in the document where you want to add the drawing, and choosing **Paste** from the **Edit** menu.

Click **Drawing** in the **New Document** window, then click **OK**. (Refer to step 1 of Task 2 if you need help opening this window.)

Click on a shape in the toolbox that you want to add to your diagram or chart.

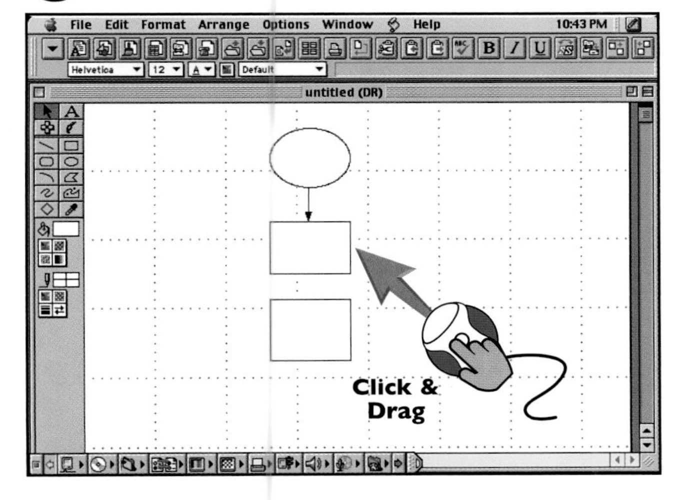

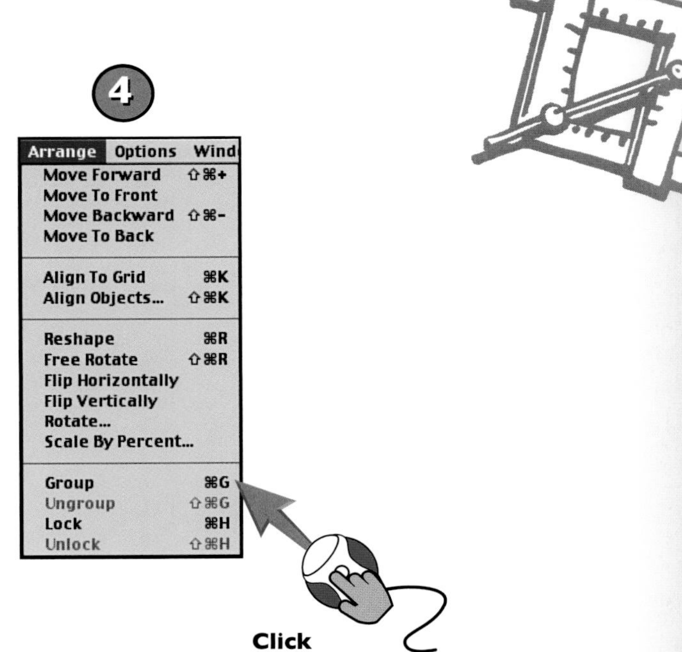

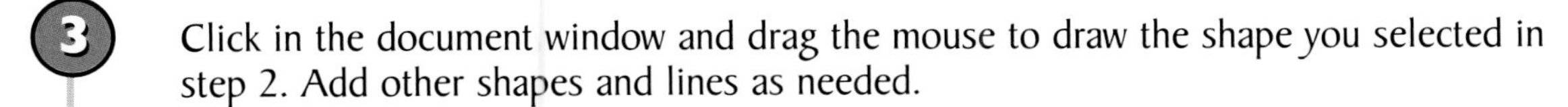

3. Click in the document window and drag the mouse to draw the shape you selected in step 2. Add other shapes and lines as needed.

4. To group shapes together, click one or more shapes, and then choose **Group** from the **Arrange** menu.

Task 6: Creating a Database with AppleWorks

Documents and spreadsheets are great tools for creating and viewing information. The best thing about putting information into a database is that you can store a good amount of information in one file, but view it in a variety of ways. For example, you can create a database of all your documents and spreadsheets to keep track of them. A more common use of a database is for storing name, address, and phone number information.

Start Here

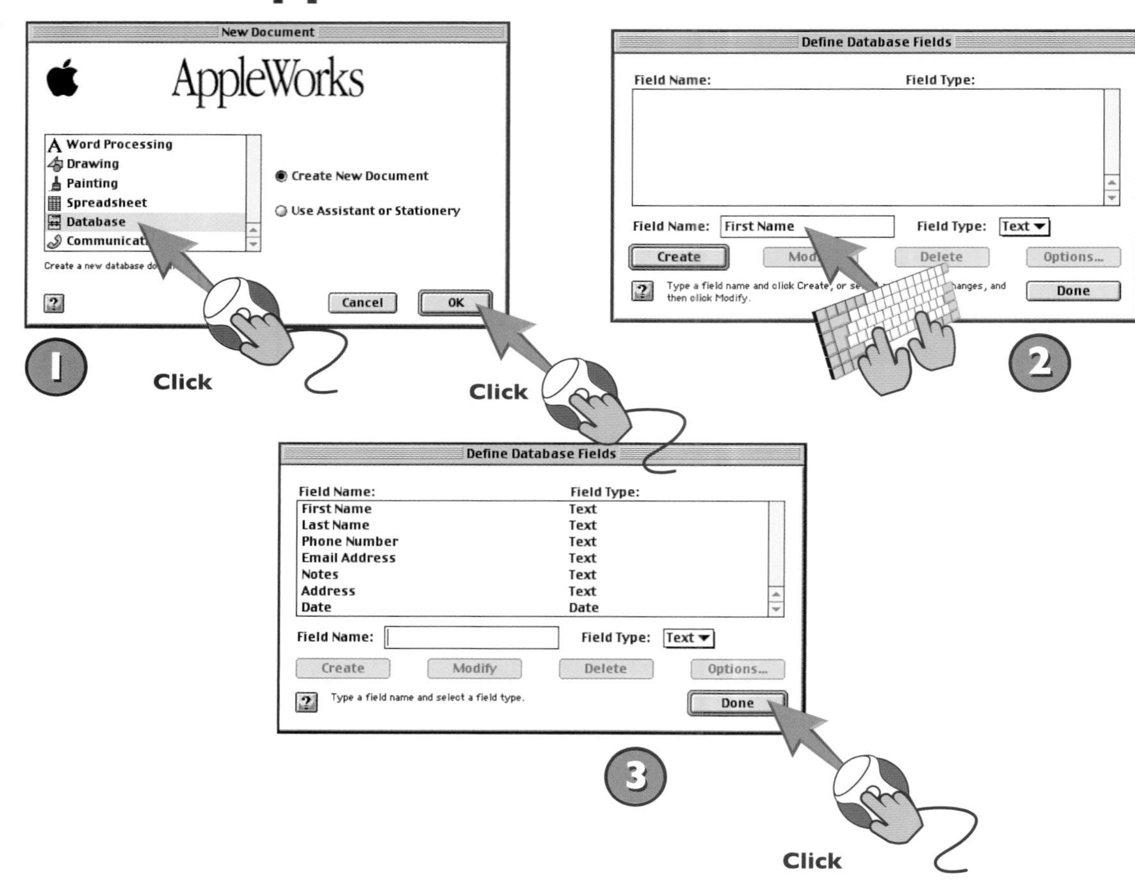

- **Most businesses use a database to track inventory and product sales.**
- **You can use AppleScript to automate information that is placed in a database from the word processor or spreadsheet areas of AppleWorks.**

1. Click **Database** in the **New Document** window, then click **OK**. (Refer to step 1 of Task 2 if you need help opening this window.)
2. Type the name of a field you want to use in your database (in this case, **First Name**).
3. Create any other fields you want to use, and then click **Done**.

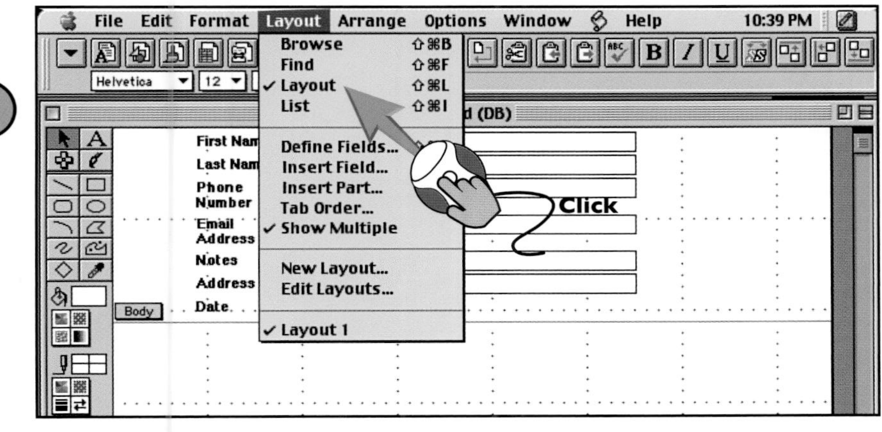

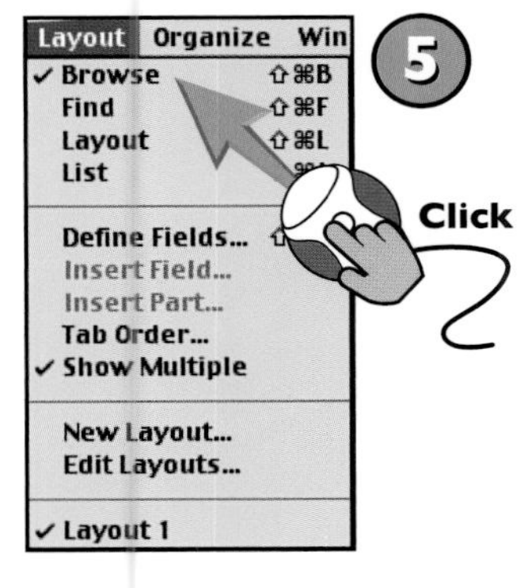

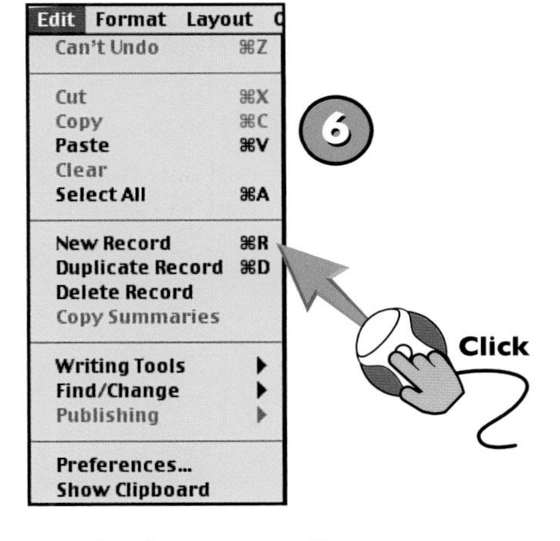

Click **Layout** and choose **Layout** to lay out your database manually. You can use your mouse to move any of the database items.

Click **Layout** and choose **Browse** to browse database records, or to enter or view information in the database.

Click **Edit** and choose **New Record** to add new files to your database; click the **Notepad** icon in the toolbox to move to the previous or next database record.

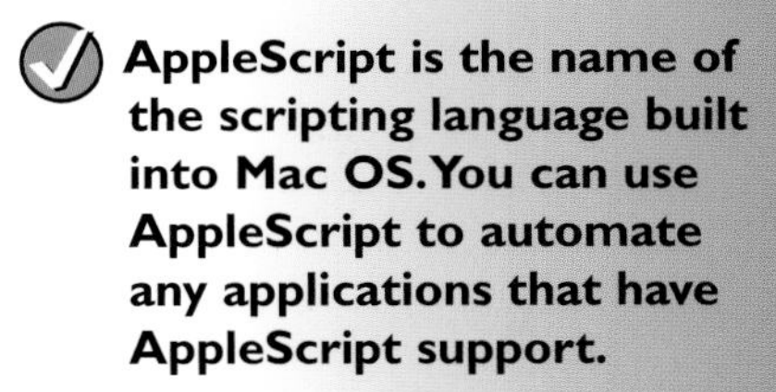

AppleScript is the name of the scripting language built into Mac OS. You can use AppleScript to automate any applications that have AppleScript support.

Many Web sites use databases to link a wide range of information, such as for shopping on the Internet or for storing phone numbers.

Task 7: Drawing Freehand with AppleWorks

You don't need to be an artist to use the paint tools in AppleWorks. Many of the tools, such as the paint bucket, text, paintbrush, and shapes work in the same way as in the draw window.

Start Here

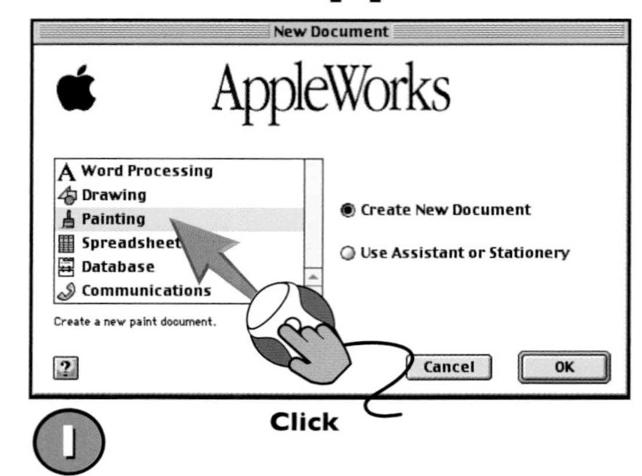

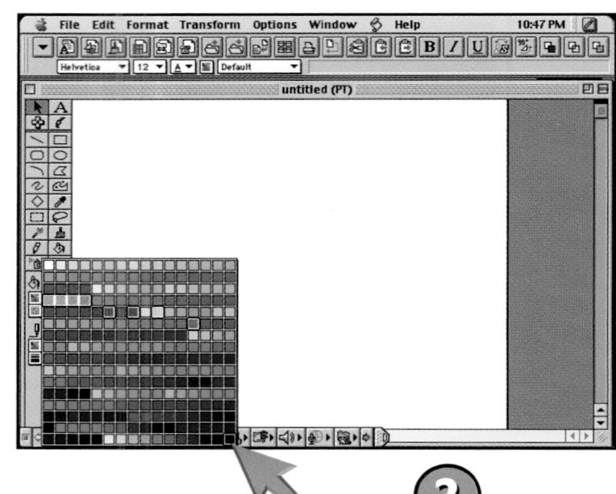

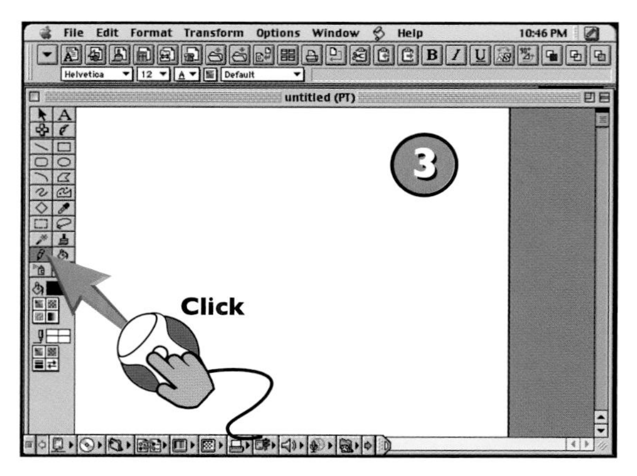

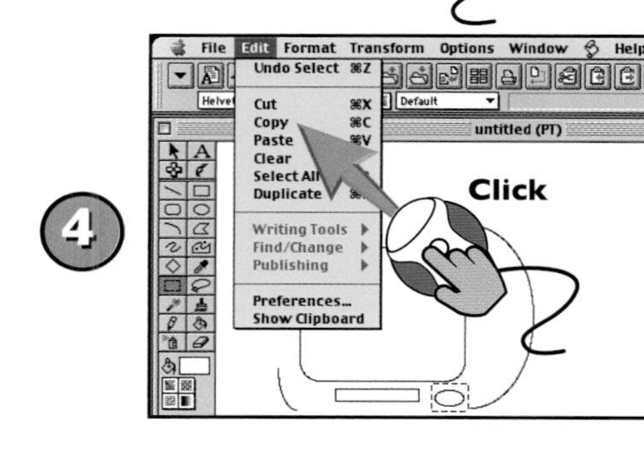

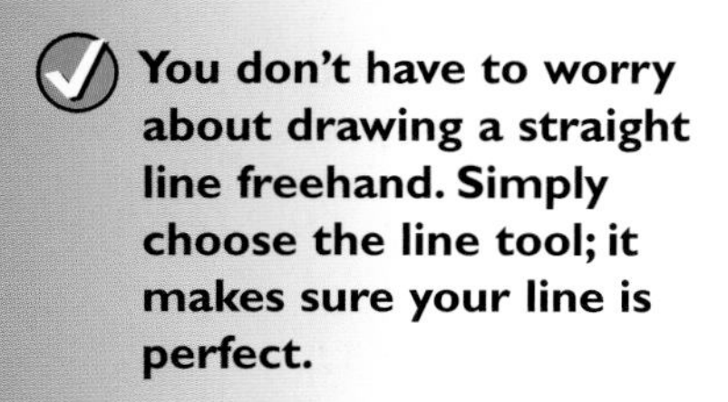

You don't have to worry about drawing a straight line freehand. Simply choose the line tool; it makes sure your line is perfect.

1. Click **Painting** in the **New Document** window, then click **OK**. (Refer to step 1 of Task 2 if you need help opening this window.)

2. Choose a color from the paint pop-up palette in the toolbar.

3. Select a shape or tool in the toolbar.

4. To draw, click the document window and drag the mouse. Click **Edit** and choose **Copy** to duplicate any artwork in the document window.

End Task

Task 8: Playing Nanosaur

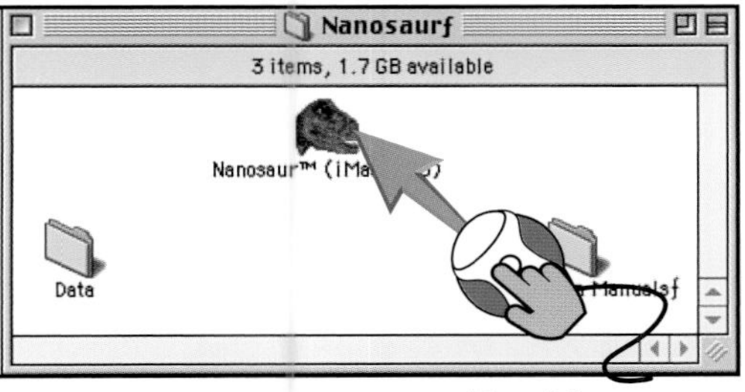

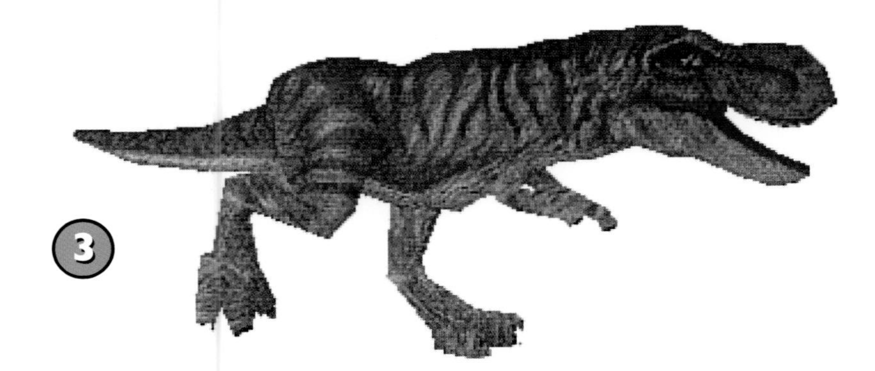

Your iMac comes with a dinosaur game, Nanosaur, which is a full color, 3D game. In it, you are a dinosaur who must collect different dinosaur eggs and avoid being killed by other dinosaurs in order to move to higher levels of adventure.

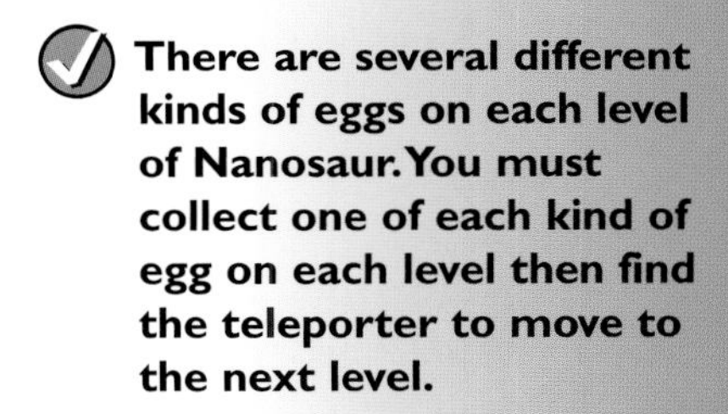

✓ There are several different kinds of eggs on each level of Nanosaur. You must collect one of each kind of egg on each level then find the teleporter to move to the next level.

✓ If you want to view the key controls, press the **left-** or **right-arrow** key and choose the question mark before you start a game. Press the **Spacebar** to exit the help screen.

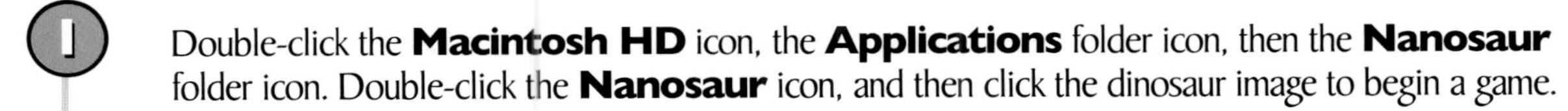

1. Double-click the **Macintosh HD** icon, the **Applications** folder icon, then the **Nanosaur** folder icon. Double-click the **Nanosaur** icon, and then click the dinosaur image to begin a game.
2. Press the **arrow keys** to make the dinosaur walk and turn; press the **Command** key to jump. Press the **Option** key to pick up eggs.
3. Press the **Spacebar** to fire the gun. Watch out for those Tyrannosaurus Rex!

Task 9: Working with Kai's Photo Soap

If you have a digital camera, or you want to touch up images before you send them to a friend or put them on your Web site, you can use Kai's Photo Soap. Unlike most Mac OS applications, Kai's Photo Soap has menus and buttons that appear as you move the mouse cursor over them. What might appear to be a blank area on your screen may be a menu, button to access help, or an image-editing feature in the application. This task provides a brief overview of some of the tools available. To find out more about the features in Kai's Photo Soap, click the Help button in any window of the application.

Once Kai's Photo Soap is running, you cannot use the menu bar or control strip modules. You must quit Kai's Photo Soap to return to Mac OS.

Start Here

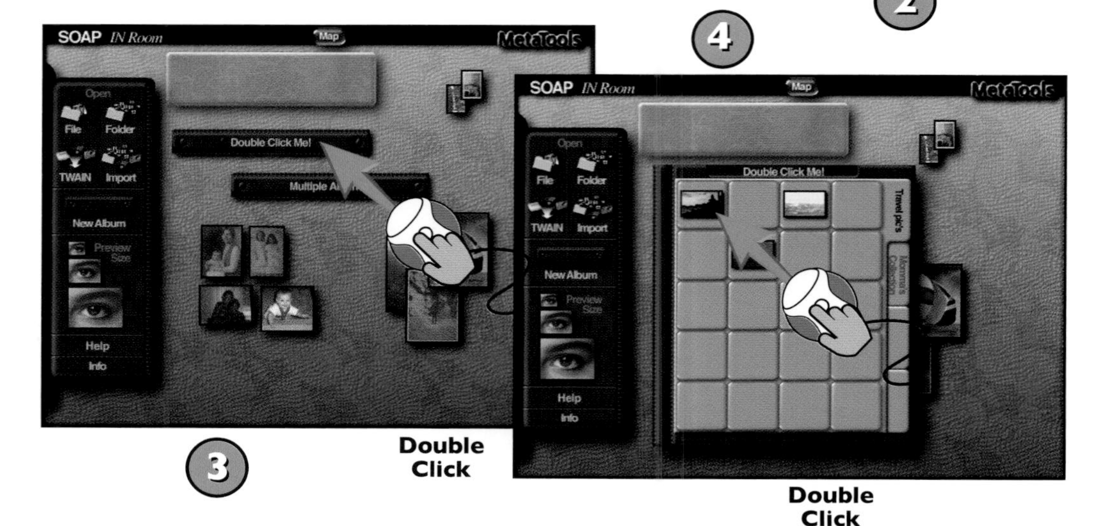

1. After you insert the Kai's Photo Soap CD-ROM into your iMac, double-click the **Kai's Photo Soap** installer icon and follow the directions.
2. Double-click the **Macintosh HD** icon, then double-click the **Applications** folder icon. Finally, double-click the **Kai's Photo Soap** icon.
3. Double-click the **Double Click Me!** Button.
4. Double-click on an image you want to work with.

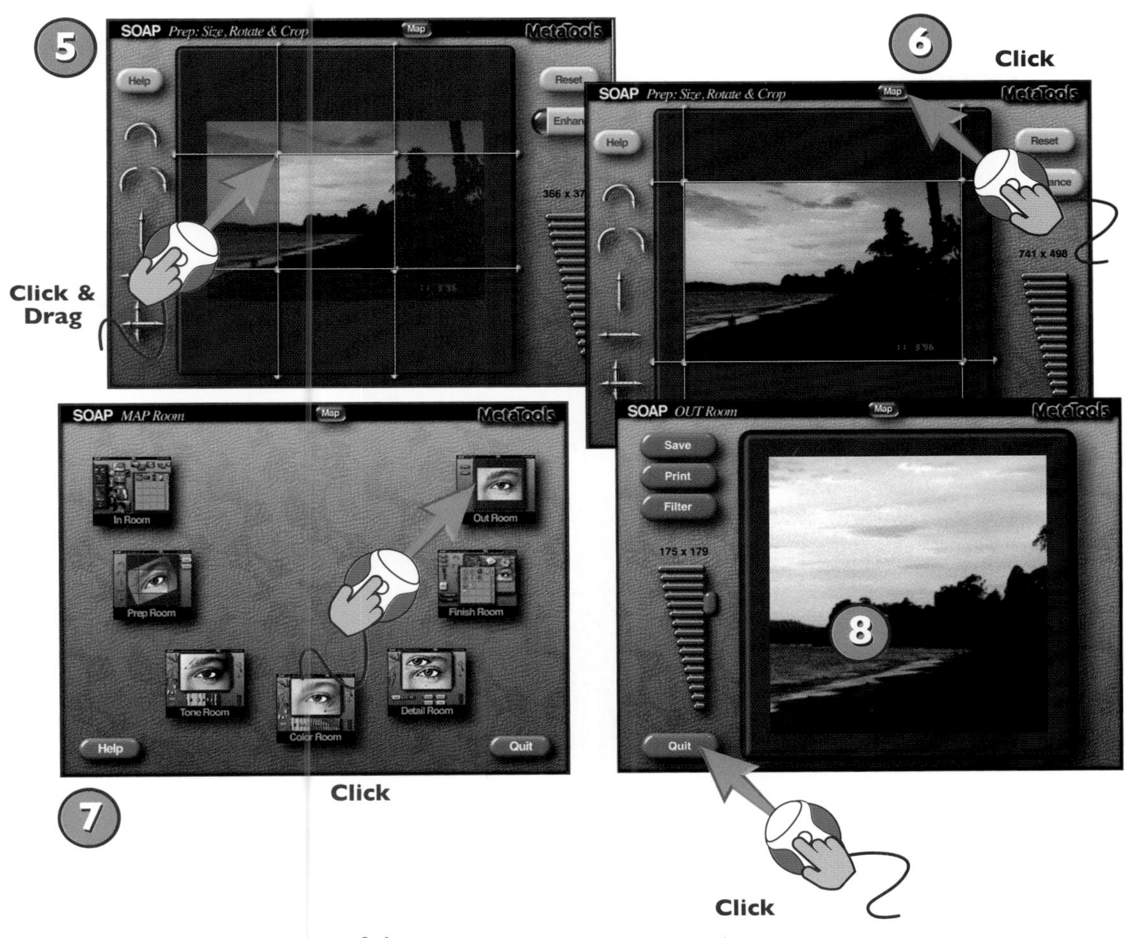

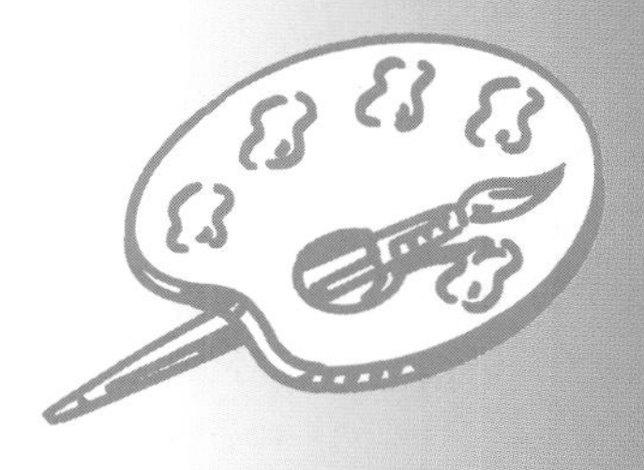

5. Click and drag the corners of the image to resize or rotate it.

6. Click the **Map** button to view the other image editing rooms available to you. Click any room button to go there.

7. Click the **Out Room** button.

8. Click the **Save** or **Print** button to save or print the final image. Click the **Quit** button to exit Kai's Photo Soap.

For more information about how to install applications onto your iMac, see Task 9, "Installing Applications," in Part 8, "Setting Up Applications."

Task 10: Creating a Web Page with PageMill 3.0

You can turn your iMac into a Web server using the Personal Web Server software included with Mac OS. Some ISPs provide Web site space when you sign up with their Internet service, but no matter how you set up your Web site, you can use PageMill to create Web pages for it. The best part is you don't need to learn how to program in order to create a Web page.

Start Here

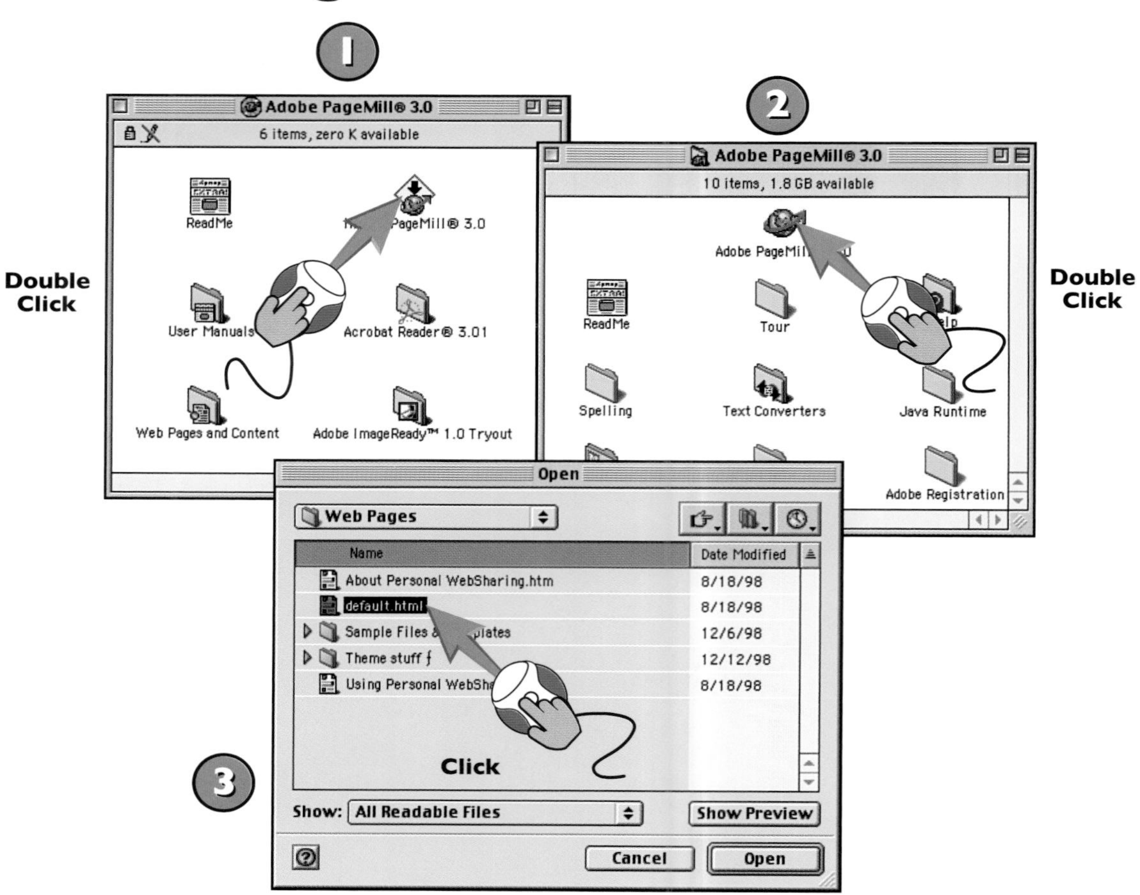

1. Insert the PageMill 3.0 CD-ROM into your iMac's CD-ROM drive, double-click the **PageMill 3.0** installer application, and follow the directions.
2. Double-click the **PageMill 3.0** icon.
3. In the **File** menu, click **Open** and navigate to the **Web Pages** folder on your hard drive. Double-click on an HTML file (in this case, **default.html**).

You can save an existing document as an HTML file, and then use PageMill to add images and format the document for your Web site.

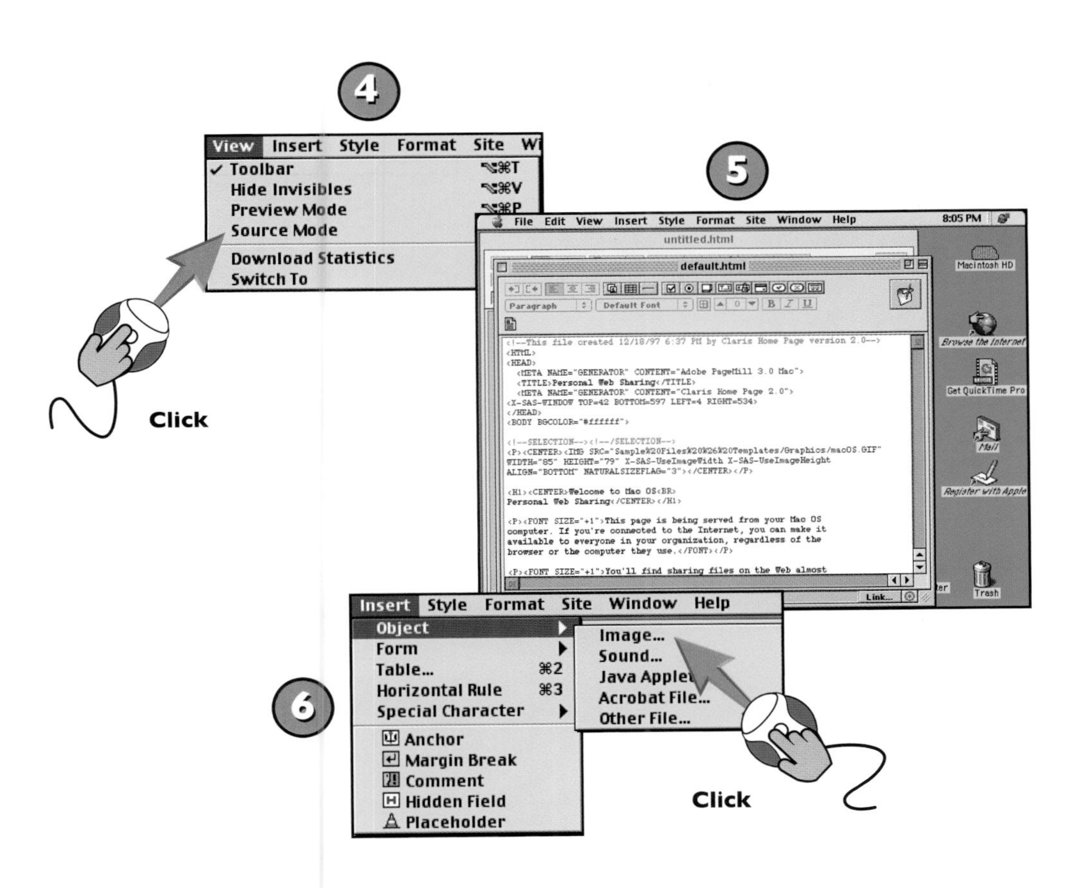

4. Click **View** and choose **Source Mode** to view the HTML code for the page you are viewing.

5. You can edit text and add files in this mode. Click **View** and choose **Source Mode** a second time to return the page to its default mode.

6. Click **Insert**, choose **Object**, then choose a menu command (**Image**, **Sound**, **Java Applet**, **Acrobat File**, or **Other File**) to place an object on the Web page.

In addition to editing HTML source, you can edit any Web page as a regular text document in PageMill. PageMill will save the document as an HTML file, which you can use on your Web site.

Task 11: Managing Your Finances with Quicken 98

Start Here

Quicken 98 is the latest version of Quicken, one of the most popular software applications for computers today. Quicken 98 can be used to track everything from the checks you write to your investments, assets, debts, and financial planning.

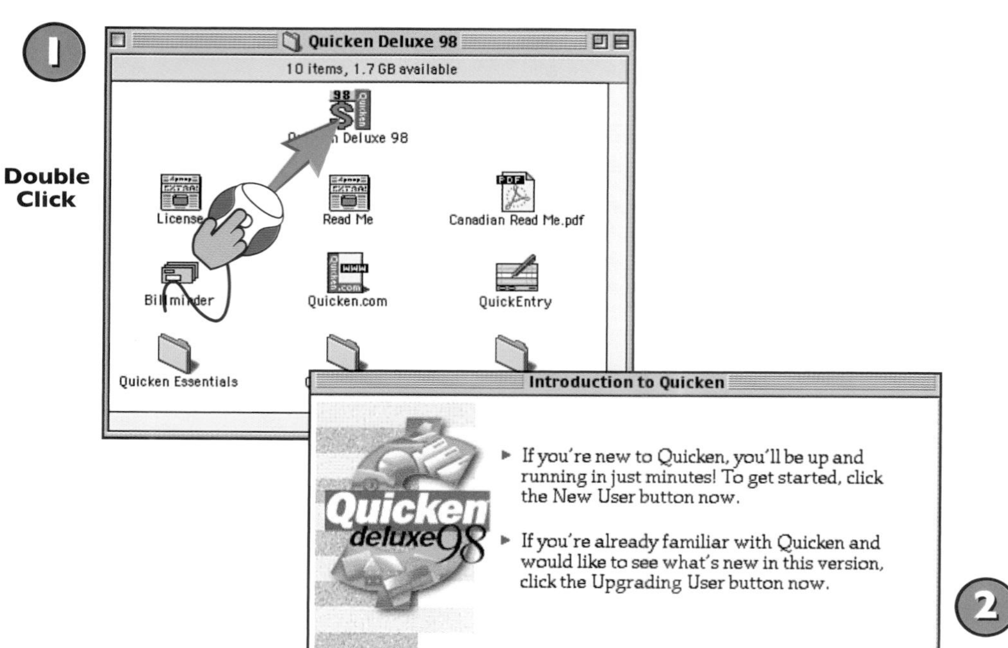

✓ You can password-protect any Quicken file to keep your financial information secure. To add a password, click **Edit** and choose **Preferences**. Then click the **Passwords** icon and type a password for your file.

1. Insert the Quicken 98 CD-ROM, double-click the installer application, and follow the directions to install Quicken 98. Finally, double-click the **Quicken 98** icon.
2. Type your name to personalize your copy of Quicken, and then click **OK**. In the **Introduction to Quicken** window, click the **New User** button.

Next Step

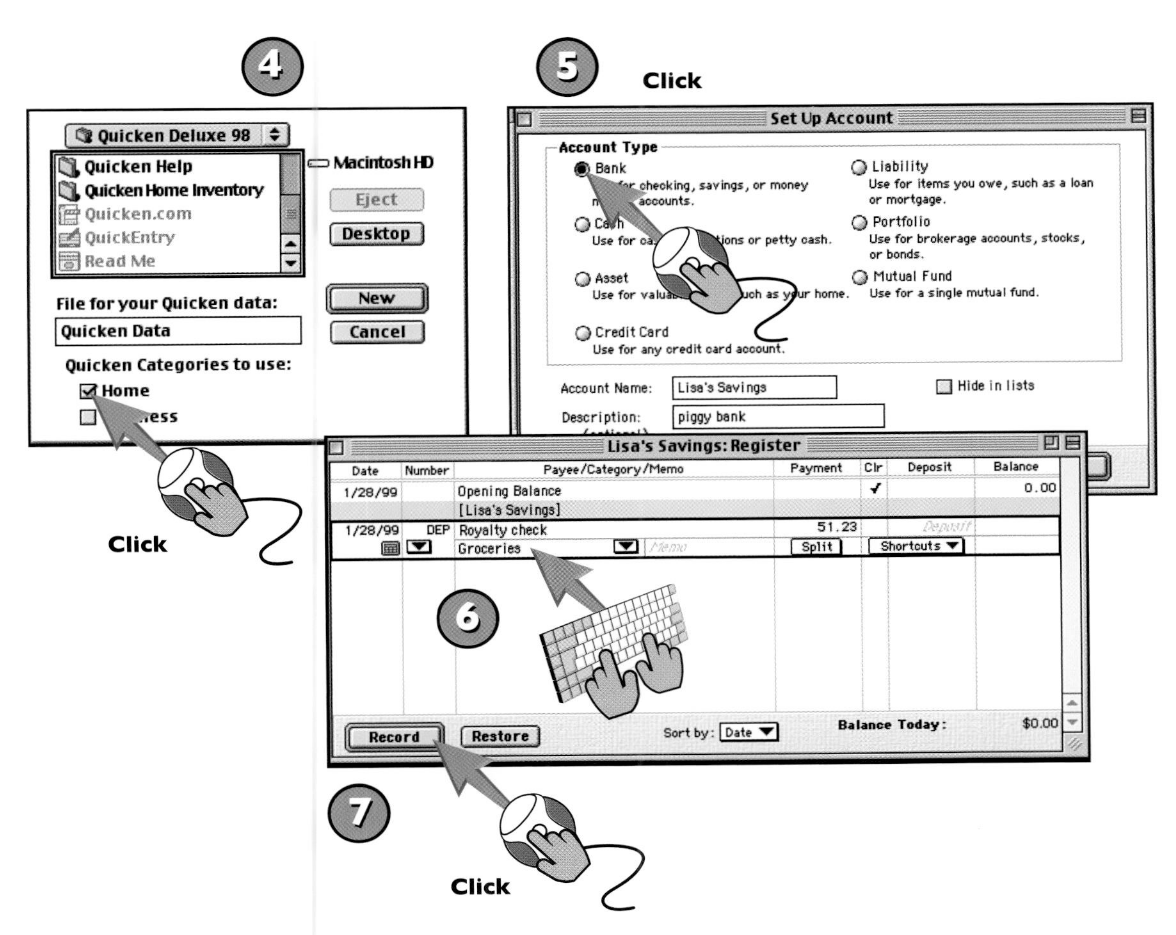

4. Click a category check box (in this case, **Home**), and then click the **OK** button.

5. Click the **Bank** radio button, and then click the **Create** button to create a new account.

6. Type a new entry into the account window.

7. Click **Record** to add the entry to the account.

Quicken 98 uses a help window to walk you through setting up your accounts and entering your financial information. If you do not want to use this window information, click its Close box.

Task 12: Searching for Recipes with Williams Sonoma's Good Cooking

The Williams Sonoma Good Cooking CD-ROM contains hundreds of recipes. You can search, sort, and view any recipe. If you need to find specific ingredient amounts, Williams Sonoma Good Cooking will reproportion the recipe to fit the number of people for whom you plan to cook.

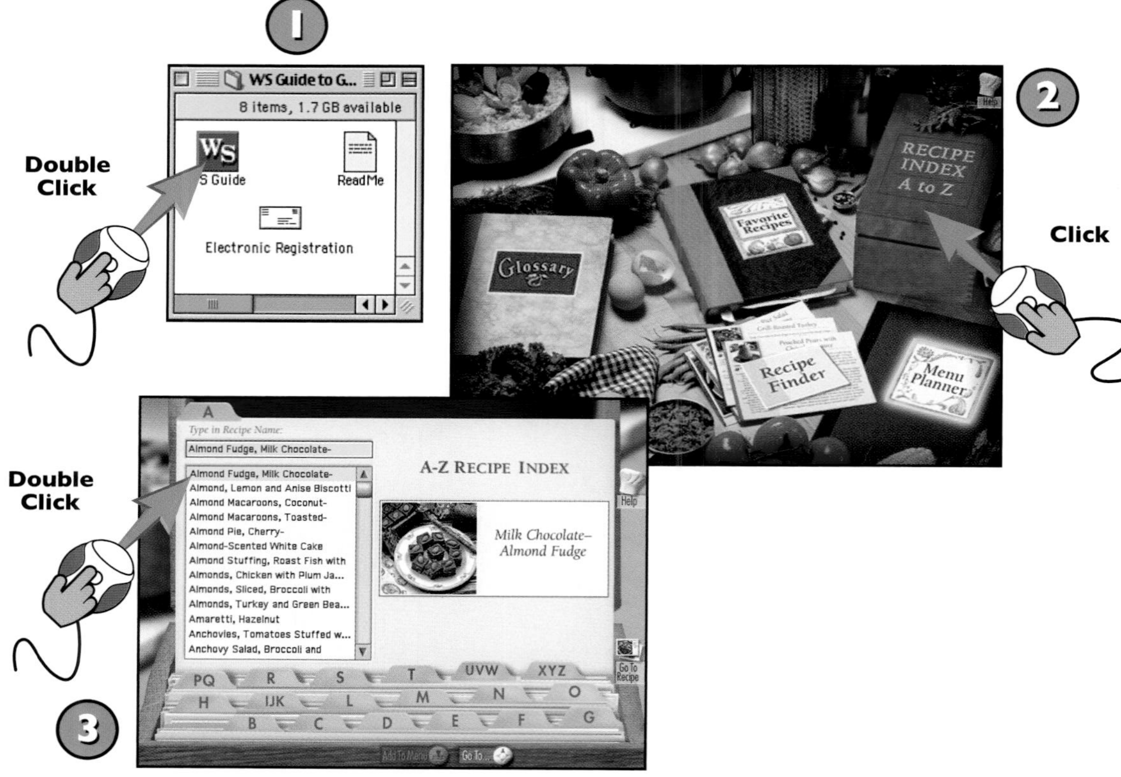

Be sure to put the Williams Sonoma Good Cooking CD-ROM into your iMac before you start its application on the hard drive.

Turn file sharing off before starting Williams Sonoma Good Cooking. If you leave file sharing on, the software may crash when you try to start it.

Click at the top of the screen to access the menu bar.

1. Insert the Williams Sonoma Good Cooking CD-ROM, double-click the installer application, and follow the onscreen directions. Finally, double-click the **WS Guide** icon.

2. Click the **Recipe Index** image.

3. Click an alphabet character, then double-click a recipe in the list window.

4 Click the **See recipe** button to view the recipe.

5 Click the **Serves** button to view additional serving options for that recipe.

A

accessory One of the applications that comes free with iMac. Examples include Note Pad, Scrapbook, and Apple Audio CD Player.

active window The window you're currently using. You can tell a window is active by looking at its title bar: If the bar shows dark letters on a gray background, the window is active. Inactive windows show gray letters on a light gray background.

AppleScript The name of Apple's scripting language, which built into Mac OS. You can automate applications and tasks in Mac OS using AppleScript scripts.

application Software that accomplishes a specific set of tasks or functions. This term is used interchangeably with the term *program*.

application window A window that contains a running application, such as Internet Explorer or SimpleText.

ASCII text file A file that uses only the American Standard Code for Information Interchange character set (techno-lingo for the characters you see on your keyboard).

B

back up The process of making a copy of your files. The backup copy can be restored to replace the original.

blueberry The shade of blue of revC iMacs.

boot To start your computer. The term *booting* comes from the phrase "pulling oneself up by one's bootstraps," which refers to the fact that your computer can load everything it needs to operate properly without any help from you.

bondi blue The shade of blue of your revA and revB iMac, keyboard, and mouse.

bps Bits per second. The rate at which a modem or other communications device spits data through a phone line or cable.

browser An application you use to surf sites on the World Wide Web. The browsers that come with your iMac are called *Internet Explorer* and *Netscape Navigator*.

byte A single character of information

C

CD-ROM drive A special computer disk drive that's designed to handle CD-ROM disks, which resemble audio CDs. CD-ROMS have enormous capacity (about 500 times that of a typical floppy disk), so they're most often used to hold large applications, graphics libraries, huge collections of shareware, or your local backup if you have a CD recorder.

channel A special World Wide Web site that features changing content that is sent automatically to your computer at predefined intervals. AOL departments are also called channels. See also *subscription*.

character formatting Changing the look of text characters by altering their font, size, style, color, and more.

check box A square-shaped switch that toggles a dialog box option on or off. The option is toggled on when a check mark appears in the box.

click To quickly press and release the mouse button.

clipboard An area of memory that holds data temporarily during cut-and-paste operations.

Collapse box Hides all window content except for the window title bar. This box is located in the upper right corner of any **Finder** window, and most document windows. See also *Uncollapse box*.

commands The options you see in a pull-down menu. You use these commands to tell the application what you want it to do next.

D

data files The files used by you on your programs. See also *program files*.

delay The amount of time it takes for a second character to appear when you press and hold down a key.

desktop A metaphor for the iMac screen. Starting a Mac OS application is similar to putting a folder full of papers (the application window) on your desk. To do some work, you pull some papers out of the folder (the document windows) and place them on the desktop.

device driver A small program that controls the way a device (such as a printer or external drive) works with your iMac

dialog box A window that pops up on the screen to ask you for information or to seek confirmation of an action you requested.

digital camera A special camera that saves pictures using digital storage (such as a memory card) instead of film.

directory See *folder*.

disk cache A specific amount of hard drive space used to store small amounts of frequently used data in order to increase the overall performance of software on your iMac.

document window A window opened in an application. Document windows hold whatever you're working on in the application.

double-click To quickly press and release the mouse button twice in succession.

double-click speed The maximum amount of time Mac OS allows between the mouse clicks of a double-click.

drag To press and hold down the mouse button and then move the mouse.

drag-and-drop A technique you can use to run commands or move things around; you use your mouse to drag files or folders to a document window or to the desktop and drop them there to add or convert them to a format compatible with the application.

DVD drive DVD stands for *Digital Video Display*. A DVD drive is similar to a CD-ROM drive, but is capable of storing up to 15GB of data. See also *CD-ROM drive*.

E

email Short for *electronic mail*. Email is a tool for communicating across networks as well as on the Internet. Email applications enable their users to exchange messages with each other.

Erase Disk A command in the Special menu that formats floppies or hard drives to work with your iMac. See also *formatting*.

Ethernet A network protocol commonly used to transfer data between two or more networked computers. Your iMac has a 10/100BaseT Ethernet connector.

F

favorite A Web site you add to your Favorites menu in a browser, such as Internet Explorer, or in the Apple menu on your iMac.

file An organized unit of information stored on your hard disk.

file sharing A feature in Mac OS software that enables you to share the files on your iMac with other Macintoshes or AppleTalk computers.

file system The technology used to create, track, and modify files and folders stored on your hard disk. Your iMac uses the Mac OS File System, which comes in two flavors: the Hierarchical File System (HFS), also known as the Mac OS standard format, and HFS Plus, also known as the Mac OS extended format. Your iMac hard disk is formatted with the extended format.

floppy disk A portable storage medium that consists of a flexible disk protected by a plastic case. Floppy disks are available in a variety of sizes and capacities.

folder A storage location on your hard disk in which you keep related files together.

font A character set of a specific typeface, type style, and type size.

Format bar A series of text boxes and buttons that enable you to format the characters in your document. The Format bar typically appears under the toolbar.

formatting The process of setting up a disk so that a drive can read its information and write information to it (not to be confused with character formatting).

fragmented When a single file is chopped up and stored in separate chunks scattered around a hard disk. You can fix this by running Norton Utilities' Speed Disk application.

full backup Backs up all the files in a current backup job. See also *incremental backup*.

G

gigabyte 1,024 megabytes. Also referred to as a *gig* when spoken, or abbreviated as *GB* when written. Also see *byte*, *kilobyte*, and *megabyte*.

grape The shade of purple of revC iMacs.

Grow box Enlarge or shrink any Finder window and most document windows by clicking and dragging the lower right corner of a window.

H

hard disk The main storage area inside your iMac.

home page The first page that loads when you start a browser, or the first page of a Web site.

hover To place the mouse pointer over an object for a few seconds. If you have Balloon Help on, for example, a help balloon appears over most Finder items, such as icons and window controls.

HTML Hypertext Markup Language. This is the language used to create Web pages.

hub A network device that contains jacks (such as Ethernet or USB jacks). A hub enables you to expand the number of devices that can be connected together.

hyperlink Highlighted text or graphic on a Web page that points to another location on the document, or a different document.

I

icons The little pictures that Mac OS uses to represent applications, folders, and files.

incremental backup Backs up only files in the current backup job that have changed since the last full backup.

infrared port A communications port, usually found on notebook computers and some printers. Infrared ports enable two devices to communicate by using infrared waves instead of cables. This port is only available on revA and revB iMacs.

insertion point cursor The blinking vertical bar you see inside a text box or in a word-processing application, such as SimpleText. It indicates where the next character you type will appear.

Internet A network of networks that extends around the world. By setting up an account with an Internet service provider, you can access this network.

intranet The implementation of Internet technologies for use within a corporate organization rather than for connection to the Internet as a whole.

IR Short for infrared. See also *infrared port*.

IrDA Short for Infrared Data Association, a group of manufacturers who specialize in designing and making infrared devices.

J-K

Java An Internet technology that enables one application to be created for a variety of computer platforms.

Kbps One thousand bits per second (bps). Today's modern modems transmit data at 28.8Kbps, 33.6Kps, or 56Kbps.

kilobyte 1,024 bytes. This is often abbreviated to *K* or *KB*. See also *megabyte* and *gigabyte*.

L

LAN See *local area network*.

Lime The shade of green of revC iMacs.

link See *hyperlink*

local area network A network in which all the computers occupy a relatively small geographical area, such as a department, an office, a home, or a building. All the connections between computers are made via network cables as opposed to via a modem or other hardware device. Two computers can also be connected with a crossover or null modem cable.

list box A small window that displays a list of items such as file names or directives.

log off To disconnect from the Internet or network.

log on To connect to the Internet or a network by entering a valid user name and password.

M

Macintosh HD The name of the hard disk icon on your iMac. You can rename your hard disk, too.

maximize To increase the size of a window to its largest form. A maximized application window fills the entire screen (except for the taskbar). A maximized document window fills the entire application window.

Mbps One million bits per second (bps).

megabyte 1,024 kilobytes, or 1,048,576 bytes. This is often abbreviated in writing as *M* or *MB* and is often referred to as a *meg* in speech. See also *gigabyte*.

Menu bar The bar at the top of your iMac screen. The menu bar contains pull-down menus which enable you to execute commands.

minimize To reduce the size of a window.

modem An electronic device that enables two computers to exchange data over phone lines.

multitasking The capability to run several programs at the same time.

N-O

network A collection of computers and printers connected via special cables or other network hardware (such as modems, or infrared parts) to process network transactions, such as print job, or share files, folders, disks, peripherals, and applications. See also *local area network*.

newsgroup An Internet discussion group devoted to a single topic. These discussions progress by messages being posted to the group.

Open Transport Apple's networking technology. Open Transport is used to connect to an Internet service provider as well as to connect with other computers on a network.

P

Page Holder A window in Internet Explorer 4.5 used to store a Web page for quick access.

plug-in A software component commonly used with software applications. Specifically used with Internet browsers to add functionality, such as the capability to play back QuickTime movies on a Web page, or to play sound over the Internet on your iMac.

point To place the mouse pointer so that it rests on a specific screen location.

pop-up window A Finder window located at the bottom of your desktop.

port The connection into which you plug the cable from a device such as a mouse or printer.

program files The files that run your programs. See also *data files*.

pull-down menus Hidden menus that you open from an application's menu bar to access the commands and features of the application.

Q-R

QuickTime Apple's multimedia technology. Enables applications which use QuickTime to play animation, movies, and sounds.

QuickDraw 3D Apple's 3D technology. Enables applications such as games to show three dimensional objects and fonts.

radio button A dialog box option that appears as a small circle, often in groups of two or more.

RAM Stands for *random access memory*. The memory in your iMac that Mac OS uses to run your applications.

RAM disk A specific amount of memory used as a hard disk on your desktop. You can run applications or store files on a RAM disk.

repeat rate After the initial delay, the rate at which characters appear when you press and hold down a key.

Reset switch A hardware switch that restarts your iMac. It is located inside the right door of your iMac

resolution The number of dots per inch of your desktop (example: 800×600).

S

scalable font A font in which each character exists as an outline that can be scaled to different sizes. Mac OS includes such scalable fonts as Arial, Courier New, and Times New Roman. Scalable fonts can either be PostScript or TrueType fonts.

scrollbar A bar that appears at the bottom or on the right side of a window when the window is too small to display all its contents.

serial port A type of hardware port not found on an iMac. Hardware peripherals with serial ports can use a USB-to-serial port adapter to connect to an iMac.

SDRAM The type of memory your iMac uses to run Mac OS and its applications.

SGRAM The type of video memory your iMac uses to bring images to its screen.

spring-loaded folders The behavior of Finder folders when you drag and hover an item over a folder icon.

strawberry The shade of red of revC iMacs.

subscription A method of checking for new or changed data on a World Wide Web site or channel. The subscription sets up a schedule for checking a particular site to see whether it has changed in any way since the last time it was checked.

surf To travel from site to site on the World Wide Web.

T

tangerine The shade of orange of revC iMacs.

text box A screen area in which you type text information, such as a description or a file name.

text editor An application that lets you edit files that contain only text. AppleWorks, SimpleText, Note Pad, and Stickies are all text editors included with your iMac.

title bar The area on the top line of a window that displays the window's title.

toolbar A series of application-specific buttons that typically appears beneath the menu bar.

tracking speed The speed at which the mouse pointer moves across the screen when you move the mouse on its pad.

TrueType A scalable font technology that comes with Mac OS.

type size A measure of the height of a font. Type size is measured in *points*; there are 72 points in an inch.

type style Character attributes, such as normal, bold, and italic. Other type styles are underline, shadow, and outline.

typeface A distinctive graphic design of letters, numbers, and other symbols.

U

Uncollapse box If the window area is collapsed, clicking this box displays the previous hidden window area below the window title bar. This box is located in the upper right corner of any Finder window. See also *Collapse box*.

URL Uniform resource locator, or the Internet address you type into a Web browser's Address text field to go from one Web site to another.

USB Universal Serial Bus. The port iMacs use to enable peripheral devices such as mice, keyboards, cameras, printers, scanners, joysticks, hard drives, and hubs to connect to your iMac.

V-W

virtual memory A method for managing memory on your iMac, using the hard drive to swap data to available memory (RAM) in order to run software applications and Mac OS.

window A rectangular screen area in which Mac OS displays applications and documents.

World Wide Web Also known as the Internet and the Information superhighway. A global network of computers that provides information, entertainment, and services for just about anything you can think of.

word wrap A word-processor feature that automatically starts a new line when your typing reaches the end of the current line.

Write protection A hardware or software setting that prevents Mac OS from writing data to a hard drive or removable medium, such as a Zip or floppy disk.

Z

Zip drive A special disk drive that uses portable disks (slightly larger than a floppy disk), which hold 100MB of data.

Zoom box Located next to the Collapse box in a Finder window title bar. Clicking the Zoom box once resizes a window to its maximum size. Clicking it again resizes it to the previous size selected.

iMac Products

If you are wondering what kinds of USB products are available for your iMac, or if you are looking for a particular USB product, this appendix will help you. You can connect a wide range of USB devices to your iMac, including adapters, printers, cameras, speakers, and scanners, along with the basics such as a keyboard, mouse, joystick, or trackball.

USB Drives

You can connect several types of drives to your USB port. The most common type is the removable media drive, such as a floppy drive or Iomega's Zip drive. You can also purchase PC card drives and DVD-ROM drives in addition to the more traditional external hard drive. Table B.1 shows some information about various USB drives, including prices (when available):

TABLE B.1 USB Drives

Manufacturer	Device	Description	Price
Ariston	USB Reader	Flash card for cameras	
	PC Card Reader	Flash card for cameras	
Imation	SuperDisk	An external drive that holds up to 120MB	$149
Iomega	Zip	An external drive that holds up to 100MB	$149
La Cie	USB CD-RW	Readable/writeable CD-ROM drive	TBA
	USB DVD drive	Reads DVD-ROM disks	TBA
	USB hard drives	4, 6, and 8GB drives	TBA
Microtech	Mii Zip 100 Drive	External 100MB Zip Drive	$190
Newer	uDrive Floppy	USB 1.44MB floppy drive	$99

USB Input Devices

The most familiar USB devices are input devices, such as keyboards, mice, joysticks, trackballs, scanners, and cameras. The list below contains a sampling of input devices. If you have a RevB or a RevC iMac (one that shipped after January 1999 or it isn't Bondi Blue), you have 6MB of VRAM and 3D acceleration. If you play a lot of 3D games, consider purchasing a joystick. Prices range from $50 to $100.

- Ariston Ares joystick
- Thrustmaster Top Gun joystick
- Kernel Joyport USB
- CH GameStick 3D, F16 Combatstick
- Evolution Mouse Trak trackball
- Mac Ally 1 button mouse, iMouse, iBall, iKey, and trackball
- BTC, Cherry keyboards
- Ariston Hermes Gamepad, Podiki mouse, iSee camera
- Imaccessories iPad reversible controller, keyboard, mouse, and flight command stick
- Interex mouse
- iPoint mouse
- Wacom Pen Partner
- iTrack ProBall

Cameras

If you've been waiting to purchase a digital camera, now may be a great time to buy. You can use your iMac's USB port to transfer digital pictures from your camera to your iMac. Alternatively, you can purchase a PC card adapter and a PC card reader and view your digital images from your desktop without the USB connection to the camera. Table B.2 lists a couple of cameras and their prices.

TABLE B.2 Digital Cameras

Manufacturer	Model	Price
Logitech	QuickCam VC	Starting at $125
	Pro	Starting at $125
Kodak	DC 220 still camera	$799
	DC 260 still camera	$999

Scanners

If you prefer analog cameras, or if you like creating your own artwork, a scanner can be a handy tool. If you haven't purchased you iMac yet, you might want to see if there are any iMac bundles that include a scanner in addition to digitizing software for your iMac. Table B.3 lists a few scanners on the market.

TABLE B.3 Scanners

Manufacturer	Model	Price
Umax	1220U	$179
Microtek	TBA	TBA
Agfa	1212u	$179

USB Adapter Devices

If you do not have a USB device but have a serial, SCSI, ADB, or parallel device that is compatible with Mac OS 8.5, you can purchase a variety of adapters for printers, keyboard, mice, and many other types of devices so you can connect them to your iMac's USB port. You'll find USB-to-parallel port, USB-to-serial, and USB-to-ADB adapters and converters on the market ranging in price from $30 to $100. Altogether, these adapters enable you to connect over 1,500 additional devices to your iMac; Table B.4 lists only a few of them.

TABLE B.4 USB Adapter Devices

Manufacturer	Device	Price
Ariston	USB Parallel printer converter	$59
Griffon Technology	iMage (USB to ADB)	$29
Epson	Parallel to USB	$49
Farallon	iPrint serial to USB adapter	$110
Hewlett-Packard	HP/USB Connectivity Kit (parallel to USB)	$69
Keyspan	USB to serial	$79
InfoWare	Power Print USB (parallel to USB)	$99
Momentum	uPrint (USB to serial printer)	$99
Momentum	uConnect (USB to serial adapter)	$69
Newer Technology	uSCSI (USB to SCSI adapter)	$79

USB Printers

Table B.5 lists companies that make USB printer products. More printers can be connected using a parallel or serial adapter. See the previous section about USB adapters for more information about USB adapters.

TABLE B.5 USB Printers

Manufacturer	Model	Price
Epson	USB Stylus 740	$299
Alps	MB1300	$549
	MB1000	$299
Brother	1040iM Laser Printer	TBA
Tektronix	Phaser 850	TBA

USB Hubs

If you plan on using many USB peripherals, a USB hub can reduce the cable clutter and help organize your USB devices. USB hubs either have four or seven ports and come in many shapes, sizes, colors and prices. Table B.6 lists a few of the hubs available today.

TABLE B.6 USB Hubs

Manufacturer	Device	Price
ADS Technologies	Four-port hub	$89
Ariston	Four-port hub	$89
Belkin	Express Hub (four ports)	$99
Entrega	Four-port hub	$80
	Seven-port hub	$130
Peracom	USB Quad Hub	$99
Computer Access Technology	Andromeda USB hub (four ports)	$100
Future Technology Devices	seven-port hub	$189
UnixTar	USB Hub UT	$95
USB Stuff	four-port hub	$100
Newer Technology	uHub (seven-ports)	$89
	seven-port hub	$200
Philips	four-port hub	$100
	seven-port hub	$200
Interex	four-port hub	$99
Mac Ally	iHub (four ports)	$79

Symbols

A

C

D

E

F

G - H

I

J - K - L

M

P

Q - R

S

U - V

W - X - Y - Z

Notes